An Introduction to Operating Systems

Revised First Edition

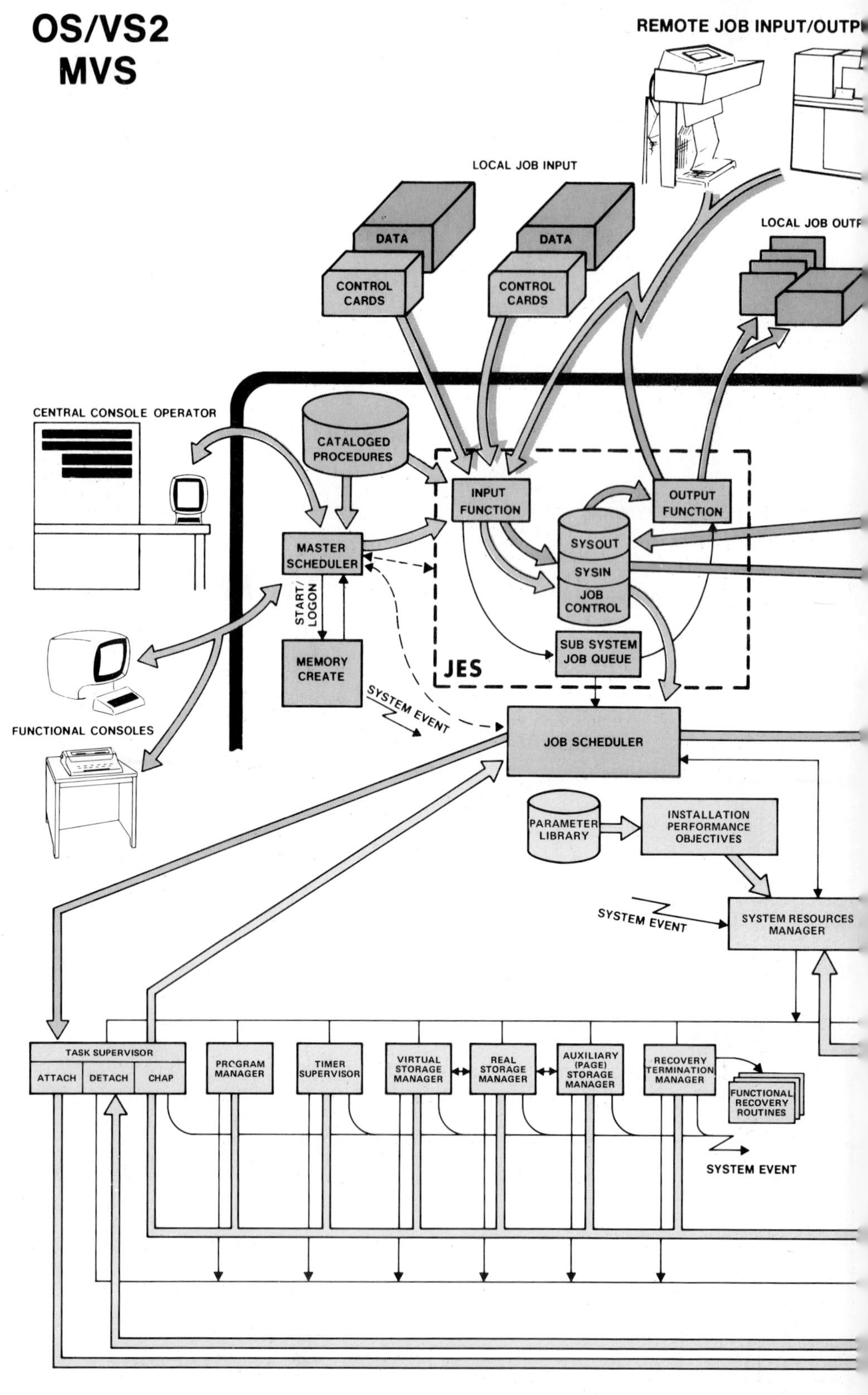

OS/VS2
MVS
REMOTE JOB INPUT/OUTP
LOCAL JOB INPUT
DATA
CONTROL CARDS
DATA
CONTROL CARDS
LOCAL JOB OUTP
CENTRAL CONSOLE OPERATOR
CATALOGED PROCEDURES
INPUT FUNCTION
OUTPUT FUNCTION
SYSOUT
SYSIN
JOB CONTROL
MASTER SCHEDULER
START/ LOGON
MEMORY CREATE
SUB SYSTEM JOB QUEUE
JES
SYSTEM EVENT
FUNCTIONAL CONSOLES
JOB SCHEDULER
PARAMETER LIBRARY
INSTALLATION PERFORMANCE OBJECTIVES
SYSTEM EVENT
SYSTEM RESOURCES MANAGER
TASK SUPERVISOR
ATTACH
DETACH
CHAP
PROGRAM MANAGER
TIMER SUPERVISOR
VIRTUAL STORAGE MANAGER
REAL STORAGE MANAGER
AUXILIARY (PAGE) STORAGE MANAGER
RECOVERY TERMINATION MANAGER
FUNCTIONAL RECOVERY ROUTINES
SYSTEM EVENT

ONLINE USERS

REMOTE TERMINALS

LOCAL TERMINALS

ACCESS METHOD ROUTINES

CONTROL PROGRAM SERVICE ROUTINES

COMMON STORAGE AREA

SCHEDULER WORK AREA

USER

NUCLEUS

VIRTUAL STORAGE

USER

USER

USER

NUCLEUS

REAL STORAGE

EXTERNAL (AUXILIARY) PAGE STORAGE

CATALOGS

IPL-NUCLEUS

CONTROL PROGRAM ROUTINES

LOGS

SYSTEM DATA SETS

DATA BASE AND PROGRAM LIBRARIES

CPU 2

CPU 1

CPU 1

CPU 2

EXTERNAL

MACHINE

PROGRAM

I/O

SVC

INTERRUPT HANDLERS

ERROR

RECOVERY MGR SUPPORT

AUTOMATIC CPU RECOVERY

EM

US

DIRECT ACCESS DEVICE SPACE MANAGER

VIO

EXCP PROCESSOR

VSAM PROCESSOR

OLTEP PROCESSOR

VTAM PROCESSOR

MSS PROCESSOR

IOS

QUEUED REQUESTS FOR CPU SERVICE

DISPATCHER

TO CPU 1

TO CPU 2

Courtesy of International Business Machines Corporation.

An Introduction to Operating Systems

Revised First Edition

HARVEY M. DEITEL
Boston College

ADDISON-WESLEY PUBLISHING COMPANY

Reading, Massachusetts • Amsterdam • London
Manila • Singapore • Sydney • Tokyo

WORLD STUDENT SERIES

Sponsoring Editor: William B. Gruener
Production Editor: William J. Yskamp

Text Designer: Herb Caswell
Illustrator: ANCO/Boston
Cover Designer: Gary Fujiwara
Art Coordinator: Susanah H. Michener

Production Manager: Susan Zorn
Production Coordinator: Helen M. Wythe

The text of this book was composed in
Times Roman by International Computaprint Corporation

ISBN 0-201-14502-2
DEFGHIJ-HA-89876

To my wife, Barbara,
and to my children, Paul and Abbey:
You are the joys of my life.

Preface

This text is intended primarily for the one-semester operating systems course that universities offer to juniors, seniors, and first-year graduate students in computer science. It contains sufficient material to be useful as the main text for courses CS6 and CS10 in ACM Curriculum 78. Chapter 15, Analytic Modeling, is heavily mathematical; this chapter should be included by instructors in "hard-core" computer science schools, but it may be omitted without loss of continuity in less formal programs.

The text contains approximately 300 charts, diagrams, and illustrations, 504 exercises, 22 chapters, and five detailed case studies. Each chapter lists extensive literature—577 books and papers are referenced. Over 1200 terms are highlighted in the end-of-chapter terminology sections.

Five detailed case studies are included on operating systems that will have great importance in the 1980s, namely, the UNIX system, VAX/VMS, CP/M, MVS, and VM. Each of these systems has a certain "flavor" that I have worked hard to convey. Each of them is intended for a different portion of the operating systems marketplace.

Eight major parts are included; each part contains several related chapters. The text is handsomely illustrated (thanks to the skills of Sue Michener of Addison-Wesley). Each chapter begins with an outline so that the reader may approach the material in "top-down" fashion. One or more quotes are used in introducing each chapter—some are humorous; some are thought-provoking; all are intended to humanize the text and add a touch of the philosophical.

Significant terms, major concepts, and important statements are italicized. Each chapter includes a summary of important concepts and ideas for review. Terminology sections are included; key terms are presented alphabetically. Each chapter includes many exercises varying in difficulty from simple review of the material to complex reasoning from basic principles. Literature sections are localized; each chapter ends with a listing of relevant texts and papers. An Author Index at the end of the text lists all of the authors and co-authors mentioned in the text; an extensive conventional Subject Index provides rapid access to virtually any portion of the text by keyword.

Part One introduces the notion of operating systems, presents a history of operating systems, and discusses hardware, software, and firmware. Chapter 2 includes a case study on microprogramming; this is especially important to the operating systems student—in future designs much (and in some cases all) of the operating system will migrate into microcode. Portions of Chapter 1 are based upon "A History of Operating Systems" by N. Weizer, *Datamation,* January 1981. This material is reprinted with permission of *Datamation*® magazine, © Copyright by Technical Publishing Company, A Dun & Bradstreet Company, 1981, all rights reserved.

Part Two presents the notions of process, process state transitions, interrupts, context switching, operating systems structure, asynchronism, mutual exclusion, monitors, and deadlock. Chapter 3 introduces various process concepts and discusses the interrupt structure of the large-scale IBM processors; this material is critical to the discussions of the MVS and VM operating systems in the case studies later in the text. Chapter 4 presents the notion of asynchronism. The problems encountered in concurrent access to shared resources are discussed, and various mutual exclusion techniques, both hardware- and software-oriented, are presented for dealing with these problems. Chapter 5 discusses monitors and how they may be used to solve certain classical problems in concurrency; monitor implementations of the Ring Buffer as well as Readers and Writers are presented. The chapter continues with an introduction to concurrent programming in Ada, the emerging language whose development has been sponsored by the United States government.

Many of the Ada program segments presented are based on examples in *Preliminary Ada Reference Manual,* SIGPLAN NOTICES, Vol. 14, No. 6, June 1979, Part A, and *Rationale for the Design of the Ada Programming Language,* by J. D. Ichbiah, J. C. Heliard, O. Roubine, J. G. P. Barnes, B. Krieg-Brueckner, and B. A. Wichmann, SIGPLAN NOTICES, Vol. 14, No. 6, June 1979, Part B ("The Government of the United States of America grants free permission to reproduce this document for the purpose of evaluating and using the Ada language"). (Ada® is a registered trademark of the United States Government, Ada Joint Program Office.)

Chapter 6 explains the notion of deadlock in which various processes cannot proceed because they are waiting for events that will never happen. The chapter discusses the major areas of deadlock research, and presents various means of dealing with deadlock and the related problem of indefinite postponement. The chapter includes a detailed discussion of deadlock avoidance with Dijkstra's Banker's Algorithm.

Part Three discusses storage management for both real storage and virtual storage systems. Chapter 7 traces the development of real storage systems from single user dedicated systems through the various forms of partitioned multiprogramming systems. Chapters 8 and 9 deal with virtual storage organization and management, respectively. Chapter 8 motivates the concept of virtual storage, and discusses the reduction of mapping information by the block mapping techniques and paging and segmentation. A detailed discussion of virtual storage organization and address translation in paged/segmented systems is presented. Chapter 9 discusses the various strategies for managing virtual storage systems. Fetch, placement, and replacement strategies are considered; both demand fetch and anticipatory fetch strategies are discussed. The chapter concentrates on page replacement strategies; it considers the Principle of Optimality, and the random, FIFO, LRU, LFU, and NUR strategies. Then, Denning's working set theory of program behavior is presented, and working set page replacement is analyzed.

Part Four deals with processor management, in particular the issues of processor scheduling and multiprocessing. Chapter 10 concentrates on scheduling strategies; it discusses high-level, intermediate-level, and low-level scheduling, scheduling objectives and criteria, priority scheduling, static vs. dynamic priorities, earned vs. bought priorities, and deadline scheduling. Various scheduling algorithms are presented including FIFO, RR, SJF, SRT, and HRN. The chapter ends with a thorough analysis of multilevel feedback queueing mechanisms. Chapter 11 explains multiprocessing, motivated as a means of improving performance and reliability. The exploitation of parallelism is considered; the techniques of loop distribution, tree height reduction, and the "never wait" rule are discussed. Various multiprocessor hardware organizations and operating systems organizations are analyzed. This material has strong ties to the material on networks in Chapter 16.

Part Five considers auxiliary storage management. Chapter 12 discusses disk scheduling; it explains the operation of moving-head disk storage, motivates the need for disk scheduling, and presents the popular disk scheduling strategies including FCFS, SSTF, SCAN, N-step SCAN, C-SCAN, the Eschenbach scheme and rotational optimization. A number of systems considerations that might affect the usefulness of disk scheduling are examined.

Chapter 13 considers file and database management systems. The chapter discusses file system functions and operations; the data hierarchy; blocking and buffering; sequential, indexed sequential, direct, and partitioned file organizations; queued and basic access methods; hierarchical file system structure; contiguous and noncontiguous allocation; linked allocation, file mapping, file descriptors, access control; and backup and recovery. The importance of database systems, especially in the context of operating systems, is emphasized; the discussion considers the advantages of database systems, data independence, database languages, the database administrator, distributed database, and data dictionary concepts. The chapter ends with a discussion of the hierarchical, network, and relational database models.

Part Six deals with the issues of computer system performance. Chapter 14 considers the issues of performance measurement, monitoring, and evaluation. The chapter discusses timings, instruction mixes, kernel programs, analytic models, benchmarks, synthetic programs, simulation, and performance monitoring. Bottleneck isolation and removal are examined. Both negative and positive feedback mechanisms are analyzed. The chapter includes a very large complement of exercises, many of which are suitable as term projects, particularly in simulation-oriented courses.

Chapter 15 presents a mathematical treatment of analytic modeling; both queueing models and Markov processes are considered. The chapter may be omitted without loss of continuity, but it is highly recommended for students who have had some background in calculus, probability, and statistics. The queueing theory portion of the chapter discusses the notions of source, arrivals, Poisson arrivals, service times, queue capacity, multiple servers, queue disciplines, traffic intensity, server utilization, steady state vs. transient solutions, and Little's Result. Two case studies are presented: analyzing an M/M/1 queueing system, and analyzing an M/M/c queueing system. The section of the chapter on Markov processes concentrates on the special case of birth and death models; a rather detailed case study analyzes the performance of a disk subsystem. Portions of the presentation on queueing theory are based on material in Chapter 5 of *Probability, Statistics, and Queueing Theory with Computer Science Applications* by Arnold O. Allen. Copyright 1978 by Academic Press, Inc., New York. Adapted with permission.

Part Seven considers computer networks and security issues. Chapter 16, Network Operating Systems, discusses network categories including resource sharing networks, distributed computation networks, and remote communication networks. A detailed discussion of packet switching is presented; included is the ISO OSI layered architecture, the X.25 standard, and the datagram and virtual circuit models. Network operating systems are examined as well as the primitive operations required to service them—user communication, job migration, data migration, and control primitives. The popular network organizations are examined including the star, ring, and mesh topologies. Notions of security, privacy, encryption, and authentication are discussed; this is preliminary to the more detailed presentation in Chapter 17. Local networking is considered in depth; the techniques of CSMA/CD, token passing, and message slots are explained. The operation of Ethernet is discussed. The chapter ends with a case study of Digital Equipment Corporation's DECnet and its DNA (Digital Network Architecture). This case study emphasizes the functions and capabilities provided in a major network operating system, especially those of file handling and interprocess communication.

Chapter 17 deals with computer security and its importance in operating systems. The chapter discusses security requirements, the need for a total approach to security, external security, operational security, surveillance, threat monitoring, amplification, password protection, auditing, access controls, security kernels, hardware security, and survivable systems. It continues with a detailed discussion of the capabilities-based, object-oriented systems that are receiving so much attention today as the means for achieving systems that afford greater security. A case study is presented on the object-oriented architecture of the IBM System/38. Cryptography is discussed; a cryptographic privacy system is illustrated; cryptanalysis, public key systems, digital signatures, and the DES and RSA schemes are explained; numerous applications of cryptography are listed. The DES standards document published by the United States Government is included as an appendix to the text. Operating system penetration is considered in depth; generic system functional flaws and generic operating system attacks are categorized. The chapter concludes with a case study examining the successful penetration of an existing operating system.

Part Eight presents five detailed case studies on important operating systems, namely, the UNIX system, VAX/VMS, CP/M, MVS, and VM. The body of the text discusses general principles; the case studies deal with the real issues of real operating systems.

Chapter 18 discusses the UNIX operating system developed by Bell Laboratories. The UNIX system has been nothing less than a phenomenon of its time. It was developed primarily by two people for their own use. Now it is used in universities and industrial environments throughout the world. Versions developed for personal computers are becoming quite popular; some enthusiasts believe the UNIX system will eventually displace CP/M as the de facto standard personal computer operating system. (This issue is investigated further in Chapter 20.) The case study includes a discussion of the interesting UNIX input/output system, and the UNIX-originated concepts of pipes and filters. Within the UNIX system case study is another case study on Microsoft's XENIX system—a version of the UNIX system developed for 16-bit microcomputers. Microsoft supplies a XENIX-like system for the IBM Personal Computer.

Chapter 19 discusses Digital Equipment Corporation's top-of-the-line operating system, VAX/VMS. VAX extends the 16-bit architecture of DEC's successful PDP-11 series into the realm of today's popular 32-bit virtual storage systems. The case study focuses on storage management, process scheduling, input/output, record management services, interprocess communication, and process synchronization. VAX is quite typical of today's efforts by minicomputer manufacturers to produce systems that challenge the power of large mainframe systems. Major portions of the VAX case study are based upon *Computer Programming and Architecture: The VAX-11* by H. M. Levy and R. H. Eckhouse, Jr., Digital Press, 1980, and *VAX-11 Software Handbook*, Digital Equipment Corporation, 1981. The author is grateful for permission granted to use these materials.

Chapter 20 discusses Digital Research's CP/M operating system for microcomputers. Initially developed for the 8-bit micros that served at the heart of early personal computers like Radio Shack's TRS-80 Model I, CP/M has been extended considerably to compete in the 16-bit arena—it is offered as CP/M-86 for the 16-bit IBM Personal Computer. The case study discusses PL/M, portability, table-driven systems, memory allocation, logical-to-physical device mapping, the Console Command Processor (CCP), the Basic Input/Output System (BIOS), the Basic Disk Operating System (BDOS), and the file system. The chapter includes two case-studies-within-case-studies: one on MP/M, a multiuser CP/M-based timesharing system, and one on CP/NET, a networking system for CP/M-based and MP/M-based microcomputers.

Chapter 21 discusses IBM's top-of-the-line operating system, MVS, designed for very large-scale processors. The chapter traces the history of IBM operating systems development since the announcement of the System/360. Important aspects of IBM hardware architecture are reviewed. Then, many aspects of MVS are examined in detail—MVS functions, the Supervisor, the Master Scheduler, the Job Entry Subsystem, the System Management Facility, the System Activity Measurement Facility, the Timesharing Option, data management, the Real Storage Manager, the Auxiliary Storage Manager, the Virtual Storage Manager, the System Resources Manager, storage organization, resource control, locking, Enqueue, Reserve, tasks, service requests, multiprocessing, performance, and monitoring system activity.

Chapter 22 discusses what is perhaps the most "exotic" of the operating systems in the case studies, namely IBM's VM virtual machine operating system. It enables one computer system to execute several operating systems simultaneously. This capability allows an installation to run dramatically different operating systems at once, or to run different versions of the same system—perhaps allowing a new release to be tested while a production system continues operation. VM has particularly interesting ramifications in networking, as is evidenced by IBM's Hydra concept and Spartacus Computers' Kangaroo (*Datamation*, August 1981). The chapter discusses the history of VM, the Control Program (CP), demand paging, minidisks, console management, user privilege classes, the VM directory, the Conversational Monitor System (CMS), the Remote Spooling and Communications System, performance considerations, the Virtual Machine Assist Feature, the Extended Control Program Support Feature, performance measurement, performance analysis, reliability, availability, and serviceability. The case study ends with a discussion of why VM may emerge as IBM's banner operating system for large-scale processors for the mid-to-late 1980s.

The richness of the case studies provides the material for comparing and contrasting the different design and implementation philosophies used in contemporary operating systems. The case studies span the full range from "tiny" operating systems like CP/M to massive systems like MVS. They include mainframe operating systems like MVS and VM, minicomputer operating systems like VAX/VMS and UNIX, and microcomputer operating systems like CP/M and XENIX. They include real storage systems and virtual storage systems, real machine systems and virtual machine systems, single user systems and multiuser systems, stand-alone systems, multiprocessing systems, and networked systems.

It is a pleasure to acknowledge the many people who have contributed to this project. The most important acknowledgment is to the hundreds of authors represented in the literature sections in the chapters; their fine papers and texts have provided the diversity of interesting material that makes operating systems such a fascinating area. The book was reviewed by experts in many fields. The core of the review team consisted of James Peterson of the University of Texas at Austin, Richard Wexelblatt of Sperry Univac, Paul Ross of Millersville State College, and Anthony Lucido of Intercomp.

The sections of the book dealing with computer hardware, microprogramming, and computer security were reviewed by Steve Paris of Prime Computer. Bart Guerreri, president of DSD Laboratories, contributed considerable hardware expertise. Nathan Tobol, consulting engineer for Codex Corporation and chairman of the IEEE 802 Local-Area Networking subcommittee, reviewed Chapter 16, Network Operating Systems, and contributed valuable material from one of his forthcoming papers. Larry Nelson, Chief of Systems Support at AVCO Services, contributed most of the material in the MVS case study, and provided many useful insights into VM. Barry Shein, who administered UNIX and VAX systems for Harvard University, contributed many useful suggestions that helped me refine those case studies. William Blocher, president of The Bit Bucket, provided insights on CP/M.

Eliezer Gafni of MIT, and Anat Gafni and Josefina Bondoc of Boston University scrupulously examined Chapter 15, on Analytic Modeling; the material on queueing theory and Markov processes was polished considerably by the incorporation of their numerous suggestions.

Others who provided assistance and inspiration throughout the writing effort were Julius Zigman, Miriam Zigman, Stephanie Guerreri, Eric Shoemaker, Mary Wiles, Steven Broderick, Richard Miles, and Shirley Spas.

My production editor, William Yskamp of Addison-Wesley, has done an impeccable job bringing this book to publication. His dedication to the project never wavered, his influence on the form and style of the finished product was truly substantial, and his leadership was critical to the timely publication of the text.

My wife, Barbara, and my children, Paul and Abbey, provided the incredible support and understanding without which this text could never have come to fruition. They collectively contributed 2000 hours of researching, sorting, copying, word processing, and proofreading. Their efforts helped me trim one year from the writing schedule for the text.

William B. Gruener, Executive Editor, the computer sciences, Addison-Wesley Publishing Company, has been my mentor in publishing since 1978. Bill is truly responsible for the fact that this book happened. He and Addison-Wesley placed impressive resources at my disposal. I hope this work merits the trust and confidence they have shown in me.

Any effort of this scope is bound to have its flaws. I assume complete responsibility for any remaining defects. I am currently researching and writing the next edition of this work, and would be most grateful for your comments, criticisms, and corrections. Any correspondence should be sent to Harvey M. Deitel (author), c/o Computer Science Editor, Addison-Wesley Publishing Company, Reading, Mass. 01867. I will acknowledge all correspondence immediately.

H. M. D.

Framingham, Massachusetts
August 1983

Contents

PART 2
PROCESS MANAGEMENT

CHAPTER 3
PROCESS CONCEPTS 53

CHAPTER 4
ASYNCHRONOUS CONCURRENT PROCESSES 73

CHAPTER 5
CONCURRENT PROGRAMMING: MONITORS; THE ADA RENDEZVOUS 101

PART 7
NETWORKS AND SECURITY

CHAPTER 16
NETWORK OPERATING SYSTEMS 415

CHAPTER 17
OPERATING SYSTEMS SECURITY 445

PART 8
CASE STUDIES

CHAPTER 18
CASE STUDY: UNIX SYSTEMS 479

CHAPTER 19
CASE STUDY: VAX 505

CHAPTER 20
CASE STUDY: CP/M 535

ABOUT THE AUTHOR

Dr. Harvey M. Deitel has 22 years experience in the computer field. He participated in the research and development of several large-scale operating systems and in the design and implementation of numerous commercial systems. He received the Bachelor of Science and Master of Science Degrees from the Massachusetts Institute of Technology where he did extensive development work on the Multics operating system. He received the Doctor of Philosophy Degree from Boston University where his dissertation research examined the problems of developing very large-scale, structured software systems.

Since 1965, Dr. Deitel has been interested in operating systems. He worked on the teams that developed IBM's OS, IBM's TSS, and M.I.T.'s Multics. He has consulted for Epson, Advanced Computer Techniques Corporation, Computer Usage Corporation, Harbridge House, Inc., American Express, IBM Systems Development Division, IBM Advanced Systems Development Division, IBM Thomas J. Watson Research Center, M.I.T.'s Project MAC, and numerous energy and real estate companies.

Dr. Deitel is currently on the Computer Science Faculty of Boston College where he teaches courses in systems programming, computer architecture, operating systems, software engineering, and computer networking. He has received numerous teaching commendations, and has been rated nationally among the top computing teachers in the country.

Dr. Deitel is a member of several professional honoraries including Tau Beta Pi, Eta Kappa Nu, and Sigma Xi. He holds the CDP Certification of the Institute for the Certification of Computer Professionals, and is a member of various professional societies including the Association for Computing Machinery, and the Computer Society of the Institute of Electrical and Electronics Engineers.

Dr. Deitel's publications include *Absentee Computations in a Multiple-Access Computer System,* MAC-TR-52 1968 Advanced Research Projects Agency, Department of Defense; *Introduction to Computer Programming with the BASIC Language,* Prentice-Hall, 1977; *Structured Software Development,* Ph.D. dissertation published by University Microfilms, 1980; *Operating Systems* (with Harold Lorin of the IBM Systems Research Institute), Addison-Wesley, 1980, and "Functions of Operating Systems," (with Harold Lorin) *Software World,* Vol. 12, No. 2, pp. 2–13, 1981.

An Introduction to Operating Systems

Revised First Edition

Part 1
Overview

1
Introduction*

The last thing one knows in constructing a work is what to put first.

Blaise Pascal

"Where shall I begin, please your Majesty?" he asked. "Begin at the beginning," the King said, gravely, "and go on till you come to the end: then stop."

Alice's Adventures in Wonderland,
Lewis Carroll

A morsel of genuine history is a thing so rare as to be always valuable.

Thomas Jefferson

*This chapter incorporates several facts and ideas from N. Weizer, "A History of Operating Systems," *Datamation*® magazine (January 1981).

Outline

1.1 OPENING REMARKS

Only a few people who will read this text can recall a time when there were no operating systems. Operating systems today are used on computers ranging in size from giant *mainframes* to small *personal computers.* Operating systems often shape the user's view of a computer even more than the hardware itself. In the personal computing field, for example, the *CP/M®* operating system (see Chapter 21) has become a de facto standard, and a very large number of computer manufacturers build hardware to support CP/M. The user sees the hardware's packaging such as the CRT and the keyboard, but the functional view is provided by CP/M.*

In the 1960s one might have defined operating system as the *software that controls the hardware.* But today there is a significant trend for functions to migrate from software into *firmware,* i.e., *microcode* (see Chapter 2). This trend has become so pronounced that it is likely the functions coded in firmware may soon exceed those in software on some systems.

It is clear that a better definition of operating system is needed. *We view an operating system as the programs, implemented in either software or firmware, that make the hardware usable. Hardware provides "raw computing power." Operating systems make this power conveniently available to users.* They also manage the hardware carefully to achieve good performance (see Part 6 of the text).

However we choose to define them, operating systems are an integral part of the computing environment, and they must be understood to some degree by every computer user.

Some of the operating systems available today consume a very large part of a computer's resources as they function. Some users view this as a conspiracy by hardware manufacturers to sell more hardware. In fact, most hardware manufacturers view operating systems as a necessary evil without which their hardware would not sell at all. These views are being tempered somewhat by the availability of microprocessor-based systems and personal computers with relatively simple operating systems. Instead of providing only the all-encompassing, large-scale, general-purpose operating systems the industry thought necessary in the 1960s and early 1970s, vendors (and independents) now also supply simpler operating systems that provide convenient computing environments meeting the specific needs of individual users.

An operating system is primarily a resource manager, and the primary resource it manages is computer hardware. It provides many features including

- defining the "user interface"
- sharing the hardware among users
- allowing users to share data among themselves

---

*CP/M® is a Registered Trademark of Digital Research.

- scheduling resources among users
- facilitating input/output
- recovering from errors

The key resources an operating system manages are

- processors
- storage
- input/output devices
- data

The operating system interfaces with

- computer operators
- applications programmers
- systems programmers
- administrative personnel
- programs
- hardware
- users (such as bank tellers)

Users are the customers in a computing environment who utilize the computer to perform useful work. *Computer operators* are people charged with the responsibility of monitoring the operating system, responding to requests for intervention, mounting and dismounting tapes and disks, loading and unloading cards, making sure that the right forms are placed on printers and that the forms are properly aligned, etc. Operators are integral to the smooth operation of a system. They provide those functions that have not as yet been automated.

Systems programmers are generally concerned with maintaining the operating system, tailoring it to the needs of the installation, and modifying it to support new types of devices.

Systems administrators are people who set policy and interface with the operating system to ensure that those policies are properly implemented.

Programs interface with operating systems via special instructions variously called *supervisor calls, monitor calls, executive requests,* etc. These instructions allow the users to obtain services from the operating system without compromising its integrity.

The operating system is generally given the status of *most trusted user.* It is allowed to access all features of the hardware, all user programs and data, etc. In some systems, portions of the operating system are less trusted because the people and programs with access to these portions do not require carte blanche access, and so it is best not to give it to them (see Chapter 17).

1.2 GENERATIONS OF OPERATING SYSTEMS

Operating systems, like computer hardware, have undergone a series of revolutionary changes called *generations.* In computer hardware, generations have been marked by major advances in componentry from vacuum tubes (first generation), to transistors (second generation), to integrated circuitry (third generation), to large-scale and very large-scale integrated circuitry (fourth generation). The successive hardware generations have each been accompanied by dramatic reductions in costs, size, heat emission, and energy consumption, and by dramatic increases in speed and storage capacity.

1.2.1 The Zeroth Generation (1940s)

Early computing systems had no operating system. Users had complete access to the machine language. They hand-coded all instructions.

1.2.2 The First Generation (1950s)

The operating systems of the 1950s were designed to smooth the transition between jobs. Before the systems were developed, a great deal of time was lost between the completion of one job and the initiation of the next. This was the beginning of *batch processing systems* in which jobs were gathered in groups or *batches.* Once a job was running, it had total control of the machine. As each job terminated (either normally or abnormally), control was returned to the operating system that "cleaned up after the job" and read in and initiated the next job.

1.2.3 The Second Generation (Early 1960s)

The second generation of operating systems was characterized by the development of shared systems with *multiprogramming* (see Chapter 7), and the beginnings of *multiprocessing* (see Chapter 11). In multiprogramming systems several user programs are in main storage at once and the processor is switched rapidly between the jobs. In multiprocessing systems, several processors are used on a single computer system to increase the processing power of the machine.

Device independence began to appear. In first generation systems, a user wishing to write data on tape had to reference a particular tape drive specifically. In second generation systems, the user program specified only that a file was to be written on a tape drive with a certain number of tracks and a certain density. The operating system located an available tape drive with the desired characteristics and instructed the operator to mount a tape on that drive.

Timesharing systems were developed in which users could interface directly with the computer through typewriterlike *terminals.* Timesharing systems operate in an *interactive or conversational mode* with users. The user types a request to the computer, the computer processes the request as soon as it can (often within a second or less), and a response (if any) is typed on the user's terminal. Conversational computing made possible great strides in the program development process. A timesharing user could locate and correct errors in seconds or minutes, rather than suffering the delays, often hours or days, in batch processing environments.

Real-time systems emerged in which computers were used to control industrial processes such as gasoline refining. Military real-time systems were developed to monitor thousands of points at once for possible enemy air attacks. *Real-time systems are characterized by supplying immediate response.* For example, a measurement from a gasoline refinery indicating that temperatures are getting too high might demand immediate attention to avert an explosion. *Real-time systems are often heavily underutilized—it is far more important for such systems to be available when needed and to respond quickly than it is for them to be busy a large portion of the time. This fact helps explain their great cost.*

1.2.4 The Third Generation (Mid-1960s to Mid-1970s)

The third generation of operating systems effectively began with the introduction of the IBM System/360 family of computers in 1964. Third generation computers were designed to be *general-purpose systems.* They were large, often ponderous, systems purporting to be all things to all people. The concept sold a lot of computers, but it took its toll. Users running particular applications that did not require this kind of power payed heavily in increased run-time overhead, learning time, debugging time, maintenance, etc.

Third generation operating systems were *multimode systems.* Some of them simultaneously supported batch processing, timesharing, real-time processing, and multiprocessing. *They were large and expensive. Nothing like them had ever been constructed before, and many of the development efforts finished well over budget and long after scheduled completion.* (A notable exception to this is the UNIX system developed at Bell Laboratories. UNIX systems are discussed in depth in Chapter 18.)

These systems introduced to computer environments a greater complexity—a complexity to which users were, at first, unaccustomed. The systems interposed a *software layer* between the user and the hardware. This software layer was often so thick that a user lost sight of the hardware and saw only the view created by the software. To get one of these systems to perform the simplest useful task, users had to become familiar with complex *job control languages* to specify the jobs and their resource requirements. Third generation operating systems represented a great step forward, but a painful one for many users.

1.2.5 The Fourth Generation (Mid-1970s to Present)

Fourth generation systems are the current state of the art. (See the case studies in Chapters 18 through 22.) Many designers and users are still smarting from their experiences with third generation operating systems and are careful before getting involved with complex operating systems.

With the widespread use of *computer networking* (see Chapter 16) and *on-line processing,* users gain access to networks of geographically dispersed computers through various types of terminals. The microprocessor has made possible the development of the personal computer, one of the most important developments of social consequence in the last several decades. Now many users have dedicated computer systems available for their own use at any time of the day or night. Computer power that cost hundreds of thousands of dollars in the early 1960s is now available for less than a thousand dollars.

Personal computers are often equipped with data communications interfaces, and also serve as terminals. The user of a fourth generation system is no longer confined to communicating with a single computer in a timeshared mode. Rather the user may communicate with geographically dispersed systems. Security problems have increased greatly with information now passing over various types of vulnerable communications lines (see Chapter 17). *Encryption* is receiving much attention—it has become necessary to encode highly proprietary or personal data so that, even if the data is compromised, it is of no use to anyone other than the intended receivers (or possessors of the *decryption keys*).

The percentage of the population with access to computers in the 1980s is far greater than ever before and growing rapidly. It is common to hear the term *user friendly* denoting systems that give users of average intelligence easy access to computer power. The highly symbolic, mnemonic, acronym-oriented user environments of the 1960s and 1970s are being replaced in the 1980s by *menu-driven* systems that guide the user through various options expressed in simple English.

The concept of *virtual machines* (see Chapter 22) has become widely used. The user is no longer concerned with the physical details of the computer systems (or network) being accessed. Instead the user sees a view called a virtual machine created by the operating system. Today's user is more concerned with accomplishing work with a computer, and is generally not interested in the internal functioning of the machine.

Database systems have gained central importance. Ours is an information-oriented society, and the job of database systems is to make information conveniently accessible in a controlled fashion to those who have a right to access it. Thousands of on-line databases have become available for access via terminals over communications networks.

The concept of *distributed data processing* (see Chapter 16) has become firmly entrenched. We are now concerned with bringing the computer power to the site at which it is needed, rather than bringing the data to some central computer installation for processing.

1.3 EARLY HISTORY OF OPERATING SYSTEMS

The General Motors Research Laboratories are credited with implementing the first operating system in the early 1950s for their IBM 701. In 1955, GM and North American Aviation cooperated in the production of an operating system for the

IBM 704. The IBM user organization, SHARE, fostered discussion on operating systems, and by 1957 many home-grown operating systems for the 704 had been developed.

These early operating systems were concerned mostly with reducing time ordinarily wasted while jobs were placed on a computer system (*setup time*) and removed from the computer system (*teardown time*). Before these systems were developed, jobs were individually loaded, usually from cards, and occupied the entire machine for their duration. Each job would either run to completion or terminate because of some error situation. An operator would then load a program to dump memory, and would remove tapes, cards, and printed outputs. Eventually, the next job would be loaded, and the cycle would start again. While jobs were being set up or torn down, the system sat idle.

The earliest operating systems tried to minimize this idle time by smoothing job-to-job transitions. These systems achieved their performance improvements by processing jobs in groups or batches rather than individually. Jobs were loaded to tape, often by a small *satellite computer,* and then processed on a large machine. As each job finished, it would branch back to a location in the operating system causing the next job to be loaded. This greatly reduced job-to-job transition time.

The concept of *system file names* emerged in early operating systems as a means of achieving some degree of device independence. The user no longer had to *hard code* physical device numbers, but could now refer to the *standard system input file* as the place from which control cards were read, or the *standard system output file* as the device that printed outputs. Standard file names made it possible to smooth the transition from assemblers and compilers to the linkers and loaders that processed their outputs.

By the late 1950s, the major computer vendors were supplying operating systems with the following characteristics.

- single stream batch processing
- standard input/output routines so that users did not have to be concerned with the messy details of machine-level coding of the input and output processes
- program-to-program transition capabilities to reduce the overhead involved in starting a new job
- error recovery techniques that automatically "cleaned up" after a job terminated abnormally and allowed the next job to be initiated with minimal operator intervention
- job control languages that allowed users to specify much of the detail for defining their jobs and the resources the jobs required

Operating systems were generally used on large systems in these years. Many of the smaller commercial systems such as the IBM 1400 series functioned without an operating system. It was common for users of these small systems to load their own *IOCS (input/output control system*), a small package of routines to facilitate input/output operations. Actually, IOCS as run on these early systems was the beginning of the operating system as we know it today. Some early operating systems functions were designed to get better utilization of the hardware, but IOCS packages were designed to make programming easier by reducing the amount of time needed to write complex input/output routines. In today's operating systems, a far greater emphasis is placed on making programmers and users more productive, especially because of the fact that labor represents a much larger portion of the total cost of today's systems than hardware does.

1.4 DEVELOPMENTS OF THE EARLY 1960s

In the early 1960s, vendors began supplying operating systems with much more powerful capabilities. Some of the competitors of the time were

- Bendix
- Burroughs
- Control Data Corporation
- General Electric
- Honeywell
- IBM
- NCR
- Philco
- RCA
- Sperry Univac

The operating systems of this period were batch-oriented and were concerned mostly with improving *throughput* (i.e., work processed per unit time) on expensive hardware. Multiprogramming was commonly employed in which several programs were resident in primary storage at once, and the processor was rapidly switched between programs. *The key to the success of the multiprogramming concept as a means of increasing system throughput is the mismatch in speeds between input/output devices and the processor.* A program that generates an input/output request and cannot proceed until the I/O completes caused a single user dedicated system's processor to sit idle waiting for the I/O. This was a waste of the most precious resource of the system, and often the system might lose 50,000 processor cycles while it idled waiting for the I/O to complete. Designers realized that by keeping several programs in primary storage at once these processor cycles could be put to use by switching the processor to another program ready to execute (and not waiting for input/output completion).

Multiprocessing systems (see Chapter 11) emerged in which several processors cooperate, sometimes as independent computer systems communicating with one another, and sometimes as multiple processors sharing a common memory. Such systems were capable of increasing throughput over the single CPU versions.

One of the most significant developments of this period was the implementation and successful operation of the American Airlines SABRE reservations system. It was the first major *transaction processing system* in which users from remote locations communicated with the central computer system via typewriter terminals. Transaction processing systems involve a dialog between the user and the computer system in which the user makes relatively simple requests (like "Is a seat available on today's flight 404?") and the computer responds quickly. Such user terminals are said to be *on-line* (directly connected) to the computer.

Transaction processing systems introduced a whole new series of considerations into operating systems. Now computers had to operate conversationally with their users, and thus human factors issues like response times and the *user friendliness* of the interface became important. Rather than merely processing one or a few batch jobs at once, computers had to respond quickly to requests coming from possibly hundreds or even thousands of terminals at diverse locations. *Direct access storage organizations* (see Chapters 12 and 13) received much attention as a means of referencing data quickly. Interfacing with telephone lines and higher-speed data communication links became important. The marriage of computers and communications may very well have been the most significant development of the period.

In 1963, Burroughs released its Master Control Program operating system (MCP) for its B5000 system that contained many features now commonly provided in today's systems.

- multiprogramming
- multiprocessing
- virtual storage
- operating system written in a high-level language
- source language debugging capability

1.5 THE IBM SYSTEM/360 FAMILY OF COMPUTERS

In April 1964, IBM announced its System/360 series of computers, *probably the most significant event in the history of operating systems.*

Computer users of the period seemed to have an insatiable hunger for more and more capability. As they outgrew each system, they were forced to move up to a more powerful system, often of a completely different design and operating system. The conversions between systems were slow, awkward, and plagued with the problems of incompatibility.

Recognizing these problems, IBM designed the System/360 series of computers to be architecturally compatible, to use the same operating system (OS/360), and to offer greater computer power as the user moved upward in the series. This *family concept of computers* has become permanently embedded in the industry. Once a user was committed to the 360 series, it was possible to stay with it for many years. The obvious problem was how to get users to commit themselves to the 360 series in the first place because these machines were incompatible with other systems of the period.

IBM solved this problem by providing the largest assortment of machine *simulators* and *emulators* ever assembled. Simulators and emulators make one computer appear to be another. For example, a user of an IBM 1401 could now switch easily to the 360 by running 1401 programs directly on the 360 as if the 360 were a 1401. Simulators are primarily software-driven: emulators actually contain hardware modifications. Simulators generally are very slow but relatively economical to produce. Emulators cost more to produce but can run the old programs much faster. Users were thus able to switch to the 360 equipment immediately, and could convert their programs to 360 format at their convenience.

Even though the 360 series did not include some of the more advanced features that other manufacturers like Burroughs were already supplying, it did excel in one very important area, namely *customer support.* The simulators and emulators were convenient for the customers, and OS/360 contained the largest array of *utility programs* ever supplied for facilitating computer usage.

1.6 INDUSTRY REACTION TO THE SYSTEM/360

The shock of the 360 announcement sent the other computer manufacturers back to their drawing boards. Their managers and planners knew that they had to develop strategies to compete with this major development.

One strategy was literally to copy the 360 architecture and provide operating systems similar to OS/360, and then to sell these systems at a much lower cost than IBM was charging. This strategy was followed domestically by RCA with its Spectra/70 series. Industrial giants Siemans in Germany and Hitachi in Japan also followed this approach.

These vendors believed that they would be able to draw customers from IBM's huge customer base. But their strategy failed. In fact, RCA failed so spectacularly that it soon exited the computer industry and took a $500,000,000 tax writeoff, the largest such loss in corporate history up to that time. Why did RCA's apparently clever strategy fail? RCA, though a huge and respected company, did not command credibility among computer circles in which conservative bankers and data processing management had to make the commitment decisions. Also, RCA discovered the task of duplicating OS/360 and its associated programs to be almost impossible. RCA was able to copy the hardware but greatly underestimated how difficult and costly the production of an OS/360-like operating system would be. RCA's operating system was in some ways superior to OS/360, but the system's reliability was poor and RCA did not provide good customer support.

Another strategy of the period, used by vendors such as Burroughs and General Electric, was to develop products that were not compatible with the 360 series but that were more powerful and more cost effective. This strategy, too, sounded good. However, developing the products turned out to be a more formidable task than GE had anticipated and that company soon followed RCA out of the industry.

Some of the manufacturers of the time adopted a more conservative strategy. They developed improved systems more like IBM's older 1400 and 7000 lines. These vendors hoped to attract IBM customers who wanted to avoid the difficult conversion to the 360. Univac and Control Data were moderately successful in attracting some of IBM's 7000 line customers. Honeywell attracted many previous 1400 line users.

IBM's hope for a single operating system for its 360 series was frustrated by the varying degrees of sophistication among its users. Small computer users did not want a complex operating system with an endless array of features. In fact the smaller systems suffered severe performance degradation under OS/360.

Larger users demanded more functions and capabilities. Their powerful hardware was able to support more operating system. So instead of the single operating system, OS/360, IBM ultimately delivered four major systems during the 1960s.

- DOS/360 for the smaller 360s
- OS/MFT for the medium and large 360s
- OS/MVT for the large 360s
- CP-67/CMS for the powerful 360/67 timesharing, virtual storage system

1.7 TIMESHARING SYSTEMS

In the late 1950s and early 1960s, researchers in industry and the universities developed a number of timesharing systems. These systems allow several users to converse with a computer directly from terminals. They differ from the transaction processing systems such as the American Airlines SABRE system in that they are actually general-purpose computer systems. They provide users with a full range of computing capabilities. Timesharing users generally spend most of their time developing programs, or running specially designed applications packages.

Perhaps the most significant timesharing system of the era was CTSS (the Compatible Time-Sharing System) developed at the Massachusetts Institute of Technology by a government funded research group called Project MAC. CTSS ran on an IBM 7094 with specially modified hardware. It supported a large number of interactive users from 1961 through the late 1960s. *It proved the value of timesharing systems in the support of program development activities, and revealed the tremendous impact that sharing of programs and data among users had on the productivity and creativity of computing communities.*

The proof of the value of timesharing in a program development environment came at M.I.T. as CTSS was used to implement M.I.T.'s next generation timesharing system, namely Multics (for Multiplexed Information and Computing Service). Multics was a joint effort by M.I.T.'s Project MAC, Bell Laboratories, and General Electric (later Honeywell) to develop a large-scale, general-purpose, timesharing computer utility based upon the *virtual storage* concept. One notable aspect of the Multics system was that it was written largely in a high-level language, EPL, an early version of IBM's PL/I. Programs were maintained and edited on the CTSS system and sent to the GE-645 for execution.

A number of such systems were developed by many groups during the mid to late 1960s. These included

- Multics
- IBM's TSS for the 360/67
- IBM's CP-67/CMS also for the 360/67
- RCA's VMOS
- CDC's KRONOS for its 6000 series

These projects helped researchers gain important insights into the use and management of virtual storage. But the projects were of more developmental interest than they were commercial successes. The TSS system, for example, proved to be a costly, but valuable, learning experience for IBM.

1.8 THE EMERGENCE OF A NEW FIELD: SOFTWARE ENGINEERING

Many operating systems were developed during the 1960s. They were huge conglomerations of software written by people who really didn't understand that software, as well as hardware, had to be engineered to be reliable, understandable, and maintainable. Endless hours and countless dollars were spent tracking bugs that should never have entered the systems in the first place. Errors in the earliest phases of the projects were not located until long after the products were delivered to customers. These errors were enormously expensive to correct. People turnover on the projects often resulted in large numbers of software modules being scrapped and then rewritten by new people because the existing modules couldn't be understood. So much attention was given to these problems that eventually computer scientists and industry people began devoting considerable resources to the problems of constructing software systems. This spawned the development of the field of *software engineering*.

Software engineering is now considered so important that most universities require it in computer systems curricula, and several degree programs have been instituted. The IEEE publishes a journal entitled *Transactions on Software Engineering*. Software developers are often given titles like software engineer, senior software engineer, etc. Doctoral dissertations have been written in the area (De80). The emergence of the field of software engineering and the recognition of the importance of developing a disciplined and structured approach to the construction of reliable, understandable, and maintainable software were truly fostered by the devastating experiences on many of the operating systems development efforts of the 1960s (Br75).

1.9 UNBUNDLING OF SOFTWARE AND HARDWARE

Through the early 1970s, computer vendors generally sold one type of product, namely hardware. Operating systems, support programs, applications systems, and documentation and educational manuals were often supplied to users at no (or nominal) charge. One interesting consequence of this was that the vendors tended to view software as a "giveaway" item, and refused to take much responsibility for its quality. Also, users receiving a vendor's software for free would rarely consider it worthwhile to purchase software from outside sources, or to expend time and money to develop home-grown versions.

As an interesting exercise, the reader might try to locate some of the vendor-written contracts from the late 1960s. These generally included precisely worded disclaimers placing the burden and consequences of using the software strictly on the users' shoulders.

Vendors published long lists of known bugs as a "courtesy" to their customers. Customers calling the vendor and complaining about a problem were occasionally chided that if they had looked in the known bug list they would have avoided using that feature in the first place.

In the early 1970s, IBM *unbundled* its software from its hardware. This meant that it charged separately for each, although it continued to supply some basic software at no charge. The consequences upon the industry were significant.

- Now it was much more difficult for computer vendors to insert the lengthy disclaimers in their contracts. Somehow, when you charge money for a product, the user seems to feel more strongly about that product functioning properly, and about your responsibility to ensure that it does so.
- An independent software industry was created almost overnight as a response to unbundling. If an independent vendor could supply software that was cheaper than IBM's and perhaps had more powerful features than IBM's software, then there was a real chance to sell non-IBM software to IBM customers.
- Other manufacturers followed suit and unbundling rapidly became industry-wide.
- Users were given a big incentive to shop around for their software with many competitive products available.
- An important consequence of unbundling was that vendors began designing their software more modularly so that it could be sold or licensed as individual units.
- The IBM-compatible computer market got a big boost. Many companies, called PCMs (for plug compatible mainframers) now copy IBM hardware. They produce models that are more powerful and cost less than corresponding IBM models. Users have a greater incentive to buy PCM computers now that they can obtain IBM software.

1.10 FUTURE TRENDS

A number of clear trends seem to be pointing the way to future systems.

- Computer hardware will continue to decline in price, while processor speeds increase, storage capacities increase, and the physical size of processors and memories decreases.

- The "scale of integration" will continue to increase with VLSI (very large-scale integration) moving to ULSI (ultra large-scale integration) over the next decade.
- Multiprocessing will become much more common.
- Many of the operating systems functions now performed by software will migrate into microcode.
- Hardware architectures of the future will distribute control into localized processors.
- Languages are being developed to exploit concurrency, and hardware and operating systems are being designed to execute concurrent programs more efficiently (see Chapters 3, 4, 5, 6, and 10).
- Massive parallelism will become common. It will become possible to execute parallel programs with great speed because of the very high degree of concurrency.
- Computers and their operating systems will be designed to foster the operation of virtual machines. Real machines will be hidden from the user.
- The family concept of computers as first introduced in the IBM 360 series will endure. Users will be able to run their applications on many different members of a family of computers, and these applications will see only virtual machines.
- As new generations of computers are introduced by the manufacturers, existing programs will run on the new equipment as is, or with nominal conversion effort.
- Developments in software engineering will result in operating systems that are more maintainable, reliable, and understandable.
- The cost of data communications will continue to decrease, and data transmission speeds will increase.
- Computers will be tied increasingly into networks, and work performed for a user may be done on a computer of which the user is unaware. This will continue to emphasize the importance of the views of virtual machines.
- The concept of virtual storage will endure.
- The previous view of an operating system as a resource manager will endure but the resources being managed will change. In particular, data will be viewed increasingly as a resource to be managed.
- The concept of distributed processing will cause the development of dispersed operating systems in which operating systems functions are distributed among many processors throughout large networks.
- Personal computers will become omnipresent. Utilization of the resource will mean less than its availability, reliability, flexibility, and "user friendliness."

SUMMARY

An operating system consists of programs implemented in either software or firmware that make the hardware usable. An operating system is primarily a resource manager; it manages processors, storage, input/output devices, and data.

Operating systems have envolved through a series of generations. The zeroth generation computer systems of the 1940s had no operating system. First generation systems of the 1950s had batch processing capabilities. Second generation systems of the early 1960s introduced multiprogramming, multiprocessing, device independence, timesharing, and real-time processing. Third generation systems of the mid 1960s to the mid 1970s were primarily general-purpose systems featuring multimode operation. They interposed a software layer between the hardware and the user. The current state of the art is fourth generation systems including computer networking, personal computers, virtual machine operating systems, database systems, and distributed data processing systems.

In 1964, IBM introduced its System/360 series of computers. The 360 family included a series of increasingly powerful computers. Users could begin with a small 360 and then easily convert to more powerful systems as their needs grew. IBM provided a vast array of simulators and emulators to help users convert to the 360s.

M.I.T.'s Project MAC was instrumental in developing timesharing systems, first with CTSS in the early 1960s, and then, with Multics in the late 1960s.

Many of the large operating systems development efforts of the 1960s experienced great difficulties. The abundance of problems in these projects led researchers to investigate the problems of constructing reliable, maintainable, and understandable software systems. This spawned the field of software engineering.

IBM's unbundling of software and hardware in the early 1970s led to a number of dramatic changes in the computer industry. For the most part, these changes fostered the development of better quality software, and increased competition. One group that benefited greatly from unbundling was the plug compatible mainframers.

Future trends include the continued decline in the cost of computing, movement from VLSI to ULSI components, increased multiprocessing, migration of operating systems functions from software to microcode, use of localized processors, further exploitation of concurrency, increased use of the virtual machine concept, continued use of the family concept, better software construction methodologies, decreased cost of data communications and increasing data transmission speeds, increased computer networking, continued use of the virtual storage concept, increasing emphasis on the importance of data, greater use of distributed processing, and the increasing availability of personal computers in our homes and businesses.

TERMINOLOGY

batch of jobs
batch processing
computer networking
computer operator
conversational mode
CP-67/CMS

CP/M
CTSS
database systems
decryption
device independence
direct access storage organization
distributed data processing
DOS/360
emulator
encryption
executive request
family of computers
firmware
first generation operating systems
fourth generation operating systems
General Motors Research Laboratories
general-purpose systems
generations
hard coding physical device numbers
IBM 701
IBM System/360
IEEE Transactions on Software Engineering
interactive mode
IOCS (input/output control system)
job control language
job-to-job transition
KRONOS
mainframe
Master Control Program (MCP)
menu-driven
microcode
M.I.T.'s Project MAC
monitor call
most trusted user
Multics
multimode systems
multiprocessing
multiprogramming
on-line processing
OS/MFT
OS/MVT
PCM (plug compatible mainframer)
personal computer
physical device numbers
real-time system
SABRE
satellite computer
second generation operating systems
setup time
SHARE
simulator
software engineering
software layer
standard system input file
standard system output file
supervisor call
system file names
systems administrator
systems programmer
teardown time
terminal
third generation operating systems
throughput
timesharing
transaction processing system
TSS 360/67
unbundling
user
user friendly
virtual machine
virtual storage
VMOS

EXERCISES

1.1 Why is the definition of operating system as "the software that controls the hardware" inadequate? Give a better definition.

1.2 List the various entities with which an operating system must interface. Briefly describe the nature of each of these interfaces.

1.3 What does it mean for the operating system to be granted the status of "most trusted user"?

1.4 Distinguish between multiprogramming and multiprocessing.

1.5 What is device independence? Why is it important to users?

1.6 Define, compare, and contrast each of the following terms.

a) on-line
b) real-time
c) timesharing
d) interactive computing
e) conversational computing
f) transaction processing

1.7 What is the software layer? How does it affect the user's view of a computer?

1.8 What does user friendly mean? Why is it important?

1.9 What were the primary goals of the earliest operating systems?

1.10 What are standard file names? Why are they useful?

1.11 What is the motivation for multiprogramming?

1.12 Give several reasons why IBM's System/360 was a significant development in the history of operating systems.

1.13 What are simulators and emulators? Which might you prefer to facilitate conversion between computer systems quickly and economically? Why might you prefer if you had to run large production runs on the new computer using the old computer's programs?

1.14 What major strategies were followed by IBM's competitors in reaction to the System/360 series?

1.15 When IBM originally announced the System/360, they hoped to deliver a single operating system, namely OS/360, that would run on all machines in the series. Why instead were they forced to deliver many operating systems?

1.16 The following systems were mentioned in this chapter. Briefly discuss the significance of each.

a) American Airlines SABRE
b) Burroughs Master Control Program
c) CP-67/CMS
d) CP/M
e) CTSS
f) DOS/360
g) IOCS
h) KRONOS
i) Multics
j) OS/360
k) OS/MFT
l) OS/MVT
m) TSS
n) VMOS

1.17 What factors led to the emergence of the field of software engineering?

1.18 What is unbundling? How did it change the computer industry?

1.19 List several trends pointing the way to future operating systems designs. How will each affect the nature of future systems.

1.20 State several key differences between personal computer operating systems and large computer operating systems.

LITERATURE

(Ba64) Barnett, N. L., and A. K. Fitzgerald, "Operating System for the 1410/7010," *Datamation,* May 1964.

(Bo64) Bouvard, J., "Operating System for the 800/1800," *Datamation,* May 1964.

(Br75) Brooks, F. P., Jr., *The Mythical Man-Month: Essays on Software Engineering,* Reading, Mass.: Addison-Wesley, 1975.

(Cr64) Crisman, P. A., et al. (eds.), *The Compatible Time-Sharing System,* Cambridge, Mass.: M.I.T. Press, 1964.

(Ct63) Critchlow, A. J., "Generalized Multiprocessing and Multiprogramming Systems," *Proc. AFIPS, FJCC,* Vol. 24, New York: Spartan Books, 1963, pp. 107–125.

(De80) Deitel, H. M., *Structured Software Development,* Ph.D. Dissertation, Boston University, May 1980.

(Gr77) Grosch, H. R. J., "The Way It Was in 1957," *Datamation,* September 1977.

(Me66) Mealy, G. H.; B. I. Witt; and W. A. Clark, "The Functional Structure of OS/360," *IBM Systems Journal,* Vol. 5, No. 1, 1966, pp. 3–51.

(My70) Meyer, R. A., and L. H. Seawright, "A Virtual Machine Time-Sharing System," *IBM Systems Journal,* Vol. 9, No. 3, 1970.

(Ol64) Oliphint, C., "Operating System for the B5000," *Datamation,* May 1964.

(Pa72) Parmelee, R. P., et al., "Virtual Storage and Virtual Machine Concepts," *IBM Systems Journal,* Vol. 11, No. 2, 1972.

(Ro67) Rosen, S., (ed.), *Programming Systems and Languages,* New York: McGraw-Hill, 1967.

(Ro69) Rosen, S., "Electronic Computers: A Historical Survey," *ACM Computing Surveys,* Vol. 1, No. 1, March 1969.

(Rn69) Rosin, R. F., "Supervisory and Monitor Systems," *ACM Computing Surveys,* Vol. 1, No. 1, March 1969.

(Sh59) The SHARE 709 System, *JACM,* Vol. 6, No. 2, April 1959, pp. 123–155.

(St64) Steel, T. B., Jr., "Operating Systems: An Introduction," *Datamation,* Vol. 10, No. 5, May 1964, pp. 26–28.

(We81) Weizer, N., "A History of Operating Systems," *Datamation,* January 1981, pp. 119–126.

2
Hardware, Software, Firmware

I have sacrificed time, health, and fortune, in the desire to complete these Calculating Engines. I have also declined several offers of great personal advantage to myself. But, notwithstanding the sacrifice of these advantages for the purpose of maturing an engine of almost intellectual power, and after expending from my own private fortune a larger sum than the government of England has spent on that machine, the execution of which it only commenced, I have received neither an acknowledgment of my labors, nor even the offer of those honors or rewards which are allowed to fall within the reach of men who devote themselves to purely scientific investigations. . . .

If the work upon which I have bestowed so much time and thought were a mere triumph over mechanical difficulties, or simply curious, or if the execution of such engines were of doubtful practicability or utility, some justification might be found for the course which has been taken; but I venture to assert that no mathematician who has a reputation to lose will ever publicly express an opinion that such a machine would be useless if made, and that no man distinguished as a civil engineer will venture to declare the construction of such machinery impracticable. . . .

And at a period when the progress of physical science is obstructed by that exhausting intellectual and manual labor, indispensable for its advancement, which it is the object of the Analytical Engine to relieve, I think the application of machinery in aid of the most complicated and abstruse calculations can no longer be deemed unworthy of the attention of the country. In fact, there is no reason why mental as well as bodily labor should not be economized by the aid of machinery.

Charles Babbage
Passage from the Life of a Philosopher

The units of which computers are made are getting smaller, shrinking beyond the range of ordinary microscopes into the infinities of the molecular world.

Christopher Evans

Software stands between the user and the machine.

Harlan D. Mills

Microprogramming is the implementation of hopefully reasonable systems through interpretation on unreasonable machines!

R.F. Rosin

Microprogramming an inefficient algorithm does not make it efficient.

Rauscher's Law

Outline

2.1 Introduction
2.2 Hardware
- **2.2.1** Storage Interleaving
- **2.2.2** Relocation Register
- **2.2.3** Interrupts and Polling
- **2.2.4** Buffering
- **2.2.5** Peripheral Devices
- **2.2.6** Storage Protection
- **2.2.7** Timers and Clocks
- **2.2.8** On-line and Off-line Operation; Satellite Processors
- **2.2.9** Input/Output Channels
- **2.2.10** Cycle Stealing
- **2.2.11** Base-plus-Displacement Addressing
- **2.2.12** Problem State, Supervisor State, Privileged Instructions
- **2.2.13** Virtual Storage
- **2.2.14** Multiprocessing
- **2.2.15** Direct Memory Access
- **2.2.16** Pipelining
- **2.2.17** Storage Hierarchy

2.3 Software
- **2.3.1** Machine Language Programming
- **2.3.2** Assemblers and Macro Processors
- **2.3.3** Compilers
- **2.3.4** Input/Output Control System (IOCS)
- **2.3.5** Spooling
- **2.3.6** Procedure-Oriented Languages vs. Problem-Oriented Languages
- **2.3.7** Quick-and-Dirty Compilers vs. Optimizing Compilers
- **2.3.8** Interpreters
- **2.3.9** Absolute and Relocating Loaders
- **2.3.10** Linking Loaders and Linkage Editors

2.4 Firmware

2.4.1 Horizontal and Vertical Microcode

2.4.2 Deciding What Functions to Implement in Microcode

2.4.3 Emulation

2.4.4 Microdiagnostics

2.4.5 Personalized Computers

2.4.6 Microcode Assists

2.4.7 Microprogramming and Operating Systems

2.4.8 Microprogramming: A Case Study

2.1 INTRODUCTION

In this chapter we consider hardware, software, and firmware. All of these contribute to the operation and control of computer systems. *Hardware* consists of the devices of a computer system—its processors, its storages, its input/output devices, and its communications connections. *Software* consists of the programs of machine language instructions and data that are interpreted by the hardware. Some common types of software are compilers, assemblers, loaders, linkage editors, linking loaders, user applications programs, database management systems, data communications systems, and operating systems. *Firmware* consists of microcode programs executed from very high-speed control storage. Commonly used object programs "burned" into read-only memories (ROMs and PROMs) are also sometimes called firmware. The last portion of this chapter discusses microprogramming and its importance in today's computer architectures and operating systems.

2.2 HARDWARE

In the next several sections various hardware items of importance to operating systems are discussed. The reader who needs more detail than is presented here should consult texts on computer architecture such as (Ba80) (Il82) and (Le80).

2.2.1 Storage Interleaving

Storage interleaving is used to speed the accessing of primary storage. Ordinarily while any one of the locations in a *primary storage bank* is being accessed, no other references may be in progress. Storage interleaving places adjacent storage locations in different storage banks so that multiple references may be in progress at the same time. Two-way interleaving, for example, would place the odd-numbered storage addresses in one storage bank and the even-numbered addresses in another. In simple sequential references to primary storage, locations are referenced in order. Thus storage interleaving allows several locations to be referenced at once as long as they are in different storage banks.

2.2.2 Relocation Register

A *relocation register* allows programs to be relocated dynamically. The base address of the program in primary storage is placed in the relocation register. The contents of the relocation register are added to each address developed by a running program. The user is able to program as if the user's program begins at location zero. At execution time, as the program runs, all address references involve the relocation register; this allows the program to reside in locations other than those which it was translated to occupy.

2.2.3 Interrupts and Polling

One technique for allowing a unit to check the status of another independently functioning unit is *polling*; the first unit checks whether the second is in a certain status—if it isn't, then the first unit proceeds with what it was doing. Polling can be a high-overhead operation.

Interrupts allow one unit to gain the immediate attention of another so that the first unit may report a status change. The interrupt causes the interrupted unit's *state* to be saved before the interrupt is processed. Then the interrupt is processed and the state of the interrupted unit is restored. Interrupts are discussed in detail in Chapter 3.

2.2.4 Buffering

A *buffer* is an area of primary storage for holding data during input/output transfers. As an input/output transfer progresses, its speed depends on many factors related to input/output hardware, but normally unrelated to processor operation. On input, for example, the data is placed in the buffer by an input/output channel; when the transfer is complete the data may be accessed by the processor.

With *single-buffered* input, the channel deposits data in a buffer, the processor processes that data, the channel deposits the next data, etc. While the channel is depositing data, no processing on that data may occur; while the data is being processed, no additional data may be deposited. A *double-buffering* system allows overlap of input/output operations with processing; while the channel is depositing data in one buffer, the processor may be processing the data in the other buffer. When the processor is finished processing the data in one buffer, it may process the data in the second buffer while the channel deposits new data back into the first buffer. This alternating use of the buffers is sometimes called *flip-flop buffering.* Communication between channels and processors will be discussed shortly.

2.2.5 Peripheral Devices

Peripheral devices allow the storage of massive amounts of information outside the primary storage of the computer. Tape drives are inherently *sequential devices* that read and write data on a long strip of magnetic tape. Tapes can be as long as 3600 feet on a 12-inch reel. Information may be recorded on tape at various *recording densities.* Early systems recorded 200 characters per inch (cpi) of tape, then 556 cpi became popular, then 800 cpi, then 1600 cpi, and now commonly 6250 cpi. Greater densities will certainly be supported in future systems.

Perhaps the most significant peripheral device as far as operating systems are concerned is the magnetic disk drive. Disks are *direct access devices*—they allow reference to individual data items without the need to search all data items on the disk in order. Early disk devices stored several million characters. Each of today's units stores as many as a billion characters. Units to be designed in the near future will provide even greater capacities. Chapters 12 and 13 examine the operation of disk storage and its importance to operating systems.

2.2.6 Storage Protection

Storage protection is essential in multiuser computer systems. It limits the range of addresses a program may reference. Storage protection may be implemented for a program in a contiguous block of storage locations by *bounds registers* that define the lower and upper addresses of the block of storage. As a program executes, all referenced storage addresses are checked to see that they are between the addresses in the bounds registers. Storage protection may also be implemented by the use of *storage protection keys* attached to areas in primary storage; a program may reference storage locations only in those areas with keys matching that program's key.

2.2.7 Timers and Clocks

An *interval timer* is useful in multiuser systems for preventing one user from monopolizing a processor. After a designated interval, the timer generates an interrupt to gain the attention of the processor; the processor may then be assigned to another user.

A *time-of-day clock* provides a means for the computer to keep track of *wall clock time* in increments as fine as or finer than millionths of a second.

2.2.8 On-line and Off-line Operation; Satellite Processors

Some peripherals have been equipped for either *on-line operation* in which they are connected to the processor or *off-line operation* in which they are run by control units not connected to the central computer system. *Off-line control units* are appealing because they make it possible to drive peripheral devices without placing a burden directly on the processor. Card-to-tape, tape-to-card, and tape-to-print operations are frequently performed by off-line units.

In 1959, IBM announced its 1401 "low-end" computer system (which eventually became the best-selling computer system of its time). The 1401 was a complete computer system supporting a wide variety of conventional peripheral devices. Interestingly, one of the most popular uses of the 1401 was handling off-line input/output operations for larger systems. In this mode of an operation, a computer is called a *satellite processor* or a *stand-alone processor.*

2.2.9 Input/Output Channels

As the computing demands placed on early systems increased, particularly in commercial data processing environments, systems tended to become input/output bound. While input/output was in progress, processors were tied up handling the

I/O. On some systems only a single input/output operation could be handled at once. An important improvement to modify this situation was the development of *I/O channels*. A channel is a special-purpose computer system devoted to handling input/output independently of the main processor of the computer system. A channel can access primary storage directly to store or retrieve information.

Early systems handled communication between processors and channels by processor instructions such as

- Branch if a channel is in operation.
- Wait until a channel command completes.
- Store contents of channel control registers into primary storage for subsequent interrogation by the processor.

In today's interrupt-driven systems, a processor executes a *startio* instruction to initiate an I/O transfer over a channel; the channel issues an *I/O completion interrupt* to inform a processor of the completion of an I/O operation.

The real significance of channels is that they greatly increase the amount of concurrent hardware activity possible on a computer, and they remove most of the burden of handling input/output from the processor.

A *selector channel* is used for high-speed data transfers between devices and primary storage. Selector channels have only a single *subchannel*; they can service only one device at a time.

Multiplexor channels have many subchannels; they can interleave many data streams at once. A *byte-multiplexor channel* interleaves the transmissions of slow devices such as terminals, card readers and punches, printers, and low-speed communications lines. A *block-multiplexor channel* interleaves the transmission of several high-speed devices such as laser printers and disk drives.

2.2.10 Cycle Stealing

One point of conflict between channels and the processor is the accessing of primary storage. Since only one access (to a primary storage bank) may be in progress at one time, and since it is possible for channels and the processor to want to access primary storage simultaneously, the channels are normally given priority. This is called *cycle stealing*; the channel literally steals storage cycles from the processor. The channels use only a small percentage of the cycles, but giving them priority in this manner causes better utilization of input/output devices. This type of logic has been transported into today's operating systems; I/O-bound programs are generally given priority over processor-bound programs by the operating system's scheduling mechanisms.

2.2.11 Base-plus-Displacement Addressing

As the need for larger primary storages became apparent, computer architectures were modified to accommodate a very large range of addresses. A system designed to support 16M bytes (M=1,048,576) would require 24-bit addresses. Incorporating such lengthy addresses into every instruction on a machine with single-address instructions would be costly; on a machine with multiple-address instructions it would be intolerable. So to achieve very large address ranges, systems use *base-plus-displacement addressing* in which all addresses are added to the contents of a *base register.* This scheme has the additional advantage of making programs *location-independent,* a particularly valuable property for programs in multiuser environments in which a program may have to be placed at different locations in primary storage each time it is loaded.

2.2.12 Problem State, Supervisor State, Privileged Instructions

Computer systems generally have several different *execution states.* Varying the state of a machine makes it possible to build more secure systems. Normally, when the machine is in a particular state only some subset of its instructions is executable by a running program. For user programs, the subset of instructions the user may execute in *problem state* precludes, for example, the direct execution of input/output instructions; a user program allowed to perform arbitrary input/output could dump the system's master list of passwords, print the information of any other user, or destroy the operating system. The operating system ordinarily runs with *most trusted user* status in a *supervisor state*; it has access to all of the instructions in the machine's instruction set. Such a problem state/supervisor state dichotomy has been adequate for most modern computing systems. In the case of highly secure systems, however, it is desirable to have more than two states. This allows a finer *granularity of protection.* It also allows access to be granted by the *principle of least privilege*: Any particular user should be granted the least amount of privilege and access that user needs to accomplish its designated tasks.

It is interesting that as computer architectures have evolved, the number of *privileged instructions,* i.e., those instructions not accessible in problem state, has tended to increase. This indicates a definite trend toward the incorporation of more operating systems functions in hardware. Some microprocessors already have complete operating systems in firmware; many have much operating system functionality in hardware.

2.2.13 Virtual Storage

Virtual storage systems allow programs to reference addresses that need not correspond to the real addresses available in primary storage. The virtual addresses developed by running programs are translated dynamically (i.e., at execution time) by the hardware into the addresses of instructions and data in primary storage. Virtual storage systems allow programs to reference address spaces much larger than the address spaces available in primary storage. They allow users to create programs independent (for the most part) of the constraints of primary storage, and they facilitate the operation of shared multiuser systems.

Virtual storage systems use the techniques of *paging* fixed-sized blocks of data back and forth between primary storage and secondary storage, and *segmentation* which identifies logical units of programs and data to facilitate access control and sharing. These techniques are sometimes used individually and are sometimes combined. Virtual storage systems are considered in Chapters 8 and 9.

2.2.14 Multiprocessing

In *multiprocessing* systems several processors share a common primary storage and a single operating system. Multiprocessing introduces the potential for certain types of conflicts that do not occur in uniprocessor systems. It is necessary to *sequentialize* access to a shared storage location so that two processors do not attempt to modify it at the same time, possibly scrambling its contents. Sequentialization is also necessary when one processor is attempting to modify a location and another wants to read it. Chapter 11 discusses these issues in depth. The case study on MVS in Chapter 21 explains how multiprocessing is handled in IBM's large-scale systems. Sequentialization is also necessary in uniprocessor systems. Chapters 3, 4, and 5 discuss this in detail.

2.2.15 Direct Memory Access (DMA)

One key to obtaining good performance in computer systems is minimizing the number of interrupts that occur while a program executes. *Direct Memory Access* (*DMA*) requires only a single interrupt for each block of characters transferred in an I/O operation. It is thus significantly faster than the method in which the processor is interrupted for each character transferred.

Once an I/O operation is initiated, characters are transferred to primary storage on a cycle stealing basis—the channel temporarily usurps the processor's path to storage while a character is being transferred; then the processor continues operation.

When a device is ready to transmit one character of the block, it "interrupts" the processor. But with DMA the processor's state does not have to be saved; the processor is more delayed than it is interrupted. Under the control of special hardware, the character is transferred to primary storage. When the transfer is complete, the processor resumes operation.

DMA is a performance feature particularly useful in systems that support a very large volume of I/O transfers. The hardware responsible for stealing cycles and operating the I/O devices in DMA mode is called a *DMA channel.*

2.2.16 Pipelining

Pipelining is a hardware technique used in high-performance computer systems to exploit certain types of parallelism in instruction processing. Quite simply, the processor is arranged very much like a production line in a factory; several instructions may be in different stages of execution simultaneously. This overlap requires more extensive hardware but it can greatly reduce the total execution time of a sequence of instructions.

2.2.17 Storage Hierarchy

Today's systems have several levels of storage including primary storage, secondary storage, and cache storage. Instructions and data must be placed in primary storage to be referenced by a running program. Secondary storage consists of tapes, disks, cards, and other media designed to hold information that will eventually be accessed in primary storage. Cache is very fast storage designed to increase the execution speed of running programs; it is generally transparent to user programs. On computer systems with cache storage, the current portion of a program is placed in cache where it can execute much faster than in primary storage. These levels of storage create a *storage hierarchy*; the various levels from cache, to primary, to secondary storage have decreasing cost and speed, and increasing capacity.

Storage is ordinarily divided into bytes (characters) or words (consisting of a fixed number of bytes). Each location in storage has an address; the set of all addresses available to a program is called an *address space.*

2.3 SOFTWARE

Software consists of the programs of instructions and data that define for the hardware the algorithms for solving problems. A huge variety of programming languages exists.

2.3.1 Machine Language Programming

Machine language is the programming language that a computer can understand directly. Each machine language instruction is interpreted by the hardware that performs the indicated functions. Machine language instructions have generally been quite primitive; it is the arrangement of these instructions into machine language programs that enables the specification of useful algorithms. Today's machine language instruction sets often include some very powerful capabilities. (See, for example, the case study on VAX in Chapter 19.)

Machine language is said to be *machine-dependent*; a machine language program written on one vendor's computer cannot ordinarily be run on another vendor's system unless its machine language is identical (or larger) than that of the first vendor's system. Another indication of machine dependence is the flavor of the instructions themselves; machine language instructions name specific registers of the computer system and process data in the physical form in which that data exists in that computer system. Most early computer systems were programmed directly in machine language; today very few programs are written in machine language.

2.3.2 Assemblers and Macro Processors

Machine language programming is time-consuming and error-prone. *Assembly languages* were developed to speed the programming process and reduce coding errors. Assembly languages use meaningful abbreviations and words to replace the strings of numbers used to write machine language programs. But assembly language programs are not directly understandable by computers. The programs must first be translated into machine language. This translation is performed by a program called an *assembler.*

Assembly languages are also machine-dependent. Their instructions correspond roughly one-to-one with the instructions in a machine language program. To speed the assembly program coding process, *macro processors* were developed and incorporated into assemblers. A *macro instruction* is written by a programmer to indicate the performance of a task that requires several assembly language instructions. When the macro instruction processor reads a macro during program translation, it performs a *macro expansion*—it generates a series of assembly language instructions corresponding to the macro instruction. The programming process is considerably speeded because the programmer writes fewer instructions to define the same algorithm.

2.3.3 Compilers

The trend to make instructions more powerful led to the development of some very sophisticated macro processors and macro languages to support assembly language programmers. But augmenting assemblers by adding macro processors still does not solve the problem of machine-dependence. This led to the development of *high-level languages.*

High-level languages allow users to write programs in a *machine-independent* manner. Most users are interested in the computer as a means for implementing applications systems. High-level languages let the users be concerned primarily with the problems unique to their applications; users are not even aware of any machine dependencies that may exist. This greatly speeds the programming process, makes programs transportable between systems of different vendors, and allows people to write useful applications systems without having to be thoroughly familiar with the internal structure of a computer system.

High-level languages are translated into machine language by programs called *compilers*. Both compilers and assemblers are generically referred to as *translators*. In the translation process, the user-written program that is input to the translator is called the *source program*; the machine language program produced by the translator is called the *object program* or the *target program*.

2.3.4 Input/Output Control System (IOCS)

The detailed channel programs, necessary to control input/output, and the various routines for coordinating the operation of channels and processors are complex. The development of a supervisory program for handling the complexities of input/output removed this burden from the applications programmer. This supervisory program is called the *input/output control system* (*IOCS*).

In the 1950s, users would actually include IOCS source code with their assembly language program statements. The IOCS package, already written and debugged, was actually reassembled as part of each individual program. However, this greatly lengthened program translation time. Therefore, on many systems *preassembled IOCS routines* were often used. The assembly language programmer wrote statements sensitive to the locations of key routines in the preassembled IOCS code.

Another problem with the IOCS concept was the fact that the complete IOCS package often occupied a significant portion of primary storage leaving much less space for user applications code. Some users overlayed certain portions of the IOCS that were not needed. Others wrote their own slimmer packages. Ultimately, users realized the importance of leaving the burden of input/output control to IOCS, and they were simply forced to add more (expensive) primary storage to their computer systems. This trend has become firmly established; operating systems have taken over more and more of the system-oriented code so that applications developers can concentrate on producing applications-oriented code. This has caused operating systems to require increasing amounts of primary storage. Fortunately, the cost of primary storage has been decreasing steadily.

2.3.5 Spooling

In *spooling* (*Simultaneous Peripheral Operation On Line*), a high-speed device like a disk is interposed between a running program and a slow-speed device involved with the program in input/output. Instead of writing lines directly to the line printer, for example, the lines are written to a disk. The program can run to completion faster, and other programs can be initiated sooner. When the printer becomes available, the lines may be printed. The name spooling is quite appropriate for this procedure; it is much like thread being spun onto a spool so that it may later be unwound as needed.

2.3.6 Procedure-Oriented Languages vs. Problem-Oriented Languages

High-level languages are either *procedure-oriented* or *problem-oriented.* Procedure-oriented high-level languages are general-purpose languages that may be used to solve a wide variety of problems. Problem-oriented languages are specifically geared to solving particular types of problems. Languages like Pascal, COBOL, FORTRAN, BASIC, and PL/I are generally considered to be procedure-oriented; languages like GPSS (for simulation), and SPSS (for performing statistical calculations) are considered to be problem-oriented.

2.3.7 Quick-and-Dirty Compilers vs. Optimizing Compilers

In program development environments, compilations are performed frequently and programs are run briefly until a bug appears. For this purpose *quick-and-dirty compilers* are useful. They produce an object program quickly but the code may be quite inefficient both in terms of its storage consumption and execution speed. Once a program has been debugged and is ready to be put into production, an *optimizing compiler* is used to produce highly efficient machine code. An optimizing compiler runs more slowly but the quality of the object code it produces is very high.

Through the 1970s, it was commonly believed that a good assembly language programmer could produce much better code than an optimizing compiler. Today optimizing compilers are so effective that the code they generate matches or exceeds the quality of the code produced by a highly skilled assembly language programmer. Programs that need to be really efficient (such as operating systems) no longer have to be written in assembly language. Most large operating systems today are written in high-level languages and translated by very high-quality optimizing compilers into efficient machine code.

2.3.8 Interpreters

One interesting and popular form of translator, an *interpreter,* does not produce an object program. Rather, it actually runs a source program directly. Interpreters are particularly popular in program development environments in which programs run only briefly before a bug is found. Interpreters avoid the overhead of assembling or compiling. They are also popular with personal computers. But interpreters run slowly compared with compiled code; they must translate an instruction each time it is executed.

2.3.9 Absolute and Relocating Loaders

Programs must be placed in primary storage in order to be executed. Associating instructions and data items with particular primary storage locations is an enormously important task. The burden of this association is sometimes placed on the user, sometimes on the translator, sometimes on a systems program called a *loader,* and sometimes on the operating system. The association of instructions and data items with particular storage locations is called *binding*. In machine language programming, binding is performed at the moment of coding. The trend has been to defer binding as much as possible; today's virtual storage systems perform binding dynamically as a program executes. Associated with the delay of binding is an increase in flexibility for both the user and the system, but this occurs at the cost of increasingly sophisticated translators, loaders, hardware, and operating systems.

A loader is a program that places a program's instructions and data into primary storage locations. An *absolute loader* places these items into the precise locations indicated in the machine language program. A *relocating loader* may load a program at various places in primary storage depending perhaps on the availability of primary storage at the moment of loading (called *load time*).

2.3.10 Linking Loaders and Linkage Editors

In early computing environments, a programmer would produce a machine language program that contained every instruction needed to solve a particular problem. Even the complex and awkward control of input/output had to be hand-coded into each machine language program.

Today, user programs often contain only a small portion of the instructions and data needed to solve a given problem. Large *subroutine libraries* are supplied so that a programmer wanting to perform certain common operations may use system-supplied routines to do so. Input/output in particular is normally handled by routines outside of the user program. Therefore, the machine language program produced by a translator must normally be combined with other machine language programs to form a useful execution unit. This process of *program combination* is performed by *linking loaders* and *linkage editors* prior to program execution time.

At load time, a linking loader combines whatever programs are required and loads them directly into primary storage. A linkage editor also performs this program combination, but it creates a load image that it preserves on secondary storage for future reference. The linkage editor is particularly useful in production environments; when a program is to be executed, the load image produced by the linkage editor may be loaded immediately without the overhead (often extensive) of recombining program pieces.

2.4 FIRMWARE

The concept of microprogramming is generally attributed to Professor Maurice Wilkes. His 1951 paper (Wi51) presented the concepts that form the basis of current microprogramming techniques. However, it wasn't until the System/360 appeared in the mid-1960s that microprogramming was used on a wide scale. During the 1960s computer manufacturers used microprogramming to implement machine language instruction sets (Hu70).

Dynamic microprogramming appeared in the late 1960s and early 1970s; it allows new microprograms to be loaded easily into the control storage from which microprograms are executed. Thus machine instruction sets can now be varied dynamically and frequently. It is not inconceivable that future multiprogramming systems might allow different users to use different instruction sets, and that a part of switching the processor between programs would involve also switching the instruction set of the machine to that desired by the next user.

Microprogramming introduces a layer of programming below a computer's machine language. As such, it makes it possible to define machine language instructions. This is integral to modern computer architectures and has enormous significance in operating systems performance and security considerations.

Microprograms are run in a special very high-speed *control storage.* They are formed from individual *microinstructions* that are much more elementary in nature and sparser in function than conventional machine language instructions. On systems in which the machine language instruction set is implemented by microprogramming, each machine language instruction is implemented by a complete, and possibly large, microprogram. This immediately implies that for microprogramming to be useful the control store must be much faster than primary storage.

2.4.1 Horizontal and Vertical Microcode

Microcode instructions may be classified as either *horizontal* or *vertical.* Executing vertical microinstructions is very much like executing machine language instructions. A typical vertical instruction specifies the movement of one (or a few) data items between registers.

Horizontal microcode is quite different. Each instruction requires many more bits since it can specify the parallel operation of data movement between many or all data registers in the control unit. Horizontal microinstructions are more powerful than vertical ones, but the resultant programs can be more difficult to code and debug.

2.4.2 Deciding What Functions to Implement in Microcode

An important design decision is what computer systems functions to implement in microcode. Microcode presents a real opportunity to improve the execution performance of a computer system. By placing frequently executed instruction sequences in firmware instead of software, designers have realized dramatic performance improvements. As readers become familiar with operating systems functions while progressing through the text, they should carefully consider which of these functions might be implemented usefully in microcode.

2.4.3 Emulation

Emulation is a technique in which one machine is made to appear as if it were another. The machine language instruction set of the machine to be emulated is microprogrammed on the *host machine.* Then the machine language programs of the emulated machine may be run directly on the host. Computer vendors often make extensive use of emulation when they introduce new systems. Users who are committed to older computers, for example, are able to run their established programs directly on the new computers without alteration. This smoothes the conversion process.

2.4.4 Microdiagnostics

Microprograms have access to more of the hardware than do machine language programs. So it is possible to perform more extensive error detection and correction, and to perform these operations at a finer level. Some systems interleave *microdiagnostics* with machine language program instructions. This makes it possible to avoid potential problems and have more reliable operation.

2.4.5 Personalized Computers

Because of the expense of designing, building, and marketing a computer system, vendors have concentrated on producing general-purpose machines. The massive investment it takes to bring out a new system means that large sales are necessary to recoup costs and make a profit. Vendors have tended to avoid building special-purpose, one-of-a-kind systems; this has been left to the universities in which such systems are constructed primarily for their research value.

Computer users have thus been faced with the task of customizing computers to their own needs; traditionally this customizing has been performed via software. The hardware provides a general-purpose environment for running software programs; the software programs tailor the computer system to the users' needs.

On some systems, users can perform this customization via microcode. They can either use vendor-supplied microcode, or they can write their own—both options are popular.

2.4.6 Microcode Assists

Vendors often supply performance improvement options in microcode. IBM has done this quite successfully with its VM operating system. (See Chapter 22.) As will be seen in the case study on VM, this operating system implements multiple virtual machines by careful utilization of the interrupt mechanism. The *microcode assists* implement a number of the more frequently executed interrupt handling routines in microcode to achieve significant performance improvements.

2.4.7 Microprogramming and Operating Systems

Portions of the operating system are among the most frequently executed sequences of instructions in most computer systems. In an interactive transaction processing system, for example, the dispatching mechanism that selects the next unit of work to which the processor will be assigned might be executed hundreds of times per second. Such a dispatching mechanism must execute efficiently—placing it in microcode is one way of making it faster.

Some of the functions often implemented in microcode include

- interrupt handling
- maintaining various types of data structures
- synchronization primitives that control access to shared data and other resources
- partial word operations that allow bit manipulation operations to be handled efficiently
- "context switching," i.e., rapidly switching a processor between users in a multiuser system
- procedure call and return sequences

Implementing operating systems functions in microcode can improve performance, reduce program development costs, and improve system security. (See Chapter 17.)

Readers wishing to investigate further the use of microprogramming in operating systems should consult (Br77) (Bu81) and (So75).

2.4.8 Microprogramming: A Case Study

This section considers a small hypothetical microprogrammed computer system. Our goal is to convey the flavor of microprogramming, and especially how it may be used to implement a computer's machine language instruction set. This example is based on that presented by Rauscher and Adams in their excellent tutorial paper (Ra80).

The machine language instruction set for a hypothetical small simple computer system, the ITSIAC, is shown in Fig. 2.1.

Instruction	Explanation
ADD	ACC ← ACC + (A)
SUB	ACC ← ACC − (A)
LOAD	ACC ← (A)
STORE	(A) ← ACC
BRANCH	BRANCH to A
COND BRANCH	If ACC = 0 BRANCH to A

Fig. 2.1 Machine language instruction set for the ITSIAC.

The ITSIAC has an Accumulator register (ACC) that is involved in all arithmetic operations. Each instruction in the machine language has two 8-bit fields—an operation code (opcode) and a storage address, A. The processor has an arithmetic and logic unit (ALU) for performing certain arithmetic calculations. The ITSIAC's registers and their functions are shown in Fig. 2.2.

The machine operates as follows. The microprogram is first loaded into control storage. Each instruction in the microprogram resides in one location of control storage. The CSIAR points to the next microinstruction to be executed. This instruction is fetched from control storage and placed in the MIR. The instruction is then decoded, and control is transferred to the appropriate routine in the microprogram to interpret this microinstruction. The CSIAR is then adjusted to point to the next microinstruction to be executed; the entire process then repeats. The microprogram gets the primary storage address of the next machine language instruction to be interpreted from the PSIAR. After interpreting a machine language instruction, the microprogram adjusts the PSIAR to point to the location in primary storage of the next machine language instruction to be executed.

Register	Function
ACC	Accumulator—This register is involved in all arithmetic operations. One of the operands in each arithmetic operation must be in the accumulator; the other must be in primary storage.
PSIAR	Primary Storage Instruction Address Register—This register points to the location in primary storage of the next machine language instruction to be executed.
SAR	Storage Address Register—This register is involved in all references to primary storage. It holds the address of the location in primary storage being read from or written to.
SDR	Storage Data Register—This register is also involved in all references to primary storage. It holds the data being written to or receives the data being read from primary storage at the location specified in the SAR.
TMPR	Temporary Register—This register is used to extract the address portion (rightmost 8-bits) of the machine instruction in the SDR so that it may be placed in the SAR. (The machine does not allow a direct SDR to SAR transfer.)
CSIAR	Control Storage Instruction Address Register—This register points to the location of the next microinstruction (in control storage) to be executed.
MIR	Microinstruction Register—This register contains the current microinstruction being executed.

Fig. 2.2 ITSIAC registers.

The decoded microinstructions correspond directly to the primitive operations the hardware can perform; they are much simpler than machine language instructions.

The microoperations that the machine can perform are shown in Fig. 2.3.

These microoperations are combined in sequences to implement the machine language instructions of our simple machine. The microprogram that performs these machine language instructions is shown in Fig. 2.4. Execution of the microprogram begins at location 00 with the routine that fetches the next machine language instruction to be executed.

The microprogrammed machine operates as follows. Initially, the CSIAR is set to 0 that is the location of the microcode routine that performs a machine language instruction fetch. The next machine language instruction to be executed is fetched from the location whose address is in the PSIAR. The READ operation causes this instruction to be loaded from primary storage into the SDR. The instruction

```
CSIAR ← decoded SDR
```

sets the CSIAR to the address of the proper microcode routine in control storage for interpreting the machine language instruction; it merely examines the opcode and does the equivalent of a table lookup with the opcode as a search key. The next microinstruction execution cycle causes control to be transferred to the microcode routine.

Register tranfers (REG is ACC, PSIAR, or TMPR):

```
SDR ← REG
REG ← SDR
SAR ← REG
```

Primary storage operations:

`READ` (from primary storage location to SDR)
`WRITE` (from SDR to primary storage location)

Sequencing operations:

`CSIAR ← CSIAR + 1` (assumed as normal case)
`CSIAR ← decoded SDR`
`CSIAR ← constant`
`SKIP` (Add 2 to CSIAR if ACC = 0; add 1 otherwise.)

Operations involving the accumulator:

```
ACC ← ACC + REG
ACC ← ACC - REG
ACC ← REG
REG ← ACC
ACC ← REG + 1
```

Fig. 2.3 ITSIAC microoperations.

Instruction fetch:

```
(00) SAR    ← PSIAR
(01) READ
(02) CSIAR ←  decoded SDR
```

ADD:

```
(10) ACC   ← PSIAR + 1
(11) PSIAR ←  ACC
(12) TMPR  ← SDR
(13) SAR   ← TMPR
(14) READ
(15) TMPR  ← SDR
(16) ACC   ← ACC + TMPR
(17) CSIAR ←  0
```

SUB:

```
(20) ACC   ← PSIAR + 1
(21) PSIAR ←  ACC
(22) TMPR  ← SDR
(23) SAR   ← TMPR
(24) READ
(25) TMPR  ← SDR
(26) ACC   ← ACC − TMPR
(27) CSIAR ←  0
```

LOAD:

```
(30) ACC   ← PSIAR + 1
(31) PSIAR ←  ACC
(32) TMPR  ← SDR
(33) SAR   ← TMPR
(34) READ
(35) TMPR  ← SDR
(36) ACC   ← TMPR
(37) CSIAR ←  0
```

STORE:

```
(40) ACC   ← PSIAR + 1
(41) PSIAR ←  ACC
(42) TMPR  ← SDR
(43) SAR   ← TMPR
(44) SDR   ← ACC
(45) WRITE
(46) CSIAR  ←  0
```

BRANCH:

```
(50) PSIAR ←  SDR
(51) CSIAR ←  0
```

COND BRANCH:

```
(60) SKIP
(61) CSIAR ←  0
(62) PSIAR ←  SDR
(63) CSIAR ←  0
```

Fig. 2.4 Microprogram that interprets ITSIAC machine language programs.

If the machine instruction being interpreted is

```
ADD 50
```

then the contents of location 50 in primary storage are to be added to the contents of the accumulator. Let's follow the microcode that accomplishes this.

```
(10) ACC ← PSIAR + 1
(11) PSIAR ← ACC
(12) TMPR ← SDR
(13) SAR ← TMPR
(14) READ
(15) TMPR ← SDR
(16) ACC ← ACC + TMPR
(17) CSIAR ← 0
```

Instructions (10) and (11) adjust the PSIAR to point to the next sequential location in primary storage. Instructions (12) and (13) extract the primary storage address from the instruction in the SDR and transfer it to the SAR. (Again, it is necessary to use TMPR because the machine does not allow a direct SDR to SAR transfer.) After (13) is performed, the SAR contains 50. The READ in (14) causes the contents of the location specified in the SAR to be loaded into the SDR. Instruction (15) causes this data to be placed in TMPR, and (16) causes it to be added to the contents of the accumulator. Instruction (17) resets the CSIAR to the address of the microinstruction fetch routine, so that the next microinstruction execution cycle will begin the process of fetching the next machine language instruction to be executed.

SUMMARY

Hardware consists of the devices of a computer system, software consists of the instructions interpreted by the hardware, and firmware consists of microcode instructions resident in high-speed control storage.

Storage interleaving allows simultaneous access to successive locations in primary storage by placing alternating sets of locations in different storage banks. Interrupts are useful in environments in which many operations may progress asynchronously, but in which occasional synchronization is needed. Multiple buffering facilitates the overlap of processing with input/output.

Spooling disassociates a running program from the slow operation of devices like printers and card readers. Input/output is directed instead to fast devices like disks; the data is actually read or written when the card readers and printers are available. Storage protection is essential to the isolation of users from one another in multiuser systems; it may be implemented in several ways including the use of bounds registers or protection keys.

The use of a standard I/O interface makes it much easier to add new devices to a system. On-line peripherals are connected to the processor; off-line peripherals are controlled by units independent of the processor. Stand-alone computer systems that perform card-to-tape, tape-to-print, etc. operations for larger systems are said to be satellite processors.

A channel is a special-purpose computer system for performing input/output independently of the processor. Communication between a processor and a channel is ordinarily handled by polling or by interrupts. Some common types of channels are selector channels, byte-multiplexor channels, and block-multiplexor channels.

An input/output control system (IOCS) is a software package designed to remove the burden of handling the details of input/output from the user. IOCS packages are an important component of today's operating systems.

Base-plus-displacement addressing makes it possible to address very large address spaces without the need to extend the size of a machine word; at execution time all addresses are formed by adding a displacement to the contents of a base register. This also facilitates ease of program relocation.

Multiple machine states provide protection. In supervisor state, all instructions (including privileged instructions) may be executed; in problem state only nonprivileged instructions may be executed. These states define the boundary between user capabilities and operating system capabilities. Some machines have more than two machine states.

Virtual storage systems normally allow programs to reference a much larger range of addresses than the range available in primary storage. This helps free the programmer from the constraints of primary storage.

Direct Memory Access eliminates the need to interrupt the processor as each byte of a block is transmitted during input/output operations. A single interrupt is generated when the transmission of the entire block is completed. Characters are transmitted to and from primary storage on a cycle stealing basis; the channel is given priority while the processor waits.

Pipelining is used in high-performance computer architectures; it allows several instructions to be in different stages of execution simultaneously.

Today's computer systems use hierarchical storage consisting of cache, primary storage, and secondary storage; these have increasing capacities and decreasing cost-per-character of storage in the order shown.

Software consists of programs of instructions that are interpreted by the hardware; these instructions define the algorithms for solving problems. Computers may be programmed in machine language, assembly language, or high-level languages. Machine languages are rarely used directly by programmers but machine language programs are produced by assemblers and compilers. Macro processors make it possible for assembly language programmers to write macro instructions that generate many assembly language instructions. Compilers translate high-level language programs into machine language. Interpreters execute source programs directly; they do not generate object programs.

Procedure-oriented languages are general-purpose; problem-oriented languages are geared to handling specific classes of problems. Quick-and-dirty compilers operate quickly but generate relatively inefficient code; optimizing compilers generate efficient code, but they run more slowly than quick-and-dirty compliers. Interpreters execute source language programs directly without producing object programs.

Absolute loaders load programs into the specific locations for which they were compiled; relocating loaders can place programs in various free areas of storage. Binding in absolute environments occurs at translation time; binding in relocatable environments occurs at load time, or even at execution time.

Linking loaders combine program pieces into a single executable unit; the executable unit is placed in primary storage ready to execute. Linkage editors also combine programs, but the executable unit is preserved on secondary storage for future reference.

Microprogramming is the writing of programs that effect the primitive operations of the hardware; it is critical to today's computer architectures and operating systems. In dynamic microprogramming, new microprograms may be loaded easily into the control storage from which microprograms are executed.

Vertical microcode instructions are very much like machine language instructions; a typical vertical microinstruction indicates that a certain operation is to be performed with certain data. Horizontal microcode has more powerful instructions that can indicate the simultaneous execution of many operations on many data items.

Microprogramming is often used in emulation to make one computer appear as if it were another. Emulation is particularly useful when installations convert from one system to another.

Microprograms may produce microdiagnostics that test for errors on a much finer level than is possible with machine language instructions.

Microprogramming may be used to personalize a computer to the needs of its users. Microcode assists are supplied by vendors as performance improvement options; often the placing of frequently executed sequences of instructions in microcode makes them execute more quickly. Many operating systems functions in today's systems are implemented in firmware instead of software; these functions normally execute faster and are more secure.

TERMINOLOGY

absolute loader
address space
assembler
assembly language
asymmetrical multiprocessing
base-plus-displacement addressing
base register
binding
block-multiplexor channel
buffer
bounds registers
byte-multiplexor channel

cache storage
channel
compilers
control storage
cycle stealing
direct access device
DMA (Direct Memory Access)
double buffering
emulated machine
emulation
emulator
execution states
firmware
fixed-length field
flip-flop buffering
front end
granularity of protection
hardware
hidden buffer
horizontal microcode
interpreter
IOCS (input/output control system)
I/O completion interrupt
I/O device controller
I/O interface
interrupts
interval timer
linkage editor
linking loader
load time
loader
location-independent program
machine-dependent
machine-independent
machine language
macro expansion
macro instruction
macro processor
microcode
microcode assists
microdiagnostics
microinstruction
microprogram
microprogramming
multiplexor channels
multiprocessing
object program
off-line
on-line
optimizing compiler
paging
pipelining
polling
preassembled IOCS
primary storage
principle of least privilege
privileged instructions
problem-oriented
problem state
procedure-oriented
program combination
quick-and-dirty compiler
recording density
relocating loader
relocation register
satellite processor
secondary storage
segmentation
selector channel
sequential device
single-address instructions
single buffering
software
source program
spooling
standard I/O interface
stand-alone processor
storage hierarchy
storage interleaving
storage protection
storage protect keys
subchannel
supervisor state
target program
three-address instructions
time-of-day clock

translator
two-address instructions
variable-length field
vertical microcode
virtual storage

EXERCISES

2.1 Distinguish among hardware, software, and firmware.

2.2 Explain the concept of storage interleaving.

2.3 What is double buffering? Explain in detail how a triple-buffering scheme might operate. In what circumstances would triple buffering be effective?

2.4 What is spooling? How would an input spooling system designed to read punched cards from a card reader operate?

2.5 Explain the concepts of DMA and cycle stealing.

2.6 Describe several techniques for implementing storage protection.

2.7 Describe two different techniques for handling the communication between a processor and a channel.

2.8 Give several motivations for the concept of base-plus-displacement addressing.

2.9 Relate the principle of least privilege to the concepts of problem state, supervisor state, and privileged instructions.

2.10 Distinguish among selector channels, byte-multiplexor channels, and block-multiplexor channels.

2.11 Distinguish among machine, assembly, and high-level languages.

2.12 What is a macro processor?

2.13 Distinguish between problem-oriented and procedure-oriented languages.

2.14 In what circumstances is it appropriate to use a quick-and-dirty compiler? When should an optimizing compiler be used?

2.15 How do interpreters differ from assemblers and compilers? When is it preferable to use an interpreter rather than a compiler?

2.16 Compare and contrast absolute loaders with relocating loaders.

2.17 What is binding? Why does delaying binding time increase both the user's and the system's flexibility?

2.18 How do linkage editors differ from linking loaders?

2.19 What is microprograming? Why is the term "firmware" appropriate for describing microcode resident in control storage?

2.20 Distinguish between horizontal and vertical microcode.

2.21 What factors might influence a designer's choice to implement certain functions in microcode?

2.22 What is emulation? Why is microprogramming particularly important in the construction of emulators?

2.23 Explain how microprogramming might be used to personalize a computer. Why might this be useful?

2.24 Explain why an understanding of microprogramming is of great importance to operating systems designers.

EXERCISES FOR THE MICROPROGRAMMING CASE STUDY (SECTION 2.4.8)

2.25 Write a machine language program for the ITSIAC that will total the numbers stored in locations 50 to 99 and place the result in location 100. Trace the execution of this program as it is interpreted by the ITSIAC microprogram supplied in the text.

2.26 Write a high-level language program to simulate the operation of the ITSIAC. Use a 256 element array to simulate primary storage. Each word of storage has 16 bits. Use variables to represent the various registers including the ACC, PSIAR, SAR, SDR, TMPR, CSIAR, and MIR. Use high-level language statements to implement each microoperation. For example, adding the contents of the temporary register to the accumulator can be accomplished by the Pascal statement

ACC:=ACC+TMPR

Add a HALT instruction that prints the contents of all registers and all locations in the ITSIAC's storage and then the ending message "EOJ." Run the program that you wrote in Exercise 2.25 on your ITSIAC simulator.

LITERATURE

(Ba80) Baer, J. L., *Computer Systems Architecture*, Rockville, Md.: Computer Science Press, 1980.

(Be81) Belady, L. A.; R. P. Parmelee; and C. A. Scalzi, "The IBM History of Memory Management Technology," *IBM J. Res. Develop.*, Vol. 25, No. 5, September 1981, pp. 491–503.

(Br77) Brown, G. E., et al., "Operating System Enhancement through Firmware," *SIGMICRO Newsletter*, Vol. 8, September 1977, pp. 119–133.

(Bs81) Bashe, C. J.; W. Buchholtz; G. V. Hawkins; J. J. Ingram; and N. Rochester, "The Architecture of IBM's Early Computers," *IBM J. Res. Develop.*, Vol. 25, No. 5, September 1981, pp. 363–375.

(Bu81) Bucci, G.; G. Neri; and F. Baldassarri, "MP80: A Microprogrammed CPU with a Microcoded Operating System Kernel," *Computer*, October 1981, pp. 81–90.

(Ca80) Campbell-Kelley, M., "Programming the EDSAC," *Annals of the History of Computing*, Vol. 2, 1980, pp. 7–36.

(Da78) Davidson, S., and B. D. Shriver, "An Overview of Firmware Engineering," *Computer*, May 1978, pp. 21–31.

(Il82) Iliffe, J. K., *Advanced Computer Design*, Englewood Cliffs, N.J.: Prentice-Hall, 1982.

(Ka73) Kaplan, K. R., and R. O. Winder, "Cache-Based Computer Systems," *Computer*, Vol. 6, No. 3, 1973, pp. 30–36.

(Ko77) Kogge, P. M., "The Microprogramming of Pipelined Processors," *Proc. Fourth Annual Symposium on Computer Architecture*, March 1977, pp. 63–69.

(Le80) Levy, H. M., and R. H. Eckhouse, Jr., *Computer Programming and Architecture: The VAX-11*, Bedford, Mass.: Digital Press, Digital Equipment Corporation, 1980.

(Lo80) Love, H. H., Jr. "The Highly Parallel Supercomputers: Definitions, Applications, and Predictions," *Proc. NCC*, 1980, pp. 181–190.

(Ma75) Mallach, E. G., "Emulator Architecture," *Computer*, Vol. 8, August 1975, pp. 24–32.

(Pa81) Padegs, A., "System/360 and Beyond," *IBM J. Res. Develop.*, Vol. 25, No. 5, September 1981, pp. 377–390.

(Ph80) Phelps, B. E., "Early Electronic Computer Developments at IBM," *Annals of the History of Computing*, Vol. 2, 1980, pp. 253–267.

(Po81) Pohm, A. V., and T. A. Smay, "Computer Memory Systems," *Computer*, October 1981, pp. 93–110.

(Ra76) Rauscher, T. G., and A. K. Agrawala, "Developing Application-Oriented Computer Architectures on General-Purpose Microprogrammable Machines," *Proc. of 1976 NCC*, Montvale, N.J.: AFIPS Press, pp. 715–722.

(Ra78) Rauscher, T. G., and A. K. Agrawala, "Dynamic Problem-Oriented Redefinition of Computer Architecture via Microprogramming," *IEEE Trans. on Computers*, Vol. C-27, November 1978, pp. 1006–1014.

(Ra80) Rauscher, T. G., and P. N. Adams, "Microprogramming: A Tutorial and Survey of Recent Developments," *IEEE Trans. on Computers*, Vol. C-29, No. 1, January 1980, pp. 2–20.

(So75) Sockut, G. H., "Firmware/Hardware Support for Operating Systems: Principles and Selected History," *SIGMICRO Newsletter*, Vol. 6, December 1975, pp. 17–26.

(St81) Stankovic, J. A., "The Types and Interactions of Vertical Migrations of Functions in a Multilevel Interpretive System," *IEEE Trans. on Computers*, Vol. C-30, No. 7, July 1981, pp. 505–513.

(Tu65) Tucker, S. G., "Emulation of Large Systems," *CACM*, Vol. 8, 1965, pp. 753–761.

(Wi51) Wilkes, M. V., *The Best Way to Design an Automatic Calculating Machine*, Report of the Manchester University Computer Inaugural Conference, Electrical Engineering Department of Manchester University, Manchester, England, July 1951, pp. 16–18. Reprinted in Earl E. Swartzlander, Jr. (ed.), *Computer Design Development—Principal Papers*, Rochelle Park, N.J.: Hayden Book Co., 1976, pp. 266–270.

(Wi69) Wilkes, M. V., "The Growth of Interest in Microprogramming: A Literature Survey," *Comput. Surveys*, Vol. 1, No. 3, September 1969, pp. 139–145.

Part 2
Process Management

3
Process Concepts

It was surprising that Nature had gone tranquilly on with her golden process in the midst of so much devilment.

The Red Badge of Courage
Stephen Crane

To be awake is to be alive.

Walden
Henry David Thoreau

Outline

3.1 Introduction
3.2 Definitions of "Process"
3.3 Process States
3.4 Process State Transitions
3.5 The Process Control Block
3.6 Operations on Processes
3.7 Suspend and Resume
3.8 Interrupt Processing
  3.8.1 Interrupt Types
  3.8.2 Context Switching
3.9 The Nucleus of the Operating System
  3.9.1 A Summary of Nucleus Functions
  3.9.2 Enabling and Disabling Interrupts
  3.9.3 Hierarchical System Structure
  3.9.4 Migration of the Nucleus to Microcode

3.1 INTRODUCTION

In this chapter we introduce the notion of *process* that is central to the understanding of today's multiuser computer systems. Several of the more popular definitions are presented, but no "perfect" definition of process has as yet appeared in the literature.

The concept of discrete *process states* is presented, as well as a discussion about how processes make transitions between states. A number of basic operations that may be performed upon processes are considered.

The definitions and concepts introduced here serve as a basis for the discussions of asynchronous concurrent processes and process scheduling in later chapters.

3.2 DEFINITIONS OF "PROCESS"

The term process was first used by the designers of the Multics system in the 1960s. Since that time, process, used somewhat interchangeably with *task*, has been given many definitions. Some of these follow.

- a program in execution
- an asynchronous activity
- the "animated spirit" of a procedure
- the "locus of control" of a procedure in execution
- that which is manifested by the existence of a "process control block" in the operating system
- that entity to which processors are assigned
- the "dispatchable" unit

Many other definitions have been given. There is no universally agreed upon definition but the "program in execution" concept seems to be most frequently referenced.

3.3 PROCESS STATES

During its existence, a process goes through a series of discrete states. Various events can cause a process to change states.

A process is said to be *running* (i.e., in the *running state*) if it currently has the CPU. A process is said to be *ready* (i.e., in the *ready state*) if it could use a CPU if one were available. A process is said to be *blocked* (i.e., in the *blocked state*) if it is waiting for some event to happen (such as an I/O completion, for example) before it can proceed. There are other process states but for the present the discussion will concentrate on these three.

Let's consider a single CPU system for simplicity, although the extension to multiprocessing is not difficult. Only one process may be running at a time but several processes may be ready, and several may be blocked. We therefore establish a *ready list* of ready processes, and a *blocked list* of blocked processes. The ready list is maintained in priority order so that the next process to receive the CPU is the first process on the list. The blocked list is unordered—processes do not become unblocked (i.e., ready) in priority order; rather they unblock in the order in which the events they are awaiting occur.

3.4 PROCESS STATE TRANSITIONS

When a job is admitted to the system, a corresponding process is created and then inserted at the back of the ready list. The process gradually moves to the head of the ready list as the processes before it complete. When the process reaches the head of the list, and when the CPU becomes available, the process is given the CPU and is said to make a *state transition* from the ready state to the running state (Fig. 3.1). The assignment of the CPU to the first process on the ready list is called *dispatching*, and is performed by a system entity called the *dispatcher*. We indicate this transition as follows.

dispatch(processname): ready → running

While the process has the CPU, it is said to be running. To prevent any one process from monopolizing the system, either accidentally or maliciously, the operating system sets a hardware *interrupting clock* to allow this user to run for a specific time interval or *quantum*. If the process does not voluntarily relinquish the CPU before the interval expires, the clock generates an interrupt causing the operating

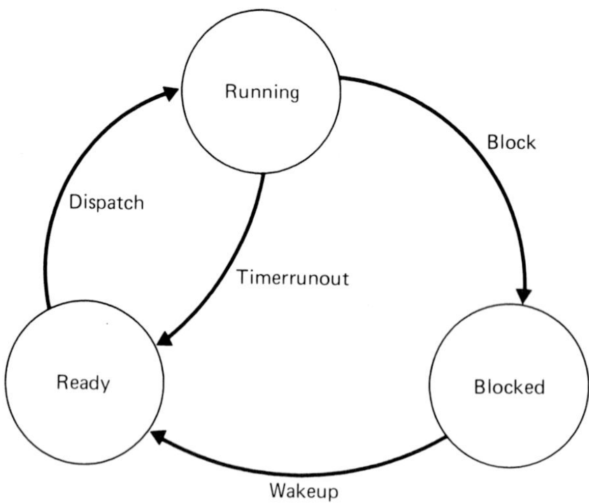

Fig. 3.1 Process state transitions.

system to regain control. The operating system then makes the previously running process ready, and makes the first process on the ready list running. These state transitions are indicated as

timerrunout(processname): running → ready

and

dispatch(processname): ready → running

If a running process initiates an input/output operation before its quantum expires, the running process voluntarily relinquishes the CPU (i.e., the process blocks itself pending the completion of the input/output operation). This state transition is

block(processname): running → blocked

The only other allowable state transition in our three-state model occurs when an input/output operation (or some other event the process is waiting for) completes. The process makes the transition from the blocked state to the ready state. The transition is

wakeup(processname): blocked → ready

Thus we have defined four possible state transitions:

dispatch(processname): ready → running
timerrunout(processname): running → ready
block(processname): running → blocked
wakeup(processname): blocked → ready

Note that *the only state transition initiated by the user process itself is block—the other three transitions are initiated by entities external to the process.*

3.5 THE PROCESS CONTROL BLOCK

The manifestation of a process in an operating system is a *process control block (PCB).* The PCB is data structure containing certain important information about the process including

- the current state of the process
- unique identification of the process
- the process's priority
- pointers to locate the process's memory
- pointers to allocated resources
- a register save area

The PCB is a central store of information that allows the operating system to locate all key information about a process. When the operating system switches the attention of the CPU among processes, it uses the save areas in the PCB to hold the information it needs to restart each process when the process next gets the CPU.

Thus the PCB is the entity that defines a process to the operating system. Because PCBs need to be manipulated quickly by the operating system, many computer systems contain a hardware register that always points to the PCB of the currently executing process. Hardware instructions are often available that load state information into the PCB and restore the information quickly.

3.6 OPERATIONS ON PROCESSES

Systems that manage processes must be able to perform certain operations on processes. These include

- create a process
- destroy a process
- suspend a process
- resume a process
- change a process's priority
- block a process
- wakeup a process
- dispatch a process.

Creating a process involves many operations including

- name the process
- insert it in the system's list of known processes
- determine the process's initial priority
- create the process control block
- allocate the process's initial resources

A process may *spawn a new process.* If it does, the creating process is called the *parent process* and the created process is called the *child process.* Only one parent is needed to create a child. Such creation yields a *hierarchical process structure* like that in Figure 3.2 in which each child has only one parent, but each parent may have many children.

Destroying a process involves obliterating it from the system. Its resources are returned to the system, it is purged from any system lists or tables, and its process control block is erased.

A suspended process cannot proceed until another process resumes it. Suspension is an important operation and has been implemented in a variety of ways on

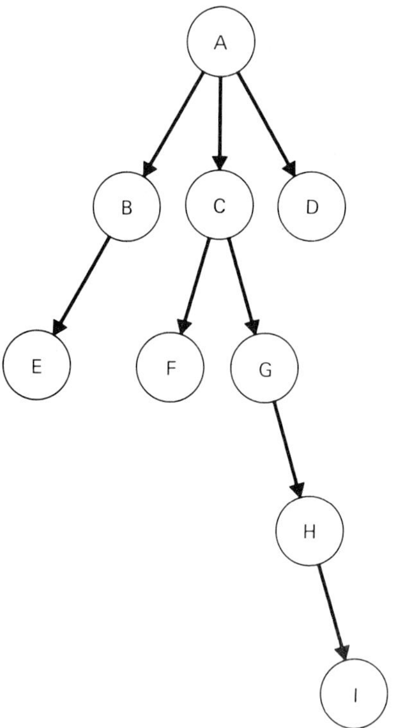

Fig. 3.2 Process creation hierarchy.

many different systems. Suspensions normally last only brief periods of time. They are often performed by the system to remove certain processes temporarily during a peak loading situation. For long-term suspensions, the process's resources should be freed. The decision about freeing resources depends very much on the nature of the resource. Primary memory should be freed immediately when a process is suspended. A tape drive may be retained by a process suspended only briefly but should be released by a process suspended for a lengthy or indefinite period.

Resuming (or activating) a process involves restarting it from the point at which it was suspended.

Destruction of a process is more complicated when the process has spawned other processes. In some systems, a spawned process is destroyed automatically when its parent is destroyed; in other systems, spawned processes proceed independently of their parents, and the destruction of a parent has no effect on the destroyed parent's children.

Changing the priority of a process normally involves nothing more than modifying the priority value in the process's control block.

3.7 SUSPEND AND RESUME

In the previous section the notions of suspending and resuming processes were introduced. These operations are important for several reasons.

- If a system is functioning poorly and may fail, then current processes may be suspended to be resumed after the problem is corrected.
- A user suspicious about the partial results of a process may suspend it (rather than aborting it) until the user can ascertain whether or not the process is functioning correctly.
- In response to short-term fluctuations in system load, some processes may be suspended and resumed later when the load settles back to normal levels.

Figure 3.3 shows the process state transition diagram modified to include suspend and resume. Two new states have been added, namely *suspendedready* and *suspendedblocked*; there is no need for a *suspendedrunning* state. Above the dashed line in the figure are the *active states*; below it are the *suspended states.*

A suspension may be initiated either by the process itself or by another process. On a uniprocessor system a running process may suspend itself; no other process could be running at the same moment to issue the suspend. On a multiprocessor system, a running process may be suspended by another process running on a different processor.

A ready process may be suspended only by another process. It makes the transition

suspend (processname): ready → suspendedready

A suspendedready process may be made ready by another process. It makes the transition

resume (processname): suspendedready → ready

A blocked process may be suspended by another process. It makes the transition

suspend (processname): blocked → suspendedblocked

A suspendedblocked process may be resumed by another process. It makes the transition

resume (processname): suspendedblocked → blocked

One could argue that instead of suspending a blocked process, it is better to wait until the I/O completion or event completion occurs and the process becomes ready. Unfortunately, the completion may never come, or it may be delayed indefinitely. So the designer is faced with either performing the suspension of the blocked process or setting up a mechanism such that when the completion occurs, the suspension will be made from the ready state. Because suspension is often a high-priority activity, it should be performed immediately. When the completion finally occurs (if indeed it does), the suspendedblocked process makes the transition

completion (processname): suspendedblocked → suspendedready

The use of suspend and resume by the operating system to balance the system load is discussed in Chapter 10.

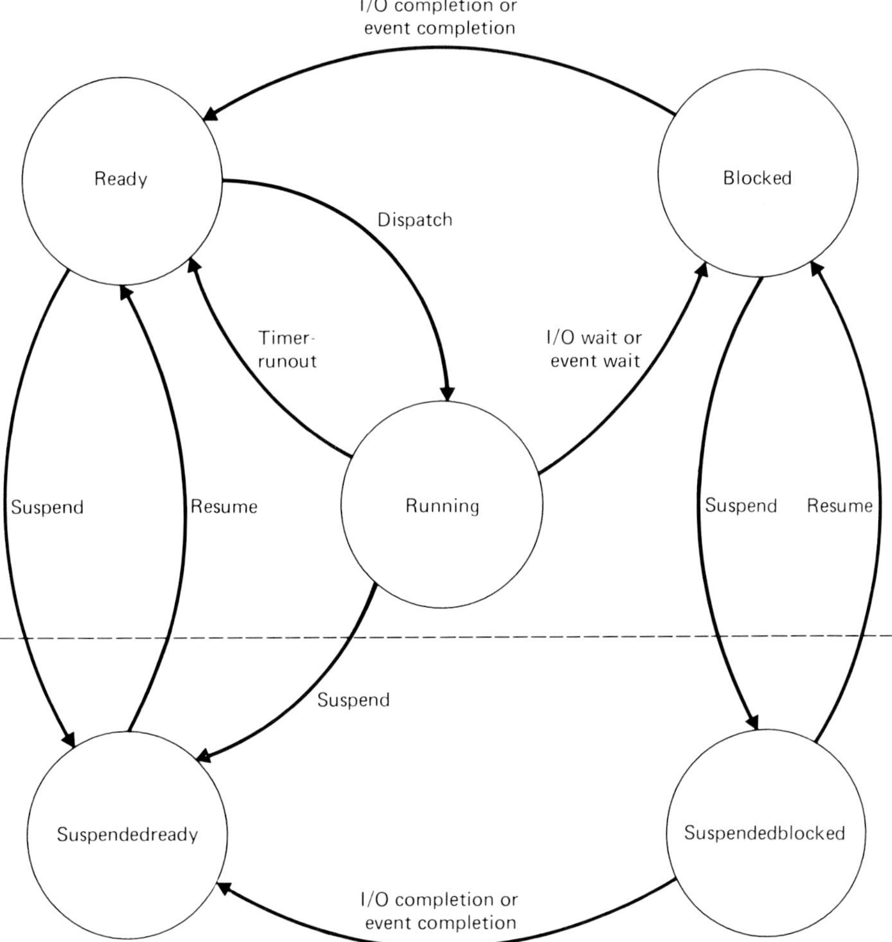

Fig. 3.3 Process state transitions with suspend and resume.

3.8 INTERRUPT PROCESSING

Figure 3.4 shows an example of interrupt processing with which we are certainly familiar. On a computer system, an *interrupt* is an event that alters the sequence in which a processor executes instructions. It is generated by the hardware of the computer system. When an interrupt occurs

- The operating system gains control.
- The operating system saves the state of the interrupted process. In many systems this information is stored in the interrupted process's process control block.
- The operating system analyzes the interrupt and passes control to the appropriate routine to handle the interrupt.

An interrupt may be specifically initiated by a running process, or it may be caused by some event that may or may not be related to the running process.

Fig. 3.4 Real-life interrupt processing.

3.8.1 Interrupt Types

In this section the interrupt scheme of the large-scale IBM processors is discussed. This information is especially useful later in the text when case studies of IBM's MVS and VM operating systems are presented.

There are six interrupt types. These are

- *SVC (supervisor call)* interrupts. These are initiated by a running process that executes the SVC instruction. An SVC is a user-generated request for a particular system service such as performing input/output, obtaining more storage, or communicating with the system operator. The SVC mechanism helps keep the operating system secure from the users. A user may not arbitrarily enter the operating system; rather the user must request a service through an SVC. The operating system is thus aware of all user attempts to cross its borders, and it may refuse certain requests if the user does not have appropriate privileges.
- *I/O interrupts.* These are initiated by the input/output hardware. They signal to the CPU that the status of a channel or device has changed. I/O interrupts are caused when an I/O operation completes, when an error occurs, or when a device is made ready, for example.
- *External interrupts.* These are caused by various events including the expiration of a quantum on an interrupting clock, the pressing of the console's interrupt key by the operator, or the receipt of a signal from another processor on a multiprocessor system.
- *Restart interrupts.* These occur when the operator presses the console's *restart button,* or when a *restart SIGP (signal processor) instruction* arrives from another processor on a multiprocessor system.
- *Program check interrupts.* These are caused by various types of errors experienced by a running process such as an attempt to divide by zero, an attempt by a user process to execute a privileged instruction, an attempt to execute an invalid operation code, etc.
- *Machine check interrupts.* These are caused by malfunctioning hardware.

3.8.2 Context Switching

The operating system includes routines called *interrupt handlers (IHs)* to process each different type of interrupt. Thus there are six interrupt handlers (IHs)—the *SVC IH,* the *I/O IH,* the *external IH,* the *restart IH,* the *program check IH,* and the *machine check IH.* When an interrupt occurs, the operating system saves the status of the interrupted process, and routes control to the appropriate interrupt handler. This is accomplished by a technique called *context switching.*

Program status words (PSWs) control the order of instruction execution and contain various information about the state of a process. There are three types of PSWs, namely *current PSWs, new PSWs,* and *old PSWs.*

The address of the next instruction to be executed is kept in the current PSW which also indicates the types of interrupts currently *enabled* and those currently *disabled.* The CPU allows enabled interrupts to occur; disabled interrupts either remain *pending,* or in some cases are ignored. The processor may never be disabled for SVC, restart, or some types of program interrupts. The reasons for enabling or disabling interrupts will soon become clear.

On a uniprocessor system, there is only one current PSW, but there are six new PSWs (one for each interrupt type) and six old PSWs (again, one for each interrupt type). The new PSW for a given interrupt type contains the permanent hardware address at which the interrupt handler for that interrupt type resides. When an interrupt occurs (Fig. 3.5), if the processor is not disabled for that type of interrupt, then the hardware automatically switches PSWs by

- storing the current PSW in the old PSW for that type of interrupt,
- storing the new PSW for that type of interrupt into the current PSW.

After this *PSW swap*, the current PSW now contains the address of the appropriate interrupt handler. The interrupt handler then processes the interrupt.

When the processing of the interrupt is complete the CPU is dispatched to either the process that was running at the time of the interrupt, or to the highest priority ready process. This depends on whether the interrupted process is *preemptive* or *nonpreemptive*. If the process is nonpreemptive, it gets the CPU again. If the process is preemptive, it gets the CPU only if there are no ready processes.

There are many significant interrupt schemes other than that described here. The reader interested in exploring them further should consult texts on computer

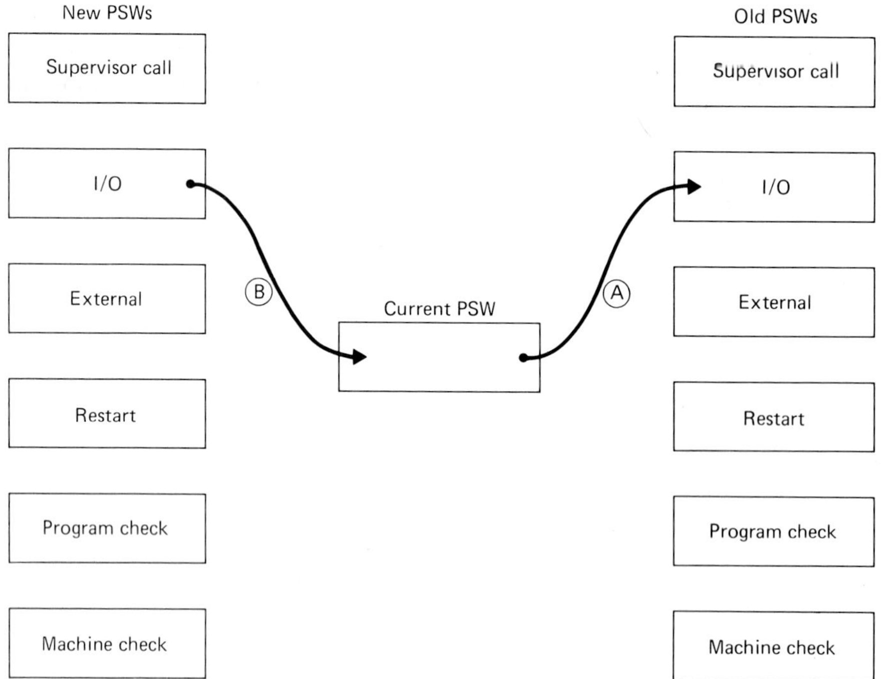

Fig. 3.5 PSW swapping in interruption processing.

organization and computer architecture such as (Ba80) (Le80) (Ha78) (Hy78) (St75) (Ge74).

3.9 THE NUCLEUS OF THE OPERATING SYSTEM

All of the operations involving processes are controlled by a portion of the operating system variously called its *nucleus, core,* or *kernel* (Lo81, Br70, Sc77, Sh75, Wu74). The nucleus represents only a small portion of the code of the entire operating system, but it is among the most intensively used code. For this reason, the nucleus ordinarily remains in primary storage while other portions of the operating system are shuttled to and from secondary storage as needed.

One of the most important functions included in the nucleus is interrupt processing. In large, multiuser systems, there is a constant flood of interrupts directed at the processor. Rapid response to these interrupts is essential to keeping the resources of the system well utilized, and to providing acceptable response times to interactive users.

The nucleus disables interrupts while it is responding to an interrupt; interrupts are again enabled after the processing of an interrupt is complete. With a steady flow of interrupts, it is possible that the nucleus could have interrupts disabled for a large portion of the time; this could result in poor response to interrupts. Therefore, nuclei are designed to do the "bare minimum" amount of processing that is possible on each interrupt, and then to pass the remaining processing of each interrupt to an appropriate system process that can operate while the nucleus is enabled for further interrupts. This ultimately means that interrupts may be enabled a much larger percentage of the time, and that the system is more responsive.

3.9.1 A Summary of Nucleus Functions

An operating system nucleus normally contains the code to perform the following functions.

- Interrupt handling.
- Process creation and destruction.
- Process state switching.
- Dispatching. (See also Chapter 10.)
- Process suspension and resumption. (See also Chapter 10.)
- Process synchronization. (See Chapters 4 and 5.)
- Interprocess communication. (See Chapters 4 and 5.)
- Manipulation of process control blocks.
- Support of input/output activities. (See the case studies of Chapters 18 through 22. Input/output is generally unique to each different type of computer system.)
- Support of storage allocation and deallocation. (See Chapters 7, 8, and 9.)

- Support of the file system. (See Chapter 13.)
- Support of a procedure call/return mechanism.
- Support of certain system accounting functions. (See Chapter 21.)

The reader interested in a detailed explanation of the structure and operation of the nucleus should refer to Chapter 6 of the text by Lorin and Deitel (Lo81).

3.9.2 Enabling and Disabling Interrupts

The nucleus is normally entered by an interrupt. The nucleus disables interrupts while it responds to the interrupt. Once the cause of the interrupt is determined, the nucleus passes the processing of the interrupt to a specific system process designed to handle that type of interrupt.

In some systems, all of the processing of each interrupt is done by a large, one-piece operating system. In such systems, interrupts are disabled for a larger percentage of the time, but the systems are conceptually simpler. Such a design is useful in small systems that support a limited number of processes; in large multiuser systems the nucleus approach yields far better performance.

3.9.3 Hierarchical System Structure

The literature includes papers (Di68) that advocate a hierarchical approach to designing operating systems. At the base of the hierarchy is the computer hardware itself, sometimes called the "raw machine" or "naked iron." At the next level up in the hierarchy (or the next several levels in some designs) are the various nucleus functions. These are viewed as creating an *extended machine*, i.e., a computer that offers not only its machine language in support of the operating system and its users but also a group of additional capabilities provided by the nucleus functions. These additional capabilities are often called *primitives.*

Above the nucleus in the hierarchy are the various operating system processes that operate in support of user processes—for example, the device manager processes that actually supervise the input/output operations for system devices in behalf of various users. At the top of the hierarchy are the user processes themselves.

Such hierarchical designs have proven easier to debug, modify, and to prove correct (Di68). In designs in which the nucleus itself is spread over several levels of the hierarchy, the choice of which nucleus function is to be placed at which level requires careful thought. Often in such designs, the restriction is imposed that only downward calls in the hierarchy are allowed; each level may call upon only those functions it sees in the level directly below.

3.9.4 Migration of the Nucleus to Microcode

One definite trend that has emerged in recent systems is for the placement of much of the nucleus into microcode. This is an effective security technique, and with careful microcoding can make the nucleus functions execute more quickly.

SUMMARY

The most common notion of process is a program in execution. A process that has a processor is running. A process that could use a processor if one was available is ready. A process waiting for some event to occur before it can proceed is blocked.

A running process becomes ready if its quantum expires before it voluntarily releases the processor. A running process becomes blocked if it initiates an I/O operation (or some other event) that must complete before it can proceed. A blocked process becomes ready when the event it is waiting for occurs. A ready process becomes running when the processor is assigned to it by the dispatcher.

A process control block (PCB) is a data structure containing information that allows the operating system to locate all key information about a process including its current state, identification, priority, memory, resources, register values, etc. The PCB defines the process to the operating system.

Operating systems contain mechanisms to perform various operations on processes such as create, destroy, suspend, resume, change priority, block, wakeup, and dispatch a process. A process may spawn another process in which case the spawning process is the parent and the spawned process is the child. When only one parent is needed to create a child, a hierarchical process structure results.

Suspending and resuming processes is particularly useful to the operating system in its efforts to balance the system load.

Interrupt processing is important in computer systems that support devices and processes operating concurrently. When an interrupt occurs, the operating system gives it immediate attention. After processing an interrupt, the next process is dispatched. This may be the interrupted process itself if this process is nonpreemptive.

The interrupt scheme for the large-scale IBM processors allows six types of interrupts: SVC, I/O, external, restart, program check, and machine check. For each type of interrupt, the operating system contains a routine called an interrupt handler (IH) that processes interrupts of that type. When an interrupt occurs, PSW swapping or context switching occurs; control is switched from the running process to the operating system. The IBM scheme involves a current PSW containing the address of the next instruction to be executed, a set of old PSWs (one per interrupt type) providing save areas for the current PSW when interrupts of that type occur, and a set of new PSWs (one per interrupt type) containing the addresses of the appropriate interrupt handlers.

The nucleus is a small portion of the operating system that contains intensively used code and resides in primary storage. Its functions generally include interrupt handling, process manipulation, process control block manipulation, dispatching, process synchronization, interprocess communication, support of input/output activities, storage allocation and deallocation, support of the file system, a procedure call/return mechanism, and certain system accounting functions.

In hierarchical system structures, the nucleus is above the computer system itself, and the next levels up contain system processes and user processes. Hierarchical structures have proven easier to debug, modify, and prove correct.

There is a trend toward the migration of major portions of the nucleus to microcode; this yields greater security and faster execution.

TERMINOLOGY

activate a process
active states
block
child process
context switching
core
create a process
current PSW
destroy a process
device manager process
disabled interrupts
dispatch
dispatch a process
enabled interrupts
extended machine
external interrupt
hierarchical process structure
hierarchical system structure
interrupt
interrupt handler (IH)
I/O interrupt
kernel
machine check interrupt
naked iron
new PSW
nonpreemptive process
nucleus
old PSW
parent process
preemptive process
primitives
process
process control block (PCB)
process state transitions
process states
program check interrupt
program status word (PSW)
PSW swapping
raw machine
ready a process
ready queue
ready state
restart interrupt
resume a process
running process
running state
spawn a process
supervisor call (SVC) interrupt
suspend a process
suspended process
suspended states
suspendedblock state
suspendedready state
SVC instruction
switching CPU control
terminated process
wakeup a process

EXERCISES

3.1 Give several definitions of process. Why, do you suppose, is there no universally accepted definition?

3.2 Define each of the following terms: program, procedure, processor, process, user, task, job.

3.3 Sometimes the terms user, job, and process are used interchangeably. Define each of the terms. In what circumstances do these terms have similar meanings?

3.4 Why doesn't it make sense to maintain the blocked list in priority order? In what circumstances, however, might it be useful to do so?

3.5 The ability of one process to spawn a new process is an important capability, but it is not without its dangers. Consider the consequences of allowing a user to run the following process.

```
errant: process;
        do forever;
           spawn a new process just like me;
        end;
```

a) Assuming that a system allowed such a process to run, what would the consequences be?
b) Suppose that you as an operating systems designer have been asked to build in safeguards against such processes. We know (from the "Halting Problem" of computability theory) that it is impossible, in the general case, to predict the path of execution a program will take. What are the consequences of this basic result from computer science on your ability to prevent processes like the above from running?
c) Suppose you decide that it is inappropriate to reject certain processes, and that the best approach is to place certain run-time controls on them. What controls might the operating system use to detect processes like the above at run-time? Would the controls you propose hinder a process's ability to spawn new processes? How would the implementation of the controls you propose affect the design of the system's process handling mechanisms?

3.6 In single user dedicated systems, it is generally obvious when a program goes into an infinite loop. But in multiuser systems running tens or hundreds of processes, it cannot easily be determined that an individual process is not progressing.

a) Can the operating system determine that a process is in an infinite loop?
b) What reasonable safeguards might be built into an operating system to prevent processes in infinite loops from running indefinitely?

3.7 Choosing the correct quantum size is important to the effective operation of an operating system. Later in the text we will consider the issue of quantum determination in depth. For now, let's anticipate some of the problems.

Consider a single processor timesharing system that supports a large number of interactive users. Each time a process gets the processor, the interrupting clock is set to interrupt after the quantum expires. Assume a single quantum for all processes on the system.

a) What would be the effect of setting the quantum at a very large value, say ten minutes?
b) What if the quantum were set to a very small value, say a few processor cycles?
c) Obviously, an appropriate quantum must be between the values in (a) and (b). Suppose you could turn a dial and vary the quantum. How would you know when you had chosen the "right" value? What factors make this value right from the user's standpoint? What factors make it right from the system's standpoint?

3.8 In a block/wakeup mechanism, a process blocks itself to wait for an event to occur. Another process must detect that the event has occurred, and wakeup the blocked process. It is possible for a process to block itself to wait for an event that will never occur.

a) Can the operating system detect that a blocked process is waiting for an event that will never occur?

b) What reasonable safeguards might be built into an operating system to prevent processes from waiting indefinitely for an event?

3.9 System A runs exactly one process per user. System B can support many processes per user. Discuss the organizational differences between operating systems A and B with regard to support of processes.

3.10 Ultimately, all resources must be paid for by users. As a system runs, there are various operations it performs that are difficult to attribute to a particular user. How might the system charge user processes for such system overhead?

3.11 One reason for using a quantum to interrupt a running process after a "reasonable" period of time is to allow the operating system to regain the processor and dispatch the next process. Suppose a system does not have an interrupting clock, and that the only way a process can lose the processor is to relinquish it voluntarily. Suppose also that no dispatching mechanism is provided in the operating system. Describe how a group of user processes could cooperate among themselves to effect a user-controlled dispatching mechanism. What potential dangers would be inherent in this scheme? What are the advantages to the users over a system-controlled dispatching mechanism?

3.12 In some systems, a spawned process is destroyed automatically when its parent is destroyed; in other systems spawned processes proceed independently of their parents, and the destruction of a parent has no effect on its children. Discuss the advantages and disadvantages of each approach.

3.13 When interrupts are disabled, on most types of devices they remain pending until they can be processed when interrupts are again enabled. No further interrupts are allowed. The functioning of the devices themselves is temporarily halted. But in real-time systems, the environment that generates the interrupts is often disassociated from the computer system. When interrupts are disabled on the computer system, the environment keeps on generating interrupts anyway. These interrupts are often lost. Discuss the consequences of lost interrupts. In a real-time system, is it better to lose occasional interrupts or to halt the system temporarily until interrupts are again enabled?

3.14 Give an example of each of the following types of interrupts.

a) SVC
b) I/O
c) external
d) restart
e) program check
f) machine check

3.15 What does it mean for a process to be preemptive? nonpreemptive? Can the processor handle interrupts while a nonpreemptive process is running? Give an example of a process that would probably be preemptive. What type of process would probably be nonpreemptive?

3.16 Discuss an interrupt scheme other than that described in this chapter. Compare the two schemes.

3.17 What is the nucleus or kernel of an operating system? Why is the nucleus ordinarily maintained in primary storage? What functions are normally performed by the nucleus?

3.18 Why does the nucleus ordinarily run with interrupts disabled?

3.19 What is an extended machine? What are primitives?

3.20 Give several reasons why it is effective to place major portions of the nucleus in microcode.

LITERATURE

(Ba80) Baer, J., *Computer Systems Architecture*, Rockville, Md.: Computer Science Press, 1980.

(Br70) Brinch Hansen, P., "The Nucleus of a Multiprogramming System," *CACM*, Vol. 13, No. 4, April 1970, pp. 238–241.

(Di68) Dijkstra, E. W., "The Structure of the T.H.E. Multiprogramming System," *CACM*, Vol. 11, No. 5, May 1968, pp. 341–346.

(Ge74) Gear, C. W., *Computer Organization and Programming* (2nd ed.), New York: McGraw-Hill, 1974.

(Ha78) Hamacher, V. C.; Z. G. Vranesic; and S. G. Zaky, *Computer Organization*, New York: McGraw-Hill, 1978.

(Hy78) Hayes, J. P., *Computer Architecture and Organization*, New York: McGraw-Hill, 1978.

(Ho78) Holt, R. C.; G. S. Graham; E. D. Lazowska; and M. A. Scott, *Structured Concurrent Programming with Operating Systems Applications*, Reading, Mass.: Addison-Wesley, 1978.

(Hr73) Horning, J. J., and B. Randell, "Process Structuring," ACM *Computing Surveys*, Vol. 5, No. 1, March 1973, pp. 5–29.

(La78) Lauer, H. C., and R. M. Needham, "On the Duality of Operating System Structures." In D. Lanciaux (ed.), *Operating Systems: Theory and Practice*, Amsterdam: North-Holland, 1979, pp. 371–384.

(Le80) Levy, H. M., and R. H. Eckhouse, Jr., *Computer Programming and Architecture: The VAX-11*, Maynard, Mass.: Digital Press, 1980.

(Lo81) Lorin, H., and H. M. Deitel, *Operating Systems*, Reading, Mass.: Addison-Wesley, 1981, pp. 161–186.

(Sc77) Schroeder, M. D.; D. Clark; and J. H. Saltzer, "Multics Kernel Design Project," Proceedings of the Sixth Annual Symposium on Operating Systems Principles, *Operating Systems Review*, Vol. 11, No. 5, November 1977.

(Sh74) Shaw, A. C., *The Logical Design of Operating Systems*, Englewood Cliffs, N. J.: Prentice-Hall, 1974.

(Sh75) Shaw, A., et al., "A Multiprogramming Nucleus with Dynamic Resource Facilities," *Software Practice and Experience*, Vol. 5, 1975, pp. 245–267.

(St75) Stone, H. S., *Introduction to Computer Architecture*, Chicago: SRA, 1975.

(Wu74) Wulf, W. A., et al., "Hydra: The Kernel of a Multiprocessor Operating System," *CACM*, Vol. 17, No. 6, 1974, pp. 337–345.

4 Asynchronous Concurrent Processes

A person with one watch knows what time it is; a person with two watches is never sure.

Proverb

Outline

4.1 INTRODUCTION

Processes are *concurrent* if they exist at the same time. Concurrent processes can function completely independently of one another, or they can be *asynchronous* which means that they require occasional synchronization and cooperation. Asynchronism is a complex topic—this chapter and Chapter 5 discuss the organization and management of systems that support asynchronous concurrent processes.

Many important asynchronism problems are presented. Their solutions are presented as concurrent programs that use a program notation similar to, although not identical to, that of the language Concurrent Pascal developed by Brinch Hansen (Br75, Br77). Another popular Pascal-based concurrent language is Modula developed by Wirth (Wi77). Chapter 5 discusses the concurrent programming features of the emerging language Ada (Ad82), certain to become the leading concurrent programming language of the 1980s.

4.2 PARALLEL PROCESSING

As computer hardware continues to decrease in size and cost, there will be a distinct trend toward multiprocessing and eventually toward massive parallelism. If certain operations can logically be performed in parallel, then future computers will physically perform them in parallel, even if the *level of parallelism* is thousands or perhaps millions of concurrent activities.

Parallel processing is interesting for several reasons. People seem better able to focus their attention on one activity at a time than to think in parallel. (The reader might try to read two books at once, reading a line from one, a line from the other, the second line from the first, etc.)

It is difficult to determine what activities can and cannot be performed in parallel. Parallel programs are much more difficult to debug then sequential programs—after a bug is supposedly fixed, it may be impossible to reconstruct the sequence of events that exposed the bug in the first place, so it would be inappropriate to certify, in some sense, that the bug has been corrected.

Asynchronous processes must occasionally interact with one another and these interactions can be complex. We discuss many examples of process interaction in this and the next several chapters.

Finally, parallel programs are much more difficult to prove correct than sequential programs, and it is widely believed that proving correctness must eventually displace exhaustive testing if real strides are to be made in developing highly reliable software systems.

4.3 A CONTROL STRUCTURE FOR INDICATING PARALLELISM: PARBEGIN/PAREND

Many programming language constructs for indicating parallelism have appeared in the literature. These generally involve pairs of statements as follows.

- One statement, indicating that sequential execution is to split off into several parallel execution sequences (*threads of control*).
- One statement indicating that certain parallel execution sequences are to merge and sequential execution is to resume.

These statements occur in pairs and are commonly called *parbegin/parend* (for begin and end parallel execution), or *cobegin/coend* (for begin and end concurrent execution). In this text we use parbegin/parend as suggested by Dijkstra (Di65). Its general form is shown in Fig. 4.1.

```
parbegin
   statement1;
   statement2;
       .
       .
       .
   statementn
parend
```

Fig. 4.1 The parbegin/parend parallelism construct.

Suppose a program currently executing a single sequence of instructions encounters the preceding parbegin construct. This causes the single thread of control to split into n separate threads of control—one for each statement in the parbegin/parend construct. These may be simple statements, procedure calls, blocks of sequential statements delineated by begin/end, or combinations of these. Each of the separate threads of control eventually terminates and reaches the parend. When all of the parallel threads of control finally terminate, a single thread of control is resumed and the system proceeds past the parend.

As an example consider the calculation of one root of a quadratic equation as follows.

$$x := (-b + (b ** 2 - 4 * a * c) ** .5)/(2 * a)$$

This assignment might be evaluated on a sequential processor (possessing an exponentiation instruction) as follows.

1 $b ** 2$
2 $4 * a$
3 $(4 * a) * c$
4 $(b ** 2) - (4 * a * c)$
5 $(b ** 2 - 4 * a * c) ** .5$
6 $-b$
7 $(-b) + ((b ** 2 - 4 * a * c) ** .5)$
8 $2 * a$
9 $(-b + (b ** 2 - 4 * a * c) **.5)/(2 * a)$

Here, each of the nine operations is executed one at a time in a sequence determined by a system's rules of operator precedence.

On a system that supports parallel processing, the expression might be evaluated as follows.

```
1     parbegin
         temp1 := -b;
         temp2 := b ** 2;
         temp3 := 4 * a;
         temp4 := 2 * a
      parend;
2        temp5 := temp3 * c;
3        temp5 := temp2 - temp5;
4        temp5 := temp5 ** .5;
5        temp5 := temp1 + temp5;
6        x := temp5 / temp4
```

Here, the four operations within the parbegin/parend construct are evaluated in parallel—the remaining five operations must still be performed sequentially. By performing the calculations in parallel, it is possible to reduce real execution time substantially.

4.4 MUTUAL EXCLUSION

Consider a system with many timesharing terminals. Assume that users end each line they type to the system with a carriage return. Suppose it is desired to monitor continuously the total number of lines that users have entered since the day began. Assume each user terminal is monitored by a different process. Each time one of these processes receives a line from a user terminal it increments a systemwide global shared variable, LINESENTERED, by 1. Consider what happens if two processes attempt to increment LINESENTERED simultaneously. Assume each process has its own copy of the code

```
LOAD   LINESENTERED
ADD    1
STORE  LINESENTERED
```

Suppose LINESENTERED is currently 21687. Now suppose the first process executes the LOAD and ADD instructions, thus leaving 21688 in an accumulator. Then the process loses the processor (through a quantum expiration) to the second process. The second process now executes all three instructions, thus setting LINESENTERED to 21688. It loses the processor to the first process which then continues by executing the STORE instruction—also placing 21688 into LINESENTERED. Because of the uncontrolled access to the shared variable LINESENTERED, the system has essentially lost track of one of the lines—the correct total should have been 21689.

This problem can be solved by giving each process exclusive access to LINESENTERED. While one process increments the shared variable, all other processes desiring to do so at the same moment should be kept waiting; when that process is finished accessing the shared variable, one of the processes waiting to do so should be allowed to proceed. In this fashion, each process accessing the shared data excludes all others from doing so simultaneously. This is called *mutual exclusion.*

4.5 CRITICAL SECTIONS

Mutual exclusion needs to be enforced only when processes access shared data—when processes are performing operations that do not conflict with one another they should be allowed to proceed concurrently. When a process is accessing shared data, the process is said to be in its *critical section* (or *critical region* (Di65)). Clearly, to prevent the kind of problem experienced in the last section, it must be ensured that when one process is in its critical section, all other processes (at least those that access the same shared data) are excluded from their own critical sections.

While a process is in its critical section, other processes may certainly continue executing outside their critical sections. When a process leaves its critical section, then one other process waiting to enter its own critical section should be allowed to proceed (if indeed there is a waiting process). Enforcing mutual exclusion is one of the key problems in concurrent programming. Many solutions have been devised: some software solutions and some hardware solutions; some rather low-level and some high-level; some requiring voluntary cooperation among processes, and some demanding rigid adherence to strict protocols.

Being inside a critical section is a very special status accorded to a process. The process has exclusive access to shared data, and all other processes currently requiring access to that data are kept waiting. Therefore critical sections must execute as quickly as possible, a process must not block within its critical section, and critical sections must be carefully coded (to avoid the possibility of infinite loops, for example).

If a process in a critical section terminates, either voluntarily or involuntarily, then the operating system, in performing its *termination housekeeping* must release mutual exclusion so that other processes may enter their critical sections.

4.6 MUTUAL EXCLUSION PRIMITIVES

The concurrent program in Fig. 4.2 properly implements the line counting mechanism of the previous section. For simplicity, we shall assume only two concurrent processes in the programs presented in this and the next several sections. Handling n concurrent processes is considerably more complex.

```
program mutualexclusion;
var linesentered: integer;
procedure processone;
   while true do
      begin
         getnextlinefromterminal;
         entermutualexclusion;
            linesentered := linesentered + 1;
         exitmutualexclusion;
         processtheline
      end;
procedure processtwo;
   while true do
      begin
         getnextlinefromterminal;
         entermutualexclusion;
            linesentered := linesentered + 1;
         exitmutualexclusion;
         processtheline
      end;
begin
   linesentered := 0;
   parbegin
       processone;
       processtwo
    parend
 end.
```

Fig. 4.2 Using mutual exclusion primitives.

The constructs, *entermutualexclusion* and *exitmutualexclusion* introduced in Fig. 4.2 *encapsulate* the code in each process that accesses the shared variable linesentered, i.e., these constructs delineate critical sections. These operations are sometimes called *mutual exclusion primitives*; that is, they invoke the most fundamental operations inherent in mutual exclusion.

In the two-process case, these primitives operate as follows. When processone executes entermutualexclusion, if processtwo is not in its critical section, then processone enters its critical section, accesses the shared variable, and then executes exitmutualexclusion to indicate that it has left its critical section.

If processtwo is in its critical section when processone executes entermutualexclusion, then processone is made to wait until processtwo executes exitmutualexclusion. Processone may then proceed to enter its own critical section.

If processone and processtwo simultaneously execute entermutualexclusion, then one will be allowed to proceed and one will be kept waiting. We shall assume that the "winner" is selected at random.

4.7 IMPLEMENTING MUTUAL EXCLUSION PRIMITIVES

We seek an implementation of entermutualexclusion (*mutual exclusion entry code*) and exitmutualexclusion (*mutual exclusion exit code*) that satisfies the following four constraints.

- The solution is implemented purely in software on a machine without specially designed mutual exclusion instructions. Each machine language instruction is executed *indivisibly*; i.e., once started each instruction completes without interruption. If multiple processors try to access the same data item, we shall assume that a hardware feature called *storage interlock* resolves any conflicts. Storage interlock *sequentializes* the conflicting references by the separate processors, i.e., the references are made to happen one at a time. We assume that the separate references are serviced in random order.
- No assumptions may be made about the relative speeds of asynchronous concurrent processes.
- Processes operating outside of their critical sections cannot prevent other processes from entering their own critical sections.
- Processes must not be indefinitely postponed from entering their critical sections.

An elegant software implementation of mutual exclusion was first presented by the Dutch mathematician Dekker. In the next section we follow Dijkstra's development of *Dekker's Algorithm* (Di65).

4.8 DEKKER'S ALGORITHM

Figure 4.3 shows a first effort at specifying the code for enforcing mutual exclusion in the context of a concurrent program with two processes. The parbegin/parend construct causes processone and processtwo to operate as concurrent processes. Each of these processes loops indefinitely, repeatedly entering and reentering its critical section. In Fig. 4.3, entermutualexclusion is implemented as a single while loop that keeps looping until processnumber becomes equal to the number of the process; exitmutualexclusion is implemented as a single instruction that sets processnumber to the number of the other process.

Processone executes the while do. Since processnumber is initially 1, processone enters its critical section. Processtwo finds processnumber equal to 1 and remains locked in its while do. Whenever processtwo gets the processor, it simply loops waiting for processnumber to be set to 2, so processtwo does not enter its critical section and mutual exclusion is guaranteed.

Eventually, processone finishes executing in its critical section (we must assume no infinite loops) and it sets processnumber to 2 thus allowing processtwo to enter its own critical section.

```
program versionone;
var processnumber: integer;
procedure processone;
   begin
      while true do
         begin
            while processnumber = 2 do;
            criticalsectionone;
            processnumber := 2;
            otherstuffone
         end
   end;
procedure processtwo;
   begin
      while true do
         begin
            while processnumber = 1 do;
            criticalsectiontwo;
            processnumber := 1;
            otherstufftwo
         end
   end;
begin
   processnumber := 1;
   parbegin
      processone;
      processtwo
   parend
end.
```

Fig. 4.3 Version one of mutual exclusion primitives.

Mutual exclusion is guaranteed, but the price is high. Processone must go first, so if processtwo is ready to enter its critical section, it may be considerably delayed. After processone enters and leaves its critical section, then processtwo must go—even if processone wants to reenter and processtwo is not ready. Thus the processes must enter and leave their critical sections in strict alternation. If one process needs to do so many times more frequently than the other, it is constrained to operate at a much slower speed than it requires. The system cannot become completely deadlocked—at least one process can proceed if both are simultaneously attempting to enter their critical sections. If one of the processes is terminated, then eventually the other will not be able to proceed.

In the first solution, there was only a single global variable and this forced the *lockstep synchronization* problem. So in version two (Fig. 4.4), we use two variables —p1inside that is true if processone is inside its critical section, and p2inside that is true if processtwo is inside its critical section.

```
program versiontwo;
var p1inside, p2inside: boolean;
procedure processone;
   begin
      while true do
         begin
            while p2inside do;
            p1inside := true;
            criticalsectionone;
            p1inside := false;
            otherstuffone
         end
   end;
procedure processtwo;
   begin
      while true do
         begin
            while p1inside do;
            p2inside := true;
            criticalsectiontwo;
            p2inside := false;
            otherstufftwo
         end
   end;
begin
   p1inside := false;
   p2inside := false;
   parbegin
      processone;
      processtwo
   parend
end.
```

Fig. 4.4 Version two of mutual exclusion primitives.

Now processone remains locked in a busy wait as long as p2inside is true. Eventually processtwo leaves its critical section, and performs its own mutual exclusion exit code setting p2inside to false. Processone then sets p1inside true and enters its critical section. While p1inside is true, processtwo may not enter its own critical section.

Again, the subtleties of concurrent programming surface. Because processone and processtwo are concurrent processes, they could both attempt their respective mutual exclusion entry code sequences simultaneously. Initially, both p1inside and p2inside are false. Processone could test p2inside and find it false—then, before processone can set p1inside to true, processtwo can test p1inside and find it false. At this point processone sets p1inside to true and enters its critical section, and processtwo sets p2inside to true and enters its critical section. Both processes are in their critical sections simultaneously, so version two doesn't even guarantee mutual exclusion.

```
program versionthree;
var p1wantstoenter, p2wantstoenter: boolean;
procedure processone;
   begin
      while true do
         begin
            p1wantstoenter := true;
            while p2wantstoenter do;
            criticalsectionone;
            p1wantstoenter := false;
            otherstuffone
         end
   end;
procedure processtwo;
   begin
      while true do;
         begin
            p2wantstoenter := true;
            while p1wantstoenter do;
            criticalsectiontwo;
            p2wantstoenter := false;
            otherstufftwo
         end
   end;
begin
   p1wantstoenter := false;
   p2wantstoenter := false;
   parbegin
      processone;
      processtwo
   parend
end.
```

Fig. 4.5 Version three of mutual exclusion primitives.

In version two, there was difficulty because between the time a process determines in the while test that it can go ahead and the time that the process sets a flag to say it is in its critical section, there is enough time for the other process to test its flag and slip into its critical section. Therefore, once one process attempts the while test it must be assured that the other process cannot proceed past its own while test. Version three (Fig. 4.5) attempts to resolve this by having each process set its own flag prior to performing the while.

One problem has been solved, but another has been introduced. If each process sets its flag before proceeding to the while test, then each process will find the other's flag set and will loop forever in the while do. This is an example of a two-process *deadlock*.

```
program versionfour;
var p1wantstoenter, p2wantstoenter: boolean;
procedure processone;
   begin
      while true do
         begin
            p1wantstoenter := true;
            while p2wantstoenter do
               begin
                  p1wantstoenter := false;
                  delay (random, fewcycles);
                  p1wantstoenter := true
               end;
            criticalsectionone;
            p1wantstoenter := false;
            otherstuffone
         end
   end;
procedure processtwo;
   begin
      while true do
         begin
            p2wantstoenter := true;
            while p1wantstoenter do
               begin
                  p2wantstoenter := false;
                  delay (random, fewcycles);
                  p2wantstoenter := true
               end;
            criticalsectiontwo;
            p2wantstoenter := false;
            otherstufftwo
         end
   end;
begin
   p1wantstoenter := false;
   p2wantstoenter := false;
   parbegin
      processone;
      processtwo
   parend
end.
```

Fig. 4.6 Version four of mutual exclusion primitives.

The problem with version three is that each of the processes can get locked up in its respective while do loop. We need a way to "break out" of these loops. Version four (Fig. 4.6) accomplishes this by forcing each looping process to set its flag false repeatedly for brief periods—this would allow the other process to proceed past its while with its own flag still on.

Mutual exclusion is guaranteed and deadlock cannot occur, but another potentially devastating problem could develop, namely, *indefinite postponement.* Let's see how. Because we cannot make any assumptions about the relative speeds of asynchronous concurrent processes, we must consider all possible execution sequences. The processes could, for example, proceed in tandem. Each process can set its flag to true, then make the while test, then enter the body of the while loop, then set its flag to false, then set its flag to true, and then repeat the sequence beginning with the while test. As they do this, the tested conditions will remain true. Of course, such operation would occur with very low probability—but it *could* occur. Therefore, version four is unacceptable. If a system using this type of mutual exclusion were controlling a space flight, a heart pacemaker, or an air traffic control system, the possibility of indefinite postponement and consequent system failure would loom.

In just a few lines of code, Dekker's Algorithm (Fig. 4.7) elegantly handles two-process mutual exclusion without the need for any special hardware instructions.

Dekker's Algorithm resolves the possibility of indefinite postponement experienced in version four. Let's see how. Processone indicates its desire to enter its critical section by setting its flag on. It then proceeds to the while test where it checks if processtwo also wants to enter. If processtwo's flag is off, then processone skips the body of the while loop and enters its critical section.

Suppose, however, that when processone performs the while test, it discovers that processtwo's flag is set. This forces processone into the body of its while loop. Here it looks at the variable, favoredprocess, that is used to resolve the conflicts that ensue when both processes simultaneously want to enter their critical sections. If processone is the favored process, it skips the body of the if and repeatedly executes the while test waiting for processtwo to turn off its flag. (We will soon see that processtwo must eventually do this.)

If processone determines that processtwo is the favored process, then processone is forced into the body of the if where it sets its own flag off, and then loops inside the following while do as long as processtwo remains the favored process. By turning off its flag, processone allows processtwo to enter its own critical section.

Eventually, processtwo will leave its critical section and execute its mutual exclusion exit code. These statements set the favored process back to processone and set processtwo's flag off. Processone may now pass the inner while and set its own flag on. Processone then executes the outer while test. If processtwo's flag (which was recently set off) is still off, then processone enters its critical section. If, however, processtwo has quickly tried to reenter its critical section, then processtwo's flag will be on and processone is once again forced into the body of the outer while.

```
program dekkersalgorithm;
var favoredprocess: (first, second);
   p1wantstoenter, p2wantstoenter: boolean;
procedure processone;
   begin
      while true do
         begin
            p1wantstoenter := true;
            while p2wantstoenter do
               if favoredprocess = second then
                  begin
                     p1wantstoenter := false;
                     while favoredprocess = second do;
                     p1wantstoenter := true
                  end;
            criticalsectionone;
            favoredprocess := second;
            p1wantstoenter := false;
            otherstuffone
         end
   end;
procedure processtwo;
   begin
      while true do
         begin
            p2wantstoenter := true;
            while p1wantstoenter do
               if favoredprocess = first then
                  begin
                     p2wantstoenter := false;
                     while favoredprocess = first do;
                     p2wantstoenter := true
                  end;
            criticalsectiontwo;
            favoredprocess := first;
            p2wantstoenter := false;
            otherstufftwo
         end
   end;
begin
   p1wantstoenter := false;
   p2wantstoenter := false;
   favoredprocess := first;
   parbegin
      processone;
      processtwo
   parend
end.
```

Fig. 4.7 Dekker's Algorithm for implementing mutual exclusion primitives.

This time, however, processone is "in the driver's seat" because it is now the favored process (remember that as processtwo left its critical section it set favoredprocess to first). So processone skips the body of the if, and repeatedly executes the outer while test until processtwo "humbly" sets its flag off allowing processone to enter its critical section.

Consider the following interesting possibility. As processone comes out of the inner busy wait loop, it is possible for it to lose the processor, and for processtwo to loop around and reattempt to enter its critical section. Processtwo will then set its flag on first—and will reenter its critical section. When processone gets the processor back, it sets its flag on. Because it will be processone's turn, if processtwo tries to reenter, it will then set its own flag off, be forced into the inner busy wait, and processone will be able to enter its critical section. So this tricky timing will not result in indefinite postponement.

4.9 *N*-PROCESS MUTUAL EXCLUSION

Dijkstra was the first to present a software solution for implementation of *n*-process mutual exclusion primitives (Di65a). Knuth (Kn66) responded with a solution that eliminated the possibility of indefinite postponement in Dijkstra's algorithm, but still allowed a process to experience a (potentially) lengthy delay. This generated a series of efforts to find algorithms with shorter delays. Eisenberg and McGuire (Ei72) presented a solution guaranteeing that a process will enter its critical section within $n - 1$ tries. Lamport (La74) developed a solution that is particularly applicable to distributed processing systems. The algorithm uses a "take a ticket" system like those employed in busy bakeries, and has been dubbed *Lamport's Bakery Algorithm.* Brinch Hansen (Br78a) also discusses control of concurrency among distributed processes.

4.10 A HARDWARE SOLUTION TO MUTUAL EXCLUSION: THE TESTANDSET INSTRUCTION

Dekker's Algorithm is a software solution to the mutual exclusion problem. This section presents a hardware solution.

The key to success here is to have a single hardware instruction that reads a variable, stores its value in a save area, and sets the variable to a certain value. This instruction, often called *testandset,* once initiated will complete all of these functions without interruption. The indivisible testandset instruction

```
testandset (a,b)
```

reads the value of boolean *b,* copies it into *a,* and then sets *b* to true—all within the span of a single uninterruptible instruction. Testandset may be used as in Fig. 4.8 to enforce mutual exclusion.

```
program testandsetexample;
var active: boolean;
procedure processone;
   var onecannotenter: boolean;
   begin
      while true do
         begin
            onecannotenter := true;
            while onecannotenter do
               testandset (onecannotenter, active);
            criticalsectionone;
            active := false;
            otherstuffone
         end
   end;
procedure processtwo;
   var twocannotenter: boolean;
   begin
      while true do;
         begin
            twocannotenter := true;
            while twocannotenter do
               testandset (twocannotenter, active);
            criticalsectiontwo;
            active := false;
            otherstufftwo
         end
   end;
begin
   active := false;
   parbegin
      processone;
      processtwo
   parend
end.
```

Fig. 4.8 Mutual exclusion with testandset.

The boolean variable, active, is true if either process is in its critical section, and false otherwise. Processone bases its decision to enter its critical section on its local boolean variable, onecannotenter. It sets onecannotenter to true and then repeatedly testandsets the global boolean variable, active. If processtwo is not in its critical section, active will be false. The testandset will store this value in onecannotenter, and will set active to true. The while test will become false and processone will enter its critical section. Because active has been set to true, processtwo cannot enter its critical section.

Now suppose processtwo is already in its critical section when processone wants to enter. Processone sets onecannotenter to true and then repeatedly testandsets active. Because processtwo is in its critical section, active remains true. Each testandset finds active true, sets onecannotenter to true, and sets active to true. Therefore processone continues its busy waiting until processtwo eventually leaves its critical section and sets active to false. At this point the testandset will find active false (and set it to true to keep processtwo out) and set onecannotenter to false, thus allowing processone to enter its critical section.

This solution can suffer from indefinite postponement, but this is highly unlikely, especially if there are multiple processors. As soon as a process leaving its critical section sets active to false, the other process's testandset is likely to "grab" active (by setting it true) before the first process can loop around and set active to true.

4.11 SEMAPHORES

Dijkstra abstracted the key notions of mutual exclusion in his concept of *semaphores* (Di65). A semaphore is a *protected variable* whose value can be accessed and altered only by the operations *P* and *V* and an initialization operation we shall call *semaphoreinitialize. Binary semaphores* can assume only the value 0 or the value 1. *Counting semaphores* can assume nonnegative integer values.

The P operation on semaphore S, written P(S), operates as follows.

```
If S > 0
   then S := S - 1
   else (wait on S)
```

The V operation on semaphore S, written V(S), operates as follows.

```
If (one or more processes are waiting on S)
   then (let one of these processes proceed)
   else S := S + 1
```

We shall assume a first-in-first-out queueing discipline for processes waiting to complete a P(S).

Like testandset, P and V are indivisible. Mutual exclusion on the semaphore, S, is enforced within P(S) and V(S). If several processes attempt a P(S) simultaneously, only one will be allowed to proceed. The others will be kept waiting.

Semaphores and semaphore operations can be implemented in software or hardware. They are commonly implemented in the nucleus of the operating system where process state switching is controlled.

Figure 4.9 shows how semaphores may be used to enforce mutual exclusion. Here P(active) is equivalent to entermutualexclusion and V(active) is equivalent to exitmutualexclusion.

```
program semaphoreexampleone;
var active: semaphore;
procedure processone;
   begin
      while true do
         begin
            preliminarystuffone;
            P(active);
               criticalsectionone;
            V(active);
            otherstuffone
         end
   end;
procedure processtwo;
   begin
      while true do
         begin
            preliminarystufftwo;
            P(active);
               criticalsectiontwo;
            V(active);
            otherstufftwo
         end
   end;
begin
   semaphoreinitialize(active,1);
   parbegin
      processone;
      processtwo
   parend
end.
```

Fig. 4.9 Using a semaphore and the P and V primitives to enforce mutual exclusion.

4.12 PROCESS SYNCHRONIZATION WITH SEMAPHORES

When a process issues an I/O request, it blocks itself to await the completion of the I/O. Some other process must awaken the blocked process. Such an interaction is an example of a *block/wakeup* protocol.

More generally, suppose one process wants to be notified about the occurrence of some event. Suppose some other process is capable of detecting that this event has occurred. Figure 4.10 shows how semaphore operations may be used to implement a simple two-process block/wakeup synchronization mechanism.

Processone executes some preliminarystuffone and then executes P(eventofinterest). The semaphore has been initialized to zero so the process must wait. Eventually processtwo executes V(eventofinterest) to signal that the event has occurred. This allows processone to proceed.

Note that this mechanism works even if processtwo detects and signals the event before processone executes P(eventofinterest)—the semaphore will have been

```
program blockandwakeup;
var eventofinterest: semaphore;
procedure processone;
   begin
      preliminarystuffone;
      P(eventofinterest);
      otherstuffone
   end;
procedure processtwo;
   begin
      preliminarystufftwo;
      V(eventofinterest);
      otherstufftwo
   end;
begin
   semaphoreinitialize(eventofinterest,0);
   parbegin
      processone;
      processtwo
   parend
end.
```

Fig. 4.10 Block/wakeup process synchronization with semaphores.

incremented from 0 to 1, so P(eventofinterest) will simply decrement the semaphore from 1 to 0, and processone will proceed without waiting for the event.

4.13 THE PRODUCER–CONSUMER RELATIONSHIP

In a sequential program, when one procedure calls another and passes data, the procedures are part of a single process—they do not operate concurrently. But when one process passes data to another process, the problems are much more complex. Such transmission is an example of *interprocess communication.*

Consider the following producer–consumer relationship. Suppose one process, a *producer,* is generating information that a second process, a *consumer,* is using. Suppose they communicate by a single shared integer variable, numberbuffer. The producer does some calculations and then writes the result into numberbuffer; the consumer reads the data from numberbuffer and prints it.

It is possible that the producer and consumer processes could run quite nicely in tandem, or their speeds could be grossly mismatched. If every time the producer deposits a result in numberbuffer the consumer immediately reads it and prints it, then the printed output would faithfully represent the stream of numbers generated by the producer.

But suppose the speeds of the processes are mismatched. If the consumer is operating faster than the producer, the consumer could read and print the same number twice (or many times for that matter) before the producer deposits the next number. If the producer is operating faster than the consumer, the producer could overwrite its previous result before the consumer has had a chance to read it and print it; a very fast producer could in fact do this several times so that many results would be lost.

Obviously, the behavior we desire here is for the producer and the consumer to cooperate in such a manner that data written to numberbuffer are neither lost nor duplicated. Enforcing such behavior is an example of *process synchronization.*

Figure 4.11 shows a concurrent program that uses semaphore operations to implement a producer–consumer relationship.

```
program producerconsumerrelationship;
var exclusiveaccess: semaphore;
    numberdeposited: semaphore;
    numberbuffer: integer;
procedure producerprocess;
   var nextresult: integer;
   begin
      while true do
         begin
            calculatenextresult;
            P(exclusiveaccess);
            numberbuffer := nextresult;
            V(exclusiveaccess);
            V(numberdeposited)
         end
   end;
procedure consumerprocess;
   var nextresult: integer;
   begin
      while true do
         begin
            P(numberdeposited);
            P(exclusiveaccess);
            nextresult := numberbuffer;
            V(exclusiveaccess);
            write (nextresult)
         end
   end;
begin
   semaphoreinitialize(exclusiveaccess,1);
   semaphoreinitialize(numberdeposited,0);
   parbegin
      producerprocess;
      consumerprocess
   parend
end.
```

Fig. 4.11 Producer–consumer relationship implemented with semaphores.

Here we have used two semaphores: exclusiveaccess is used to enforce mutually exclusive access to the shared variable, and numberdeposited is used for process synchronization.

4.14 COUNTING SEMAPHORES

Counting semaphores are particularly useful when a resource is to be allocated from a pool of identical resources. The semaphore is initialized to the number of resources in the pool. Each P operation decrements the semaphore by 1 indicating that another resource has been removed from the pool and is in use by a process. Each V operation increments the semaphore by 1 indicating that a process has returned a resource to the pool, and the resource may be reallocated to another process. If a P operation is attempted when the semaphore has been decremented to zero, then the process must wait until a resource is returned to the pool by a V operation.

4.15 IMPLEMENTING SEMAPHORES, P AND V

Given Dekker's Algorithm and/or the availability of a testandset machine instruction, it is straightforward to implement P and V with busy waiting. But busy waiting can be wasteful.

In Chapter 3 we studied the process state switching mechanisms implemented in the nucleus of an operating system. It was observed that a process requesting an I/O operation voluntarily blocks itself pending completion of the I/O. The blocked process does not busy wait. Instead it relinquishes the processor, and the nucleus threads the process's PCB into the blocked list. The process thus remains asleep until it is awakened by the nucleus that removes the process from the blocked list and threads it into the ready list.

Semaphore operations can also be implemented in the nucleus to avoid busy waiting. A semaphore is implemented as a protected variable and a queue in which processes can wait for V operations. When a process attempts a P operation on a semaphore whose current value is zero, the process relinquishes the processor and blocks itself to await a V operation on the semaphore. The nucleus threads the process's PCB into the queue of processes waiting on that semaphore. (We assume a first-in-first-out queue discipline. Other disciplines, including priority queueing, have been investigated.) The nucleus then reassigns the processor to the next ready process.

The process in the semaphore queue eventually moves to the head of the queue. Then the next V operation removes the process from the semaphore queue and places it on the ready list. Of course, processes attempting simultaneous P and V operations on a semaphore are guaranteed exclusive access to the semaphore by the nucleus.

Note that in the special case of uniprocessor systems, the indivisibility of P and V can be ensured by simply disabling interrupts while P and V operations are manipulating a semaphore. This prevents the processor from being usurped until the manipulation is complete (at which point interrupts are again enabled).

SUMMARY

Processes are concurrent if they exist at the same time. Asynchronous concurrent processes require occasional synchronization and cooperation.

Systems that support parallel activities are interesting to study because of the trends toward multiprocessing and massive parallelism, because it is difficult to determine what activities can and cannot be performed in parallel, because parallel programs are much more difficult to debug than sequential programs, because the interactions between asynchronous processes can be complex, and because proving program correctness is much more difficult for parallel programs than for sequential programs.

The parbegin/parend construct is used to indicate that a single thread of control is to split into multiple threads of control, and that eventually these are to merge back into a single thread of control. Its general form is

```
parbegin
   statement1;
   statement2;
         .
         .
         .
   statementn
parend
```

indicating that each of the statements may be executed in parallel.

When processes cooperate in a manner such that while one process is accessing shared data all others are excluded from doing so, this is called mutual exclusion. When a process is accessing shared data, the process is said to be in its critical section. When processes cooperate over the use of shared variables, when one process is in its critical section, all other processes must be excluded from their critical sections.

Critical sections must execute as quickly as possible, a process must not block within its critical section, and critical sections must be carefully coded (to avoid the possibility of infinite loops, for example).

A process desiring to enter its critical section executes entermutualexclusion, a primitive operation that makes this process wait if another process is in its critical section. A process leaving its critical section executes exitmutualexclusion to allow a waiting process to proceed.

Dekker's Algorithm, a software implementation of mutual exclusion primitives, has the following properties.

- It requires no special hardware instructions.
- A process operating outside its critical section cannot prevent another process from entering its own critical section.
- A process desiring to enter its critical section will do so without the possibility of indefinite postponement.

Dekker's Algorithm is applicable for two-process mutual exclusion. Software solutions have been developed for *n*-process mutual exclusion; these solutions are generally quite complex.

The indivisible testandset instruction, testandset (*a, b*), reads the value of boolean *b*, copies it into *a*, and then sets *b* to true. It cannot be used to enforce mutual exclusion.

A semaphore is a protected variable whose value can be accessed and altered only by the operations P and V and an initialization operation (called semaphore-initialize in the text). Binary semaphores can assume only the value 0 or the value 1. Counting semaphores can assume nonnegative integer values.

The P operation on semaphore S, written P(S), operates as follows.

```
If S > 0
   then S := S - 1
   else (wait on S)
```

The V operation on binary semaphore S, written V(S), operates as follows.

```
If (one or more processes are waiting on S)
   then (let one of these processes proceed)
   else S := S + 1
```

Semaphores may be used to implement a block/wakeup synchronization mechanism: one process blocks itself (via P(S) with S initially zero) to await the occurrence of an event; another process detects the event and awakens the blocked process (via V(S)).

In a producer–consumer relationship one process, a producer, generates information that a second process, a consumer, uses. This is an example of interprocess communication. If these processes communicate through a shared buffer, the producer must not produce when the buffer is full and the consumer must not consume when the buffer is empty. Enforcing these restrictions is an example of process synchronization.

Counting semaphores are particularly useful when a resource is to be allocated from a pool of identical resources. Each P operation indicates that a resource has been allocated; each V operation indicates that a resource has been returned to the pool.

Semaphore operations can be implemented with busy waiting, but this can be wasteful. Semaphore operations can be implemented in the nucleus to avoid busy waiting.

TERMINOLOGY

asynchronism
asynchronous concurrent processes
binary semaphore
block/wakeup protocol
busy wait
cobegin/coend
concurrency
concurrent programming
counting semaphore
critical region
critical section
deadlock

Dekker's Algorithm
Dijkstra
encapsulation
entermutualexclusion
exitmutualexclusion
indefinite postponement
indivisible operations
Lamport's Bakery Algorithm
level of parallelism
lockstep synchronization
mutual exclusion
mutual exclusion entry code
mutual exclusion exit code
mutual exclusion primitives
n-process mutual exclusion
P operation
parallel processing
parbegin/parend
process synchronization
protected variable
semaphore
sequentialization
shared data
shared resource
storage interlock
testandset instruction
thread of control
two-process mutual exclusion
V operation

EXERCISES

4.1 Give several reasons why the study of concurrency is appropriate and important for students of operating systems.

4.2 Rewrite the following expression using parbegin/parend to achieve maximum parallelism.

```
3 * a * b + 4 / (c + d) ** (e - f)
```

4.3 Rewrite the following parallel computation as a simple sequence of calculations.

```
a := b + c;
parbegin
    d := b * c - x;
    e := a/6 + n ** 2
parend
```

4.4 Why might the following be unacceptable?

```
parbegin
    a := b + c;
    d := b * c - x;
    e := a/6 + n ** 2
parend
```

4.5 Give several reasons why the following statement is false: When several processes access shared information in primary storage, mutual exclusion must be enforced to prevent the production of indeterminate results.

4.6 Dekker's Algorithm, testandset, and the semaphore operations P and V may all be used to enforce mutual exclusion. Compare and contrast these various schemes. Consider their respective advantages and disadvantages.

4.7 When two processes simultaneously attempt entermutualexclusion, we have assumed that the "winner" is selected at random. Discuss the ramifications of this assumption.

4.8 Comment on the following use of mutual exclusion primitives.

```
dosomestuffone;
entermutualexclusion;
   dosomestufftwo;
   entermutualexclusion;
      dosomestuffthree;
   exitmutualexclusion;
   dosomestufffour;
exitmutualexclusion;
dosomestufffive
```

4.9 What is the real significance of Dekker's Algorithm?

4.10 Perform an exhaustive timing analysis of Dekker's Algorithm. Does it have any weaknesses?

4.11 Without referencing the published solutions, develop your own solution to the implementation of n-process mutual exclusion primitives. (This is a very difficult problem.)

4.12 The solution for n-process mutual exclusion presented by Eisenberg and McGuire (Ei72) guarantees that a process will enter its critical section within $n - 1$ tries. Should one hope for better performance with n processes?

4.13 Mutual exclusion primitives can be implemented with busy waiting or with blocking. Discuss the applicability and relative merits of each approach.

4.14 Explain in detail how semaphores and semaphore operations can be implemented in the nucleus of an operating system.

4.15 Explain how the disabling and enabling of interrupts is useful in implementing mutual exclusion primitives on uniprocessor systems.

4.16 Why must the V operation be done indivisibly?

4.17 In the program of Fig. 4.11, what would be the effect of reversing the two P operations in the consumer process? What would be the effect of reversing the two V operations in the producer process?

4.18 Use counting semaphores to rewrite the program of Fig. 4.9 so that it controls access to a pool of five identical resources.

4.19 As mentioned in the text, critical sections that reference nonintersecting sets of shared variables may indeed be executed simultaneously. Suppose the mutual exclusion primitives are each modified to include a parameter list of the particular shared variables to be referenced in a critical section.

a) Comment on the following use of these new mutual exclusion primitives.

```
dosomestuffone;
entermutualexclusion(a);
   dosomestuffwitha;
   entermutualexclusion(b);
      dosomestuffwithaandb;
   exitmutualexclusion(b);
   dosomemorestuffwitha;
exitmutualexclusion(a);
dosomestufftwo;
```

b) Suppose the two processes below operate concurrently. What are the possible outcomes?

```
PROCESSONE:                          PROCESSTWO:
   . . .                                . . .
entermutualexclusion(a);             entermutualexclusion(b);
   . . .                                . . .
   entermutualexclusion(b);             entermutualexclusion(a);
      . . .                                . . .
   exitmutualexclusion(b);              exitmutualexclusion(a);
   . . .                                . . .
exitmutualexclusion(a);              exitmutualexclusion(b);
   . . .                                . . .
```

4.20 Many computer systems implement mutual exclusion primitives in microcode. Give several reasons why this is desirable.

4.21 In Dekker's Algorithm, what (if anything) would happen if the two assignment statements in the mutual exclusion exit code were reversed?

LITERATURE

(Ad82) "Reference Manual for the Ada Programming Language (Draft Revised Mil-Std 1815)," *ACM Special Publication*, July 1982, ACM Order No. 825820.

(Br70) Brinch Hansen, P., "The Nucleus of a Multiprogramming System," *CACM*, Vol. 13, No. 4, April 1970, pp. 238–241, 250.

(Br72) Brinch Hansen, P., "Structured Multiprogramming," *CACM*, Vol. 15, No. 7, July 1972, pp. 574–578.

(Br73a) Brinch Hansen, P., *Operating Systems Principles*, Englewood Cliffs, N.J.: Prentice-Hall, 1973.

(Br73b) Brinch Hansen, P., "Concurrent Programming Concepts," *ACM Computing Surveys*, Vol. 5, No. 4, December 1973, pp. 223–245.

(Br75) Brinch Hansen, P., "The Programming Language Concurrent Pascal," *IEEE Trans. of Soft. Eng.*, Vol. SE-1, No. 2, June 1975, pp. 199–207.

(Br77) Brinch Hansen, P., *The Architecture of Concurrent Programs*, Englewood Cliffs, N.J.: Prentice-Hall, 1977.

(Br78a) Brinch Hansen, P., "Distributed Processes—a Concurrent Programming Concept," *CACM*, Vol. 21, No. 11, November 1978, pp. 934–941.

(Br78b) Brinch Hansen, P., "Multiprocessor Architectures for Concurrent Programs," *ACM 78 Conf. Proc.*, Washington, D.C., December 1978, pp. 317–323.

(Br79) Brinch Hansen, P., "A Keynote Address on Concurrent Programming," *IEEE Computer Magazine*, May 1979, pp. 50–56.

(Co71) Courtois, P. J.; F. Heymans; and D. L. Parnas, "Concurrent Control with Readers and Writers," *CACM*, Vol. 14, No. 10, October 1971, pp. 667–668.

(De81) Denning, P.J.; T. D. Dennis; and J. A. Brumfield, "Low Contention Semaphores and Ready Lists," *CACM*, Vol. 24, No. 10, October 1981, pp. 687–699.

(Di65) Dijkstra, E.W., "Cooperating Sequential Processes," Technological University, Eindhoven, Netherlands, 1965. (Reprinted in F. Genuys (ed.), *Programming Languages*, Academic Press, New York, 1968).

(Di65a) Dijkstra, E.W., "Solution of a Problem in Concurrent Programming Control," *CACM*, Vol. 8, No. 5, September 1965, p. 569.

(Di68) Dijkstra, E.W., "The Structure of the T.H.E Multiprogramming System," *CACM*, Vol. 11, No. 5, May 1968, pp. 341–346.

(Di71) Dijkstra, E.W., "Hierarchical Ordering of Sequential Processes," *Acta Informatica*. Vol. 1, 1971, pp. 115–138.

(Ea72) Easton, W.B., "Process Synchronization without Long-Term Interlock," Proc. Third ACM Symp. Operating Systems Principles. *ACM Operating Systems Review*, Vol. 6, No. 1, June 1972, pp. 50–95.

(Ei72) Eisenberg, M.A., and M.R. McGuire, "Further Comments on Dijkstra's Concurrent Programming Control Problem," *CACM*, Vol. 15, No. 11, November 1972, p. 999.

(Gr75) Greif, I., "Semantics of Communicating Parallel Processes," *M.I.T. Project MAC TR-154*, September 1975.

(Ha72) Habermann, A. N., "Synchronization of Communicating Processes," *CACM*, Vol. 15, No. 3, March 1972, pp. 171–176.

(Ho72) Hoare, C.A.R., "Towards a Theory of Parallel Programming," In C.A.R. Hoare (ed.), *Operating Systems Techniques*, New York: Academic Press, 1972.

(Ho78) Hoare, C.A.R., "Communicating Sequential Processes," *CACM*, Vol. 21, No. 8, August 1978, pp. 666–667.

(Ka76) Kaubisch, W.H.; R.H. Perrott; and C.A.R. Hoare, "Quasi-parallel programming," *Software Practice and Experience*, Vol. 6, pp. 341–356, 1976.

(Kn66) Knuth, D., "Additional Comments on a Problem in Concurrent Programming Control," *CACM*, Vol. 9, No. 5, May 1966, pp. 321–322.

(La74) Lamport, L., "A New Solution of Dijkstra's Concurrent Programming Problem," *CACM*, Vol. 17, 1974, pp. 453–455.

(La76) Lamport, L., "Synchronization of Independent Processes," *Acta Informatica*, Vol. 7, No. 1, pp. 15–34, 1976.

(La77) Lamport, L., "Concurrent Reading and Writing," *CACM*, Vol. 20, No. 11, November 1977, pp. 806–811.

(La78) Lamport, L., "Time, Clocks, and the Ordering of Events in a Distributed System," *CACM*, Vol. 21, No. 7, July 1978, pp. 558–565.

(Ow76) Owicki, S., and D. Gries, "Verifying Properties of Parallel Programs: An Axiomatic Approach," *CACM*, Vol. 19, No. 5, May 1976, pp. 279–288.

(Pa71) Patil, S.S., "Limitations and Capabilities of Dijkstra's Semaphore Primitive for Coordination among Processes," *M.I.T. Proj. MAC Computational Structures Group Memo 57*, February 1971.

(Re79) Reed, D.P., and R.K. Kanodia, "Synchronization with Eventcounts and Sequencers," *CACM,* Vol. 22, No. 2, February 1979, pp. 115–123.

(Tr79) Treleaven, P. C., "Exploiting Program Concurrency in Computing Systems," *IEEE Computer Magazine,* January 1979, pp. 42–50.

(Wi77) Wirth, N., "Modula: A Language for Modular Programming," *Software Practice and Experience,* Vol. 7, No. 1, January–February 1977, pp. 3–35.

5
Concurrent Programming: Monitors; The Ada* Rendezvous

Minotaur, n —1: Class. Myth. A monster, the offspring of Pasiphaë and the Cretan bull, that had the head of a bull on the body of a man; housed in the Cretan Labyrinth, it was fed on human flesh until Theseus, helped by Ariadne, killed it. 2: Any person or thing that devours or destroys.

The Random House Dictionary of the English Language

You see but you do not observe.

Sir Arthur Conan Doyle
The Memoirs of Sherlock Holmes

We may say most aptly that the Analytical Engine weaves algebraical patterns just as the Jacquard loom weaves flowers and leaves.

Ada Lovelace

*Ada® is a registered trademark of the United States Government, Ada Joint Program Office.

Outline

5.1 INTRODUCTION

In the last chapter we presented Dekker's Algorithm for the implementation of mutual exclusion primitives, and we studied Dijkstra's semaphores. But these methods have a number of weaknesses. They are so primitive that it is difficult to express the solutions to more complex concurrency problems, and their presence in concurrent programs increases the already difficult problem of proving program correctness. The misuse of these primitives, either intentional or accidental, could corrupt the operation of a concurrent system. Therefore researchers have been prompted to seek out higher-level mutual exclusion constructs that

- facilitate expressing the solutions to complex concurrency problems,
- facilitate proving program correctness,
- are difficult (if not impossible) for the user to misuse or corrupt.

Perhaps the most important of these constructs is the *monitor* suggested by Dijkstra (Di71), then Brinch Hansen (Br72, Br73), and then refined by Hoare (Ho74).

5.2 MONITORS

A monitor is a concurrency construct that contains both the data and procedures needed to perform allocation of a particular shared resource or group of shared resources. To accomplish a resource allocation function, a process must call a particular *monitor entry*. Many processes may want to enter the monitor at various times. But mutual exclusion is rigidly enforced at the monitor boundary. Only one process at a time is allowed to enter. Processes desiring to enter the monitor when it is already in use must wait. This waiting is automatically managed by the monitor. Since mutual exclusion is guaranteed, the nasty concurrency problems (such as indeterminate outcomes) discussed in Chapter 4 are avoided.

The data inside the monitor may be either global to all procedures within the monitor or local to a specific procedure. All of this data is accessible only from within the monitor; there is simply no way for processes outside the monitor to access monitor data. This is called *information hiding*—a system structuring technique that greatly facilitates the development of more reliable software systems.

If the process calling the monitor entry finds the resource already allocated, the monitor procedure calls *wait*. The process could remain inside the monitor, but this would violate mutual exclusion if another process then entered the monitor. Therefore, the process calling *wait* is made to wait outside the monitor for the resource to be released.

Eventually, the process that has the resource will call a monitor entry to return the resource to the system. This entry could merely accept the returned resource and wait for another requesting process to arrive. But there may be processes waiting for the resource, so the monitor entry calls *signal* to allow one of the waiting processes to acquire the resource and leave the monitor. If a process signals the return (sometimes called the release) of the resource, and no processes are waiting, then the signal has no effect (but, of course, the monitor has recaptured the resource). Clearly, a process waiting for a resource must do so outside the monitor to allow another process into the monitor to return the resource.

To ensure that a process waiting for a resource eventually does get it, the monitor gives priority to the waiting process over a new requesting process attempting to enter the monitor. Otherwise a new process could grab the resource before the waiting process reenters the monitor. If this unfortunate sequence were to occur repeatedly, then a waiting process could be indefinitely postponed.

Actually, processes may wish to (need to) wait outside a monitor for many different reasons as we will see in the examples. So the notion of a *condition variable* is introduced. A separate condition variable is associated with each distinct reason that a process might need to wait. The wait and signal operations are then modified to include the name of the condition variable being waited upon or signaled

```
wait (conditionvariablename)
signal (conditionvariablename)
```

Condition variables are very different from the "conventional" variables with which we are familiar. When a condition variable is defined, a queue is established. A process calling *wait* is threaded into the queue; a process calling *signal* causes a waiting process to be removed from the queue and to enter the monitor. We may assume a first-in-first-out queue discipline, although priority schemes can be useful in certain situations.

5.3 SIMPLE RESOURCE ALLOCATION WITH MONITORS

Suppose several processes need access to a certain resource that may be used by only one process at a time. A simple monitor for handling the assignment and deassignment of such a resource is shown in Fig. 5.1.

```
monitor resourceallocator;
var resourceinuse: boolean;
    resourceisfree: condition;
procedure getresource;
   begin
      if resourceinuse then
         wait(resourceisfree);
      resourceinuse := true
   end;
procedure returnresource;
   begin
      resourceinuse := false;
      signal(resourceisfree)
   end;
begin
   resourceinuse := false
end;
```

Fig. 5.1 Simple resource allocation with a monitor.

The beauty of the resourceallocator is that it performs exactly as a binary semaphore; getresource functions as the P operation; returnresource functions as the V operation. Because the simple one-resource monitor can be used to implement semaphores, monitors are at least as powerful as semaphores.

5.4 MONITOR EXAMPLE: THE RING BUFFER

Operating systems today are generally implemented as sets of asynchronous concurrent processes controlled by a nucleus. These processes manage parallel activities quite independently, but occasional communication between processes is needed. In this section we discuss the *ring buffer* and how it is useful in situations in which a producer process passes data to a consumer process.

The producer will occasionally want to produce data when the consumer is not ready to consume, and the consumer will occasionally want to consume data that the producer has not yet produced. Thus synchronization between a producer and a consumer is important.

Operating systems often allow some reasonable fixed amount of storage for buffering communications between producer and consumer processes. This can be simulated by an array of the designated size. The producer deposits data in the successive elements of the array. The consumer removes them in the order in which they were deposited. The producer can be several items ahead of the consumer. Eventually, the producer fills the last element of the array. When it produces more data, it must "wrap around" and again begin depositing data in the first element of the array (assuming of course that the consumer has removed the data previously put there by the producer). The array effectively closes in a circle, thus the term ring buffer.

Because of the fixed size of the ring buffer, the producer will occasionally find all of the array elements full; in this case the producer must be made to wait until the consumer empties an array element. Similarly, there will be times when the consumer wants to consume, but the array will be empty; in this case the consumer must be made to wait until the producer deposits data into an array element. The monitor ringbuffermonitor in Fig. 5.2 (based on that in (Ho74)) implements a ring buffer and the appropriate synchronization mechanism to handle the producer–consumer relationship.

We shall assume that the array contains slots (supplied as a constant) consisting of data type stuff (also to be supplied). Variables nextslottofill and nextslottoempty indicate where the next item is to be placed and from where the next item is to be removed. Condition variable ringbufferhasspace is waited upon by the producer finding ringbuffer completely full; it is signaled by the consumer who has just emptied a slot. Condition variable ringbufferhasdata is waited upon by the consumer finding ringbuffer empty; it is signaled by the producer who has just deposited data in a slot.

A ring buffer mechanism is appropriate for implementing *spooling* control in operating systems. One common example of spooling occurs when a process generates

```
monitor ringbuffermonitor;
var ringbuffer: array [0..slots-1] of stuff;
    slotinuse: 0..slots;
    nextslottofill: 0..slots-1;
    nextslottoempty: 0..slots-1;
    ringbufferhasdata, ringbufferhasspace: condition;
procedure fillaslot (slotdata:stuff);
   begin
      if slotsinuse = slots
         then wait (ringbufferhasspace);
      ringbuffer [nextslottofill] := slotdata;
      slotinuse := slotinuse+1;
      nextslottofill := (nextslottofill + 1) mod slots;
      signal(ringbufferhasdata)
   end;
procedure emptyaslot (var slotdata:stuff);
   begin
      if slotinuse = 0 then wait(ringbufferhasdata);
      slotdata := ringbuffer[nextslottoempty];
      slotinuse := slotinuse - 1;
      nextslottoempty := (nextslottoempty + 1) mod slots;
      signal(ringbufferhasspace)
   end;
begin
   slotinuse := 0;
   nextslottofill := 0;
   nextslottoempty := 0
end;
```

Fig. 5.2 A monitor implementation of a ring buffer.

lines to be printed on a relatively slow output device such as a line printer. Because the process can produce the lines much faster than the printer can print them, and because it is desired for the process to run as quickly as possible, the process's output lines are directed to a ring buffer mechanism. The ring buffer may be in primary storage, or more likely on disk. This first process is often called a *spooler.* Another process reads lines from the ringbuffer and writes them on the printer. But this second process, often called a *despooler,* runs at the slower speed of the printer. The ringbuffer has sufficient storage to "take up the slack" resulting from the mismatch in the speeds of the spooler and despooler processes.

5.5 MONITOR EXAMPLE: READERS AND WRITERS

In computer systems, it is common to have some processes (called readers) that read data and others (called writers) that write it. For example, in an airline reservation system there may be many more readers than writers—many inquiries will be made against the database of available flight information before the customer actually selects and commits to seats on a particular flight.

Because readers do not change the contents of the database, many readers may access the database at once. But a writer can modify the data, so it must have exclusive access. When a writer is active, no other readers or writers may be active. This exclusion needs only to be enforced at the record level. It is not necessary to grant a writer exclusive access to the entire database.

The problem of designing a concurrent program to control access of readers and writers to a database was first posed and solved by Courtois, Heymans, and Parnas (Co71). The solution in Fig. 5.3 is based on that developed by Hoare and Gorman (Ho74).

The monitor readersandwriters may be used to control access to an entire database, a subset of the database consisting of many or few records, or even a single record. In any of these cases, the following discussion applies. Only one writer may be active at once; when a writer is active, the boolean variable someoneiswriting is true. No readers may be active when a writer is active. The variable, readers, indicates the number of active readers. When the number of readers is reduced to zero, then a waiting writer may become active. The condition variable readingallowed is waited upon by a new reader that cannot proceed. The condition variable writingallowed is waited upon by a new writer that cannot proceed.

When a reader wishes to read it calls monitor entry beginreading; a reader that has finished calls finishedreading. In beginreading, a new reader can proceed as long as no process is writing and no writer process is waiting to write. The later condition is important for preventing indefinite postponement of waiting writers. Note that procedure beginreading ends by signaling readingallowed to allow another waiting reader to begin reading. This, of course, causes this next reader to become active and signal the next waiting reader to proceed. In fact, this chain reaction will continue until all waiting readers have become active. While this chaining is progressing, all arriving processes are forced to wait. The chaining makes good sense. Because the readers don't interfere with one another, and because they can be run in parallel on multiple processor systems, this is an efficient way to service these processes. Note that while the chaining is in progress even arriving readers cannot enter the monitor because we observe the rule that signaled processes are serviced before arriving processes.

When a process is done reading, it calls finishedreading where it decrements the number of readers by 1. Eventually, this decrementing causes the number of readers to become zero at which point the process signals writingallowed to allow a waiting writer to proceed.

When a writer wishes to proceed, it calls monitor procedure beginwriting. Because a writer must have completely exclusive access, if there are any readers or if there is an active writer, this writer must wait on condition variable writingallowed. When the writer is able to proceed, someoneiswriting is set to true. This keeps out any other readers and writers.

```
monitor readersandwriters;
var
   readers: integer;
   someoneiswriting: boolean;
   readingallowed, writingallowed: condition;
procedure beginreading;
   begin
      if someoneiswriting or queue(writingallowed)
         then wait(readingallowed);
      readers := readers + 1;
      signal(readingallowed)
   end;
procedure finishedreading;
   begin
      readers := readers - 1;
      if readers = 0 then signal(writingallowed)
   end;
procedure beginwriting;
   begin
      if readers > 0 or someoneiswriting
         then wait(writingallowed);
      someoneiswriting := true
   end;
procedure finishedwriting
   begin
      someoneiswriting := false;
         if queue(readingallowed)
            then signal(readingallowed)
            else signal(writingallowed)
      end;
   begin
      readers := 0;
      someoneiswriting := false
   end;
```

Fig. 5.3 A monitor for solving the Readers and Writers Problem.

When a writer finishes, it sets someoneiswriting to false to allow other processes in. It then must signal some other waiting process to proceed. Should it give preference to a waiting reader or a waiting writer? If it gives preference to a waiting writer, then it will be possible for a steady stream of incoming writers to cause the indefinite postponement of waiting readers. Therefore as a writer finishes it first checks if there is a waiting reader. If there is, then readingallowed is signaled and the waiting reader proceeds. If there is no waiting reader, then writingallowed is signaled and a waiting writer is allowed to proceed.

5.6 ADA: THE CONCURRENT PROGRAMMING LANGUAGE FOR THE 1980s

The remainder of this chapter discusses concurrent programming with the emerging language Ada (Ad79a, Ad79b, Ad82). Most of today's popular languages were designed for writing sequential programs. They do not provide the special features needed for writing concurrent programs.

Ada allows an individual user to establish many separate threads of control that operate in behalf of the user. This is called *multitasking.*

5.7 MOTIVATION FOR ADA MULTITASKING

Military command and control systems often require the monitoring of many concurrent activities. Keeping track of the status of the world's naval vessels, controlling air traffic, and watching the skies for enemy missiles are all examples of systems that must monitor many concurrent activities, and respond quickly to unpredictable changes in the monitored activities. Writing effective software for the computer components of these systems is greatly facilitated by the use of a concurrent programming language. It is for this reason that the United States Government sponsored the development of Ada.

Concurrent programs are normally more difficult to write, debug, and prove correct than sequential programs. But in many situations they are actually easier to develop because they can more naturally express the relationships inherent in the highly parallel systems being modeled.

With uniprocessor computers, there isn't much motivation to develop and use concurrent languages except perhaps as research curiosities. But with multiprocessors, concurrent programs can be executed much more efficiently. So it is reasonable to expect a tremendous surge in interest in concurrent programming languages in the near future.

5.8 CORRECTNESS OF CONCURRENT PROGRAMS

A program is said to be *correct* if it meets its specification, i.e., if it does what it is supposed to do. Previously, implementors established the correctness of their programs by exhaustive testing. But correctness has assumed a new dimension in recent years, namely, the notion of a program being correct in a mathematical sense. Researchers in the field of software engineering have focused their attention on this issue: how does one demonstrate (prior to even attempting to execute or test a program) that a program is correct? Establishing the correctness of concurrent programs is generally much more difficult than establishing the correctness of sequential programs (La77, La79, Ow76, Pu81). The designers of Ada were concerned with developing a language that would facilitate demonstrating the correctness of concurrent programs.

5.9 THE ADA RENDEZVOUS*

The designers of Ada chose to incorporate a technique called a *rendezvous* for enforcing mutual exclusion and task synchronization. Exactly two tasks may rendezvous at once in Ada—a *caller* and a *server.* The caller calls an entry in the server. The server, when it is ready to do so, issues an *accept statement* to receive the call. If the caller calls an entry for which the server has not as yet issued an accept, then the caller waits until the accept is issued. If the server issues an accept for an entry that the caller has not as yet called, then the server waits (at the accept) for the caller to call the entry.

When a call has been accepted, the rendezvous occurs. The caller passes data to the server through parameters in the entry call. The data are processed by the statements within the accept statement body. Results, if any, are passed back to the caller through the entry parameters.

The caller waits while the server executes within the accept statement. When this processing is complete, parameters are passed back to the caller, the rendezvous ends, and the caller and server tasks resume independent operation.

One interesting aspect of the Ada rendezvous is that the caller must know of the existence of the server and the various server entries. But the server accepts calls from any caller. Many callers may attempt to call one server. In this sense, the rendezvous is asymmetric.

Mutual exclusion is guaranteed by underlying system mechanisms; only one caller at a time may rendezvous with the server. Other callers attempting a simultaneous rendezvous are kept waiting. Synchronization of the tasks is implicit during the rendezvous. After a rendezvous, any waiting callers are processed first-come-first-served.

5.10 THE ACCEPT STATEMENT

Figure 5.4 shows an Ada task, RESOURCECONTROLLER, designed to control access to a single shared resource. The task loops indefinitely alternately accepting calls to entries GETCONTROL and RELINQUISHCONTROL.

---

*Ada is a large language and we simply don't have room in an operating systems text to define it. Therefore, we have tried to illustrate concurrency features of the language in a way that a reader familiar with Pascal should be able to comprehend. An abundance of literature is available for the reader interested in studying Ada.

At the time of this writing, Ada compilers were not as yet in wide use. The Ada program segments in this chapter have not been compiled, therefore they should be viewed as academic examples that may need further refinement when implemented. The material may not follow Ada syntax precisely.

Note: The examples that follow are based on those presented in certain Ada documents issued by the United States Government (Ad79a, Ad79b). Material in these documents may be used freely without permission, to encourage the evaluation and use of the Ada Language.

```
task RESOURCECONTROLLER is
   entry GETCONTROL;
   entry RELINQUISHCONTROL;
end RESOURCECONTROLLER;
task body RESOURCECONTROLLER is
begin
   loop
      accept GETCONTROL;
      accept RELINQUISHCONTROL;
   end loop;
end RESOURCECONTROLLER;
         .
         .
         .
RESOURCECONTROLLER.GETCONTROL;
   -- use the resource
RESOURCECONTROLLER.RELINQUISHCONTROL;
         .
         .
         .
```

Fig. 5.4 Controlling access to a single resource with the Ada rendezvous.

Tasks voluntarily cooperate in their use of RESOURCECONTROLLER to ensure mutual exclusion. If several tasks call GETCONTROL simultaneously, only one call will be accepted and the other calls will wait in a first-come-first-served queue.

This is essentially the same as a binary semaphore mechanism. If one task ignores the cooperative protocol or misuses it, then mutual exclusion cannot be guaranteed. For example, a malicious task that wants to grab control of the resource can do so by issuing

```
   .
   .
   .
RESOURCECONTROLLER.RELINQUISHCONTROL
RESOURCECONTROLLER.GETCONTROL
```

and the task will be able to access the resource (as long as no other task was previously waiting on GETCONTROL).

5.11 ADA EXAMPLE: PRODUCER–CONSUMER RELATIONSHIP

As one simple example of a producer–consumer relationship, consider a producer task that deposits an 80-character card image in a buffer, and a consumer task that removes the characters from the buffer one at a time until the buffer is empty. The producer may not deposit the next line in the buffer until the consumer has completely processed all 80 characters in the line; the consumer may not begin removing characters from the buffer until a line has been deposited. Also, after the consumer processes all the characters in one line, it must wait for the producer to deposit the next line. Otherwise the consumer would process the same line more than once. Figure 5.5(a) shows a task for synchronizing the producer and consumer tasks that are shown in Fig. 5.5(b).

```
task CONVERTCARDIMAGE is
   type CARDIMAGE is array (1..80) of CHARACTER;
   entry DEPOSITCARD (CARD: in CARDIMAGE);
   entry READCHARACTER (NEXTCHARACTER: out
                                   CHARACTER);
end;
task body CONVERTCARDIMAGE is
   CARDBUFFER: CARDIMAGE;
begin
   loop
      accept DEPOSITCARD (CARD: in CARDIMAGE) do
         CARDBUFFER := CARD;
      end DEPOSITCARD;
      for POSITION in 1..80 loop
       accept READCHARACTER(NEXTCHARACTER:out
                                     CHARACTER) do
          NEXTCHARACTER := CARDBUFFER(POSITION);
       end READCHARACTER;
      end loop;
   end loop;
end;
```

(a)

```
task PRODUCER;
task body PRODUCER is
   use CONVERTCARDIMAGE;
   NEWCARD: CARDIMAGE;
begin
   loop
      -- create NEWCARD
      DEPOSITCARD (NEWCARD);
   end loop;
end;
task CONSUMER;
task body CONSUMER is
   use CONVERTCARDIMAGE;
   NEWCHARACTER: CHARACTER;
begin
   loop
      READCHARACTER (NEWCHARACTER);
      -- process NEWCHARACTER
   end loop;
end;
```

(b)

Fig 5.5 (a) Task for synchronizing a producer task and a consumer task. (b) Producer and consumer tasks.

5.12 THE SELECT STATEMENT

Entry calls need not necessarily be accepted in some prespecified and rigid fashion. Ada provides the *select statement* to enable tasks to accept entry calls in a more flexible manner. A common form of the select statement is

```
select
   when CONDITION1 => accept ENTRY1
      sequence of statements;
   or when CONDITION2 => accept ENTRY2
      sequence of statements;
   or . . .
   else
      sequence of statements;
end select;
```

The select statement is executed as follows.

- Each of the conditions (also called *guards* (see Di75)) is evaluated to be true or false. Each condition that evaluates to true causes the following accept sequence of statements to be considered *open*. If a condition is not written before an accept, then the accept is always open.
- There may be several open accept statements. Of these, in turn, several may be ready for a rendezvous; i.e., the appropriate entries have been called by other tasks. One of these is selected arbitrarily, i.e., Ada does not specify which one, and the associated rendezvous occurs.
- If there is an else part and no entry calls to open accept statements, the else is executed. If there is no else part, the task waits for an entry call.
- If there are no open accepts, the else part is executed. If there is also no else, then a SELECT-ERROR occurs.

5.13 ADA EXAMPLE: THE RING BUFFER

Figure 5.6 shows an Ada implementation of a ring buffer. The select statement allows the task to service appropriate entry calls. The guard BUFFERSINUSE < BUFFERS allows a call to WRITEPACKET to be accepted whenever space is available. The guard BUFFERSINUSE > 0 allows a call to READPACKET to be accepted whenever the buffer contains data.

```
task RINGBUFFER is
   type DATAPACKET is array (1..80) of CHARACTER;
   entry READPACKET (PACKET: out DATAPACKET);
   entry WRITEPACKET (PACKET: in DATAPACKET);
end;
task body RINGBUFFER is
   BUFFERS: constant INTEGER := 20;
   RING: array (1..BUFFERS) of DATAPACKET;
   BUFFERSINUSE: INTEGER range 0..BUFFERS := 0;
   NEXTIN,NEXTOUT: INTEGER range 1..BUFFERS := 1;
```

Fig. 5.6 Ada implementation of a ring buffer.

```
begin
   loop
      select
         when BUFFERSINUSE < BUFFERS =>
           accept WRITEPACKET(PACKET: in DATAPACKET) do
             RING(NEXTIN) := PACKET;
           end;
           BUFFERSINUSE := BUFFERSINUSE + 1;
           NEXTIN := NEXTIN mod BUFFERS + 1;
         or when BUFFERSINUSE > 0 =>
           accept READPACKET(PACKET: out DATAPACKET) do
             PACKET := RING(NEXTOUT);
           end;
           BUFFERSINUSE := BUFFERSINUSE - 1;
           NEXTOUT := NEXTOUT mod BUFFERS + 1;
      end select;
   end loop;
end RINGBUFFER;
```

Fig. 5.6 (*Continued*)

5.14 ADA EXAMPLE: READERS AND WRITERS

In this section, Ada solutions to the Readers and Writers problem are presented.

```
task READERSANDWRITERS is
   procedure READER (READVALUE: out INTEGER);
   entry WRITER (WRITEVALUE: in INTEGER);
end;
task body READERSANDWRITERS is
   SHAREDVARIABLE: INTEGER;
   READERS: INTEGER := 0;
   entry BEGINREADING;
   entry FINISHEDREADING;
   procedure READER (READVALUE: out INTEGER) is
   begin
      BEGINREADING;
      READVALUE := SHAREDVARIABLE;
      FINISHEDREADING;
   end;
   begin
      accept WRITER (WRITEVALUE: in INTEGER) do
         SHAREDVARIABLE := WRITEVALUE;
      end;
      loop
         select
            accept BEGINREADING;
            READERS := READERS + 1;
```

Fig. 5.7 Ada solution to Readers and Writers: version one.

```
            or
               accept FINISHEDREADING;
               READERS := READERS - 1;
            or
               when READERS = 0 =>
                  accept WRITER (WRITEVALUE: in INTEGER) do
                     SHAREDVARIABLE := WRITEVALUE;
                  end;
            end select;
         end loop;
      end READERSANDWRITERS;
```

Fig. 5.7 *(Continued)*

In this first solution (Fig. 5.7), a WRITER must write to SHAREDVARIABLE before any READER can access it. This ensures that the value of SHAREDVARIABLE is defined before the first read.

After the first WRITER finishes, the task will loop indefinitely. If no WRITER is active, then any number of additional READERs can be initiated. This of course could result in indefinite postponement of WRITERs. The next WRITER can be initiated only when there are no active READERs, but even if a WRITER is waiting, the random choice inherent in the SELECT might allow a waiting READER to proceed first. This solution does enforce mutual exclusion, but processes may be indefinitely postponed.

Note that READER is a procedure rather than an entry. This allows many tasks to be reading at once.

```
task READERSANDWRITERS is
   procedure READER (READVALUE: out INTEGER);
   entry WRITER (WRITEVALUE: in INTEGER);
end;
task body READERSANDWRITERS is
   SHAREDVARIABLE: INTEGER;
   READERS: INTEGER := 0;
   entry BEGINREADING;
   entry FINISHEDREADING;
   procedure READER (READVALUE: out INTEGER) is
   begin
      BEGINREADING;
      READVALUE := SHAREDVARIABLE;
      FINISHEDREADING;
   end;
begin
   accept WRITER (WRITEVALUE: in INTEGER) do
      SHAREDVARIABLE := WRITEVALUE;
   end;
```

Fig. 5.8 Ada solution to Readers and Writers: version two.

```
   loop
      select
         when WRITER'COUNT = 0 =>
            accept BEGINREADING;
            READERS := READERS + 1;
         or
            accept FINISHEDREADING;
            READERS := READERS - 1;
         or
            when READERS = 0 =>
              accept WRITER (WRITEVALUE: in INTEGER) do
                SHAREDVARIABLE := WRITEVALUE;
              end;
              loop
                 select
                   accept BEGINREADING;
                   READERS := READERS + 1;
                 else
                   exit;
                 end select;
              end loop;
      end select;
   end loop;
end READERSANDWRITERS;
```

Fig. 5.8 *(Continued)*

Version two (Fig. 5.8) also forces a WRITER to write once before any READERs can proceed. Now let's consider the main loop that loops indefinitely.

The first guard tests WRITER'COUNT to determine if there are any waiting WRITERs. If not, then a new READER will be initiated. In fact, as long as there are no waiting WRITERs, more READERs may continue to be initiated.

The second accept in the main loop, accept FINISHEDREADING, has no guard so it is always open. Thus a finishing READER will always be accepted; this, of course, facilitates reducing the number of READERs to zero so that another WRITER may eventually be initiated.

When the number of READERs is finally reduced to zero and there is a waiting WRITER, then a waiting WRITER is initiated. Immediately after this WRITER terminates, all READERs trying to proceed are allowed to do so.

The rendezvous is always in effect when a WRITER is active so mutual exclusion is guaranteed. So the real key is how version two handles the READERs.

No READER can be active when a WRITER is active because the rendezvous guarantees mutual exclusion. So let's consider what happens when no WRITER is active.

If no WRITER is waiting, then READERs will continue to be initiated. As soon as a WRITER starts waiting, then no more READERs will be initiated. All calls to FINISHEDREADING will be accepted until READERs is reduced to zero. At this point, the guard READERS=0 becomes true and the first waiting WRITER is accepted. When this WRITER completes, all READERs that have arrived since the WRITER began are initiated in the inner loop. This mass initiation of READERs will stop as soon as one iteration of the loop executes accept BEGINREADING and no READER is ready to go. This causes the else clause to be executed and the loop to be exited.

There is still a weakness in version two. In the inner loop, it is possible for waiting WRITERs to be indefinitely postponed by a rapid influx of READERs. As long as the READERs arrive faster than the loop can accept them, WRITERs are delayed. It is possible to develop a better solution of READERSANDWRITERS with Ada. This task is left to the exercises.

SUMMARY

A monitor is a concurrency construct that contains both the data and the procedures needed to perform allocation of a shared resource or group of shared resources.

The monitor enforces information hiding—processes calling the monitor have no knowledge of, nor access to, data inside the monitor.

Mutual exclusion is rigidly enforced at the monitor boundary—only one process at a time is allowed to enter.

If a process inside the monitor cannot proceed until a certain condition becomes true, the process calls wait(conditionvariablename) and waits outside the monitor on a queue for conditionvariablename to be signaled by another process.

To ensure that a process already waiting for a resource eventually does get it, the monitor gives priority to the waiting process over a new requesting process attempting to enter the monitor.

A separate condition variable is associated with each distinct reason that a process might need to wait. When a condition variable is defined, a queue is established. A process calling **wait** is threaded into the queue; a process calling *signal* causes a waiting process to be removed from the queue and to enter the monitor.

The ring buffer is a data structure commonly used in operating systems for buffering communications between producer and consumer processes. In the monitor implementation of the ring buffer, a producer finding the buffer full calls wait(ringbufferhasspace); a consumer finding the buffer empty calls wait (ringbufferhasdata). A producer depositing data calls signal(ringbufferhasdata); a consumer removing data calls signal(ringbufferhasspace).

The Readers and Writers problem was discussed and a solution with a monitor was presented. A writer must be given exclusive access to the database; any number of readers may be active at once. A reader wishing to begin reading may do so only if there is no active writer and no waiting writers (the latter condition presents indefinite postponement of writers by an influx of readers). A finishing reader reduces the number of active readers by one; when no more active readers remain, the finishing reader signals a waiting writer (if there is one) to proceed. A writer wishing to write waits if there are active readers or if there is an active writer; otherwise it proceeds. A finishing writer gives preference to waiting readers over waiting writers; this prevents indefinite postponement of readers by an influx of writers.

The emerging language Ada was specifically designed to facilitate concurrent programming. Ada allows an individual user to establish many separate threads of control; this is called multitasking. Each thread of control in Ada is called a task.

The trends toward multiprocessing and computer networking point to the need for concurrent programming languages like Ada. A program is said to be correct if it meets its specification; Ada was designed to facilitate proving program correctness.

In Ada, mutual exclusion and task synchronization are enforced by a technique called rendezvous. A caller task may call an entry of another task; a server task issues an accept statement to accept a call to one of its entries. When a call is accepted, the rendezvous occurs. The caller passes data to the server through parameters in the entry call; results are also passed back through call parameters. The caller waits while the server does its processing.

Ada provides the select statement to enable tasks to accept entry calls in a flexible manner. A common form of the select statement is

```
select
   when CONDITION1 => accept ENTRY1
      sequence of statements;
   or when CONDITION2 => accept ENTRY2
      sequence of statements;
   or ...
   else
      sequence of statements;
end select;
```

Each of the conditions (or guards) is evaluated. A true condition causes the following accept sequence of statements to be considered open. If a condition is not written before an accept statement, then the accept is always open. Of the open accepts whose entries have been called, one is selected at random and the associated rendezvous occurs. If no open accepts are ready for a rendezvous, the else part is executed. If there is no else part, the task waits for an entry call.

TERMINOLOGY

accept statement in Ada
Ada
Brinch Hansen
caller task in Ada
concurrent programming language
condition variable

correctness
despooler process
Dijkstra
global data in a monitor
guard in Ada
higher-level mutual exclusion
constructs
Hoare
indefinite postponement
information hiding
local data in a monitor
monitor
monitor entry
multitasking
open accept statement in Ada
producer–consumer relationship
readers and writers
rendezvous
ring buffer
select statement in Ada
server task in Ada
signal (conditionvariablename)
spooler process
task
thread of control
wait (conditionvariablename)

EXERCISES

5.1 Compare and contrast the use of monitors and semaphore operations.

5.2 When a resource is returned by a process calling a monitor, the monitor gives priority to a waiting process over a new requesting process. Why?

5.3 How do condition variables differ from conventional variables? Does it make sense to initialize condition variables?

5.4 In the text it has been stated repeatedly that no assumptions should be made about the relative speeds of asynchronous concurrent processes. Why?

5.5 What factors, do you suppose, would affect a designer's choice of the number of slots a ring buffer should have?

5.6 Compare and contrast multitasking and multiprogramming.

5.7 Why is it considerably more difficult to test, debug, and prove program correctness for concurrent programs than for sequential programs?

5.8 Explain the rendezvous technique used in Ada for task synchronization, intertask communication, and mutual exclusion.

5.9 Why is the Ada rendezvous said to be an asymmetric technique?

5.10 Referring to the producer/consumer relationship shown in Section 5.11, explain why a third task is used to synchronize the producer and consumer tasks.

5.11 Show the general form of the Ada select statement. Explain how select statements are executed.

5.12 Consult the literature on Ada and develop a better Ada solution to the Readers and Writers problem than that presented in the text.

5.13 The Dining Philosophers. One of Dijkstra's more delightful contributions is his problem of the Dining Philosophers (Di71). It illustrates many of the subtle problems inherent in concurrent programming. The problem is this.

Five philosophers sit around a circular table. Each of the five philosophers leads a simple life alternating between thinking and eating spaghetti. In front of each philosopher is a dish of spaghetti that is constantly replenished by a dedicated server. There are exactly five forks on the table, one between each adjacent pair of philosophers. Eating spaghetti (in the most proper manner) requires that a philosopher use both forks (simultaneously) which are adjacent to his plate.

Your goal is to devise a concurrent program (with a monitor) that simulates the behavior of the philosophers. Your program should be free of deadlock and indefinite postponement—otherwise one or more philosophers would soon starve. Your program must, of course, enforce mutual exclusion—two philosophers cannot use the same fork at once.

A typical philosopher behaves as follows.

```
procedure typicalphilosopher;
   begin
      while true do
         begin
            think;
            eat
         end
   end;
```

Comment on each of the following implementations of a typical philosopher.

a)
```
procedure typicalphilosopher;
   begin
      while true do
         begin
            thinkforawhile;
            pickupleftfork;
            pickuprightfork;
            eatforawhile;
            putdownleftfork;
            putdownrightfork
         end
   end;
```

b)
```
procedure typicalphilosopher;
   begin
      while true do
         begin
            thinkforawhile;
            pickupbothforksatonce;
            eatforawhile;
            putdownbothforksatonce;
         end
   end;
```

c)
```
procedure typicalphilosopher;
   begin
      while true do
         begin
            thinkforawhile;
            repeat
               pickupleftfork;
               if rightforknotavailable
                  then putdownleftfork
                  else pickuprightfork
            until holdingbothforks;
            eatforawhile;
            putdownleftfork;
            putdownrightfork
         end
   end;
```

5.14 Use a monitor to implement a solution to the Dining Philosophers problem that allows at most four philosophers to be eating or attempting to eat at once. Comment on the effectiveness of this solution.

5.15 The text states that information hiding is a system structuring technique that contributes to the development of more reliable software systems. Why, do you suppose, is this so?

5.16 Refer to the monitor, ringbuffermonitor, shown in Fig. 5.2 and answer each of the following questions.

a) Which procedure places data into the ring buffer?
b) Which procedure removes data from the ring buffer?
c) Which queueing discipline best describes the operation of the ring buffer?
d) Is this true: nextslottofill > = nextslottoempty?
e) Which statements perform monitor initialization?
f) Which statement(s) can "wake up" a process waiting on a condition variable?
g) Which statement(s) can put a process "to sleep"?
h) Which statement(s) ensure that the buffer "wraps around"?
i) Which statement(s) modify a shared critical variable to indicate that another slot in the buffer is available?

LITERATURE

(Ad79a) "Preliminary Ada Reference Manual," *ACM SIGPLAN Notices,* Vol. 14, No. 6, June 1979, Part A.

(Ad79b) "Rationale for the Design of the Ada Programming Language," *ACM SIGPLAN Notices,* Vol. 14, No. 6, June 1979, Part B.

(Ad82) "Reference Manual for the Ada Programming Language (Draft Revised Mil-Std 1815)," *ACM Special Publication,* July 1982, ACM Order No. 825820.

(Br72) Brinch Hansen, P., "Structured Multiprogramming," *CACM,* Vol. 15, No. 7, July 1972, pp. 574–577.

(Br73) Brinch Hansen, P., *Operating System Principles,* Englewood Cliffs, N.J.: Prentice-Hall, 1973.

(Br75) Brinch Hansen, P., "The Programming Language Concurrent Pascal," *IEEE Trans. of Soft. Eng.,* Vol. 1, No. 2, June 1975, pp. 199–207.

(Br76) Brinch Hansen, P., "The Solo Operating System: Processes, Monitors, and Classes," *Software—Practice and Experience,* Vol. 6, 1976, pp. 165–200.

(Br78) Brinch Hansen, P., "Distributed Processes: A Concurrent Programming Concept," *CACM,* Vol. 21, No. 11, November 1978, pp. 934–941.

(Co71) Courtois, P. J.; F. Heymans; and D. L. Parnas, "Concurrent Control with Readers and Writers," *CACM,* Vol. 14, No. 10, October 1971, pp. 667–668.

(Ca74) Campbell, R. H., and A. N. Habermann, "The Specification of Process Synchronization by Path Expressions," *Lecture Notes in Computer Science,* Vol. 16, Springer (1974), pp. 89–102.

(Da72) Dahl, O. J., and C. A. R. Hoare, "Hierarchical Program Structures," in *Structured Programming,* New York: Academic Press, 1972.

(Di65) Dijkstra, E. W., "Cooperating Sequential Processes," Technological University, Eindhoven, Netherlands, 1965. (Reprinted in F. Genuys (ed.), *Programming Languages,* Academic Press, New York, 1968).

(Di71) Dijkstra, E. W., "Hierarchical Ordering of Sequential Processes," *Acta Informatica,* Vol. 1, 1971, pp. 115–138.

(Di72) Dijkstra, E. W., "Information Streams Sharing a Finite Buffer," *Information Processing Letters,* Vol. 1, No. 5, October 1972, pp. 179–180.

(Di75) Dijkstra, E. W., "Guarded Commands, Nondeterminacy, and Formal Derivation of Programs," *CACM,* Vol. 18, 1975, pp. 453–457.

(Ho72a) Hoare, C. A. R., "Proof of Correctness of Data Representations," *Acta Informatica,* 1972, pp. 271–281.

(Ho72b) Hoare, C. A. R., "Towards a Theory of Parallel Programming," *Operating Systems Techniques,* New York: Academic Press, 1972.

(Ho74) Hoare, C. A. R., "Monitors: An Operating System Structuring Concept," *CACM,* Vol. 17, No. 10, October 1974, pp. 549–557. Corrigendum, *CACM,* Vol. 18, No. 2, February 1975, p. 95.

(Ho78) Hoare, C. A. R., "Communicating Sequential Processes," *CACM,* Vol. 21, No. 8, August 1978, pp. 666–677.

(Hw76a) Howard, J. H., "Proving Monitors," *CACM,* Vol. 19, No. 5, May 1976, pp. 273–279.

(Hw76b) Howard, J. H., "Signaling in Monitors," *Second Int. Conf. on Software Eng.,* San Francisco, October 1976, pp. 47–52.

(Ka74) Kahn, G., "The Semantics of a Simple Language for Parallel Programming," *Proc. IFIP Congress 74,* North Holland (1974).

(Ke78) Keedy, J., "On Structuring Operating Systems with Monitors," *Australian Computer Journal,* Vol. 10, No. 1, February 1978, pp. 23–27. Reprinted in *Operating Systems Review,* Vol. 13, No. 1, January 1979, pp. 5–9.

(La77) Lamport, L., "Proving the Correctness of Multiprocess Programs," *IEEE Trans. on Soft. Eng.,* Vol. SE–3, 1977, pp. 127–143.

(La79) Lamport, L., "A New Approach to Proving the Correctness of Multiprocess Programs," *ACM Trans. on Prog. Lang. and Sys.,* Vol. 1, 1979, pp. 84–97.

(La80) Lampson, B. W., and D. D. Redell, "Experience with Processes and Monitors in MESA," *CACM,* Vol. 23, No. 2, February 1980, pp. 105–117.

(Li75) Liskov, B. H., and S. N. Zilles, "Specification Techniques for Data Abstractions," *1975 Int. Conf. on Reliable Software,* Los Angeles, pp. 72–87.

(Ls76) Lister, A. M., and K. J. Maynard, "An Implementation of Monitors," *Software—Practice and Experience,* Vol. 6, No. 3, July 1976, pp. 377–386.

(Mi79) Mitchell, J. G., W. Maybury, and R. Sweet, *Mesa Language Manual,* Palo Alto, Calif.: Xerox Research Center, 1979.

(Ow76) Owicki, S., and D. Gries, "Verifying Properties of Parallel Programs: An Axiomatic Approach," *CACM,* Vol. 19, 1976, pp. 279–285.

(Pn81) Pnueli, A., "The Temporal Semantics of Concurrent Programs," *Theoretical Computer Science,* Vol. 13, 1981, pp. 45–60.

(Ra80) Ravn, A. P., "Device Monitors," *IEEE Trans. on Soft. Eng.,* Vol. SE-6, No. 1, January 1980, pp. 49–53.

(Re80) Redell, D., et al., "Pilot: An Operating System for a Personal Computer," *CACM,* Vol. 23, No. 2, February 1980.

(Ro75) Robinson L; K. N. Levitt; P. G. Neumann; A. R. Saxena, "On Attaining Reliable Software for a Secure Operating System," *1975 Int. Conf. on Reliable Software,* Los Angeles, pp. 267–284.

(Sa75) Saxena, A. R., and T. H. Bredt, "A Structured Specification of a Hierarchical Operating System," *SIGPLAN Notices,* Vol. 10, No. 6, June 1975, pp. 310–318.

(Si75) Sintzoff, M., and A. van Lamsweerde, "Constructing Correct and Efficient Concurrent Programs," *1975 Int. Conf. on Reliable Software,* Los Angeles, pp. 267–284.

(Wi77) Wirth, N., "Modula: A Language for Modular Multiprogramming," *Software—Practice and Experience,* Vol. 7, No. 1, January 1977, pp. 3–36.

6
Deadlock

Delay is the deadliest form of denial.

C. Northcote Parkinson

Break the embraces, dance while you can.

Wystan Hugh Auden

A quarrel is quickly settled when deserted by one party; there is no battle unless there be two.

Seneca

Outline

6.1 INTRODUCTION

A process in a multiprogramming system is said to be in a state of *deadlock* (or *deadlocked*) if it is waiting for a particular event that will not occur. In a system deadlock, one or more processes are deadlocked.

In multiprogrammed computing systems, resource sharing is one of the primary goals of the operating system. When resources are shared among a population of users, each of whom maintains exclusive control over particular resources allocated to that user, it is possible for deadlocks to develop in which the processes of some users will never be able to finish.

This chapter discusses the problem of deadlock and summarizes the major research results in the areas of *deadlock prevention, avoidance, detection,* and *recovery.* Also considered is the closely related problem of *indefinite postponement* in which a process, even though not deadlocked, could wait for an event that may never occur because of biases in the resource scheduling policies of a system.

The trade-offs between the overhead of deadlock correction mechanisms and the anticipated benefits are considered. In some cases, the price that must be paid to make a system deadlock free is high. In other cases, such as in real-time process control, there is no choice but to pay the price because allowing a deadlock to develop could be catastrophic.

6.2 EXAMPLES OF DEADLOCK

Perhaps the simplest manner in which to create a deadlocked process was illustrated by Holt (Ho72) in a PL/I program designed to cause a deadlock under OS/360.

```
REVENGE: PROCEDURE OPTIONS (MAIN, TASK);
         WAIT(EVENT);
END REVENGE;
```

The process associated with the program above will wait forever for EVENT to occur; however, no provision has been made in the program to SIGNAL the event. The system would have to detect that this process is "hung up" (deadlocked) and would break the deadlock by cancelling the job. Deadlocks such as this are extremely difficult to detect.

6.2.1 A Traffic Deadlock

Figure 6.1 illustrates a kind of deadlock that occasionally develops in our cities. A number of automobiles are attempting to drive through a busy section of the city, but the traffic has become completely snarled. Traffic comes to a complete halt, and it is necessary for the police to come in and unwind the jam by slowly and carefully backing cars out of the congested area. Eventually the traffic begins to flow normally, but not without much annoyance, effort, and the loss of considerable time.

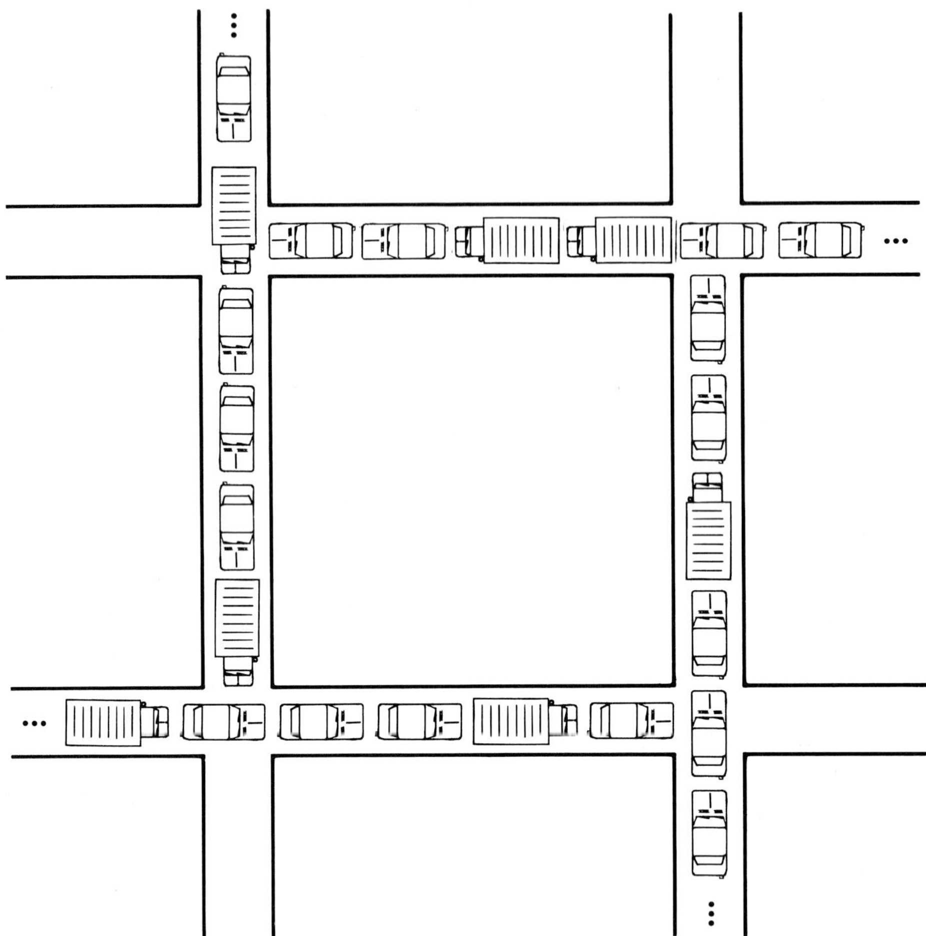

Fig. 6.1 A traffic deadlock.

6.2.2 A Simple Resource Deadlock

Most deadlocks in operating systems develop because of the normal contention for dedicated resources (i.e., resources that may be used by only one user at a time, sometimes called *serially reusable resources*). A simple example of a resource deadlock is illustrated in Fig. 6.2. This *resource allocation graph* shows two processes as rectangles and two resources as ovals. An arrow from a resource to a process indicates that the resource belongs to or has been allocated to the process. An arrow from a process to a resource indicates that the process is requesting, but has not as yet been allocated, the resource. The diagram illustrates a deadlocked system: Process A holds Resource 1 and needs Resource 2 to continue. Process B holds Resource 2 and needs Resource 1 to continue. Each process is waiting for the other to

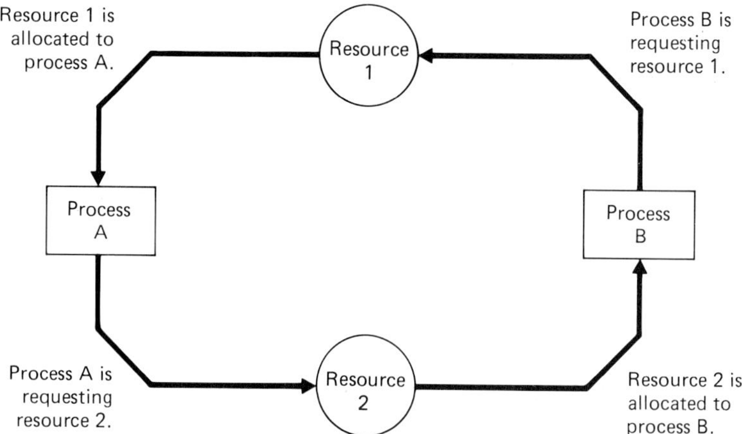

Fig. 6.2 A simple deadlock. This system is deadlocked because each process holds a resource being requested by the other process and neither process is willing to release the resource it holds.

free a resource that it will not free until the other frees its resource that it will not do until the other frees its resource, etc. This *circular wait* is characteristic of deadlocked systems.

6.2.3 Deadlock in Spooling Systems

Spooling systems are often prone to deadlock. A spooling system is used to improve system throughput by dissociating a program from the slow operating speeds of such devices as card readers and printers. For example, if a program sending lines to the printer must wait for each line to be printed before it can transmit the next line, then the program will execute slowly. To speed the program's execution, output lines are routed to a much faster device such as a disk drive where they are temporarily stored until they may be printed. In some spooling systems, the complete output from a program must be available before actual printing can begin. Thus several partially completed jobs generating print lines to a spool file could become deadlocked if the available space fills before any job completes. Unwinding, or recovering, from such a deadlock might involve restarting the system with a loss of all work performed so far. If the system deadlocks in a manner that leaves the operator in control, then a less drastic approach to recovery might be to kill one or more jobs until sufficient spooling space becomes available for the remaining jobs to complete.

When an operating system is generated by the systems programmer, the amount of space for spooling files is specified. One way to make spooling deadlocks less likely is to provide considerably more space for spooling files than is anticipated will be needed. This solution is not always feasible if space is at a premium. A more common solution is to collar the input spoolers so that they will not read in more jobs when the spooling files begin to reach some saturation threshold such as 75 percent full. This may reduce system throughput, but it is the price paid to reduce the likelihood of deadlocks.

Today's systems are more sophisticated than this. They might allow printing to begin before the job is completed so that a full, or nearly full, spooling file can be emptied or partially cleared even while a job is still executing. In many systems, allocation of spooling space has been made more dynamic so that if existing space starts to fill, then more space may be made available. The benefits of spooling generally outweigh the problems we have presented here, but our concern is that the reader be aware of potential difficulties in operating systems design.

6.3 A RELATED PROBLEM: INDEFINITE POSTPONEMENT

In any system that keeps processes waiting while it makes resource allocation and process scheduling decisions, it is possible to delay indefinitely the scheduling of a process while other processes receive the system's attention. This situation, called *indefinite postponement,* can often be as devastating as deadlock.

Indefinite postponement may occur because of biases in a system's resource scheduling policies. When resources are scheduled on a priority basis, it is possible for a given process to wait for a resource indefinitely as processes with higher priorities continue arriving. Waiting is a part of our lives and is certainly an important aspect of what goes on inside computer systems. Systems should be designed to manage waiting processes fairly as well as efficiently. In some systems, indefinite postponement is prevented by allowing a process's priority to increase as it waits for a resource. This is called *aging.* Eventually, that process's priority will exceed the priorities of all incoming processes, and the waiting process will be serviced.

Mathematical queueing theory provides the formal treatment of systems that manage waiting entities. Queueing theory is introduced in this text in Chapter 15, "Analytic Modeling."

6.4 RESOURCE CONCEPTS

An operating system is primarily a resource manager. It is responsible for the allocation of a vast array of resources of various types. The richness of resource types is part of what makes operating systems such an interesting topic. We consider resources that are "preemptible" such as the CPU and main memory; a user program currently occupying a particular range of locations in main memory may be removed or preempted by another program. A user program that has requested input/output cannot make effective use of the main memory during the long delay until the input/output is complete. The CPU is perhaps the most preemptible resource on a computer system. The CPU must be rapidly switched (multiplexed) among a large number of processes competing for system service to keep all of those processes progressing at a reasonable pace. Whenever a particular process reaches a point at which the CPU cannot be effectively used (such as during a long wait for input/output completion), control of the CPU is removed from that process and given to another process. *Preemption is thus extremely critical to the success of multiprogrammed computer systems.*

Certain resources are *nonpreemptible* and cannot be removed from the processes to which they are assigned. For example, tape drives are normally assigned to a particular process for periods of several minutes or hours. While a tape drive belongs to one process, it may not be taken from that process and given to another.

Some resources may be shared among several processes while others are dedicated to single processes. Disk drives are sometimes dedicated to single processes, but often contain files belonging to many processes. Main memory and the CPU are shared among many processes.

Data and programs are certainly resources that need to be controlled and allocated. On multiprogramming systems, many users may simultaneously want to use an editor program. It would waste main memory to bring in a separate copy of the editor for each program. Instead, one copy of the code is brought in and several copies of the data are made, one for each user. Since the code may be in use by many people at once, it cannot change. Code that cannot be changed while in use is said to be *reentrant.* Code that may be changed but is reinitialized each time it is used is said to be *serially reusable.* Reentrant code may be shared by several processes simultaneously whereas serially reusable code may be used by only one process at a time.

When we call particular resources shared, we must be careful to state whether they may be used by several processes simultaneously, or whether they may be used by several processes, but only by one at a time. The latter are the resources that become involved in deadlocks most commonly.

6.5 FOUR NECESSARY CONDITIONS FOR DEADLOCK

Coffman, Elphick, and Shoshani (Co71) stated the following four necessary conditions that must be in effect for a deadlock to exist.

- Processes claim exclusive control of the resources they require (*mutual exclusion* condition).
- Processes hold resources already allocated to them while waiting for additional resources (*wait for* condition).
- Resources cannot be removed from the processes holding them until the resources are used to completion (*no preemption* condition).
- A circular chain of processes exists in which each process holds one or more resources that are requested by the next process in the chain (*circular wait* condition).

6.6 MAJOR AREAS OF DEADLOCK RESEARCH

Deadlock has been one of the more productive research areas in computer science and operating systems. The results of deadlock research have been "nice" in that clean-cut methods have been found to handle many of the common problems. Primarily, there are four areas of interest in deadlock research. These are

- deadlock prevention,
- deadlock avoidance,
- deadlock detection,
- deadlock recovery.

In *deadlock prevention* our concern is to condition a system to remove any possibility of deadlocks occurring. Prevention is a clean solution as far as deadlock itself is concerned, but prevention methods can often result in poor resource utilization. Nevertheless, deadlock prevention methods are widely practiced.

In *deadlock avoidance* the goal is to impose less stringent conditions than in deadlock prevention in an attempt to get better resource utilization. Avoidance does not precondition the system to remove all possibility of deadlock. Instead, avoidance methods allow the possibility of deadlock to loom, but whenever a deadlock is approached, it is carefully sidestepped. (See the discussion of Dijkstra's Banker's Algorithm later in this chapter.)

Deadlock detection methods are used in systems that allow deadlocks to occur, either willingly or unwillingly. The goal of deadlock detection is to determine if a deadlock has occurred, and to determine precisely those processes and resources involved in a deadlock. Once this is determined, the deadlock can be cleared from the system.

Deadlock recovery methods are used to clear deadlocks from a system so that it may proceed to operate free of the deadlock, and so that the deadlock processes may complete and their resources may be freed. Recovery is a messy problem at best and most systems recover from deadlock by flushing one or more of the deadlocked processes completely. Then, the flushed processes are normally restarted from the beginning, with much if not all previous work done by these processes lost.

6.7 DEADLOCK PREVENTION

By far, the most frequent approach used by designers in dealing with the problem of deadlock is deadlock prevention. In this section, the various methods of deadlock prevention are considered, and the effects on both users and systems, especially from the standpoint of performance, are examined.

Havender (Hv68) concluded that if any of the four necessary conditions is denied, it is impossible for a deadlock to occur. Havender suggested the following strategies for denying various necessary conditions.

- Each process must request all its required resources at once and cannot proceed until all have been granted.
- If a process holding certain resources is denied a further request, that process must release its original resources and, if necessary, request them again together with the additional resources.
- Imposition of a linear ordering of resource types on all processes; i.e., if a process has been allocated resources of a given type, it may subsequently request only those resources of types later in the ordering.

Note that Havender presents three strategies, and not four. Each of the above, as we will see in the following sections, is designed to deny one particular necessary condition. The first necessary condition, namely that processes claim exclusive use of the resources they require, is not one that we want to break because we specifically want to allow *dedicated* resources.

6.7.1 Denying the "Wait for" Condition

Havender's first strategy requires that all of the resources a process will need must be requested at once. The system must grant them on an "all or none" basis. If the set of resources needed by a process is available, then the system may grant all of those resources to the process at one time and the process will be allowed to proceed. If the complete set of resources needed by a process is not currently available, then the process must wait until the complete set is available. While the process waits, however, it may not hold any resources. Thus the "wait for" condition is denied and deadlocks simply cannot occur.

This sounds good but it can lead to serious waste of resources. For example, a program requiring ten tape drives at one point in its execution must request, and receive, all ten tape drives before it begins executing. If all ten drives are needed throughout the execution of the program, then there is no serious waste. But, consider the case in which the program needs only one tape drive to begin execution (or worse yet, none at all) and then does not need the remaining tape drives for several hours. The requirement that the program must request, and receive, all of these tape drives before execution begins means that substantial computer resources will sit idle for several hours.

One approach frequently used by systems implementors to get better resource utilization in these circumstances is to divide a program into several program steps that run relatively independently of one another. Then resource allocation can be controlled by step rather than for the entire process. This can reduce waste, but it involves a greater overhead in the design of applications systems, as well as in their execution.

This strategy can cause indefinite postponement since not all of the required resources may become available at once. The computer system must allow a sufficient number of jobs to complete and free their resources before the waiting job can proceed. While the required resources are being accumulated they cannot be allocated to other jobs, and the resources are wasted. There is some controversy over whom to charge for these unused resources. Because the resources are being accumulated for a specific user, some designers feel this user should pay for them, even during the period the resources sit idle. Other designers say this would destroy the *predictability of resource charges*; if the user tries to run the job on a busy day, the charges would be much higher than when the machine is lightly loaded.

6.7.2 Denying the "No-Preemption" Condition

Havender's second strategy, considered here independently of the others, denies the "no-preemption" condition. Suppose a system does allow processes to hold resources while requesting additional resources. As long as sufficient resources remain available to satisfy all requests, the system cannot deadlock. But consider what happens when a request cannot be satisfied. Now a process holds resources a second process may need in order to proceed while the second process may hold the resources needed by the first process. This is deadlock.

Havender's second strategy requires that when a process holding resources is denied a request for additional resources, that process must release its held resources and, if necessary, request them again together with the additional resources. Implementation of this strategy effectively denies the "no-preemption" condition. Resources can be removed from the processes holding them prior to the completion of those processes.

Here, too, the means for preventing deadlock is not without cost. A process using certain resources for some time, when it releases those resources may lose all of its work to that point. This may seem to be a high price to pay, but the real question is "How often does this price have to be paid?" If this occurs infrequently, then a relatively low-cost means of preventing deadlocks is provided. If, on the other hand, this occurs frequently, then the cost is substantial and the effects are disruptive, particularly when high-priority or deadline processes cannot be completed on time.

One serious consequence of this strategy is the possibility of indefinite postponement. A process might be held off indefinitely as it repeatedly requests and releases the same resources. If this occurs, the system might need to remove the process so that other processes could proceed. The possibility that the process being indefinitely postponed might not be very "visible" to the system cannot be ignored. In this case, the process might consume substantial computer resources and degrade the system's performance.

6.7.3 Denying the "Circular Wait" Condition

Havender's third strategy denies the possibility of a circular wait. Because all resources are uniquely numbered, and because processes must request resources in ascending order, it is impossible for a circular wait to develop.

This strategy has been implemented in a number of operating systems, but not without difficulties.

- Resources must be requested in ascending order by resource number. Resource numbers are assigned for the installation and must be "lived with" for long periods (i.e., months or even years). If new resource types are added at an installation, existing programs and systems may have to be rewritten.
- Clearly, when the resource numbers are assigned, they should reflect the normal ordering in which most jobs actually use resources. For jobs matching this ordering, efficient operation may be expected. But for jobs that need the resources in a different order than that assumed at the installation, resources must be acquired and held, possibly long before they are actually used. This results in waste because these resources are held but unused.
- One of the most important goals in today's operating systems is to create user-friendly environments. Users should be able to develop their applications with a minimal pollution of their environments by awkward hardware and software restrictions. Havender's linear ordering truly eliminates the possibility of a circular wait, yet it is certainly a polluting effect upon a user's ability to freely and easily write applications code.

6.8 DEADLOCK AVOIDANCE AND THE BANKER'S ALGORITHM

If the necessary conditions for a deadlock to occur are in place, it is still possible to avoid deadlock by being careful when resources are allocated. Perhaps the most famous deadlock-avoidance algorithm is Dijkstra's Banker's Algorithm (Di65), called by this interesting name because it involves a banker who makes loans and receives payments from a given source of capital. We paraphrase the algorithm here in the context of operating systems resource allocation.

6.8.1 Dijkstra's Banker's Algorithm

When we refer to resources in the following, we mean resources of the same type. The Banker's Algorithm is easily extendable to pools of resources of several different types. For example, consider the allocation of a quantity, t, of identical tape drives.

> An operating system shares a fixed number of equivalent tape drives, t, among a fixed number of users, u. Each user specifies in advance the maximum number of tape drives he or she will need during the execution of his or her job on the system.
>
> The operating system will accept a user's request if that user's maximum need for tape drives does not exceed t.
>
> A user may obtain or release tape drives one by one. Sometimes, a user may have to wait to obtain an additional tape drive, but the operating system guarantees a finite wait. The current number of tape drives allocated to a user will never exceed that user's stated maximum need.

If the operating system is able to satisfy a user's maximum need for tape drives, then the user guarantees that the tape drives will be used and released to the operating system within finite time.

The current state of the system is called *safe* if it is possible for the operating system to allow all current users to complete their jobs within a finite time. (Again, it is assumed that tape drives are the only resources requested by users). If not, then the current system state is called *unsafe.*

Now suppose there are n users.

Let 1 (i) represent user i's current loan of tape drives. If user 5, for example, has been allocated four tape drives, then $1(5) = 4$. Let m (i) be the maximum need of user i so that if user 3 has a maximum need of two tape drives then m $(3) = 2$. Let c (i) be the current claim of a user where a user's claim is equal to his maximum need minus his current loan. If, for example, user 7 has a maximum need of six tape drives and a current loan of four tape drives, then we have

$$c(7) = m(7) - 1(7) = 6 - 4 = 2.$$

The operating system controls t tape drives. Let a be the number of tape drives still available for allocation. Then a is t minus the sum of the loans to the various users.

Dijkstra's Banker's Algorithm says to allocate tape drives to users only when the allocations result in safe states rather than in unsafe states. A safe state is one in which the total resource situation is such that all users would eventually be able to finish. An unsafe state is one that might eventually lead to deadlock.

6.8.2 Example of a Safe State

Suppose a system has twelve equivalent tape drives, and three users sharing the drives as in State I.

State I

	Current loan	Maximum need
User(1)	1	4
User(2)	4	6
User(3)	5	8
Available	2	

This state is "safe" because it is still possible for all three users to finish. Note that User(2) currently has four tape drives allocated to him and will eventually need a maximum of six, or two additional drives. The system has twelve drives of which ten are currently in use and two are available. If these two available drives are given to User(2) fulfilling User(2)'s maximum need, then User(2) may run to completion. User(2) upon finishing will release all six tape drives that the system may assign to User(1) and User(3). User(1) has one tape drive and will need three more eventually. User(3) has five and will need three more eventually. If User(2) returns six, then three may be given to User(1) who may then finish and return four tape drives to the system. The system may then give three drives to User(3) who may now also finish. Thus the key to a state being safe is that there is a way for all users to finish.

6.8.3 Example of an Unsafe State

Assume a system's twelve tape drives are allocated as in State II.

State II

	Current loan		Maximum need
User(1)	8		10
User(2)	2		5
User(3)	1		3
Available		2	

Here eleven of the system's twelve tape drives are currently in use and only one drive is available for allocation. At this point, no matter which user requests the available drive, we cannot guarantee that all three users will finish. In fact, suppose User(1) requests and is granted the last available drive. A three-way deadlock could occur if indeed each process needs to request at least one more drive before releasing any drives to the pool.

It is important to note here that *an unsafe state does not imply the existence, or even the eventual existence, of deadlock. What an unsafe state does imply is simply that some unfortunate sequence of events might lead to a deadlock.*

6.8.4 Example of Safe State to Unsafe State Transition

That a state is known to be safe does not imply that all future states will be safe. Our resource allocation policy must carefully consider all resource requests before granting them. For example, suppose the current state of a system is as in State III.

State III

	Current loan		Maximum need
User(1)	1		4
User(2)	4		6
User(3)	5		8
Available		2	

Now suppose that User(3) requests an additional resource. If the system were to grant this request, then the new state would be State IV.

State IV

	Current loan	Maximum need
User(1)	1	4
User(2)	4	6
User(3)	6	8
Available	1	

Certainly, State IV is not necessarily deadlocked. But the state has gone from a safe one to an unsafe one. The State IV characterizes a system in which completion of all user processes cannot be guaranteed. One resource is available. A minimum of two resources must be available to ensure that either User(2) or User(3) could complete, return its resources to the system, and ultimately allow the other users to finish.

6.8.5 The Banker's Algorithm Resource Allocation

Now it should be clear how resource allocation operates under Dijkstra's Banker's Algorithm. The "mutual-exclusion," "wait-for," and "no-preemption" conditions are allowed. Processes do claim exclusive use of the resources they require. Processes are indeed allowed to hold resources while requesting and waiting for additional resources, and resources may not be preempted from a process holding those resources. Users ease on to the system by requesting one resource at a time. The system may either grant or deny each request. If a request is denied, that user holds any allocated resources and waits for a finite time until that request is eventually granted. *The system grants requests that result in safe states only.* A user's request that would result in an unsafe state is denied until it can eventually be satisfied. Of course, because the system is always maintained in a safe state, sooner or later (i.e., in a finite time) all requests can be satisfied and all users can finish.

6.8.6 Weaknesses in the Banker's Algorithm

The Banker's Algorithm is of interest to us because it provides a way of allocating resources to avoid deadlock. It allows jobs to proceed that under a deadlock prevention situation would have had to wait. But the algorithm contains a number of serious weaknesses that might cause a designer to choose another approach to the deadlock problem.

- The algorithm requires that there be a fixed number of resources to allocate. Since resources frequently require service, either because of breakdowns or preventive maintenance, we cannot count on the number of resources constantly remaining fixed.

- The algorithm requires that the population of users remain fixed. This, too, is unreasonable. In today's multiprogrammed systems, the user population is constantly changing. On a large timesharing system, for example, it is not unusual to service 100 or more users simultaneously. But the population of users changes constantly, perhaps as often as every few seconds.
- The algorithm requires that the Banker guarantee all requests will be granted within finite time. Clearly, much better guarantees than this are needed in real systems.
- Similarly, the algorithm requires that clients (i.e., jobs) guarantee that loans will be repaid (i.e., resources will be returned) within finite time. Again, much better guarantees than this are needed in real systems.
- The algorithm requires that users state their maximum needs in advance. With resource allocation becoming increasingly dynamic, it is becoming more difficult to know a user's maximum need. In fact, as systems provide more user-friendly interfaces, it is becoming common to have users who don't have the slightest idea what their resource needs are.

6.9 DEADLOCK DETECTION

Deadlock detection is the process of actually determining that a deadlock exists, and of identifying the processes and resources involved in the deadlock. Deadlock detection algorithms are generally used in systems in which the first three necessary conditions for deadlock to occur are allowed. These algorithms then determine if a circular wait exists.

The use of deadlock detection algorithms involves certain run-time overhead. Thus we once again face the trade-off considerations so prevalent in operating systems. Does the overhead involved in deadlock detection algorithms more than compensate for the potential savings from locating and breaking up deadlocks? For the moment, we shall ignore this issue and concentrate instead on the development of algorithms capable of detecting deadlocks.

6.9.1 Resource Allocation Graphs

To facilitate the detection of deadlocks, a popular notation is used in which a directed graph indicates resource allocations and requests. Squares represent processes and large circles represent classes of identical resources. Small circles drawn inside large circles indicate the number of identical resources of each class. For example, a large circle labeled "R1" containing three small circles indicates that there are three equivalent resources of type R1 available for allocation in this system.

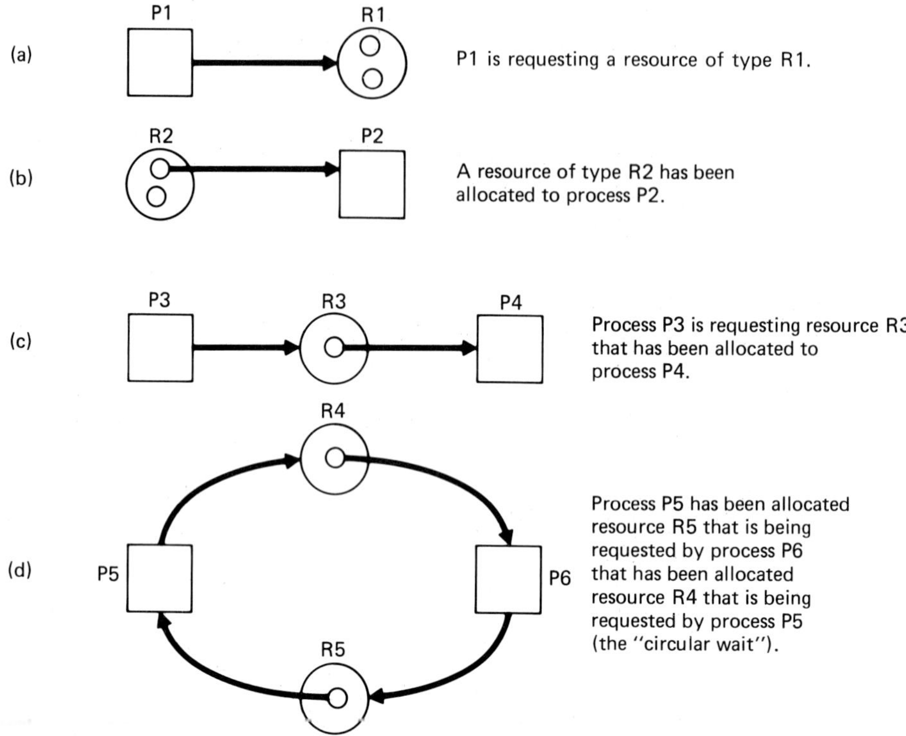

Fig. 6.3 Resource allocation and request graph.

Figure 6.3 indicates the relationships that may be indicated in a resource allocation and request graph. In Fig. 6.3(a), process P1 is requesting a resource of type R1. The arrow from P1 touches only the extremity of the large circle indicating that the resource request is currently under consideration.

In Fig. 6.3(b), process P2 has been allocated a resource of type R2 (of which there are two equivalent resources). The arrow is drawn from the small circle within the large circle R2 to the square P2.

Figure 6.3(c) indicates a situation somewhat closer to a potential deadlock. Resource R3 is being requested by process P3, but R3 has been allocated to process P4.

Figure 6.3(d) indicates a small deadlocked system in which resource R4 is being requested by process P5 that has been allocated resource R5 that is being requested by process P6 that has been allocated resource R4 that is being requested by process P5; an example of the "circular wait" typical of a deadlocked system.

Resource allocation and request graphs change as processes request resources, acquire them, and eventually release them to the operating system.

6.9.2 Reduction of Resource Allocation Graphs

Deadlock detection is concerned with determining whether a deadlock exists. One technique useful for detecting deadlocks involves graph reductions in which the processes that may complete and the processes that will remain deadlocked are determined.

If a process's resource requests may be granted, then we say that a graph may be *reduced* by that process. This reduction is equivalent to showing the graph if this process is allowed to complete and return its resources to the system. The reduction of a graph by a particular process is shown by removing the arrows to that process from resources (i.e., resources allocated to that process), and by removing arrows from that process to resources (i.e., current resource requests of that process). *If a graph can be reduced by all its processes, then there is no deadlock. If a graph cannot be reduced by all its processes, then the "irreducible" processes constitute the set of deadlocked processes in the graph.*

Figure 6.4 shows a series of graph reductions that eventually demonstrates that a particular set of processes is not deadlocked. Figure 6.3(d) shows a set of processes that is irreducible and thus constitutes a deadlocked system.

It is important to note here that the order in which the graph reductions are performed does not matter: the final result will always be the same. This result is relatively easy to demonstrate and it is left to the reader as an exercise.

6.10 DEADLOCK RECOVERY

Once a system has become deadlocked, the deadlock must be broken by removing one or more of the necessary conditions. Usually, several processes will lose some or all of the work they have accomplished. This may be a small price to pay compared with leaving the deadlock in place. Recovery from deadlock is made difficult by a number of factors.

- It may not be clear that the system has become deadlocked in the first place.
- Most systems have poor facilities for suspending a process indefinitely, removing it from the system, and resuming it at a later time. In fact, some processes such as real-time processes that must function continuously are simply not amenable to being suspended and resumed.
- Even if effective suspend/resume capabilities existed, they would most certainly involve considerable overhead and might require the attention of a highly skilled operator. Such an operator is not always available.
- Recovering from a deadlock of modest proportions might involve a reasonable amount of work; a deadlock on a grand scale (i.e., tens or even hundreds of processes) could require an enormous amount of work.

In current systems, recovery is ordinarily performed by forcibly removing a process from the system and reclaiming its resources. The removed process is ordinarily

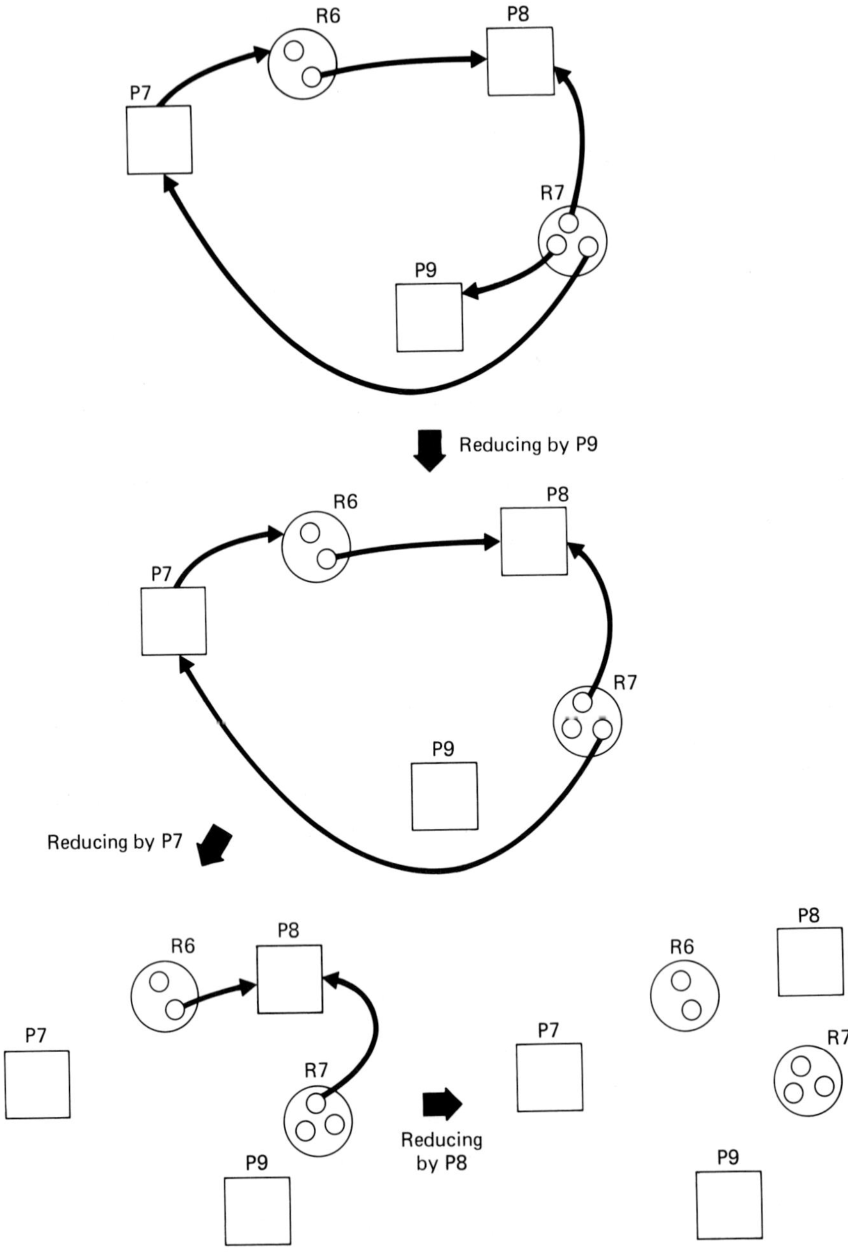

Fig. 6.4 Graph reductions.

lost, but the remaining processes may now be able to complete. Sometimes it is necessary to remove several processes until sufficient resources have been reclaimed to allow the remaining processes to finish. Recovery somehow seems like an inappropriate term here. It's like recovering from a sore hand by amputation of a finger!

Processes may be removed according to some priority order. Here, too, we face several difficulties.

- The priorities of the deadlocked processes may not exist so the operator may need to make an arbitrary decision.
- The priorities may be incorrect or somewhat muddled by special considerations, such as *deadline scheduling* in which a relatively low-priority process has a temporarily high priority because of an impending deadline.
- The optimum choice of processes to remove may require considerable effort to determine.

It would seem that the most desirable approach to deadlock recovery would be an effective suspend/resume mechanism. This would allow us to put temporary holds on processes, and then to resume the held processes without loss of productive work. Research in this area is important for reasons other than deadlock recovery. For example, it may become necessary to shut down a system temporarily and start up the system again from that point without loss of productive work. Suspend/resume would be useful here. The checkpoint/restart features available on many systems facilitate suspend/resume with a loss of the work only since the last checkpoint (i.e., a save of the state of the system) was taken. But many systems are designed without taking advantage of checkpoint/restart capabilities. It normally requires conscious effort on the part of applications systems developers to incorporate checkpoint/restart, and unless the jobs to be run require many hours of operation, its use is rare.

Deadlocks could have horrendous consequences in certain real-time systems. A real-time process control system monitoring a gasoline refinery simply must continue to function for the safety and proper operation of the refinery. Deadlocks can not be risked in such environments. What would happen if a deadlock did develop? Clearly, it would have to be detected and removed instantaneously. But is this always possible? These are some of the considerations that keep operating systems designers from restful sleep.

6.11 DEADLOCK CONSIDERATIONS IN FUTURE SYSTEMS

In recent computer systems, deadlock has generally been viewed as a limited annoyance. Most systems implement the basic deadlock prevention methods suggested by Havender, and these methods seem to be satisfactory.

In future systems, however, deadlock will be a far more critical consideration for several reasons.

- Future systems will be oriented more toward asynchronous parallel operation than toward the serial systems of the past. Multiprocessing will be common and parallel computation will be prevalent. There will, quite simply, be more operations going on concurrently.
- In future systems, resource allocation will tend to be dynamic. Processes will be able to acquire and release resources freely as needed. Users will not have to know much about their resource needs in advance of their execution. In fact, with the anticipated user-friendly interfaces of the future, most users will not be terribly concerned with the resource consumption of their processes.
- With the increasing tendency of operating systems designers to view data as a resource the number of resources operating systems must manage will increase dramatically.

Thus the burden of deadlock-free resource allocation in future computer systems should be on the operating system. With computing resources becoming cheaper, it is reasonable for the computer and the operating system to assume such an expanded role.

SUMMARY

Deadlock and the related problem of indefinite postponement are important considerations in operating systems. One process may deadlock by waiting for an event that will never occur. Two or more processes may become involved in a resource deadlock in which each process holds resources requested by the others while it in turn requests resources held by the others. Spooling systems are prone to deadlock if allotted spool file space fills before processes finish.

Preemptible resources may be removed from a process; nonpreemptible resources may not. Dedicated resources are allocated to one process at a time. Reentrant code does not change while it is in execution; it may be shared simultaneously by several executing processes to conserve main storage space. Serially reusable code may be used by only one process at a time start-to-finish; the code may change while in execution, but it reinitializes itself for each new process.

The four necessary conditions for a deadlock to exist are "mutual exclusion," "wait for," "no-preemption," and "circular wait." "Mutual exclusion" means that processes claim exclusive control of their resources; "wait for" means that processes may hold resources while waiting for additional requested resources to be allocated; "no-preemption" means that resources may not be forcibly removed from processes; and "circular wait" means that a chain of processes exists in which each process holds a resource being requested by another process that holds a resource being requested by another process, etc.

The major areas of deadlock research are prevention in which by denying one or more of the necessary conditions, any possibility of deadlock occurring is completely removed from the system; avoidance in which deadlock is allowed to loom but is carefully sidestepped (hoping to get better resource utilization); detection in which existing deadlocks are isolated for the attention of operators and the system; and recovery in which deadlocks are removed (almost always with the loss of work).

Deadlocks may be prevented by denying one or more of the necessary conditions for deadlock. Only the mutual exclusion condition cannot be denied since we must allow mutually exclusive use of many types of system resources. The wait for condition may be denied by requiring that users request all resources they will need in advance; the system either grants the request as a group or denies the request and makes the user wait until the entire group of resources becomes available. The no-preemption condition may be denied by requiring that a user who holds some resources and is denied a request for additional resources must release all held resources and again request all required resources; this is unpleasant at best. The circular-wait condition may be denied by requiring that users request resources in a prearranged installation-defined order; it is easily shown that this prevents circuits from developing in the resource allocation graph.

Dijkstra's Banker's Algorithm provides a basis for implementing deadlock-avoidance algorithms. The state of a system in the Banker's Algorithm is said to be safe if it is possible for all users to finish and return their resources to the system; a state is unsafe if it is not possible to guarantee completion of all users. An unsafe state does not necessarily lead to deadlock; a system in an unsafe state could finish if events occur for the best. The Banker's Algorithm contains several serious weaknesses that preclude its use in today's operating systems, but it is of theoretical interest, possibly as the basis of more workable deadlock-avoidance algorithms for future operating systems.

Resource allocation graphs are useful for showing the "resource state" of a system. The technique of graph reductions is useful for detecting deadlock.

Deadlock recovery is generally accomplished by flushing one or more of the deadlocked processes from the system, freeing their resources so that they may be given to other processes. Recovery in today's systems is messy. Improved suspend/resume capabilities would greatly improve the deadlock recovery process.

Deadlock in today's systems is generally viewed as an infrequent annoyance. In future systems, deadlock could become a far more important consideration because these systems will operate with much more dynamic resource allocation and more processes will run concurrently.

TERMINOLOGY

checkpoint/restart
"circular wait" condition
deadlock
deadlock avoidance
deadlock detection
deadlock prevention

deadlock recovery
dedicated resource
Dijkstra's Banker's Algorithm
dynamic resource allocation
indefinite postponement
irreducible process
mutual exclusion condition
necessary conditions for deadlock
nonpreemptible resource
"no-preemption" condition
preemptible resource
predictability of resource charges
reducible process
reduction of a resource allocation graph
reentrant procedure
resource allocation graph
safe state
serially reusable resource
Standard Allocation Pattern of Havender
unsafe state
"wait for" condition

EXERCISES

6.1 Define deadlock.

6.2 Give an example of a deadlock involving only a single process.

6.3 Give an example of a simple resource deadlock involving three processes and three resources. Draw the appropriate resource allocation graph.

6.4 Discuss the motivation for spooling systems. Why are spooling systems often prone to deadlock?

6.5 Suppose a spooling system is susceptible to deadlock. As an operating systems designer, what features might you provide in this operating system to help an operator unwind deadlocks without loss of work done so far by any of the deadlocked user processes?

6.6 Today's spooling systems often allow printing to begin even before a process has finished execution. Suppose a process has generated 1000 lines of printing and that these lines were accepted by the spooling mechanisms and placed on disk. Suppose the process will continue to execute and will eventually generate 19,000 remaining lines of a printed report. After the first 1000 lines have been generated, a printer becomes available, and the printing of the first 1000 lines is initiated. What do you suppose happens when the printing of these lines has completed in each of the following cases.

a) The process has completed spooling the remaining 19,000 lines to disk.
b) The process is still executing.

Be careful to consider that the printed report must not show any interruptions; it must appear as if all 20,000 lines had been printed continuously.

6.7 Many early spooling systems operated with a fixed amount of spooling space. Today's systems are more dynamic in that more spooling space may be obtained by the operating system while the system is executing. How does this help decrease the chance of deadlock? Such a system could still deadlock. How?

6.8 What is indefinite postponement? How does it differ from deadlock? How is it similar?

6.9 Suppose a given system allows for indefinite postponement of certain entities. How would you as a systems designer provide a means for preventing indefinite postponement?

6.10 Discuss the consequences of indefinite postponement in each of the following types of systems.

a) batch processing b) timesharing c) real-time

6.11 Why is preemption critical to the success of multiprogrammed computer systems?

6.12 Discuss each of the following resource concepts.

a) preemptible resource b) nonpreemptible resource
c) shared resource d) dedicated resource
e) reentrant code f) serially reusable code

6.13 State the four necessary conditions for a deadlock to exist. Give a brief intuitive argument for the reason each individual condition is necessary.

6.14 Consider the traffic deadlock illustrated in Fig. 6.1. Discuss each of the necessary conditions for deadlock in the context of the traffic deadlock.

6.15 What are the four areas of deadlock research mentioned in the text? Discuss each briefly.

6.16 Havender's method for denying the "wait for" condition requires that processes must request all of the resources they will need before the system may let them proceed. The system grants resources on an "all or none" basis. This is one of the most widely implemented methods for preventing deadlock. Discuss its pros and cons.

6.17 Havender's method for denying the "no-preemption" condition is not a popular means for preventing deadlock. Why is this true?

6.18 Havender's method for denying the "circular wait" condition has been implemented in many systems. Discuss its pros and cons.

6.19 Show that Havender's Standard Allocation Pattern for denying the "circular wait" condition actually prevents circuits from developing in resource allocation graphs.

6.20 Explain the intuitive appeal of deadlock avoidance over deadlock prevention.

6.21 In the context of Dijkstra's Banker's Algorithm discuss whether each of the following states is safe or unsafe. If a state is safe, show how it is possible for all processes to complete. If a state is unsafe, show how it is possible for deadlock to occur.

State A

	Current loan	Maximum need
User(1)	2	6
User(2)	4	7
User(3)	5	6
User(4)	0	2
Available	1	

State B

	Current loan	Maximum need
User(1)	4	8
User(2)	3	9
User(3)	5	8
Available	2	

6.22 Just because a state is unsafe does not necessarily imply that the system will deadlock. Explain why this is true. Give an example of an unsafe state and show how all of the processes could complete without a deadlock occurring.

6.23 Dijkstra's Banker's Algorithm has a number of weaknesses that preclude its effective use in real systems. Comment on why each of the following restrictions may be considered a weakness in the Banker's Algorithm.

a) The number of resources to be allocated remains fixed.
b) The population of users remains fixed.
c) The operating system guarantees that resource requests will be serviced in finite time.
d) Users guarantee that they will return held resources within finite time.
e) Users must state maximum resource needs in advance.

6.24 In a system in which it is possible for a deadlock to occur, under what circumstances would you use a deadlock detection algorithm.

6.25 In the deadlock detection algorithm employing the technique of graph reductions, show that the order in which the graph reductions are performed is immaterial; the same final result will be achieved.

6.26 Why is deadlock recovery such a difficult problem?

6.27 Why is it difficult to choose which processes to "flush" in deadlock recovery?

6.28 In this chapter, we state that an effective suspend/resume capability is useful in deadlock recovery. The "suspend/resume" problem is of great interest to operating systems designers, and it has not as yet been solved satisfactorily.

a) Discuss why suspend/resume is such an important feature to provide.
b) Discuss why suspend/resume is so difficult to implement.

6.29 Why will deadlock probably be a more critical problem in future operating systems than it is today?

6.30 Given that the first three necessary conditions for a deadlock to occur are in place, comment on the feasibility of the following strategy: All processes are given unique priorities. When more than one process is waiting for a resource and the resource becomes available, allocate the resource to the waiting process with the highest priority.

6.31 Given that all resources are identical, they can be acquired and released strictly one at a time, and no process ever needs more than the total resources on the system, state whether deadlock can occur in each of the following systems.

	Number of processes	Number of resources
a)	1	1
b)	1	2
c)	2	1
d)	2	2
e)	2	3

Now suppose that no process ever needs more than two resources. State whether deadlock can occur in each of the following systems.

	Number of processes	Number of resources
f)	1	2
g)	2	2
h)	2	3
i)	3	3
j)	3	4

6.32 Sometimes enough information about the maximum resource needs of processes is available to enable deadlock avoidance without considerable run-time overhead. For example, consider the following situation (R. C. Holt): A set of m processes shares n identical resources. Resources may be acquired and released strictly one at a time. No process ever needs more than n resources. The sum of the maximum needs for all of the processes is strictly less than $m + n$. Show that no deadlocks can develop in this system.

LITERATURE

(Ch80) Chang, E., "n-Philosophers: An Exercise in Distributed Control," *Computer Networks,* Vol. 4, April 1980, pp. 71–76.

(Co71) Coffman, E. G., Jr.; M. Elphick; and A. Shoshani, "System Deadlocks," *Computing Surveys,* Vol. 3, No. 2, June 1971, pp. 67–78.

(Di65) Dijkstra, E. W., *Cooperating Sequential Processes,* Technological University, Eindhoven, The Netherlands, 1965.

(Di68) Dijkstra, E. W., "The Structure of the T.H.E. Multiprogramming System," *CACM,* Vol. 11, No. 5, May 1968, pp. 341–346.

(Fo71) Fontao, R. O., "A Concurrent Algorithm for Avoiding Deadlocks," *Proc. Third ACM Symposium on Operating Systems Principles,* October 1971, pp. 72–79.

(Fr73) Frailey, D. J., "A Practical Approach to Managing Resources and Avoiding Deadlock," *CACM,* Vol. 16, No. 5, May 1973, pp. 323–329.

(Ge81) Gelernter, D., "A DAG Based Algorithm for Prevention of Store-and-Forward Deadlock in Packet Networks," *IEEE Trans. on Computers*, Vol. 30, October 1981, pp. 709–715.

(Ha69) Habermann, A. N., "Prevention of System Deadlocks," *CACM*, Vol. 12, No. 7, July 1969, pp. 373–377, 385.

(Ha78) Habermann, A. N., "System Deadlocks," *Current Trends in Programming Methodology*, Vol. III, Englewood Cliffs, N. J.: Prentice-Hall, 1978, pp. 256–297.

(Hv68) Havender, J. W., "Avoiding Deadlock in Multitasking Systems," *IBM Systems Journal*, Vol. 7, No. 2, 1968, pp. 74–84.

(He70) Hebalkar, P. G., "Deadlock-Free Sharing of Resources in Asynchronous Systems," *M.I.T. Project MAC TR-75*, September 1970.

(Ho71) Holt, R. C., "Comments on the Prevention of System Deadlocks," *CACM*, Vol. 14, No. 1, January 1971, pp. 36–38.

(Ho71a) Holt, R. C., *On Deadlock Prevention in Computer Systems*, Ph.D. Thesis, Ithaca, N. Y.: Cornell University, 1971.

(Ho71b) Holt, R. C., "Some Deadlock Properties of Computer Systems," *Proc. Third ACM Symposium on Operating Systems Principles*, October 1971, pp. 64–71.

(Ho72) Holt, R. C., "Some Deadlock Properties of Computer Systems," *ACM Computing Surveys*, September 1972, pp. 179–196.

(Hw73) Howard, J. H., "Mixed Solutions for the Deadlock Problem," *CACM*, Vol. 16, No. 7, July 1973, 427–430.

(Ka80) Kameda, T., "Testing Deadlock-Freedom of Computer Systems," *JACM*, Vol. 27, April 1980, pp. 280–290.

(Lo80) Lomet, D., "Subsystems of Processes with Deadlock Avoidance," *IEEE Trans. on Soft. Eng.*, Vol. 6, May 1980, pp. 297–303.

(Ne80) Nezu, K., "System Deadlocks Resolution," *AFIPS Conf. Proc.*, Vol. 49, 1980, pp. 257–260.

(Se75) Sekino, L. C., "Multiple Concurrent Updates," In D. Kerr (ed.), *Proc. Intl. Conf. on Very Large Data Bases*, September 1975, pp. 505–507.

(Sh69) Shoshani, A., and A. J. Bernstein, "Synchronization in a Parallel-Accessed Data Base," *CACM*, Vol. 12, No. 11, 1969, pp. 604–607.

Part 3
Storage Management

7
Real Storage

Nothing ever becomes real till it is experienced—even a proverb is no proverb to you till your life has illustrated it.

John Keats

Outline

7.1 INTRODUCTION

The organization and management of the *main memory* or *primary memory* or *real memory* of a computer system has been one of the most important factors influencing operating systems design. The terms *memory* and *storage* have been used interchangeably in the literature. Of the two terms, storage is more fashionable today. Programs and data must be in main storage in order to be run or referenced directly. Secondary storage, most commonly disk, drum, and tape, provides massive, inexpensive capacity for the abundance of programs and data that must be kept readily available for processing.

In this and subsequent chapters, many popular schemes for organizing and managing a computer's storage are discussed. This chapter deals with *real storage*; the next several chapters discuss *virtual storage*. The schemes are presented approximately as they evolved historically.

7.2 STORAGE ORGANIZATION

Historically, main storage has been viewed as an expensive resource. As such, it has demanded the attention of systems designers; it has been necessary to squeeze the maximum use out of this costly resource. Early systems were concerned with organizing and managing main storage for optimal use.

By storage organization we mean the manner in which the main storage is viewed. Do we place only a single user in the main storage, or do we place several users in it at the same time? If several user programs are in main storage at the same time, do we give each of them the same amount of space, or do we divide main storage into portions, called *partitions*, of different sizes? Do we partition the main storage in a rigid manner with partitions defined for extended periods of time, or do we provide for a more dynamic partitioning allowing the computer system to adapt quickly to changes in the needs of user jobs? Do we require that user jobs be designed to run in a specific partition, or do we allow jobs to run anywhere they will fit? Do we require that each job be placed in one contiguous block of storage locations, or do we allow jobs to be parcelled up into separate blocks and placed in any available slots in main storage?

Systems have been built implementing each of these schemes. This chapter discusses how each of these schemes is implemented.

7.3 STORAGE MANAGEMENT

Regardless of what storage organization scheme we adopt for a particular system, we must decide what strategies to use to obtain optimal performance. Storage management strategies determine how a particular storage organization performs under various policies: When do we get a new program to place in the memory? Do we get it when the system specifically asks for it, or do we attempt to anticipate the system's requests? Where in main storage do we place the next program to be run? Do we place programs as tightly as possible into available memory slots to minimize wasted space, or do we place programs as quickly as possible to minimize execution time?

If a new program needs to be placed in main storage and if main storage is currently full, which of the other programs do we displace. Should we replace the oldest programs, or should we replace those that are least frequently used, or those that are least recently used? Systems have been implemented using each of these storage management strategies.

7.4 STORAGE HIERARCHY

In the 1950s and 1960s, main storage, usually magnetic core memory, was very expensive. A decision about how much main storage to place on a computer system was made carefully. An installation couldn't buy more than it could afford, but it had to buy enough to support the operating system and a given number of users. The goal was to buy the minimum amount that could adequately support the anticipated user loads within the economic constraints of the installation.

Programs and data need to be in main storage in order to be executed or referenced. Programs or data not needed immediately may be kept on secondary storage until needed and then brought into the main storage for execution or reference. Secondary storage media such as tape or disk are generally less costly than main storage and have much greater capacity. Main storage may generally be accessed much faster than secondary storage.

In systems with several levels of storage, a great deal of shuttling goes on in which programs and data are moved back and forth between the various levels. This shuttling consumes system resources such as CPU time that could otherwise be put to productive use.

In the 1960s it became clear that the storage hierarchy could be extended by one more level with dramatic improvements in performance and utilization. This additional level, the *cache,* is a high-speed storage that is much faster than the main storage. Cache storage is extremely expensive compared with main storage and therefore only relatively small caches are used. Figure 7.1 shows the relationship between cache, primary storage, and secondary storage.

Cache storage imposes one more level of shuttling on the system. Programs in the main storage are shuttled to the very high-speed cache before being executed. In the cache, they may be executed much faster than in main storage. The hope of designers using the cache concept is that the overhead involved in shuttling programs back and forth will be much smaller than the performance increase obtained by the faster execution possible in the cache.

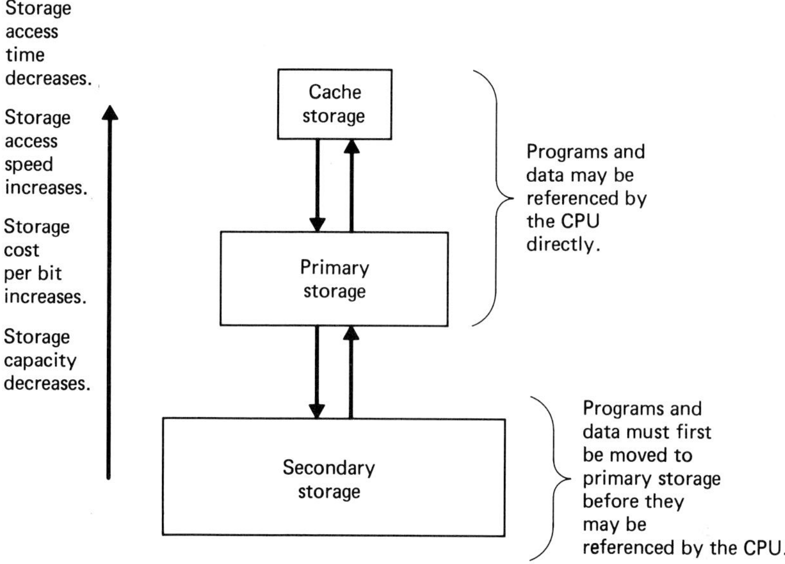

Fig. 7.1 Hierarchical storage organization.

7.5 STORAGE MANAGEMENT STRATEGIES

Expensive resources are managed intensively to achieve better use. Storage management strategies are geared to obtaining the best possible use of the main storage resource. Storage management strategies are divided into the following categories.

1. Fetch strategies
   a) Demand fetch strategies
   b) Anticipatory fetch strategies
2. Placement strategies
3. Replacement strategies

Fetch strategies are concerned with when to obtain the next piece of program or data for insertion into main storage. For many years, the conventional wisdom has been *demand fetch* in which the next piece of program or data is brought in to the main storage when it is referenced by a running program. It was believed that since we cannot generally predict where program control will go next, the overhead involved in making guesses and anticipating the future would far exceed expected benefits. Today many researchers feel that anticipatory fetching will yield improved system performance.

Placement strategies are concerned with determining where in main storage to place an incoming program. In this chapter, we shall consider the *first-fit, best-fit,* and *worst-fit* storage placement strategies.

Replacement strategies are concerned with determining which piece of program or data to displace to make room for incoming programs.

7.6 CONTIGUOUS VS. NONCONTIGUOUS STORAGE ALLOCATION

The earliest computing systems required *contiguous storage allocation*—each program had to occupy a single contiguous block of storage locations. It wasn't until variable partition multiprogramming was attempted that it became clear noncontiguous storage allocation might be useful.

In *noncontiguous storage allocation,* a program is divided into several blocks or *segments* that may be placed throughout main storage in pieces not necessarily adjacent to one another. It is more difficult for an operating system to control noncontiguous storage allocation. The benefit is that if main storage has many small holes available instead of a single large hole, then the operating system can often load and execute a program that would otherwise need to wait.

In the next several chapters the virtual storage systems so popular today are studied. They all involve noncontiguous storage allocation.

7.7 SINGLE USER CONTIGUOUS STORAGE ALLOCATION

The earliest computer systems allowed only a single person at a time to use the machine. All of the machine's resources were at the user's disposal. Billing for the use of the computer was straightforward—because the user had the entire machine, the user was charged for all of the resources whether or not the job used those resources. In fact, the normal billing mechanisms were based upon *wall clock* time. A user was given the machine for some time interval and was charged a flat hourly rate. Some of today's shared systems have far more complex billing algorithms.

Originally each user wrote all of the code necessary to implement a particular application, including the highly detailed machine level input/output instructions. Very quickly, the input/output coding needed to implement basic functions was consolidated into an *input/output control system (IOCS).* Users wishing to do input/output no longer had to code the instructions directly. Instead, they called IOCS routines to do the real work. This greatly simplified and speeded the coding process. The implementation of input/output control systems may have been the beginning of today's concept of operating systems. Figure 7.2 illustrates the storage organization for a typical *single user contiguous allocation system.*

Programs are limited in size to the amount of main storage, but it is possible to run programs larger than the main storage by using *overlays.* Figure 7.3 illustrates this concept. If a particular program section is not needed for the duration of the

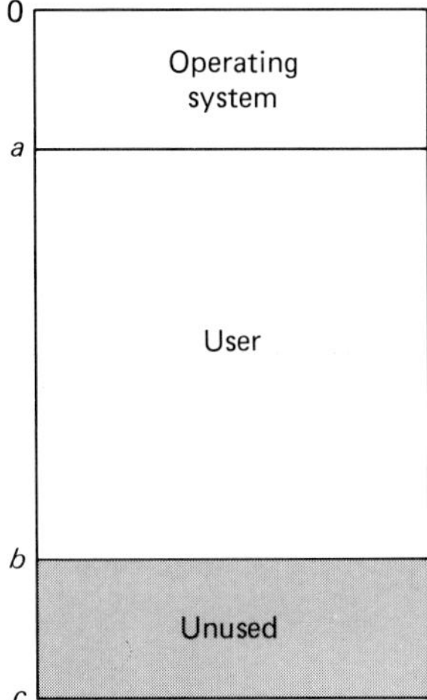

Fig. 7.2 Single user contiguous storage allocation.

program's execution, then another section of program may be brought in from secondary storage to occupy the storage used by the program section that is no longer needed.

Overlay gives the programmer a way to extend limited main storage. But manual overlay requires careful and time-consuming planning. A program with a sophisticated overlay structure can be difficult to modify. As we will see in subsequent chapters, virtual storage systems have obviated the need for programmer-controlled overlays.

7.7.1 Protection in Single User Systems

In single user contiguous allocation systems, the user has complete control over all of main storage. Storage is divided into a portion holding operating system routines, a portion holding the user's program, and an unused portion. The question of protection is simple. How should the operating system be protected from destruction by the user's program?

If the user's program goes astray, it can destroy the operating system. If this is fatal and the user cannot proceed, then the user will know something is wrong, will terminate execution, fix the problem, and retry the job. In these circumstances, the need for protecting the operating system is not apparent.

But suppose the user destroys the operating system more "gently." For example, suppose certain input/output routines are accidentally changed. Then all output records might be truncated. The job could still run. If the results are not examined until it completes, then the machine resource will be wasted. Worse yet, the damage

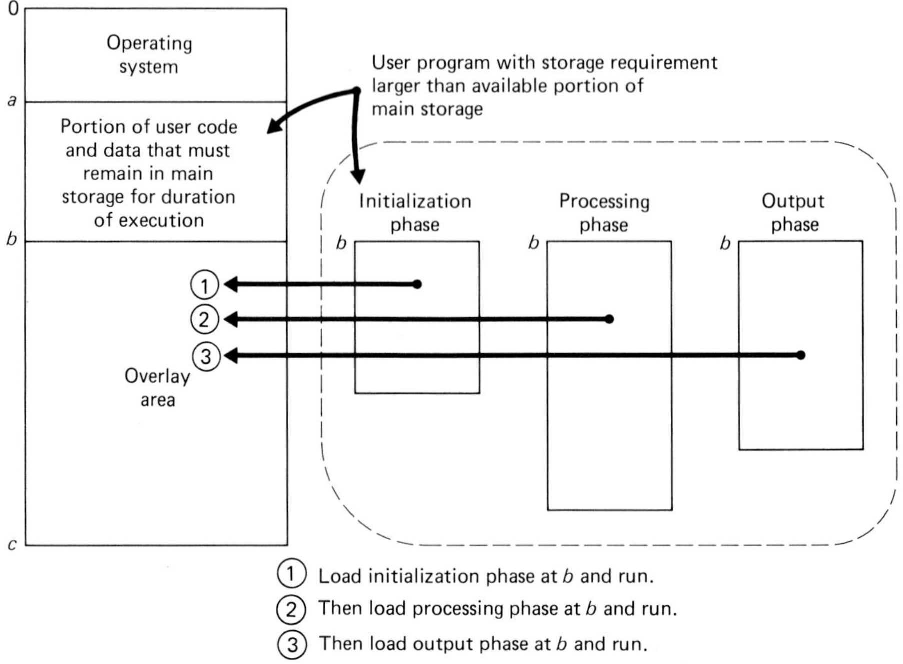

Fig. 7.3 A typical overlay structure.

to the operating system might cause outputs to be produced that can not easily be determined to be inaccurate.

It surely is clear that the operating system should be protected from the user. Protection is implemented by the use of a single *boundary register* built into the CPU, as in Fig. 7.4. Each time a user program refers to a storage address, the boundary register is checked to be certain that the user is not about to destroy the operating system. The boundary register contained the address of the highest instruction used by the operating system. If the user tried to enter the operating system, then the instruction is intercepted and the job terminates with an appropriate error message.

Of course, the user needs to enter the operating system from time to time to obtain services such as input/output. This problem is solved by giving the user a specific instruction with which to request services from the operating system (i.e., a *supervisor call* instruction). The user wanting to read from tape will issue an instruction asking the operating system to do so in the user's behalf. The operating system will perform the desired function, and then return control to the user program.

As operating systems have become more complex, it has been necessary to implement far more sophisticated mechanisms to protect the operating system from the users and to protect the users from one another. We shall discuss these mechanisms in detail later.

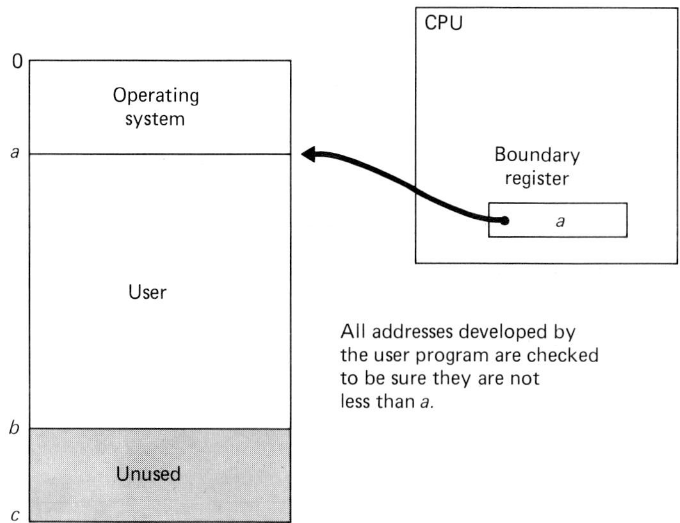

Fig. 7.4 Storage protection with single user contiguous storage allocation.

7.7.2 Single Stream Batch Processing

Single user systems are dedicated to one job for more than the job's execution time. Jobs generally require considerable setup time during which the operating system is loaded, tapes and disk packs are mounted, card decks are placed in the reader, appropriate forms are placed in the printer, time cards are "punched in," etc. When jobs complete, they require a considerable amount of *teardown time* as tapes, card decks, and disk packs are removed, forms are removed, time cards are "punched out," etc. During job setup and job teardown the computer sits idle.

Designers realized that if they could automate *job-to-job transition*, then they could reduce considerably the amount of time wasted between jobs. This led to the development of *batch processing* systems. In *single stream batch processing*, jobs are grouped in *batches* by placing their control cards back-to-back in the card reader, (or by loading the jobs consecutively onto tape or disk). A *job stream processor* reads the *job control language* statements, and facilitates the *setup* of the next job. It issues directives to the system operator, and performs many functions automatically that were previously performed manually. When the current job terminates, the job stream reader automatically reads in the control language statements for the next job, and performs appropriate *housekeeping* chores to facilitate the transition to the next job. Batch processing systems greatly improved the use of computer systems and helped demonstrate the real value of operating systems and intensive resource management.

Because reading cards is a relatively slow operation, it was common in large computer installations to use small *satellite computers* to prepare the batches for the large system. Job decks would arrive at the computer center, be grouped into batches, and loaded to tape on the satellite systems. The tapes would then be brought to the large system. This was an effective way to reduce job transition time on the large system and get better use of the computer. Single stream batch processing systems were the state of the art in the early 1960s.

7.8 FIXED PARTITION MULTIPROGRAMMING

Even with batch processing operating systems, single user systems still waste a considerable amount of the computing resource. Figure 7.5 illustrates this situation. The program consumes the CPU resource until an input or output is needed. When the I/O request is issued, the job often cannot continue until the requested data is either sent or received. Input and output speeds are extremely slow compared with CPU speeds. For example, a card reader reading 1000 cards per minute requires 60,000 microseconds to read a single card and make it available for processing. During that time, the CPU sits idle.

Designers saw that they could once again considerably increase the utilization of the CPU by intensive management. This time, they chose to implement *multiprogramming* systems in which several users simultaneously compete for system resources. The job currently waiting for I/O will yield the CPU to another job ready to do calculations if, indeed, another job is waiting. Thus both input/output and CPU calculations can occur simultaneously. This greatly increases CPU utilization and system throughput.

To take maximum advantage of multiprogramming, it is necessary for several jobs to reside in the computer's main storage at once. Thus when one job requests

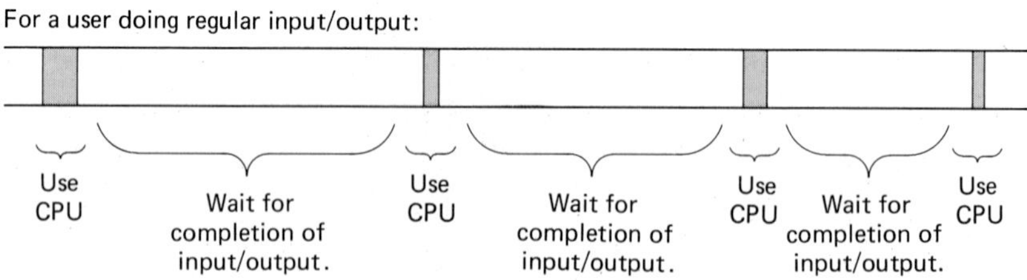

Fig. 7.5 CPU utilization on a single user system. Note: In many single user jobs, the length of the input/output waits is much larger relative to the length of periods of CPU utilization than is indicated in this diagram.

input/output, the CPU may be immediately switched to another, and may do calculations without delay. When this new job yields the CPU, another may be ready to use it.

Multiprogramming often requires more storage than a single user system. However, the improved resource use for the CPU and the peripheral devices more than justifies the expense of additional storage. Many multiprogramming schemes have been implemented. We discuss these in the next several sections.

7.8.1 Fixed Partition Multiprogramming: Absolute Translation and Loading

In the earliest multiprogramming systems, main storage was divided into a number of fixed-size *partitions.* Each partition could hold a single job. The CPU was switched rapidly between users to create the illusion of simultaneity.

Jobs were translated with absolute assemblers and compilers to run only in a specific partition (Fig. 7.6). If a job was ready to run and its partition was occupied, then that job had to wait, even if other partitions were available (Fig. 7.7). This resulted in waste of the storage resource, but the operating system was relatively straightforward to implement.

7.8.2 Fixed Partition Multiprogramming: Relocatable Translation and Loading

Relocating compilers, assemblers, and loaders are used to produce relocatable programs that can run in any available partition that is large enough to hold them. (Fig. 7.8). This scheme eliminates some of the storage waste inherent in multiprogramming with absolute translation and loading. Relocatable translators and loaders are more complex than their absolute counterparts.

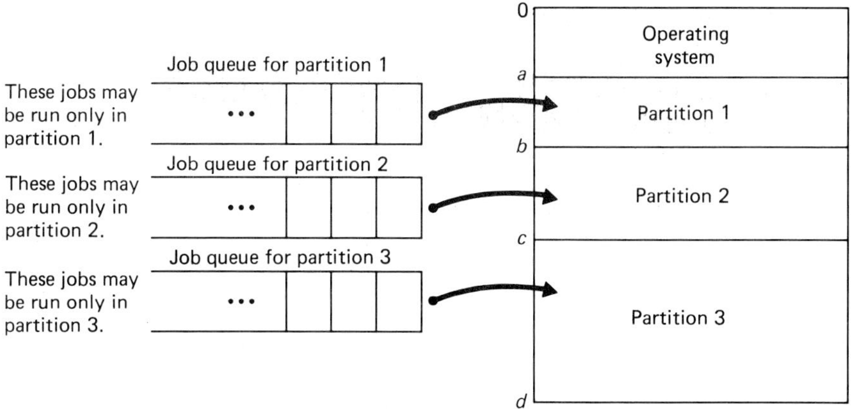

Fig. 7.6 Fixed partition multiprogramming with absolute translation and loading.

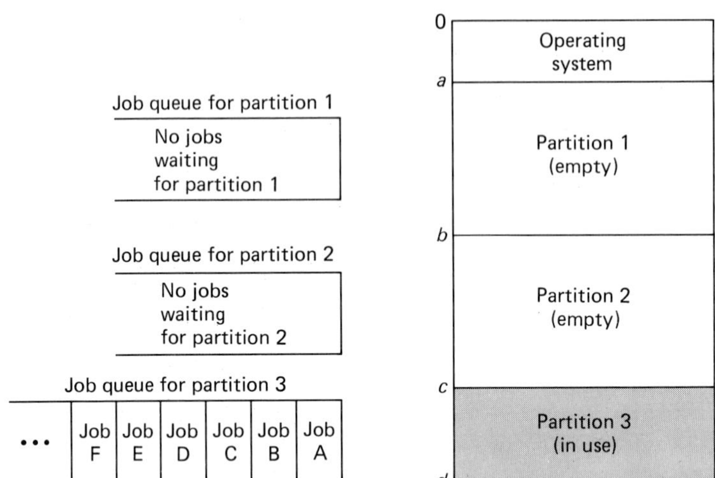

Fig. 7.7 An extreme example of poor storage utilization in fixed partition multiprogramming with absolute translation and loading. Jobs waiting for partition 3 are small and could "fit" in the other partitions. But with absolute translation and loading, these jobs may run only in partition 3. The other two partitions remain empty.

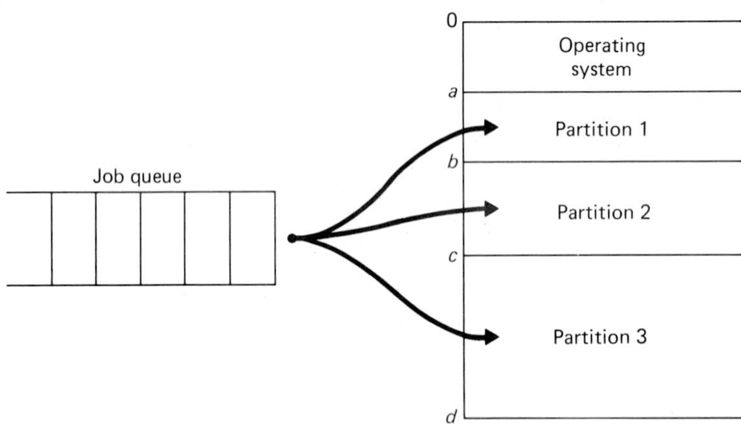

Fig. 7.8 Fixed partition multiprogramming with relocatable translation and loading.

7.8.3 Protection in Multiprogramming Systems

In contiguous allocation multiprogramming systems, protection is often implemented with several *bounds registers.* With two registers the low and high boundaries of a user partition can be delineated (Fig. 7.9), or the low boundary (high boundary) and the length of the region can be indicated. The user needing to call upon the operating system uses a supervisor call instruction to do so. This allows the user to cross the boundary of the operating system and request its services.

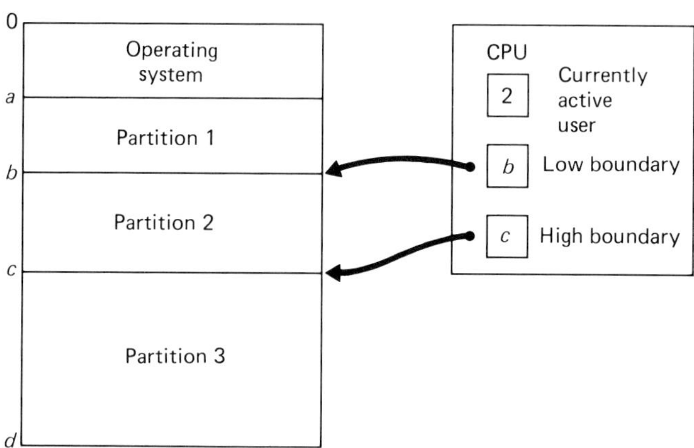

Fig. 7.9 Storage protection in contiguous allocation multiprogramming systems. While the user in partition 2 is active, all storage addresses developed by the running program are checked to be sure they fall between *b* and *c*.

7.8.4 Fragmentation in Fixed Partition Multiprogramming

Storage *fragmentation* occurs in every computer system regardless of its storage organization. In fixed partition multiprogramming systems, fragmentation occurs either because user jobs don't completely fill their designated partitions or when a partition remains unused if it is too small to hold a waiting job.

7.9 VARIABLE PARTITION MULTIPROGRAMMING

Operating systems designers observing the problems with fixed partition multiprogramming decided that an obvious improvement would be to allow jobs to occupy as much space (short of the full real storage) as they needed. No fixed boundaries would be observed. Instead, jobs would be given as much storage as they required. This scheme is called *variable partition multiprogramming.* Initial partition assignment in variable partition multiprogramming is illustrated in Fig. 7.10.

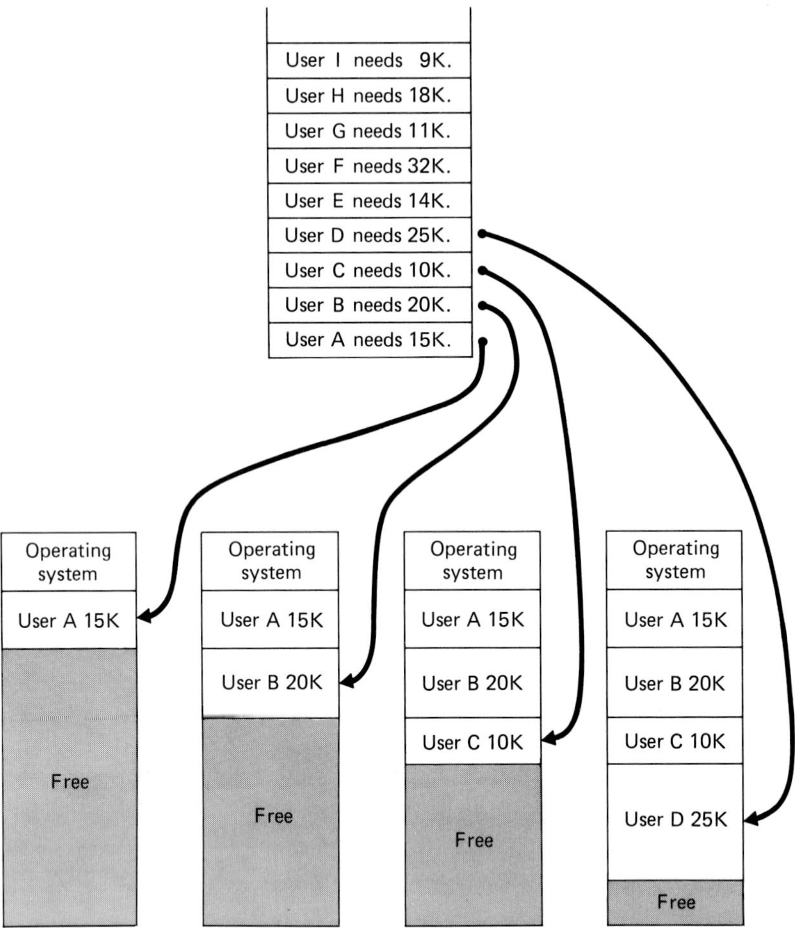

Fig. 7.10 Initial partition assignments in variable partition programming.

We continue to discuss only *contiguous allocation schemes* here: a job must occupy adjacent storage locations. In variable partition multiprogramming, we make no assumptions about how large jobs will be (except that they must be no greater than the size of the computer's available main storage). As jobs arrive, if the scheduling mechanisms decide that they should proceed, they are given as much storage as they need. There is no waste—a job's partition is exactly the size of the job.

But every storage organization scheme involves some degree of waste. In variable partition multiprogramming, the waste does not become obvious until jobs start to finish and leave *holes* in the main storage as shown in Fig. 7.11. These holes can be used for other jobs, but even as this happens, the remaining holes get smaller. So in variable partition multiprogramming waste does occur.

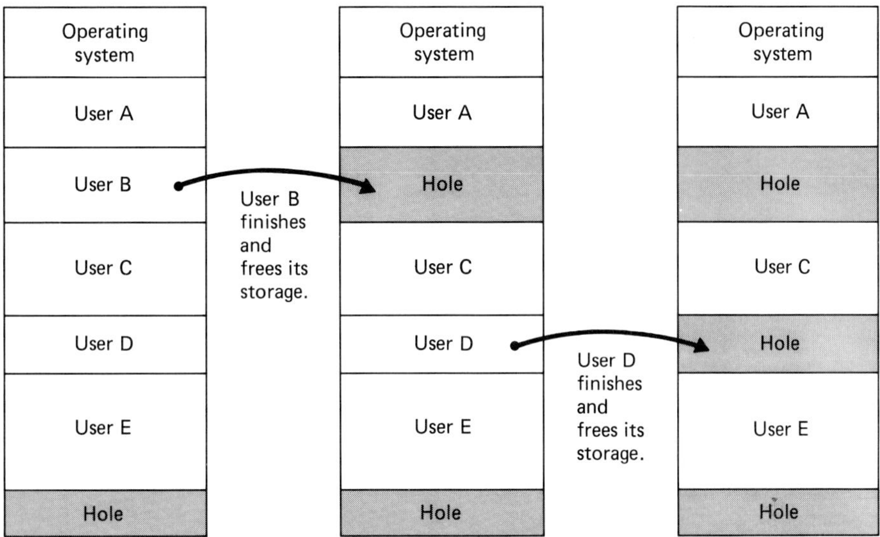

Fig. 7.11 Storage "holes" in variable partition multiprogramming.

7.9.1 Coalescing Holes

When a job finishes in a variable partition multiprogramming system, we can check whether the storage being freed borders on other free storage areas (*holes*). If it does, then we may record in the free storage list either (1) an additional hole or (2) a single hole reflecting the merger of the existing hole and the new adjacent hole.

The process of merging adjacent holes to form a single larger hole is called *coalescing* and is illustrated in Fig. 7.12. By coalescing holes, we reclaim the largest possible contiguous blocks of storage.

7.9.2 Storage Compaction

Even as holes are coalesced, it is often the case that the separate holes distributed throughout the main storage constitute a significant amount of storage. Sometimes when a job requests a certain amount of main storage no individual hole is large enough to hold the job, even though the sum of all the holes is larger than the storage needed by the new job.

The technique of storage *compaction* (Fig. 7.13) involves moving all occupied areas of storage to one end or the other of main storage. This leaves a single large free storage hole instead of the numerous small holes common in variable partition multiprogramming. Now all of the available free storage is contiguous so that a waiting job can run if its memory requirement is met by the single hole that results from compaction. Sometimes, storage compaction is colorfully referred to as *burping the storage.* More conventionally, it is called *garbage collection.*

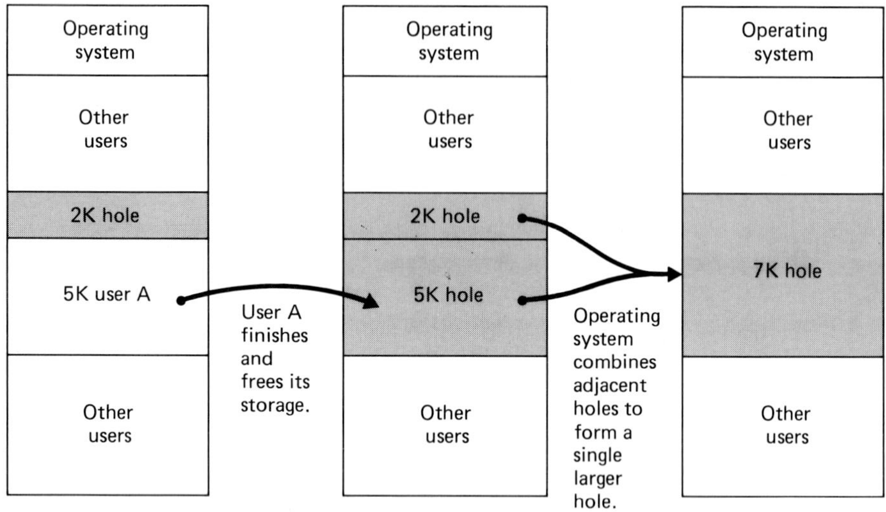

Fig. 7.12 Coalescing storage "holes" in variable partition multiprogramming.

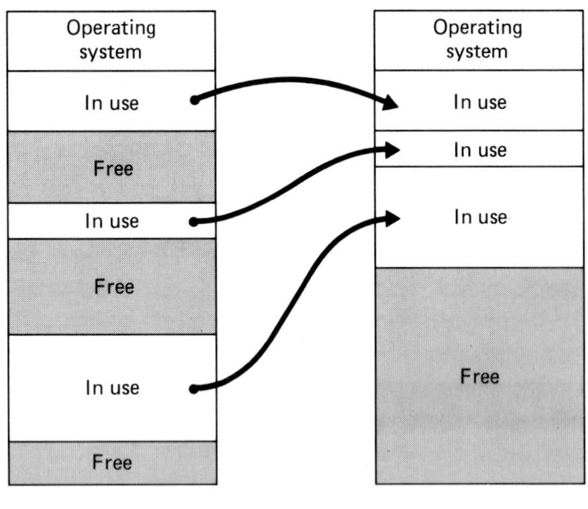

Fig. 7.13 Storage compaction in variable partition multiprogramming.

Compaction is not without drawbacks.

- It consumes system resources that could otherwise be used productively.
- The system must stop everything while it performs the compaction. This can result in erratic response times for interactive users and could be devastating in real-time systems.
- Compaction involves relocating the jobs that are in storage. This means that relocation information, ordinarily lost when a program is loaded, must now be maintained in readily accessible form.
- With a normal, rapidly changing job mix, it is necessary to compact frequently. The consumed system resources might not justify the benefits from compacting.

7.9.3 Storage Placement Strategies

Storage placement strategies are used to determine where in the main storage to place incoming programs and data. The three strategies most frequently discussed in the literature are illustrated in Fig. 7.14.

- *Best-fit strategy*—An incoming job is placed in the hole in main storage in which it fits most tightly and leaves the smallest amount of unused space. To many people, best fit seems to be the most intuitively appealing strategy.
- *First-fit strategy*—An incoming job is placed in the main storage in the first available hole large enough to hold it. First fit also has intuitive appeal in that it allows the placement decision to be made quickly.
- *Worst-fit strategy* —At first, this appears to be a whimsical choice. After closer examination, worst fit also has strong intuitive appeal. Worst fit says to place a program in main storage in the hole in which it fits worst, i.e., the largest possible hole. The intuitive appeal is simple: after placing the program in this large hole, the remaining hole often is also large and is thus able to hold a relatively large new program.

7.10 MULTIPROGRAMMING WITH STORAGE SWAPPING

In each of the multiprogramming schemes discussed so far, user programs remain in main memory until completion. Another scheme, called *swapping* does not have this requirement.

In some swapping systems (Fig. 7.15), one job occupies the main storage at once. That job runs until it can no longer continue and then it relinquishes both the storage and the CPU to the next job. Thus the entire storage is dedicated to one job for a brief period, that job is then removed (i.e., *swapped out*) and the next job is brought in (i.e., *swapped in*). A job will normally be swapped in and out many times before it is completed.

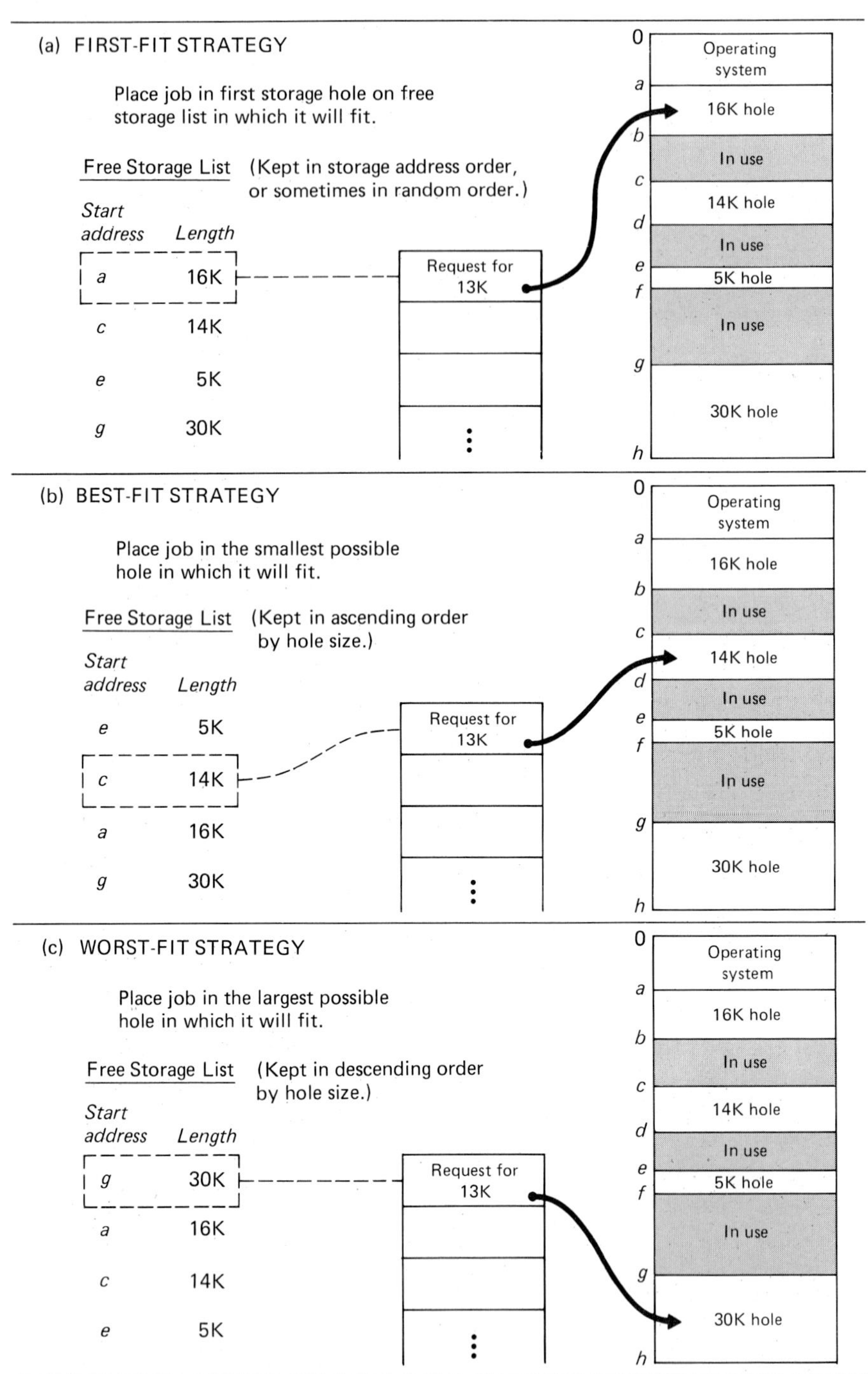

Fig. 7.14 First-fit, best-fit, and worst-fit storage placement strategies.

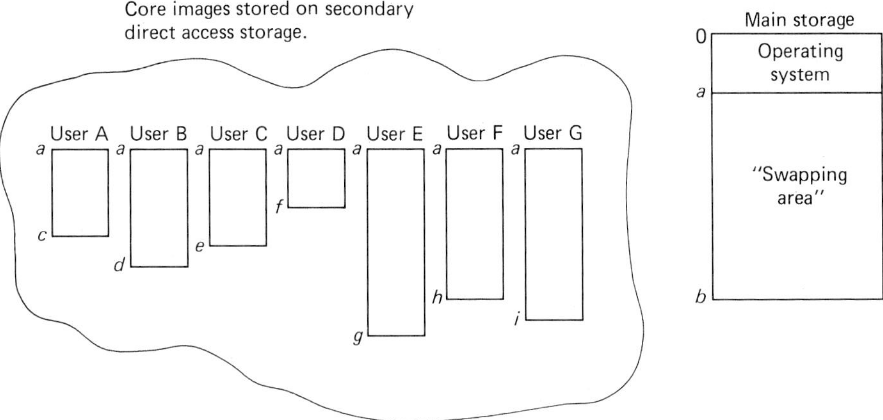

1. Only one user at a time is in main storage.
2. That user runs until
   a) I/O is issued,
   b) timer runout,
   c) voluntary termination.
3. Swapping area ("core image") for that user is then copied to secondary storage (i.e., "swapped out").
4. Core image for next user is read into the swapping area (i.e., "swapped in") and that user runs until it is eventually swapped out and the next user is swapped in, etc.
5. This scheme was common in early timesharing systems.

Fig. 7.15 Multiprogramming in a swapping system in which only a single user at a time is in main storage.

Many early timesharing systems were implemented with this swapping technique. It was possible to guarantee reasonable response times for relatively few users but designers knew that better techniques would be needed to handle large numbers of users. The swapping systems of the early 1960s led to the paging systems in common use today. Paging is considered in detail in the next several chapters.

More sophisticated swapping systems have been developed that allow several user images to remain in main storage at once. In these systems, a user image is swapped out only when its storage is needed for an incoming user image. With a sufficient amount of storage, these systems greatly reduce the time spent swapping.

SUMMARY

Historically, the organization and management of the computer's main storage has greatly affected operating systems evolution. Storage organization is the manner in which the main storage is viewed; in this chapter several popular storage organizations for real storage systems were discussed.

- single user systems
- fixed partition multiprogramming with absolute translation and loading
- fixed partition multiprogramming with relocatable translation and loading
- variable partition multiprogramming
- storage swapping systems

Storage management strategies seek to achieve the best possible use of and performance from the expensive main storage resource. Three types of storage management strategies were discussed.

- fetch strategies
- placement strategies
- replacement strategies

Fetch strategies are concerned with when the next piece of program or data is to be brought into the main storage. In demand fetch strategies, program and data pieces are brought in specifically when they are requested. In anticipatory fetch strategies, the system attempts to anticipate a program's needs and have the appropriate program and data pieces loaded into main storage before they are actually needed; when they are requested they will be available and the program may continue without delay.

Placement strategies are concerned with where in the main storage to place an incoming program. Three placement strategies were discussed.

- First fit
- Best fit
- Worst fit

First fit places the program in the first storage hole that can be found and that is large enough to hold it. Best fit places the program in the "tightest" fitting hole, i.e., the smallest of the available storage holes that can hold it. Worst fit places the program or data piece in the largest available hole that will hold it. First fit is a low overhead strategy. Best fit is intuitively appealing to most people. Worst fit appeals because it avoids creating small storage holes.

Computer storage systems have become hierarchical consisting of several levels of storage. Secondary storage is relatively inexpensive, but large. Primary storage is expensive but less abundant than secondary storage. Programs and data must be in primary storage to be used by the CPU. Programs and data not needed immediately may be kept on secondary storage, generally disk or drum. Cache storage is extremely expensive but offers high-speed execution of program instructions and referencing of data items.

Contiguous allocation systems require that an entire program must occupy one block of adjacent storage locations in order to execute. Noncontiguous allocation systems allow programs and data to be separated into several smaller blocks that may be placed in any available free storage holes, even if these holes are not adjacent to one another. Virtual storage systems generally involve noncontiguous allocation and will be considered in the next several chapters.

The first computer systems were dedicated to one user at a time. These single user systems contained the earliest operating systems, generally input/output control systems to facilitate machine-level input/output programming. Protection was accomplished by a single boundary register that separated the user from the operating system. Single stream batch processing systems were developed to facilitate job-to-job transition and thus obtain increased throughput.

Eventually, it became clear that several users could share a machine at once, but they had to be protected from one another. In fixed partition multiprogramming with absolute translation and loading, user programs are prepared to run in specific partitions. If the partition for a particular user program is unavailable, then that user has to wait, even if another sufficiently large partition goes unused. In fixed partition multiprogramming with relocatable translation and loading, a program can be loaded into any available partition that is large enough to hold it.

Protection is accomplished in contiguous allocation multiprogramming systems with two boundary registers that are part of the CPU. Every storage reference by a given program is checked to be sure that it is within the range of main storage addresses that program is allowed to access. The user wishing to enter the operating system to have input/output or other functions performed does so with the use of a supervisor call instruction. This instruction allows the user program to cross the operating system boundary to obtain certain services. After the operating system performs these services, it returns control to the user program.

Fixed partition multiprogramming systems waste a considerable amount of main storage when the user programs are much smaller than their designated partitions. In variable partition multiprogramming, a user program is assigned exactly as much storage as it needs (short of the main storage size). But as user programs finish in this scheme, many storage holes are left scattered throughout the main storage.

Adjacent holes are coalesced to reclaim the largest possible contiguous blocks of main storage. Occasionally, a job arrives with a storage requirement larger than any available hole but smaller than the total of all free storage holes. In this case, storage may be compacted to create a hole sufficiently large to hold the program. In compaction, all user programs are relocated to be adjacent to one another so that a single large storage hole remains.

Once the fetch strategy determines that a new program should be brought into the main storage, the placement strategy must decide where to put it. Sometimes, no storage hole is available and a program in main storage must be removed to make room. Storage replacement strategies make this decision.

Multiprogramming may also be implemented via swapping in which only a single user is in the main storage at once. The user program runs until it cannot continue. It is then swapped out of main storage, the next user is swapped in and this user runs until it cannot continue. The storage swapping technique is useful when main storage is limited. It was used in many early timesharing systems that supported relatively few users. More sophisticated storage swapping systems allow several programs to remain in storage at once.

TERMINOLOGY

anticipatory fetch
best-fit storage placement strategy
boundary registers
"burping" the memory
cache storage
coalescing holes
compaction of storage
contiguous storage allocation
demand fetch
fetch strategy
fixed partition multiprogramming with absolute translation and loading
fixed partition multiprogramming with relocatable translation and loading
first-fit storage placement strategy
fragmentation
free storage list
garbage collection
holes
input/output control system (IOCS)
job setup
job teardown
noncontiguous storage allocation
overlay
placement strategy
primary storage
real storage
real storage multiprogramming
replacement strategy
secondary storage
segments
single stream batch processing systems
single user dedicated systems
storage hierarchy
storage management
storage management strategies
storage organization
storage protection
supervisor call instruction
swapping
variable partition multiprogramming
worst-fit storage placement strategy

EXERCISES

7.1 In hierarchical storage systems, a certain amount of overhead is involved in moving programs and data between the various levels of the hierarchy. Discuss why the benefits derived from such systems justify the overhead involved.

7.2 A certain computer system may execute programs in either its main storage or its cache. Programs may be moved between the main storage and the cache in fixed sized blocks only. The overhead of such a move is a constant. The cache runs programs faster than the main storage.

a) In what circumstances should programs be executed in the cache storage?
b) In what circumstances should programs be executed in the main storage?

c) Suppose you have been given the responsibility of determining how large a cache storage to purchase for your installation. You know that the cache is expensive but that it runs programs much faster than the main storage. What considerations would affect your decision?

7.3 Why has demand fetch endured as the conventional wisdom for so long? Why are anticipatory fetch strategies receiving so much more attention today than they did ten years ago?

7.4 Discuss how storage fragmentation occurs in each of the storage organization schemes presented in this chapter.

7.5 In what circumstances is overlay useful? When may a section of main storage be overlayed? How does overlay affect program development time? How does overlay affect program modifiability?

7.6 Discuss the motivations for multiprogramming. What characteristics of programs and machines make multiprogramming desirable? In what circumstances is multiprogramming undesirable?

7.7 You are given a hierarchical storage system consisting of four levels—cache, primary storage, secondary storage, and tertiary storage. Assume that programs may be executed in any of the storage levels. Assume that each level consists of an identical amount of real storage, and that the range of storage addresses in each level is identical. Tertiary storage runs programs the slowest, cache runs programs the fastest, primary storage is ten times slower than the cache, secondary storage is ten times slower than primary storage, and tertiary storage is ten times slower than secondary storage. There is only one CPU and it may execute only one program at a time.

a) Assume that programs and data may be shuttled from any level to any other level under the operating system's control. The time it takes to transfer items between two particular levels is dependent upon the speed of the lowest (and slowest) level involved in the transfer. Why might the operating system choose to shuttle a program from cache directly to secondary storage thus bypassing primary storage? Why would items be shuttled to slower levels of the hierarchy? Why would items be shuttled to faster levels of the hierarchy?

b) The scheme above is somewhat unconventional. It is more common for programs and data to be moved only between adjacent levels of the hierarchy. Give several arguments against allowing transfers directly from the cache to any level other than primary storage.

7.8 As a systems programmer in a large computer installation using a fixed partition multiprogramming system, you have been given the task of determining if the current partitioning of the system should be altered.

a) What information would you need to help you make your decision?

b) If you had this information readily available, how would you determine the ideal partitioning?

c) What are the consequences of repartitioning such a system?

7.9 One simple scheme for relocating programs in multiprogramming environments involves the use of a single relocation register. All programs are translated to locations beginning at zero, but every address developed as the program executes is modified by adding to it the contents of the CPU's relocation register. Discuss the use and control of the relocation register in variable partition multiprogramming. How might the relocation register be used in a protection scheme?

7.10 Placement strategies determine where in the main storage incoming programs and data should be loaded. Suppose a job waiting to begin execution has a storage requirement that can be fulfilled immediately. Should the job be loaded and begin execution immediately?

7.11 Charging for resources in multiprogramming systems can be complex.

a) In a dedicated system, the user is normally charged for the entire system. Suppose in a multiprogramming system only one user is currently on the system. Should that user be charged for the entire system?
b) Multiprogramming operating systems generally consume substantial system resources as they manage multiple user environments. Who should pay for this overhead?
c) Most people agree that charges for computer system usage should be fair, but few of us can define precisely what "fairness" is. Another attribute of charging schemes, but one which is easier to define is predictability. We want to know that if a job costs a certain amount to run once, it will cost approximately the same amount to run the job again in similar circumstances. Suppose that in a multiprogramming environment we charge by wall clock time, i.e., the total real time involved in running the job from start to completion. Would such a scheme yield predictable charges? Why?

7.12 Discuss the advantages and disadvantages of noncontiguous storage allocation.

7.13 Many designers believe that the operating system should always be given a most trusted status. Some designers feel that even the operating system should be curtailed, particularly in its ability to reference various areas of memory. Discuss the pros and cons of allowing the operating system to access the full range of real addresses in a computer system at all times.

7.14 Developments in operating systems have generally occurred in an evolutionary rather than revolutionary fashion. For each of the following transitions, describe the primary motivations of operating systems designers that led them to produce the new type of system from the old.

a) single user dedicated systems to multiprogramming
b) fixed partition multiprogramming systems with absolute translation and loading to fixed partition multiprogramming systems with relocatable translation and loading
c) fixed partition multiprogramming to variable partition multiprogramming
d) contiguous storage allocation systems to noncontiguous storage allocation systems
e) single user dedicated systems with manual job-to-job transition to single user dedicated systems with single stream batch processing systems

7.15 Consider the problem of jobs waiting in a queue until sufficient memory becomes available for them to be loaded and executed. If the queue is a simple first-in-first-out structure, then only the job at the head of the queue may be considered for placement in storage. On the other hand, with a more complex queueing mechanism, it might be possible to examine the entire queue to choose the next job to be loaded and executed. Show how the latter discipline, even though more complex, might yield better throughput than the simple first-in-first-out strategy.

7.16 One pessimistic operating systems designer says it really doesn't matter what storage placement strategy is used. Sooner or later a system achieves steady state and all of the strategies perform similarly. Do you agree? Explain.

7.17 Another pessimistic designer asks why we go to the trouble of defining a strategy with an offical-sounding name like first fit. This designer claims that a first-fit strategy is equivalent to nothing more than random storage placement. Do you agree? Explain.

7.18 Consider a swapping system with several partitions. The absolute version of such a system would require that programs be repeatedly swapped in and out of the same partition. The relocatable version of such a system would allow programs to be swapped in and out of any available partitions large enough to hold them, possibly different partitions on successive swaps. Assuming that real storage is many times the size of the average job, discuss the advantages of this multiple user swapping scheme over the single user swapping scheme described in the text.

LITERATURE

(Ba80) Baer, J. L., *Computer Systems Architecture*, Rockville, Md.: Computer Science Press, 1980.

(De71) Denning, P. J., "Third Generation Computer Systems," *ACM Computing Surveys*, Vol. 3, No. 4, December 1971, pp. 175–216.

(Ha78) Hayes, J. P., *Computer Architecture and Organization*, New York: McGraw-Hill, 1978.

(Li72) Lin, Y. S., and R. L. Mattson, "Cost-Performance Evaluation of Memory Hierarchies," *IEEE Trans. Magn.*, MAG-8, No. 3, September 1972, p. 390.

(Ma77) Matick, R. E., *Computer Storage Systems and Technology*, New York: Wiley, 1977.

(Mi74) Mitra, D., "Some Aspects of Hierarchical Memory Systems," *JACM*, Vol. 21, No. 1, January 1974, p. 54.

(Ri74) Ritchie, D. M., and K. T. Thompson, "The UNIX Time-sharing System," *CACM*, Vol. 17, No. 7, July 1974.

(Ro69) Rosen, S., "Electronic Computers: A Historical Survey," *ACM Computing Surveys*, Vol. 1, No. 1, March 1969, pp. 7–36.

(Rn69) Rosin, R. F., "Supervisory and Monitor Systems," *ACM Computing Surveys*, Vol. 1, No. 1, March 1969, pp. 37–54.

8 Virtual Storage Organization

The fancy is indeed no other than a mode of memory emancipated from the order of time and space.

Samuel Taylor Coleridge

Outline

- **8.1** Introduction
- **8.2** Evolution of Storage Organizations
- **8.3** Virtual Storage: Basic Concepts
- **8.4** Multilevel Storage Organization
- **8.5** Block Mapping
- **8.6** Paging: Basic Concepts
  - **8.6.1** Paging Address Translation by Direct Mapping
  - **8.6.2** Paging Address Translation by Associative Mapping
  - **8.6.3** Paging Address Translation with Combined Associative/Direct Mapping
  - **8.6.4** Sharing in a Paging System
- **8.7** Segmentation
  - **8.7.1** Access Control in Segmentation Systems
  - **8.7.2** Segmented Address Translation by Direct Mapping
  - **8.7.3** Sharing in a Segmentation System
- **8.8** Paging/Segmentation Systems
  - **8.8.1** Dynamic Address Translation in Paging/Segmentation Systems
  - **8.8.2** Sharing in a Paging/Segmentation System

8.1 INTRODUCTION

The term *virtual storage* is normally associated with the ability to address a storage space much larger than that available in the primary storage of a particular computer system. Virtual storage is not a new concept. It first appeared in the Atlas computer system constructed at the University of Manchester in England in 1960. The widespread use of virtual storage systems is relatively recent.

The two most common methods of implementing virtual storage are *paging* and *segmentation,* both of which are discussed in detail in this chapter. Some virtual storage systems use one technique or the other. Some systems use both.

All virtual storage systems have the attribute that the addresses developed by running programs are not necessarily those addresses available in primary storage. In fact, virtual addresses are normally selected from a much larger set of addresses than is available in primary storage.

8.2 EVOLUTION OF STORAGE ORGANIZATIONS

Figure 8.1 shows how storage organizations have evolved from real storage systems dedicated to a single user, to virtual storage systems combining the techniques of paging and segmentation. Real storage organizations were discussed in the previous chapter. Because virtual storage is far more complex, the discussion has been split into two chapters. In this chapter, the various virtual storage organizations are examined. In the next chapter, the techniques and strategies for managing them are discussed.

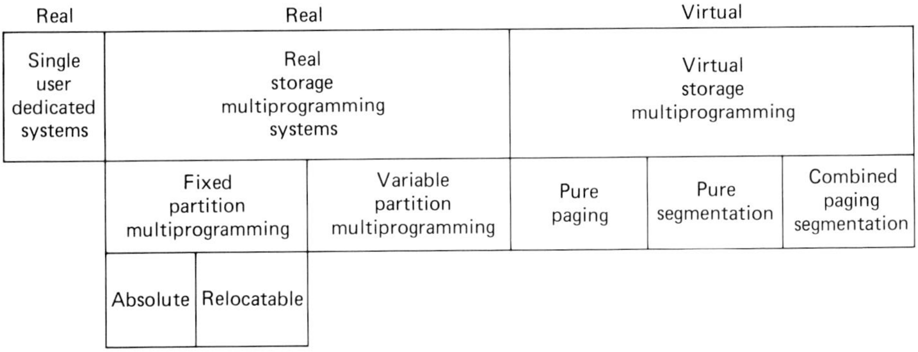

Real
Single user dedicated systems

Real
Real storage multiprogramming systems
Fixed partition multiprogramming
Absolute
Relocatable
Variable partition multiprogramming

Virtual
Virtual storage multiprogramming
Pure paging
Pure segmentation
Combined paging segmentation

Fig. 8.1 Evolution of storage organizations.

8.3 VIRTUAL STORAGE: BASIC CONCEPTS

The key to the virtual storage concept is disassociating the addresses referenced in a running process from the addresses available in primary storage.

The addresses referenced by a running process are called *virtual addresses.* The addresses available in primary storage are called *real addresses.* The range of virtual addresses a running process may reference is called that process's *virtual address space,* V. The range of real addresses available on a particular computer system is called that computer's real address space, R.

Even though processes reference only virtual addresses, they must actually run in real storage. Thus *virtual addresses must be mapped into real addresses as a process executes.* This must be done quickly, or else the performance of the computer system would degrade to intolerable levels, thus eliminating many gains from using the virtual storage concept in the first place (Fig. 8.2).

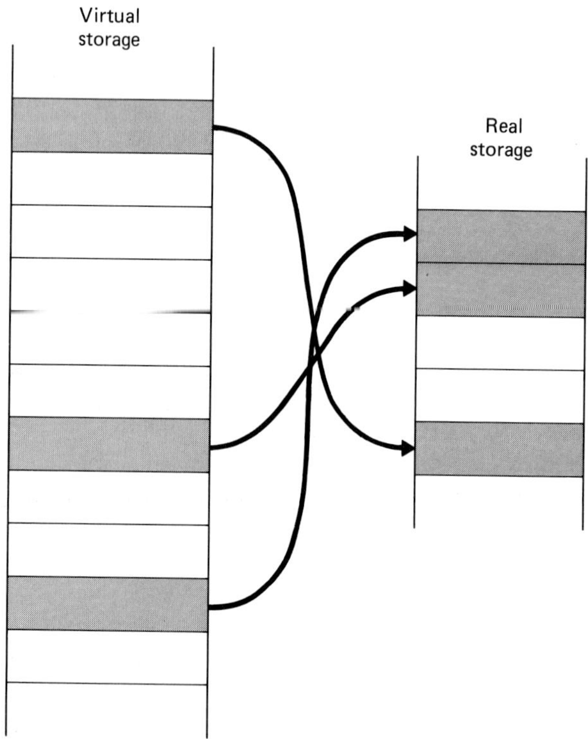

Fig. 8.2 Item mapping from virtual address space to real address space.

Various means have been developed for associating virtual addresses with real addresses. *Dynamic address translation (DAT)* mechanisms convert virtual addresses to real addresses as a process executes. All of these systems exhibit the property

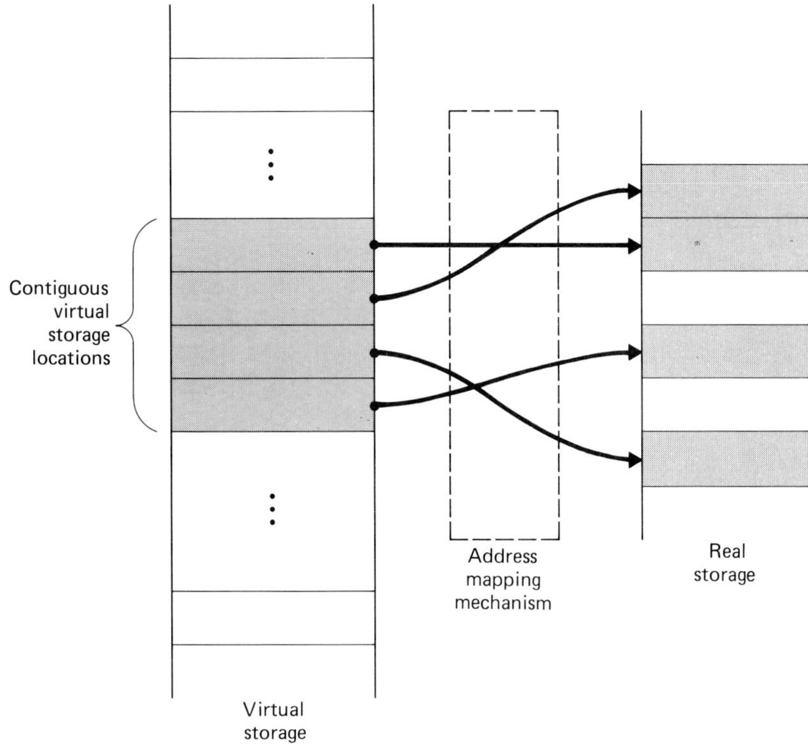

Fig. 8.3 Artificial contiguity. Items that are contiguous in virtual storage are mapped to items in real storage that are not necessarily contiguous.

that the addresses contiguous in a process's virtual address space need not be contiguous in real storage—this is called *artificial contiguity* (Fig. 8.3). Thus the user is freed from concern about where procedures and data are positioned in real storage. The user is able to write programs in the most natural manner, considering details of algorithm design and program structure, but ignoring details of the underlying hardware structure. The computer is (or can be) viewed in a logical sense as an implementor of algorithms rather than in a physical sense as a device with unique characteristics, some of which may impede the program development process.

8.4 MULTILEVEL STORAGE ORGANIZATION

If we are to permit a user's virtual address space to be larger than the real address space and certainly if we are to multiprogram a system effectively with many users sharing the real storage resource, then we must provide a means for retaining programs and data in a large auxiliary storage. This is normally accomplished by using

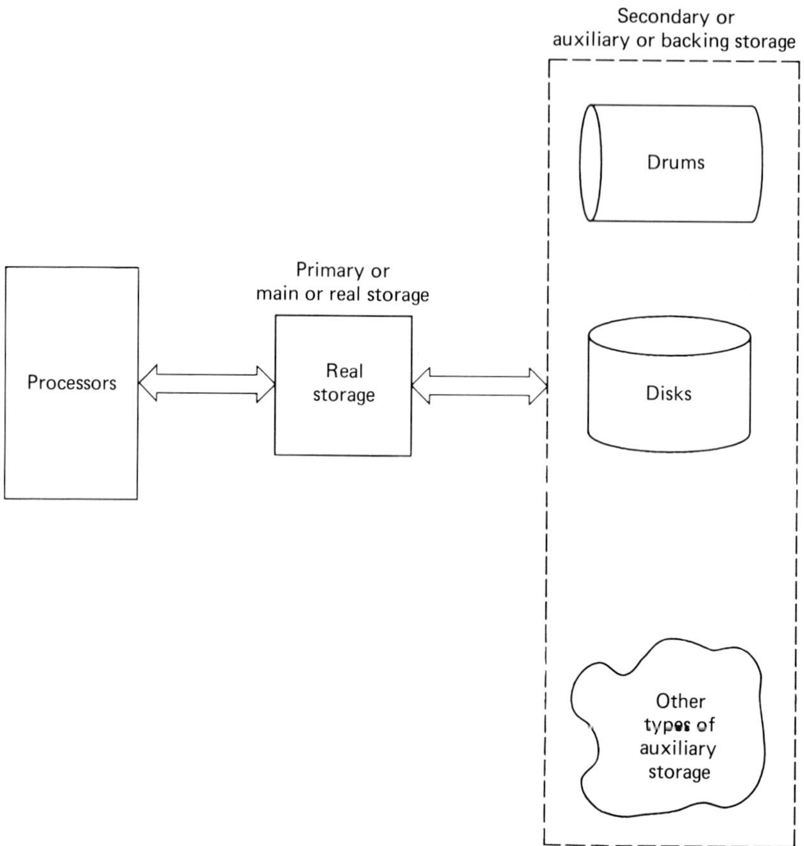

Fig. 8.4 Two-level storage.

a two-level storage scheme (Fig. 8.4). The first level is the real storage in which processes execute and in which data must be in order to be referenced by a running process. The second level consists of large capacity storage media such as disks or drums capable of holding the programs and data that cannot all fit in the limited real storage at once. This second level of storage is generally called *auxiliary, secondary,* or *backing* storage. When a process is to be run, its code and data are brought to the main storage. The details of how this is done will be explained thoroughly in this and the next chapter.

Because the real storage is shared among many processes, and because each process may have a virtual address space much larger than real storage, then only a small portion of each process's programs and data may be maintained in real storage at a time. Figure 8.5 illustrates a two-level storage system in which items from various users' virtual storages have been placed in the real storage.

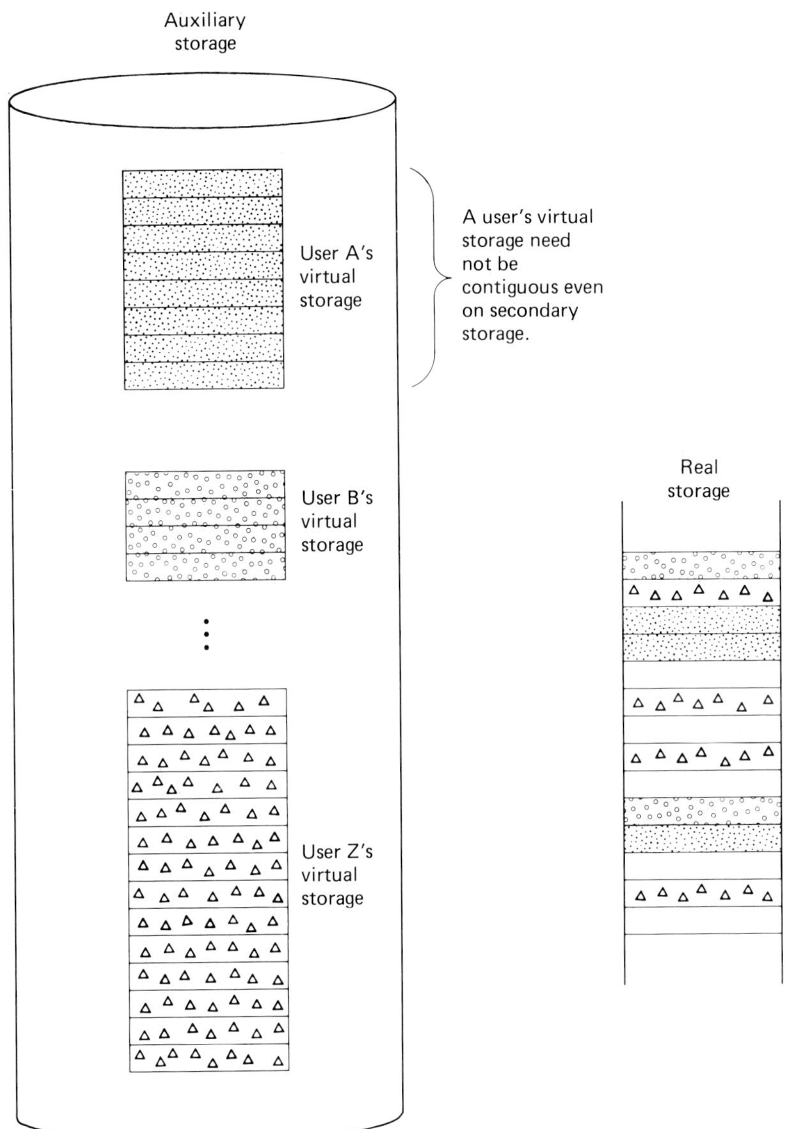

Figure 8.5

8.5 BLOCK MAPPING

The dynamic address translation mechanism must maintain maps illustrating which virtual storage locations are currently in real storage, and where they are. If this mapping were performed on a word-by-word or byte-by-byte basis, then the mapping information would be so voluminous that it would require as much or more real storage than the processes themselves need. A method is needed to reduce the amount of mapping information in order to make implementation of virtual storage worthwhile.

Thus we cannot afford to map items individually. Therefore, information is grouped into *blocks,* and the system keeps track of where in real storage the various virtual storage blocks have been placed. The larger the block size, the smaller the fraction of real storage that must be devoted to storing mapping information.

Making blocks large will lower the storage overhead of the mapping mechanism. But large blocks take longer to transfer between secondary and primary storage, and consume more real storage, possibly limiting the number of processes that can share the real storage.

There is some question as to whether the blocks should all be the same size, or of different sizes. When blocks are the same size, they are called *pages* and the associated virtual storage organization is called *paging.* When the blocks may be of different sizes, they are called *segments,* and the associated virtual storage organization is called *segmentation.* Some systems combine the two techniques implementing segments as variable sized entities composed of fixed sized pages.

Addresses in a block mapping system are *two-dimensional.* To refer to a particular item, a program specifies the block in which the item resides, and the *displacement* of the item from the start of the block (Fig. 8.6). A virtual address, v, is denoted by an ordered pair (b,d) where b is the block number in which the referenced item resides, and d is the displacement from the start of the block.

Fig. 8.6 Virtual address format in a block mapping system.

The translation from a virtual storage address $v = (b,d)$ to a real storage address, r, proceeds as follows (Fig. 8.7). Each process has its own *block map table* maintained by the system in real storage. A special register in the processing unit, called the *block table origin register* is loaded with the real address, a, of the block map table. The block map table contains one entry for each block of the process, and the entries are kept in sequential order for block 0, block 1, etc. Now the block number, b, is added to the base address, a, of the block table to form the real address of the entry in the block map table for block b. This entry contains the real address, b', for block b. The displacement, d, is added to the block start address, b', to form the desired real address, $r = b' + d$.

The block mapping techniques employed in segmentation, paging, and combined paging/segmentation systems are all similar to the mapping shown in Fig. 8.7.

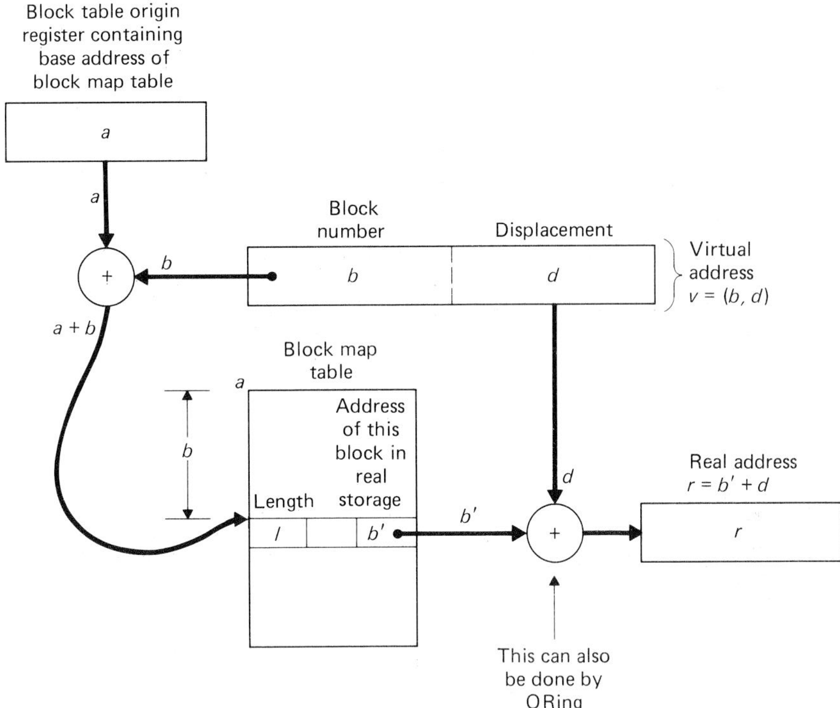

Fig. 8.7 Virtual address translation with block mapping.

It is important to note that block mapping is performed dynamically as a process runs. If not implemented efficiently, its overhead could cause performance degradation that would eliminate much of the benefit obtained by using virtual storage.

8.6 PAGING: BASIC CONCEPTS

Recalling the complexity of managing variable sized blocks under variable partition multiprogramming, let us begin by considering fixed size block mapping, i.e., paging. In this section we consider *pure paging* as distinguished from paging in a system with combined segmentation and paging.

A virtual address in a paging system is an ordered pair (p,d) where p is the page number in virtual storage on which the referenced item resides, and d is the displacement within page p at which the referenced item is located (Fig. 8.8). A pro-

Page number p	Displacement d	Virtual address $v = (p, d)$

Fig. 8.8 Virtual address format in a pure paging system.

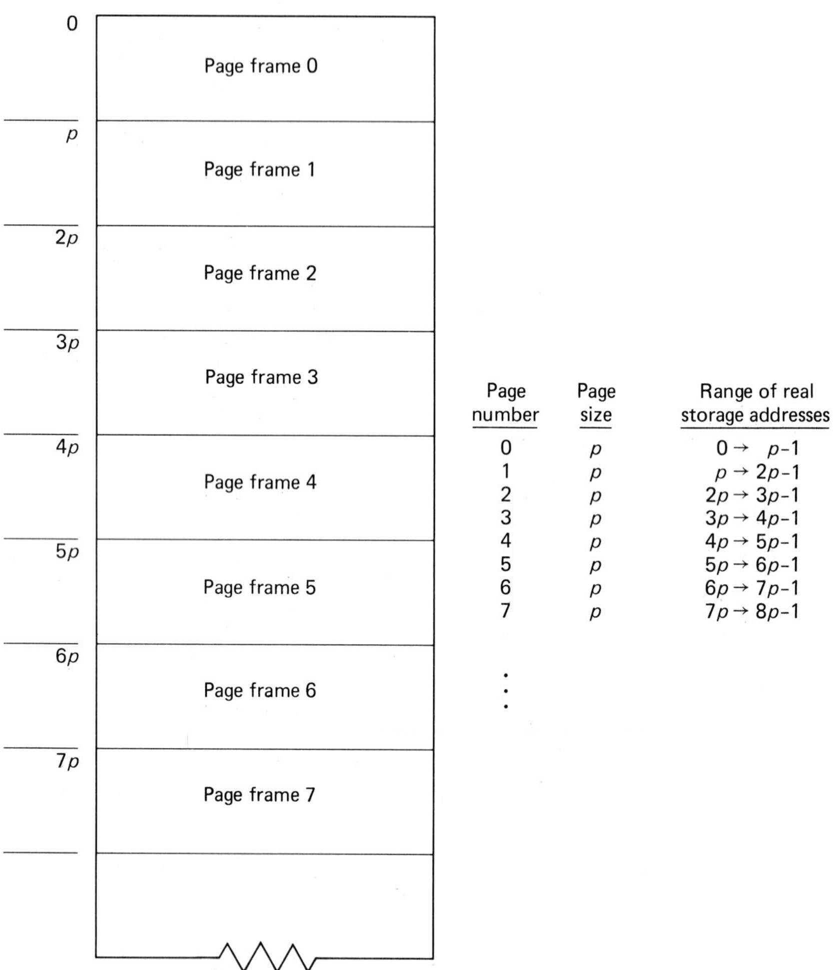

Fig. 8.9 Real storage divided into page frames.

cess may run if its current page is in primary storage. Pages are transferred from secondary to primary storage and placed in primary storage in blocks called *page frames* that are the same size as the incoming pages. Page frames begin at real storage addresses that are integral multiples of the fixed page size (Fig. 8.9). An incoming page may be placed in any available page frame.

Dynamic address translation under paging proceeds as follows. A running process references a virtual storage address $v = (p,d)$. A page mapping mechanism, Fig. 8.10, looks up page p in a *page map table*, and determines that page p is in page frame p'. The real storage address is then formed by concatenating p' and d.

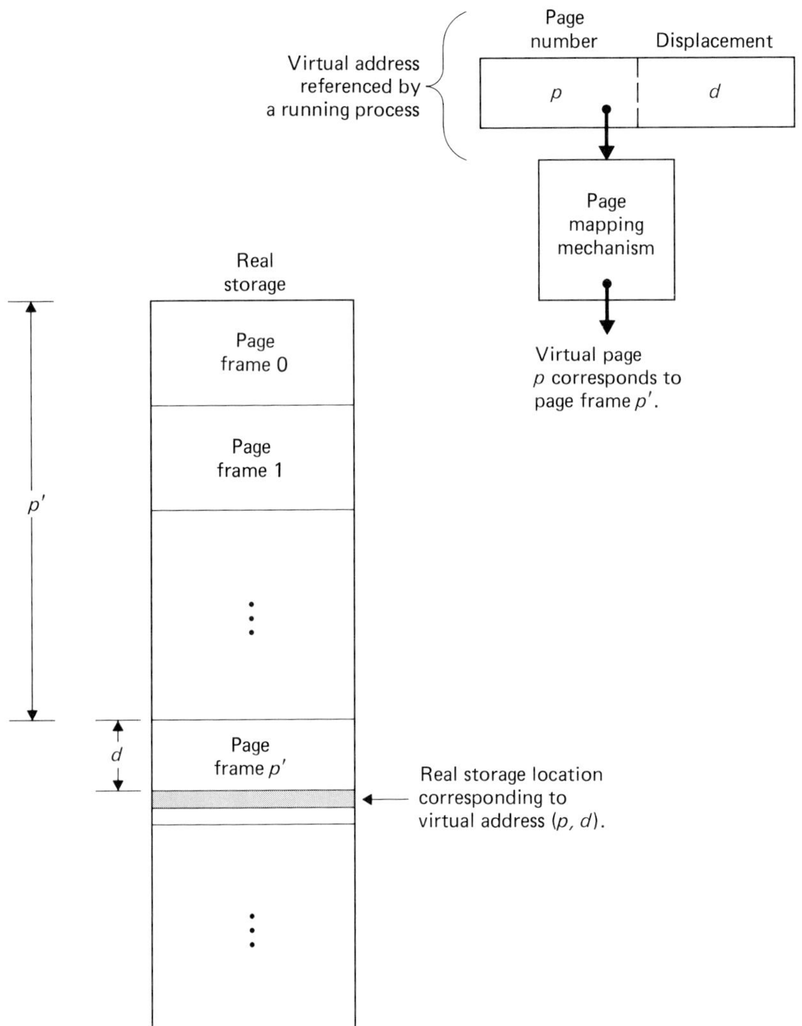

Fig. 8.10 Correspondence between virtual storage addresses and real storage addresses in a paging system.

Now consider this process in more detail. In particular, because not every page of the process is ordinarily in primary storage at the same time, the page map table must indicate whether or not the referenced page is in primary storage; if it is, where it is; and if it isn't, where it may be found in secondary storage. Figure 8.11 shows a typical page map table entry. A page residence bit, r, is set to 0 if the page is not in primary storage and set to 1 if the page is in primary storage. If the page

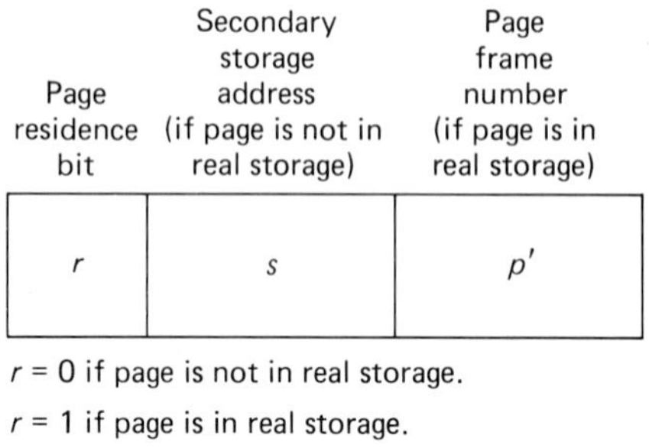

Page residence bit	Secondary storage address (if page is not in real storage)	Page frame number (if page is in real storage)
r	s	p'

r = 0 if page is not in real storage.

r = 1 if page is in real storage.

Fig. 8.11 A page map table entry.

is not in primary storage, then s is its secondary storage address. If the page is in primary storage, then p' is its page frame number. Note that p' is not an actual primary storage address. The primary storage address, a, at which page frame p' begins (assuming page size p) is given by

$$a = (p)\,(p')$$

(assuming page frames are numbered 0, 1, 2, etc.).

If main storage is at a premium, the secondary storage addresses of pages may be omitted from the page map table.

8.6.1 Paging Address Translation by Direct Mapping

In this and the next several sections, we consider several techniques for performing page mapping. First we consider *direct mapping* as is illustrated in Fig. 8.12.

A running process references virtual address $v = (p,d)$. Before a process begins running, the operating system loads the primary storage address of the page map table into the page map table origin register. The base address, b, of the page map table is added to the page number, p, to form the address in primary storage, $b + p$, of the entry in the page map table for page p. This entry indicates that page frame p' corresponds to virtual page p. Then p' is concatenated with the displacement, d, to form real address, r. *This is said to be an example of direct mapping because the page map table contains an entry for every page in this process's virtual storage.* If the process has n pages in its virtual storage, then the direct mapping page map table for the process contains entries successively for page 0, page 1, page 2, . . ., page $n - 1$.

The virtual address being translated and the base address of the page map table are both kept in high-speed registers in the control processor, so the operations involving them can be performed quickly within a single instruction execution cycle. But the direct mapped page map table, which can be quite large, is ordinarily kept in primary storage. Consequently, the reference to the page map table requires one complete primary storage cycle. Because the primary storage cycle time ordinarily represents the largest part of an instruction execution cycle, and because we require

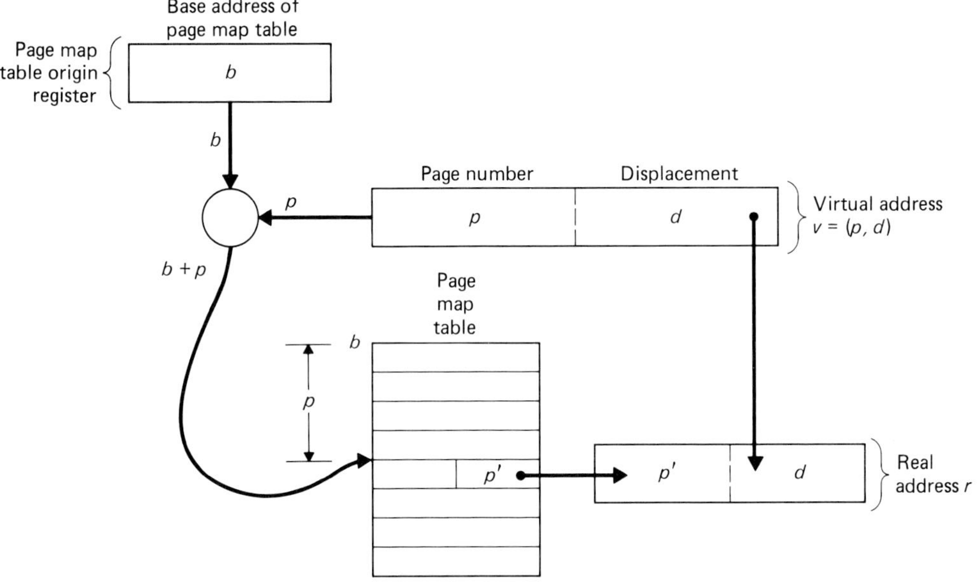

Fig. 8.12 Paging address translation by direct mapping.

another primary storage execution cycle for page mapping, then the use of direct mapping page address translation can cause the computer system to run programs at about half speed! This is intolerable. Therefore, faster translation methods must be used. This does not completely invalidate the usefulness of direct mapping because some systems implement the complete direct mapped page map table in very high-speed cache storage.

8.6.2 Paging Address Translation by Associative Mapping

One way of speeding dynamic address translation is to place the entire page map table into an *associative storage* that has a cycle time perhaps an order of magnitude faster than primary storage. Figure 8.13 illustrates how dynamic address translation proceeds with pure *associative mapping.* A running program refers to virtual address $v = (p,d)$. Every entry in the associative storage is searched simultaneously for page p. It returns p' as the page frame corresponding to page p, and p' is concatenated with d, forming the real address, r. Note that the arrows into the associative map actually enter every cell of the map. This indicates that every cell of the associative storage is searched simultaneously for a match on p. This is what makes associative storage expensive.

Again, the dilemma faced is that dynamic address translation must proceed quickly to make the concept of virtual storage feasible. But using a cache storage to

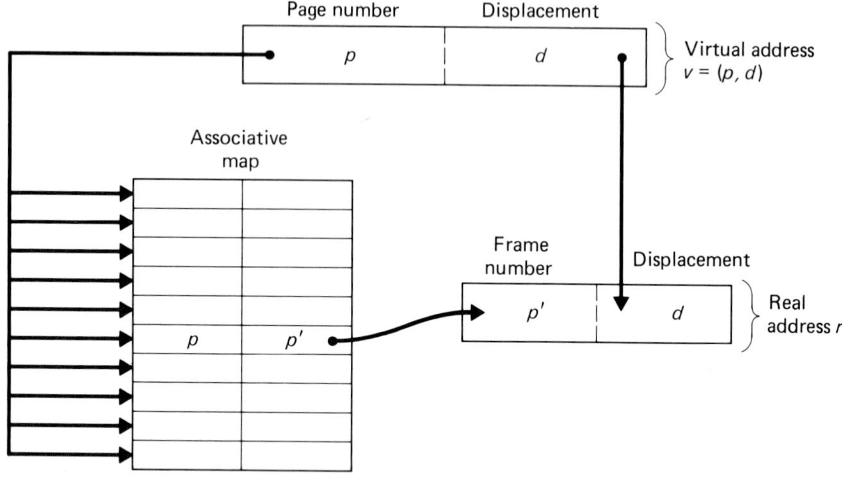

Fig. 8.13 Paging address translation with pure associative mapping.

implement pure direct mapping or using an associative storage to implement pure associative mapping is too costly. We need a compromise scheme that offers most of the advantages of the cache or associative storage approach but at a more modest cost.

8.6.3 Paging Address Translation with Combined Associative/Direct Mapping

Much of the discussion to this point has dealt with the computer hardware it takes to implement virtual storage efficiently. The hardware view presented has been logical rather than physical. We are concerned not with the precise structure of the devices but with their functional organization and relative speeds. This view of hardware is typical of that which the operating systems designer must have, especially in development environments in which hardware designs may be modified.

Improvements in hardware over the last three decades have come at a much more dramatic pace than improvements in software. It has actually come to the point that designers are reluctant to commit themselves to a particular hardware technology because they expect a better technology will soon be available. Operating systems designers generally have little choice in these matters because they must implement operating systems with existing technologies. They must also deal with the realities and economics of today's hardware. Currently, cache and associative storage are far more expensive than direct access primary storage. This leads us to our compromise page mapping mechanism.

An associative storage capable of holding only a small percentage of the complete page map for a process (Fig. 8.14) is used. The page entries maintained in this map correspond to the most recently referenced pages only, using the heuristic that a page referenced recently in the past is likely to be referenced again in the near future. Today's systems using a partial associative page map have achieved perfor-

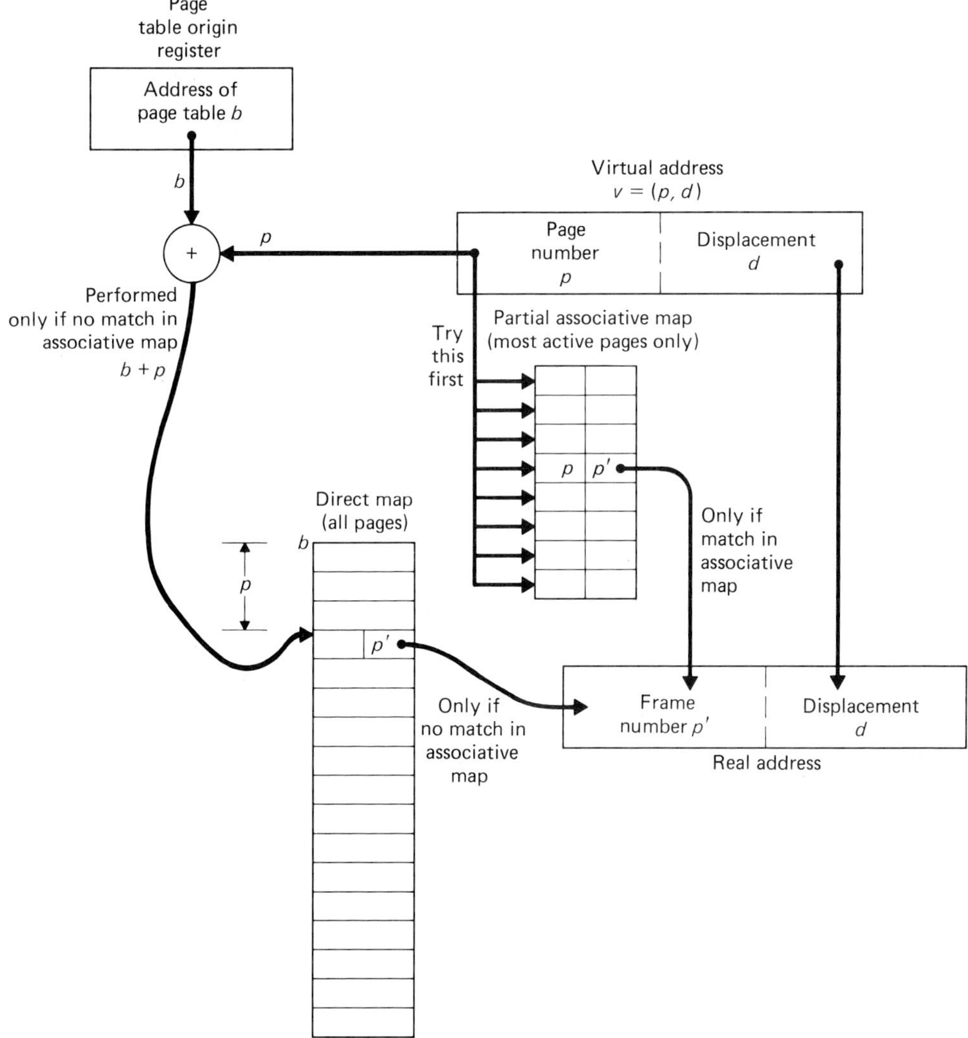

Fig. 8.14 Paging address translation with combined associative/direct mapping.

mances of 90 percent and higher of that performance possible with a complete associative page map.

Dynamic address translation proceeds as follows. A running program references virtual address $v = (p,d)$. The address translation mechanism first tries to find page p in the partial associative page map. If p is there, then the associative map returns p' as the frame number corresponding to virtual page p, and p' is concatenated with the displacement d to form the real address r that corresponds to virtual address $v = (p,d)$.

If there is no match for page p in the associative page map, a conventional direct map is used. The address, b, in the page table origin register is added to p to locate the appropriate entry for page p in the direct mapping page map table in primary storage. The table indicates that p' is the page frame corresponding to virtual page p, and p' is concatenated with the displacement, d, to form the real address r corresponding to virtual address $v = (p,d)$.

The partial associative page map does not need to be large to achieve good performance. In fact, systems using this technique with only eight or sixteen associative storage registers often achieve 90 percent or more of the performance possible with a complete associative map, which on today's systems might require 100 times as many entries. This occurs because of the phenomenon of *locality*, a property of running processes we shall consider in the next chapter.

Using a combined associative/direct mapping mechanism is an engineering decision based on the economics of existing hardware technologies. Hardware technologies change quickly. Therefore, it is important for operating systems students to be aware of emerging hardware technologies. Books on computer architecture, such as (Ba80), are a good source for this material.

8.6.4 Sharing in a Paging System

In multiprogrammed computer systems, especially in timesharing systems, it is common for many users to be executing the same programs. If individual copies of these programs were given to each user, then much of primary storage would be wasted. The obvious solution is to share those pages that can be shared.

Sharing must be carefully controlled to prevent one process from modifying data that another process is reading. In most of today's systems that implement sharing, programs are divided into separate procedure and data areas. Nonmodifiable procedures are called *pure procedures* or *reentrant procedures.* Modifiable data clearly cannot be shared. Nonmodifiable data (such as fixed tabular information, for example) can be shared. Modifiable procedures cannot be shared.

All of this discussion points to the need to identify each page as either sharable or nonsharable. Once each process's pages have been categorized in this fashion, then sharing in pure paging systems is implemented as in Fig. 8.15. By having page map table entries of different processes point to the same page frame, then that page

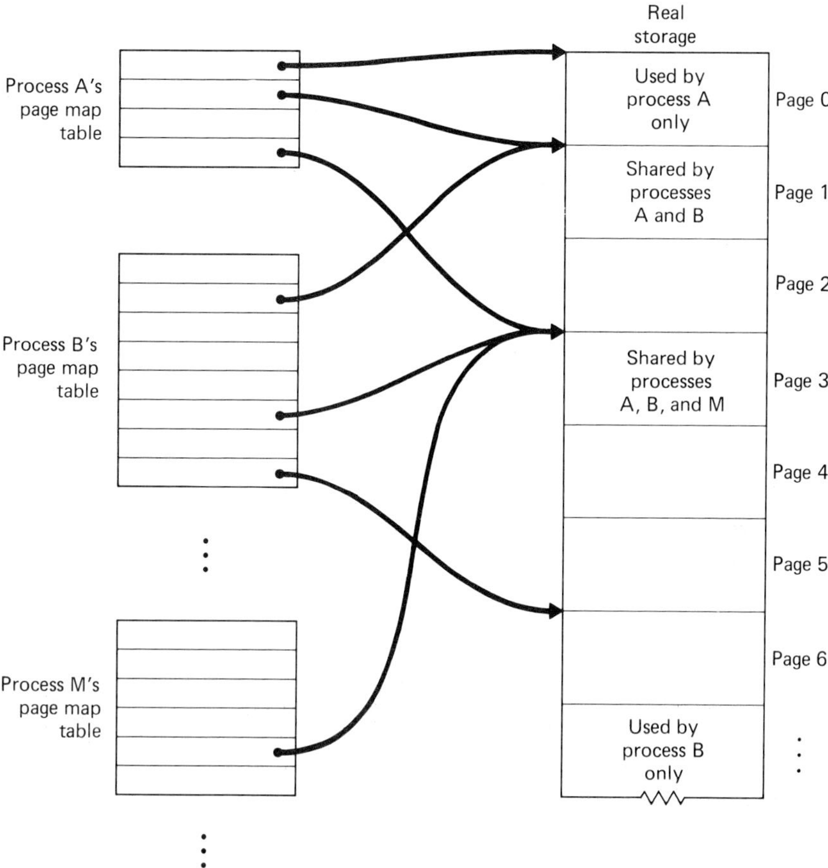

Fig. 8.15 Sharing in a pure paging system.

frame is shared among those processes. Sharing reduces the amount of primary storage needed for a group of processes to run efficiently, and can make it possible for a given system to support more users. In the next chapter, the issues of how sharing affects virtual storage management will be considered.

8.7 SEGMENTATION

From the chapter on real storage, we recall that in variable partition multiprogramming, placing programs in storage is often performed on a first-fit, best-fit, or worst-fit basis. But we are still restricted to running programs in one block of contiguous locations of real storage.

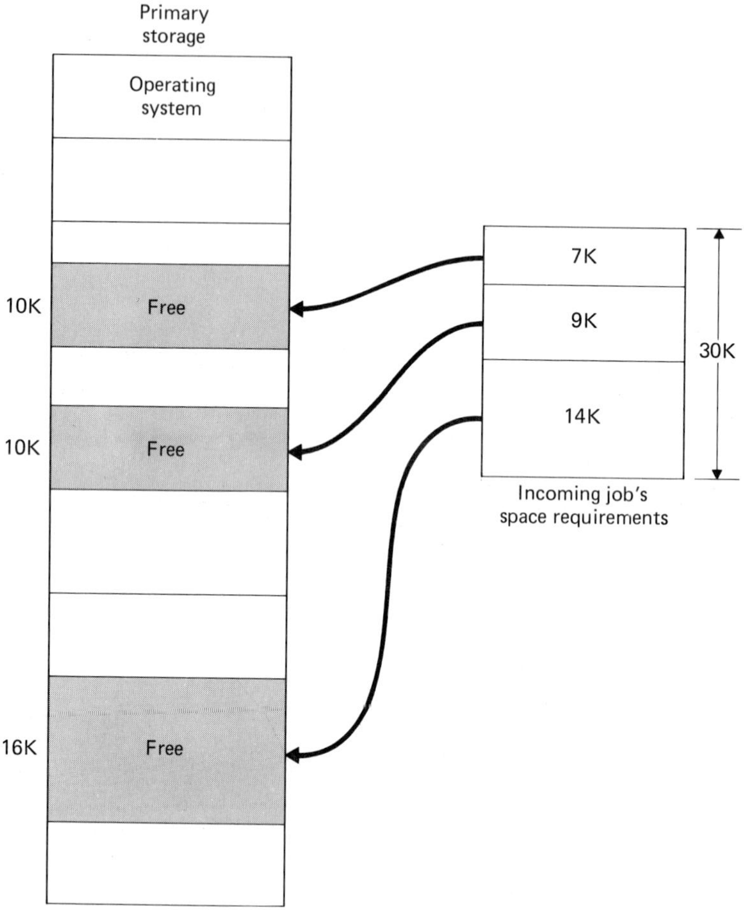

Fig. 8.16 Noncontiguous storage allocation.

In *segmentation* systems, this restriction is removed and a program (and its data) are allowed to occupy many separate blocks of real storage (Fig. 8.16). The blocks themselves need not be the same size and must still consist of contiguous locations, but the separate blocks need not be adjacent to one another.

This introduces several interesting problems. For example, the problem of protecting each user from destruction by other users now becomes more complex. A pair of bounds registers no longer suffices. Similarly, it becomes more difficult to limit the range of access of any given program. One scheme for implementing storage protection in segmentation systems is the use of storage protection keys as shown in Fig. 8.17.

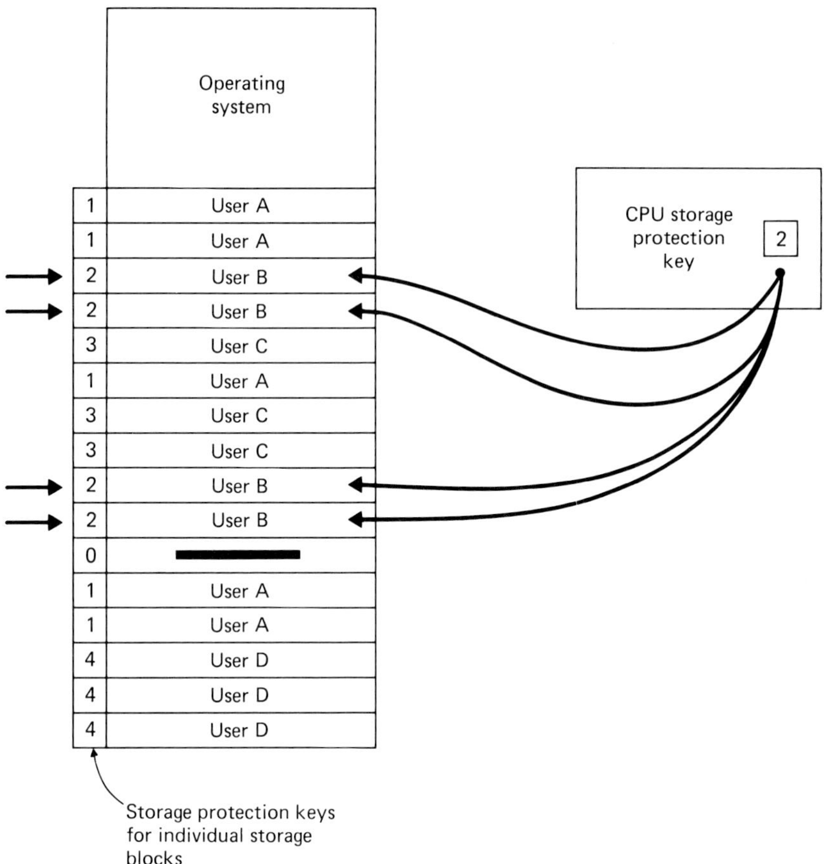

Fig. 8.17 Storage protection with keys in noncontiguous storage allocation multiprogramming systems. While the storage protection key in CPU is 2, corresponding to User B, User B's program may refer only to other blocks of storage with the same storage protection key of 2. These keys are strictly under the control of the operating system.

A virtual address in a segmentation system is an ordered pair $v = (s,d)$ where s is the segment number in virtual storage in which the referenced items resides, and d is the displacement within segment s at which the referenced item is located (Fig. 8.18). A process may run only if its current segment (as a minimum) is in primary

Segment number s	Displacement d	Virtual address $v = (s, d)$

Fig. 8.18 Virtual address format in a pure segmentation system.

storage. Segments are transferred from secondary to primary storage as complete units. All of the locations within a segment are placed in contiguous locations in primary storage. An incoming segment may be placed in any available set of contiguous locations in primary storage large enough to hold the segment. The placement strategies for segmentation are identical to those used in variable partition multiprogramming with first fit and best fit being most common.

Dynamic address translation under segmentation proceeds as follows. A running process references a virtual storage address $v = (s,d)$ (Fig. 8.19). A segment mapping mechanism looks up segment s in the *segment map table* and determines that segment s is in real storage beginning at location s'. The real storage address corresponding to virtual storage address $v = (s,d)$ is then formed by adding s' to d. We will examine this process in more detail in the next several sections.

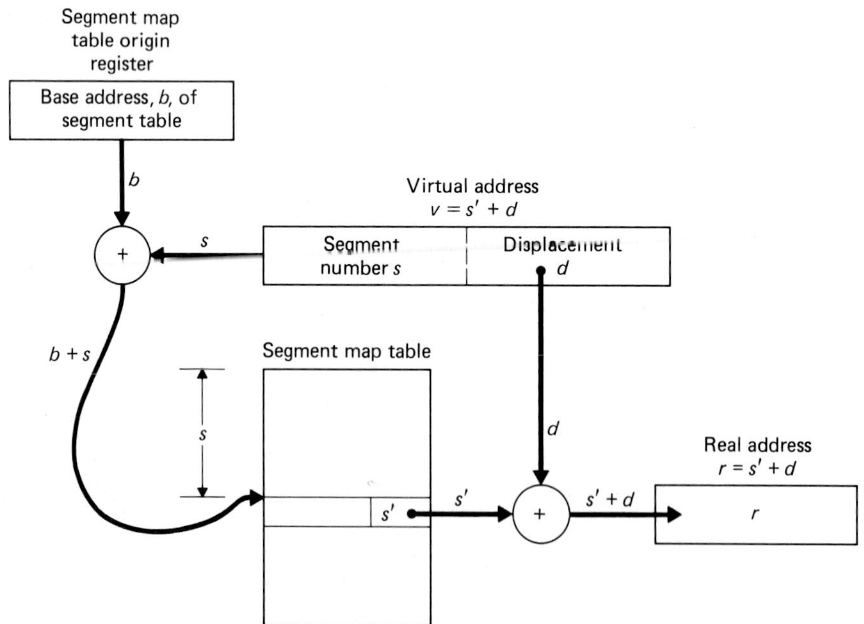

Fig. 8.19 Virtual address translation in a pure segmentation system.

8.7.1 Access Control in Segmentation Systems

It is unwise to give each process unlimited access to every segment in the system. In fact, one of the attractions in segmentation systems is the careful access control that is possible. This is provided by giving each process certain access rights to each segment and by, in fact, completely denying access to many segments.

Figure 8.20 lists the most common access control types in use in today's systems. If a process has *read access* to a segment, then the process may obtain any item of information contained in that segment. The process may make a complete copy of the segment if it so desires.

Type of access	Abbreviation	Explanation
Read	R	This block may be read.
Write	W	This block may be modified.
Execute	E	This block may be executed.
Append	A	This block may have information added to it at its end.

Fig. 8.20 Access control types.

If a process is given *write access* to a segment, then the process may modify any of the contents of the segment, and may place additional information in the segment. The process may destroy all of the information in the segment if it so desires.

A process given *execute access* to a segment may run that segment as a program. Execute access to a data segment is normally denied.

A process given *append access* to a segment may write additional information at the end of the segment, but may not modify existing information.

In a system with these four access control types, by either allowing or denying each type, it is possible to create sixteen different *access control modes*. Some of these are interesting, while others don't make sense. For simplicity, consider the eight different combinations of read, write, and execute access as shown in Fig. 8.21.

In mode 0, no access is permitted to the segment. This is useful in security schemes in which the segment is not to be accessed by a particular process.

In mode 1, a process is given *execute only access* to the segment. This mode is useful when a process is to be allowed to use a program contained in the segment, but may not copy or modify it.

	Read	Write	Execute	Explanation	Application
Mode 0	No	No	No	No access permitted	Security
Mode 1	No	No	Yes	Execute only	A program made available to users who cannot modify it or copy it, but who can run it.
Mode 2	No	Yes	No	Write only	These possibilities are not useful; it doesn't make sense to grant write access while denying read access.
Mode 3	No	Yes	Yes	Write/execute but cannot be read	
Mode 4	Yes	No	No	Read only	Information retrieval
Mode 5	Yes	No	Yes	Read/execute	A program can be copied or executed but cannot be modified.
Mode 6	Yes	Yes	No	Read/write but no execution	Protects data from an erroneous attempt to execute it.
Mode 7	Yes	Yes	Yes	Unrestricted access	This access is granted to trusted users.

Fig. 8.21 Combining read, write, and execute access to yield useful protection modes.

Modes 2 and 3 are not useful—it doesn't make sense to give a process the right to modify a segment without also giving it the right to read the segment.

Mode 4 allows a process *read only access* to a segment. This is useful in information retrieval applications in which a process is to have access to information, but may not modify it.

Mode 5 allows a process *read/execute access* to a segment. This is useful in situations in which a process is allowed to use the program contained in the segment, but may not modify the original copy. The process may, however, make its own copy of the segment that it may then modify.

Mode 6 allows a process *read/write access* to a segment. This is useful when the segment is data that may be read or written by the process but that must be protected from accidental execution (since the segment is not a program).

Mode 7 allows a process *unrestricted access* to a segment. This is useful for allowing a process complete access to its own segments, and for giving it most-trusted status to other users' segments.

The simple access control mechanism described in this section is the basis of segment protection in many implemented systems.

8.7.2 Segmented Address Translation by Direct Mapping

Just as in paged systems, there are many strategies for implementing segmented address translation. It can be done by direct mapping, by associative mapping, or by combined direct/associative mapping. It can be done with cache storages large enough to hold the entire segment map table, or it can be done with partial cache storages large enough to hold entries for only the most recently referenced segments. In this section, we consider segmented address translation using direct mapping with the complete segment map table maintained in a fast access cache storage. A typical segment map table entry is shown in detail in Fig. 8.22.

First, we consider the case in which the address translation proceeds normally, and then we consider several problems that may arise. A running process references virtual address $v = (s,d)$. The segment number, s, is added to the base address, b, in the segment map table origin register to form the real storage address, $b + s$, of the entry for segment s in the segment map table. The segment map table contains the primary storage address, s', at which the segment begins. The displacement, d, is added to s' forming the real address, $r = d + s'$, corresponding to virtual address $v = (s,d)$.

Figure 8.22 shows a typical segment map table entry in detail. A *residence bit, r,* indicates whether or not that segment is currently in primary storage. If the segment is in primary storage, then s' is the primary storage address at which the segment begins. If the segment is not in primary storage, then a is the secondary storage address from which the segment must be retrieved before the process may proceed. All references to the segment are checked against the segment length, l, to be sure that they fall within the range of the segment. Each reference to the segment is also checked against the protection bits to determine if the operation being attempted is allowed. Now, during dynamic address translation, once the segment map table entry for segment s has been located, first r is examined to be sure the segment is in primary storage. If the segment is not in primary storage, then a *missing segment fault* is generated causing the operating system to get control and load

Segment residence bit	Secondary storage address (if not in real storage)	Segment length	Protection bits				Base address of segment (if segment is in storage)
r	a	l	R	W	E	A	s'

$r = 0$ if segment is not in primary storage
$r = 1$ if segment is in primary storage

Protection bits: (1—yes, 0—no)

R—read access
W—write access
E—execute access
A—append access

Fig. 8.22 Segment map table entry.

the referenced segment from secondary storage address a. Once the segment is loaded, address translation proceeds with checking that the displacement, d, is less than or equal to the segment length, l. If it is not, then a *segment overflow fault* is generated causing the operating system to get control, and terminate execution of this process. If the displacement is within the range of the segment, then the protection bits are checked to be sure that the operation being attempted is allowed. If it is, then finally the base address, s', of the segment in primary storage is added to the displacement, d, to form the real storage address $r = s' + d$ corresponding to virtual storage address $v = (s,d)$. If the operation being attempted is not allowed, then a *segment protection fault* is generated causing the operating system to get control and terminate execution of this process.

8.7.3 Sharing in a Segmentation System

One of the advantages of segmentation over paging is that it is a logical rather than a physical concept. In their most general form, segments are not arbitrarily constrained to a certain size. Instead, they are allowed to be (within reasonable limits) as large as they need to be. A segment corresponding to an array is as large as the array. A segment corresponding to a dynamic data structure may grow and shrink in size as the data structure itself grows and shrinks. A segment corresponding to procedural code generated by a compiler is as large it needs to be to hold the code.

Sharing segments is quite straightforward when compared to sharing in a pure paging system. If an array in a pure paging system is three and one-half pages long, then instead of having simple entries that indicate "share this array," we must now have separate entries for each of the pages on which the array resides. Handling the partial page can be awkward. The situation is even worse with a dynamic data structure. When a dynamic data structure grows into a new page, the sharing indications must be adjusted at execution time. In a segmentation system, once the segment is declared as shared, then data structures may grow and shrink at will without changing the logical fact that they reside on shared segments.

Figure 8.23 illustrates how sharing is accomplished in a pure segmentation system. Two processes may share a segment by simply having entries in their segment tables that point to the same segment in primary storage.

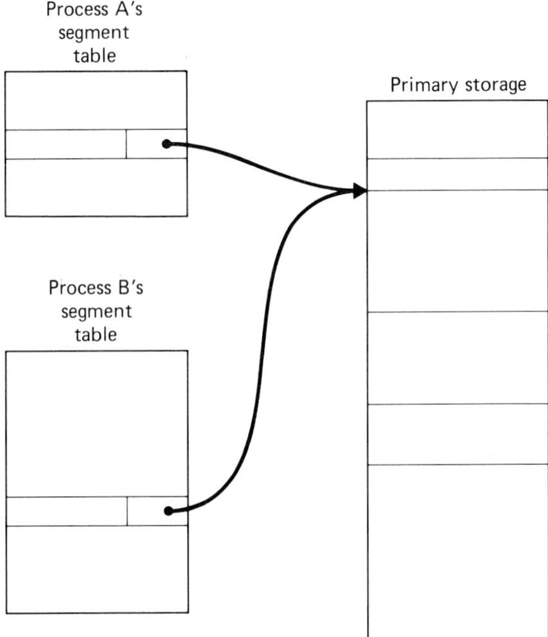

Fig. 8.23 Sharing in a pure segmentation system.

8.8 PAGING/SEGMENTATION SYSTEMS

Both segmentation and paging offer significant advantages as virtual storage organizations. Beginning with systems in the mid-1960s, in particular Multics and IBM's TSS, many computer systems have been built that combine paging and segmentation (Da68) (De71) (Do76). These systems offer the advantages of both virtual storage organization techniques. Segments are usually multiples of pages in size, it is not necessary for all of the pages of a segment to be in primary storage at once, and virtual storage pages that are contiguous in virtual storage need not be contiguous in real storage. Addressing is three-dimensional with a virtual storage address, v, being an ordered triple $v = (s,p,d)$ where s is the segment number, p is the page number, and d is the displacement within the page at which the desired item is located (Fig. 8.24).

Segment number s	Page number p	Displacement d	Virtual address $v = (s, p, d)$

Fig. 8.24 Virtual address format in a paged and segmented system.

8.8.1 Dynamic Address Translation in Paging/Segmentation Systems

Now consider the dynamic address translation of virtual addresses to real addresses in a paging/segmentation system using combined associative/direct mapping as is illustrated in Fig. 8.25.

A running process references virtual address $v = (s,p,d)$. The most recently referenced pages have entries in an associative storage. An associative search is performed to attempt to locate (s,p) in the associative storage. If (s,p) is found, then the page frame, p', at which this page resides in primary storage is concatenated to the displacement, d, to form the real storage address, r, corresponding to virtual address $v = (s,p,d)$ and the address translation is complete.

Normally, most address translation requests are satisfied by this associative storage search. When a request is not satisfied by searching the associative storage, then a complete direct mapping occurs as follows. The base address, b, of the segment table is added to the segment number, s, to form the address, $b + s$, of the entry in the segment map table for segment s in primary storage. The segment map table entry indicates the base address, s', of the page table for segment s. The page number, p, is added to s' to form the address, $p + s'$, of the entry in the page table for page p of segment s. This table yields the fact that p' is the frame number corresponding to virtual page p. The frame number, p', is concatenated with the displacement, d, to form the real address, r, corresponding to virtual address $v = (s,p,d)$.

This translation process has, of course, assumed that every piece of information is exactly where it's supposed to be. But there are many steps along the way where the translation process may fail. The segment map table search may indicate that segment s is not in primary storage, thus generating a *missing segment fault* and causing the operating system to locate the segment on secondary storage, create a page table for the segment, and load the appropriate page into primary storage, possibly replacing an existing page of this or some other process. If the segment is in primary storage, then the reference to the page map table may indicate that the de-

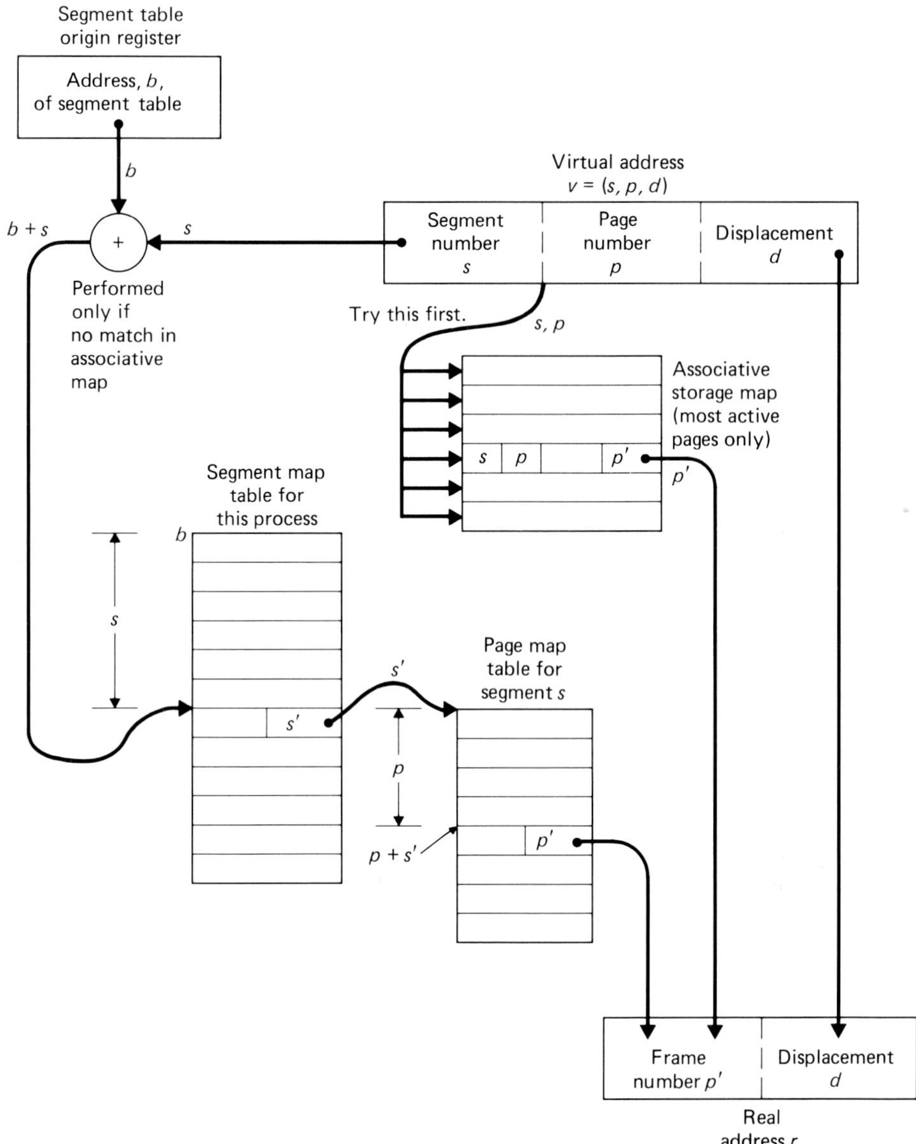

Fig. 8.25 Virtual address translation with combined associative/direct mapping in a paged and segmented system.

sired page is not in primary storage. This would generate a *missing page fault* causing the operating system to gain control, locate the page on secondary storage, and load the page (again, possibly replacing another page). Just as in pure segmentation, a virtual storage address may be past the end of a segment, thus generating a *segment overflow fault.* Or the protection bits may indicate that the indicated operation to be performed on the referenced virtual address is not allowed, thus generating a *segment protection fault.* The operating system must handle all of these eventualities.

The associative storage (or similarly, a high-speed cache storage) is critical to the efficient operation of the dynamic address translation mechanism. If a purely direct mapping mechanism is used with the complete map maintained in primary storage, the average virtual storage reference would require a storage cycle to access the segment map table, a second storage cycle to reference the page map table, and a third storage cycle to reference the desired item in real storage. Thus every reference to an item would involve three storage cycles, and the computer system would run only at approximately one-third its normal speed, with two-thirds of its time being spent in address translation! It is interesting that with only eight or sixteen associative registers, many systems achieve operating speeds 90 percent and higher of the full processing speed of their control processors.

Figure 8.26 indicates the detailed table structure required by paged/segmented systems. At the top level is a *process table* containing an entry for every process known to the system. The process table entry for a given process points to that process's segment map table. Each entry of a process's segment map table points to the page map table for the associated segment, and each entry in a page map table points either to the page frame in which that page resides or to the secondary storage address at which the page may be found. In a system with a large number of processes, segments, and pages, this table structure can consume a significant portion of primary storage. The trade-off here is that address translation proceeds more quickly at execution time if all of the tables are in primary storage, but with more tables in primary storage, the system supports fewer processes, and thus productivity declines. Operating systems designers must evaluate many such trade-offs to achieve the delicate balance needed for a system both to run efficiently and to provide responsible service to its users.

8.8.2 Sharing in a Paging/Segmentation System

In a paging/segmentation system the advantages of segment sharing become important. Sharing is implemented by having entries in segment map tables for different processes point to the same page map table as is indicated in Fig. 8.27.

Sharing, whether it be in paged systems, segmented systems, or paged/segmented systems, requires careful management by the operating system. In particular, the reader should consider what would happen if an incoming page were to replace a page shared by many processes.

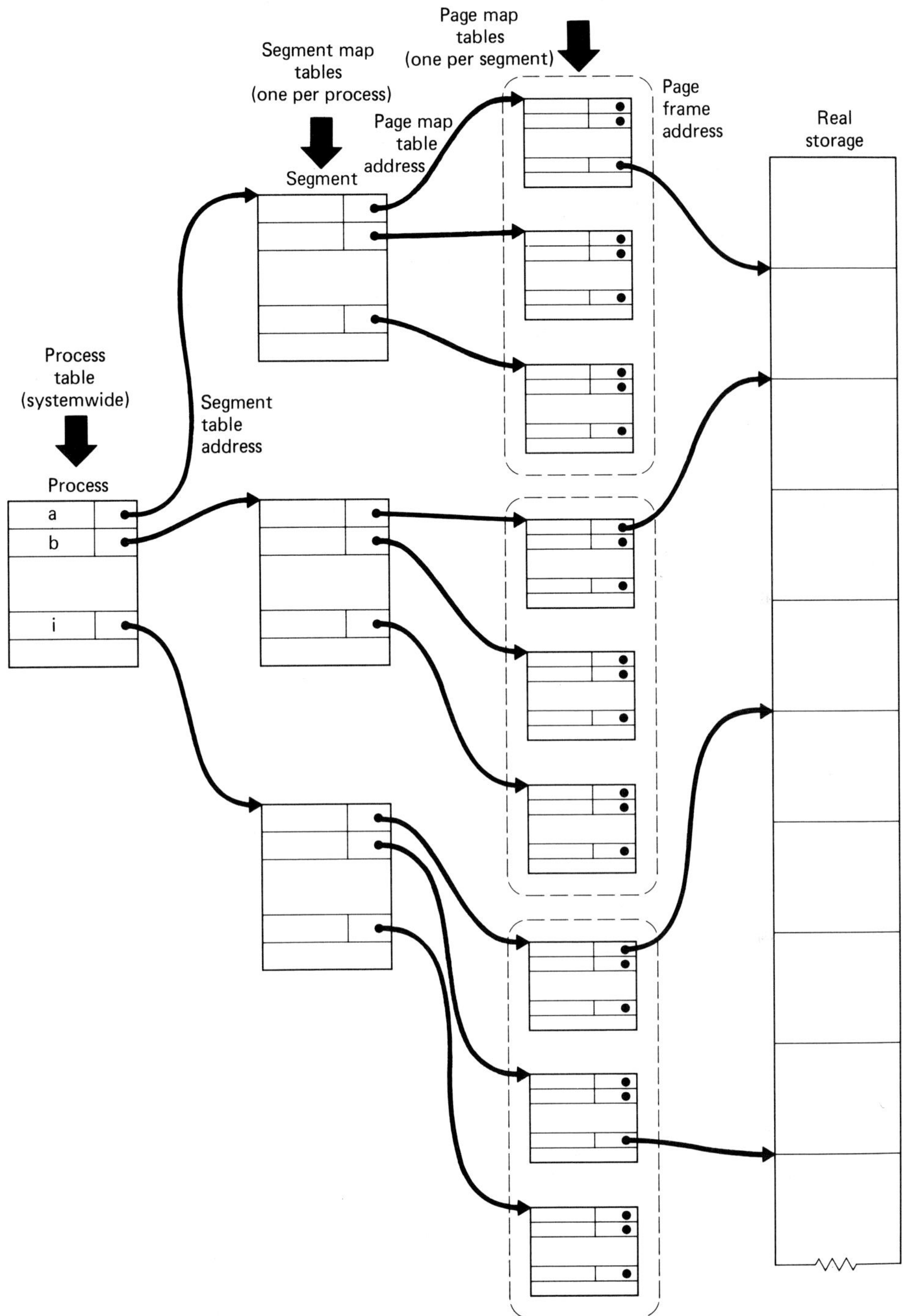

Fig. 8.26 Table structure for a paged and segmented system.

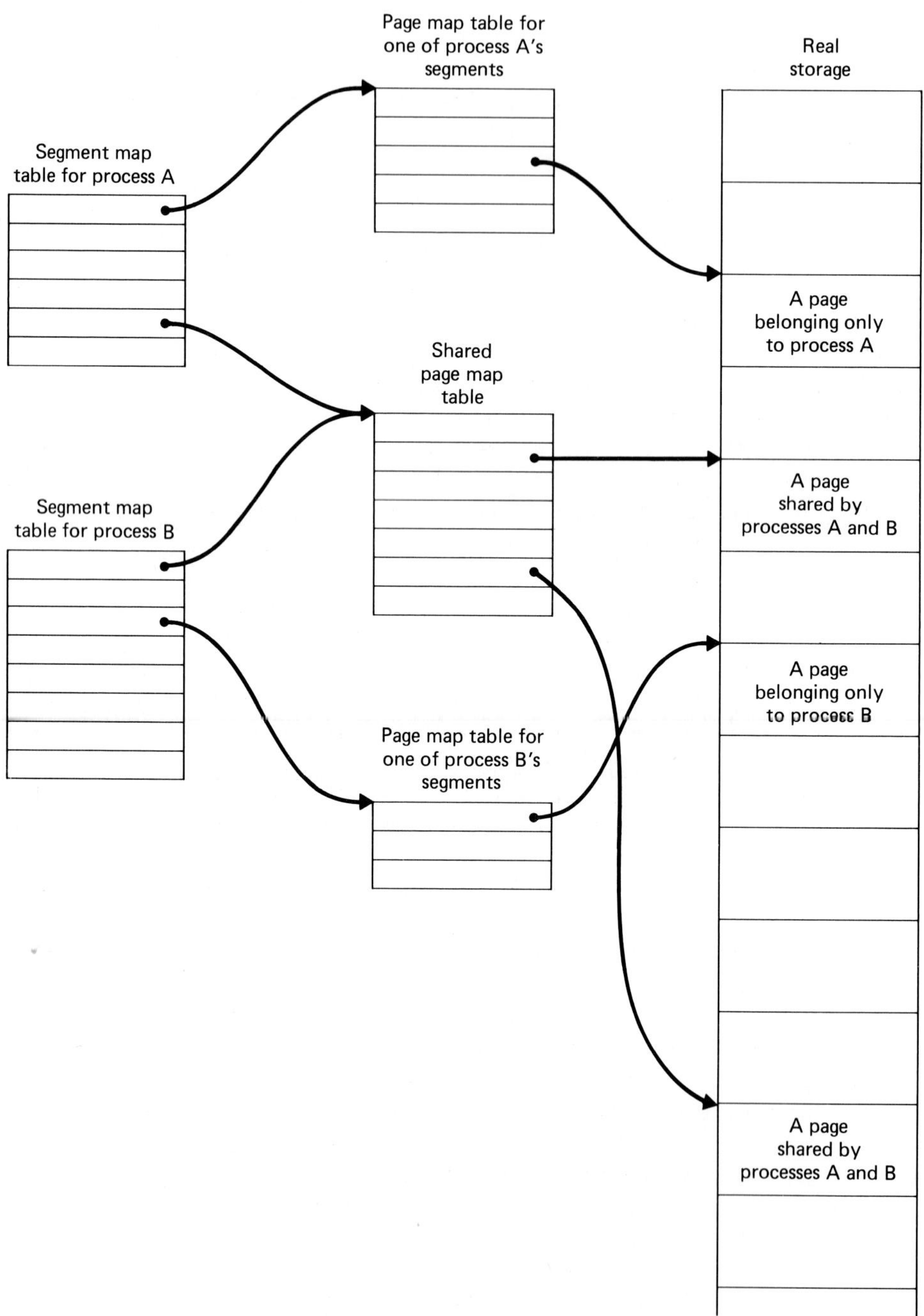

Fig. 8.27 Two processes sharing in a paged and segmented system.

SUMMARY

The two most common methods of implementing virtual storage are paging and segmentation. Virtual addresses are normally selected from a much larger set of addresses than is available in primary storage.

The key to the virtual storage concept is disassociating the virtual addresses referenced in a running process from the addresses available in primary storage, real addresses. The range of virtual addresses a running process may reference is called that process's virtual address space, V. The range of real addresses available on a particular computer system is called that computer's real address space, R.

Converting virtual addresses to real addresses is called dynamic address translation. It is performed by the system and is transparent to the user. Artificial contiguity means that addresses contiguous in V need not be contiguous in R.

Only a small portion of each process's procedures and data is normally in real storage at once. The remainder is kept on fast access secondary storage devices.

Virtual storage systems require maps from virtual addresses to real addresses. A key issue in virtual storage systems is minimizing the amount of mapping information that must be maintained in primary storage, while at the same time guaranteeing satisfactory performance. Block mapping helps accomplish this goal.

Fixed-size blocks are called pages; variable size blocks are called segments. Some systems combine the two techniques using segments that are integral multiples in length of fixed size pages. In block mapping schemes, addresses may be thought of as ordered pairs $v = (b,d)$ where b is the block in which virtual address v is contained, and d is v's displacement from the start of block b.

In a block mapping system, virtual addresses are translated to real addresses by the use of a block mapping table. For speed, this table is often implemented in a fast access cache or associative storage.

A virtual address in a paging system is an ordered pair $v = (p,d)$ where p is the page containing v, and d is the displacement of v from the start of p. Primary storage is divided into page frames the same size as virtual pages. A page may be placed in any available page frame.

Dynamic address translation under paging involves mapping the page number p to a page frame p'. The mapping may be direct, in which case a complete page map table is maintained in either primary storage or fast access cache storage. The mapping may be associative, in which case a complete page map table is maintained in a fast access associative storage. Or because of the high costs of associative and cache storages, the mapping may be combined associative/direct with only the most recent pages maintained in the associative storage, and direct mapping used when an associative search fails. This last technique is often implemented with a cache storage rather than the associative storage.

Sharing in a paging system is accomplished by having page map table entries of different processes point to the same page frame. Sharing in this manner is awkward because processes really share logical entities like procedures and data, which can often occupy several pages and grow and shrink as a process executes.

Segmentation uses variable size blocks. Each block, within reasonable limits, is as large as it needs to be to hold a logical entity such as a procedure or a data structure. A process's segments need not all be in primary storage at once, nor must they be contiguous in primary storage. A process may run if its current segment (as a minimum) is in primary storage.

A virtual address in a segmentation system is an ordered pair $v = (s,d)$ where s is the segment in which v resides and d is v's displacement within s. Dynamic address translation can be performed with essentially the same types of direct, associative, and combined direct/associative mapping performed in paging systems. Because segments vary in length, the displacement d must be checked to see that it is within the range of the segment.

Protection in segmentation systems is more natural than it is in paging systems because logical rather than physical entities are being protected. Processes are given various combinations of read, write, execute, and append access to various segments. Sharing is also more natural in a segmentation system. The segment table entries of different processes are made to point to the shared segment.

Many systems employ both paging and segmentation. A virtual address in a paging/segmentation system is an ordered triple $v = (s,p,d)$ with s the segment in which v resides, p the page within s that contains v, and d the displacement of v within p. Dynamic address translation is complex in such systems with segment map table entries pointing to page map tables, and page map table entries pointing to page frames. A fast access associative storage or cache storage is almost always used in such systems to prevent the dynamic address translation from causing serious performance degradation.

Sharing in a paging/segmentation system is accomplished by having entries in different segment map tables point to the page map table of the shared segment.

TERMINOLOGY

address map
address space
append access
artificial contiguity
associative mapping
associative storage
block
block map table
block mapping
block table origin register
cache storage
combined associative/direct mapping
combined paging/segmentation
direct mapping
displacement
dynamic address translation (DAT)
execute access
missing item fault
missing page fault
missing segment fault
multilevel storage organization
page
page frame
page map table
page transport
page wait

paging
process table
protection
pure paging
pure procedure
pure segmentation
read access
real address
real address space
reentrant procedure
residence bit
segment
segment map table
segment overflow fault
segment protection fault
segmentation
segmentation with paging
segmented name space
sharing of code and data
three-dimensional addressing
translation lookaside buffer
two-dimensional addressing
virtual address
virtual address space
virtual storage
write access

EXERCISES

8.1 Give several reasons why it is useful to separate a process's virtual storage space from its real storage space.

8.2 Some systems in use today actually implement virtual storage constrained to be smaller than the underlying real storage. Discuss the advantages and disadvantages of such a scheme.

8.3 One of the attractions of virtual storage is that users no longer have to restrict the size of their programs to make them fit into limited real storage. Programming style becomes a freer form of expression. Discuss the effects of such a free programming style on performance in a multiprogramming virtual storage environment. List both positive and negative effects.

8.4 Explain the various techniques used for mapping virtual addresses to real addresses under paging.

8.5 Discuss the relative merits of each of the following virtual storage mapping techniques.

a) direct mapping
b) associative mapping
c) combined direct/associative mapping

8.6 Explain the mapping of virtual addresses to real addresses under segmentation.

8.7 Explain how storage protection is implemented in virtual storage systems with segmentation.

8.8 Discuss the various hardware features useful for implementing virtual storage systems.

8.9 Discuss how fragmentation manifests itself in each of the following types of virtual storage systems.

a) segmentation
b) paging
c) combined segmentation/paging

8.10 In any computer system, regardless of whether it is a real storage system or a virtual storage system, the computer will rarely reference all of the instructions or data brought into real storage. Let us call this *chunk* fragmentation because it is the result of handling storage items in blocks or chunks rather than individually. Chunk fragmentation might very well account for more waste of real storage than all other types of fragmentation combined.

a) Why, then, has chunk fragmentation not been given the same amount of treatment in the literature as other forms of fragmentation?
b) How do virtual storage systems with dynamic storage allocation greatly reduce the amount of chunk fragmentation over that experienced in real storage systems?
c) What effect would smaller page sizes have on chunk fragmentation?
d) What considerations, both practical and theoretical, prevent the complete elimination of chunk fragmentation?
e) What can each of the following do to minimize chunk fragmentation?
    i) the programmer
    ii) the hardware designer
    iii) the operating system designer

8.11 Explain the mapping of virtual addresses to real addresses under combined segmentation/paging.

8.12 In multiprogramming environments, sharing of code and data can greatly reduce the real storage needed by a group of processes to run efficiently. For each of the following types of systems, outline briefly how sharing can be implemented.

a) fixed partition multiprogramming
b) variable partition multiprogramming
c) paging
d) segmentation
e) combined segmentation/paging

8.13 Why is sharing of code and data so much more natural in virtual storage systems than in real storage systems?

8.14 Discuss the similarities and differences between paging and segmentation.

8.15 Compare and contrast pure segmentation with segmentation/paging combined.

8.16 Suppose you are asked to implement segmentation on a machine that has paging hardware but no segmentation hardware. You may use only software techniques. Is this possible? Explain your answer.

8.17 Suppose you are asked to implement paging on a machine that has segmentation hardware but no paging hardware. You may use only software techniques. Is this possible? Explain your answer.

8.18 As the chief designer of a new virtual storage system you have been given the choice of implementing either paging or segmentation, but not both. Which would you choose? Why?

8.19 Suppose that economical associative storage were to become available. How might such associative storage be incorporated into future computer architectures to improve the performance of the hardware, the operating system, and user programs?

8.20 Some paged virtual storage systems do I/O with systemwide buffers. Other systems do I/O directly with user buffer areas in each user's paged virtual storage. Discuss the relative merits of each approach.

LITERATURE

(Ba80) Baer, J., *Computer Systems Architecture,* Rockville, Md.: Computer Science Press, 1980.

(Da68) Daley, R. C., and J. B. Dennis, "Virtual Memory, Processes and Sharing in Multics," *CACM,* Vol. 11, No. 5, May 1968, pp. 306–311.

(De70) Denning, P. J., "Virtual Memory," *ACM Computing Surveys,* Vol. 2, No. 3, September 1970, pp. 153–189.

(De71) Denning, P. J. , "Third Generation Computing Systems," *ACM Computing Surveys,* Vol. 3, No. 4, December 1971, pp. 175–216.

(Ds65) Dennis, J. B., "Segmentation and the Design of Multiprogrammed Computer Systems," *JACM,* Vol. 12, No. 4, October 1965, pp. 589–602.

(Do76) Doran, R. W., "Virtual Memory," *Computer,* October 1976, pp. 27–37.

(Fo76) Foster, C. C., *Computer Architecture* (2nd ed.), New York: Van Nostrand Reinhold, 1976.

(Ma77) Matick, R., *Computer Storage Systems and Technology,* New York: Wiley-Interscience, 1977.

(Or72) Organick, E. I., *The Multics System: An Examination of Its Structure,* Cambridge, Mass.: M.I.T. Press, 1972.

(Or73) Organick, E. I., *Computer System Organization: The B5700/B6700 Series,* New York: Academic Press, 1973.

(Ra68) Randell, B., and C. J. Kuehner, "Dynamic Storage Allocation Systems," *CACM,* Vol. 11, No. 5, May 1968, pp. 297–304.

(St75) Stone, H. S., (ed.), *Introduction to Computer Architecture,* Chicago: SRA, 1975.

9
Virtual Storage Management

What we anticipate seldom occurs; what we least expect generally happens.

Benjamin Disraeli

Outline

9.1 INTRODUCTION

In the last chapter, the various virtual storage organizations that have been implemented were discussed, namely

- paging,
- segmentation, and
- segmentation and paging combined.

We discussed the hardware and software mechanisms for implementing virtual storage. In this chapter, we consider strategies for managing virtual storage systems, and we examine the behavior of virtual storage systems operating under these strategies.

9.2 VIRTUAL STORAGE MANAGEMENT STRATEGIES

The chapter on real storage discussed fetch, placement, and replacement storage management strategies. These are reconsidered here in the context of virtual storage systems.

- Fetch strategies—These are concerned with when a page or segment should be brought from secondary to primary storage. Demand fetch strategies wait for a page or segment to be referenced by a running process before bringing the page or segment to primary storage. Anticipatory fetch schemes attempt to determine in advance what pages or segments will be referenced by a process. If the likelihood of reference is high and if space is available, then the page or segment will be brought to primary storage before it is explicitly referenced.
- Placement strategies—These are concerned with where in primary storage to place an incoming page or segment. *Paging systems trivialize the placement decision because an incoming page may be placed in any available page frame.* Segmentation systems require placement strategies like those we discussed in the context of variable partition multiprogramming systems.
- Replacement strategies—These are concerned with deciding which page or segment to displace to make room for an incoming page or segment when primary storage is already fully committed.

9.3 PAGE REPLACEMENT STRATEGIES

It is common in paging systems for all page frames to be in use. In this case operating system storage management routines must decide which page in primary storage to displace to make room for an incoming page. We consider each of the following page replacement strategies.

- The Principle of Optimality
- Random page replacement
- First-in-first-out
- Least-recently-used
- Least-frequently-used
- Not-used-recently
- Working set

9.3.1 The Principle of Optimality

The *Principle of Optimality* (De70) states that to obtain optimum performance the page to replace is the one that will not be used again for the furthest time into the future. It is possible to demonstrate the optimality of this strategy, but of course the strategy is not realizable since we cannot predict the future.

Thus to achieve good performance we attempt to approach the Principle of Optimality by using page replacement techniques that approximate optimal page replacement.

9.3.2 Random Page Replacement

If we seek a low overhead page replacement strategy that does not discriminate against particular users, one simple technique is to choose the page to be replaced at random. All pages in main storage thus have an equal likelihood of being selected for replacement. This strategy could select any page for replacement, including the next page to be referenced (which is, of course, the worst page to replace). Because of its hit-or-miss approach, this scheme is rarely used.

9.3.3 First-In-First-Out (FIFO) Page Replacement

In the first-in-first-out page replacement, we time-stamp each page as it enters primary storage. When a page needs to be replaced, we choose the one that has been in storage the longest. The intuitive appeal of this strategy seems reasonable; namely that this page has had its chance and it's time to give another page a chance. Unfortunately, first-in-first-out is likely to replace heavily used pages because the reason a page has been in primary storage for a long time may well be that it is in constant use. For example, on large timesharing systems it is common for many users to share a copy of a text editor as they type and correct programs. First-in-first-out page replacement on such a system might choose a heavily used editor page to replace. This would certainly be a poor choice. This page would be recalled to main storage almost immediately.

9.3.3.1 *FIFO Anomaly*

It would seem reasonable that the more page frames allocated to a process, the fewer page faults the process will experience. Belady, Nelson, and Shedler (Be69b) discovered that under FIFO page replacement, certain page reference patterns actually cause more page faults when the number of page frames allocated to a process is increased. This phenomenon is called the *FIFO Anomaly.*

Consider Fig. 9.1. The leftmost column indicates the page reference pattern of a process. The first table shows how this page reference pattern causes pages to be loaded into storage and replaced under FIFO when three page frames are allocated to the process. The second table shows how this process behaves in these same circumstances, but instead with four page frames allocated to it. To the left of each table we indicate whether the new page reference causes a page fault or not. When the

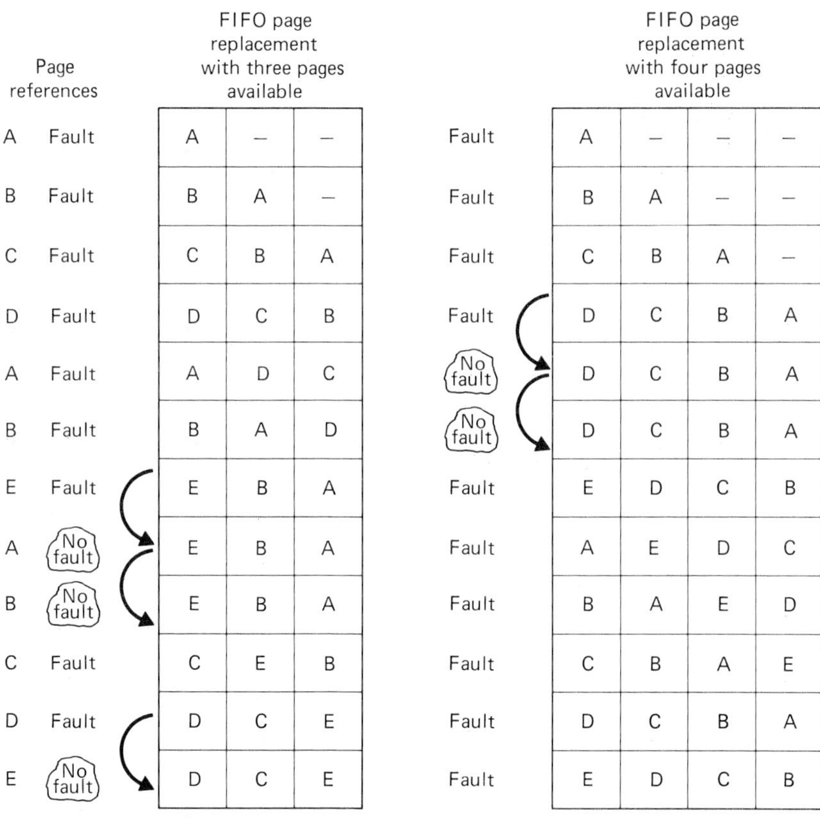

Fig. 9.1 The FIFO Anomaly.

process runs in four pages, it actually experiences one more page fault than when it runs in three pages, an observation certainly contrary to intuition.

The FIFO Anomaly is considered to be more of a curiosity than an important result. Perhaps its real significance to the operating systems student is to serve as a warning that operating systems are complex entities that sometimes defy intuition.

9.3.4 Least-Recently-Used (LRU) Page Replacement

This strategy selects that page for replacement that has not been used for the longest time. Here we rely on the heuristic that the recent past is a good indicator of the near future. LRU requires that each page be time-stamped whenever it is referenced. This could require substantial overhead, and thus the LRU strategy, although appealing, is not often implemented in current systems. Instead, lower overhead strategies that approximate LRU are used.

We must always be careful when applying heuristic reasoning in operating systems. For example, in the LRU strategy, the page least recently used could in fact be the next to be used as a program cycles its way around a large loop involving several pages. By replacing the LRU page we would find ourselves paging it right back into main storage almost immediately.

9.3.5 Least-Frequently-Used (LFU) Page Replacement

One approximation to LRU is the least-frequently used (LFU) strategy. Here we are concerned with how intensive the use of each page has been. The page to replace is that page that is least frequently used or least intensively referenced. Here again the intuitive appeal is real. However, the wrong page could quite easily be selected for replacement. For example, the least frequently used page could be the page brought into main storage most recently. The page has been used once whereas all other pages in main storage could have been used more than once. Now the page replacement mechanism replaces this page when in fact it would be highly likely to be used immediately.

It certainly seems as though every page replacement scheme runs some danger of making bad decisions. This is true simply because we cannot accurately predict the future. Thus a page replacement strategy that makes reasonable decisions most of the time and has low overhead is desired.

9.3.6 Not-Used-Recently (NUR) Page Replacement

One popular scheme for approximating LRU with little overhead is not-used-recently (NUR). Pages not used recently are not likely to be used in the near future and they may be replaced with incoming pages.

Because it is desirable to replace a page that has not been changed while in primary storage, the NUR strategy is implemented with the addition of two hardware bits per page. These are

a) *referenced bit* = 0 if the page has not been referenced
= 1 if the page has been referenced

b) *modified bit* = 0 if the page has not been modified
= 1 if the page has been modified

The modified bit is often called the *dirty bit.* The NUR strategy works as follows. Initially, the referenced bits of all pages are set to 0. As a reference to a particular page occurs, the referenced bit of that page is set to 1. Initially, the modified bits on all pages are 0. Whenever a page is modified, its modified bit is set to 1. When a page is to be replaced, we first try to find a page which has not been referenced (because we're approximating LRU). Otherwise we have no choice but to replace a referenced page. If a page has not been referenced, then we check to see whether or not it has been modified. If it has not been modified, we replace it on the basis that there is less overhead involved than in replacing a modified page that must be written back to secondary storage. Otherwise we must replace a modified page.

Of course, main storage will be actively referenced in a multiple user system, and sooner or later most of the referenced bits will be set on. We then lose our ability to distinguish the most desirable pages to replace. One technique that has been widely implemented to avoid this problem is to periodically set all the referenced bits to 0 to get a fresh start, and then to allow referenced bits to be set to 1 again under normal referencing patterns. This makes even active pages vulnerable to replacement, but only for a brief moment after the bits are reset. Active pages will have their referenced bits set to 1 again almost immediately.

The NUR scheme as described above results in the existence of four groups of pages.

Group 1	unreferenced	unmodified
Group 2	unreferenced	modified
Group 3	referenced	unmodified
Group 4	referenced	modified

The pages in the lowest numbered groups should be replaced first, and those in the highest numbered groups should be replaced last. Note that Group 2 seems to describe an unrealistic situation, namely pages that have been modified but not referenced. Actually, this is a simple consequence of the periodic resetting of the referenced bits (but not of the modified bits), and is perfectly reasonable.

9.4 LOCALITY

Central to most storage management strategies is the concept of *locality*—that *processes tend to reference storage in nonuniform, highly localized patterns.*

Locality manifests itself in both time and space. *Temporal locality* is locality over time. For example, if the weather is sunny at 3 P.M., then there is a good chance (but certainly no guarantee) that the weather was sunny at 2:30 P.M., and will be sunny at 3:30 P.M. *Spatial locality* means that nearby items tend to be similar. Again, considering the weather, if it's sunny in one town, then it's likely (but not guaranteed) that it will be sunny in nearby towns.

Locality is also observed in operating systems environments, particularly in the area of storage management. It is an empirical (observed) property rather than a theoretical one. It is never guaranteed but is often highly likely. For example, in paging systems, we observe that processes tend to favor certain subsets of their pages, and that these pages often tend to be adjacent to one another in a process's virtual address space. This doesn't mean that a process won't make a reference to a new page—if this were the case, then processes could not start running in the first place. It does mean that a process will tend to concentrate its references in a time interval to a particular subset of its pages.

Actually, locality is quite reasonable in computer systems, when one considers the way programs are written and data is organized. In particular,

1. Temporal locality—means that storage locations referenced recently are likely to be referenced in the near future. Supporting this observation are
   a) looping,
   b) subroutines,
   c) stacks, and
   d) variables used for counting and totaling.
2. Spatial locality—means that storage references tend to be clustered so that once a location is referenced, it is highly likely that nearby locations will be referenced. Supporting this observation are
   a) array traversals,
   b) sequential code execution, and
   c) the tendency of programmers to place related variable definitions near one another.

Perhaps the most significant consequence of storage reference locality is that a program can run efficiently as long as its favored subset of pages is in primary storage. Denning formulated the *working set theory of program behavior* (De68) (De68a) based upon observations of locality. We discuss Denning's working set theory in the next section.

Many studies have been performed that illustrate the phenomenon of locality. Figure 9.2 shows a graph of a process's storage reference pattern across its pages (Ha72). The darkened areas show which storage areas were referenced during con-

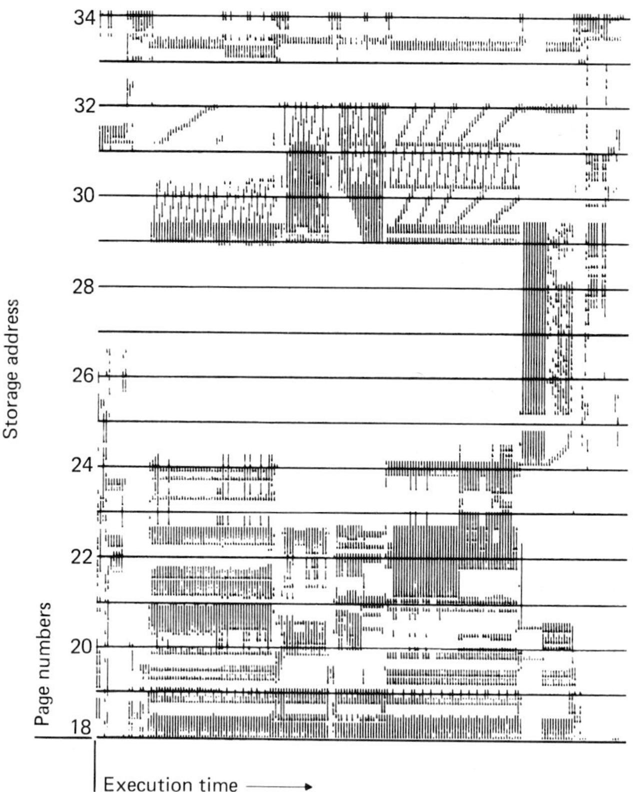

Fig. 9.2 Storage reference pattern exhibiting locality (Reprint by permission from *IBM Systems Journal.* © 1971 by International Business Machines Corporation.)

secutive time intervals. The figure vividly illustrates how this process tends to favor a subset of its pages during certain execution intervals.

Figure 9.3 also supports the existence of the phenomenon of locality. It shows how a process's page fault rate depends on the amount of primary storage available for its pages. The straight line shows how this relationship would appear if processes exhibited random reference patterns uniformly distributed over their various pages. The curved line shows how most processes actually behave when observed in operation. As the number of page frames available to a process is reduced, there is some interval over which it does not dramatically affect the page fault rate. But at a certain point when the number of page frames is further reduced, the number of page faults experienced by the running process rises dramatically. What is being observed here is that as long as the favored subset of the process's pages remains in primary storage, the page fault rate does not change much. But as soon as pages in the favored subset are removed from storage the process's paging activity greatly increases as it constantly references and recalls these pages to primary storage. All of

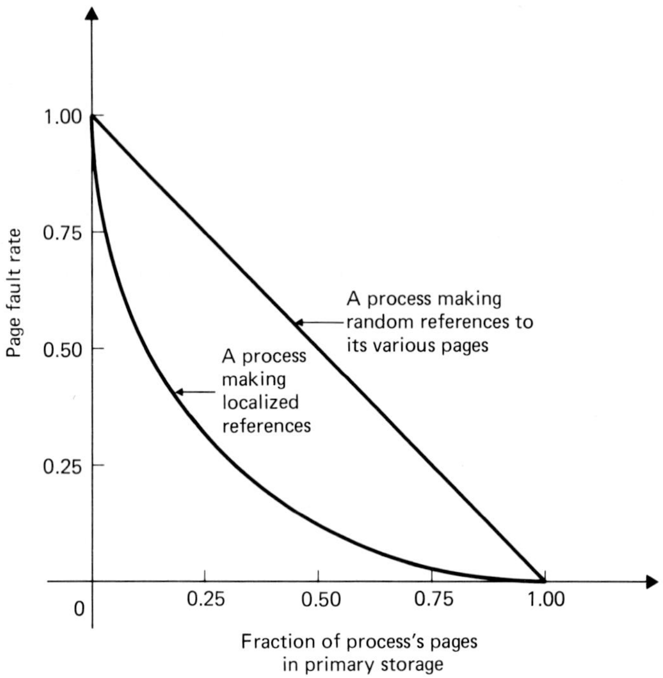

Figure 9.3

this supports Denning's working set concept that is considered in the next section. (Note that this discussion also applies to the establishment of working sets in cache memories as well.)

9.5 WORKING SETS

Denning (De68) developed a view of program paging activity called the *working set theory of program behavior.* Informally, a working set is a collection of pages a process is actively referencing. Denning maintained that for a program to run efficiently, its working set of pages must be maintained in primary storage. Otherwise, excessive paging activity called *thrashing* (De68b) might occur as the program repeatedly requests pages from secondary storage.

A *working set storage management policy* seeks to maintain the working sets of active programs in primary storage. The decision to add a new process to the active set of processes (i.e., to increase the level of multiprogramming) is based on whether sufficient space is available in primary storage to accommodate the working set of pages of the new process. This decision especially in the case of freshly initiated processes is often made by the use of heuristics because it is impossible for the system to know in advance how large a given process's working set will be.

The working set of pages of a process, $W(t,w)$ at time t, is the set of pages referenced by the process during the process time interval $t - w$ to t. (See Fig. 9.4.) Process time is the time during which a process has the CPU. The variable w is called the *working set window size*, and the determination of just how large w should be is critical to the effective operation of a working set storage management strategy. Figure 9.5 illustrates how working set size increases as w increases. This is a consequence of the mathematical definition of working set, and is not an indication of empirically observable working set sizes. *The real working set of a process is the set of pages that must be in primary storage for a process to execute efficiently.*

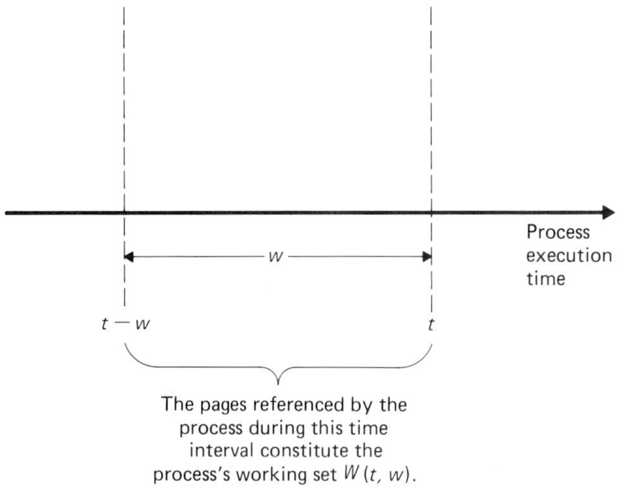

Fig. 9.4 One definition of a process's working set of pages.

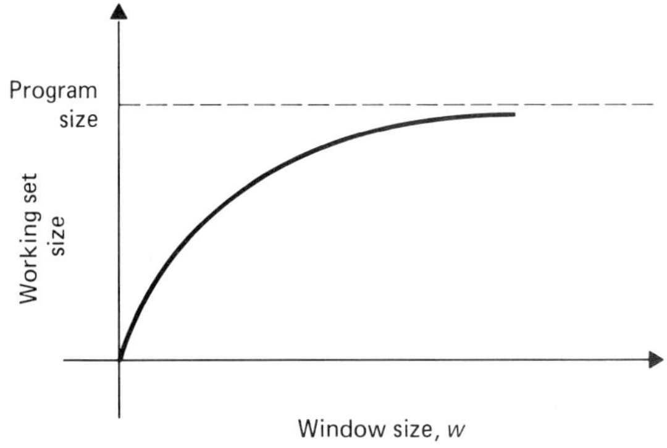

Fig. 9.5 Working set size as a function of window size.

Working sets change as a process executes. Sometimes pages are added or deleted. Sometimes dramatic changes occur when the process enters a phase of execution requiring a completely different working set. Thus any assumptions about the size and content of a process's initial working set do not necessarily apply to the subsequent working sets the process will accumulate. This complicates precise storage management under a working set strategy.

Figure 9.6 shows how a process running under a working set storage management strategy might use primary storage. First, as the process demand pages in its working set one page at a time, the process gradually receives enough storage to hold its working set. At this point, its storage use stabilizes as it actively references the pages in its first working set. Eventually, the process will make a transition to the next working set, as indicated by the curved line from first working set to second working set. At first, the curved line rises above the number of pages in the first working set because the process is rapidly demand paging in its new working set. The system has no way of knowing whether this process is expanding its working set or changing working sets. Once the process stabilizes in its next working set, the system sees fewer page references in the window and reduces the primary storage allocation of the process to the number of pages in its second working set. Each time a transition between working sets occurs, this rising and then falling curved line shows how the system adapts to the transition.

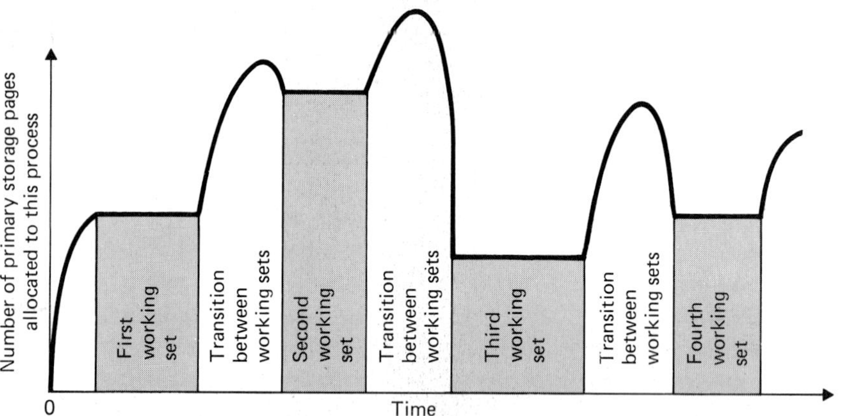

Fig. 9.6 Primary storage allocation under working set storage management.

The figure illustrates one of the difficulties with a working set storage management strategy, namely that *working sets are transient, and a process's next working set may differ substantially from its previous working set.* A storage management strategy must carefully consider this fact in order to prevent overcommitment of primary storage, and consequent thrashing.

9.6 DEMAND PAGING

It is the conventional wisdom that a process's pages should be loaded on demand. No page should be brought from secondary to primary storage until it is explicitly referenced by a running process. There are several reasons for the appeal of this strategy.

- Computability results, specifically the *halting problem* (Mi67) (He77), tell us that the path of execution a program will take cannot be accurately predicted. Therefore any attempt to preload pages in anticipation of their use might result in the wrong pages being loaded.
- Demand paging guarantees that the only pages brought to main storage are those actually needed by processes.
- The overhead involved in deciding which pages to bring to main storage is minimal. Anticipatory page fetch strategies might require substantial execution time overhead.

Demand paging is not without its problems, as indicated in Fig. 9.7. A process must accumulate its pages one at a time. As each new page is referenced, the process must wait while the new page is transferred to primary storage. Depending on

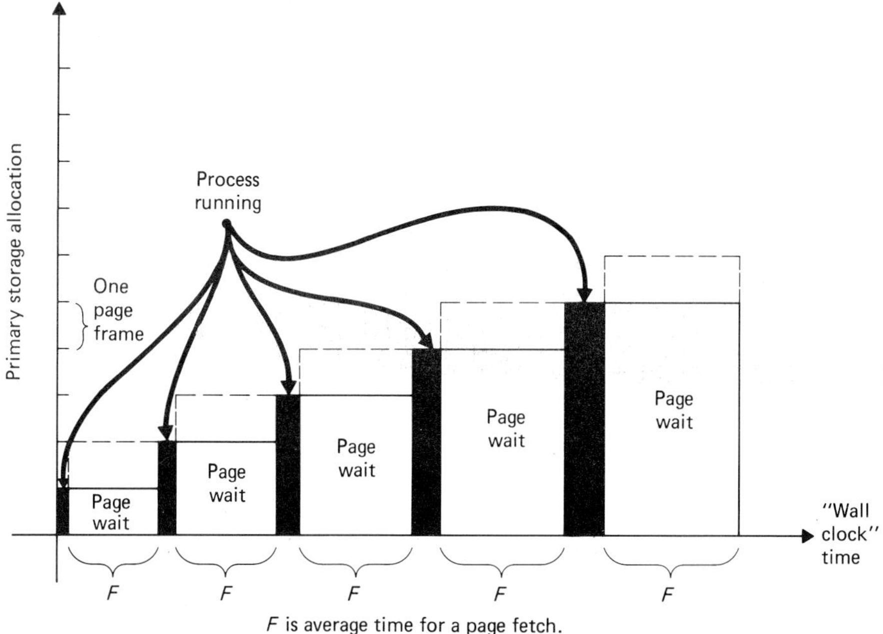

Fig. 9.7 Space–time product under demand paging.

how many pages of this process are already in primary storage, these waits become increasingly costly as greater amounts of storage are occupied by waiting processes. The figure illustrates the concept of a *space–time product* often used in operating systems to assess a process's storage usage. The space–time product corresponds to the area under the "curve" in the figure. It reflects both the amount of storage a process uses, and how long it is used. *Reducing the space–time product of a process's page waits is an important goal of storage management strategies.*

9.7 ANTICIPATORY PAGING

A central theme in resource management is that *the relative value of a resource influences just how intensively the resource should be managed.* Hardware costs have been decreasing dramatically. The relative value of machine time to people time has been considerably reduced. Now operating systems designers are concerned with methods of reducing the amount of time people must wait for results from a computer. *Anticipatory paging* is one technique that holds promise.

In anticipatory paging, the operating system attempts to predict the pages a process will need, and then preloads these pages when space is available. If correct decisions are made, the total run time of the process can be reduced considerably. While the process runs with its current pages, the system loads new pages that will be available when the process requests them.

Anticipatory paging offers the following advantages.

- If correct decisions can be made in a large majority of the cases, the running time of a process will be reduced considerably. Therefore, it is worth trying to develop anticipatory paging mechanisms even though they cannot be 100 percent accurate.
- Accurate decisions can be made in many cases. If this decision making can be implemented with relatively low overhead, then the execution of a given process can be considerably speeded without adversely affecting other active processes.
- With computer hardware becoming more economical, the consequences of a bad decision are less serious. We can buy extra main storage to support the accumulation of the excess pages an anticipatory mechanism would bring to main storage.

9.8 PAGE RELEASE

Under working set storage management, programs tell us what pages they want to use by explicit reference. Programs that no longer need specific pages have to pass those pages from their working sets. There is usually a period of time during which the pages no longer needed remain in main storage.

When it becomes clear that a page will no longer be needed, a user could issue a *voluntary page release* to free the page frame. This would eliminate the delay period caused by letting the process gradually pass the page from its working set.

Voluntary page release could eliminate waste, and speed program execution. But most users of today's computer systems don't even know what a page is, and these users should not be asked to make system-level decisions. The incorporation of page release commands into user programs might considerably slow applications development.

The real hope in this area is for compilers and operating systems to detect page release situations automatically, and much sooner than is possible under working set strategies.

9.9 PAGE SIZE

In paging systems, real storage is normally divided into fixed size page frames. How large should these page frames be? How large should a page be? Should all of the pages in a system be the same size, or should several different page sizes be used? If several sizes are used, should the larger page sizes be integral multiples of the smaller page sizes?

These questions require judgment and a careful understanding of the hardware, software, and intended applications for a particular system. There are no universal answers. There is no pressing need for all computer systems to have the same page size, or a single page size for that matter.

What considerations determine whether a page should be large or small? Several are summarized here.

- The smaller the page size, the more pages and page frames there are and the larger the page tables need to be. On systems in which page tables occupy primary storage, this points to the need for larger pages. The waste of storage due to excessively large tables is called *table fragmentation.* We note here that this argument is less valid today with the availability of very large and economical memories.
- With large page sizes, large amounts of information that ultimately may not be referenced are paged into primary storage. This points to the need for smaller pages.
- Because I/O transfers from disk are relatively time-consuming, we wish to minimize the number of transfers a program will experience as it runs. This seems to point to the need for large page sizes.
- Programs tend to exhibit the property of locality of reference, and these localities tend to be small. Thus a smaller page size would help a program establish a tighter working set, i.e., the working set pages maintained in real storage would contain more intensively referenced items.

- Because procedure and data units rarely comprise an integral number of pages, paging systems experience internal fragmentation as illustrated in Fig. 9.8. A segment of length *s* is just as likely to have its last page nearly full as nearly empty, and thus, on the average, there is one-half page of internal fragmentation (with the restriction that a page may not contain portions of more than one segment). The smaller the page size, the less the internal fragmentation.

Most results in the literature (De80), both theoretical and empirical, point to the need for small pages. Figure 9.9 shows the page sizes used in several popular computers. Note the page size chosen for the VAX 11/780, one of the more recent systems.

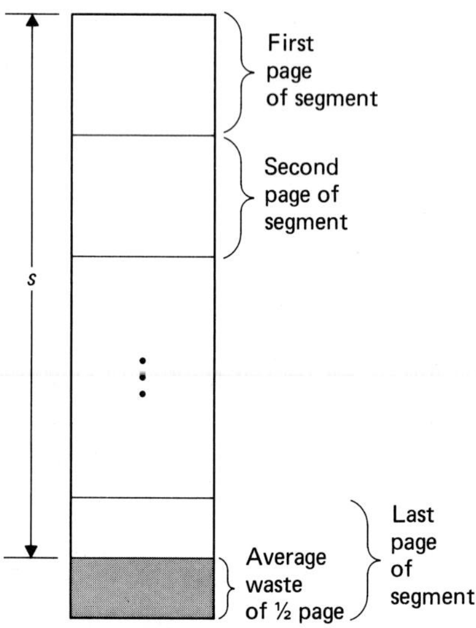

Fig. 9.8 Internal fragmentation in a paged system.

Manufacturer	Model	Page Size	Unit
Honeywell	Multics	1024	36-bit word
IBM	360/67	1024	32-bit word
IBM	370/168	1024 or 512	32-bit word
DEC	PDP-10 PDP-20	512	36-bit word
DEC	VAX 11/780	128	32-bit word

Fig. 9.9 Some common page sizes.

9.10 PROGRAM BEHAVIOR UNDER PAGING

Paging is a valuable concept, and it will probably continue to be integrated into computer systems for the next several decades. Many studies have been performed examining the behavior of processes in paging environments (Be66) (Co68) (Ha72) (Sp72) (Ol74) (Sa75) (Ba76) (Po77) (Sp77) (Fr78) (De80). In this section, some qualitative results of these studies are shown.

Figure 9.10 shows the percentage of a typical process's pages referenced from the time the process begins execution. The initial sharp upward slope indicates that a process tends to reference a significant portion of its pages immediately after it begins execution. With time, the slope diminishes, and the graph asymptotically approaches 100 percent. Certainly some processes reference 100 percent of their pages but the graph is drawn in the indicated manner to reflect that many processes may execute for a long time without referencing 100 percent of their pages. This is often the case when certain error processing routines are rarely invoked.

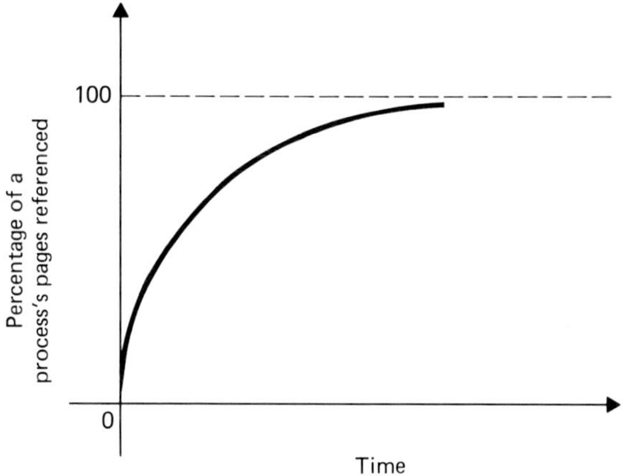

Figure 9.10

Figure 9.11 indicates the effects of varying the page size when the amount of primary storage is held constant. The graph shows that the number of page faults experienced by a running process tends to increase as the page size increases. This occurs because as page size increases more procedures and data that will not be referenced are brought into a fixed size primary storage. Thus there is a decrease in the percentage of a process's limited primary storage occupied by procedures and data that will be referenced. Because the referencing pattern of the process is essentially independent of the amount of primary storage allocated, more page faults are generated to bring the required procedures and data into primary storage throughout the process's execution.

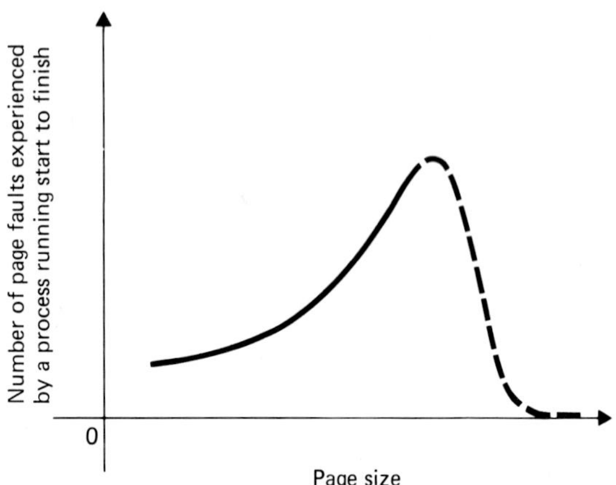

Figure 9.11

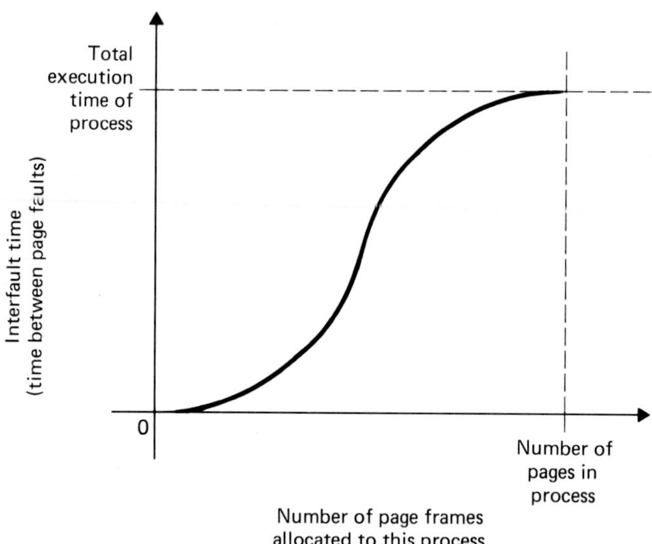

Figure 9.12

Figure 9.12 shows how the average interfault time (i.e., the time between page faults) varies as the number of page frames allocated to a process increases. The graph is monotonically increasing—the more page frames a process has, the longer the time between page faults. But the graph bends at one point, and its slope reduces sharply. This is the point at which the process has its entire working set in primary storage. Initially, the interfault time grows very quickly as more of the working set may be kept in primary storage. Once the primary storage allotment is sufficient to hold the working set, the curve bends sharply indicating that the effect

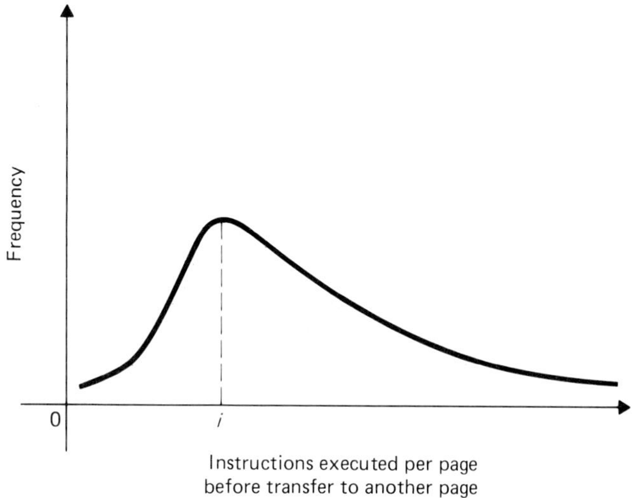

Figure 9.13

of allocating additional page frames on increasing the interfault time is not as great. The key is to get the working set into primary storage.

Figure 9.13 shows what percentage of the instructions on a page are executed before control transfers to another page. In one particular experiment, the maximum of the curve occurred at about 200 instructions for a page size of 1024 words. Results like this seem to point to the need for smaller page sizes.

The qualitative discussions of this section generally point to the validity of the working set concept, and the need for smaller page sizes. As computer architecture evolves, these results will need to be reevaluated.

SUMMARY

Virtual storage management strategies are divided into three categories. Fetch strategies are concerned with when to bring the next page or segment to primary storage. Demand fetch does so upon explicit reference; anticipatory fetch does so in advance when it is likely that a page or segment will soon be referenced. Placement strategies are concerned with where in primary storage to place the incoming page or segment. Replacement strategies are concerned with which page or segment to replace to make room for an incoming page or segment when primary storage is fully committed.

Some of the page replacement strategies discussed in the chapter are

- Principle of Optimality—replaces the page which will not be used until furthest time into the future.
- Random—pages are selected at random.

- FIFO—the page in primary storage the longest is selected.
- LRU—the least-recently-used page is selected.
- LFU—the least-frequently-used page is selected.
- NUR—an inexpensive and efficient approximation of LRU that replaces a page not-used-recently.
- Working set—replaces a page if it is not in the favored subset of a process's pages.

The FIFO Anomaly occurs when increasing the number of page frames available to a process increases the page fault rate of the process.

Locality is a property exhibited by running processes, namely that processes tend to favor a subset of their pages during an execution interval. Temporal locality means that if a process references a page, it will probably reference that page again soon. Spatial locality means that if a process references a page, it will probably reference adjacent pages in its virtual address space. Locality is expected because of the way programs are written using loops, subroutines, stacks, counting and totaling variables, array traversals, sequential code execution, and also because of the tendency of programmers to place related variables near one another.

Denning developed the concept of working sets to explain program behavior in terms of locality. Working set storage management strategies attempt to keep a process's working set of pages, i.e., the most recently referenced pages, in primary storage so that the process will run quickly. New processes may be initiated only if there is room in primary storage for their working sets. Denning defined the working set $W(t,w)$ at time t as the set of pages referenced by a process in the process time interval from $t - w$ to t. Processes attempting to execute without sufficient space for their working sets often experience thrashing, a phenomenon in which they continually replace pages and then immediately recall the replaced pages back to primary storage.

Demand paging has been the conventional wisdom for some time because

- computability results tell us that we cannot implement completely accurate anticipatory paging schemes because we can't predict the future,
- only the pages actually needed by a process are brought to primary storage, and
- the fetch overhead is nominal.

But demand paging is wasteful of primary storage because processes must wait while each referenced page is brought in.

Proponents of anticipatory paging argue that good decisions can be made a large portion of the time, and that processes will execute more quickly when their pages are already in primary storage when referenced.

Some systems provide a page release capability which allows a running process to inform the system explicitly that a particular page is no longer needed. Page release helps rid primary storage of pages that are no longer needed.

A number of issues affect the determination of optimum page size for a given system.

- A small page size causes larger page tables, and consequent table fragmentation.
- A large page size causes instructions and data that will not be referenced to be brought into primary storage.
- I/O transfers are more efficient with large pages.
- Localities tend to be small.
- Internal fragmentation is reduced with small pages.

In the balance, most designers feel that these factors point to the need for small pages.

Many experiments have examined the behavior of paged computer systems, and the results have been interesting.

- When a process begins executing, it normally references a large percentage of its pages quickly.
- The number of page faults experienced by a running process tends to increase as page size is increased, assuming that the primary storage allocated to the process remains constant.
- The interfault time (time between page faults) experienced by a running process increases as the amount of page frames allocated to the process increases. Once a sufficient number of page frames has been allocated to the process to hold its working set, the rate of increase diminishes.
- The number of instructions executed on a page before control leaves the page tends to be small.

TERMINOLOGY

anticipatory paging
demand paging
fetch strategy
first-in-first-out (FIFO) page replacement
FIFO Anomaly
internal fragmentation
least-frequently-used (LFU) page replacement
least-recently-used (LRU) page replacement
locality
not-used-recently (NUR) page replacement
optimal page replacement
page replacement strategy
Principle of Optimality
random page replacement
space–time product
spatial locality
table fragmentation
temporal locality
thrashing
voluntary page release
working set of pages
working set page replacement
working set storage management policy
working set theory of program behavior
working set window size

EXERCISES

9.1 Discuss the goals of each of the following storage management strategies in the context of virtual storage systems with paging.

a) fetch strategy b) placement strategy c) replacement strategy

9.2 Explain why storage management in pure segmentation systems is quite similar to storage management in variable partition multiprogramming systems.

9.3 Give several reasons why demand paging has been the conventional wisdom in page fetch strategies for many years.

9.4 One particular virtual storage computer system with combined segmentation and paging supports a level of multiprogramming of 10. Instruction pages (reentrant code) are maintained separately from data pages (modifiable). You have studied the system in operation and have made the following observations. (1) Most procedure segments are many pages long and (2) most data segments use only a small fraction of a page.

Your associate has proposed that one way to get better utilization out of storage is to pack several of each user's data segments onto an individual page. Comment on this proposal considering issues of

a) storage use
b) execution efficiency
c) indefinite postponement
d) protection
e) sharing

9.5 Today there is much interest in anticipatory paging and in anticipatory resource allocation in general. What useful information might each of the following supply to an anticipatory paging mechanism?

a) the programmer
b) the language translator
c) the operating system
d) a log of past executions of the program

9.6 It is known that in the general case we cannot predict the path of execution of an arbitrary program. If we could, then we would be able to solve the halting problem—which is known to be unsolvable. Explain the ramifications of this upon the effectiveness of anticipatory resource allocation mechanisms.

9.7 Suppose a storage manager has narrowed its page replacement decision to one of two pages. Suppose that one of the pages is shared by several processes, and the other page is in use only by a single process. Should the storage manager replace the nonshared page? Explain.

9.8 Discuss each of the following unconventional page replacement schemes in the context of a virtual storage multiprogramming system servicing both batch and interactive users.

a) "Global LIFO"—The page brought into real storage most recently is replaced.
b) "Local LIFO"—The page brought in most recently by the process which requested the incoming page is replaced.
c) "Tired Page"—The most heavily referenced page in the system is replaced. (Consider both the global and local variants of this scheme.)
d) "Battered Page"—The most heavily modified page in the system is replaced. (Consider both the global and local variants of this scheme.)

9.9 Some types of processes perform well under certain page replacement strategies and poorly under others. Discuss the possibility of implementing a storage manager that would dynamically determine the type of a process, and then select and use the appropriate page replacement strategy for that process.

9.10 Suppose a storage manager decides which page to replace solely on the basis of examining the referenced and modified bits for each page frame. List several incorrect decisions the storage manager might make.

9.11 List several reasons why it is necessary to prevent certain pages from being paged out of real storage.

9.12 Why is it generally more desirable to replace an unmodified page rather than a modified one? In what circumstances might it be more desirable to replace a modified page?

9.13 For each of the following pairs of replacement strategies show a page reference string that would result in both strategies choosing (1) the same page for replacement and (2) a different page for replacement.

a) LRU, NUR
b) LRU, LFU
c) LRU, FIFO
d) NUR, LFU
e) LFU, FIFO
f) NUR, FIFO.

9.14 The Optimal (OPT) Page Replacement strategy is unrealizable because it is impossible to predict the future. There are circumstances, however, in which OPT can be implemented. What are they?

9.15 The overhead of moving a modified page to secondary storage in order that a new page may be brought into primary memory is so large that it should be avoided whenever possible. Suppose a storage manager has chosen a modified page for replacement. This page must be pushed to secondary storage before the new page may be placed in its page frame. Therefore, the storage manager schedules this page for a push. An entry is made in a list of pages waiting to be pushed. Thus the page will remain in real storage for some time before being pushed. Now suppose that while the page is waiting a running process requests it. How should the storage manager react? Be sure to consider the possibility of indefinite postponement, and the need to guarantee good response times for interactive users.

9.16 FIFO page replacement is relatively easy to implement, and has low overhead. But FIFO can easily replace a heavily used page. Design a simple modification to FIFO that is also easy to implement, has low overhead, and prevents a heavily used page from being replaced.

9.17 Show an example of the FIFO Anomaly different from that in the text.

9.18 Design an experiment for a paged system to demonstrate the phenomenon of locality.

9.19 A programmer who writes programs specifically to exhibit good locality can expect marked improvement in the execution efficiency of the programs. List several strategies a programmer can use to improve locality. In particular, what high-level language features should be emphasized? What features should be avoided?

9.20 Suppose you put a tap on an I/O channel and observe heavy page traffic. Does this imply thrashing? Explain.

9.21 Why might a global replacement policy be more susceptible to thrashing than a local page replacement policy?

9.22 Discuss the trade-offs between giving each process more page frames than it needs (to prevent thrashing), and the resulting fragmentation of real storage.

9.23 Design several heuristics that a storage manager might use to determine if main storage has become overcommitted.

9.24 The working set of a process may be defined in several ways. Discuss the merits of each of the following schemes for deciding which pages constitute a process's working set.

a) those pages that a process has referenced in the last *w* seconds of wall clock time
b) those pages that the process has referenced in the last *w* seconds of virtual time (i.e., time during which the process was actually running on a CPU)
c) the last *k* different pages referenced by the process
d) those pages on which a process made its last *r* instruction or data references
e) those pages that the process has referenced in the last *w* seconds of virtual time with a frequency greater than *f* times per virtual second.

9.25 Give an example in which a working set page replacement strategy would replace

a) the best possible page
b) the worst possible page

9.26 One difficulty in implementing a working set storage management strategy is that when a process requests a new page, it is difficult to determine whether that process is changing to a new working set, or is expanding its current working set. In the first case it is better for the storage manager to replace one of the process's pages; in the latter case it is better for the storage manager to add a page to the process's page allocation. How might a storage manager decide which case is appropriate?

9.27 Just because a page is a member of a process's working set does not necessarily imply that it is being referenced frequently. Similarly, the pages in a process's working set are not necessarily being referenced at the same frequency. Propose a modification to the working set page replacement strategy that, when a working set page is to be replaced, chooses the page for replacement via one of the other schemes such as FIFO, LRU, LFU, NUR, etc. Compare this new page replacement strategy with the pure working set strategy.

9.28 Suppose all of the processes included in the level of multiprogramming have established their working sets in main storage. As localities change, working sets could grow and main storage could become overcommitted causing thrashing. Discuss the relative merits of each of the following strategies for preventing this.

a) Never initiate a new process if real storage is already 80 percent or more committed.
b) Never initiate a new process if real storage is already 97 percent or more committed.
c) When a new process is initiated, assign it a maximum working set size beyond which it will not be allowed to grow.

9.29 The interaction between the various components of an operating system is critical to achieving good performance. Discuss the interaction between the storage manager and the job initiator in a virtual storage multiprogramming system. In particular, suppose the storage manager uses a working set storage management approach.

9.30 Consider the following experiment and explain the observations.

A program is run by itself on a paged machine. The program begins execution with its first procedure page. As it runs, the pages it needs are demand paged into available page frames. The number of available page frames is much larger than the number of pages in the program. But there is a dial external to the computer that allows a person to set the maximum number of page frames the program may use.

Initially, the dial is set at two frames and the program is run to completion. The dial is then set at three frames and again the program is run to completion. This process is continued until the dial is eventually set to the number of available page frames in real storage, and the program is run for the last time. For each run, the run time of the program is recorded.

Observations:

As the dial is changed from two to three to four, the run times improved dramatically. From four to five to six, the run times still improved each time, but less dramatically. With dial settings of seven and higher, the run time remained essentially constant.

9.31 An operating systems designer has proposed the PD storage management strategy that operates as follows. Exactly two page frames are allocated to each active process. These frames hold the most recently referenced procedure page, P-page, and the most recently referenced data page, D-page. When a page fault occurs, if the referenced page is a procedure page, it replaces P-page, and if the referenced page is a data page, it replaces D-page.

The designer says that the chief virtue of the scheme is that it trivializes all aspects of storage management, and thus has very low overhead.

a) How are each of the following storage management strategies handled under the PD scheme?

   i) fetch
   ii) placement
   iii) replacement

b) In what circumstances would PD actually yield better results than working set storage management?
c) In what circumstances would PD yield poor results?

9.32 Describe how the sharing of code and data affects each of the following.

a) fetch strategy
b) placement strategy
c) replacement strategy
d) "local locality" (i.e., within a process)
e) "global locality" (i.e., over all processes)
f) thrashing
g) charging for resources
h) fragmentation

   i) internal
   ii) external
   iii) chunk

9.33 Summarize the arguments for and against (1) small page sizes and (2) large page sizes.

9.34 The Multics system was originally designed to manage 64-word pages and 1024-word pages (the dual-page-size scheme was eventually abandoned).

a) What factors do you suppose motivated this design decision?
b) What effect does this dual-page-size approach have on storage management strategies?

9.35 Discuss the use of each of the following hardware features in virtual storage systems.

a) dynamic address mapping mechanisms
b) associative storage
c) cache storage

d) "page referenced" bit
e) "page modified" bit
f) "page in transit" bit (signifying that a page is currently being input to a particular page frame)

9.36 Discuss the issue of how programming style affects performance in a paging system. Consider each of the following.
a) top-down approach
b) minimal use of GOTOs
c) modularity
d) recursion
e) iteration

9.37 If programs are carefully organized in a paged system so that references are highly localized to small groups of pages, the resulting performance improvements can be impressive. But because most programs today are being written in high-level languages, the programmer does not generally have access to information sufficiently rich to aid in producing programs with good organization. Because the path of execution a program will take cannot be predicted, it is difficult to know precisely which sections of code will be used intensively.

One hope for improving program organization is called dynamic program restructuring. Here, the operating system monitors the execution characteristics of a program, and rearranges the code and data so that more active items are placed together on pages.
a) What execution characteristics of a large program should be monitored to facilitate dynamic program restructuring?
b) How would a dynamic program restructuring mechanism use this information to make effective restructuring decisions?

9.38 Charging for resource use is a complex problem. Consider each of the following in the context of a virtual storage multiprogramming system with paging.
a) Should a process be charged more for generating excessive page faults?
b) Should a process be charged more for having a large working set?
c) Should a process receive credits for experiencing service degradation caused by thrashing?
d) Should a process be charged for operating system overhead involved in managing virtual storage?

LITERATURE

(Ah71) Aho, A. V.; P. J. Denning; and J. D. Ullman, "Principles of Optimal Page Replacement," *JACM,* Vol. 18, No. 1, January 1971, pp. 80–93.

(Ba76) Baer, J., and G. R. Sager, "Dynamic Improvement of Locality in Virtual Memory Systems," *IEEE Trans. on Soft. Eng.*, Vol. SE-1, March 1976, pp. 54–62.

(Ba70) Batson, A. P.; S. Ju; and D. Wood, "Measurements of Segment Size," *CACM,* Vol. 13, No. 3, March 1970, pp. 155–159.

(Ba77) Batson, A. P., and R. G. Bundage, "Segment Sizes and Lifetimes in ALGOL 60 Programs," *CACM,* Vol. 20, January 1977, pp. 36–44.

(Be66) Belady, L. A., "A Study of Replacement Algorithms for Virtual Storage Computers," *IBM Systems Journal,* Vol. 5, No. 2, 1966, pp. 78–101.

(Be69) Belady, L. A., and C. J. Kuehner, "Dynamic Space Sharing in Computer Systems," *CACM,* Vol. 12, No. 5, May 1969, pp. 282–288.

(Be69b) Belady, L. A.; R. A. Nelson; and G. S. Shedler, "An Anomaly in Space-Time Characteristics of Certain Programs Running in a Paging Environment," *CACM,* Vol. 12, No. 6, June 1969, pp. 349–353.

(Br68) Brawn, B., and F. G. Gustavson, "Program Behavior in a Paging Environment," *AFIPS Conf. Proc.,* Vol. 33, 1968 FJCC, pp. 1019–1032.

(Br75) Bryant, P., "Predicting Working Set Sizes," *IBM Journal of R&D,* Vol. 19, No. 3, May 1975, pp. 221–229.

(Ch73) Chamberlin, D. D.; S. H. Fuller; and L. Liu, "An Analysis of Page Allocation Strategies for Virtual Memory Systems," *IBM Journal of R&D,* Vol. 17, 1973, pp. 404–412.

(Ch76) Chu, W. W., and Opderbeck, H., "Program Behavior and the Page-Fault-Frequency Replacement Algorithm," *Computer,* November 1976, pp. 29–38.

(Co73) Coffman, E. G., Jr., and P. J. Denning, *Operating Systems Theory,* Englewood Cliffs, N.J.: Prentice-Hall, 1973.

(Co68) Coffman, E. G., Jr., and L. C. Varian, "Further Experimental Data on the Behavior of Programs in a Paging Environment," *CACM,* Vol. 11, No. 7, July 1968, pp. 471–474.

(De68) Denning, P. J., "The Working Set Model for Program Behavior," *CACM,* Vol. 11, No. 5, May 1968, pp. 323–333.

(De68a) Denning, P. J., *Resource Allocation in Multiprocess Computer Systems,* Ph.D. Thesis, Report MAC-TR-50 M.I.T. Project MAC, May 1968.

(De68b) Denning, P. J., "Thrashing: Its Causes and Prevention" *AFIPS Conf. Proc.,* Vol. 33, 1968 FJCC, pp. 915–922.

(De70) Denning, P. J., "Virtual Memory," *ACM Computing Surveys,* Vol. 2, No. 3, September 1970, pp. 153–189.

(De72) Denning, P. J., and S. C. Schwartz, "Properties of the Working Set Model," *CACM,* Vol. 15, No. 2, March 1972, pp. 191–198.

(De72a) Denning, P. J., "On Modeling Program Behavior," *AFIPS Conf. Proc.,* Vol. 40, 1972 *SJCC,* pp. 937–944.

(De75) Denning, P. J., and G. S. Graham, "Multiprogrammed Memory Management," *Proc. IEEE,* Vol. 63, June 1975, pp. 924–939.

(De75) Denning, P. J., and K. C. Kahn, "A Study of Program Locality and Lifetime Functions," *Proc. 5th ACM Symp. Operating Systems Principles,* November 1975, pp. 207–216.

(De78) Denning, P. J., "Optimal Multiprogrammed Memory Management," In K. M. Chandy and R. Yeh (eds.), *Current Trends in Programming Methodology,* Vol. III, Englewood Cliffs, N.J.: Prentice-Hall, 1978, pp. 298–322.

(De80) Denning, P. J., "Working Sets Past and Present," *IEEE Trans. on Soft. Eng.,* Vol. SE-6, No. 1, January 1980, pp. 64–84.

(Ea77) Easton, M. C., and B. T. Bennett, "Transient-Free Working Set Statistics," *CACM,* Vol. 20, No. 2, February 1977, pp. 93–99.

(Fe74) Ferrari, D., "Improving Locality by Critical Working Sets," *CACM,* Vol. 17, No. 11, November 1974, pp. 614–620.

(Fe75) Ferrari, D., "Tailoring Programs to Models of Program Behavior," *IBM Journal of R&D,* Vol. 19, No. 3, May 1975, pp. 244–251.

(Fe76) Ferrari, D., "The Improvement of Program Behavior," *IEEE Computer,* Vol., 9, No. 11, November 1976, pp. 39–47.

(Fo74) Fogel, M. "The VMOS Paging Algorithm," *Operating Systems Review,* Vol. 8, 1974, pp. 8–16.

(Fr78) Franklin, M. A.; G. S. Graham; and R. K. Gupta, "Anomalies with Variable Partition Paging Algorithms," *CACM,* Vol. 21, No. 3, March 1978, pp. 232–236.

(Gu78) Gupta, R. K., and M. A. Franklin, "Working Set and Page Fault Frequency Replacement Algorithms: A Performance Comparison," *IEEE Trans. on Computers,* Vol. C-27, August 1978, pp. 706–712.

(Ha71) Hatfield, D., and J. Gerald, "Program Restructuring for Virtual Memory" *IBM Systems Journal,* Vol. 10, 1971, pp. 168–192.

(Ha72) Hatfield, D., "Experiments on Page Size, Program Access Patterns, and Virtual Memory Performance," *IBM Journal of R&D,* Vol. 16, No. 1, January 1972, pp. 58–62.

(He77) Hennie, F., *Introduction to Computability,* Reading, Mass.: Addison-Wesley, 1977.

(Ma76) Madison, A. W., and A. P. Batson, "Characteristics of Program Localities," *CACM,* Vol. 19, No. 5, May 1976, pp. 285–294.

(Ma70) Mattson, R. L.; J. Gecsei; D. R. Slutz; and I. L. Traiger, "Evaluation Techniques for Storage Hierarchies," *IBM Systems Journal,* Vol. 9, No. 2, 1970, pp. 78–117.

(Mi67) Minsky, M. L., *Computation: Finite and Infinite Machines,* Englewood Cliffs, N.J.: Prentice-Hall, 1967.

(Mo72) Morris, J. B., "Demand Paging through the Use of Working Sets on the Maniac II," *CACM,* Vol. 15, No. 10, October 1972 pp. 867–872.

(Ol74) Oliver, N. A., "Experimental Data on Page Replacement Algorithms," *Proc. AFIPS,* 1974 NCC 43, Montvale, N.J.: AFIPS Press, 1974, pp. 179–184.

(Op74) Operdeck, H., and W. W. Chu, "Performance of the Page Fault Frequency Algorithm in a Multiprogramming Environment," *Proc. IFIP Congress,* 1974, pp. 235–241.

(Po81) Pohn, A. V., and T. A. Smay, "Computer Memory Systems," *IEEE Computer Magazine,* October 1981, pp. 93–110.

(Pr76) Prieve, B. G., and R. S. Fabry, "VMIN—An Optimal Variable Space Page Replacement Algorithm," *CACM,* Vol. 19, No. 5, May 1976, pp. 295–297.

(Po77) Potier, D., "Analysis of Demand Paging Policies with Swapped Working Sets," *Proc. 6th ACM Symposium on Operating Systems Principles,* November 1977, pp. 125–131.

(Ro73) Rodriguez-Rosell, J., and J. P. Dupuy, "The Design, Implementation, and Evaluation of a Working Set Dispatcher," *CACM,* Vol. 16, No. 4, April 1973, pp. 247–253.

(Sa75) Sadeh, E., "An Analysis of the Performance of the Page Fault Frequency (PFF) Replacement Algorithm," *Proc. 5th ACM Symposium on Operating Systems Principles,* November 1975, pp. 6–13.

(Sl74) Slutz, D. R., and I. L. Traiger, "A Note on the Calculation of Average Working Set Size," *CACM,* Vol. 17, No. 10, October 1974, pp. 563–565.

(Sm76) Smith, A. J., "A Modified Working Set Paging Algorithm," *IEEE Trans. on Computers,* Vol. C-25, No. 9, September 1976, 907–914.

(Sm78) Smith, A. J., "Sequential Program Prefetching in Memory Hierarchies," *Computer,* Vol. 11, No. 12, December 1978, pp. 7–21.

(Sn78) Snyder, R., "On *a Priori* Program Restructuring for Virtual Memory Systems," *Proc. 2nd Intl. Colloq. on Operating Systems,* IRIA, October 1978.

(Sp72) Spirn, J. R., and P. J. Denning, "Experiments with Program Locality," *AFIPS Conf. Proc.,* Vol. 41, 1972 *FJCC,* pp. 611–621.

(Sp77) Spirn, J. R., *Program Behavior: Models and Measurement,* Elsevier/North-Holland, 1977.

(Tr76) Trivedi, K. S., "Prepaging and Applications to Array Algorithms," *IEEE Trans. on Computers,* Vol. C-25, September 1976, pp. 915–921.

(Vo81) Vogt, P.D., "Virtual Memory Extension for an Existing Minicomputer," *Computer Design,* July 1981, pp. 151–156.

(We69) Weizer, N., and G. Oppenheimer, "Virtual Memory Management in a Paging Environment" *AFIPS Conf. Proc.,* Vol. 34, 1969 *SJCC* p. 234.

(Wi73) Wilkes, M. V., "The Dynamics of Paging," *Computer Journal,* Vol. 16, February 1973, pp. 4–9.

Part 4
Processor Management

10
Job and Processor Scheduling

Nothing in progression can rest on its original plan. We may as well think of rocking a grown man in the cradle of an infant.

Edmund Burke

For every problem there is one solution which is simple, neat, and wrong.

H. L. Mencken

Don't tell me how hard you work. Tell me how much you get done.

James J. Ling

There is nothing more requisite in business than dispatch.

Joseph Addison

Outline

10.1 INTRODUCTION

It is the assignment of physical processors to processes that allows processes to accomplish work. That assignment is a complex problem handled by the operating system. In this chapter we discuss the problems of determining when processors should be assigned, and to which processes. This is called *processor scheduling.*

10.2 SCHEDULING LEVELS

Three important levels of scheduling are considered (Fig. 10.1).

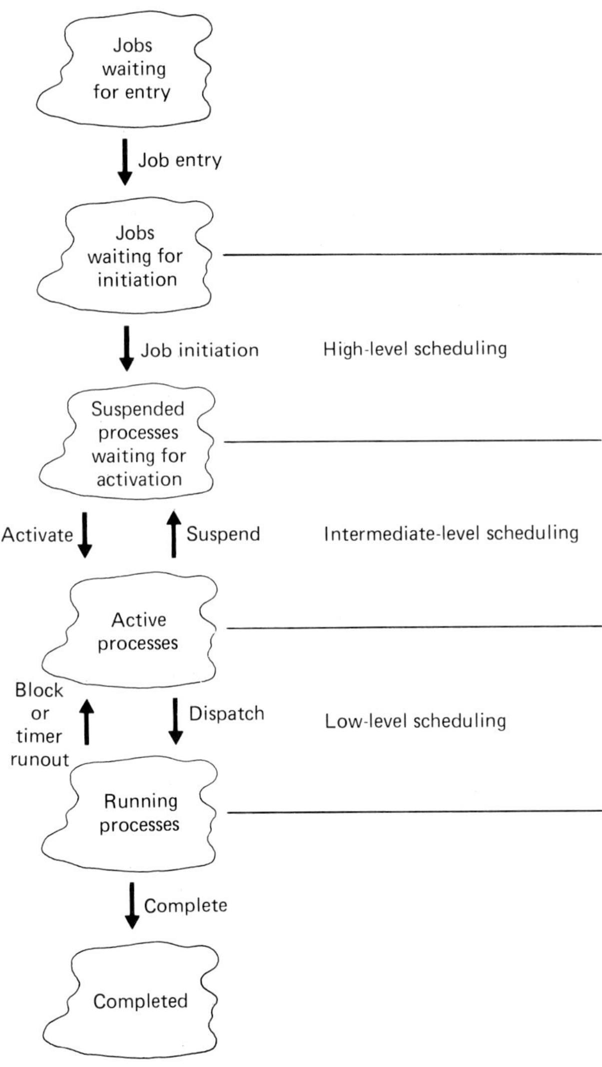

Fig. 10.1 Scheduling levels.

- *High-level scheduling*—Sometimes called *job scheduling,* this determines which jobs shall be allowed to compete actively for the resources of the system. This is sometimes called *admission scheduling* because it determines which jobs gain admission to the system. Once admitted, jobs become processes or groups of processes.
- *Intermediate-level scheduling*—This determines which processes shall be allowed to compete for the CPU. The intermediate-level scheduler responds to short-term fluctuations in system load by temporarily *suspending* and *activating* (or resuming) processes to achieve smooth system operation and to help realize certain systemwide performance goals. Thus the intermediate-level scheduler acts as a buffer between the admission of jobs to the system, and the assigning of the CPU to these jobs.
- *Low-level scheduling*—This determines which ready process will be assigned the CPU when it next becomes available, and actually assigns the CPU to this process (i.e., it *dispatches* the CPU to the process). Low-level scheduling is performed by the *dispatcher* that operates many times per second. The dispatcher must therefore reside at all times in primary storage.

In this chapter we discuss many of the scheduling policies that have been used in operating systems and the *scheduling mechanisms* that implement them. Many of the policies are useful for both job and process scheduling.

10.3 SCHEDULING OBJECTIVES

A scheduling discipline should

- Be fair—A scheduling discipline is fair if all processes are treated the same, and no process can suffer indefinite postponement.
- Maximize throughput—A scheduling discipline should attempt to service the largest possible number of processes per unit time.
- Maximize the number of interactive users receiving acceptable response times (i.e., at most a few seconds).
- Be predictable—A given job should run in about the same amount of time and at about the same cost regardless of the load on the system.
- Minimize overhead—Interestingly, this is not generally considered to be one of the most important objectives. Overhead is commonly viewed as wasted resources. But a certain portion of system resources invested as overhead can greatly improve overall system performance.
- Balance resource use—The scheduling mechanisms should keep the resources of the system busy. Processes that will use underutilized resources should be favored.

- Achieve a balance between response and utilization—The best way to guarantee good response times is to have sufficient resources available whenever they are needed. The price to be paid for this strategy is that overall resource utilization will be poor. In real-time systems, fast responses are essential, and resource utilization is less important. In other types of systems, the economics often makes effective resource utilization imperative.
- Avoid indefinite postponement—In many cases, indefinite postponement can be as bad as deadlock. Avoiding indefinite postponement is best accomplished by *aging*, i.e., as a process waits for a resource, its priority should grow. Eventually, the priority will become so high that the process will be given the resource.
- Enforce priorities—In environments in which processes are given priorities, the scheduling mechanism should favor the higher-priority processes.
- Give preference to processes holding key resources—Even though a low-priority process may be holding a key resource, the resource may be in demand by high-priority processes. If the resource is nonpreemptible, then the scheduling mechanism should give the process better treatment than it would ordinarily receive so that the process will release the key resource sooner.
- Give better service to processes exhibiting desirable behavior (low paging rates, for example).
- Degrade gracefully under heavy loads—A scheduling mechanism should not collapse under the weight of a heavy system load. Either it should prevent excessive loading by not allowing new processes to be created when the load is heavy, or it should service the heavier load by providing a moderately reduced level of service to all processes.

Many of these goals are in conflict with one another thus making scheduling a complex problem.

10.4 SCHEDULING CRITERIA

To realize the scheduling objectives a scheduling mechanism should consider

- The I/O-boundedness of a process—When a process gets the CPU, does it use the CPU only briefly before generating an I/O request?
- The CPU-boundedness of a process—When a process gets the CPU, does it tend to use the CPU until its time quantum expires?
- Whether a process is batch or interactive—Interactive users generally submit trivial requests that should receive immediate service to guarantee good response times. Batch users are not present and can generally suffer reasonable delays.
- How urgent a fast response is—An overnight batch process will not need immediate response. A real-time process control system monitoring a gasoline refinery requires fast response, possibly to prevent an explosion.

- Process priority—High-priority processes should receive better treatment than those of lower priority.
- How frequently a process is generating page faults—Presumably, processes generating few page faults have accumulated their working sets in main storage. Processes experiencing large numbers of page faults have not yet established their working sets. The conventional wisdom is to favor processes that have established their working sets. Another viewpoint is that processes with high page fault rates should receive priority because they use the CPU only briefly before generating an I/O request.
- How frequently a process has been preempted by a higher priority process—Frequently preempted processes should receive less favored treatment. The point is that every time the operating system invests the overhead to get this process running, the short run-time before preemption does not justify the overhead of getting the process running in the first place.
- How much real execution time the process has received—Some designers feel that a process that has received little execution time should be favored. Others believe a process that has received much execution time should be near completion and should be favored to help it reach completion and leave the system as soon as possible.
- How much more time the process needs to complete—Average waiting times can be minimized by running those processes first that require the minimum run-time until completion. Unfortunately, it is rarely known exactly how much more time each process needs to complete.

10.5 PREEMPTIVE VS. NONPREEMPTIVE SCHEDULING

A scheduling discipline is *nonpreemptive* if, once a process has been given the CPU, the CPU cannot be taken away from that process. A scheduling discipline is *preemptive* if the CPU can be taken away.

Preemptive scheduling is useful in systems in which high-priority processes require rapid attention. In real-time systems, for example, the consequences of missing an interrupt could be devastating. In interactive timesharing systems, preemptive scheduling is important in guaranteeing acceptable response times.

Preemption is not without cost. Context switching involves overhead. To make preemption effective, many processes must be kept in main storage so that the next process is normally ready for the CPU when it becomes available. Keeping nonrunning programs in main storage also involves overhead.

In nonpreemptive systems, short jobs are made to wait by longer jobs, but the treatment of all processes is fairer. Response times are more predictable because incoming high-priority jobs can not displace waiting jobs.

In designing a preemptive scheduling mechanism, one must carefully consider the arbitrariness of virtually any priority scheme. We may build a sophisticated mechanism to implement a priority preemption scheme faithfully when, in fact, the priorities themselves are not meaningfully assigned. It is not uncommon in operating systems to have fancy mechanisms supporting somewhat arbitrary schemes. The designer would be wise to evaluate every proposed mechanism carefully before implementing it. "Keep it simple" has great appeal, but if you can't keep it simple, you should at least insist on making it effective and meaningful!

10.6 THE INTERVAL TIMER OR INTERRUPTING CLOCK

The process to which the CPU is currently assigned is said to be running. If it is an operating system process, then the operating system is running, and it can make decisions influencing the operation of the system. To prevent users from monopolizing the system (either maliciously or accidentally), the operating system has mechanisms for taking the CPU away from the user.

The operating system sets an *interrupting clock* or *interval timer* to generate an interrupt at some specific future time (or at some elapsed time into the future). The CPU is then dispatched to the next process. The process retains control of the CPU until it voluntarily releases the CPU, or the clock interrupts, or some other interrupt diverts the attention of the CPU. If the user is running and the clock interrupts, the interrupt causes the operating system to run. The operating system then decides which process should get the CPU next.

The interrupting clock helps guarantee reasonable response times to interactive users, prevents the system from getting hung up on a user in an infinite loop, and allows processes to respond to *time-dependent events*. Processes that need to run periodically depend on the interrupting clock.

10.7 PRIORITIES

Priorities may be assigned automatically by the system or they may be assigned externally. They may be earned or they may be bought. They may be static or they may be dynamic. They may be rationally assigned, or they may be arbitrarily assigned in situations in which a system mechanism needs to distinguish between processes but doesn't really care which one is truly more important.

10.7.1 Static vs. Dynamic Priorities

Static priorities do not change. Static priority mechanisms are easy to implement and have relatively low overhead. They are not, however, responsive to changes in environment, changes that might make it desirable to adjust a priority.

Dynamic priority mechanisms are responsive to change. The initial priority assigned to a process may have only a short duration after which it is adjusted to a better value. Dynamic priority schemes are more complex to implement and have greater overhead than static schemes. The overhead is hopefully justified by the increased responsiveness of the system.

10.7.2 Purchased Priorities

An operating system must provide competent and reasonable service to a large community of users but must also provide for those situations in which a member of the user community needs special treatment.

A user with a rush job may be willing to pay a premium for a higher level of service. This extra charge is merited because resources may need to be withdrawn from other paying customers. If there were no extra charge, then all users would request the higher level of service.

10.8 DEADLINE SCHEDULING

In *deadline scheduling* certain jobs are scheduled to be completed by a specific time or deadline. These jobs may have very high value if delivered on time and may be worthless if delivered later than the deadline. The user is often willing to pay a premium to have the system ensure on-time completion. Deadline scheduling is complex for many reasons.

- The user must supply the precise resource requirements of the job in advance. Such information is rarely available.
- The system must run the deadline job without severely degrading service to other users.
- The system must carefully plan its resource requirements through to the deadline. This may be difficult because new jobs may arrive and place unpredictable demands on the system.
- If many deadline jobs are to be active at once, scheduling could become so complex that sophisticated optimization methods might be needed to ensure that the deadlines are met.
- The intensive resource management required by deadline scheduling may generate substantial overhead. Even if deadline users are willing to pay a sufficiently high fee for the services received, the net consumption of system resources may be so high that the rest of the user community could suffer degraded service. Such conflicts must be considered carefully by operating systems designers.

10.9 FIRST-IN-FIRST-OUT (FIFO) SCHEDULING

Perhaps the simplest scheduling discipline is first-in-first-out (FIFO) (Fig. 10.2). Processes are dispatched according to their arrival time on the ready queue. Once a process has the CPU, it runs to completion. FIFO is a nonpreemptive discipline. It is fair in the formal sense but somewhat unfair in that long jobs make short jobs wait, and unimportant jobs make important jobs wait. FIFO offers a relatively small variance in response times and is therefore more predictable than most other schemes. It is not useful in scheduling interactive users because it cannot guarantee good response times.

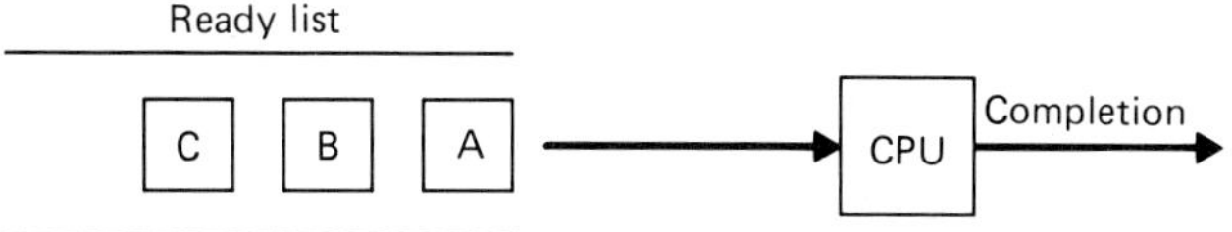

Fig. 10.2 First-in-first-out scheduling.

FIFO is rarely used as a master scheme in today's systems but it is often embedded within other schemes. For example, many scheduling schemes dispatch processes according to priority, but processes with the same priority are dispatched FIFO.

10.10 ROUND ROBIN (RR) SCHEDULING

In *round robin (RR)* scheduling (Fig. 10.3), processes are dispatched FIFO but are given a limited amount of CPU time called a *time-slice* or a *quantum*. If a process does not complete before its CPU time expires, the CPU is preempted and given to the next waiting process. The preempted process is then placed at the back of the ready list.

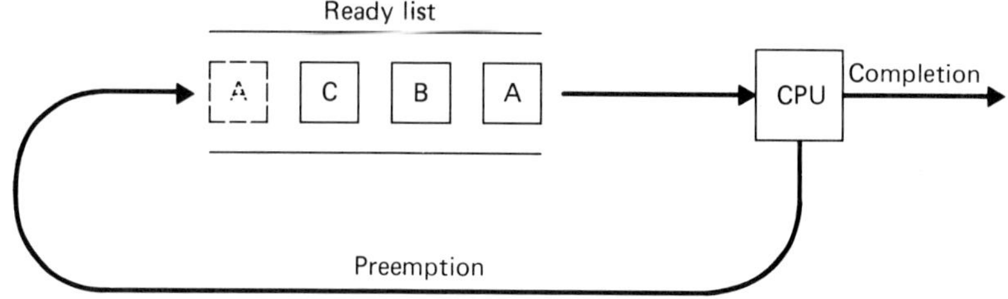

Fig. 10.3 Round robin scheduling.

Round robin is effective in timesharing environments in which the system needs to guarantee reasonable response times for interactive users. The preemption overhead is kept low by efficient context switching mechanisms and by providing adequate storage for the processes to reside in main storage at the same time.

10.11 QUANTUM SIZE

Determination of quantum size is critical to the effective operation of a computer system. Should the quantum be large or small? Should it be fixed or variable? Should it be the same for all users, or should it be determined separately for each user?

First, let's consider the behavior of the system as the quantum gets either very large or very small. As the quantum gets very large, each process is given as much time as it needs to complete, so the round robin scheme degenerates to first-in-first-out. As the quantum gets very small, context switching overhead becomes a dominant factor and the performance of the system eventually degrades to the point that most of the time is spent switching the processor, with little, if any, time spent performing users' computations.

Just where between zero and infinity should the quantum be set? Consider the following experiment. Suppose there is a circular dial marked in readings from $q =$ 0 to $q =$ infinity. We begin with the knob positioned at zero. As the knob is turned, the quantum for the system changes. Assume the system is operational and that there are many interactive users. As the knob is initially rotated, the readings are near zero and the context switching overhead consumes most of the CPU resource. The interactive users experience a sluggish system with poor response times. As the knob is turned further thus increasing the quantum, the response times improve. At least the point has been reached at which the percentage of CPU consumed by overhead is small enough that the users receive some CPU service. But response times are still not very good.

As the knob is turned more, response times continue to improve. At one point, the users are getting prompt responses from the system. But it is still not clear if the quantum setting is optimal. The knob is turned a bit further, and response times become slightly better. But then, as the knob is turned more, the response times become sluggish again. As the quantum gets larger, it is becoming sufficiently large for each user to run to completion upon receiving the CPU. The scheduling is degenerating to FIFO in which longer processes make shorter ones wait, and the average waiting time increases as the longer processes run to completion before yielding the CPU.

Consider the supposedly optimal value of the quantum that yielded good response times. It is a small fraction of a second. Just what does this quantum represent? It is large enough so that the vast majority of interactive requests require less time than the duration of the quantum. When an interactive process begins executing, it normally uses the CPU long enough to generate an I/O request. Once the I/O is generated, that process yields the CPU to the next process. Because the quantum is larger than this compute-until-I/O time, the user processes are kept working at top speed. Each time a user process gets the CPU, there is great likelihood that it will run until it generates an I/O. This minimizes preemption overhead, maximizes I/O utilization, and provides relatively rapid response times.

Just what is this optimal quantum? Clearly, it varies from system to system, and it varies under different loads. It also varies from process to process, but our experiment isn't geared to measuring differences in processes.

When all processes are CPU-bound, it makes little sense to preempt processes. The point is that the additional overhead involved in preemption only detracts from system performance. As long as any interactive users are in the multiprogramming mix, however, the CPU must still be preempted periodically to guarantee interactive response times.

10.12 SHORTEST-JOB-FIRST (SJF) SCHEDULING

Shortest-job-first (SJF) is a nonpreemptive scheduling discipline in which the waiting job (or process) with the smallest estimated run-time-to-completion is run next. SJF reduces average waiting time over FIFO. The waiting times, however, have a larger variance (i.e., are more unpredictable) then FIFO, especially for large jobs.

SJF favors short jobs (or processes) at the expense of longer ones. Many designers advocate that the shorter the job, the better service it should receive. There is not universal agreement on this, especially when job priorities must be considered.

SJF selects jobs for service in a manner that ensures the next job will complete and leave the system as soon as possible. This tends to reduce the number of waiting jobs, and also reduces the number of jobs waiting behind large jobs. As a result, SJF can minimize the average waiting time of jobs as they pass through the system.

The obvious problem with SJF is that it requires precise knowledge of how long a job or process will run, and this information is not usually available. The best SJF can do is to rely on user estimates of run times. In production environments where the same jobs run regularly, it may be possible to provide reasonable estimates. But in development environments users rarely know how long their programs will execute.

Relying on user estimates has an interesting ramification. If users know that the system is designed to favor jobs with small estimated run-times, they may give small estimates. The scheduler can be designed, however, to remove this temptation. The user can be forewarned that if the job runs longer than estimated, it will be terminated and the user will be charged for the work. A second option is to run the job for the estimated time plus a small percentage extra, and then to *shelve* it (De68), i.e., preserve it in its current form so that it may be restarted at a later time. The user, of course, would pay for the shelving and unshelving (i.e., restarting) overhead, and would suffer a delay in the completion of the job. Another solution is to run the job for the estimated time at normal billing rates, and then to charge a premium rate, well above the normal charges, for additional execution time. Under this arrangement, the user providing unrealistically low run-time estimates to get better service will ultimately pay a sharp premium.

SJF, like FIFO, is nonpreemptive and thus not useful in timesharing environments in which reasonable response times must be guaranteed.

10.13 SHORTEST-REMAINING-TIME (SRT) SCHEDULING

SRT is the preemptive counterpart of SJF and is useful in timesharing. In SRT, the process with the smallest estimated run-time to completion is run next, including new arrivals. In SJF, once a job begins executing, it runs to completion. In SRT a running process may be preempted by a new process with a shorter estimated run-time. Again, SRT requires estimates of the future to be effective, and the designer must provide for potential user abuse of system scheduling strategies.

SRT has higher overhead than SJF. It must keep track of the elapsed service time of the running job, and must handle occasional preemptions. Arriving small processes will run almost immediately. Longer jobs, however, have an even longer mean waiting time and variance of waiting times than in SJF.

SRT requires that elapsed service times be recorded, and this contributes to the scheme's overhead. Theoretically, SRT offers minimum waiting times. But because of preemption overhead it is possible that SJF might actually perform better in certain situations.

Suppose a running job is almost complete, and a new job with a very small estimated service time arrives. Should the running job be preempted? The pure SRT discipline would perform the preemption, but is it really worth it? This situation may be handled by building in a threshold value so that once a running job needs less than this amount of time to complete, the system guarantees it will run to completion uninterrupted.

Suppose a job arrives whose estimated service time is only slightly less than that remaining for a running job with much processing remaining. Here, too, pure SRT would perform the preemption. But if the preemption overhead is greater than the difference in service times of the two jobs, preempting the running job actually results in poorer performance. The point of all this is that *the operating systems designer must carefully weigh the overhead of resource management mechanisms against the anticipated benefits.*

10.14 HIGHEST-RESPONSE-RATIO-NEXT (HRN) SCHEDULING

Brinch Hansen (Br71) developed the *highest-response-ratio-next (HRN)* strategy that corrects some of the weaknesses in SJF, particularly the excessive bias against longer jobs and the excessive favoritism toward short new jobs. HRN is a nonpreemptive scheduling discipline in which the priority of each job is a function not only of the job's service time but also of the amount of time the job has been waiting for service. Once a job gets the CPU, it runs to completion. Dynamic priorities in HRN are calculated according to the formula

$$\text{priority} = \frac{\text{time waiting} + \text{service time}}{\text{service time}}.$$

Because the service time appears in the denominator, shorter jobs will get preference. But because time waiting appears in the numerator, longer jobs that have been waiting will also be given favorable treatment. Note that the sum

$$\text{time waiting} + \text{service time}$$

is the system's response time to the job if the job were to be initiated immediately.

10.15 MULTILEVEL FEEDBACK QUEUES

When a process gets the CPU, especially when it has not as yet had a chance to establish a behavior pattern, the scheduler has no idea of the precise amount of CPU time the process will need. I/O-bound processes might use the CPU only briefly before generating an I/O request. CPU-bound processes might use the CPU for hours at a time if it is made available on a nonpreemptible basis.

A scheduling mechanism should

- favor short jobs
- favor I/O-bound jobs to get good I/O device utilization
- determine the nature of a job as quickly as possible and schedule the job accordingly

Multilevel feedback queues (Fig. 10.4) provide a structure that accomplishes these goals. A new process enters the queueing network at the back of the top queue. It moves through that queue FIFO until it gets the CPU. If the job completes or relinquishes the CPU to wait for I/O completion or completion of some event, the job leaves the queueing network. If the quantum expires before the process voluntarily relinquishes the CPU, the process is placed at the back of the next lower-level queue. The process is next serviced when it reaches the head of that queue if the first queue is empty. As long as the process continues using the full quantum provided at each level, it continues to move to the back of the next lower queue. Usually there is some bottom-level queue through which the process circulates round robin until it completes.

In many multilevel feedback schemes, the quantum given to the process as it moves to each lower-level queue becomes larger. Thus the longer a process has been in the queueing network, the larger quantum it is assigned each time it gets the CPU. But it may not get the CPU very often because processes in the higher queues are given higher priority. A process in a given queue cannot run unless all higher-level queues are empty. A running process is preempted by a process arriving in a higher queue.

Now that the operation of the queueing network has been described, consider how such a mechanism responds to different types of processes. The mechanism should favor I/O-bound processes to achieve good device utilization and responsiveness to interactive users. Indeed it will because the I/O-bound process will enter the network with very high priority and will be given the CPU quickly. The quantum in the first queue is chosen to be large enough so that the vast majority of I/O-bound jobs will issue an I/O request before the first quantum expires. When the process requests I/O, it leaves the network, and it has truly received favored treatment—as desired.

Now consider a CPU-bound job that needs a large amount of CPU time. It enters the network at the highest queue with very high priority. It does receive its first shot at the CPU quickly, but its quantum expires, and the process is moved to the

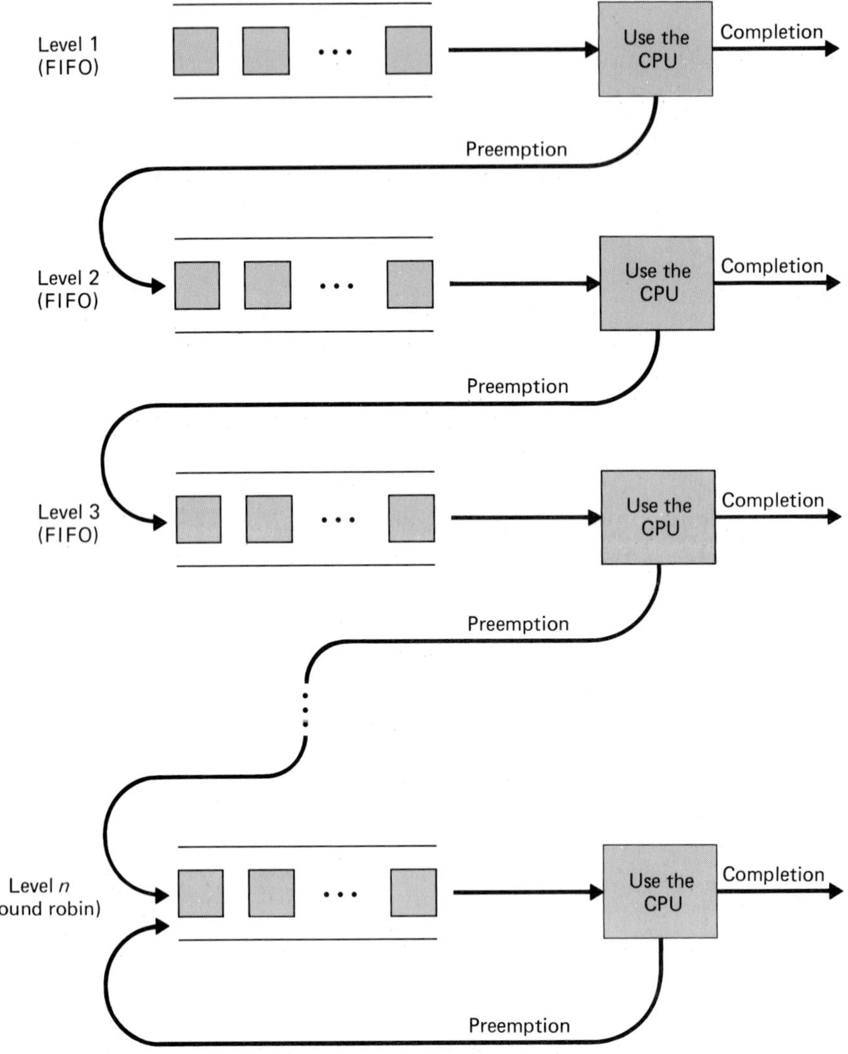

Fig. 10.4 Multilevel feedback queues.

next lower queue. Now the process gets a lower priority as incoming processes, particularly the I/O-bound ones, get the CPU first. Eventually, the CPU-bound process does get the CPU, is given a larger quantum than in the highest queue, and again uses its full quantum. It is then placed at the back of the next lower queue. The process continues moving to lower queues, waits longer between time slices, and uses its full quantum each time it gets the CPU (unless preempted by an arriving process). Eventually, the CPU-bound process gets to the lowest-level queue where it circulates round robin until it completes.

Multilevel feedback queues are ideal for separating processes into categories based upon their need for the CPU. In a timesharing system, each time a process leaves the queueing network, it can be "stamped" with the identity of the lowest-level queue in which it resided. When the process reenters the queueing network, it is sent directly to the queue in which it last completed operation. Here the scheduler is using the heuristic that a process's recent past behavior is a good indicator of its near future behavior. So a CPU-bound process returning to the queueing network is not put into the higher-level queues where it would interfere with service to high-priority short processes or I/O-bound processes.

If processes are always put back in the network at the lowest queue they occupied the last time through, it will be impossible for the system to respond to changes in a process, for example, from being CPU-bound to being I/O-bound. This problem can be solved by also stamping the process with its duration through the network last time. When it reenters the network, it can then be placed in the correct queue. Then if the process is entering a new phase in which it will change from being CPU-bound to I/O-bound, initially the process will experience some sluggish treatment as the system determines that the nature of the process is changing. But the scheduling mechanism will respond to this change quickly. Another way to make the system responsive to changes in a process's behavior is to allow the process to move up one level in the feedback queueing network each time it voluntarily gives up the CPU before its quantum expires.

The multilevel feedback queueing mechanism is a good example of an *adaptive mechanism,* one that responds to the changing behavior of the system it controls. Adaptive mechanisms generally require more overhead than nonadaptive ones, but the resulting sensitivity to changes in the system makes the system more responsive and helps to justify the increased overhead.

One common variation of the multilevel feedback queueing mechanism is to have a process circulate round robin several times through each queue before it moves to the next lower queue. Usually the number of cycles through each queue is increased as the process moves to the next lower queue.

SUMMARY

Processor scheduling determines when processors should be assigned to which processes. High-level scheduling or job scheduling determines which jobs to admit to the system. Upon admission, these jobs become processes or groups of processes. Low-level scheduling or dispatching determines which ready process gets the CPU next. Intermediate-level scheduling determines which processes shall be allowed to compete for the CPU and which shall be temporarily suspended in response to short-term fluctuations in system load.

A scheduling discipline should be fair, maximize throughput, maximize the number of interactive users receiving acceptable response times, be predictable, minimize overhead, balance resource use, achieve a balance between response vs. utilization, avoid indefinite postponement, enforce priorities, give preference to processes holding key resources, give better service to processes exhibiting desirable behavior, and degrade gracefully under heavy loads. Many of these goals conflict with one another thus making scheduling a complex problem.

To realize its goals a scheduling mechanism should consider the I/O-boundedness of a process, the CPU-boundedness of a process, whether a process is batch or interactive, the urgency of a fast response, the priority of each process, the rate at which each process generates page faults, the frequency of preemption of lower priority processes by higher-priority processes, the priorities of process waiting for already assigned resources, the length of time each process has been waiting, the accumulating execution time of each process, and the estimated amount of time each process needs to complete.

A scheduling discipline is nonpreemptive if the CPU cannot be taken away from a process; it is preemptive if the CPU can be taken away. Preemptive scheduling is important in multiprogramming systems in which some processes must receive fast responses, and is especially important in real-time systems and timesharing systems.

The interval timer or interrupting clock is useful in preemptive systems. Upon the expiration of a designated time interval, the clock generates an interrupt that causes the CPU to be switched from the current process to the operating system. The operating system may then dispatch the next process.

Static priorities remain the same throughout the duration of a process; dynamic priorities change in response to changing system conditions. Some systems give the user the option of purchasing high priorities.

In deadline scheduling, certain processes are scheduled to be completed by a certain time. Deadline scheduling is a complex problem, particularly in environments in which additional work may arrive in the interim between the time the process begins execution and its intended completion deadline.

First-in-first-out (FIFO) is a nonpreemptive scheduling discipline with processes dispatched according to their arrival time on the ready list. It is a common job scheduling discipline in batch processing systems, but it cannot guarantee good response times to interactive users.

Round robin (RR) scheduling is essentially the preemptive version of FIFO. Processes are dispatched FIFO, but they are given the CPU only for a limited amount of time called a time-slice or quantum. If a process's quantum expires before it voluntarily relinquishes the CPU, the CPU is preempted and then dispatched to the next ready process. Round robin is commonly used to guarantee reasonable response times to interactive users.

Determining quantum size is a complex problem. It is critical to achieving good system utilization and reasonable response times. A very large quantum size causes any preemptive scheduling discipline to approximate its nonpreemptive counterpart. A very small quantum can waste CPU time by performing excessive context switching among processes. Generally the quantum is chosen to be just large enough for the vast majority of trivial requests to complete within one quantum. On an I/O-bound system, for example, the quantum is just large enough for most processes to be able to issue their next I/O request within one quantum.

Shortest-job-first (SJF) scheduling is a nonpreemptive discipline used primarily for scheduling batch jobs. It minimizes the average waiting times for jobs, but long jobs can experience lengthy waits.

Shortest-remaining-time (SRT) is the preemptive counterpart of SJF. In SRT a running process may be preempted by a new process with a shorter estimated run time. SRT has a higher overhead than SJF, but it gives better service to arriving short jobs. It further reduces average waiting times for all jobs, but long jobs can suffer even greater delays than under SJF.

Brinch Hansen's highest-response-ratio-next (HRN) is a nonpreemptive discipline that corrects some of the weaknesses in SJF, particularly the excessive bias against longer jobs and the excessive favoritism toward short new jobs.

One of the most sophisticated scheduling mechanisms in use today is the multilevel feedback queueing network. It is a preemptive process scheduling discipline that is particularly useful in systems with diversified job mixes. New processes enter the network with very high priority and get fast service if they are either interactive or I/O-bound. Processes that are CPU-bound consume their full quantum and then are placed at the back of the next lower-priority queue. The longer a process uses the CPU, the lower its priority becomes, until it reaches the lowest-priority queue in the network where it circulates round robin until it completes. Normally, the quantum increases as the process moves to each lower priority queue.

A multilevel feedback queueing network is an example of an adaptive mechanism that responds to the changing behavior of the system it controls.

TERMINOLOGY

adaptive mechanism
admission scheduling
deadline scheduling
dispatcher
dispatching
dynamic priorities
first-in-first-out (FIFO)
high-level scheduling
highest-response-ratio-next (HRN)
intermediate-level scheduling
interrupting clock
interval timer
low-level scheduling (dispatching)
nonpreemptive scheduling
predictability
preemption
preemptive scheduling
priority scheduling
processor scheduling
quantum
quantum determination
response time
response vs. utilization
scheduler
scheduling
scheduling criteria
scheduling disciplines
scheduling levels
scheduling objectives
shelve a process
shortest-job-first (SJF)
shortest-remaining-time (SRT)
static priorities
time-dependent events

EXERCISES

10.1 Distinguish among the following three levels of schedulers.

a) job scheduler
b) intermediate-level scheduler
c) dispatcher

10.2 Which level of scheduler should make a decision on each of the following questions?

a) Which ready process should be assigned the CPU when it next becomes available?
b) Which of a series of waiting batch jobs that have been spooled to disk should next be initiated?
c) Which processes should be temporarily suspended to relieve a short-term burden on the CPU?
d) Which temporarily suspended process is known to be I/O-bound and should be activated to balance the multiprogramming mix?

10.3 Distinguish between a scheduling policy and a scheduling mechanism.

10.4 The following are common scheduling objectives.

a) to be fair
b) to maximize throughput
c) to maximize the number of interactive users receiving acceptable response times
d) to be predictable
e) to minimize overhead
f) to balance resource utilization
g) to achieve a balance between response and utilization
h) to avoid indefinite postponement
i) to obey priorities
j) to give preference to processes that hold key resources
k) to give a lower grade of service to high overhead processes
l) to degrade gracefully under heavy loads

Which of the preceding objectives most directly applies to each of the following?

i) If a user has been waiting for an excessive amount of time, favor that user.
ii) The user who runs a payroll job for a 1000-employee company expects the job to take about the same amount of time each week.
iii) The system should admit jobs to create a mix that will keep most devices busy.
iv) The system should favor important jobs.
v) An important process arrives but cannot proceed because an unimportant process is holding the resources the important process needs.
vi) During peak periods, the system should not collapse from the overhead it takes to manage a large number of processes.

10.5 The following are common scheduling criteria.

a) I/O-boundedness of a process
b) CPU-boundedness of a process
c) is the process batch or interactive?
d) urgency of a fast response

e) process priority
f) page fault frequency
g) frequency of a process being preempted by higher priority processes
h) priorities of processes waiting for resources held by other processes
i) accumulated waiting time
j) accumulated execution time
k) estimated run-time to completion.

For each of the following, indicate which of the preceding scheduling criteria is most appropriate.

i) In a real-time spacecraft monitoring system, the computer must respond immediately to signals received from the spacecraft.
ii) Even though a process has been receiving occasional service, it is making only nominal progress.
iii) How often does the process voluntarily give up the CPU for I/O before its quantum expires?
iv) Is the user present and expecting fast interactive response times, or is the user absent?
v) One goal of processor scheduling is to minimize average waiting times.

10.6 A process is known to be generating a large number of page faults. Argue both for and against giving the process high priority for the CPU.

10.7 State which of the following are true and which are false. Justify your answers.

a) A process scheduling discipline is preemptive if the CPU cannot be forcibly removed from a process.
b) Real-time systems generally use preemptive CPU scheduling.
c) Timesharing systems generally use nonpreemptive CPU scheduling.
d) Response times are more predictable in preemptive systems than in nonpreemptive systems.
e) One weakness of priority schemes is that the system will faithfully honor the priorities, but the priorities themselves may not be meaningful.

10.8 Why shouldn't users be allowed to set the interrupting clock?

10.9 Complete the following sentences using the phrases "static priorities" and "dynamic priorities."

a) ______________________ are easier to implement than ______________________.
b) ______________________ require less run-time overhead than ______________________.
c) ______________________ are more responsive to changes in a process's environment than ______________________.
d) ______________________ require more careful deliberation over the initial priority value chosen than ______________________.

10.10 Purchased priorities do not necessarily cost the user more than normal service. In fact, some systems allow users to purchase a very low priority (i.e., the "economy queue") for jobs that don't need to be run quickly. In what circumstances might a user who does need fast service actually request low priority at a cheaper rate?

10.11 Give several reasons why deadline scheduling is very difficult.

10.12 Give an example showing why FIFO is not an appropriate CPU scheduling scheme for interactive users.

10.13 Using the example from the previous problem show why round robin is a better scheme for interactive users.

10.14 Determining the quantum is a complex and critical task. Assume that the average context switching time between processes is s, and the average amount of time an I/O-bound process uses before generating an I/O request is t ($t \gg s$). Discuss the effect of each of the following quantum settings.

a) q = infinity
b) q is slightly greater than zero
c) $q = s$
d) $s < q < t$
e) $q = t$
f) $q > t$

10.15 Discuss the effect of each of the following methods of assigning q.

1. q fixed and identical for all users
2. q fixed and unique to each user
3. q variable and identical for all users
4. q variable and unique to each user

a) Arrange the schemes above in order from lowest to highest run-time overhead.
b) Arrange the schemes in order from least to most responsive to variations in individual processes and system load.
c) Relate your answers in (a) and (b) to one another.

10.16 State why each of the following is incorrect.

a) SRT always has a lower average response time than SJF.
b) SJF is fair.
c) The shorter the job, the better the service it should receive.
d) Because SJF gives preference to short jobs, it is useful in timesharing.

10.17 State some weaknesses in SRT. How would you modify the scheme to get better performance?

10.18 Answer each of the following questions about Brinch Hansen's HRN strategy.

a) How does HRN prevent indefinite postponement?
b) How does HRN decrease the favoritism shown by other strategies to short new jobs.
c) Suppose two jobs have been waiting for about the same time. Are their priorities about the same? Explain your answer.

10.19 Show how multilevel feedback queues accomplish each of the following scheduling goals.

a) favor short jobs.
b) favor I/O-bound jobs to get good I/O device utilization.
c) determine the nature of a job as quickly as possible and schedule the job accordingly.

10.20 One heuristic often used by CPU schedulers is that a process's past behavior is a good indicator of its future behavior. Give an example of a situation in which a CPU scheduler following this heuristic would make a bad decision.

10.21 An operating systems designer has proposed a multilevel feedback queueing network in which there are ten levels. The quantum in the first level is 1/2 second. Each lower level has a quantum twice the size of the quantum at the previous level. A process cannot be preempted until its quantum expires. The system runs both batch and interactive jobs, and these, in turn, consist of both CPU-bound and I/O-bound jobs.

a) Why is this scheme deficient?
b) What minimal changes would you propose to make the scheme more acceptable for its intended job mix.

LITERATURE

(Ab70) Abell, U. A.; S. Rosen; and R. E. Wagner, "Scheduling in a General-Purpose Operating System," *Proc. AFIPS, FJCC,* Vol. 37, 1970, pp. 89–96.

(Ba76) Babad, J. M., "A Generalized Multi-Entrance Time-Sharing Priority Queue," *JACM,* Vol. 22, No. 2, April 1976, pp. 231–247.

(Bh79) Bhat, U. N., and R. E. Nance, *JACM,* Vol. 26, No. 4, October 1979, pp. 761–778.

(Bl76) Blevins, P. R., and C. V. Ramamoorthy, "Aspects of a Dynamically Adaptive Operating System," *IEEE Trans. on Computers,* Vol. 25, No. 7, July 1976, pp. 713–725.

(Br70) Brinch Hansen, P., "The Nucleus of a Multiprogramming System," *CACM,* Vol. 13, No. 4, 1970, pp. 238–241.

(Br71) Brinch Hansen, P., "Short-Term Scheduling in Multiprogramming Systems," *Third ACM Symposium on Operating Systems Principles,* Stanford University, October 1971, pp. 103–105.

(Br73) Brinch Hansen, P., *Operating System Principles,* Englewood Cliffs, N. J.: Prentice-Hall, 1973.

(Br74) Bruno, J.; E. G. Coffman, Jr.; and R. Sethi, "Scheduling Independent Tasks to Reduce Mean Finishing Time," *CACM,* Vol. 17, No. 7, July 1974, pp. 382–387.

(Bu76) Bunt, R. B., "Scheduling Techniques for Operating Systems," *Computer,* Vol. 9, No. 10, October 1976, pp. 10–17.

(Bw72) Browne, J. C.; J. Lan; and F. Baskett, "The Interaction of Multiprogramming Job Scheduling and CPU Scheduling," *Proc. AFIPS, FJCC,* Vol. 41, 1972, pp. 13–22.

(Bz71) Buzen, J. P., *Queuing Network Models of Multiprogramming,* Ph.D. Dissertation, Harvard University, 1971.

(Co68) Coffman, E. G., Jr., and L. Kleinrock, "Computer Scheduling Methods and Their Countermeasures," *Proc. AFIPS, SJCC,* Vol. 32, 1968, pp. 11–21.

(De68) Deitel, H. M., "Absentee Computations in a Multiple Access Computer System," *M.I.T. Project MAC, MAC-TR-52,* Advanced Research Projects Agency, Department of Defense, 1968.

(Di68) Dijkstra, E. W., "The Structure of the T.H.E. Multiprogramming System," *CACM,* Vol. 11, No. 5, 1968, pp. 341–346.

(Go77) Gonzalez, M. J., Jr., "Deterministic Processor Scheduling," *ACM Computing Surveys,* Vol. 9, No. 3, September 1977.

(Ho73) Horning, J. J., and B. Randall, "Process Structuring," *ACM Computing Surveys,* Vol. 5, No. 1, 1973, pp. 5–30.

(Kl70) Kleinrock, L., "A Continuum of Time-Sharing Scheduling Algorithms," *Proc. AFIPS, SJCC,* 1970, pp. 453–458.

(La68) Lampson, B. W., "A Scheduling Philosophy for Multiprocessing Systems," *CACM,* Vol. 11, No. 5, 1968, pp. 347–360.

(Li72) Liskov, B. H., "The Design of the Venus Operating System," *CACM,* Vol. 15, No. 6, 1972, pp. 144–149.

(Mc79) McKell, Lynn J.; James V. Hansen; and Lester E. Heitger "Charging for Computer Resources," *ACM Computing Surveys,* Vol. 11, No. 2, June 1979, pp. 105–120.

(My69) McKinney, J. M., "A Survey of Analytical Time-Sharing Models," *ACM Computing Surveys,* Vol. 1, No. 2, June 1969, pp. 105–116.

(Mu75) Muntz, R. R. "Scheduling and Resource Allocation in Computer Systems." In P. Freeman, *Software Systems Principles,* Chicago, Ill.: SRA, 1975.

(Po76) Potier, D.; E. Gelenbe; and J. Lenfant, "Adaptive Allocation of Central Processing Unit Quanta," *JACM,* Vol. 23, No. 1, January 1976, pp. 97–102.

(Ri74) Ritchie, D. M., and K. Thompson, "The UNIX Time Sharing System," *CACM,* Vol. 17, No. 7, 1974, pp. 365–375.

(Ru77) Ruschitzka, M., and R. S. Fabry, "A Unifying Approach to Scheduling," *CACM,* Vol. 20, No. 7, pp. 469–477.

(Va71) Varney, R. C., "Short-Term Scheduling in Multiprogramming Systems," *Third ACM Symposium on Operating System Principles,* Stanford University, October 1971, pp. 106–108.

(Wu74) Wulf, W. A.; E. Cohen; W. Corwin; A. Jones et al., "HYDRA: The Kernel of a Multiprocessor Operating System," *CACM,* Vol. 17, No. 6, 1974, pp. 337–345.

11
Multiprocessing

One friend in a lifetime is much; two are many; three are hardly possible. Friendship needs a certain parallelism of life, a community of thought, a rivalry of aim.

Henry Brooks Adams

He that would govern others, first should be the master of himself.

Philip Massinger

No man can serve two masters.

Matt. 6:24

Outline

11.1 INTRODUCTION

One significant trend in the computer field today is toward the greater use of *multiprocessing,* i.e., configuring a computing system with several processors (Fig. 11.1). Multiprocessing has been used in systems for several decades, but it is again receiving intense interest because of the availability of inexpensive microprocessors.

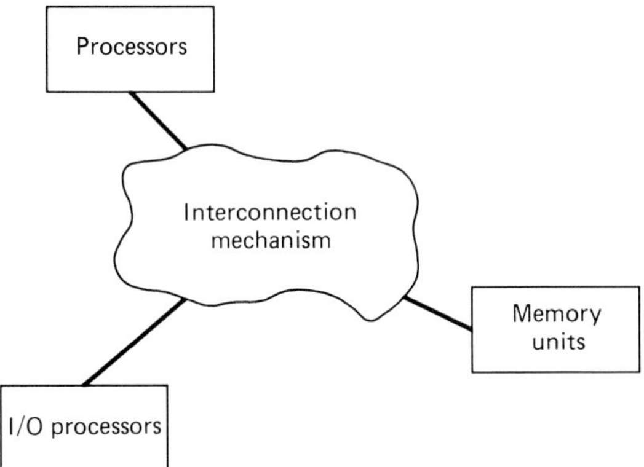

Fig. 11.1 A simplified view of a multiprocessor organization.

Microprocessors have made it possible to obtain processor cycles for a nominal cost, and their small size makes it reasonable to consider packaging many of them in a single system. It is not unreasonable today to conceive of a system built with several hundred microprocessors. With future technology, it may be reasonable to construct systems with thousands and even millions of processors.

The view of the processor as the most precious resource on a given computer system, a view common for the first two decades of modern computing, is no longer applicable. With multiprocessing, it is now more important to consider the issues of reliability, parallelism in computation, optimal connection schemes, and contention between processors attempting to access the same resources.

11.2 RELIABILITY

One appeal of multiprocessing systems is that if a processor fails, then the remaining processors can continue operating. This is not automatic. It requires careful design. A failing processor must somehow inform the other processors that they must take over. Functioning processors must be able to detect a processor that has failed. The operating system must note that a particular processor has failed and is no longer available for allocation. Similarly, because the system now has less capacity, the operating system must adjust its resource allocation strategies to prevent the system from becoming overcommitted.

11.3 EXPLOITING PARALLELISM

It is interesting to note that *most multiprocessing systems have as their central goal increasing throughput.* Programming remains an essentially sequential activity, and few programs are written to exploit concurrency. There are many reasons for this.

- People think sequentially. The human mind is simply not geared to thinking about parallelism.
- No human language provides for the convenient expression of parallelism. There are several computer languages in use such as Ada, CSP/k, Concurrent Pascal, and Modula, but none of these has yet achieved wide acceptance.
- Because multiprocessing itself has not generally been used to exploit parallelism, there is little experience with the problems of doing so.
- Computer hardware is oriented toward sequential operation.
- It is extremely difficult to debug parallel programs.
- Proving the correctness of parallel programs is far more complex than proving the correctness of sequential programs.

The hardware is available to perform operations in parallel, but it will be a long time before parallel programming is understood well enough for large numbers of parallel programs to be written. These difficulties explain why today's multiprocessors are not often used for exploiting parallelism. Real progress in this area will probably occur when compilers and operating systems can be built to detect and implement parallelism automatically.

11.4 MASSIVE PARALLELISM

One key to exploiting parallelism in future systems will certainly be the availability of a sufficient number of processors so that all operations which may be performed in parallel may be assigned to separate processors. Instead of talking about multiprocessing in today's sense, i.e., two (or perhaps a few more) processors, we now commonly talk about *massive parallelism.*

Massive parallelism offers us a way to run a given program to completion in the shortest possible time. The theoretical question of interest is: "Given the availability of massive parallelism, what is the minimum time required to execute a particular algorithm?"

11.5 GOALS OF MULTIPROCESSING SYSTEMS

By utilizing many CPUs, systems may realize many goals. Among these are very high reliability and availability, and increased computer power.

Reliability is improved because if a processor fails, the other processors may continue functioning. The system will continue to operate, although with reduced capabilities. Increased computer power is made possible by combining the processing power of several processors.

With decreasing hardware costs, it has become common to connect a large number of microprocessors to form a multiprocessor (Ch79) (Si78a) (Si78b) (Jo77). In this way, large-scale computer power can be achieved without the use of costly ultrahigh-speed processors.

Multiprocessing can provide a means for significantly increasing the computing capacity of a single processor computer system without substantial increases in cost.

It is sometimes more attractive to convert to multiprocessing to increase capacity rather than to add additional complete systems. Multiple systems can involve significant space problems, can require additional labor to support them, etc.

Multiprocessing systems provide important flexibility in computer systems. Their modular design can make it easy to expand an installation's capacity by adding processors as needed.

11.6 AUTOMATIC DETECTION OF PARALLELISM

Multiprocessors make it possible to exploit parallelism. Most programs are written for sequential execution. Computer systems achieve the benefits of concurrent processing more by multiprogramming several processes than by exploiting parallelism within a single process. The detection of parallelism—by the programmer, the language translator, the hardware, or the operating system—is a complex problem of intense interest today. Regardless of how such parallelism is eventually detected, multiprocessors make it possible to exploit it by executing the parallel portions of computations simultaneously.

Parallelism in programs may be either *explicit* or *implicit.* Explicit parallelism is specifically indicated by a programmer using a concurrency construct such as COBEGIN/COEND as follows.

```
COBEGIN;
     statement-1;
     statement-2;
     ...
     statement-n;
COEND;
```

In a multiprocessing system designed to exploit this concurrency, separate processors might be used to execute each of the statements so that the computation could be completed more quickly than if the statements were executed sequentially.

Explicit indication of parallelism places certain responsibilities with the programmer. It is a time-consuming operation, and the programmer may erroneously indicate that certain operations can be performed in parallel when in fact they cannot. The programmer may miss many situations in which parallelism may be exploited. It is likely that the programmer will detect and code explicit parallelism only for the more obvious situations. But many instances of parallelism in algorithms are hard to detect by manual inspection, so they will be missed.

One rather serious consequence of explicit expression of parallelism is that programs may become more difficult to modify. Modifying a program with a great deal of explicit parallelism could easily introduce bugs and, in fact, particularly subtle ones.

The real hope is the automatic detection of implicit parallelism, i.e., parallelism intrinsic to the algorithm, but not explicitly stated by the programmer. Detection mechanisms would be included in compilers, operating systems, and computer hardware to exploit implicit parallelism. This is more likely than explicit specification of parallelism to result in fast executing and correct programs.

Two common techniques used by compilers for exploiting implicit parallelism are *loop distribution* and *tree height reduction.*

11.6.1 Loop Distribution

A looping structure or repetition structure involves repeating a series of statements called the loop body until some terminating condition occurs. In certain cases, the statements within the loop body are such that parallel execution may be possible. Consider the following

```
FOR I = 1 TO 4 DO
    A(I) - B(I) + C(I);
```

that adds the corresponding elements of arrays B and C and places the element sums in array A. This loop causes a sequential processor to perform the following statements in sequence.

```
A(1) = B(1) + C(1);
A(2) = B(2) + C(2);
A(3) = B(3) + C(3);
A(4) = B(4) + C(4);
```

These statements may be performed concurrently by four processors in a multiprocessor system, thus greatly reducing the run time of the loop. A compiler geared to automatic detection of implicit parallelism might convert the loop above into

```
COBEGIN;
   A(1) = B(1) + C(1);
   A(2) = B(2) + C(2);
   A(3) = A(3) + C(3);
   A(4) = A(4) + C(4);
COEND;
```

thus indicating the parallelism to the computer system. This technique is called loop distribution and is relatively easy to implement. Of course, many loops involve substantially more than four iterations, so it is common for the loop distribution method to indicate a greater degree of parallelism than the number of processors available. The operating system and the computer hardware would then decide which subset of the parallel computations to perform at the same time.

11.6.2 Tree Height Reduction

By making use of the associative, commutative, and distributive properties of arithmetic, compilers may detect implicit parallelism in algebraic expressions and produce object code for multiprocessors indicating the operations that may be performed simultaneously. Compilers must perform operations according to the rules of operator precedence. Not all compilers use the same rules, but many use precedence rules similar to the following.

1. Perform operations in nested parentheses first and, in particular, perform those operations first which are most deeply nested.
2. Perform operations in parentheses next.
3. Perform exponentiations next.
4. Perform multiplications and divisions next.
5. Perform additions and subtractions next.
6. Whenever an expression contains several operations to be performed next "on the same level of precedence" perform those operations in left-to-right order.

These rules of operator precedence make it possible for the compiler to assign a unique sequential ordering to the operations within an algebraic expression, and the compiler may then proceed to generate machine code implementing the algebraic expression.

Often, the uniqueness and the sequential ordering is not necessary. For example, since addition and multiplication are both commutative operations, a compiler generating code to multiply p and q may generate either $p * q$ or $q * p$; the results of the computations will be identical. Similarly, adding p and q may be accomplished by either $p + q$ or $q + p$. Taking advantage of commutativity, and also associativity and distributivity, it is possible for a compiler to rearrange expressions so that they are more amenable to parallel computation.

Figure 11.2 illustrates how an algebraic expression would be translated by a conventional compiler and how it might be manipulated by a compiler designed to locate implicit parallelism. The diagram at the left of the figure shows a tree structure indicating how a conventional compiler might generate code to perform the indicated operations. The numbers 1, 2, and 3 are used to indicate the order in which the various operations should be performed. By taking advantage of the associative property of addition, it is possible to manipulate the expression

$$((p + q) + r) + s$$

to yield the expression

$$(p + q) + (r + s)$$

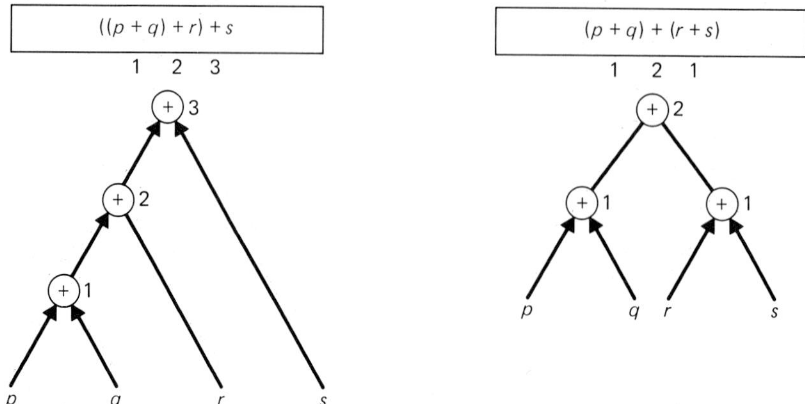

Fig. 11.2 Tree height reduction by associativity.

that is more amenable to parallel execution. The first expression requires three levels in the tree structure while the second expression only requires two and thus may be executed more quickly on a multiprocessor.

The goal of many future systems will be to run computations in the shortest possible time regardless of how many processors need to be put to work on them. So they will have mechanisms that convert previously sequential algorithms into parallel algorithms containing steps that may be performed simultaneously by multiprocessors.

Figure 11.3 illustrates how the commutative property of addition may be used to convert a sequential computation involving three levels in the tree structure to a parallel computation involving only two levels. Figure 11.4 shows how the distribu-

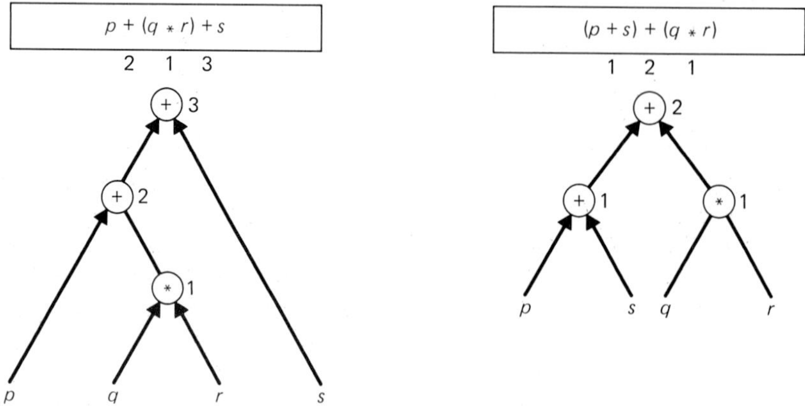

Fig. 11.3 Tree height reduction by commutativity.

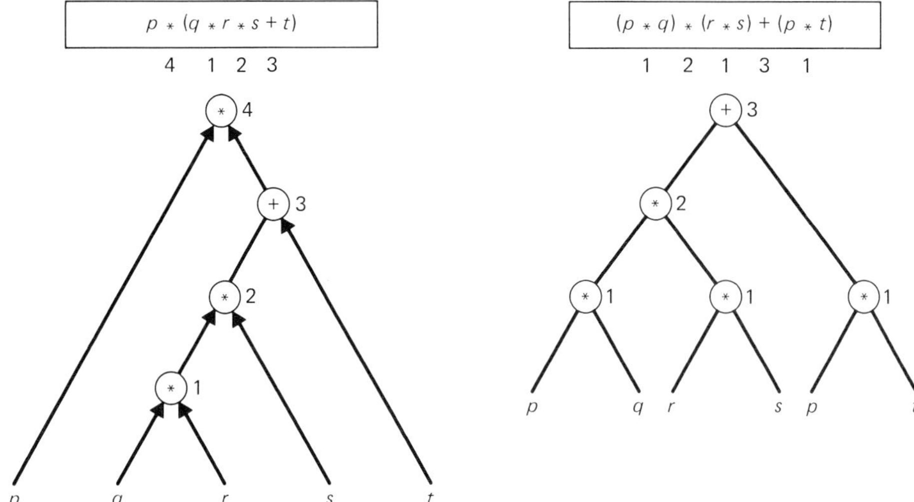

Fig. 11.4 Tree height reduction by distributivity.

tive property of multiplication across addition may be used to reduce the depth of the associated tree structure from four to three.

Using these compilation techniques to optimize programs for execution on multiprocessing systems is not without its costs. The trade-off is that more time and resources are expended at compilation time to reduce the amount of execution time consumed by a given computation. This trade-off must be carefully evaluated in individual circumstances. For example, in production environments it makes sense to optimize the execution time of programs. But in development environments in which a program may be executed only once or twice before being altered and recompiled, such optimization may cost more than the value obtained.

11.7 THE "NEVER WAIT" RULE

It sometimes makes sense to have processors performing computations that may never be needed if indeed the possibility that they are used will speed the execution of a given computation.

The Never Wait Rule states that it is better to give a processor a task that may or may not be used eventually than it is to let the processor sit idle. The point is that if the task is eventually needed, then it will be possible to perform computations faster. Consider the following example

```
A = B * C;
IF A = 9 THEN D = 10;
E = D * F
```

Based upon the result of the first statement, the second statement may alter the value of D, or it may leave D as is. If D is left as is, then the third statement could have been performed in parallel with the first statement. If D is altered, then the third statement needs to use this new value. The strategy of "never wait" is to perform the third statement in parallel with the first statement. If D changes, then the third statement will have to be recalculated. But if D doesn't change, then the third statement has already been performed, so the computation, in this case, may run to completion faster.

11.8 MULTIPROCESSOR HARDWARE ORGANIZATION

One of the key problems in the design of multiprocessor systems is determining the means of connecting the multiple processors and input/output processors to the storage units. Several popular schemes have evolved.

We are concerned in the next several sections only with true multiprocessors that may be characterized as follows (En77).

- A multiprocessor contains two or more processors of approximately comparable capabilities.
- All processors share access to common storage.
- All processors share access to input/output channels, control units, and devices.
- The entire system is controlled by one operating system providing interaction between processors and their programs at the job, task, step, data set, and data element levels.

The three most common multiprocessor system organizations are

- *timeshared* or *common bus*
- *crossbar-switch matrix*
- *multiport storage*

11.8.1 Timeshared or Common Bus

The timeshared or common bus organization, shown in Fig. 11.5, uses a single communication path between all of the functional units, namely the processors, the storage units, and the I/O processors. In this simple scheme, the common bus is essentially a passive unit, i.e., transfer operations between the functional units are controlled by the bus interfaces of the units themselves.

The processor or I/O processor wishing to transfer data must check the availability of the bus and the availability of the destination unit, inform the destination unit of what is to be done with the data, and initiate the actual data transfer. Receiving units must be able to recognize that messages on the bus are addressed to them, and they must follow and acknowledge the control signals received from the sending unit.

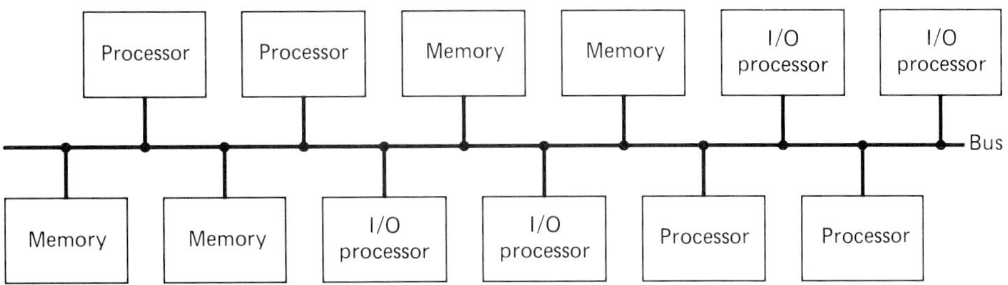

Fig. 11.5 Timeshared, common bus multiprocessor organization.

The common bus organization makes it easy to add new units by simply attaching them directly to the bus. For communications to occur, each unit must know what other units are on the bus, but this is generally handled in software.

The most serious disadvantages come from the single communications path.

- The entire system fails if the bus fails (i.e., a *catastrophic failure*).
- The net transmission rate of the system is constrained by the net transmission rate of the bus.
- Contention for the use of the bus in a busy system can cause serious performance degradation.

This system is economical, simple, and flexible, but the limitations of the common bus confine its use to smaller multiprocessing systems.

11.8.2 Crossbar-Switch Matrix

Increasing the number of buses in a common bus system to the number of storage units creates a multiprocessor organization called the *crossbar-switch matrix* in which there is a separate path to every storage unit (Fig. 11.6). With this scheme, references to two different storage units may occur simultaneously—one cannot block the other. In fact, a crossbar-switch matrix system can support simultaneous transmissions for all storage units. Crossbar switches were first used in telephone switching systems many decades ago.

The hardware required to build a crossbar switch can become complex. For example, the switch must be capable of resolving conflicts for the same storage unit. But the complexity of the switch actually makes the interfaces at the functional units much simpler.

The multiplicity of transmission paths can yield very high transmission rates. Adding functional units in a crossbar-switch system normally results in better throughput increases than those that occur within the other schemes.

The crossbar switch can contain redundant logic to increase reliability. The multiplicity of transmission paths makes it easier to partition the system. Malfunctioning units may be removed easily while the system continues functioning.

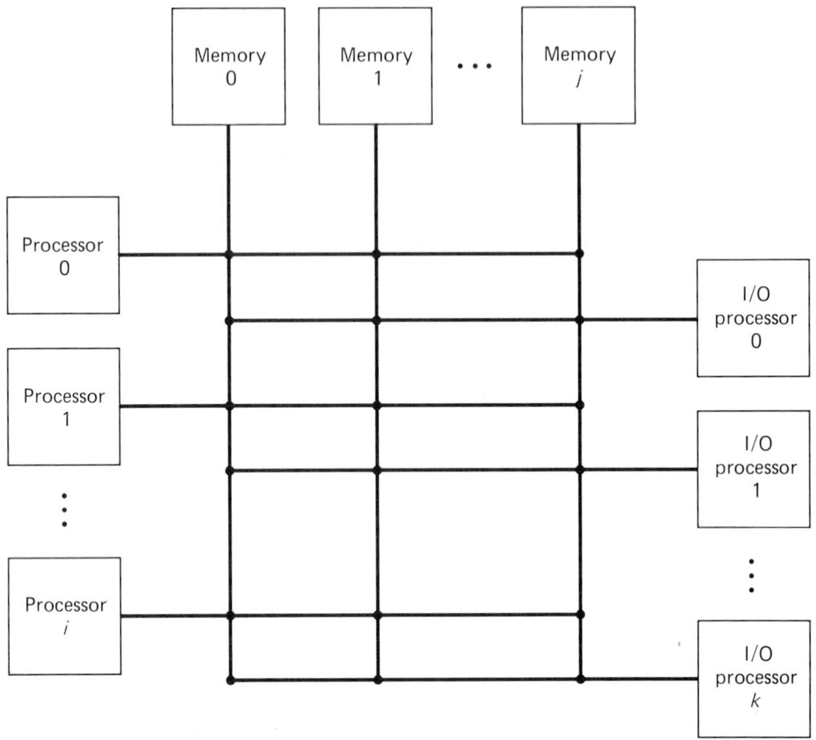

Fig. 11.6 Crossbar switch matrix multiprocessor organization.

11.8.3 Multiport Storage

By taking the control logic, switching logic, and priority arbitration logic out of the crossbar switch and placing all this logic at the interface to each storage unit, a multiport storage system (Fig. 11.7) is obtained. In this scheme, each functional unit may access each storage unit but only at a specific *storage port.* One storage port is supplied per functional unit.

Storage ports are normally assigned permanent priorities to resolve conflicts among the functional units attempting to access storage at the same time.

One interesting possibility with the multiport scheme is to restrict access to various storage units to certain subsets of the processors and I/O processors, thus creating certain private storage units. This is particularly attractive to designers of highly secure systems (Fig. 11.8). But regardless of whether all processing units can access all storage units, or access is restricted, the amount of cabling involved in multiport systems to make all necessary connections is often larger than it is with the other schemes.

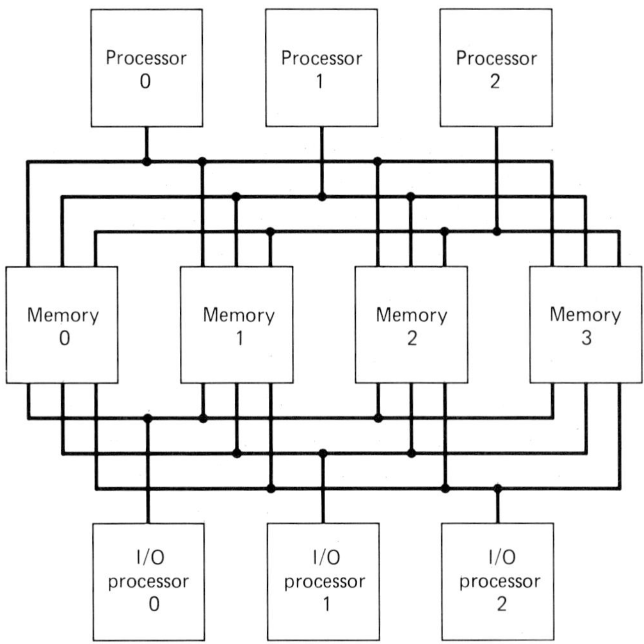

Fig. 11.7 Multiport memory system multiprocessor organization.

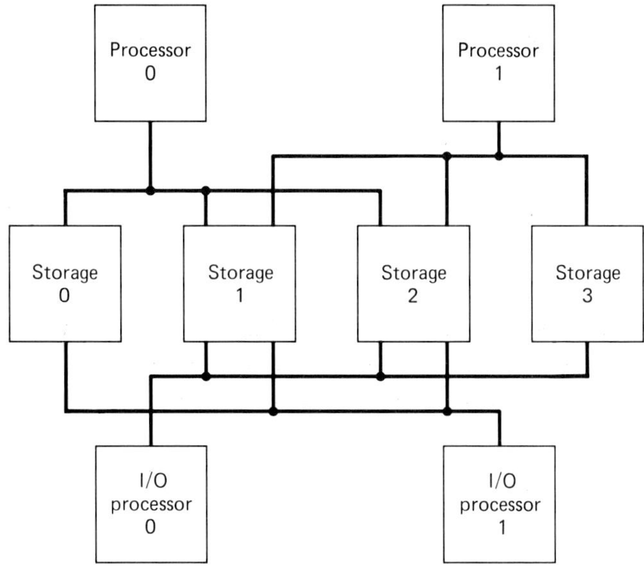

Fig. 11.8 Multiport memory system multiprocessor organization with private memories.

11.9 LOOSELY COUPLED VS. TIGHTLY COUPLED SYSTEMS

Loosely coupled multiprocessing involves connecting two or more independent computer systems via a communication link (Fig. 11.9). Each system has its own operating system and storage. The systems can function independently and can communicate when necessary. The separate systems can access each other's files across the communications link, and in some cases, they can switch tasks to more lightly loaded processors to achieve a degree of load balancing.

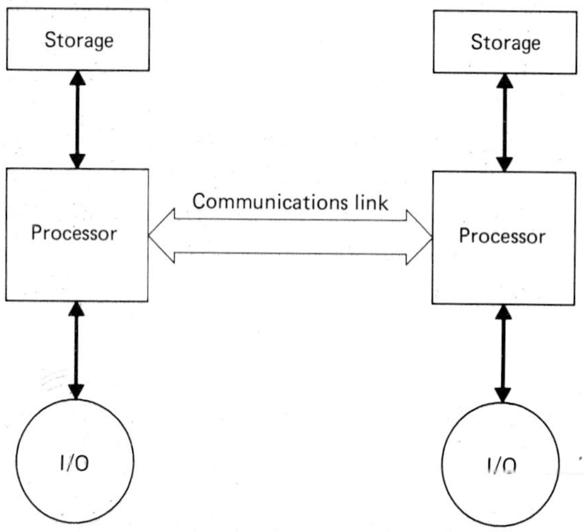

Fig. 11.9 Loosely coupled multiprocessing.

Tightly coupled multiprocessing (Fig. 11.10) uses a single storage shared by the various processors and a single operating system that controls all of the processors and system hardware.

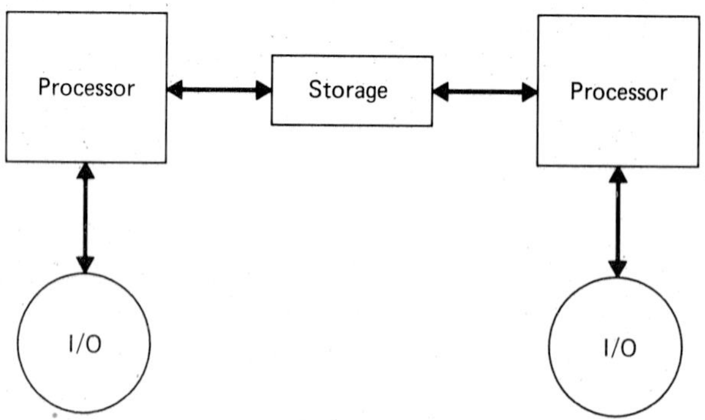

Fig. 11.10 Tightly coupled multiprocessing.

11.10 MASTER/SLAVE ORGANIZATION

In *master/slave multiprocessor organization*, one processor is designated as the *master* and the others are the *slaves*. The master is a general-purpose processor and performs input/output as well as computation. The slave processors perform only computation.

The slaves can run compute-bound jobs effectively, but I/O-bound jobs running on the slaves cause frequent calls for services only the master can perform, and this can be inefficient. From a reliability standpoint, if a slave fails, some computing capability is lost, but the system can still function. If the master fails, the system cannot perform I/O. On some systems this problem is handled by switching the I/O devices onto a slave and restarting the system with that slave redesignated as the master.

In recent years, improvements in processor speeds have far outpaced improvements in I/O speeds. This has caused jobs that were previously compute-bound to become I/O-bound since the computations they perform between successive I/Os are now done so much faster. This has caused jobs previously well suited to master/slave multiprocessing on one model of a system to be less appropriate for such processing on newer models of the hardware. Thus *the largest problem with master/slave multiprocessing is the asymmetry of the hardware.* The processors are not equivalent because only the master can do I/O as well as computation. In symmetrical multiprocessing, all of the processors are functionally equivalent and can perform I/O and computation.

11.11 MULTIPROCESSOR OPERATING SYSTEMS

The distinction between multiprogramming operating systems and multiprocessing operating systems is not as great as one might imagine. The functional capabilities of both types of systems include (En77)

- resource allocation and management
- table and data set protection
- prevention of system deadlock
- abnormal termination
- I/O load balancing
- processor load balancing, and
- reconfiguration

The last three of these are considerably different for multiprocessing systems. The ability to exploit parallelism in the hardware and in the programs is central to multiprocessing systems, and supporting this automatically is a key aspect of multiprocessor operating systems.

Adding more processors, as well as the complex connections to storage and I/O processors, adds considerably to the cost of the hardware. The burden is upon the operating system to manage this additional hardware efficiently so that the benefits derived exceed the increased costs. Certainly, the additional software costs cannot be ignored—implementing multiprocessing requires more operating system as well as more hardware.

11.12 MULTIPROCESSOR OPERATING SYSTEMS ORGANIZATIONS

One major difference between multiprocessor and uniprocessor operating systems is the organization and structure of the operating system with regard to the multiple processors. The three basic operating systems organizations for multiprocessors are:

- master/slave
- separate executive for each processor
- symmetric (or anonymous) treatment of all processors

11.12.1 Master/Slave

Master/slave is the easiest organization to implement, and is often constructed by straightforward extension of an existing multiprogramming system. As we shall soon see, master/slave organization does not achieve optimal utilization of the hardware.

In the master/slave organization (Fig. 11.11), only one particular processor, the master, may execute the operating system. A slave processor can execute only user programs. When the process executing on a slave requires the attention of the operating system, it generates an interrupt and waits for the master processor to handle the interrupt. Depending on the number of slave processors and the interrupt activity the slaves are generating, large queues could develop at the master. Interestingly, the operating system does not have to be reentrant, since it can be used by only one processor at a time, and in behalf of only one user at a time.

The mutual exclusion problem for system tables is greatly simplified because of the single processor executing the operating system. The master/slave organization is less reliable than the other organizations—a failure of the master causes a catastrophic system failure.

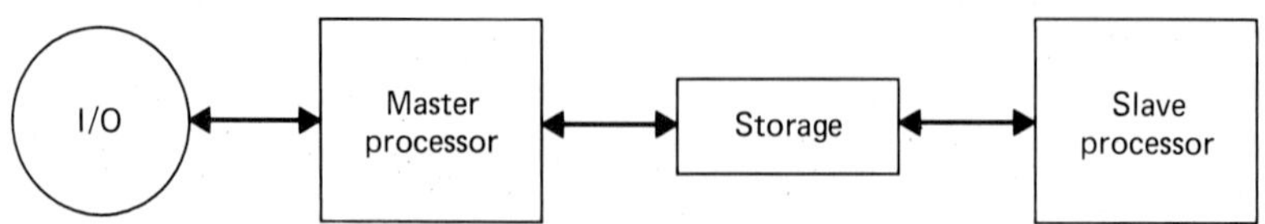

Fig. 11.11 Master/slave multiprocessing.

Utilization on a slave may be poor if the master does not service slave requests efficiently enough. This type of organization is particularly appropriate for environments with well-defined loads—the scheduling of the master can be precisely tuned. It is also appropriate for asymmetrical systems in which the slave processors are much less powerful than the master.

In master/slave, the operating system always runs in only one of the processors. This processor may be designed especially for running the operating system efficiently, or it may be similar to the other processors.

A slave processor that becomes available while the master is occupied must wait until the master assigns more work to it. If the slaves are running large numbers of short tasks, this can generate an excessive burden on the master. If the master cannot respond efficiently to these requests, then large portions of slave capacity will be wasted.

11.12.2 Separate Executives

In the *separate executives* organization, each processor has its own operating system, and responds to interrupts from users running on that processor. Some tables contain information global to the entire system (for example, the list of processors known to the system), and access to these tables must be carefully controlled using mutual exclusion techniques.

The separate executives organization is more reliable than the master/slave organization. The failure of a single processor is unlikely to cause a catastrophic system failure, but restarting the failed processor can be difficult.

Each processor controls its own dedicated resources such as files and I/O devices. Reconfiguring the I/O devices on the system may involve switching the devices to different processors with different operating systems. This can be complex and require considerable manual effort.

With separate executives organization, each processor has its own operating system and functions like a uniprocessor with its own resources. A process assigned to run on a particular processor runs to completion on that processor.

Operating systems functions are performed by each processor servicing its own requirements and those of the processes it has been assigned to execute. There is a minimal amount of contention over operating systems tables because these are distributed among the individual operating systems for their own use.

Each processor has its own private set of I/O devices it manages independently of the other processors. I/O operations requested by a process are serviced strictly by the processor to which the process is assigned. I/O interrupts return directly to the processors that initiate them. Since I/O devices are directly attached to individual processors, reconfiguration requires manual intervention.

In the separate executives organization, the processors do not cooperate on the execution of an individual process. It is possible for some of the processors to remain idle while one processor executes a lengthy process.

11.12.3 Symmetrical

Symmetrical multiprocessing is the most complex organization to implement, and the most powerful. All processors are identical. The operating system manages a pool of identical processors any one of which may be used to control any I/O device or reference any storage unit.

Because many processors may be executing the operating system at once, reentrant code and mutual exclusion are necessary. Because of the symmetry, it is possible to balance the work load more precisely than it is with the other organizations.

Conflict resolution hardware and software are important. Conflicts between processors attempting to access the same storage at the same time are ordinarily resolved by hardware. Conflicts in access to systemwide tables are ordinarily resolved by software.

Symmetrical multiprocessing systems are generally the most reliable—a failure in one processor causes the operating system to remove that processor from its pool of available processors and to notify the operator of the difficulty. The system may continue to function at reduced levels (i.e., *graceful degradation*) while repairs are made to the failed processor.

A process running on a symmetric multiprocessor may be run at different times by any of the equivalent processors. All of the processors may cooperate in the execution of a particular process.

The operating system *floats* from one processor to the next. The processor currently responsible for system tables and system functions is called the *executive processor*. Only one processor at a time may be the executive—this prevents conflicts over global system information.

Symmetrical multiprocessing offers better utilization. The load on the complete system may be balanced more easily because most work can be routed to any available processor.

Contention problems can become severe, especially because several processors may be in the supervisor state at once. Careful design of system tables is essential to prevent excessive lockouts. One technique that helps minimize contention is to divide the system data into a number of separate and independent entities that may be locked individually.

11.13 MULTIPROCESSOR SYSTEM PERFORMANCE

Even in completely symmetrical multiprocessing systems, the addition of a new processor will not cause system throughput to increase by the rated capacity of the new processor. There are many reasons for this, including

- additional operating system overhead
- increased contention for system resources

- hardware delays in switching and routing transmissions between an increased number of components

A number of performance studies have been attempted, one of which found that productivity increased by a factor of 1.8 in a two-processor system but only 2.1 in a three-processor system. Studies of this nature help explain why most multiprocessors implemented to date contain a relatively small number of processors (usually two to four). This does not mean that systems with more processors can't be built to achieve better results. It does imply, however, that current architectures will have to change if the industry hopes to achieve multiprocessing on a larger scale. Some recent multiprocessors have achieved much better performance improvements. For example, the four-processor Sperry Univac 1100/84 is about 3.6 times more productive than the single processor 1100/81.

11.14 COST EFFECTIVENESS OF MULTIPROCESSOR SYSTEMS

Choosing a multiprocessing approach to growth rather than a multiple computer approach requires careful analysis for each different organization and installation. Some advantages of the multiprocessing approach follow.

- Processors may often be added without the need for additional personnel.
- If the primary benefit to be gained is more processor capacity, i.e., if storage and I/O capabilities are sufficient, then adding processors is more economical than adding completely separate systems.
- Modularly designed symmetric multiprocessor systems make it fast and economical to add new processors.
- The additional space required for another processor is much less than that required for a complete computer system.
- System capacity may be increased smoothly in smaller increments.
- Queueing theory (see Chapter 15 on "Analytic Modeling") tells us that better throughput is obtained when a single stream of arrivals is directed to a multiple server facility than when the arrivals are divided into multiple streams and routed to single server facilities (where the servers in both types of systems have identical service rates).
- The multiprocessors are more cost effective over a wide range of work loads.

There are many disadvantages to the multiprocessor approach.

- Multiprocessing operating systems tend to be more complex than uniprocessor systems.
- Multiprocessor hardware is more complex than uniprocessor hardware.
- When the upper limit of processors on a multiprocessor system is finally reached, further expansion at the installation can be quite costly if a second multiprocessor system is obtained.

11.15 ERROR RECOVERY

One of the most important capabilities of multiprocessor operating systems is their ability to withstand equipment failures in individual processors and to continue operation. These capabilities are supported in great part by carefully designed software. Many techniques are commonly used to facilitate error recovery. These include

- Critical data for the system and the various processes should be maintained in multiple copies. These should reside in separate storage banks so that failures in individual components will not completely destroy the data.
- The operating system must be designed so that it can run the maximal configuration of hardware effectively, but it must also be able to run subsets of the hardware effectively in case of failures.
- Hardware error detection and correction capabilities should be implemented so that extensive validation is performed but without interfering with the efficient operation of the system.
- Idle processor capacity should be utilized to attempt to detect potential failures before they occur.
- The operating system should direct a functioning processor to take control of a process running on a failing processor.

11.16 SYMMETRICAL MULTIPROCESSING IN TOPS-10

In Digital Equipment Corporation's TOPS-10 system, master/slave restrictions of early versions have been eliminated by giving each processor full functional capabilities (Wi80). The resulting organization is called Symmetrical Multiprocessing (SMP) (Fig. 11.12). I/O devices can be connected to each of the processors. All monitor calls, including those for I/O, can be executed on all processors.

Because monitor calls can be executed by any processor, even if a processor is running a program that requests I/O on a device connected to a different processor, the processor can continue to run the job. The I/O is queued for initiation by the appropriate processor.

SMP considers the processor running a particular job to be the *executing processor.* The processor connected to the various devices the job is using is called the *owning processor.* A running job's requests for I/O on the executing processor are entered into that processor's I/O queues. I/O requests for the other processors cause the executing processor to issue a request to the owning processor to queue the I/O request. Immediately upon making the request, the executing processor completes the monitor call and the job is resumed—the owning processor handles the I/O. One advantage of this scheme over master/slave organization is that context-switching overhead is greatly reduced. In master/slave organization, I/O requests on the slave cause a context-switch to the master, and these can be costly.

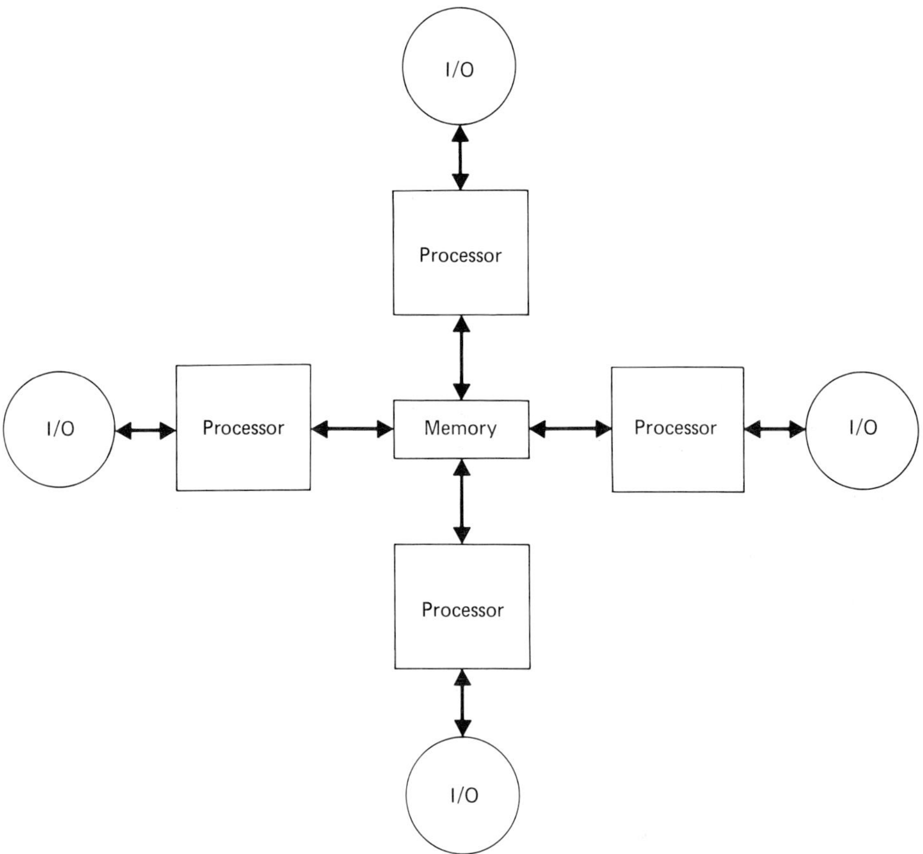

Fig. 11.12 Symmetrical multiprocessing with TOPS–10 SMP.

With SMP scheduling, each of the processors can execute the scheduler to seek the next job to run. This generally results in a particular job running on different processors at different times. The queued protocol used for I/O guarantees the correct handling of I/O requests regardless of which processor is currently executing a job and which I/O devices contain the user's files.

SMP utilizes a single job queue and each processor can select jobs from that queue for service. Thus SMP is able to perform load balancing operations not ordinarily done in the other multiprocessor organizations.

SMP scheduling in a two-processor system is performed as follows: One processor concentrates on running high-priority and interactive jobs. The other processor gives priority to background work if it can find any; otherwise this processor also handles high-priority and interactive jobs. This scheduling scheme is asymmetric; it tends to force one processor to favor interactive processes and the other to favor compute-bound processes.

Dispatching occurs frequently in uniprocessor systems and even more frequently in multiprocessor systems. Because the processors execute the same routines and examine the same data when looking for processes to run, serious contention problems may develop. To help minimize this contention in SMP, the clocks on all the processors are skewed so that clock interrupts occur at different times.

When a clock interrupts a processor to run the dispatcher, the processor also examines a global I/O request queue to determine if it must perform I/O for processes running on other processors. When I/O finishes, the waiting processes are made runnable. These processes may then be run on any available processor.

One interesting problem that develops in this multiprocessing configuration is that one processor may modify a process's data in cache storage and another processor may then attempt to run that process from primary storage with stale data. To prevent this problem, a processor must cause the updated data in the cache to replace the old data in primary storage before any other attempts are made to use the data again.

Interprocessor communication is a frequent occurrence in SMP, especially because one copy of the operating system is shared by all of the processors. SMP's designers chose a *software doorbell* approach for interprocessor communication. One processor may not interrupt another via a hardware interrupt mechanism. Rather each processor voluntarily "listens" for a doorbell when it has nothing else to do.

To improve reliability and availability SMP has been made sensitive to the condition of the storage in which it resides. When the operating system determines that the storage is malfunctioning, it simply relocates itself into a properly functioning area of storage.

11.17 C.MMP AND CM*

Researchers at Carnegie–Mellon University have developed several significant multiprocessor systems. These include C.mmp and Cm*. C.mmp (Si78a) (Si78b) (Wu80) is a 16-processor system consisting of PDP-11/40 minicomputers. The processors share 16 storage modules through a crossbar-switch matrix. Accesses from any processor to any storage module have the same cost because of the symmetry of the connection scheme. Sixteen storage references can occur concurrently provided that each is directed to a different storage port. Because the complexity of the crossbar-switch matrix increases with the square of the number of processors and storages, the C.mmp architecture is not useful for constructing very large-scale multiprocessors.

Cm* (Ar75) (Ch79) (Fu78) (Ha82) (Jo77) (Si78a) (Si78b) (Sw77a) (Sw77b) consists of 50 LSI-11 microprocessors. It is constructed from processor-storage pairs called *computer modules*. Each of these is referred to as a *Cm*. Cm's are grouped into *clusters*. Clusters are connected by *intercluster buses*. The cost of a storage reference depends on whether it is directed to a module's local storage, to the storage of another module in the same cluster, or to the storage of a module in another cluster. These three different types of storage references have a cost ratio of 1:3:9. Thus optimal performance depends on ensuring that most storage references in an application are directed to the local storages of the modules making those references.

Both of these multiprocessor systems have been used to solve a large number of problems exhibiting a high degree of inherent parallelism. In many cases, nearly linear improvements in performance (over the uniprocessor approach) have been achieved. A linear improvement means that with n processors the job will execute n times faster. This has occurred for example in certain mathematical applications such as integer programming and the solution of partial differential equations. The results of these efforts have demonstrated the importance of large-scale multiprocessing as a means of greatly reducing the execution times of highly parallel algorithms.

11.18 THE FUTURE OF MULTIPROCESSORS

Most indications are that the use of multiprocessing systems will greatly increase in the future. There are many reasons for this optimistic forecast.

- Reliability is becoming an ever-increasing consideration in computing environments.
- The cost of processors is declining rapidly because of advances in microelectronics.
- There will be a significant increase in the use of languages that allow users to express explicit parallelism. Multiprocessors may perform highly parallel programs much faster than uniprocessors. Applications will no doubt be discovered in which the true simultaneity of multiprocessors becomes important.
- Much progress is being made by researchers in the automatic detection of parallelism.
- The limitations of uniprocessors are being reached. Electromagnetic signals can travel no faster than the speed of light, and some uniprocessors already work at speeds in which electromagnetic signals may move less than one foot in the computer during the processing of an operation. Size limitations will eventually force designers to use multiprocessors to achieve throughput improvements.

Various studies of trends in computer architecture point to the development of systems that will combine both symmetric and asymmetric multiprocessing to create a hierarchy of processors within a system. The term *polyprocessors* has been used to describe such systems.

Regardless of how future multiprocessors will be structured, it is clear that operating systems of the future will be greatly influenced by multiprocessor computer architecture.

SUMMARY

A multiprocessing system employs several processors. With processor cycles becoming increasingly economical, the key concerns today in multiprocessing are reliability, parallelism in computation, optimal connection schemes, and contention between processors.

Few programs are written today to exploit concurrency. The real hope in this area is that hardware, compilers, and operating systems will automatically detect parallelism in algorithms.

In massive parallelism, sufficient processors are available so that all portions of a program that may be run concurrently may be assigned to separate processors.

Two common techniques used to exploit implicit parallelism are loop distribution and tree height reduction. In loop distribution, iterations that may be performed independently of one another are separated into concurrently executable units. Tree height reduction applies the commutative, associative, and distributive properties of arithmetic to rearrange algebraic expressions to make them amenable to concurrent execution.

The Never Wait Rule states that it is better to give a processor a task that may or may not be used eventually than to let the processor sit idle.

The three most common multiprocessor system organizations are the timeshared or common bus, the crossbar-switch matrix, and the multiport storage. The timeshared bus uses a single communication path between all of the functional units. It is the simplest of the three schemes. It facilitates the addition of new functional units. Its disadvantages are that the entire system fails if the bus fails, the net transmission rate of the system is constrained by the net transmission rate of the bus, and contention for the use of the bus in a busy system can cause serious performance degradation.

In the crossbar-switch matrix there is a separate path to every storage unit. This allows transmissions to and from all storage units simultaneously. The main disadvantage of this organization is the complexity of the crossbar switch.

In the multiport storage scheme, each functional unit may access each storage unit, but only at a specific storage port. The multiport scheme makes it possible to restrict access to various storage units to certain subsets of the processors and I/O processors. This is useful in the design of highly secure systems. The main disadvantage of the scheme is the large amount of cabling required.

Loosely coupled multiprocessing involves connecting two or more independent computer systems via a communication link. Tightly coupled multiprocessing uses a single storage shared by all the processors.

In master/slave multiprocessing, one processor is the master and the others are slaves. The master can perform input/output as well as computation. The slave processors perform only computation. The slaves are best suited to running compute-bound jobs. A slave running an I/O-bound job generates frequent interrupts to the master to perform the I/O in the slave's behalf. The largest problem with master/slave multiprocessing is the asymmetry of the hardware.

The three basic operating systems organizations for multiprocessors are master/slave, separate executives, and symmetric treatment of all processors. Master/slave is the easiest to implement. Only the master may execute the operating system. The operating system does not have to be reentrant, and mutual exclusion for system tables is greatly simplified. A failure of the master causes catastrophic system failure.

In the separate executives organization each processor has its own operating system. Mutual exclusion techniques are used to control access to global system information. The failure of a single processor is unlikely to be catastrophic. Each processor controls its own resources. A process runs to completion on the processor to which it is assigned. Utilization can be poor—it is possible for some processors to remain idle while one processor executes a lengthy process.

Symmetrical multiprocessing is the most complex organization to implement and the most powerful. The operating system manages a pool of identical processors any one of which may be used to control any I/O device or reference any storage unit. Reentrant code and mutual exclusion techniques are necessary. Better workload balancing is possible because of the symmetry. A failure of a single processor causes the operating system to remove the processor from the pool of processors, but the system continues to function. A process may be run at different times by different processors. The operating system floats between the processors. Contention can become a problem because several processors may be in the supervisor state at once.

Three multiprocessor systems were discussed briefly: DEC's TOPS-10 SMP, and the C.mmp and Cm* systems developed at Carnegie–Mellon University. SMP uses an interesting asymmetric scheduling algorithm. To help mininize contention in SMP, the clocks on all the processors are slightly skewed so that clock interrupts occur at different times. SMP uses a software doorbell approach to interprocessor communication.

C.mmp is a large-scale multiprocessor constructed by interconnecting 16 PDP-11/40 minicomputers via a crossbar-switch matrix. Cm* is a very large-scale multiprocessor formed by interconnecting 50 DEC LSI-11 microcomputers in clusters. Storage references in Cm* vary in cost depending on whether they are directed to a module's local storage, to the storage of another module in the same cluster, or to the storage of a module in another cluster. Both of these multiprocessors have achieved nearly linear improvements in performance (over the uniprocessor approach) in solving problems with a high degree of inherent parallelism.

Multiprocessing is growing in importance and is certain to be a major influence on the evolution of operating systems.

TERMINOLOGY

asymmetric multiprocessing
automatic detection of parallelism
availability
bus
catastrophic failure
cluster (in Cm*)
C.mmp
COBEGIN/COEND

Cm*
contention
crossbar-switch matrix
executing processor (in SMP)
executive processor
explicit parallelism
floating executive
graceful degradation
implicit parallelism
intercluster bus (in Cm*)
interprocessor communication
lock contention
loop distribution
loosely coupled multiprocessing
massive parallelism
master processor
master/slave
multiport storage
multiprocessing
multiprocessor
multiple server queueing system
Never Wait Rule
owning processor (in SMP)
polyprocessor
priority arbitration logic
processor load balancing
reconfiguration
recovery
redundancy
reliability
separate executives
single server queueing system
slave processor
software doorbell
storage contention
storage port
symmetric multiprocessing
tightly coupled multiprocessing
timeshared or common bus
TOPS-10 SMP system
tree height reduction

EXERCISES

11.1 What is loop distribution? In what circumstances is it practical to use this technique? What is the trade-off in the use of loop distribution vs. not using it.

11.2 What is tree height reduction? In what circumstances is it useful?

11.3 What is the Never Wait Rule? In what circumstances is it useful?

11.4 Describe the timeshared or common bus multiprocessor organization. What are its advantages and disadvantages?

11.5 What is a catastrophic failure in a multiprocessor system? What can designers do to minimize the chance of catastrophic failure?

11.6 Describe the crossbar-switch matrix multiprocessor organization. What are its advantages and disadvantages?

11.7 How should the resource allocation mechanisms of a symmetric multiprocessing system be adjusted to reflect the loss of capacity when a processor fails?

11.8 What is the central goal of most multiprocessing systems? List several advantages of multiprocessor architectures over uniprocessor architectures. List several disadvantages.

11.9 What is massive parallelism? What types of problems may be solved with this approach?

11.10 What is explicit parallelism? What are its disadvantages?

11.11 What is implicit parallelism? Discuss the importance of developing mechanisms that will automatically detect implicit parallelism.

11.12 Describe the multiport storage multiprocessor organization. What are its advantages and disadvantages?

11.13 What is loosely coupled multiprocessing? What is tightly coupled multiprocessing?

11.14 Discuss the master/slave multiprocessor organization. Compare it with symmetrical multiprocessing.

11.15 Compare and contrast the following multiprocessor operating system organizations: master/slave, separate executives, symmetrical.

11.16 What aspect of the architecture of C.mmp makes it inappropriate for the implementation of very large-scale multiprocessing? Why is Cm* a more appropriate architecture for this purpose?

11.17 Carefully examine a program you have written and indicate which operations may be performed concurrently.

a) How much time did it take you to do this?
b) How certain are you that you are correct?
c) Suppose a modification were to be made? Do you suppose it would be easier to modify the sequential program or the concurrent program? Explain.

11.18 As a computer systems designer with both hardware and software expertise, you have been given the task of designing an ultrahigh reliability multiprocessing system. Discuss the hardware and software techniques you would employ.

11.19 A job normally run on a uniprocessor LSI-11 is to be run on a Cm* type multiprocessor with n interconnected LSI-11s. Give at least two key considerations affecting whether a near linear performance improvement may be achieved.

11.20 Consider the following loop taken from a FORTRAN program

```
      DO 1,I = 1,20
         IF (X.EQ.0) Y(I) = 3.5
1        IF (X.NE.0) Y(I) = 5
```

a) Recode this program segment into assembly language.
b) Recode the FORTRAN program segment so that it will run much more efficiently on a uniprocessor.
c) Assume a four-processor symmetrical multiprocessor is available. Produce the most efficient concurrent program you can to accomplish exactly what the given FORTRAN loop does.
d) Assume the availability of a symmetric massive parallel processor. Produce the most efficient concurrent program you can to accomplish exactly what the given FORTRAN loop does.
e) Compare the execution speed of the given FORTRAN loop with the execution speeds of the programs you produced in answer to (b), (c), and (d). Assume that all of the processors have identical capabilities.

11.21 Use tree height reduction techniques to produce versions of the following expressions more amenable to parallel evaluation. In each case draw evaluation trees for the original expression and the new expression.

a) $(p + (q + (r + s)))$
b) $((a + b * c * d) * e)$
c) $(m + (n * p * q * r) + a + b + c)$
d) $(a * (b + c + d * (e + f)))$

LITERATURE

(Ar75) Arden, B.W., and A.D. Berenbaum, "A Multi-Microprocessor Computer System Architecture," *Proceedings of the Fifth Symposium on Operating Systems Principles*, Austin, November 1975.

(Ba80) Baer, J.L., "Computer Systems Architecture," Rockville, Md.: Computer Science Press, 1980, pp. 547–586.

(Ba76) Baer, J.L., "Multiprocessing Systems," *IEEE Trans. on Computers*, Vol. C-25, No. 12, December 1976, pp. 1271–1277.

(Ba68) Barnes, G., et al., "The ILLIAC IV Computer," *IEEE Trans. on Computers*, Vol. C-17, August 1968, pp. 746–757.

(Bu78) Baudet, G.M., "Asynchronous Iteractive Methods for Multiprocessors," *JACM*, Vol. 25, No. 2, April 1978, pp. 226–244.

(Be77a) Bell, G., et al., "Multiprocessor Memory Organization and Memory Interference," *CACM*, Vol. 20, No. 10, October 1977, pp. 754–761.

(Be78b) Bell, C.G., et al., "The Evolution of the DEC System 10," *CACM*, Vol. 21, No. 1, January 1978.

(Br78) Brinch Hansen, P., "Multiprocessor Architectures for Concurrent Programs," *Proceedings of 1978 ACM Annual Conference*, pp. 317–323.

(Bo73) Browne, J.L.; K.M. Chandy; J. Hagarth; and C.C. Lee, "The Effect on Throughput of Multiprocessing in a Multiprogramming Environment," *IEEE Trans. on Computers*, Vol. 22, No. 8, August 1973.

(Ca78) Case, R.P., and A. Padegs, "Architecture of the IBM System/370," *CACM*, Vol. 21, No. 1, January 1978, pp. 73–96.

(Ch79) Childs, R.E., "Multiple Microprocessor Systems: Goals, Limitations, and Alternatives," *Digest of Papers, Compcon*, Spring 1979, San Francisco, February 1979.

(En74) Comtre Corporation and P.H. Enslow (ed.), *Multiprocessors and Parallel Processing*, New York: Wiley, 1974.

(En77) Enslow, Philip H., Jr., "Multiprocessor Organization—A Survey," *CACM*, Vol. 9, No. 1, March 1977, pp. 103–129.

(Fu78) Fuller, S.H.; J.K. Ousterhout; L. Raskin; P.I. Rubinfeld, D.S. Sindhu, and R. J. Swan, "Multi-microprocessors: An Overview and Working Experience," *Proc. IEEE*, Vol. 66, No. 2, February 1978, pp. 216–228.

(Ga80) Garcia, O.N., "Parallel Processing Today," *IEEE Trans. on Computers*, Vol. C-29, No. 9, September 1980.

(Gu78) Gula, J.L., "Operating System Considerations for Multiprocessor Architecture," *Proceedings of the Seventh Texas Conference on Computing Systems*, Houston, November 1978.

(Ha82) Haynes, L.S.; R.L. Lau; D.P. Siewiorek; and D.W. Mizell, "A Survey of Highly Parallel Computing," *Computer*, January 1982, pp. 9–24.

(Ho79) Holley, L.H.; R.P. Parmelee, C.A. Salisbury, and D.N. Saul, "VM/370 Asymmetric Multiprocessing," *IBM Systems Journal*, No. 1, 1979, pp. 47–69.

(Jo77) Jones, A.K.; R.J. Chansler, Jr.; I. Durham; P. Feiler; and K. Schwans, "Software Management of Cm*—A Distributed Multiprocessor," *Proceedings AFIPS National Computer Conference*, Arlington, Va.: AFIPS Press, 1977, pp. 657–663.

(Jo79) Jones, A.K.; R.J. Chansler, Jr.; I. Durham; K. Schwans; and S.R. Vegdahl, "StarOS, a Multiprocessor Operating System for the Support of Task Forces," *Proceedings of the Seventh Symposium Operating Systems Principles (ACM)*, December 1979.

(Jo80) Jones, A.K., and P. Schwarz, "Experience Using Multiprocessor Systems—A Status Report," *ACM Computing Surveys*, Vol. 12, No. 2, June 1980, pp. 121–166.

(Ka78) Katuski, D., et al., "Pluribus—An Operational Fault-Tolerant Multiprocessor," *Proceedings of the IEEE*, Vol. 66, No. 10, October 1978, pp. 1146–1159.

(Ko77) Kober, R., "The Multiprocessor System SMS 201—Combining 128 Microprocessors into a Powerful Computer," *CompCon*, Fall 1977, ACM, 1977.

(Ku77) Kuck, D.J., "A Survey of Parallel Machine Organization and Programming," *ACM Computing Surveys*, Vol. 9, No. 1, March 1977, pp. 29–60.

(Le81) Lerner, E.J., "Fast Graphics Use Parallel Techniques," *IEEE Spectrum*, Vol. 18, No. 3, March 1981.

(Nu77) Nutt, G.J., "A Parallel Processor Operating System Comparison," *IEEE Trans. on Soft. Eng.*, Vol. SE-3, No. 6, November 1977, pp. 467–475.

(Ou80) Ousterhout, J.K.; A. Schelza; and P.S. Sindhu, "Medusa: An Experiment in Distributed Operating System Structure," *CACM*, Vol. 23, No. 2, February 1980, pp. 92–105.

(Qu78) Quaynon, N., and A. Bernstein, "Operating Systems for Hierarchical Multiprocessors," *Proceedings of the Seventh Texas Conference on Computing Systems*, Houston, November 1978, pp. 1–9 to 1–15.

(Ro80) Roberts, M., "Multiprocessing—Networks vs. Mainframes," *Mini-Micro Systems*, October 1980 (Part I), November 1980 (Part II).

(Sa80a) Satyanarayanan, M., "Commercial Multiprocessing Systems," *Computer*, May 1980, pp. 75–96.

(Sa80b) Satyanarayanan, M., "Multiprocessors: A Comparative Study," Englewood Cliffs, N.J.: Prentice-Hall, 1980.

(Sa79) Sauer, C.H.; and K.M. Chandy, "The Impact of Distributions and Disciplines on Multiprocessor Systems," *CACM*, Vol. 22, No. 1, January 1979.

(Se79) Sethi, A.S., and N. Deo, "Interference in Multiprocessor Systems with Localized Memory Access Probabilities," *IEEE Trans. on Computers*, Vol. C-28, No. 2, February 1979.

(Si80a) Siewiorek, D.P.; G. Bell; and A. Newell, "The Multiprocessor Design Space," *Computer Structures: Principles and Examples*, New York: McGraw-Hill, 1980.

(Si78a) Siewiorek, D.P., et al., "A Case Study of C.mmp, Cm* and C.vmp, Part I: Experience with Fault-Tolerance in Microprocessor Systems," *Proceedings of the IEEE*, Vol. 66, No. 10, October 1978, pp. 1178–1199.

(Si78b) Siewiorek, D.P., et al., "A Case Study of C.mmp, Cm* and C.vmp, Part II: Predicting and Calibrating Reliability of Multiprocessor Systems," *Proceedings of the IEEE*, Vol. 66, No. 10, October 1978, pp. 1200–1220.

(Sr78) Srodawa, R.J., "Positive Experiences with a Multiprocessing System," *Computing Surveys*, Vol. 10, No. 1, March 1978.

(St77) Stone, H.S., "Multiprocessor Scheduling with the Aid of Network Flow Algorithms," *IEEE Trans. on Soft. Eng.*, Vol. SE-5, No. 1, January 1977, pp. 85–93.

(Sw77a) Swan, R.J.; A. Bechtolsteim; K. Lai; and J.K. Ousterhout, "The Implementation of the Cm* Multimicroprocessor," *AFIPS Conf. Proc.*, Vol. 46, *1977 NCC*, pp. 645–655.

(Sw77b) Swan, R.J.; S.H. Fuller; and D.P. Siewiorek; "Cm*—A Modular Multi-microprocessor," *Proceedings of the AFIPS National Computer Conference*, Arlington, Va.: AFIPS Press, 1977, pp. 637–644.

(Th80) Theis, D.J., "Distributed Network and Multiprocessing Minicomputer State-of-the-art Capabilities," *NCC*, Vol. 49, 1980, pp. 93–103.

(Wa77) Walters, S.J., "Majority Verdicts in Multiprocessing—Any Two from Three," *Computer Journal*, Vol. 20, No. 3, August 1977, pp. 207–212.

(Wi80) Wilson, A.B., "More Power to You: Symmetrical Multiprocessing Gives Large-Scale Computer Power at a Lower Cost with Higher Availability," *Datamation*, June 1980, pp. 216–223.

(Wu80) Wulf, W.A.; R. Levin; and S.P. Harbison, "Hydra: An Experimental Operating System," New York: McGraw-Hill, 1980.

(Ya77) Yau, S.S., and H.S. Fung, "Associative Processor Architecture—A Survey," *Computing Surveys*, Vol. 9, No. 1, March 1977, pp. 3–25.

Part 5
Auxiliary Storage Management

12
Disk Scheduling

The wheel is come full circle.

King Lear, V, iii, 176
William Shakespeare

Treat nature in terms of the cylinder, the sphere, the cone, all in perspective.

Paul Cézanne

Ask, and it shall be given you; seek, and ye shall find; knock, and it shall be opened unto you.

Matt. 2:5–7

Outline

12.1 INTRODUCTION

In multiprogrammed computing systems, inefficiency is often caused by improper use of rotational storage devices such as disks and drums. In this chapter, the literature on managing rotational storage devices is surveyed.

We explain the operation of moving-head disks, discuss the causes of inefficiency, consider various schemes for improving efficiency, and compare and contrast the schemes in the context of several performance criteria.

We discuss various systems considerations that might influence a designer's choice on whether or not to include rotational storage device scheduling in a particular system, and we show situations in which scheduling is not useful.

12.2 OPERATION OF MOVING-HEAD DISK STORAGE

Figure 12.1 is a schematic representation of the side view of a *moving-head disk.* Data is recorded on a series of magnetic disks or *platters.* These disks are connected by a common *spindle* that spins at very high speed (some spindles rotate at speeds of 3600 revolutions per minute.)

The data is accessed (i.e., either read or written) by a series of *read–write heads,* one head per disk surface. A read–write head can only access data immediately adjacent to it. Therefore, before data can be accessed, the portion of the disk surface from which the data is to be read (or the portion on which the data is to be writ-

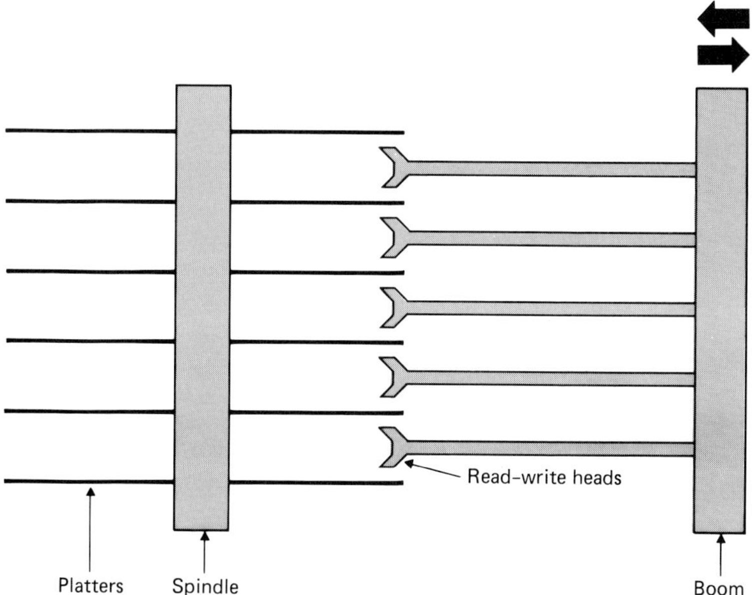

Fig. 12.1 Schematic of a moving-head disk.

ten) must rotate until it is immediately below (or above) the read–write head. The time it takes for data to rotate from its current position to a position adjacent to the read–write head is called *latency time.*

Each of the several read–write heads, while fixed in position, sketches out a circular *track* of data on a disk surface. All read–write heads are attached to a single *boom* or *moving-arm assembly.* The boom may move either in or out. When the boom moves the read–write heads to a new position, a completely different set of tracks becomes accessible. For a particular position of the boom, the set of tracks sketched out by all the read–write heads forms a vertical *cylinder.* The process of moving the boom to a new cylinder is called a *seek* operation.

Thus, in order to access a particular record of data on a moving-head disk, several operations are usually necessary (Fig. 12.2). First, the boom must be moved (i.e., a seek) to the appropriate cylinder. Then the portion of the disk on which the data record is stored must rotate until it is immediately under (or over) the read–write head (i.e., latency time). Then the record, which is of arbitrary size (up to a full circular track), must be made to spin by the read–write head. (This is called *transmission time.*) Because each of these operations involves mechanical movement, the total time it takes to access a particular record is often an appreciable fraction of a second (0.01 to 0.1 second). This is very slow compared with the very high processing speeds of the central computer system.

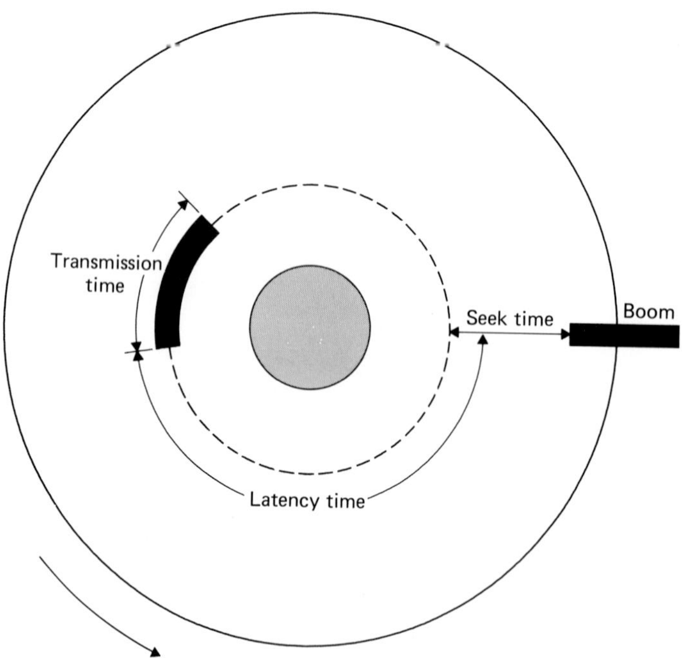

Fig. 12.2 Components of a disk access.

12.3 WHY SCHEDULING IS NECESSARY

In multiprogrammed computing systems, many processes may be generating requests for reading and writing disk records. Because these processes often make requests faster than they can be serviced by the moving-head disks, waiting lines or queues build up for each device. Some computing systems merely service these requests on a *first-come-first-served (FCFS)* basis. Whichever request for service arrives first is serviced first. FCFS is a *fair* method of allocating service, but when the *request rate* (i.e., the *load*) becomes heavy, FCFS can result in very long waiting times.

FCFS exhibits a *random seek pattern* in which successive requests can cause time-consuming seeks from the innermost to the outermost cylinders (Fig. 12.3). To minimize time spent seeking records, it seems reasonable to order the request queue in some manner other than FCFS. This process is called *disk scheduling.*

Disk scheduling involves a careful examination of pending requests to determine the most efficient way to service the requests. A disk scheduler examines the positional relationships among the waiting requests. The request queue is then reordered so that the requests will be serviced with minimum mechanical motion.

The two most common types of scheduling discussed in the literature are *seek*

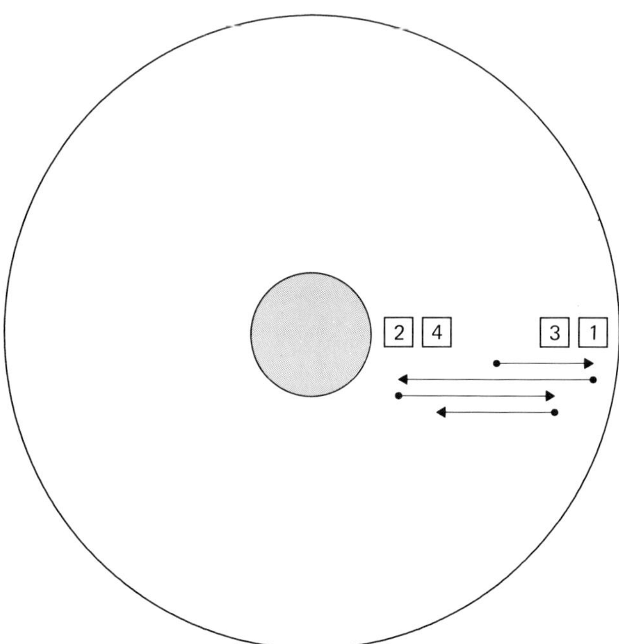

Fig. 12.3 FCFS random seek pattern. The numbers indicate the order in which the requests arrived.

optimization and *rotational* (or *latency*) *optimization. Since seek times tend to be about an order of magnitude greater than latency times, most scheduling algorithms concentrate on minimizing seek times for a set of requests.* Minimizing latency usually has very little effect on overall system performance, except under very heavy loads.

Under light loading conditions (i.e., a small average queue length), FCFS is an acceptable way to service requests. Under medium to heavy loading conditions, however, scheduling can result in much better performance than FCFS.

12.4 DESIRABLE CHARACTERISTICS OF SCHEDULING POLICIES

It has already been mentioned that FCFS is a relatively fair method of servicing requests. Several other criteria for categorizing scheduling policies are

- *throughput*
- *mean response time*
- *variance in response times* (i.e., predictability)

Clearly, a scheduling policy should attempt to maximize *throughput*, the number of requests serviced per unit time. Since scheduling policies can minimize time wasted in performing lengthy seeks, the throughput can certainly be improved over FCFS servicing. Also a scheduling policy should attempt to minimize the mean response time (or average waiting time). Again, because scheduling reduces the time spent waiting on seeks, it should certainly be able to improve upon mean response time over FCFS.

The criteria above attempt to improve overall performance, possibly at the expense of individual requests. *Scheduling often improves the total picture while reducing service levels for certain requests.*

One important measure of this phenomenon is the variance in response times. Variance is a statistical term with a precise mathematical definition. It is a measure of how far individual items tend to deviate from the average of the items. As such, we use variance to indicate predictability—the smaller the variance, the greater the predictability. We desire a scheduling policy that minimizes variance. Otherwise certain requests may experience erratic service levels. This could be intolerable, for example, in an airline reservation system where prompt service can help sell a ticket or ensure that a passenger meets a plane. If a scheduling policy merely attempts to maximize throughput without simultaneously minimizing variance, it could process the easy-to-service requests and could ignore some requests completely. The designer must be wary of this situation.

12.5 SEEK OPTIMIZATION

Figure 12.4 (Te72) summarizes some of the most popular seek optimization strategies. The next several sections discuss these strategies in detail.

- FCFS (First-come-first-served): There is no reordering of the queue.
- SSTF (Shortest-seek-time-first): Disk arm is positioned next at the request that minimizes arm movement.
- SCAN: Disk arm sweeps back and forth across the disk surface, servicing all requests in its path. It changes direction only when there are no more requests to service in the current direction.
- C-SCAN (Circular scan): Disk arm moves unidirectionally across the disk surface toward the inner track. When there are no more requests for service ahead of the arm it jumps back to service the request nearest the outer track and proceeds inward again.
- N-Step scan: Disk arm sweeps back and forth as in SCAN, but all requests that arrive during a sweep in one direction are batched and reordered for optimum service during the return sweep.
- Eschenbach scheme: Disk arm movement is circular as in C-SCAN, but with several important exceptions. Every cylinder is serviced for exactly one full track of information whether or not there is a request for that cylinder. Requests are reordered for service within a cylinder to take advantage of rotational position, but if two requests overlap sector positions within a cylinder, only one is serviced on the current sweep of the disk arm.

Fig. 12.4 Basic disk scheduling policies (T.F. Teorey, "Properties of Disk Scheduling Policies in Multiprogrammed Computer Systems," Proceedings, 1972. FJCC, Vol. 41, Part I, p. 2; AFIPS Press.)

12.5.1 FCFS (First-Come-First-Served) Scheduling

In FCFS scheduling, the first request to arrive is the first one serviced. FCFS is fair in the sense that once a request has arrived, its place in the schedule is fixed. A request cannot be displaced because of the arrival of a higher priority request.

When requests are uniformly distributed over the disk surfaces, FCFS scheduling results in a random seek pattern. It ignores positional relationships among the pending requests in the queue. It makes no attempt at optimizing the seek pattern.

FCFS is acceptable when the load on a disk is light. But as the load grows, FCFS tends to saturate the device and response times become large. FCFS does offer small variance but this is of little solace to the request sitting at the back of the disk queue while the boom rambles around in a torrid "disk dance."

12.5.2 SSTF (Shortest-Seek-Time-First) Scheduling

In SSTF scheduling, the request that results in the shortest seek distance (and thus the shortest seek time) is serviced next, even if that request is not the first one in the queue.

SSTF tends to discriminate sharply against certain requests. SSTF seek patterns tend to be highly localized with the result that the innermost and outermost tracks can receive poor service compared with the mid-range tracks (Fig. 12.5).

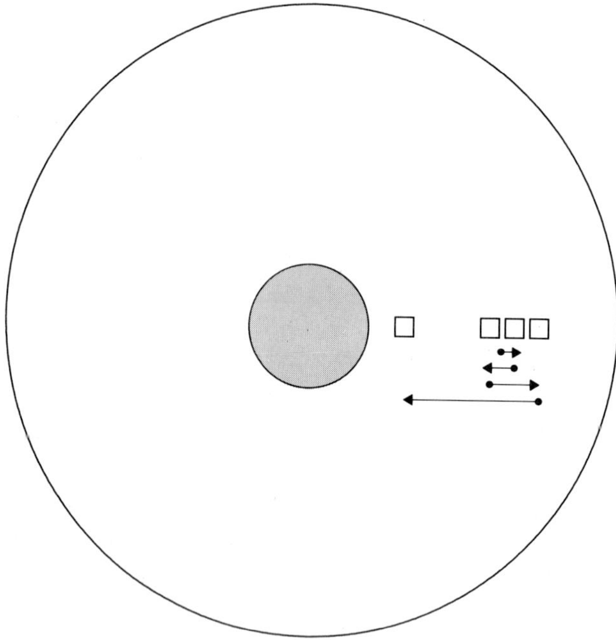

Fig. 12.5 SSTF localized seek patterns.

SSTF results in better throughput rates than FCFS, and mean response times tend to be lower for moderate loads. One significant drawback is that higher variances occur on response times because of the discrimination against the outermost and innermost tracks. When the significant improvements in throughput and mean response times are considered, this increased variance may be tolerable. SSTF is useful in batch processing systems where throughput is the major consideration. But its high variance of response times (i.e., its lack of predictability) makes it unacceptable in interactive systems.

12.5.3 SCAN Scheduling

Denning (De67) developed the SCAN scheduling strategy to overcome the discrimination and high variance in response times of SSTF.

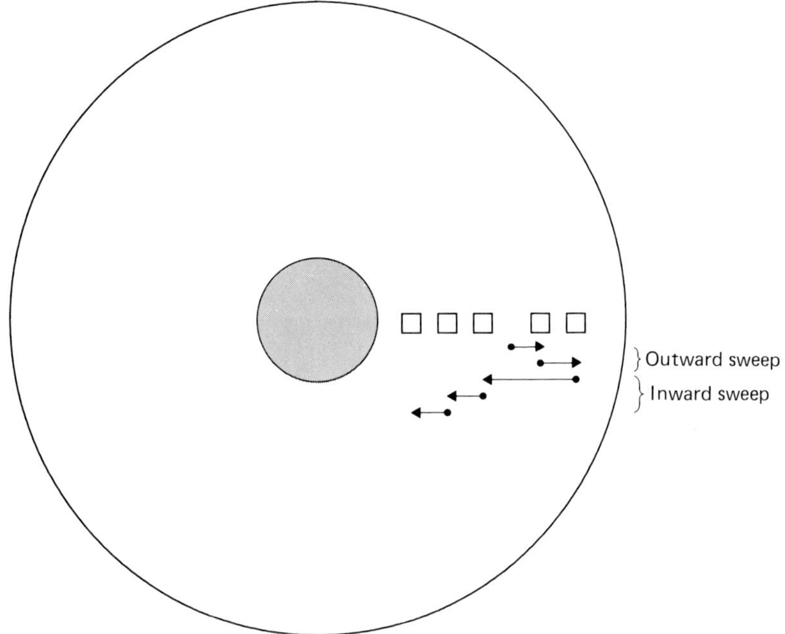

Fig. 12.6 SCAN scheduling with preferred directions.

SCAN operates like SSTF except that it chooses the request that results in the shortest seek distance in a *preferred direction* (Fig. 12.6). If the preferred direction is currently outward, then the SCAN strategy chooses the shortest seek distance in the outward direction. SCAN does not change direction until it reaches the outermost cylinder or until there are no further requests pending in the preferred direction. *SCAN has been the basis of most disk scheduling strategies actually implemented.*

SCAN behaves very much like SSTF in terms of improved throughput and improved mean response times but it eliminates much of the discrimination inherent in SSTF schemes and offers much lower variance.

Because of the oscillating motion of the read–write heads in SCAN, the outer tracks are visited less often than the mid-range tracks, but this is not as serious as the discrimination of SSTF.

12.5.4 N-Step SCAN Scheduling

One interesting modification to the basic SCAN strategy is called *N-Step Scan.* In this strategy, the disk arm moves back and forth as in SCAN except that it services only those requests waiting when a particular sweep begins. Requests arriving during a sweep are grouped together and ordered for optimum service during the return sweep (Fig. 12.7).

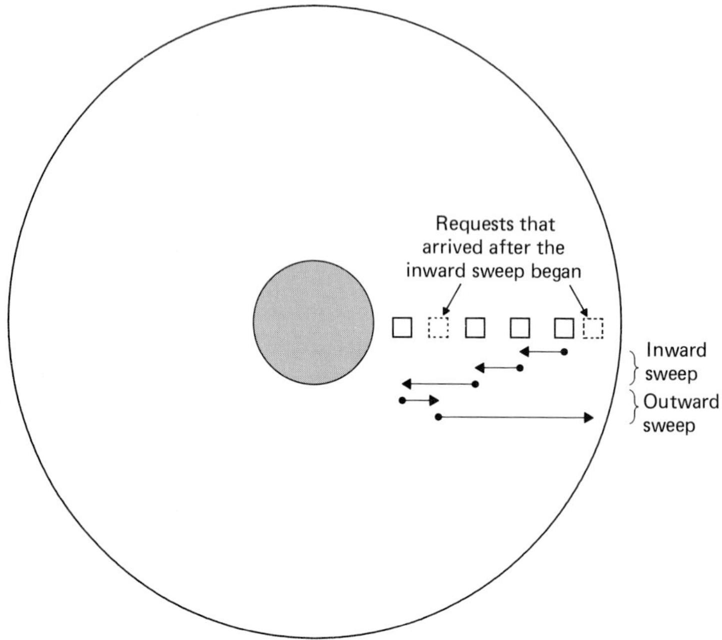

Fig. 12.7 N-Step SCAN scheduling.

N-Step SCAN offers good performance in throughput and mean response time. Its most significant characteristic is a lower variance of response times than either SSTF or conventional SCAN scheduling. N-Step SCAN avoids the possibility of indefinite postponement occurring if a large number of requests arrive for the current cylinder. It saves these requests for servicing on the return sweep.

12.5.5 C-SCAN Scheduling

Another interesting modification to the basic SCAN strategy is called *C-SCAN* (for Circular SCAN). C-SCAN eliminates the discrimination of earlier strategies against the innermost and outermost cylinders.

In the C-SCAN strategy, the arm moves from the outer cylinder to the inner cylinder servicing requests on a shortest seek basis. When the arm has completed its inward sweep, it jumps to the request nearest to the outermost cylinder, and then resumes its inward sweep processing requests. C-SCAN may be implemented so that requests arriving on the current sweep are serviced on the next sweep (Fig. 12.8). Thus C-SCAN completely eliminates the discrimination against requests for the innermost or outermost cylinders. It has a very small variance in response times.

Simulation results in the literature (Te72a) indicate that the best disk scheduling policy might operate in two stages. At low loading, the SCAN policy is best while

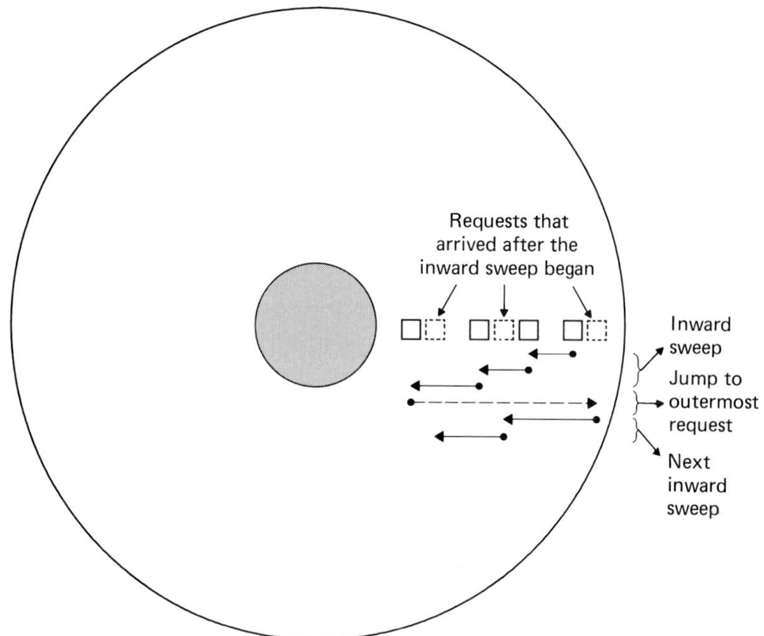

Fig. 12.8 C-SCAN scheduling.

at medium to heavy loading, C-SCAN yields the best results. C-SCAN with rotational optimization handles very heavy loading conditions effectively.

12.5.6 Eschenbach Scheme

This strategy, described in Fig. 12.4, was originally developed for an airline reservation system designed for handling very heavy loads. The scheme was one of the first to attempt to optimize not only seek time but rotational delay as well (We66). The C-SCAN strategy with rotational optimization has proven to be better than the Eschenbach scheme under all loading conditions (Te72a).

12.6 ROTATIONAL OPTIMIZATION

Under heavy loading conditions, the likelihood of several references to a particular cylinder increases, and it becomes useful to consider rotational optimization as well as seek optimization. Rotational optimization has been used with fixed-head devices such as drums for many years (Fu74) (St73).

Paralleling the SSTF strategy of seek optimization is the *SLTF* (shortest-latency-time-first) strategy for rotational optimization. Once the disk arm arrives at a

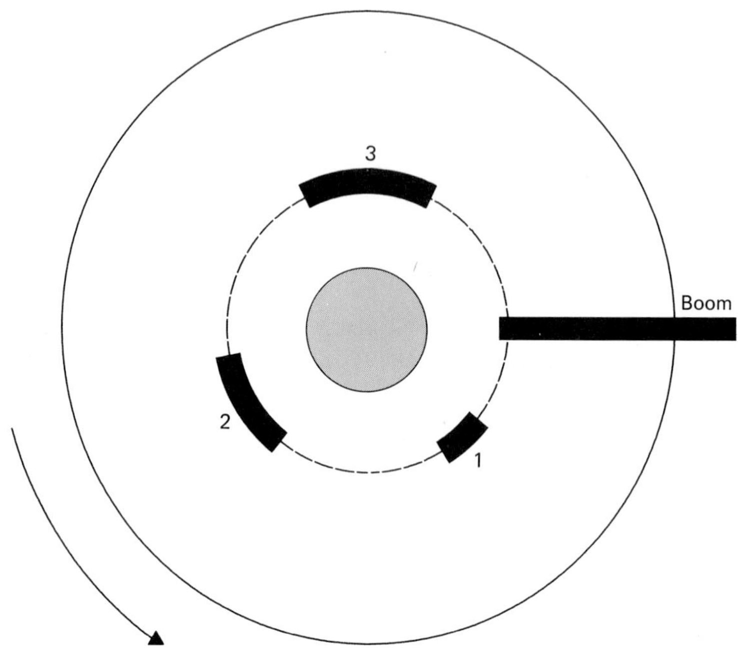

Fig. 12.9 SLTF scheduling. The requests will be serviced in the indicated order regardless of the order in which they arrived.

particular cylinder, there may be many requests pending on the various tracks of that cylinder. The SLTF strategy examines all of these requests and services the one with the shortest rotational delay first (Fig. 12.9). This strategy has been shown to be very close to the theoretical optimum (St73) and is relatively easy to implement.

12.7 SYSTEMS CONSIDERATIONS

When is disk scheduling useful? When might it degrade performance? These questions have to be answered in the context of the overall system into which disk usage has been incorporated. The following sections discuss several considerations that might influence the designer's decisions.

12.7.1 Disk Storage as Limiting Resource

When disk storage proves to be a *bottleneck,* some designers recommend adding more disks to the system. This doesn't always solve the problem because the bottleneck could be coming from a large request load on a relatively small number of disks. When this situation is detected, disk scheduling may be used as a means of improving performance and eliminating the bottleneck.

12.7.2 Level of Multiprogramming

The load on disks and the randomness of requests tend to increase with a greater degree of multiprogramming. Disk scheduling might not be useful in a batch processing system with a relatively low level of multiprogramming. Scheduling is often effective in a timesharing system with a moderate level of multiprogramming. Scheduling yields particularly significant improvements in a message switching system that handles thousands of requests.

12.7.3 Multiple Disk Subsystems

For economy and modularity, disk hardware is often built so that several physical disk units are managed by a single disk controller device. The controller, in turn, is connected to an input/output channel that ultimately transmits information from the disk unit to the central computer. One channel might support several disk controllers each of which might, in turn, support several disk drives (Fig. 12.10).

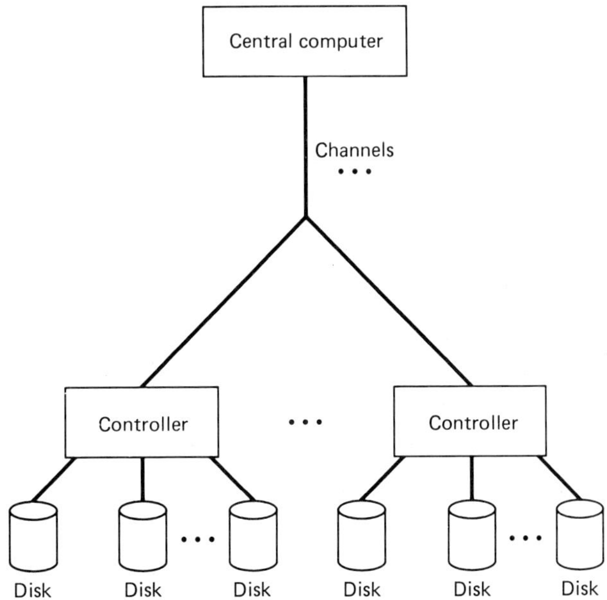

Fig. 12.10 Multiple disk subsystems.

Input/ouput channels are not connected directly to the disk units they service. This fact causes the designer to investigate a bottleneck further before deciding to incorporate disk scheduling. The bottleneck could be due to saturation of the controller or it could be caused by channel congestion. These situations can often be detected by performance monitoring software and hardware designed to measure channel and controller activity (see Chapter 14). If a controller becomes saturated, the designer may wish to rearrange the system configuration by reducing the number of disks on that controller. If the channel becomes congested, some of the devices and controllers on that channel might be moved to another channel, or an additional channel might be purchased. Thus *hardware reconfiguration* may be needed to eliminate certain bottlenecks.

To help reduce channel congestion, a technique called *rotational position sensing (RPS)* has been incorporated into many disk systems (Ib74). It reduces the time a channel is busy while searching for a record. When a record is requested, RPS allows the channel to be free until just before the record comes under the appropriate read–write head. RPS permits several requests to be active on a single channel at the same time, thereby increasing device utilization.

12.7.4 Nonuniform Request Distributions

Most of the analytical work in the literature assumes that request distributions are uniform. Conclusions drawn from this assumption may be invalid on many systems whose request distributions are not uniformly distributed over the disk surfaces. *Nonuniform request distributions* are very common in certain situations and their consequences have been investigated (Wi76) (Ly72).

One common cause of highly localized nonuniform request distributions is the use of large sequential files on dedicated disks. When an operating system allocates space for the adjacent records of a user's sequential file, it usually places adjacent records on the same track. When a track is full, additional records are placed on adjacent tracks within the same cylinder and, when a cylinder is full, additional records are placed on adjacent cylinders. Thus it is not uncommon for requests for successive records in a sequential file to cause no seeking at all. When needed, seeks are short because they are usually to immediately adjacent cylinders. Obviously, disk scheduling would be of little benefit in this situation. In particular, any overhead incurred in disk scheduling might actually result in degraded performance because scheduling is of no use here.

On some systems, when bad tracks are detected, alternate tracks are assigned. These alternates may be widely dispersed over the disk surfaces causing seeks where none might actually be expected.

12.7.5 File Organization Techniques

Sophisticated file organization techniques such as *ISAM (Index Sequential Access Method* (Ib74) can cause a proliferation of requests with large seek times. ISAM accesses can involve multiple disk references in servicing requests. In some cases, an ISAM record retrieval may involve reference to a master index, reference to a cylinder index, and then location of the actual record, a process that could encounter several seek delays. Because the master index and cylinder index are normally stored on disk (but away from the main data area), these seeks can be costly. ISAM is convenient for the applications designer but can be a real headache from an implementation and performance standpoint.

SUMMARY

Making effective use of disk storage is important in today's operating systems and will probably continue to be important throughout the next several decades. This chapter discussed the operation of moving-head magnetic disk storage, and considered techniques for optimizing the performance of disk devices in operating systems environments.

A disk access (read or write) consists of three significant actions, namely a seek, a rotational delay (latency), and record transmission. Of these, the largest by far is normally seek time. Therefore, optimization techniques generally concentrate on minimizing both the number and the length of seeks.

Arranging pending disk requests to minimize seeks is called disk scheduling. Requests may be serviced first-come-first-served (FCFS), which is generally not considered to be a scheduling strategy, or they may be serviced according to a strategy designed to minimize seeks. Some common strategies are

- SSTF that services requests according to their proximity to the last request serviced. The next request serviced is the one closest to the last request regardless of the direction in which the boom must move.
- SCAN functions like SSTF except that it continues moving in a preferred direction until all requests in that direction have been serviced; then it reverses direction.
- N-Step SCAN avoids delays and possibly indefinite postponement by forcing arriving requests to wait until the return sweep for service.
- C-SCAN eliminates SCAN's bias toward the mid-range tracks by scanning in one direction only; on the completion of a sweep, the boom jumps to the opposite end of the disk, and scanning in the same direction resumes.
- The Eschenbach scheme handles very heavy loads, but C-SCAN with rotational optimization has proven more effective under all loading conditions.

All of the strategies above are concerned with the following scheduling goals.

- maximizing throughput
- minimizing response times
- minimizing variance of response times

Rotational optimization is useful under heavy loading conditions when it is likely that several requests are pending for the same cylinder at any moment. On a drum, rotational optimization is used to schedule requests.

Disk scheduling isn't always useful because performance problems could be caused by other portions of the hardware or software. The bottlenecks could be at the disks, the controllers, or the channels. Or they could be caused by nonuniform request distributions such as those common in sequential file processing. Access methods like ISAM can be convenient for the applications designer but can require a large number of lengthy seeks as they function at run time.

TERMINOLOGY

access time
boom
channel
C-SCAN
cylinder
cylinder index
disk
disk controller
disk scheduling
disk surface
drum
Eschenbach scheme
FCFS
first-come-first-served
Index Sequential Access Method
input-output channel
ISAM
latency
latency optimization
load
localized seek pattern
master index
mean response time
moving-head magnetic disk
multiple-disk subsystem
nonuniform request distribution
N-step SCAN
predictability
preferred direction
primary storage
random seek pattern
rotational delay
rotational optimization
rotational position sensing
RPS
SCAN
seek
seek optimization
seek time
shortest-latency-time-first
shortest-seek-time-first
SLTF
spindle
SSTF
throughput
track
transmission time
uniform request distribution
variance in response times

EXERCISES

12.1 What are the essential goals of disk scheduling? Why is each important?

12.2 Suppose that on a particular model of disk drive, seek times approximate latency times. How might this affect a designer's choice to include disk scheduling on a computer system using drives of this type?

12.3 What makes a given disk scheduling discipline fair? Just how important is fairness compared to other goals of disk scheduling disciplines?

12.4 Disk scheduling disciplines that are not fair generally have a larger variance of response times than FCFS. Why is this true?

12.5 Under very light loading conditions, virtually all of the disk scheduling disciplines discussed in this chapter degenerate to which scheme? Why?

12.6 One criterion that influences the desirability of implementing disk scheduling is the run-time overhead of the disk scheduling mechanism. What factors contribute to this overhead? Suppose t is the average seek time on a system with FCFS disk scheduling. Suppose s is the approximate time it would take to schedule an average disk request if another form of disk scheduling were in use. Assume all other factors are favorable to incorporating disk scheduling on this system. For each of the following cases, comment on the potential effectiveness of incorporating disk scheduling on the system.

a) $s = 0.01t$
b) $s = 0.1t$
c) $s = t$
d) $s = 10t$
e) $s = 100t$

12.7 Latency optimization usually has little effect on system performance except under very heavy loads. Why?

12.8 On interactive systems it is essential to ensure reasonable response times to users. Minimizing the variance of response times is still an important goal, but it is not sufficient to prevent an occasional user from suffering indefinite postponement. What additional mechanism would you incorporate into a disk scheduling discipline on an interactive system to help ensure reasonable response times and to avoid the possibility of indefinite postponement.

12.9 Why is FCFS often not considered to be a scheduling discipline at all? Is there a scheme for servicing disk requests that we would be even less inclined to call disk scheduling than FCFS?

12.10 In what sense is SCAN fairer than SSTF? In what sense is C-SCAN fairer than SCAN?

12.11 Give a statistical argument for why FCFS offers a small variance of response times.

12.12 Argue why SSTF tends to favor mid-range tracks at the expense of innermost and outermost tracks.

12.13 It is possible that while a disk request for a particular cylinder is being serviced, another request for that cylinder will arrive. Some disk scheduling disciplines would service this new request immediately after processing the current request. Other disciplines preclude the servicing of the new request until the return sweep of the disk arm. What dangerous situation might occur in a disk scheduling discipline that allows immediate servicing of a new request for the same cylinder as the previous request?

12.14 Why does SCAN have a lower variance of response times than SSTF?

12.15 Compare the throughput of N-Step SCAN with that of SCAN.

12.16 Compare the throughput of C-SCAN with that of SCAN.

12.17 How does a latency optimization scheme operate?

12.18 A disk storage bottleneck may not always be removed by adding more disk drives. Why?

12.19 How does the level of multiprogramming affect the need for disk scheduling?

12.20 Suppose controller saturation is indicated. Might disk scheduling be useful? What other actions should be taken?

12.21 What actions should be taken to improve performance when channel congestion occurs?

12.22 Why is it desirable to assume uniform request distributions when considering disk scheduling disciplines? In what types of systems might you expect to observe relatively uniform request distributions?

12.23 Would disk scheduling be useful for a single user, dedicated disk in a sequential file processing application? Why?

12.24 In what circumstances might disk scheduling actually result in poorer performance than FCFS?

12.25 Compare the essential goals of disk scheduling with those of CPU scheduling. What are the similarities? What are the differences?

12.26 This chapter has concentrated on software solutions to the problem of improving performance on moving-head disk storage devices. Hardware redesign is rarely an option available to an operating systems designer, but suppose you have been given the opportunity to propose certain hardware changes to the operation of moving-head disk systems (for the benefit of future operating systems designers). What changes would you suggest? How would each of these changes affect the need for disk scheduling? If disk scheduling is still needed on your new style disks, would the disk scheduling policies discussed in this chapter be effective?

12.27 The availability of moving-head disk storage has contributed greatly to the success of modern computing systems. Disks offer relatively fast and direct access to enormous amounts of information. Industry prognosticators see a solid future for disk-based secondary storage systems and thus researchers continue developing new and improved disk scheduling disciplines. Propose several new disk scheduling schemes. Compare your schemes with those presented in this chapter.

LITERATURE

(Ab68) Abate, J.; H. Dubner; and S. B. Weinberg, "Queueing Analysis of the IBM 2314 Disk Storage Facility," *JACM*, Vol. 15, No. 4, 1968, pp. 557–589.

(Ab69) Abate, J., and H. Dubner, "Optimizing the Performance of a Drumlike Storage," *IEEE Trans. on Computers*, Vol. C-18, No. 11, 1969, pp. 992–996.

(Co68) Coffman, E. G., Jr., and A. C. McKeller, "On the Motion of an Unbounded Markov Queue in Random Access Storage," *IEEE Trans. on Computers*, Vol. C-17, No. 6, 1968, pp. 600–603.

(Co69) Coffman, E. G. Jr., "Analysis of a Drum Input/Output Queue under Scheduling Operation in a Paged Computer System," *JACM*, Vol. 16, No. 1, January 1969, pp. 73–90.

(De67) Denning, P. J., "Effects of Scheduling on File Memory Operations," *Proc. AFIPS, SJCC*, Vol. 30, 1967, pp. 9–21.

(Fi65) Fife, D. W., and J. L. Smith, "Transmission Capacity of Disk Storage Systems with Concurrent Arm Positioning," *IEEE Trans. on Computers,* Vol. EC-14, No. 8, August 1965, pp. 575–582.

(Fr69) Frank, H., "Analysis and Optimization of Disk Storage Devices for Time-Sharing Systems," *JACM,* Vol. 16, No. 4, 1969, pp. 602–620.

(Fu72) Fuller, S. H., "An Optimal Drum Scheduling Algorithm," *IEEE Trans. on Computers,* Vol. C-21, No. 11, 1972, pp. 1153–1165.

(Fu74) Fuller, S. H., "Minimal-Total-Processing-Time Drum and Disk Scheduling Disciplines," *CACM,* Vol. 17, No. 7, July 1974, pp. 376–381.

(Go73) Gotlieb, C. C., and G. H. MacEwen, "Performance of Movable-Head Disk Storage Devices," *JACM,* Vol. 20, No. 4, 1973, pp. 604–623.

(Ha74) Haughton, K., "Design Considerations of the IBM 3340 Disk File," *Proc. IEEE Comp. Sci. Conf.*, 1974, pp. 281–283.

(Ho80) Hofri, M., "Disk Scheduling: FCFS vs. SSTF Revisited," *CACM,* Vol. 23, No. 11, November 1980, pp. 645–653.

(Ib74) *Introduction to IBM/360 Direct Access Storage Devices and Organization Methods,* White Plains, N. Y.: GC20-1649-8 IBM Data Processing Division, 1974.

(Ko78) Kollias, J. G., "An Estimate of Seek Time for Batched Searching of Random or Indexed Sequential Structured Files," *Comp. Jour.*, Vol. 21, No. 2, 1978, pp. 132–133.

(Ly72) Lynch, W. L., "Do Disk Arms Move?" *Performance Evaluation Review, ACM Sigmetrics Newsletter,* Vol. 1, December 1972, pp. 3–16.

(Pe80) Perros, H. G., "A Regression Model for Predicting the Response Time of a Disc I/O System," *Comp. Jour.*, Vol. 23, No. 1, 1980, pp. 34–36.

(Se69) Seaman, P. H.; R. A. Lind; and T. L. Wilson, "An Analysis of Auxiliary-Storage Activity," *IBM Systems Journal,* Vol. 5, No. 3, 1969, pp. 158–170.

(Sm73) Smith, A., "A Performance Analysis of Multiple Channel Controllers," *Proc. First Annual SIGME Symposium of Measurement and Evaluation,* February 1973, pp. 37–46.

(Sm75) Smith, A., "A Locality Model for Disk Reference Patterns," *Proc. Tenth IEEE Comp. Science Conf.*, 1975, pp. 109–112.

(Sm78) Smith, A., "On the Effectiveness of Buffered and Multiple Arm Disks," *Proc. Fifth Symp. on Computer Architecture,* 1978, pp. 242–248.

(St73) Stone, H. S., and S. H. Fuller, "On the Near Optimality of the Shortest-Latency-Time-First Drum Scheduling Discipline," *CACM,* Vol. 16, No. 6, 1973, pp. 352–353.

(Te72) Teorey, T. J., "Properties of Disk Scheduling Policies in Multiprogrammed Computer Systems," *Proc. AFIPS, FJCC,* Vol. 41, 1972, pp. 1–11.

(Te72a) Teorey, T. J., and T. B. Pinkerton, "A Comparative Analysis of Disk Scheduling Policies," *CACM,* Vol. 15, No. 3, 1972, pp. 177–184.

(To80) Tokunaga, T.; Y. Hirai; and S. Yamamoto, "Integrated Disk Cache System with File Adaptive Control," *Proc. Distributed Computing Compcon,* Fall 1980, pp. 412–416.

(Wa73) Waters, S. J., "Estimating Magnetic Disc Seeks," *Comp. Jour.*, Vol. 18, No. 1, 1973, pp. 12–18.

(We66) Weingarten, A., "The Eschenbach Drum Scheme," *CACM,* Vol. 9, No. 7, 1966, pp. 509–512.

(We68) Weingarten, A., "The Analytical Design of Real-Time Disk Systems," *Proc. IFIPS Congr.*, 1968, pp. D131–D137.

(We79) Welch, T. A., "Analysis of Memory Hierarchies for Sequential Data Access," *IEEE Computer,* Vol. 12, No. 5, May 1979, pp. 19–26.

(Wi76) Wilhelm, N. C., "An Anomaly in Disk Scheduling: A Comparison of FCFS and SSTF Seek Scheduling Using an Empirical Model for Disk Accesses," *CACM,* Vol. 19, No. 1, January 1976, pp. 13–17.

(Wo80) Wong, C. K., "Minimizing Expected Head Movement in One-Dimensional and Two-Dimensional Mass Storage Systems," *ACM Computing Surveys,* Vol. 12, No. 2, 1980, pp. 167–178.

13
File and Database Systems

Remember thee!
Ay, thou poor ghost, while memory holds a seat
In this distracted globe. Remember thee!
Yea, from the table of my memory
I'll wipe away all trivial fond records,
All saws of books, all forms, all pressures past,
That youth and observation copied there.

Hamlet, I : v : 95
William Shakespeare

I can only assume that a "Do Not File" document is filed in a "Do Not File" file.

Senator Frank Church
Senate Intelligence Subcommittee Hearing,
1975

Outline

13.1 INTRODUCTION

A *file* is a named collection of data. It normally resides on a secondary storage device such as disk or tape. It may be manipulated as a unit by operations such as

- *open*—Prepare a file to be referenced.
- *close*—Prevent further reference to a file until it is reopened.
- *create*—Build a new file.
- *destroy*—Remove a file.
- *copy*—Create another version of the file with a new name.
- *rename*—Change the name of a file.
- *list*—Print or display the contents of a file.

Individual data items within the file may be manipulated by operations like

- *read*—Input a data item to a process from a file.
- *write*—Output a data item from a process to a file.
- *update*—Modify an existing data item.
- *insert*—Add a new data item.
- *delete*—Remove a data item from a file.

The *file system* is that portion of the overall storage management system primarily responsible for managing files on secondary storage. It is responsible for providing the means for *private storage* of information and for *sharing* of information among users in a controlled manner.

13.2 FILE SYSTEM FUNCTIONS

Some of the functions normally attributed to file systems follow.

(1) Users should be able to create, modify, and delete files.

(2) Users should be able to share each other's files in a carefully controlled manner in order to build upon each other's work.

(3) The mechanism for sharing files should provide various types of controlled access such as *read access, write access, execute access* or various combinations of these.

(4) Users should be able to structure their files in a manner most appropriate for each application.

(5) Users should be able to order the transfer of information between files.

(6) *Backup* and *recovery* capabilities must be provided to prevent against either accidental loss or malicious destruction of information.

(7) Users should be able to refer to their files by *symbolic names* rather than having to use *physical device names* (i.e., *device independence*).

(8) In sensitive environments in which information must be kept secure and private, such as in electronic funds transfer systems, criminal records systems, medical records systems, etc., the file system may also provide *encryption* and *decryption* capabilities. This makes information useful only to its intended audience (i.e., to those who possess the *decryption keys*).

(9) Most important, the file system should provide a user-friendly interface. It should give users a *logical view* of their data and the functions to be performed upon it rather than a *physical view*. The user should not have to be concerned with the particular devices on which data is stored, the form the data takes on those devices, or the physical means of transferring data to and from those devices.

13.3 THE DATA HIERARCHY

All data handled by computers is comprised of *bits*, the binary digits 0 and 1. A single bit can be set to 0 or 1 and thus is capable only of distinguishing between two entities, for example "true" or "false," or perhaps "green" or "blue." Bits are grouped together in *bit patterns* to represent virtually all data items of interest in computer systems. There are 2^n possible bit patterns for a string of n bits.

The next level up in the data hierarchy is comprised of *bytes* or *characters*, which are fixed length patterns of bits. Most computer systems today use 8-bit bytes, and thus can have 2^8 or 256 possible characters represented in their *character sets*. A *numeric character* may be any of the digits 0 through 9. An *alphabetic character* may be any of the letters of the alphabet: A–Z (the uppercase letters) or a–z (the lowercase letters). Blanks are normally treated as alphabetic characters. A *special character* is virtually any other character in the computer's character set such as the dollar sign ($), colon (:), slash (/), asterisk (*), etc.

It is sometimes useful to refer to the left or right portion of a byte. The left half of a byte is called the *left nibble*; the right half is the *right nibble* (honestly!).

The assignment of bit patterns to the characters they represent is called a *character set*. The two most popular character sets in use today are *ASCII (American Standard Code for Information Interchange)*, and *EBCDIC (Extended Binary Coded Decimal Interchange Code)*. ASCII is particularly popular in data communication systems. EBCDIC is popular for representing data internally in computer systems. Both representations are so widely used that many systems contain mechanisms to use both codes and convert freely between them.

A *field* is a group of related characters. A *numeric field* contains only digits. An *alphabetic field* contains only letters and blanks (the blank being a perfectly legitimate character in the character set). An *alphanumeric field* contains only digits, letters, and blanks. A field containing any special characters is simply called a *character field*. For example, "365" is a numeric field, "SAM JONES" is an alphabetic field, "15 WINDSOR DRIVE" is an alphanumeric field, and "$367.19" is a character field.

A *record* is a group of related fields. A student record may contain, for example, separate fields for identification number, name, address, telephone number, cumulative grade point average, major field of study, expected date of graduation, etc. A *record key* is a control field that uniquely identifies the record. In a payroll application, for example, the record key might be the employee number.

A *file* is a group of related records. For example, a student file might contain one record for each student in a university, an inventory file might contain one record for each different item sold by an automotive parts distributor, and an accounts receivable file might contain one record for each different customer of a company.

The highest level of the data hierarchy is often called a *database.* A database consists of a group of related files. Database systems are considered in detail later in this chapter.

13.4 BLOCKING AND BUFFERING

A *physical record* or *block* is the unit of information actually read from or written to a device. A *logical record* is a collection of data treated as a unit from the user's standpoint. When each physical record contains exactly one logical record, the file is said to consist of *unblocked records.* When each physical record may contain several logical records, the file is said to consist of *blocked records.* In a file with *fixed-length records,* all records are the same length; the blocksize is ordinarily an integral multiple of the record size. In a file with *variable-length records,* records may vary in size up to the blocksize. Figure 13.1 shows some common record formats.

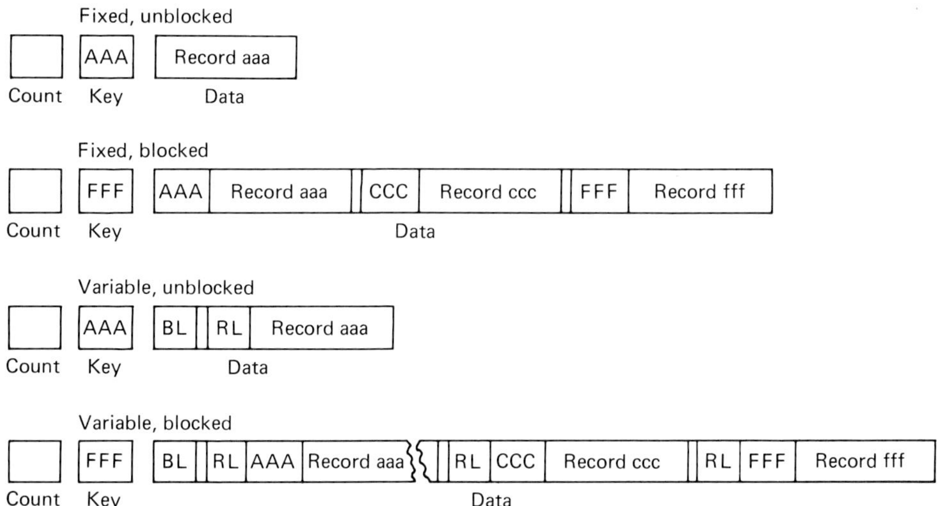

Fig. 13.1 Record formats. BL is block length. RL is record length. Count contains various control information such as cylinder number, head number, record number, length of data position of record, and error control bytes. (Courtesy of International Business Machines Corporation.)

Buffering allows computation to proceed in parallel with input/output. Spaces are provided in primary storage to hold several physical blocks of a file at once—each of these spaces is called a *buffer.* The most common scheme is called *double buffering* and it operates as follows (for output). There are two buffers. Initially, records generated by a running process are deposited in the first buffer until it is full. The transfer of the block in the first buffer to secondary storage is then initiated. While this transfer is in progress, the process continues generating records that are deposited in the second buffer. When the second buffer is full, and when the transfer from the first buffer is complete, transfer from the second buffer is initiated. The process continues generating records that are now deposited in the first buffer. This "flip-flopping" between the buffers allows input/output to occur in parallel with a process's computations.

13.5 FILE ORGANIZATION

File organization refers to the manner in which the records of a file are arranged on secondary storage. The most popular file organization schemes in use today follow.

- *Sequential*—Records are placed in physical order. The "next" record is the one that physically follows the previous record. This organization is used for files stored on magnetic tape, paper tape, punched cards, and printed output—all inherently sequential media. Disk files may also be sequentially organized.
- *Indexed sequential*—Records are arranged in logical sequence according to a key contained in each record. The system maintains an index containing the physical addresses of certain principal records. Indexed sequential records may be accessed sequentially in key order, or they may be accessed directly, by a search through the system-created index. Indexed sequential files are normally stored on disk.
- *Direct*—Records are directly (randomly) accessed by their physical addresses on a direct access storage device (DASD). The applications user places the records on the DASD in any order appropriate for a particular application. Direct files require that the applications user be familiar with the detailed physical organization of the DASDs upon which the files are stored.
- *Partitioned*—This is essentially a file of sequential subfiles (Fig. 13.2). Each sequential subfile is called a *member.* The starting address of each member is stored in the file's *directory.* Partitioned files are often used to store program libraries or macro libraries.

There are many variations of the above file organizations in common use.

The term *volume* is used to refer to the recording medium for each particular auxiliary storage device. The volume used on a tape drive is a reel of magnetic tape. The volume used on a disk drive is a disk pack.

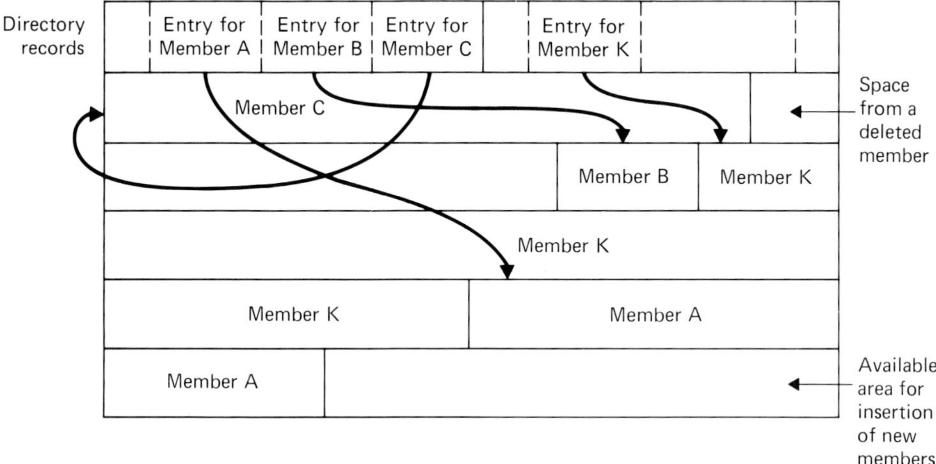

Fig. 13.2 Partitioned data set. (Courtesy of International Business Machines Corporation.)

13.6 QUEUED AND BASIC ACCESS METHODS

Large operating systems generally provide many *access methods*. These are sometimes grouped into two categories, namely *queued access methods* and *basic access methods*. The queued methods provide more powerful capabilities than the basic methods.

Queued access methods are used when the sequence in which records are to be processed can be anticipated, such as in sequential and indexed sequential accessing. The queued methods perform anticipatory buffering and scheduling of I/O operations. They try to have the next record available for processing as soon as the previous record has been processed. More than one record at a time is maintained in primary storage; this allows processing and I/O operations to be overlapped. The queued access methods also perform automatic blocking and deblocking so the user need not be concerned with these chores.

The basic access methods are normally used when the sequence in which records are to be processed cannot be anticipated, particularly with direct accessing. Also there are many situations in which user applications want to control record accesses without incurring the overhead of the queued methods. In the basic methods, the access method reads and writes physical blocks; blocking and deblocking (if appropriate to the application) is performed by the user.

13.7 FILE CHARACTERISTICS

Files may be characterized by

- *Volatility*—This refers to the frequency with which additions and deletions are made to a file. When this frequency is low, the file is called a *static file*; when the frequency is high, the file is called a *volatile file.*

- *Activity*—This refers to the percentage of a file's records processed on a given run.
- *Size*—This refers to the amount of information stored in the file.

13.8 THE FILE SYSTEM

An important component of an operating system is the *file system.* File systems generally contain

- *Access methods*—These are concerned with the manner in which data stored in files is accessed.
- *File management*—This is concerned with providing the mechanisms for files to be stored, referenced, shared, and secured.
- *Auxiliary storage management*—This is concerned with allocating space for files on secondary storage devices.
- *File integrity*—This is concerned with guaranteeing that the information in a file is uncorrupted. When file integrity is assured, whatever information is supposed to be in a file is there; information not supposed to be in a file is kept out of the file.

The file system is primarily concerned with managing secondary storage space, particularly disk storage. For the purposes of this discussion, let us assume an environment of a large-scale timesharing system supporting approximately 100 active terminals accessible to a user community of several thousand users. Each of these users may have several *accounts* on the computer which they use to distinguish work performed perhaps for various *projects.* Each of these accounts may have many files. Some files might be very small, such as a letter to be sent in an electronic mail system, for example. Other files may be large, such as a master list of parts in an inventory control application.

On large-scale timesharing systems, it is common for user accounts to contain between ten and 100 files. Thus with a user community of several thousand users the system's disks might easily contain 50,000 to 100,000 or more separate files. These files need to be accessed quickly to keep response times small.

A file system for this type of environment may be organized as follows (Fig. 13.3). A *root* is used to indicate where on disk the *root directory* begins. The root directory points to the various *user directories.* A user directory contains an entry for each of a user's files; each entry points to where the corresponding file is stored on disk.

File names need only be unique within a given user directory. The system name of a file, however, must be unique within the file system. In hierarchically structured file systems, the system name of a file is usually formed as the *pathname* from the root directory to the file. For example, in a two-level file system with users SMITH,

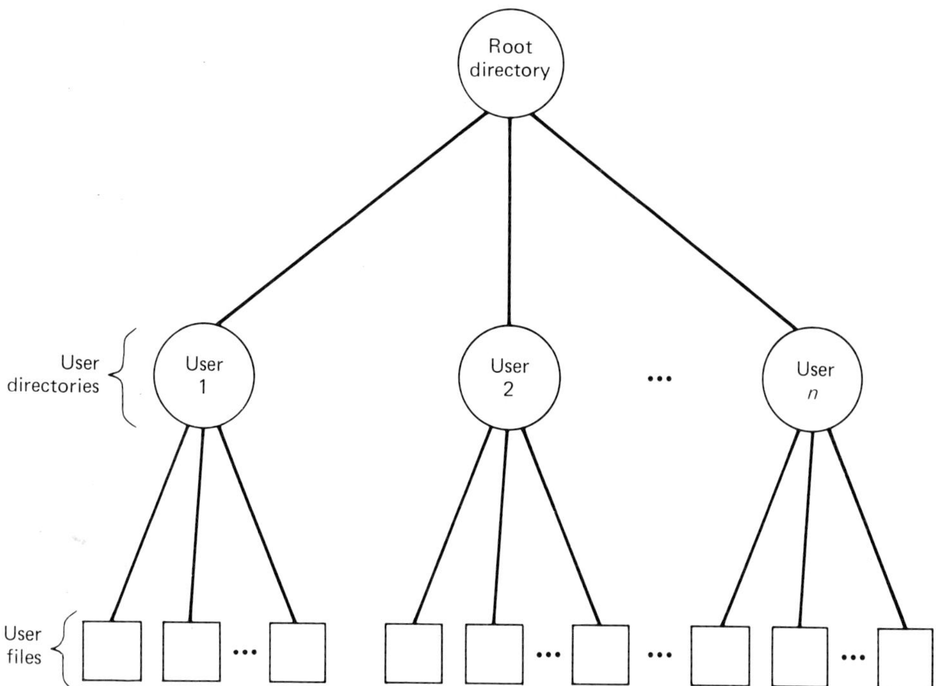

Fig. 13.3 Two-level file system.

JONES, and DOE, and in which JONES has files PAYROLL and INVOICES, the pathname for file PAYROLL might be formed as JONES : PAYROLL. Several file system structures are considered in depth in the case studies (Chapters 18–22).

13.9 ALLOCATING AND FREEING SPACE

The problem of allocating and freeing space on disks is somewhat like that experienced in primary storage allocation under variable partition multiprogramming. If it is desired to keep files in adjacent areas of the disk, then such areas need to be collected. But as files are allocated and freed it is common for the space on disk to become increasingly *fragmented.* Thus any further allocation causes files to be spread throughout widely dispersed blocks.

One technique for alleviating this problem is to perform periodic *compaction* or *garbage collection.* Files may be reorganized to occupy adjacent areas of the disk, and free areas may be collected into a single block or a group of large blocks. This garbage collection is often done during the off-hours when the system can be shut down. Some systems perform it dynamically while they continue operation. The system may choose to reorganize the files of users not currently logged in, or it may reorganize files that have not been referenced for a long time.

It may not be useful to perform garbage collection on certain systems, particularly those in which a single disk contains the files of hundreds of users. Each time a user process issues an I/O request, that process loses the processor to another process; this process may in turn issue an I/O causing a seek to a distant track on that disk. So even if successive references to data on a file are to adjacent areas on the disk, long seeks may still be necessary as the system switches between processes.

Designing a file system requires knowledge of the user community including the number of users, the average number of files per user, the average duration of user sessions, the nature of applications to be run on the system, and many other factors. These factors must be carefully considered to determine the most appropriate file organizations and directory structures.

The same locality concept we considered in virtual storage systems leads us, however, to try to store all of the data in a file contiguously. Users searching a file for information often use *file scan* options to locate the next record or the previous record. These scans should result in minimal seek activity.

In paged systems, the smallest amount of information transferred between secondary and primary storage is a page, so it makes sense to allocate secondary storage in blocks of the page size or a multiple of the page size. Locality tells us that once a process has referred to a data item on a page it is likely to reference additional data items on that page; it is also likely to reference data items on pages contiguous to that page in the user's virtual address space. Therefore it is desirable to store the logically contiguous pages of a user's virtual storage as physically contiguous pages on secondary storage.

13.9.1 Contiguous Allocation

In *contiguous allocation*, files are assigned to contiguous areas of secondary storage. A user specifies in advance the size of the area needed to hold a file to be created. If the desired amount of contiguous space is not available, the file cannot be created.

One advantage of contiguous allocation is that successive logical records are normally physically adjacent to one another. This speeds access compared to systems in which successive logical records are dispersed throughout the disk.

The file directories in contiguous allocation systems are relatively straightforward to implement. For each file it is necessary merely to retain the address of the start of the file and the file's length.

Contiguous allocation does have certain disadvantages. As files are deleted, the space they occupied on secondary storage is reclaimed. This space becomes available for allocation of new files, but these new files must fit in the available holes. Thus contiguous allocation schemes exhibit the same types of fragmentation problems inherent in variable partition multiprogramming systems—adjacent secondary storage holes must be coalesced, and periodic compaction may need to be performed to reclaim storage areas large enough to hold new files.

In environments in which files may grow and shrink over time, contiguous allocation can be difficult. To provide for anticipated expansion, users often overestimate their space needs. This causes considerable waste. When a file grows larger than its allocated slot in secondary storage, the file must be transferred to a new area large enough to hold it.

13.9.2 Noncontiguous Allocation

Because files do tend either to grow or shrink over time, and because users rarely know in advance how large their files will be, contiguous storage allocation systems are being replaced by more dynamic noncontiguous storage allocation systems. Several schemes are used to facilitate noncontiguous storage allocation.

13.9.2.1 Sector-Oriented Linked Allocation

The disk is viewed as consisting of individual sectors. Files consist of many sectors which may be dispersed throughout the disk. Sectors belonging to a common file contain pointers to one another forming a linked list. A *free space list* contains entries for all free sectors on the disk.

When a file needs to grow, the process requests more sectors from the free space list. Files that shrink return sectors to the free space list. There is no need for compaction.

Noncontiguous allocation solves some of the problems inherent in contiguous allocation schemes, but it has its own drawbacks. Because the records of a file may be dispersed throughout the disk, retrieval of logically contiguous records can involve lengthy seeks. There is execution time overhead in maintaining the linked list structure. Pointers in the list structure reduce the amount of space available for file data.

13.9.2.2 Block Allocation

One scheme which is used to manage secondary storage more efficiently and reduce execution time overhead is called *block allocation.* This is a mixture of both contiguous allocation and noncontiguous allocation methods.

In this scheme, instead of allocating individual sectors, blocks of contiguous sectors (sometimes called *extents*) are allocated. The system tries to allocate new blocks to a file by choosing free blocks as close as possible to existing blocks of the file. Each access to the file involves determining the appropriate block and then the appropriate sector within the block.

There are several common ways of implementing block allocation systems. These include *block chaining, index block chaining,* and *block-oriented file mapping.*

In block chaining (Fig. 13.4), entries in the user directory point to the first block of each file. The fixed-length blocks comprising a file each contain two portions: a data block, and a pointer to the next block. The smallest unit of allocation is a fixed-sized block that ordinarily consists of many sectors. It is common to make

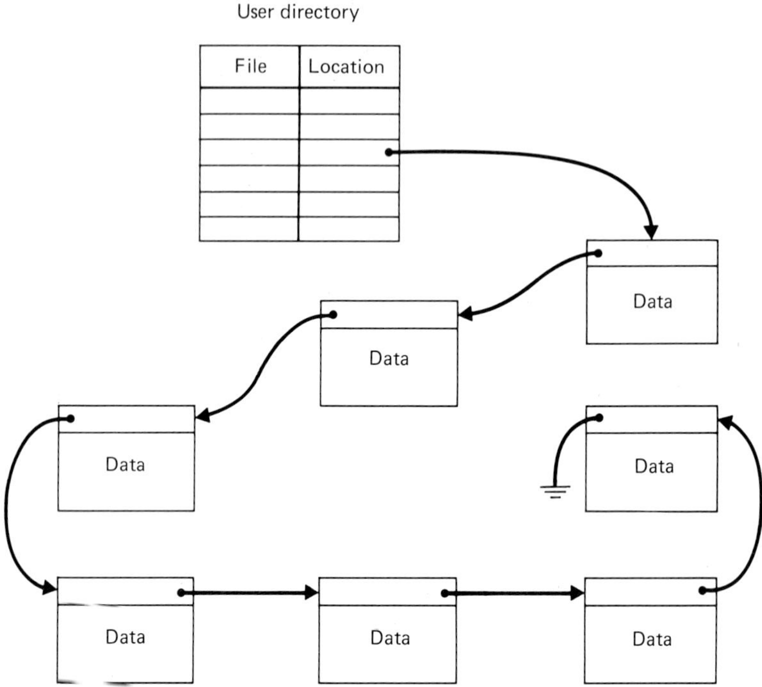

Fig. 13.4 Block chaining.

the block size one full track on a disk. Locating a particular record requires searching the block chain until the appropriate block is found, and then searching that block until the appropriate record is found. The chain must be searched from the beginning, and if the blocks are dispersed throughout the disk (which is normal), then the search process can be slow as block-to-block seeks occur. Insertion and deletion are straightforward, however. They are done by modifying the pointers in the previous block. Some systems use doubly linked lists to facilitate searching; the blocks are threaded both forwards and backwards so that a search may proceed in either direction.

With *index block chaining* (Fig. 13.5), the pointers are placed into separate index blocks. Each index block contains a fixed number of items. Each entry contains a record identifier and a pointer to that record. If more than one index block is needed to describe a file, then a series of index blocks is chained together. The big advantage of index block chaining over simple block chaining is that searching may take place in the index blocks themselves. The index blocks may be kept close together in secondary storage to minimize seeking. On some systems in which very rapid searching is needed, the index blocks can be maintained in primary storage. Once the appropriate record is located via the index blocks, the data block contain-

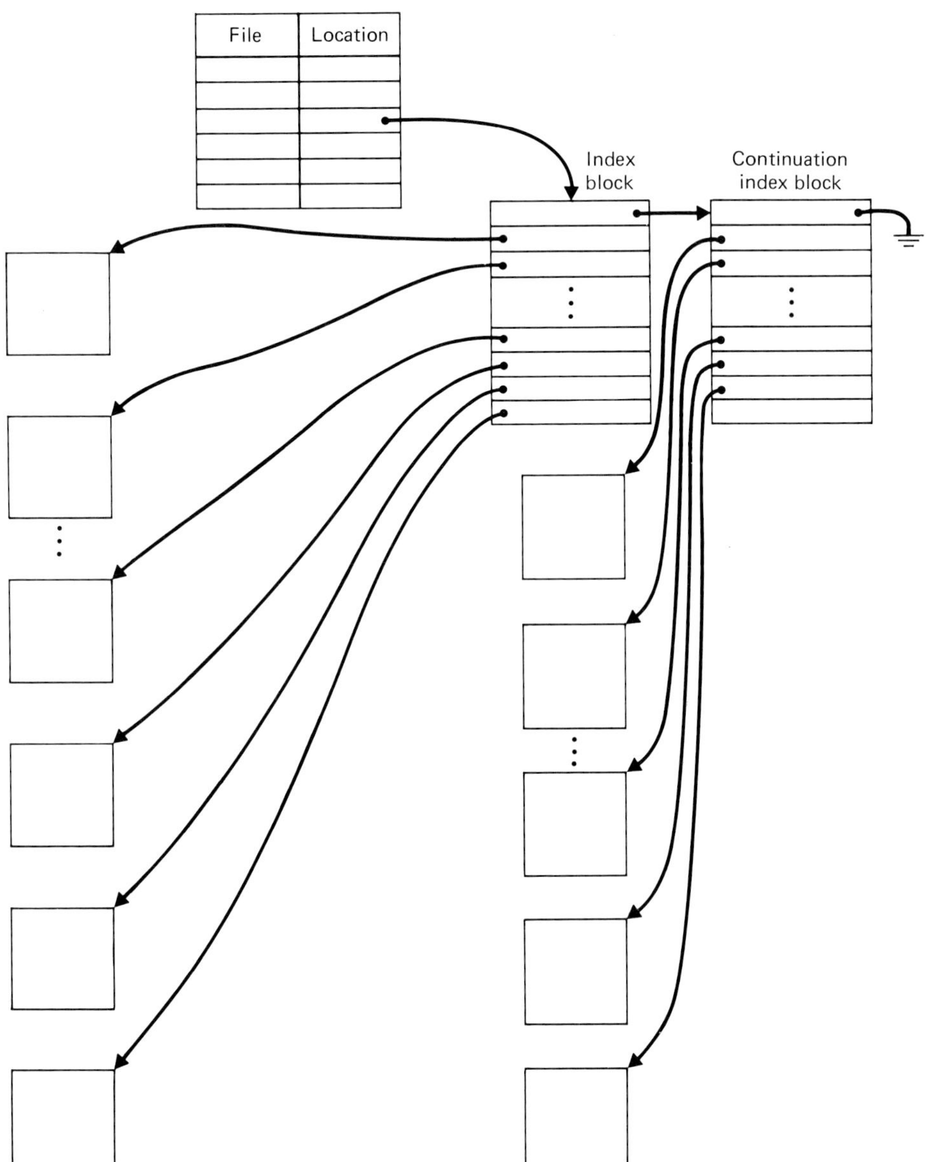

Fig. 13.5 Index block chaining.

ing that record is read into primary storage. The disadvantage of this scheme is that insertions can require the complete reconstruction of the index blocks. Some systems leave a certain portion of the index blocks empty to provide for future insertions, but once this space is exhausted, extensive reconstruction of the index block structure may be necessary.

In *block-oriented file mapping* (Fig. 13.6), instead of using pointers, the system uses block numbers. Normally, these are easily converted to actual block addresses because of the geometry of the disk. A file map is maintained containing one entry for every block on the disk. Entries in the user directory point to the first entry in the file map for each file. Each entry in the file map contains the block number of the next block in that file. Thus all of the blocks in a file may be located by following the entries in the file map.

The entry in the file map that corresponds to the last entry of a particular file is set to some sentinel value like "Nil" to indicate that the last block of a file has been reached. Some of the entries in the file map are set to "Free" to indicate that the block is available for allocation. The system may either search the file map linearly to locate a free block, or a free block list can be maintained. The file map can be modified to include record identifiers so that searching can be confined to the map for the most part. *The real advantage of this scheme is that the physical adjacencies on the disk are reflected in the file map.* When a new block is to be assigned, it is relatively easy to locate a free storage block with good proximity to the other blocks of the file. Insertions and deletions are straightforward in this scheme.

13.10 FILE DESCRIPTOR

A *file descriptor* or *file control block* is a control block containing information the system needs to manage a file. It is a highly system-dependent structure. A typical file descriptor might include

- symbolic file name
- location of file in secondary storage
- file organization (sequential, indexed sequential, etc.)
- device type
- access control data
- type (data file, object program, BASIC Source program, etc.)
- disposition (permanent vs. temporary)
- creation date and time
- destroy date
- date and time last modified
- access activity counts (number of reads, for example)

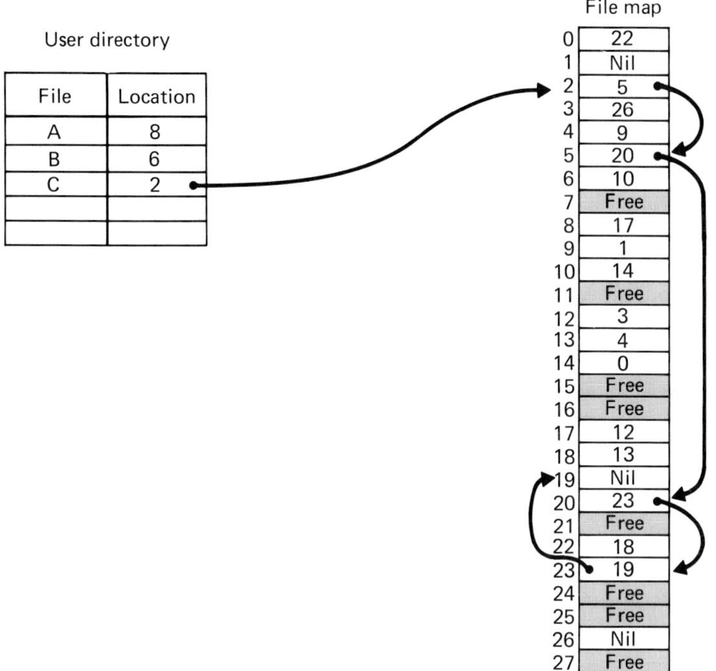

Physical blocks on secondary storage

Block 0 B(4)	Block 1 B(10)	Block 2 C(1)	Block 3 A(4)	Block 4 B(8)	Block 5 C(2)	Block 6 B(1)
Block 7 Free	Block 8 A(1)	Block 9 B(9)	Block 10 B(2)	Block 11 Free	Block 12 A(3)	Block 13 B(7)
Block 14 B(3)	Block 15 Free	Block 16 Free	Block 17 A(2)	Block 18 B(6)	Block 19 C(5)	Block 20 C(3)
Block 21 Free	Block 22 B(5)	Block 23 C(4)	Block 24 Free	Block 25 Free	Block 26 A(5)	Block 27 Free

Fig. 13.6 Block-oriented file mapping.

Ordinarily, file descriptors are maintained on secondary storage. They are brought to primary storage when a file is opened. The file descriptor is controlled by the file system—the user may not reference it directly.

13.11 ACCESS CONTROL MATRIX

One way to control access to files is to create a two-dimensional *access control matrix* (Fig. 13.7) listing all the users and all the files in the system. The entry Aij is 1 if user i is allowed access to file j; otherwise Aij = 0. In an installation with a large number of users and a large number of files, this matrix would be very large—and also very sparse. Allowing one user access to another user's files is the exception rather than the rule. To make such a matrix concept useful, it would be necessary to use codes to indicate various kinds of access such as readonly, writeonly, executeonly, readwrite, etc.

User \ File	1	2	3	4	5	6	7	8	9	10
1	1	1	0	0	0	0	0	0	0	0
2	0	0	1	0	1	0	0	0	0	0
3	0	1	0	1	0	1	0	0	0	0
4	1	0	0	0	0	0	0	0	0	0
5	1	1	1	1	1	1	1	1	1	1
6	0	0	0	0	0	1	1	0	0	0
7	1	0	0	0	0	0	0	0	0	1
8	1	0	0	0	0	0	0	0	0	0
9	1	1	1	1	0	0	0	0	1	1
10	1	1	0	0	1	1	0	0	0	1

Fig. 13.7 Access control matrix.

13.12 ACCESS CONTROL BY USER CLASSES

An access control matrix can become so large as to be impractical to maintain. A technique that requires considerably less space is to control access to various *user classes.* A common classification scheme is

- *Owner*—Normally, this is the user who created the file.
- *Specified user*—The owner specifies that another individual may use the file.

- *Group* or *project*—Users are often members of a group working on a particular project. In this case the various members of the group may all be granted access to each other's project-related files.
- *Public*—Most systems allow a file to be designated as public so that it may be accessed by any member of the system's user community. Public access normally allows users to read or execute a file, but writing is prohibited.

Chapter 17 discusses capabilities and object-oriented systems. These notions provide additional solutions to the access control problem.

13.13 BACKUP AND RECOVERY

Disks do crash, lightning does strike, power surges do occur, fires and floods happen, theft is more common than most companies are willing to admit, and vandalism (even terrorism) cannot be ignored. The point is that destruction of information, either accidental or intentional, does occur. Operating systems in general, and file systems in particular, must be designed with this in mind.

Physical safeguards can be used to prevent unauthorized access to the computer room, to filter power surges, and to turn on sprinklers in case of fire. But a simple disk head crash in which the read-write head comes in contact with the surface of the disk and scratches it can still destroy the usefulness of a disk pack.

The most common technique used to ensure the continued availability of data is to do *periodic backups*, i.e., to make one or more copies of the system's files regularly and put them in a safe place. Even periodic backups may not be sufficient, however, because all updates to a file since the last backup may be lost.

Another technique is to *log all transactions to a file* by copying them to another disk. This *redundancy* can be costly, but in case of failure, all of the lost work may be reconstructed (assuming of course that the *logging disk* isn't also destroyed).

There is no way to guarantee absolute security of files, (or anything else, for that matter). Designers must provide reasonable backup facilities that do not degrade the performance of the system, and whose costs are within the economics of the installation. In situations in which the integrity of the data must be guaranteed with very high reliability, the designers may have no choice but to use an expensive and time-consuming backup procedure. In the worst case, users would have to reconstruct all of their transactions since the last backup.

The periodic backup scheme has several weaknesses.

- The system may need to be shut down during the backup operation.
- File systems can be enormous; complete backups could require many hours.
- When a failure occurs, recovery from the last dump can be time-consuming. When it is complete, it is only current through the time of the dump. Any transactions since that time are lost.

A benefit of periodic backups is that the file system can be reorganized to allow the various blocks of user files scattered throughout the disks to be placed contiguously. This usually results in much faster access to user files when the system is restarted.

Periodic dumping of the entire file system is not sufficient in systems in which recovery needs to occur quickly and be up to the minute. A more appropriate technique is called *incremental dumping.* During a terminal session, all updated files are marked. When a user logs out, a list of these files can be passed to a system process which then dumps all modified files.

Incremental dumping is not of much use to the user in the midst of a lengthy terminal session when a system crash occurs. A better technique is to search the file directories even while a user is logged in and dump modified files more frequently.

All of the techniques discussed so far suffer from the fact that there may be significant activity between the time of the last backup and the time at which a failure occurs. In systems in which even the slightest loss of activity is unacceptable, a *transaction logging* approach may be appropriate. Here, every transaction is immediately backed up as it is occurs. This intense level of backup is somewhat easier to do in interactive systems in which activity is limited by relatively slow human response times. Even systems supporting hundreds of online interactive users can easily log every line typed at the terminals, so presumably such systems could be backed up to be quite current. But interactive commands could initiate substantial processing; substantial reconstruction time might still be required to perform the necessary recovery procedures.

13.14 DATABASE SYSTEMS

The availability of inexpensive massive direct access secondary storage has caused a tremendous amount of research and development activity in the area of database systems. Information is among any organization's most precious assets. A *database* is an integrated collection of data which is centrally controlled; a *database system* involves the data itself, the hardware on which the data resides, the software (called a *database management system* or DBMS) that controls the storing and retrieval of data, and the users themselves.

13.14.1 Advantages of Database Systems

Date (Da81) lists several important advantages of database systems.

- Redundancy can be reduced.
- Inconsistency can be avoided.
- The data can be shared.
- Standards can be enforced.
- Security restrictions can be applied.

- Integrity can be maintained.
- Conflicting requirements can be balanced.

In conventional *nondatabase* systems, each distinct application maintains its own files, often with considerable redundancy and a variety of physical formats. In database systems redundancy is considerably reduced by integrating separate files.

By reducing redundancy, the inconsistencies inherent in maintaining multiple copies of data can be reduced or avoided. There is less chance that two entries will disagree.

Sharing is one of the most important benefits of database systems. Existing applications can reference the same data; new applications can reference existing data.

Centralized control makes it possible to enforce standards rigidly. This becomes particularly important in computer networks (Chapter 16) in which data migration between systems occurs.

Security is an intriguing issue in database systems. The data may actually be more at risk because it is collected and retained in a central location rather than being dispersed throughout physically separate files in possibly many locations. To counter this, database systems must be designed with elaborate controls.

The integrity of data can be controlled better in a database environment, and in fact it *must* be; sharing implies that the effects of inaccurate and incomplete data would propagate quickly throughout the user organization.

The centralized control inherent in the database approach makes it possible to balance conflicting requirements. The database environment is geared to the needs of the entire organization. Conflicting needs of different applications can be dealt with in a context in which the total picture remains in view.

13.14.2 Data Independence

One of the most important aspects of database systems is *data independence*, i.e., applications need not be concerned with how the data is physically stored or accessed. An application is said to be *data-dependent* if the storage structure and accessing strategy cannot be changed without affecting the application significantly.

In database systems, data independence makes it convenient for different applications to have different views of the same data. From the system's standpoint, data independence makes it possible for the storage structure and accessing strategy to be modified in response to the installation's changing requirements, but without the need to modify functioning applications.

13.14.3 Database Languages

Users access a database via statements in some form of *database language*. Applications programs may use a conventional procedure-oriented, high-level language like COBOL, PL/I, or Pascal; a terminal user may use a specially designed *query language* that makes it convenient to express requests (usually in simple English) in the context of a particular application.

Such languages are referred to as *host languages.* Each host language ordinarly includes a *data sublanguage (DSL)* concerned with the specifics of database objects and operations. Each data sublanguage generally is a combination of two languages, namely a *data definition language (DDL)* that provides facilities for defining database objects, and a *data manipulation language (DML)* that provides features for specifying the processing to be performed on database objects.

13.14.4 Database Administrator

The *database administrator* is the person who controls the database system. The database administrator decides what information will be stored in the database, how the data will be stored and accessed, what authorization checks and validation procedures will be performed, what backup and recovery procedures will be used, and how the system should be tuned to meet performance goals.

13.14.5 Distributed Database

A *distributed database* is a database that is spread throughout the computer systems of a network. Ordinarily in such systems each data item is stored at the location in which it is most frequently used, but it remains accessible to other network users.

Distributed systems provide the control and economies of local processing with the advantages of information accessibility over a geographically dispersed organization. They can be costly to implement and operate, however, and they can suffer from increased vulnerability to security violations. Chapter 16 considers these issues in detail.

13.14.6 Data Dictionary

An index to all the items in an organization's database is called a *data dictionary.* A data dictionary is actually a database itself, one which contains data about the database. It lists the types of data in the database, which programs use which data, which user groups require which reports, which entities of each type exist in the system, etc.

13.15 DATABASE MODELS

Three different database models have achieved widespread popularity (1) *hierarchical database,* (2) *network database,* and (3) *relational database.*

13.15.1 Hierarchical Database

Much of the value of the database approach comes from the fact that relationships between data items may be indicated explicity. In the hierarchical model, (Fig. 13.8) data items are related in a parent/child relationship; each parent may have many children but each child may have only one parent. Hierarchical organization makes it difficult to express relationships in which children relate to more than one parent.

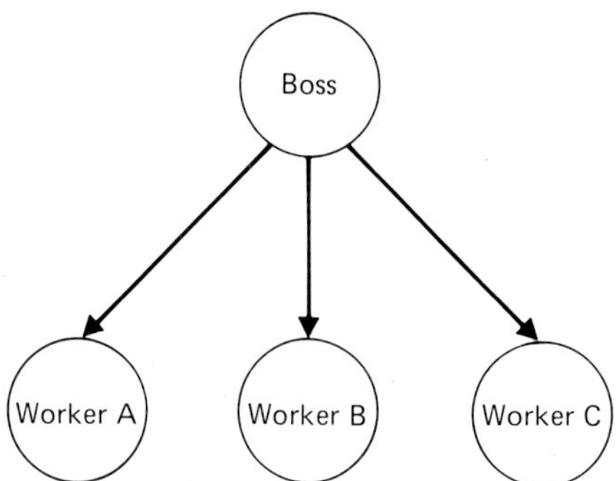

Fig. 13.8 Hierarchical database organization.

This inflexibility has led many designers to choose another model. But when the data relationships are indeed hierarchical, the database is easy to implement, modify, and search.

13.15.2 Network Database

The network model (Fig. 13.9) is more flexible than the hierarchical model. It allows children to relate to many parents, and allows very general interdependencies

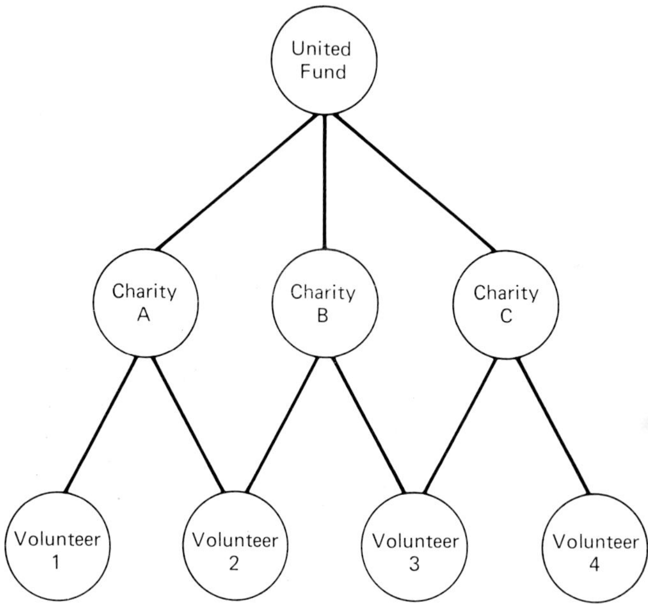

Fig. 13.9 A possible network database organization. Note that some people do volunteer work for more than one charity.

to be expressed. A disadvantage to the network approach is that some network structures begin to take on a "rat's nest" appearance with pointers going off in all directions. Such a structure can be difficult to comprehend, modify, or reconstruct in case of failure. The network structure is useful in stable environments in which the complex interdependencies of the data need to be expressed to make the database useful. In more dynamic environments in which considerable growth in the database is expected, or in which new features and relationships are likely to be added, the network approach is best avoided.

13.15.3 Relational Database

The relational database model by E.F. Codd (Co70)(Co72) has been receiving great interest in recent years. The relational model offers many advantages over the hierarchical and network models.

The relational model is a logical structure rather than a physical one; the principles of relational database management can be discussed quite conveniently without concerning oneself with the physical implementation of the data structures.

A relational database is composed of *relations.* Figure 13.10 illustrates a sample relation that might be used in a personnel system. The name of the relation is EMPLOYEE and its primary purpose is to demonstrate the relationships of various attributes of each employee with that employee. Any particular row of the relation is called a *tuple.* This relation consists of six tuples. The first field in each tuple, the employee number, is used as the *primary key* for referencing data in the relation. The tuples of the relation are ordered by primary key.

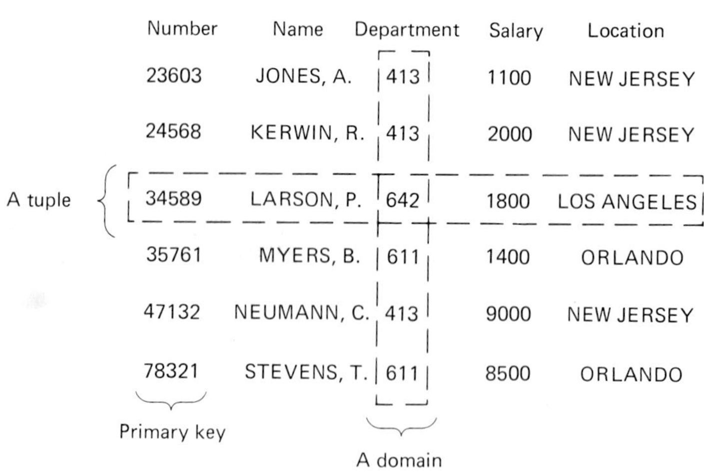

Fig. 13.10 Relational database structure.

Each column of the relation represents a different *domain.* Tuples must be unique (by primary key) within a relation, but particular domain values may be duplicated between tuples. For example, three different tuples in the example contain department number 413. The number of domains in a relation indicates the *degree of the relation.* Relations of degree 2 are *binary relations,* relations of degree three are *ternary relations,* and relations of degree *n* are *n-ary relations.*

Different users of a database will be interested in different data items and different relationships between the data items. Some users will want only certain subsets of the table columns. Other users will wish to combine smaller tables into larger ones to produce more complex relations. Codd calls the subset operation *projection,* and the combination operation *join.*

Using the relation of Fig. 13.10 we might, for example, use the projection operation to create a new relation called DEPARTMENT-LOCATOR whose purpose is to show where departments are located. This new relation is shown in Fig. 13.11.

```
        Relation: DEPARTMENT-LOCATOR
Department            Location
  413                   NEW JERSEY
  611                   ORLANDO
  642                   LOS ANGELES
```

Fig. 13.11 A relation formed by projection.

The relational database organization has many advantages over the hierarchical and network schemes.

1. The tabular representation used in the relational scheme is easy for users to comprehend and easy to implement in the physical database system.

2. It is relatively easy to convert virtually any other type of database structure into the relational scheme. Thus the scheme may be viewed as one form of universal representation.

3. The projection and join operations (among others) are easy to implement and make the creation of new relations needed for particular applications easy to do.

4. Access control to sensitive data is straightforward to implement. The sensitive data is merely placed in separate relations, and access to these relations is controlled by some sort of authority or access scheme.

5. Searches can be much faster than in schemes requiring following a string of pointers.

6. Relational structures are much easier to modify than hierarchical or network structures. In environments where flexibility is important, this becomes critical.

7. The clarity and visibility of the database improves with the relational structure. It is much easier to search tabular data than it is to unwind possibly arbitrarily complex interconnections of data elements in a pointer mechanism.

Database systems will be routinely incorporated into future operating systems to provide users with far more powerful capabilities than are available in conventional file systems. This trend has already been established with significant database capabilities integrated into both the hardware and the operating system of the IBM System/38 (Wa80a) (Wa80b), and many other recent systems.

SUMMARY

A file is a named collection of data that normally resides on secondary storage. Entire files may be manipulated by operations like open, close, create, destroy, copy, rename, and list. Individual data items (normally records) may be manipulated by operations like read, write, update, insert, and delete.

The file system manages files. It provides sharing, privacy, accessing of information, backup, recovery, device independence, and encryption/decryption capabilities.

Data is structured in increasingly complex entities including bits, bytes, fields, records, files, and databases.

Records may be unblocked (one logical record per physical block) or blocked (several logical records per physical block). Blocking minimizes the number of physical transfers involving auxiliary storage during file processing. Buffering allows input/output operations to proceed in parallel with the operation of the processor.

The most popular file organization schemes are sequential, indexed sequential, direct, and partitioned. Accessing of files is accomplished by operating systems functions called access methods. Queued access methods are used with sequentially organized files; they perform anticipatory buffering and scheduling of I/0, and they provide automatic blocking and deblocking. The basic access methods provide only physical block reading and writing.

In contiguous allocation, a file is allocated to a single area of secondary storage; in noncontiguous allocation the file may be dispersed throughout several areas of secondary storage. Contiguous allocation facilitates rapid access but suffers from serious fragmentation problems. Noncontiguous allocation is more flexible, but accessing can involve frequent seeks. Block allocation offers the flexibility of noncontiguous allocation with the fast access of contiguous allocation (at least with successive access to records in the same block). Block-oriented file mapping reflects the physical adjacencies on disk in the file map.

The file descriptor contains information the system needs to manage a file. The user may not reference file descriptors directly; file descriptors are controlled by the file system.

Controlling access to files can be handled by an access control matrix indicating which users have what types of access to which files. Access control is more commonly handled with user classes where, for example, access may be granted to "owner," "specified user," "group member," or "member of the general public."

Backup and recovery are important functions of any file system. The most common technique is periodic backups of the entire file system. With incremental dumping, the files modified by a user during a terminal session are backed up when that user logs out. Transaction logging copies every line typed by the user to a log file; recovery would involve literally reapplying all transactions logged since the last major periodic backup.

A database is an integrated collection of data which is centrally controlled. Many contemporary computer systems now provide database capabilities in both their hardware and operating systems. This gives the user far more powerful data manipulation capabilities than those ordinarily provided in conventional file systems.

Data independence allows an application to be changed and new applications to be developed without having to modify the data storage structure and accessing strategy. A distributed database is one that is spread throughout the computer systems of a network. A data dictionary describes the data in a database.

The most popular database organizations are hierarchical, network, and relational. In the hierarchical approach, data is organized according to parent/child relationships; each child has only one parent but each parent may have many children. A hierarchical database is easy to search and maintain, but it limits the user's flexibility in defining complex data interdependencies.

The network approach allows very general interdependencies to be expressed conveniently. But the resulting structures can be difficult to comprehend, modify, or reconstruct in case of failure.

The relational database approach offers many advantages over the hierarchical and network schemes. The tabular representation is easier to comprehend and implement. Databases organized according to the other schemes may easily be converted to relational organization. Convenient operations like projection and join make it easy to create new relations. Sensitive data may be secured by placing it in separate relations. Searching is generally much faster than it is within the other schemes, modification is more straightforward, and the clarity and visibility of the database is greatly improved.

TERMINOLOGY

access control matrix
access method
backup
binary relation
block allocation
block chaining
chaining
close a file
compaction
controlled information sharing
data definition language
data dependent
data dictionary
data independence

data manipulation language
data sublanguage
database
database administrator
database language
database management system (DBMS)
decryption
degree of a relation
device independence
direct file organization
distributed database
domain
dumping
encryption
encryption key
extent
file
file access control
file access rights
file control block
file descriptor
file directory
file mapping
file name
file protection
file system
fragmentation of secondary storage
free space list
garbage collection
hierarchical database
hierarchical directory structure
host language
incremental dumping
index
index block chaining
indexed sequential file organization
join
key
linked allocation
logging disk
logical view
mapped allocation
member
n-ary relation
network database
open a file
partitioned file organization
pathname
periodic backups
physical view
primary key
private storage of information
projection
query language
recovery
redundancy
relation
relational database
root directory
root node
sequential file organization
storage hierarchy
ternary relation
transaction logging
tuple
two-level, tree-structured file system
user directory
volatility of a file
volume

EXERCISES

13.1 A certain file system uses "systemwide" names, i.e., once one member of the user community uses a name, that name may not be assigned to new files. Most large file systems, however, require only that names be unique with respect to a given user—two different users may choose the same file name without conflict. Discuss the relative merits of these two schemes considering both implementation and application issues.

13.2 Some systems require files to be opened explicity. Others make the opening an implicit part of the first access to each file. Why is explicit file opening more desirable?

13.3 Some systems implement file sharing by allowing several users to read a single copy of a file simultaneously. Others provide a copy of the shared file to each user. Discuss the relative merits of each approach.

13.4 Index sequential files are popular with applications designers. Experience has shown, however, that direct access to index sequential files can be very slow. Why is this so? In what circumstances is it better to access such files sequentially? In what circumstances should the applications designer use direct files rather than indexed sequential files?

13.5 Reliability and integrity issues are becoming increasingly important as we trust more and more of the management of our lives to computers. When a computer system failure occurs, it is important to be able to reconstruct the file system quickly and accurately. Suppose a file system allows complex arrangements of pointers and interdirectory references. What measures might the file system designer take to ensure the reliability and integrity of such a system?

13.6 Some file systems support a very large number of access classes while others support only a few. Discuss the relative merits of each approach. Which is better for highly secure environments? Why?

13.7 How is allocating space for files on secondary storage similar to real storage allocation under variable partition multiprogramming?

13.8 In what circumstances is compaction of secondary storage useful? What dangers are inherent in compaction? How can these be avoided?

13.9 What are the motivations for structuring file systems hierarchically?

13.10 One problem with index sequential file organization is that additions to the file may need to be placed in overflow areas. How might this affect performance? What can be done to improve performance in these circumstances?

13.11 Pathnames in a hierarchical file system can become lengthy. Given that the vast majority of file references are made to a user's own files, what convention might the file system support to minimize the need for using lengthy pathnames?

13.12 Some file systems store information in exactly the format created by the user. Others attempt to optimize by compressing the data. For example, in systems which store user programs as 80-column card images, large portions of each card are blank. Describe how you would implement a compression/decompression mechanism. Such a mechanism necessarily trades execution time overhead against the reduced storage requirements for files. In what circumstances is this trade-off acceptable?

13.13 Suppose that a major development in primary storage technology made it possible to produce a storage so large, so fast, and so inexpensive that all of the programs and data at an installation could then be stored in a single "chip." How would the design of a file system for such a single-level storage differ from that for today's conventional hierarchical storage systems?

13.14 You have been asked to perform a security audit on a computer system. The system administrator suspects that the pointer structure in the file system has been modified to allow certain unauthorized users to access critical system information. Describe how you would attempt to determine who is responsible for the security breach and how it was possible for them to modify the pointers.

13.15 In most data processing installations, only a small portion of file backups are ever used to reconstruct a file. Thus there is a trade-off to be considered in performing backups. Do the consequences of not having a file backup available when needed justify the effort of performing the backups? What factors point to the need for performing backups as opposed to not performing them? What factors affect the frequency with which backups should be performed?

13.16 Sequential access from sequential files is much faster than sequential access from indexed sequential files. Why then do many applications designers implement systems in which indexed sequential files are to be accessed sequentially?

13.17 In a university environment how might the user access classes "owner," "group," "specified user," and "public" be used to control access to files? Consider the use of the computer system for administrative as well as academic computing. Consider also the use of the computer system in support of grant research as well as in academic courses.

13.18 File systems provide access to permanently mounted files as well as to demountable files. Demountable files are contained on volumes such as disk packs that may be mounted on a disk drive or stored off-line from the computer system. What types of files might best be stored as permanent files? as demountable files? What problems are unique to the management of demountable files?

13.19 What type and frequency of backup would be most appropriate in each of the following systems?

a) a batch-processing payroll system that runs every Thursday
b) an on-line banking system for handling teller transactions
c) a patient billing system in a hospital
d) an airline reservations system in which customers make reservations by telephone for flights as much as one year in advance
e) a timesharing program development system used by a group of 100 programmers

13.20 Most banks today use on-line teller transaction systems. Each transaction is immediately applied to customer accounts to keep balances correct and current. Errors are intolerable. But because of computer failures and power failures, these systems do "go down" occasionally. Describe how you would implement a backup/recovery capability to ensure that each completed transaction applies to the appropriate customer's account. Also, any transactions only partially completed at the time of a system failure must not apply.

13.21 Why is it useful to reorganize indexed sequential files periodically? What criteria might a file system use to determine when reorganization is needed?

13.22 Distinguish between queued access methods and basic access methods.

13.23 What is a database? What is a database system? List several of the advantages of database systems over nondatabase systems.

13.24 How might redundancy of programs and data be useful in the construction of highly reliable systems? Database systems can greatly reduce the amount of redundancy involved in storing data. Does this imply then that database systems may in fact be less reliable than nondatabase systems? Explain your answer.

13.25 Define each of the following in the context of database systems

a) database language
b) query language
c) host language
d) data sublanguage
e) data definition language
f) data manipulation language

13.26 What is a data dictionary?

13.27 Compare and contrast the hierarchical and network models for structuring databases.

13.28 Define each of the following in the context of relational database organization.

a) relation
b) tuple
c) primary key
d) domain
e) degree of a relation
f) n-ary relation
g) projection
h) join

13.29 List several advantages of the relational database organization over the hierarchical and network schemes.

LITERATURE

(Ba78) Barnett, J.K.R., "A Highly Reliable File System Which Supports Multiprocessing," *Software—Practice & Experience,* Vol. 8, No. 6, November–December 1978, pp. 645–667.

(Co70) Codd, E.F., "A Relational Model of Data for Large Shared Data Banks," *CACM,* June 1970.

(Co72) Codd, E.F., "Further Normalization of the Data Base Relational Model," In *Courant Computer Science Symposia,* Vol. 6, *Data Base Systems,* Englewood Cliffs, N.J.: Prentice-Hall, 1972.

(Da81) Date, C.J., *An Introduction to Database Systems,* Reading, Mass.: Addison-Wesley, 1981.

(De79) Denning, D., and P. Denning, "Data Security," *ACM Computing Surveys,* Vol. 11, No. 3, September 1979, pp. 227–249.

(Di78a) Digital Equipment Corporation, *Introduction to VAX-11 Record Management Services,* Maynard, Mass.: 1978.

(Di78b) Digital Equipment Corporation, *VAX-11 Record Management Services User's Guide,* Maynard, Mass.: 1978.

(Di80) Dion, Jeremy, "The Cambridge File Server," *Operating Systems Review,* Vol. 14, No. 4, October 1980, pp. 26–35.

(Fr81) Fritzson, Richard, "Data on Disk: Implementing File Systems," *Kilobaud Microcomputing,* Vol. 5, No. 1, January 1981, pp. 111–115.

(Ha80) Hansen, David, "A Portable File Directory System," *Software—Practice & Experience,* Vol. 10, No. 8, August 1980, pp. 623–636.

(Kl79a) Klein, M., "Files on Parade I: Types of Files," *Byte,* Vol. 4, No. 2, February 1979.

(Kl79b) Klein, M., "Files on Parade II: Using Files," *Byte,* Vol. 4, No. 3, March 1979.

(Ma81) Madsen, Johannes, "A Computer System Supporting Data Abstraction," *Operating Systems Review,* Vol. 15, No. 1, January 1981, pp. 45–72.

(Me79) Mendelson, H.; J.S. Pliskin; and U. Yechiali, "Optimal Storage Allocation for Serial Files," *ACM,* Vol. 22, No. 2, February 1979.

(Mi81) Miller, Barton, "XOS: An Operating System for the *X*-Tree Architecture," *Operating Systems Review,* Vol. 15, No. 2, April 1981, pp. 21–32.

(Pi75) Pirkola, Gary C., "A File System for a General-Purpose, Time-Sharing Environment," *Proc. of the IEEE,* Vol. 63, No. 6, June 1975, pp. 918–925.

(Po77) Powell, Michael, "The Demos File System," *Proc. of the Sixth ACM Symp. on Operating System Principles,* November 1977, pp. 33–42.

(Re80) Redell, David, "PILOT: An Operating System for a Personal Computer," *Communications of the ACM,* Vol. 23, No. 2, February 1980, pp. 81–92.

(Sa79) Saltzer, J.H., "Naming and Binding of Objects," In *Operating Systems: An Advanced Course,* New York: Springer-Verlag, 1979, pp. 100–208.

(Sn81) Stonebracker, Michael, "Operating Systems Support for Data Base Management," *ACM,* Vol. 24, No. 7, July 1981, pp. 412–418.

(St80) Sturgis, H.; J. Mitchell; and J. Israel, "Issues in the Design and Use of a Distributed File System," *Operating Systems Review,* Vol. 14, No. 13, July 1980, pp. 55–69.

(Wa80a) Watson, C.T., and G.F Aberle, "System/38 Machine Data Base Support," *IBM System/38 Technical Developments,* G580-0237-1, IBM Corporation, 1980, pp. 59–62.

(Wa80b) Watson, C.T.; F.E. Benson; and P.T. Taylor, "System/38 Data Base Concepts," *IBM System/38 Technical Developments,* G580-0237-1, IBM Corporation, 1980, pp.78–80.

Part 6
Performance

14 Performance Measurement, Monitoring, and Evaluation

Obviously, a man's judgment cannot be better than the information on which he has based it. Give him the truth and he may still go wrong when he has the chance to be right, but give him no news or present him only with distorted and incomplete data, with ignorant, sloppy or biased reporting, with propaganda and deliberate falsehoods, and you destroy his whole reasoning processes, and make him something less than a man.

Arthur Hays Sulzberger

Each honest calling, each walk of life, has its own elite, its own aristocracy based on excellence of performance.

James Bryant Conant

You can observe a lot just by watching.

Yogi Berra

Outline

14.1 INTRODUCTION

Because an operating system is primarily a resource manager, it is important for operating systems designers to be able to determine how effectively a particular system manages its resources. In this chapter many of the commonly used techniques for monitoring and evaluating the performance of computer systems are discussed. One of these techniques—analytic modeling—is considered in detail in the next chapter.

There is large potential for improvement in the use of existing resources, yet many installations do little if any performance monitoring and evaluation. Of those who do, many generate massive amounts of data they don't know how to interpret.

The vast majority of computer equipment is in use in commercial data processing environments. These installations are concerned with obtaining good performance, but they rarely have personnel versed in the techniques of performance analysis. For this reason, many companies have been formed to supply these installations with the needed expertise. In the projects at the end of this chapter we list several of these companies and suggest that the reader contact them to learn about their products and services.

In the early years of computer development, hardware was the dominant cost in computer systems so performance studies concentrated primarily on hardware issues. Now hardware is relatively inexpensive and becoming even more so, and software is consuming an ever-increasing portion of computing budgets. Today's computer systems come with substantial software including multiprogramming/multiprocessing operating systems, data communications systems, database management systems, and various applications support systems. The software often hides the hardware from the user, creating a virtual machine defined by the operating characteristics of the software. Cumbersome software often causes poor performance, even on systems with very powerful hardware. Therefore it is important to monitor and evaluate the performance of a system's software as well as its hardware.

14.2 IMPORTANT TRENDS AFFECTING PERFORMANCE ISSUES

Twenty years ago most of the costs in a computing environment were hardware related. With advances in hardware technology, hardware costs have been decreasing dramatically. But labor costs have continued to climb steadily, with the combination of inflation and flat productivity causing labor costs to assume a large share of the cost of computing. As a result we must rethink the previous emphasis on the performance of raw hardware, and start to measure performance in ways more sensitive to human productivity.

With the advent of the microprocessor in the 1970s, it has become possible to provide CPU cycles for a nominal cost. Now performance evaluation must shift to other areas, such as I/O device utilization, in which costs remain high.

Microprocessors made possible the development of personal computers in the 1970s. A personal computer is used primarily for the convenience of one individual.

So CPU utilization, or I/O device utilization, becomes less important than whether the computer is ready and available the moment its user needs it.

Certainly the issues of *networking* and *distributed processing* must greatly influence our views of performance evaluation. Now that personal computers are widely available in homes, and individual work station terminals are widely available in organizations, users often connect to networks rather than to specific computers. These networks may contain hundreds or even thousands of computer systems, as well as complex computer-controlled communications capabilities.

14.3 WHY PERFORMANCE MONITORING AND EVALUATION ARE NEEDED

Lucas (Lu71) mentions three common purposes for performance evaluation.

- *Selection evaluation*—Here the performance evaluator must decide if obtaining a computer system from a particular vendor is appropriate.
- *Performance projection*—The goal of the evaluator here is to estimate the performance of a system that does not exist. It may be a complete new computer system, or a new hardware or software component.
- *Performance monitoring*—The evaluator accumulates performance data on an existing system or component to be sure that the system is meeting its performance goals, to help estimate the impact of planned changes, and to provide management with the data it needs to make strategic decisions such as whether or not to modify an existing job priority system.

Performance evaluation and prediction are needed from the earliest moments in the conception of a new system, in the system's day-to-day operation after installation, and in the considerations of its modification or eventual replacement with a better system. In the early phases of a new system's development, the vendor attempts to predict

- the nature of applications that will run on the system
- the anticipated work loads these applications must handle

Once the vendor begins development and implementation of the new system, performance evaluation and prediction are used to determine

- the best hardware organization
- the resource management strategies that should be implemented in the operating system
- whether or not the evolving system meets its performance objectives

Once the product is released to the marketplace, the vendor must be prepared to answer diverse questions from potential users about whether the system can handle certain applications with certain levels of performance. Users are often concerned with choosing an appropriate configuration of a system that will service their needs. This customization is sometimes called the *configuration process.*

When the system is installed at the user's site, both the vendor and the user are concerned with obtaining optimal performance. Fine adjustments are made to make the system run at its best within the user's operating environment. This process, *system tuning,* can often cause dramatic performance improvements once the system is adjusted to the idiosyncracies of the user installation.

14.4 PERFORMANCE MEASURES

By performance, we mean the manner in which or the efficiency with which a computer system meets its goals. Thus performance is a relative rather than an absolute quantity, although we will often talk of *absolute performance measures* such as the number of jobs per hour a given computer system can service. But whenever a performance measure is taken, it is normally to be used as a basis of comparison.

Performance is often in the eye of the beholder. For example, a young music student may find a performance of Beethoven's Fifth Symphony thoroughly inspiring, whereas the conductor might be sensitive to the most minor flaws in the way the second violinist plays a certain passage. Similarly, the owner of a large timesharing system might be pleased with the high percentage utilization of the system reflected by the large billings for service, whereas an individual user might be experiencing excessive delays on such a busy system.

Some performance measures such as *ease of use* are difficult to quantify. Others such as *disk accesses per minute* are easy to enumerate. The performance evaluator must be careful to consider both types of measures, even though it may be possible to provide neatly prepared statistics only for the latter.

Some performance measures such as response time are said to be user-oriented. Others such as CPU utilization are said to be system-oriented.

Some of the common performance measures are

- *Turnaround time*—In a batch processing system, this is defined as the time from which a job is submitted until the job is returned to the user.
- *Response time*—This is the interactive system's turnaround time, and is often defined as the time from which a user presses an ENTER key until the system begins typing a response.
- *System reaction time*—In an interactive system, this is often defined as the time from which the user presses ENTER until the first time slice of service is given to that user's request.

These are probabilistic quantities, and in simulation and modeling studies of systems they are considered to be random variables. We discuss the distribution of response times, for example, because there is a wide range of response times experienced by users on a particular interactive system over some interval of operation, and this range can be described quite accurately by a probability distribution.

When we talk of the expected value of a random variable, we are referring to its mean or average value. But means can often be deceiving because a certain mean value can be produced by averaging a series of identical or nearly identical values, or it can be produced by averaging a wide variety of values, some much larger, and some much smaller than the calculated mean. So another performance measure often employed is

- *Variance in response times* (or of any of the other random variables we discuss) —The variance of response times is a measure of dispersion. A small variance indicates that the various response times experienced by users are relatively close to the mean. A large variance indicates that some users may be experiencing response times that differ widely from the mean. Some could be receiving relatively fast service, while others could be experiencing protracted delays. Thus the variance of response times is a measure of their predictability, and from a human factors standpoint, this can be a very important performance measure in an interactive system.
- *Throughput*—This is the work-per-unit-time performance measurement.
- *Work load*—This is the measure of the amount of work that has been submitted to the system, and which the system normally must process in order to be functioning acceptably.
- *Capacity*—This is a measure of the maximum throughput a system may have assuming that whenever the system is ready to accept more jobs another job is immediately available.
- *Utilization*—This is the fraction of time that a resource is in use. But utilization can be a deceptive measure. Even though a high percentage utilization seems desirable, it may be the result of inefficient usage. One way of achieving high CPU utilization, for example, is to run a series of processes all of which are in infinite loops! Another view of CPU utilization also yields interesting insights. We may view the CPU at any moment in time as being

  a) idle or

  b) in program state or

  c) in supervisor state.

  When the CPU is in program state, it is accomplishing useful work on behalf of a user, and is most likely being charged to that user. When the CPU is in the supervisor state, however, it is inside the operating system. Some of this time may be charged directly to users, but some of it such as the time spent in multiprogramming systems switching between various processes, is pure overhead. This overhead component can become large in some systems. Thus when we measure CPU utilization, we must be concerned with how much of this usage is productive and billable work on behalf of the users, and how much is system overhead.

14.5 PERFORMANCE EVALUATION TECHNIQUES

The most important performance evaluation techniques are summarized in Fig. 14.1 taken from Lucas's study (Lu71). The table shows the techniques, and their applicability for various purposes of performance evaluation. The usefulness of each technique is evaluated separately for hardware and software performance evaluation.

Evaluation technique	Purpose of Evaluation: *Selection evaluation (system exists elsewhere)*		*Performance projection (system does not yet exist)*		*Performance monitoring (system in operation)*	
	New hardware	New software	Design new hardware	Design new software	Reconfigure hardware	Change software
Timings	1	—	1	—	—	—
Mixes	1	—	1	—	—	—
Kernels	2	1	2	1	—	—
Models	2	1	2	1	2	—
Benchmarks	3	3	—	2	2	2
Synthetic programs	3	3	2	2	2	2
Simulation	3	3	3	3	3	3
Monitor (hardware and software)	2	2	2	2	3	3

—: Technique not applicable
1: Has been used but is inadequate
2: Provides some assistance but is insufficient; should be used in conjunction with other techniques
3: Satisfactory

Fig. 14.1 Applicability of various performance evaluation techniques.

14.5.1 Timings

Timings provide a means of performing quick comparisons of computer hardware. Early computer systems were often evaluated by their add times, or by their memory cycle times. Timings are useful for indicating the "raw horsepower" of a particular computer system, and it has become common to categorize a particular computer by the number of *MIPS (millions of instructions per second)* that it performs. Within a few years, some machines will be performing in the *BIPS* range *(billions of instructions per second).*

With the advent of *families of computers,* such as the IBM 360 series first introduced in 1964, it has become common for hardware vendors to offer computers that enable a user to upgrade to faster processors as the user's needs grow. The computers in a family are compatible in that they can run the same programs but at greater speeds as the user moves up in the family. Timings provide a fast means for comparing the members of a family of computers.

Timings are used mainly for quick comparisons. Other techniques should be used to evaluate more meaningfully today's complex hardware and software systems.

Timing comparisons are generally made for a few basic hardware operations. The add operation has certainly become a common basis of comparison with computers rated as capable of performing 500,000 additions per second for example. But computer systems may have instruction sets with hundreds of distinct operations. So when comparing CPUs for a particular application, timings provide too little information.

14.5.2 Instruction Mixes

The technique of *instruction mixes* uses a weighted average of various instruction timings more suited to a particular application. For example, even though a particular computer system can perform a double-precision floating point multiply instruction very quickly, that same system may still perform poorly in a commercial data processing environment in which data movement, editing, and input/output operations constitute the bulk of instructions performed.

The performance evaluator studies the job mix at a particular installation and attempts to form a weighted average of timings for those instructions most frequently used at the installation. Machines may then be compared with more validity than timings alone provide.

Here, too, mixes are useful mostly for quick comparisons, and the evaluator is cautioned that other techniques should be used before making any critical acquisition decisions. The weightings used in this technique tend to be highly subjective, and the nuances of the instruction sets of different computer systems must be carefully considered. Mixes provide little if any useful information for evaluating software.

The validity of instruction mixes is becoming more and more difficult to establish with today's complex hardware designs. With the use of cache memories and pipelining, the same instruction may execute for different amounts of time depending on its context in different executions.

14.5.3 Kernel Programs

Timings and mixes both suffer from the fact that they emphasize only a few aspects of a computer's instruction set. A *kernel program* is a typical program that might be run at an installation. Using manufacturer's instruction timing estimates, the kernel program is timed for a given machine. Comparisons between machines are then made on the basis of differences in the expected execution times of the kernel program on the different machines. So a kernel is actually "executed on paper" rather than being run on a particular computer.

Kernels give better results than either timings or instruction mixes, but they require substantial manual effort to prepare and time. One key advantage is that kernels are complete programs, and ultimately this is what the user actually runs on the computer system under consideration.

Kernels can be helpful in evaluating certain software components of a system. For example, two different compilers may produce dramatically different code, and kernels can help decide which compiler generates more efficient code. But again, the manual work involved is large, so the evaluator often chooses other means.

14.5.4 Analytic Models

Analytic models are mathematical representations of computer systems or components of computer systems. Many types of models are used, but those of *queueing theory* and *Markov processes* seem to be the most manageable and useful. In the next chapter, we present a discussion of queueing models and Markov models for computer performance evaluation.

For evaluators who are mathematically inclined, the analytic model can be relatively easy to create, and modify. A large body of mathematical results exists that evaluators can apply to help estimate the performance of a given computer system or component quickly and relatively accurately.

But there are many disadvantages. Certainly, evaluators must be skilled mathematicians, and thcse people are rare in commercial data processing environments. Secondly, "neat" solutions are available only for the simplest models. The more complex a model gets, the less likely the evaluator is to find a precise mathematical solution describing the model's behavior.

Today's systems are often so complex that the modeler is forced to make many simplifying assumptions. These can invalidate the usefulness and applicability of the model.

The performance evaluator must understand many different techniques, and must use these techniques in concert with one another. The results of an evaluation using a particular technique may sometimes be invalidated by studies using other techniques. But it often occurs that the several different evaluations tend to reinforce one another, and this helps to demonstrate the validity of the evaluator's conclusions.

14.5.5 Benchmarks

A *benchmark* is a real program that the evaluator executes on the machine being evaluated. Commonly, a benchmark is a *production program* (i.e., one that is run regularly at an installation) that is typical of many jobs at the installation. The evaluator is thoroughly familiar with the performance of the benchmark on existing equipment, and when it is run on new equipment, the evaluator may draw meaningful conclusions.

Benchmarks have the advantage that they already exist, so the evaluator merely needs to choose from among known production programs. No manual timings are taken on individual instructions. Instead the full program is run on real data on the actual machine, so the computer does most of the work. The chance of human error is minimized compared to that in timing a mix or kernel since the computer actually runs the benchmark, and the timing can be measured by the computer itself, by a stopwatch, etc.

Ultimately, the main purpose of a computer system is to run actual programs on actual data. So benchmarks have the appeal of dealing with the real items rather than pencil-and-paper versions.

Certainly, a thorough evaluation study using benchmark programs should involve the careful selection of a series of benchmarks typical of the job characteristics at the installation. This is a subjective process and is a weakness in the technique.

In complex environments with multiprogramming, timesharing, multiprocessing, database, data communications, and real-time systems, benchmarks can be particularly valuable because they run on the actual machine in real circumstances. The effects of the software may be experienced directly instead of being estimated.

Benchmarks are useful in evaluating hardware as well as software, and even under complex operating environments. They are also particularly useful in comparing the operation of a system before and after certain changes are made. They are not useful, however, in predicting the effects of proposed changes, unless another system exists with the changes incorporated on which the benchmarks may be run. Benchmarks are probably the most widely used technique among established concerns considering acquisition of equipment from several different vendors. A vendor will often make computer time available for the running of benchmark programs to help a buyer decide if the vendor's system is appropriate.

14.5.6 Synthetic Programs

Synthetic programs combine the techniques of kernels and benchmarks. They are real programs that have been custom-designed to exercise specific features of a machine. One strong advantage they have over benchmarks is that a benchmark program may not already exist which would be applicable for testing a particular feature of a new machine.

Synthetic programs are useful in development environments. As new features become available, synthetic programs may be used to test that these features are operational.

The evaluator, unfortunately, does not always have sufficient time to code and debug synthetic programs, and so the evaluator often seeks existing benchmark programs that match the desired characteristics of a synthetic program as closely as possible.

14.5.7 Simulation

Simulation is a technique in which the evaluator develops a computerized model of the system being evaluated. The model is then run on a computer system that can perform millions of detailed operations quickly and accurately thus reflecting the behavior of the system being evaluated over some simulated period of time.

With simulation it is possible to prepare a model of a system that does not exist, and then run the model to see how the system would behave in certain circumstances. Of course, the real system must eventually be built and tested to prove that the simulation is valid. Simulations can prevent the construction of poorly designed systems by illustrating their problems before they are built. Computerized simulators have become popular in the space and transportation industries, particularly because of the severe consequences of building a system that would fail.

Simulators are generally of two types.

- *Event-driven*—These are controlled by events that are made to occur in the simulator according to probability distributions.
- *Script-driven*—These are controlled by empirically derived data carefully manipulated to reflect the anticipated behavior of the simulated system.

Simulation requires substantial expertise on the part of the evaluator, and can consume large amounts of computer time. Simulators generally produce huge amounts of data that must be further analyzed either manually or by computer. A careful effort must always be made to validate a simulation model, i.e., to demonstrate that it is indeed an accurate representation of the real system being simulated. Once a simulator is developed, however, its repeated use can be useful and economical.

14.5.8 Performance Monitoring

Performance monitoring is the collection and analysis of information regarding system performance for existing systems. It is useful in determining how a system is performing in terms of throughput, response times, predictability, etc. Performance monitoring can locate bottlenecks quickly, and can help management decide how to improve performance.

Performance monitoring can be useful for determining the distribution of jobs of various types. If it is determined that most jobs are production runs, then *optimizing compilers* can be used to compile more efficient versions of production programs. If it is determined that a great deal of testing, debugging, and development is occurring, then *quick-and-dirty* compilers with good diagnostic capabilities can be obtained.

Performance monitoring can be accomplished by software or hardware techniques. Software monitors are cheap to build or acquire, but they can distort the readings of performance because they consume system resources. Hardware monitors are generally more costly, but they have the advantage that they influence the operation of the system minimally.

Monitors generally produce huge volumes of data that must be analyzed, possibly using costly computer resources. But they do indicate precisely how the system is functioning, and this information can be extremely valuable, particularly in development environments in which key design decisions may have to be made or modified based on the observed operation of the system.

Instruction execution traces, or *module execution traces,* can often reveal bottlenecks. A module execution trace might show, for example, that a small subset of the modules is being used a large percentage of the time. Thus if the designers concentrate their optimization efforts on those modules, they may be able to improve system performance considerably without expending effort and resources on infrequently used portions of the system.

14.6 BOTTLENECKS AND SATURATION

An operating system manages a collection of resources. These interface and interact in complex ways to effect the overall operation of the system. Occasionally one or more of these resources become *bottlenecks* limiting the overall performance of the system because they cannot do their share of the work. While the remaining system resources may have excess capacity, the bottlenecks may not be passing jobs or processes to these other resources fast enough to keep them busy.

A bottleneck tends to develop at a resource when the traffic of jobs or processes at that resource begins to approach its capacity. At this point we say that the resource becomes *saturated,* i.e., processes competing for the attention of the resource begin to interfere with one another. One of the classic examples of saturation in operating systems is the thrashing that occurs in paged systems when main storage has been overcommitted and the working sets of the various active processes cannot be maintained simultaneously in main storage.

How can bottlenecks be detected? Quite simply, each resource's request queue should be monitored. When a queue begins to grow quickly, then the arrival rate of requests at that resource must be larger than its service rate, and the resource has become saturated.

Isolation of bottlenecks is an important part of fine-tuning a system. The bottlenecks may be removed by increasing the capacity of the resources, or by adding more resources of that type at that point in the system. Removing a bottleneck does not always improve throughput, however, since other bottlenecks may also exist in the system. Fine-tuning a system may involve the repeated location of and elimination of bottlenecks until system performance actually improves.

14.7 FEEDBACK LOOPS

Performance in an operating system can be sensitive to the current state of the system. A *feedback loop* is a situation in which information of the current state of the system is made available to entering requests. These requests may be rerouted if the feedback indicates they may have difficulty in being serviced. Feedback may be negative, in which case arrival rates may decrease as a result of the feedback, or feedback may be positive, in which case arrival rates may increase. We consider each of these possibilities in examples in the next two sections.

14.7.1 Negative Feedback

In *negative feedback* situations, the arrival rate of new requests may actually decrease as a result of information being fed back. For example, a motorist pulling into a filling station and observing that several cars are waiting at each pump may quickly leave the station in favor of driving down the street to another less crowded station.

In operating systems, spooled outputs can be printed by any of several equivalent printers. If the queue behind one particular printer is too long, the job may be placed in a less crowded queue.

Negative feedback contributes to stability in queueing systems. If arriving jobs indiscriminately get in line behind a busy device, for example, then the queue behind that device might grow indefinitely. Instead, the negative feedback causes the queue lengths to remain near mean values.

14.7.2 Positive Feedback

In *positive feedback* situations, information fed back causes an increase rather than a decrease in some parameter. A classic example of the problems that may occur with positive feedback occurs in paged virtual memory multiprogramming systems.

Suppose the operating system detects that the CPU is underutilized. It may inform the job scheduler to admit more jobs to the multiprogramming mix anticipating that this would place a greater load on the CPU. As more jobs enter the multiprogramming mix, the amount of memory that can be allocated to each job decreases and page faults may increase. Thus as a result of the admission of more jobs the CPU utilization may actually decrease. A poorly designed operating system might decide that to increase the poor utilization of the CPU, even more jobs should be admitted. Of course, this would cause further deterioration in CPU utilization.

One truly serious problem with positive feedback is the consequent *instabilities* that might ensue. As in the example above, positive feedback might drive the system into highly unstable operation. Operating systems designers must be cautious when designing mechanisms with positive feedback to prevent the possibility of instability from developing. One means of combating the problem is to monitor the effects of each incremental change to see whether it results in an anticipated improvement. If an incremental change causes performance to deteriorate, this signals to the operating system that it may be operating in an unstable range, and that it should adjust its resource allocation strategies temporarily until stable operation resumes.

SUMMARY

This chapter discusses many of the commonly used techniques for monitoring and evaluating the performance of computer systems. Three common purposes for performance evaluation are selection evaluation, performance projection, and performance monitoring.

Performance is the manner in which or the efficiency with which a system meets its goals. Some common performance measures are turnaround time, response time, system reaction time, variance in response times, throughput, capacity, and utilization.

Timings are useful for performing quick comparisons of hardware. A computer's add time or number of additions per second has often been used for timing comparisons.

Instruction mixes use a weighted average of various instruction timings more suited to a particular application.

A kernel program is a typical program that might be run at an installation. It is timed for a given machine by using manufacturer's instruction timing estimates, and comparisons may then be made between different machines on the expected execution times of the kernel program. (Note: "Kernel" here is not meant to be confused with the kernel of the operating system.)

Analytic models are mathematical representations of computer systems or components of computer systems. The models of queueing theory and Markov processes are most useful, and are discussed in the next chapter. A large body of mathematical results exists that the evaluator can apply to help estimate the performance of a given computer system or component quickly and relatively accurately.

A benchmark is a real program that the evaluator actually submits for execution on the computer system being evaluated. The evaluator knows the performance characteristics of the benchmark on existing equipment, so when it runs on new equipment, the evaluator may draw meaningful conclusions.

Synthetic programs are real programs that have been custom-designed to exercise specific features of a computer system. They are particularly useful when benchmarks exercising those features don't already exist.

Simulation is a technique in which the evaluator develops a computerized model of the system being evaluated. The model is then run on a computer system that can perform millions of detailed operations quickly and accurately thus reflecting the behavior of the system being evaluated over some simulated period of time. Event-driven simulators are controlled by events that are made to occur in the simulator according to probability distributions. Script-driven simulators are controlled by empirically derived data carefully manipulated to reflect the anticipated behavior of the simulated system.

Performance monitoring is the collection and analysis of information regarding system performance for existing systems.

A resource becomes a bottleneck limiting the overall performance of the system when it can not handle the work being routed to it. Resources operating near their capacity tend to become saturated, i.e., processes competing for the attention of the resource begin to interfere with one another. Thrashing in a paging system is a classic example of saturation in operating systems.

In a feedback loop, information on the current state of the system is made available to entering requests. In negative feedback, the arrival rate of new requests may actually decrease as a result of the information being fed back. Negative feedback contributes to stability in queueing systems.

In positive feedback systems, information fed back causes an increase in some parameter. Positive feedback can cause instability in queueing systems, and the designer should provide controls on positive feedback mechanisms to prevent unstable operation.

TERMINOLOGY

analytic model
benchmark
BIPS (billions of instructions per second)
bottleneck
capacity
configuration process
event-driven simulator
feedback loop
hardware monitor
instability
instruction mix
kernel program
negative feedback
MIPS (millions of instructions per second)
model validation
predictability
performance evaluation
performance measurement
performance monitoring
performance projection
positive feedback
production program
response time
saturation
script-driven simulator
selection evaluation
simulation
software monitor
synthetic program
system reaction time
system tuning
thrashing
throughput
timings
turnaround time
utilization
variance of response times
work load

EXERCISES

14.1 Explain why it is important to monitor and evaluate the performance of a system's software as well as its hardware.

14.2 What does it mean for a system's software to hide the hardware from the user?

14.3 One of the factors complicating performance measurement and evaluation is that the load on a computer system varies with time. Study the load on a computer system to which you have access. Document how the load varies with time.

14.4 How do our views toward performance evaluation change in the light of microprocessors and personal computers?

14.5 When a user logs in, some timesharing systems print the total number of logged in users.

a) Why is this useful to the user?
b) In what circumstances might it not be a useful indication of load?
c) What factors tend to make this a highly reliable indication of system load on a timesharing system that supports many users?

14.6 Briefly discuss each of the following purposes for performance evaluation.

a) selection evaluation
b) performance projection
c) performance monitoring

14.7 What is the configuration process? Why are performance monitoring and evaluation critical to its success?

14.8 What is system tuning? Why is it important?

14.9 Give examples confirming that performance, indeed, is in the eyes of the beholder.

14.10 Distinguish between user-oriented and system-oriented performance measures.

14.11 What is system reaction time? Is it more critical to CPU bound or I/O-bound jobs?

14.12 In discussing random variables, why can mean values sometimes be deceiving? What other performance measure is useful in describing how closely the values of a random variable cluster about its mean?

14.13 Why is predictability such an important attribute of computer systems? In what types of systems is predictability especially critical?

14.14 Some commonly used performance measures follow.

- turnaround time
- response time
- system reaction time
- variance of response times
- throughput
- work load
- capacity
- utilization

For each of the following, indicate which performance measure is described.

a) the predictability of a system
b) the current demands on a system
c) a system's maximum capabilities
d) the percentage of a resource in use
e) the work processed per unit time
f) turnaround time in interactive systems

14.15 What performance measures will be of greatest interest to each of the following?

a) an interactive user
b) a batch processing user

c) a designer of a real-time process control system
d) installation management concerned with billing users for resource usage
e) installation managers concerned with projecting system loads for the next yearly budget cycle
f) installation managers concerned with predicting the performance improvements to be gained by adding

i) memory
ii) faster CPU
iii) disk drives
iv) channels

14.16 If users are to be billed solely for useful work performed in their behalf by a computer system, then we must separate resource consumption due to system overhead from resource consumption due to useful work.

a) List several components of resource consumption due to system overhead.
b) What measurements might be used to determine each of the overhead components mentioned in your answer to part (A)?

14.17 There is a limit to how many measurements should be taken on any system. What considerations might cause you to avoid taking certain measurements?

14.18 According to Lucas (Lu71), simulation is by far the most widely applicable performance evaluation technique.

a) Give several reasons for this.
b) Even though simulation is widely applicable, it is not as widely used as one might expect. Give several reasons why.

14.19 Some of the popular performance evaluation and monitoring techniques are

- timings
- mixes
- kernels
- models
- benchmarks
- synthetic programs
- simulations
- hardware monitors
- software monitors

Indicate which of these techniques is best defined by each of the following. (Some items can have more than one answer.)

a) their validity may be jeopardized by the making of simplifying assumptions
b) weighted average of instruction timings
c) the purview of skilled mathematicians
d) they are models that are run by a computer
e) useful for quick comparisons of "raw horsepower"
f) particularly valuable in complex software environments
g) a real program executed on a real machine
h) custom-designed programs to exercise specific features of a machine
i) a real program "executed on paper"
j) a production program
k) most commonly designed by using the techniques of queueing theory and Markov processes
l) often used when it is too costly or time-consuming to develop a synthetic program

14.20 What performance evaluation techniques are most applicable in each of the following situations? Explain your answers.

a) An insurance company has a stable work load consisting of a large number of production runs. Because of a merger, the company must increase its capacity by 50 percent. The company wishes to replace its equipment with a new computer system.
b) The insurance company described in (a) wishes to increase capacity by purchasing some additional memory and channels.
c) A computer company is designing a new, ultrahigh-speed computer system and wishes to evaluate several alternative designs.
d) A consulting firm that specializes in commercial data processing gets a large military contract requiring extensive mathematical calculations. The company wishes to determine if its existing computer equipment will process the anticipated load of mathematical calculations.
e) Management in charge of a multicomputer network needs to locate bottlenecks as soon as they develop and to reroute traffic accordingly.
f) A systems programmer expects that one of the software modules is being called upon more frequently than originally anticipated. The programmer wants to confirm this before devoting substantial effort to recoding the module to make it execute more efficiently.

14.21 On one computer system, the CPU contains a MIPS meter that records how many million instructions per second the CPU is performing at any instant in time. The meter is calibrated from 0 to 4 MIPS in increments of 0.1 MIPS. All of the terminals to this computer are currently in use. Explain how each of the following situations might occur.

a) The meter reads 3.8 MIPS and the terminal users are experiencing good response times.
b) The meter reads 0.5 MIPS and the terminal users are experiencing good response times.
c) The meter reads 3.8 MIPS and the terminal users are experiencing poor response times.
d) The meter reads 0.5 MIPS and the terminal users are experiencing poor response times.

14.22 You are a member of a performance evaluation team working for a computer manufacturer. You have been given the task of developing a generalized synthetic program to facilitate the evaluation of a completely new computer system with an innovative instruction set.

a) Why might such a program be useful?
b) What features might you provide to make your program a truly general evaluation tool?

14.23 You have been charged with the responsibility of getting a particular application running as quickly as possible at your installation. You have decided to purchase a software package from one of several reputable vendors. Your hardware is already in place. Describe how you would choose the best available software package for your application.

14.24 Distinguish between event-driven and script-driven simulators.

14.25 What does it mean to validate a simulation model? How might you validate a simulation model of a small timesharing system (which already exists) with disk storage, several CRTs, and a 100 line-per-minute printer?

14.26 In what circumstances would you use a software monitor? a hardware monitor?

14.27 What information might a performance evaluator get from an instruction execution trace? a module execution trace? Which of these is more useful for analyzing the operation of individual programs? for analyzing the operation of systems?

14.28 How can bottlenecks be detected? How can they be removed? If a bottleneck is removed, should we expect a system's performance to improve? Explain.

14.29 What is a feedback loop? Distinguish between negative and positive feedback. Which of these contributes to system stability?

14.30 Work-load characterization is an important part of any performance study. We certainly must know what a computer is supposed to be doing before we can say much about how well it is doing it. What measurements might you take to help characterize the work load in each of the following systems?

a) a timesharing system designed to support program development
b) a batch processing system used for preparing monthly bills for an electric utility with half a million customers
c) a personal computer system used solely by one engineer
d) a microprocessor implanted in a person's chest to regulate heartbeat
e) a local computer network that supports a heavily used electronic mail system within a large office building
f) an air traffic control system for collision avoidance
g) a weather forecasting computer network that receives temperature, humidity, barometric pressure and other readings from 10,000 grid points throughout the country over communications lines
h) a medical database management system that provides doctors around the world with answers to various medical questions
i) a traffic control computer network for monitoring and controlling the flow of traffic in a large city

14.31 A computer system manufacturer has a new model under development which supports multiprocessing. The system is modularly designed so that users may add new processors as they need them, but the connections are expensive. The manufacturer must provide the connections with the original machine because they are too costly to install in the field. The manufacturer wants to determine the optimal number of processor connections to provide. The chief designer says that three is the optimal number of connections. The designer believes that placing more than three processors on the system would not be worthwhile and that the contention for memory would be too great. What performance evaluation techniques would you recommend to help determine the optimal number of connections during the design stage of the project? Explain your answer.

14.32 At one installation, a channel has been assigned to handle traffic back and forth to a bank of disk drives. The channel has m disk controllers attached to it, and each of the controllers has n disk drives. A hardware monitor shows that the channel is lightly used, but the system is known to be experiencing long waits on disk requests.

a) What might the problem be? List several possibilities.
b) What measurements would you take to isolate the problem? Would hardware or software monitors be more appropriate?

14.33 At an installation that successfully timeshared 100 user terminals simultaneously, the management decided to increase the number of terminals to 130. The new terminals were installed, and immediately users began complaining of poor response times. You have been called in to do a performance evaluation on the system, and to determine how to achieve satisfactory response times.

a) List both the hardware problems and software problems that might be causing the poor response times.
b) For each of the problems listed in (a) what performance monitoring and evaluation techniques would you use to isolate the problem?
c) For each of the problems listed in (a), if indeed that problem is confirmed, how would you solve the problem most economically to improve system performance?

14.34 At one large batch processing multiprogramming installation, jobs are billed solely by wall clock time. As each batch job is initiated, the operator "punches in" the job using a conventional time clock. When the job completes, it is "punched out."

One customer has been running a certain job regularly for several months and the charges for each run have been about the same. On one particular afternoon, there was an excessively heavy load on the system when this customer's job ran, and the charges were double what the customer expected. The customer complained about the charges to the manager of the installation and asked that the charges be reduced by half.

Should the customer be charged the higher amount even though it is known that the system was heavily loaded on that day? Discuss the merits of each of the following arguments:

a) Yes. The customer agreed to be billed by elapsed wall clock time and should be charged for it.
b) No. The manager doesn't want to upset a good customer.
c) Yes. The customer occasionally runs the same job on a lightly loaded system and pays less than expected, so it all averages out anyway.
d) No. The customer should pay only for the useful work performed by the computer. This depends only on the job performed and not on the system load.
e) Yes. It is entirely possible that it was not the load on the system that determined how long the job ran, but rather that the job, in fact, was longer than normal.

14.35 The following is a list of some vendors and the popular commercial packages they supply for aiding in system simulation and modeling. Contact several of these vendors requesting literature on these and related packages they market. Also investigate other sources of information, and prepare a report summarizing commercial simulation and modeling packages.

Advanced Computer Techniques Corporation
1501 Wilson Blvd.
Arlington, VA 22209

Fast/Master—This analysis package produces reports on system utilization. It is typical of commercially available performance monitoring software.

BGS Systems Inc.
470 Totten Pond Road
Waltham, MA 02254

Best/1—A general-purpose performance prediction package for capacity planning applications. This interactive system helps evaluate the impact of changes in work load, hardware, and operating system parameters.

CACI
12011 San Vicente Blvd.
Los Angeles, CA 90049

Simscript II.5—Simscript is one of the most widely used general-purpose simulation languages, and is especially useful for designing computer system simulation models.

COSMIC
112 Barrow Hall
University of Georgia
Athens, GA 30602

Multi-Purpose System Simulator—A simulation system for evaluating performance of existing and proposed computer systems.

Information Systems Consultants, Inc.
311 Maple Avenue West
Vienna, VA 22180

Load Generator System II—A software system for emulating the work loads produced by terminals on an interactive system. User-defined "scripts" of typical terminal sessions are "run" by the simulator to generate a work load comparable to that produced by various numbers of terminals.

Performance Systems
30 Courthouse Square
Rockville, MD 20850

Scert II—A comprehensive performance prediction software package. Users specify the hardware and software environment in which particular work loads will run, and Scert projects the costs and effects of running those work loads in the specified environments.

System Development
2500 Colorado Ave.
Santa Monica, CA 90406

IMSIM—A simulation software package for analyzing the performance of computer systems and networks under various loads.

14.36 The following is a list of vendors and some of the popular commercially available hardware monitors they supply. Contact the vendors requesting their literature on these and related systems. Research other hardware monitors. Write a report discussing commercially available hardware monitors.

Computer Resources
4650 W. 160th Street
Cleveland, OH 44135

Micromeasure—This programmable microprocessor-based hardware monitor accumulates and prints statistics on terminal response times.

NCR Comten Inc.
2700 Snelling Avenue
St. Paul, MN 55113

Dynaprobe—This is actually a series of hardware monitors and associated software for analyzing the data produced by the monitors. The software produces both statistical reports and graphical outputs.

Questronics, Inc.
3565 SW. Tempe #5
Salt Lake City, UT 84115

The company produces a full range of hardware monitors and support software for measuring terminal response times and data communications network activity.

Tesdata Systems Corp.
7921 Jones Branch Drive
P.O. Box 1056
McLean, VA 22102

The company produces powerful minicomputer-based hardware monitoring and network monitoring systems. Several of their systems provide real-time reporting capabilities so that problems and bottlenecks may be detected immediately.

14.37 In this problem, you will undertake a reasonably detailed simulation study. You will write a simulation program using random number generation to produce events probabilistically, i.e., you will design an event-driven simulation.

At one large batch processing computer installation the management wants to decide what storage placement strategy will yield the best possible performance. The installation runs a large real storage computer under variable partition multiprogramming. Each user program runs in a single group of contiguous storage locations. Users state their storage requirement in advance, and the operating system allocates each user the requested storage as it initiates the user's job. A total of 100K bytes of real storage is available for user programs.

The storage requirement of jobs at this installation is distributed as follows.

10K—30 percent of the jobs
20K—20 percent of the jobs
30K—25 percent of the jobs
40K—15 percent of the jobs
50K—10 percent of the jobs

Execution times of jobs at this installation are independent of the jobs' storage requirements and are distributed as follows.

1 minute—30 percent of the jobs
2 minutes—20 percent of the jobs
5 minutes—20 percent of the jobs
10 minutes—10 percent of the jobs
30 minutes—10 percent of the jobs
60 minutes—10 percent of the jobs

This system is very busy. In particular, there is always at least one job waiting to be initiated. Jobs are processed strictly first-come-first-served.

Write a simulation program to help you decide which storage placement strategy should be used at this installation. Your program should use random number generation to produce the storage requirement and execution time for each job according to the distributions above. Investigate the performance of the installation over an eight-hour period by measuring throughput, storage utilization, and other items of interest to you for each of the following storage placement strategies.

a) first fit b) best fit c) worst fit

14.38 At the installation described in the previous problem, management suspects that the first-come-first-served job scheduling may not be optimal. In particular, they are concerned that longer jobs tend to keep shorter jobs waiting. A study of waiting jobs indicates that there are always at least ten jobs waiting to be initiated (i.e., when ten jobs are waiting and one is initiated another arrives immediately). Modify your simulation program from the previous exercise so that job scheduling is now performed on a shortest-job-first basis. How does this affect performance for each of the storage placement strategies?

14.39 At the installation described in Exercise 14.37, the management suspects that jobs with large storage requirements when processed first-come-first-served are hurting system performance. Modify your simulation program from Exercise 14.37 so that the 100K of storage is divided into two 50K areas. The first area is used to run as many 10K, 20K, and 30K jobs as will fit under variable partition multiprogramming. The second area is used exclusively to run 40K or 50K jobs. How does this affect performance assuming that a job queue exists that always contains the next ten jobs to be run, and assuming that we continue to choose jobs for each of the 50K storage areas on a first-come-first-served basis?

14.40 Propose and implement other modifications to the preceding simulations to examine the affects of other job scheduling disciplines.

LITERATURE

(Bu69) Bucholz, W., "A Synthetic Job for Measuring System Performance," *IBM Journal of R&D,* Vol. 8, No. 4, 1969, pp. 309–318.

(Ca67) Calingaert, P., "System Performance Evaluation: Survey and Appraisal," *CACM,* Vol. 10, No. 1, 1967, pp. 12–18.

(Co75) Courtois, P. J., "Decomposability, Instability, and Saturation in Multiprogramming Systems," *CACM,* Vol. 18, No. 7, 1975, pp. 371–376.

(Co77) Cohen, J., and N. Carpenter, "A Language to Inquire about the Run-Time Behavior of Programs," *Software—Practice & Experience,* Vol. 7, No. 4, July/August 1977, pp. 445–460.

(De68) Denning, P. J., "Thrashing: Its Causes and Prevention," *AFIPS Conf. Proc., FJCC 33,* Part 1, Montvale, N.J.: AFIPS Press, 1968, pp. 915–922.

(Dr73) Drummond, M. E., Jr., *Evaluation and Measurement Techniques for Digital Computer Systems,* Englewood Cliffs, N.J.: Prentice-Hall, 1973.

(Fe78) Ferrari, D., *Computer Systems Performance Evaluation,* Englewood Cliffs, N.J.: Prentice-Hall, 1978.

(Fu75) Fuller, S. H., "Performance Evaluation." In H. S. Stone (ed.), *Introduction to Computer Architecture,* Chicago: SRA, 1975, pp. 474–545.

(He75) Hellerman, H., and T. F. Conroy, *Computer System Performance,* New York: McGraw-Hill, 1975.

(Kn71) Knuth, D. E., "An Empirical Study of FORTRAN Programs," *Software—Practice & Experience,* Vol. 1, No. 2, 1971, pp. 105–133.

(Ko78) Kobayashi, H., *Modeling and Analysis: An Introduction to System Performance Evaluation Methodology,* Reading, Mass.: Addison-Wesley, 1978.

(La72) Lassettre, E., and A. Scherr, "Modeling the Performance of the OS/360 Time-Sharing Option (TSO)." In W. Freiberger (ed.), *Statistical Computer Performance Evaluation,* New York: Academic Press, 1973, pp. 57–72.

(La79) Lazowska, E. D., "The Benchmarking, Tuning, and Analytic Modeling of VAX/VMS," *Conference on Simulation, Measurement and Modeling of Computer Systems,* Boulder, Colorado, August 1979, pp. 57–64.

(Lu71) Lucas, H., "Performance Evaluation and Monitoring," *ACM Computing Surveys,* Vol. 3, No. 3, September 1971, pp. 79–91.

(Ly72) Lynch, W. C., "Operating System Performance," *CACM,* Vol. 15, No. 7, 1972, pp. 579–585.

(Mi74) Miller, E. F., "Bibliography on Techniques of Computer Performance Analysis," *IEEE Computer,* Vol. 5, No. 5, September/October 1974, pp. 39–47.

(Pe77) Perrot, R. H., and A. K. Raja, "Quasi-parallel Tracing," *Software—Practice & Experience,* Vol. 4, July/August 1977, pp. 483–492.

(Sa81) Sauer, C. H., and K. M. Chandy, *Computer Systems Performance Modeling*, Englewood Cliffs, N.J.: Prentice-Hall, 1981.

(Se72) Sekino, A., *Performance Evaluation of Multiprogrammed Time-Shared Computer Systems*, Ph.D. Dissertation, Electrical Engineering Department, M.I.T., Cambridge, Mass. June 1972.

(Sv77) Svobodova, L., *Computer Performance Measurement and Evaluation Methods: Analysis and Applications*, New York: Elsevier, 1977.

15
Analytic Modeling

Sweet Analytics, 'tis thou hast ravished me.

Doctor Faustus
Christopher Marlowe

Portions of the presentation on queueing theory are based on material in Chapter 5 of *Probability, Statistics, and Queueing Theory with Computer Science Applications* by Arnold O. Allen. Copyright 1978 by Academic Press, Inc., New York. Adapted with permission.

Outline

15.1 INTRODUCTION

This chapter presents some of the popular techniques of analytic modeling, namely queueing theory and Markov processes. Analytic models were introduced briefly in the previous chapter. They are mathematical representations of systems; they allow the performance evaluator to draw quick and accurate conclusions about a system's behavior. A large body of mathematical results has been developed and may be applied by the knowledgeable modeler.

At the very best, we have greatly oversimplified the mathematics. In many cases, we present well-known results without deriving them. Our goal is merely to familiarize the reader with the types of thinking involved in mathematical modeling. The reader interested in further study in this area should consult several of the fine texts and survey papers available (Sa81) (An78) (Kl76) (Ko78) (Mu75) (Pr76) (Re76).

This chapter may be omitted without loss of continuity, but the reader is urged to make at least a cursory scan of the material. A basic understanding of probability is a prerequisite for understanding the more mathematical sections of the chapter. Several analytic models are presented. Tables of the mathematical functions used in the models are included as Appendixes 15.1 and 15.2 on pages 410 and 411.

15.2 QUEUEING THEORY

Each of us has had to wait in line for something. When we pay a toll on a turnpike, we wait in line. When we need gasoline, we wait in line. When we go to the bakery, we "take a number" and we wait in line. The mathematical term *queue* means a waiting line, and in this chapter we introduce *queueing theory,* or the theory of waiting lines.

Why do lines develop? If there were no waiting lines, then we would receive service immediately. Of course we would prefer this—or would we? The point is that we must consider costs. To have sufficient service capability available so that we would never have to wait implies a very great cost. This is the reason we experience many of the waiting lines we are used to. We trade time for money. We spend a certain amount of time in lines waiting for service—but the costs of that service are lower because of the better utilization of the service facility. A good example is a doctor's office in which the highly skilled doctor must have enough of a waiting line to ensure that a patient is always available and the doctor is kept busy.

Figure 15.1 shows the typical arrangement of queueing systems. There is a large population of customers some of whom may eventually enter the queueing network and request service. The service could be the attention of a clerk at a bakery, receiving gasoline at a gas station or, in the case of computers, processing of a request for input/output, etc. We consider the notion of a service facility that contains a number of identical servers, each of which is capable of providing the desired service to a customer. If all of the servers are busy when a new customer enters the queueing

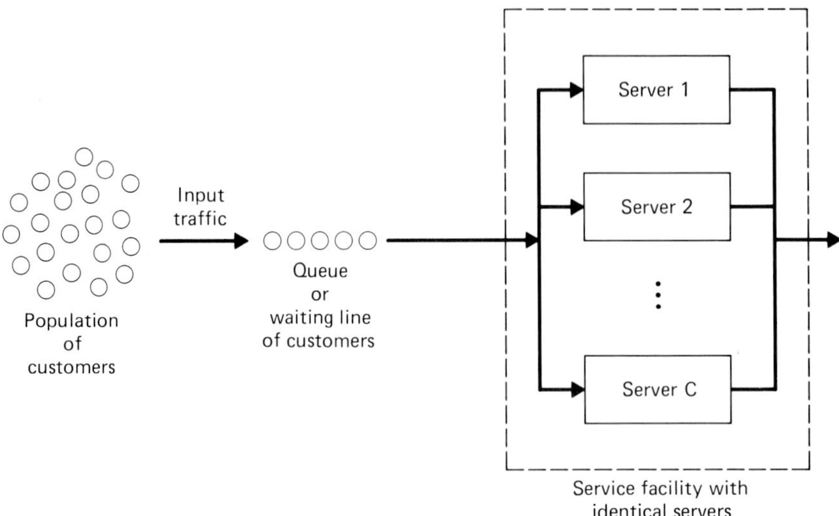

Fig. 15.1 The elements of a typical queueing system. (Adapted with permission from Fig. 5.1.1, An 78.)

network, then that customer must wait until a server becomes available—and the waiting occurs in a queue. Some queues are *unbounded,* that is, they can grow as large as necessary to hold all waiting customers. Some queues are *bounded,* that is, they can hold only some fixed number of waiting customers, possibly none at all.

When dealing with queueing problems, we must consider a number of *random variables.* Random variables can be described by *probability distributions.* Figure 15.2 shows several of the random variables of interest in queueing models. A more detailed summary of the notation used in our discussions of queueing models is given in Fig. 15.3.

We use the random variable q to represent the time a customer spends in the queue waiting for service. The random variable s represents the amount of time a customer spends in service. The random variable w represents the total time a customer spends in the queueing system, and therefore

$$w = q + s.$$

In typical queueing systems there are many items of concern and we discuss these in the next several sections.

15.2.1 Source

Customers are supplied to a queueing system from a *source* that may be infinite or finite. With an *infinite source,* the queue for service can become arbitrarily large. For a *finite source* system, the queue for service, of course, is finite.

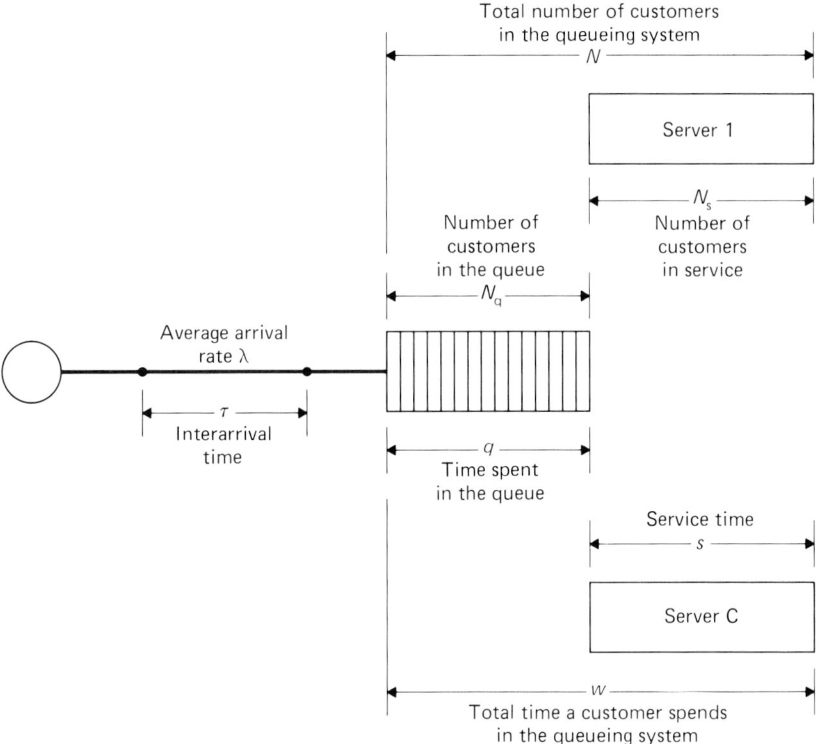

Fig. 15.2 Some of the random variables of interest in queueing models. (Adapted with permission from Fig. 5.1.2, An 78.)

When the customer source is finite but very large, it is customary to assume an infinite source. This turns out to be a reasonable approximation, and it greatly simplifies the mathematics involved. Deciding between finite and infinite models is discussed by Buzen and Goldberg (Bu74).

15.2.2 Arrivals

We will suppose that customers arrive at a queueing system randomly at times

$$t_0 < t_1 < t_2 < \ldots < t_n.$$

They arrive one at a time, and there is never a collision in which two customers attempt to enter the system at the exact same time. The random variables

$$\tau_k = t_k - t_{k-1}, \qquad (k \geq 1)$$

measure the times between successive arrivals and are called *interarrival times*. We shall assume that these random variables are *independent* and *identically distributed*. The symbol τ designates an arbitrary interarrival time.

Symbol	Definition
N	Number of customers in queueing system at steady state
N_q	Number of customers in the queue at steady state
N_s	Number of customers receiving service at steady state
q	The time a customer spends in the queue
s	The time a customer spends in service
w	The time a customer spends in the system, $w = q + s$
τ	Interarrival time—the time between two successive customers arriving for service
λ	Average arrival rate of customers to the queueing system, $\lambda = 1/E(\tau)$
λ_T	Average throughput of a computer system (= jobs/unit of time or interactions/unit of time)
$E(s)$	Expected service time for one customer
$E(\tau)$	Expected interarrival time $E(\tau) = 1/\lambda$ (λ = average interarrival rate)
μ	Average service rate for a server $\mu = 1/E(s)$
L	$L = E(N)$ = expected number of customers in the queueing system at steady state
L_q	$L_q = E(N_q)$ = expected number of customers in the queue at steady state
$\pi_q(r)$	The queueing time that is not exceeded by r percent of the customers
$\pi_w(r)$	The waiting time that is not exceeded by r percent of the customers
P_n	The probability that there are n customers in the queueing system at steady state
u	Traffic intensity $= E(s)/E(\tau) = \lambda E(s) = \lambda/\mu$
ρ	Server utilization = traffic intensity/c = $\lambda E(s)/c = (\lambda/\mu)/c$ = probability that a particular server is in use
W_q	$W_q = E(q)$ = the expected time a customer spends in the queue at steady state ($W_q = W - E(s)$)
W	$W = E(w)$ = the expected time it takes a customer to move through the system at steady state $W = W_q + E(s)$
$C(c, u)$	The probability that all c of the servers in an M/M/c queueing system are in use. (M/M/c systems will be described later in the chapter.)

Fig. 15.3 A summary of important variables used in queueing models. (Adapted with permission from Table 1, Appendix C, An 78.)

15.2.3 Poisson Arrivals

Arrivals may occur according to almost any arbitrary pattern. But in elementary queueing theory it is normally assumed that arrivals form a *Poisson arrival process.*

A Poisson arrival process is characterized by the fact that the interarrival times are distributed exponentially

$$P(\tau \leq t) = 1 - e^{-\lambda t}$$

and the probability that exactly n customers will arrive in any time interval of length t is

$$\frac{e^{-\lambda t}(\lambda t)^n}{n!}, \qquad (n = 0, 1, 2, \ldots).$$

Here λ is a constant average arrival rate expressed in "customers per unit time" and the number of arrivals per unit time is said to be *Poisson distributed* with mean λ.

15.2.4 Service Times

Just as with arrival times, it is common in queueing theory to assume that service times are random. Let s_k denote the service time that the kth arriving customer requires from the system. An arbitrary service time is referred to as s, and the distribution of service times is

$$W_s(t) = P(s \leq t).$$

Specifically, for random service with average service rate μ

$$W_s(t) = P(s \leq t) = 1 - e^{-\mu t}, \qquad (t \geq 0).$$

There are many other common service time distributions. The reader interested in investigating these should consult a text on probability such as (An78).

15.2.5 Queue Capacity

Queues may have

- *Infinite capacity*—so that every arriving customer is allowed to enter the queueing system and wait, no matter how many waiting customers there are.
- *Zero capacity*—in which case customers arriving when the service facility is busy are not admitted to the system. (These are sometimes called *loss systems.*)
- *Positive capacity*—in which case arriving customers wait only if there is still room in the queue.

15.2.6 Number of Servers in the System

Based upon the number of servers, we may categorize queueing systems as either

- *Single server systems*—which have only one server and can service only a single customer at a time, or
- *Multiple server systems*—which have c servers, all of identical capabilities, and can thus service c customers at once.

15.2.7 Queue Disciplines

A *queue discipline* is the rule used for choosing the next customer from the queue to be serviced. Many queue disciplines are in common use in operating systems, but certainly the most common is first-come-first-served (FCFS).

Figure 15.4 shows the popular *Kendall notation* used for describing the characteristics of certain common queueing systems. Figure 15.5 shows a shorthand form of Kendall notation.

$A/B/c/K/m/Z$

- A is the interarrival time distribution.
- B is the service time distribution.
- c is the number of servers.
- K is the system's queue capacity.
- m is the number of customers in the source.
- Z is the queue discipline.

Fig. 15.4 Kendall notation. (Adapted with permission from p. 157, An 78.)

$A/B/c$ is used when

- there is no limit on the length of the queue
- the source is infinite
- the queue discipline is FCFS

A and B may be

- GI for general independent interarrival time
- G for general service time
- E_k for Erlang-k interarrival or service time distribution
- M for exponential interarrival or service time distribution
- D for deterministic interarrival or service time distribution
- H_k for hyperexponential (with k stages) interarrival or service time distribution

Fig. 15.5 Abbreviated Kendal notation. (Adapted with permission from p. 157, An 78.)

15.2.8 Traffic Intensity

The *traffic intensity* in a queueing system is a measure of that system's ability to service its customers effectively. It is defined as the ratio of the mean service time $E(s)$ and the mean interarrival time $E(\tau)$. Thus traffic intensity, u, is

$$u = \frac{E(s)}{E(\tau)} = \lambda\ E(s) = \frac{\lambda}{\mu}$$

where λ is the arrival rate and μ is the service rate. The traffic intensity is useful for determining the minimum number of identical servers a system will need in order to service its customers without its queues becoming indefinitely large or having to turn customers away. For example, if $E(s)$ is 17 seconds and $E(\tau)$ is 5 seconds, then $u = 17/5$ or 3.4, and thus the system must have at least four servers. With fewer servers, customers would arrive faster than the system could service them.

One must be careful in dealing with random variables. Consider, for example, the fact that even though the arrival rate of customers in the example above is one every five seconds, that figure is an average. It is certainly possible that no customers will arrive at all for an extended period of time. Worse yet, it is possible for customers to arrive in rapid succession causing the fixed capacity of the queue to be exceeded and, consequently, customers to be turned away. Designers using fixed-size queues must be careful to provide enough capacity to handle occasional peaks in the arrival rate. Of course, this excess capacity will rarely be used, so if space is at a premium, the designer might best use a variable-length queue structure implemented with a threaded list.

15.2.9 Server Utilization

Traffic intensity is a parameter of an entire queueing system. A related parameter is the *server utilization*, ρ, that is defined as the traffic intensity per server or

$$\rho = \frac{u}{c} = \frac{\lambda}{\mu c}.$$

The server utilization is the probability that a particular server is busy. The *Law of Large Numbers* tells us that this is approximately the fraction of time that each server is in use. Note that for single-server systems, the server utilization is equal to the traffic intensity.

15.2.10 Steady State vs. Transient Solutions

We are most concerned with the operation of queueing systems that have "settled down," i.e., that are said to be operating in *steady state.* When any system is first started, it goes through some initial period of operation that is not generally indicative of its recurring behavior. For example, a car which is to be driven several hundred miles on a highway at the 55 mph speed limit must first accelerate up to that speed. This initial period of operation is not indicative of how the car runs at 55 mph—gasoline consumption is much greater, and more of the driver's attention is required. Once the car reaches cruising speed (i.e., steady state), the driver may relax a bit, and the gasoline consumption levels off.

Similarly, queueing systems also must go through some initial period of operation before they are operating smoothly and predictably. The solution and study of a queueing system is much simpler when it is known that the system is in steady state. Here a number of important parameters remain fixed, and it becomes relatively straightforward to categorize the operation of the system. *Time-dependent* or *transient solutions* are far more complex, and are beyond the scope of this text. Giffin (Gi78) discusses transient solutions for several simple queueing systems.

15.2.11 Little's Result

One of the simplest and yet most useful measures of queueing system performance is called *Little's result.* It relates the following quantities.

- W_q = mean time a customer spends in the queue.
- λ = arrival rate.
- L_q = number of customers in the queue.
- W = mean time a customer spends in the system.
- L = number of customers in the system.

Little's result may be expressed concisely as

$$L_q = \lambda W_q$$

and

$$L = \lambda W.$$

It says that the number of customers in the queue is equal to the arrival rate multiplied by the mean time a customer spends in the queue, and that the number of customers in the system is equal to the arrival rate multiplied by the mean time a customer spends in the system.

15.2.12 Summary of the Poisson Process

Suppose we are concerned with arrivals occurring at points on a continuous time scale. Define $P(k, t)$ as the probability of exactly k arrivals occurring in a time interval of length t. A process is Poisson if and only if

1. for appropriately small intervals Δt

$$P(k, t) = \begin{cases} \lambda \Delta t, & \text{for } k = 1 \ (\lambda \text{ is thus the average arrival rate}), \\ 1 - \lambda \Delta t, & \text{for } k = 0, \\ 0, & \text{for k} > 1. \end{cases}$$

2. any events that have been defined to occur on nonoverlapping time intervals are mutually independent.

Alternatively, a process is Poisson if the times between successive arrivals, i.e., the *first-order interarrival times,* are identically distributed, exponential random variables.

Figure 15.6 summarizes the following information. Using random variable k to indicate the number of arrivals, the probability of exactly k arrivals in an interval of length t is

$$P(k, t) = \frac{(\lambda t)^k e^{-\lambda t}}{k!}, \quad \Big\{ t \geq 0, \qquad k = 0, 1, 2, \ldots .$$

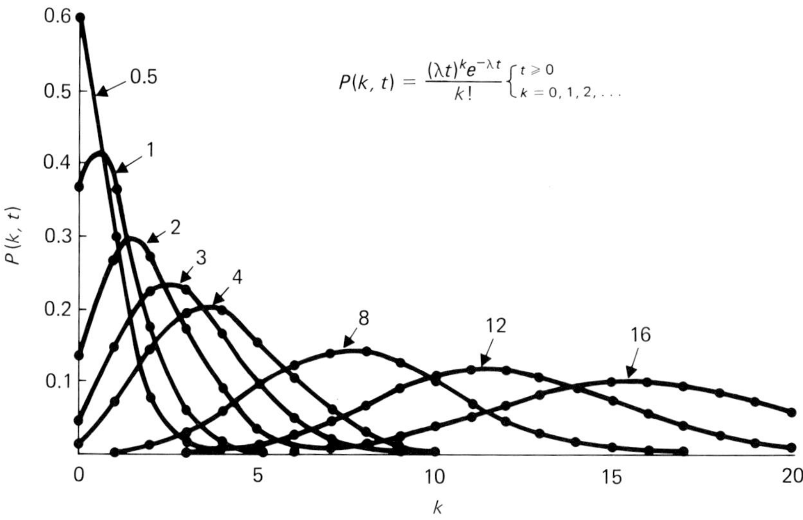

Fig. 15.6 Graphs of the Poisson distribution for various values of λt. (H. Kobayashi, *Modeling and Analysis*, © 1978. Addison-Wesley, Reading, Mass. Figure 3.4 is reprinted with permission.)

The *expectation* (*mean value*) of k is

$$E(k) = \lambda t,$$

and the *variance* of k is

$$\sigma_k^2 = \lambda t.$$

Figure 15.7 summarizes the following information. The sum of two independent Poisson random variables x and y with expectations

$$E(y) = \mu_2 = \lambda_2 t \quad \text{and} \quad E(x) = \mu_1 = \lambda_1 t$$

also describes a Poisson process. In this process, the probability of k arrivals in time t is (for $t \geq 0$, $k = 0, 1, 2, \ldots$).

$$P(k, t) = \frac{(\lambda_1 t + \lambda_2 t)^k e^{-(\lambda_1 t + \lambda_2 t)}}{k!}$$

$$= \frac{(\mu_1 + \mu_2)^k e^{-(\mu_1 + \mu_2)}}{k!}$$

$$= \frac{\mu_s^k e^{-\mu s}}{k!} = \frac{(\lambda_s t)^k e^{-\lambda_s t}}{k!}$$

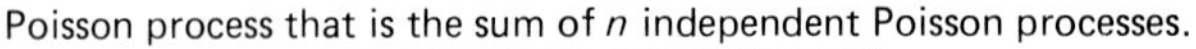

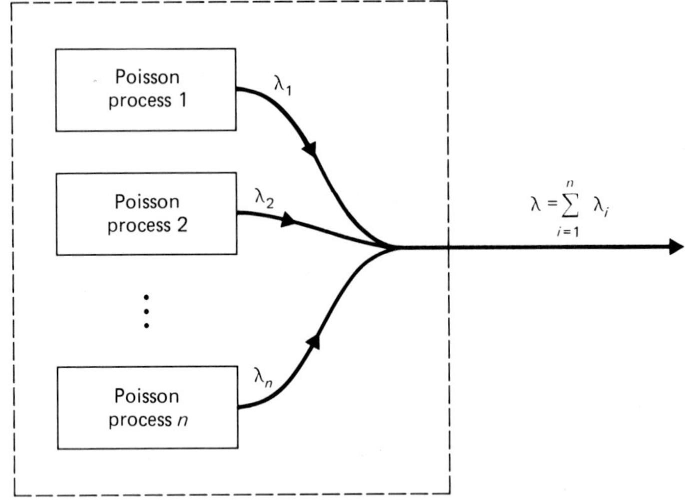

Fig. 15.7 Sum of n independent Poisson processes.

where

$$\mu_s = \mu_1 + \mu_2$$

and

$$\lambda_s = \lambda_1 + \lambda_2.$$

For a Poisson process with arrival rate λ, we may form a new Poisson process using *independent random erasures* as follows. For each arrival in the original process, accept that arrival into the new process with probability P and reject that arrival with probability $(1-P)$. The new process derived in this manner is Poisson with arrival rate λP. Figure 15.8 generalizes this result.

In a Poisson process, the probability of no arrivals in an interval of length t is

$$P(0, t) = \frac{(\lambda t)^0 e^{-\lambda t}}{0!} = e^{-\lambda t}$$

and the probability of one or more arrivals in an interval of length t is

$$1 - P(0, t) = 1 - e^{-\lambda t}.$$

The probability density function for the *first-order interarrival time* (or the time until the first arrival) is

$$f_t(t) = \lambda e^{-\lambda t}, \qquad \text{for } t \geq 0.$$

The expectation of t is

$$E(t) = \frac{1}{\lambda}$$

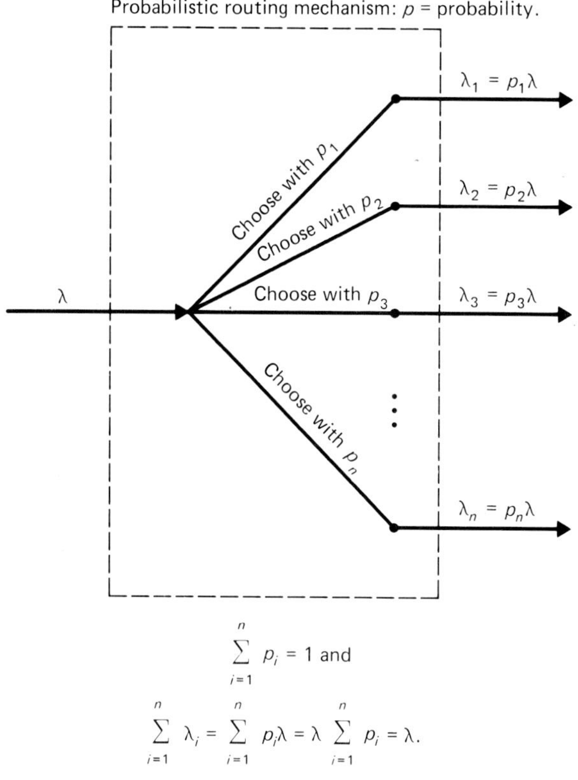

Fig. 15.8 Decomposition of a Poisson process into n independent processes.

and the variance is

$$\sigma_t^2 = \frac{1}{\lambda^2}.$$

The probability density function for the *rth-order interarrival time* (or the time until the rth arrival) is

$$f_t(t) = \frac{\lambda^r t^{r-1} e^{-\lambda t}}{(r-1)!}, \qquad t \geq 0,\ r = 1, 2, \ldots$$

with expectation

$$E(t) = \frac{r}{\lambda}$$

and standard deviation

$$\frac{r}{\lambda^2}.$$

Service facilities can provide exponential service times in which case the probability that the service time will be less than or equal to t is

$$P(S \leq t) = 1 - e^{-\mu t}, \qquad t \geq 0$$

where the mean service rate is μ and the mean service time is $1/\mu$. The probability density function for the service time t is

$$f_t(t) = \mu e^{-\mu t}, \qquad t \geq 0.$$

The mean of the service time is $E(s) = 1/\mu$ and its variance is $1/\mu^2$. A server that operates in this fashion is called an *exponential server.*

15.2.13 Problem One: Analyzing an M/M/1 Queueing System

At one computer consulting firm, programmers need to use an on-line terminal to the firm's central computer system in order to debug their programs. The firm operates 24 hours a day, and 48 programmers (on the average) need to use the terminal once a day. The programmers arrive at the terminal at random (i.e., Poisson arrivals). The time each programmer spends at the terminal is exponential and averages 20 minutes.

Each day the firm receives several complaints from the programming staff that the waits experienced at the terminal are too long and that productivity is being lost. The programmers argue that more terminals are needed. Management is concerned that the terminal is being utilized only two-thirds of the time, and thus argues that adding terminals seems wasteful.

Use queueing theory to analyze the situation at this firm, and determine if indeed additional terminals are warranted.

Solution. We use an M/M/1 queueing system to model the use of the terminal at this firm.

The equations for an M/M/c system are summarized in Fig. 15.9. The reader interested in their derivation should consult probability texts such as (An78)(Ko78).

Now let's derive the equations for an M/M/1 system from those for an M/M/c system. First we note

$$u = \frac{\lambda}{\mu} = \lambda E(s)$$

and

$$\rho = \frac{u}{c} = \frac{u}{1} = u = \lambda E(s).$$

Now

$$C(c, u) = \frac{\dfrac{u^c}{c!}}{\dfrac{u^c}{c!} + (1 - \rho) \displaystyle\sum_{n=0}^{c-1} \dfrac{u^n}{n!}}$$

$u = \frac{\lambda}{\mu} = \lambda E(s).$	Traffic intensity
$\rho = \frac{u}{c}.$	Server utilization
$C(c, u) = \dfrac{\frac{u^c}{c!}}{\frac{u^c}{c!} + (1-\rho)\sum_{n=0}^{c-1} \frac{u^n}{n!}}.$	The probability that all of the servers are currently in use, and thus an arriving customer must wait
$W_q = \dfrac{C(c, u)\,E(s)}{c(1-\rho)}.$	Mean queueing time
$W = W_q + E(s).$	Mean time in system
$\pi_q(90) = \dfrac{E(s)}{c(1-\rho)} \ln(10C(c, u)).$	The 90th percentile time in the queue

Fig. 15.9 Steady-state formulas for M/M/c queueing system. (Adapted with permission from Table 5, Appendix C, An 78.)

becomes

$$C(1, u) = \dfrac{\frac{u^1}{1!}}{\frac{u^1}{1!} + (1-\rho)\sum_{n=0}^{1-1} \frac{u^n}{n!}} = \frac{u}{u + (1-\rho)}$$

$$\therefore \boxed{C(1, u) = C(1, \rho) = u = \rho = \lambda E(s)}$$

$$W_q = \frac{C(c, u)E(s)}{c(1-\rho)} = \frac{C(1, u)E(s)}{1-\rho}$$

$$\therefore \boxed{W_q = \frac{\rho E(s)}{1-\rho}}$$

$$W = W_q + E(s) = \frac{\rho E(s)}{1-\rho} + \frac{E(s)\,(1-\rho)}{(1-\rho)}$$

$$\therefore \boxed{W = \frac{E(s)}{1 - \rho}}$$

$$\pi_q(90) = \frac{E(s)}{c(1 - \rho)} \ln (10\, C(c, u))$$

$$\therefore \boxed{\pi_q(90) = \frac{E(s)}{1 - \rho} \ln (10\rho) = W \ln (10\rho)}$$

These results are summarized in Fig. 15.10.

$$C(c, u) = \rho = \lambda E(s).$$

$$W_q = \frac{\rho E(s)}{1 - \rho}.$$

$$W = \frac{E(s)}{1 - \rho}.$$

$$\pi_q(90) = W \ln (10\rho).$$

Fig. 15.10 Steady-state formulas for M/M/1 queueing system.

The terminal utilization truly is 2/3 since

$$u = \lambda E(s) = \frac{48}{24} \cdot \frac{1}{3} = \frac{2}{3}$$

so $\rho = 2/3$ and $E(s) = 20$ minutes. The average time a programmer must wait before using a terminal is

$$W_q = \frac{\rho E(s)}{1 - \rho} = \frac{(2/3)\ 20}{(1/3)} = 40 \text{ minutes.}$$

The total time a programmer spends at the terminal facility is

$$W = W_q + E(s) = 40 + 20 = 60 \text{ minutes.}$$

The 90th percentile queueing time is

$$\begin{aligned} \pi_q(90) &= W \ln (10\rho) = 60 \ln (6.667) \\ &= 113.826 \text{ minutes.} \end{aligned}$$

Thus 10 percent of the programmers (about five per day) are indeed experiencing annoying waits. These programmers are waiting almost two hours at the terminal before being able to use it.

Little's result gives us some additional information. The arrival rate of programmers at the terminal is

$$\lambda = \frac{48}{24(60)} = \frac{1}{30} \text{ programmers per minute}$$

and thus

$$L_q = \frac{1}{30}\,40 = 1.33 \text{ programmers waiting}$$

and

$$L = \frac{1}{30}\,60 = 2 \text{ programmers in the terminal room.}$$

This completes our analysis of Problem One and confirms that the single terminal is not sufficient for handling the programmers' needs without causing excessive waits.

15.2.14 Problem Two: Analyzing an M/M/c Queueing System

After considering the preceding analysis, the firm has decided to purchase additional computer terminals. How many additional terminals should be purchased to keep the 90th percentile waiting times below ten minutes? Should these terminals be kept in a central location, or should they be located throughout the building? (*Note*: Ignore the time it takes programmers to walk to the terminals.)

Solution. First let us consider locating individual terminals at separate locations throughout the firm. Each of the terminals will be treated as an M/M/1 queueing system, and the work load will be split evenly between the terminals. Figure 15.11 shows the effects of placing two, three, four, or five terminals at separate locations.

Note that the queueing times drop off rapidly as soon as we add the second M/M/1 terminal. But the 90th percentile queueing times remain above ten minutes until we add the fifth terminal. In order to satisfy the requirement of waiting times less than ten minutes long, we must go to five terminals if we use separate M/M/1 systems.

Now let's try grouping all of the terminals at a central location. We consider a single M/M/2 queueing system and use the formulas for M/M/c systems shown in Fig. 15.9.

$$u = \frac{2}{3},$$

		Per terminal				
		One terminal	Two terminals	Three terminals	Four terminals	Five terminals
Server utilization	ρ	$\frac{2}{3}$	$\frac{1}{3}$	$\frac{2}{9}$	$\frac{1}{6}$	$\frac{2}{15}$
Expected service time	$E(s)$	20 min	20 min	20 min	20 min	20 min
Expected time in queue	W_q	40 min	10 min	5.7 min	4 min	3.1 min
Expected time in system	W	60 min	30 min	25.7 min	24 min	23 min
The 90th percentile queueing time	$\pi_q(90)$	113.8 min	36.1 min	20.5 min	12.3 min	6.6 min

Fig. 15.11 Summary of using M/M/1 queueing systems to solve Problem Two.

$$\rho = \frac{2}{3 \cdot 2} = \frac{1}{3},$$

$$C(2, u) = C\left(2, \frac{2}{3}\right),$$

$$= \frac{\dfrac{\left(\frac{2}{3}\right)^2}{2!}}{\dfrac{\left(\frac{2}{3}\right)^2}{2!} + \left(1 - \frac{1}{3}\right)\sum_{n=0}^{2-1} \dfrac{\left(\frac{2}{3}\right)^n}{n!}},$$

$$= \frac{\frac{2}{9}}{\frac{2}{9} + \frac{2}{3}\left(1 + \frac{2}{3}\right)} = \frac{1}{6},$$

$$W_q = \frac{C(c, u)\,E(s)}{c(1 - \rho)} = \frac{\frac{1}{6} \cdot 20}{2 \cdot \frac{2}{3}} = 2.5 \text{ min},$$

$$W = W_q + E(s) = 2.5 + 20 = 22.5 \text{ min},$$

$$\pi_q(90) = \frac{E(s)}{c(1 - \rho)} \ln\,(10\, C(c, u)),$$

$$= \frac{20}{2 \cdot \frac{2}{3}} \ln (1.667) = 7.66 \text{ min.}$$

It is fascinating that the 90th percentile queueing time of the M/M/2 system is below the ten minute criterion. Thus with only two centrally located terminals the firm may eliminate the serious waiting problems of the single terminal system. So it would take five M/M/1 distributed terminals or two terminals in a central M/M/2 configuration to ensure a 90th percentile queueing time of less than ten minutes. Since we are assuming negligible travel times, the firm would certainly choose the M/M/2 system.

15.3 MARKOV PROCESSES

It is often the case that it is possible to describe a system as being in one of a set of *mutually exclusive* and *collectively exhaustive* discrete *states* $S_0, S_1, S_2, \ldots, S_n$. A *Markov process* is a convenient model for describing the behavior of such a system.

In Markov processes, the *present state* of the system, and the *transition probabilities* of transitions between the various states, characterize the future behavior of the system. *Given that a Markov process is in a particular state, its future behavior is not dependent on its past history prior to entering that state.*

Many Markov processes exhibit steady-state behavior in which the probabilities that the process is in each particular state are constant in time. We will consider only those Markov processes with this nice property.

15.3.1 Some Definitions

In a Markov process, a state S_j is said to be *transient,* if from some state S_k which can be reached from S_j the system cannot return to S_j.

A state S_j is said to be *recurrent* if from every S_k reachable from S_j the system can return to S_k.

A *single chain* is a set of recurrent states such that the system can get from each state in the chain to every other state in the chain.

In a *continuous transition Markov process* state changes may occur at any instant on a continuous time scale.

15.3.2 Birth and Death Processes

An important case of Markov processes, namely *birth and death processes,* is particularly applicable in computer systems modeling. Birth and death processes are much easier to solve than are general Markov processes.

A *continuous Markov birth and death process* has the property that

$$\lambda_{ij} = 0 \qquad \text{if } (j \neq i + 1 \qquad \text{and} \qquad j \neq i - 1)$$

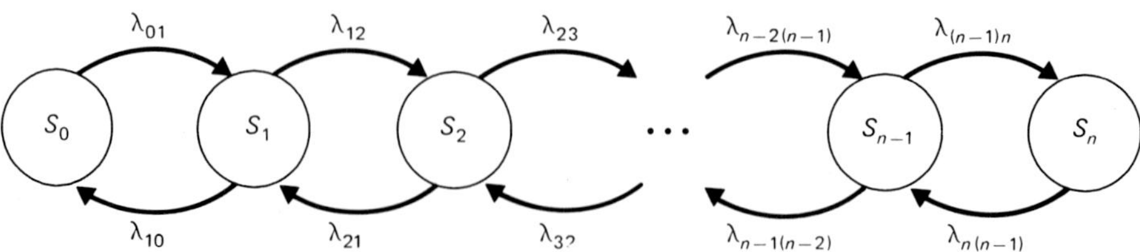

Fig. 15.12 Birth and death process.

where λ_{ij} is the rate at which transitions from state S_i to state S_j occur (Fig. 15.12).

For these processes, we use the notation (Fig. 15.13)

$$\lambda_{i(i+1)} = b_i = \textit{average birthrate} \text{ from state } S_i,$$

$$\lambda_{i(i-1)} = d_i = \textit{average death rate} \text{ from state } S_i.$$

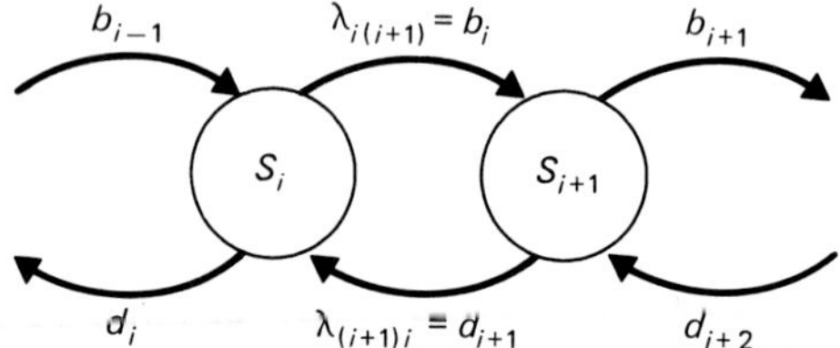

Fig. 15.13 Birth and death notation.

Let P_i be the steady-state probability that the process is in state S_i. At steady state, in any randomly chosen time interval Δt, the process is just as likely to make an $S_i \rightarrow S_{i+1}$ transition (with probability $P_i b_i$) as it is to make an $S_{i+1} \rightarrow S_i$ transition (with probability $P_{i+1} d_{i+1}$) and therefore

$$P_i b_i = P_{i+1} d_{i+1}.$$

We may solve a continuous birth and death process, i.e., determine the various P_i's, by using the relationships

$$P_{i+1} = \frac{b_i}{d_{i+1}} P_i$$

and

$$\sum_i P_i = 1.$$

Now let us consider an example that illustrates the use of birth and death processes in computer systems modeling.

15.3.3 Problem Three: Analyzing the Performance of a Disk Subsystem

Suppose that disk access requests arrive as a Poisson process with average rate λ requests per minute. If the disk is in use, the request is placed in a first-come-first-served queue to await service. When the disk becomes available, the first request on the queue is serviced. Service time is an exponentially distributed random variable with an expected value of $1/\mu$ minutes. The average service rate is μ requests per minute.

Determine, for each of the following cases, the expected value for the total number of disk requests pending (i.e., in the queue or in service), and the limiting state probabilities.

CASE I: The disk facility contains only a single arm, and can service only one request at a time. The service rate is μ.

CASE II: The disk facility contains a very large number of moving arms, each of which can service a disk request at the same rate, μ (and thus we shall assume an infinite number of requests may be serviced in parallel).

Solution (*Case I*). Let S_i be the state of the system when there are i disk requests at the disk service facility. The arrival rate of requests is independent of the state of the system, and so the probability of the transition $S_i \rightarrow S_{i+1}$ in the next time interval Δt is $\lambda \Delta t$.

We view the system as an infinite state single chain continuous birth and death process with

$$b_i = \lambda, \qquad i = 0, 1, 2, \ldots$$

and

$$d_i = \begin{cases} 0, & i = 0 \\ \mu, & i = 1, 2, 3, \ldots \end{cases}$$

since only one request may be serviced at a time, and this is serviced at rate μ.

We use the state transition diagram in Fig. 15.14.

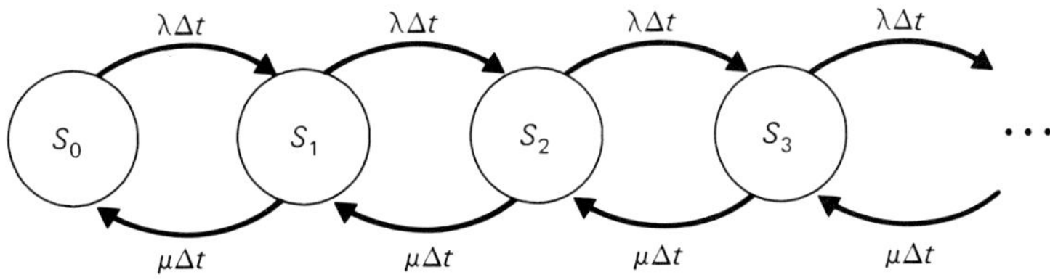

Fig. 15.14 Markov birth and death model for Case I.

We shall assume $\mu > \lambda$ (otherwise the length of the queue of waiting requests might grow indefintely). We use the relationships

$$P_{i+1} = \frac{b_i}{d_{i+1}} P_i; \qquad i = 0, 1, 2, \ldots$$

and

$$\sum_{i=0}^{\infty} P_i = 1.$$

Thus

$$P_1 = \left(\frac{\lambda}{\mu}\right) P_0,$$

$$P_2 = \left(\frac{\lambda}{\mu}\right) P_1 = \left(\frac{\lambda}{\mu}\right)^2 P_0$$

and in general

$$P_i = \left(\frac{\lambda}{\mu}\right)^i P_0,$$

$$\sum_{i=0}^{\infty} P_i = 1 = \sum_{i=0}^{\infty}\left(\frac{\lambda}{\mu}\right)^i P_0 = \frac{1}{1-\frac{\lambda}{\mu}} P_0$$

and thus the probability that the system is idle is

$$\boxed{P_0 = 1 - \frac{\lambda}{\mu}}$$

and the probability that there are i requests pending is

$$\boxed{P_i = \left(1 - \frac{\lambda}{\mu}\right)\left(\frac{\lambda}{\mu}\right)^i} \qquad i = 0, 1, 2, 3, \ldots$$

and the average number of requests pending is

$$\begin{aligned} E(i) &= \sum_{i=0}^{\infty} iP_i \\ &= \sum_{i=0}^{\infty} i\left(1-\frac{\lambda}{\mu}\right)\left(\frac{\lambda}{\mu}\right)^i = \left(1-\frac{\lambda}{\mu}\right)\sum_{i=0}^{\infty} i\left(\frac{\lambda}{\mu}\right)^i \\ &= \left(1-\frac{\lambda}{\mu}\right)\left(\frac{\lambda}{\mu}\right)\sum_{i=0}^{\infty} i\left(\frac{\lambda}{\mu}\right)^{i-1} = \left(1-\frac{\lambda}{\mu}\right)\left(\frac{\lambda}{\mu}\right)\frac{1}{\left(1-\frac{\lambda}{\mu}\right)^2} \end{aligned}$$

and thus

$$\boxed{E(i) = \frac{\lambda}{\mu}\left(1 - \frac{\lambda}{\mu}\right)^{-1}}.$$

Figure 15.15 summarizes the results for Case I.

Solution (*Case II*). With i requests currently being serviced, the probability that a particular request will finish being served in the next Δt is $\mu\Delta t$, and the probability that exactly one request (any one) will finish is $i\mu\Delta t$ (this is a good first-order approximation). This relationship holds because any of the i requests may finish and cause a state change.

Here, too, we view the system as an infinite state single chain continuous birth and death process with

$$b_i = \lambda, \qquad i = 0, 1, 2, \ldots$$

but now

$$d_i = \begin{cases} 0, & i = 0 \\ i\mu, & i = 1, 2, 3, \ldots. \end{cases}$$

Because we have an infinite number of parallel servers, no customer has to wait.

We use the state transition diagram in Fig. 15.16. Now, we again use

$$P_{i+1} = \frac{b_i}{d_{i+1}} P_i, \qquad i = 0, 1, 2, \ldots$$

and

$$\sum_{i=0}^{\infty} P_i = 1.$$

Thus

$$P_1 = \frac{\lambda}{\mu} P_0$$

$$P_2 = \frac{\lambda}{2\mu} P_1 = \frac{1}{2}\left(\frac{\lambda}{\mu}\right)^2 P_0$$

$$P_3 = \frac{\lambda}{3\mu} P_2 = \frac{1}{3\cdot 2}\left(\frac{\lambda}{\mu}\right)^3 P_0$$

and in general

$$P_i = \frac{1}{i!}\left(\frac{\lambda}{\mu}\right)^i P_0$$

$$\sum_{i=0}^{\infty} P_i = 1 = \sum_{i=0}^{\infty} \frac{1}{i!}\left(\frac{\lambda}{\mu}\right)^i P_0.$$

λ/μ	System is idle P_0	Probability of having this number of requests pending P_1	P_2	P_3	P_4	P_5	P_6	P_7	P_8	P_9	Average requests pending $E(i)$
0.1	.9000	.0900	.0090	.0009	.0001	.0000	.0000	.0000	.0000	.0000	0.11
0.2	.8000	.1600	.0320	.0064	.0013	.0003	.0001	.0000	.0000	.0000	0.25
0.3	.7000	.2100	.0630	.0189	.0057	.0017	.0005	.0002	.0000	.0000	0.43
0.4	.6000	.2400	.0960	.0384	.0154	.0061	.0025	.0010	.0004	.0002	0.67
0.5	.5000	.2500	.1250	.0625	.0313	.0156	.0078	.0039	.0020	.0010	1.00
0.6	.4000	.2400	.1440	.0864	.0513	.0311	.0187	.0112	.0067	.0040	1.50
0.7	.3000	.2100	.1470	.1029	.0720	.0504	.0353	.0247	.0173	.0121	2.33
0.8	.2000	.1600	.1280	.1024	.0819	.0655	.0524	.0419	.0336	.0268	4.00
0.9	.1000	.0900	.0810	.0729	.0656	.0590	.0531	.0478	.0430	.0387	9.00
0.91	.0900	.0819	.0745	.0678	.0617	.0562	.0511	.0465	.0423	.0385	10.11
0.92	.0800	.0736	.0677	.0623	.0573	.0527	.0485	.0446	.0411	.0378	11.50
0.93	.0700	.0651	.0605	.0563	.0524	.0487	.0453	.0421	.0392	.0364	13.29
0.94	.0600	.0564	.0530	.0498	.0468	.0440	.0414	.0389	.0366	.0344	15.67
0.95	.0500	.0475	.0451	.0429	.0407	.0387	.0368	.0349	.0332	.0315	19.00
0.96	.0400	.0384	.0369	.0354	.0340	.0326	.0313	.0301	.0289	.0277	24.00
0.97	.0300	.0291	.0282	.0274	.0266	.0258	.0250	.0242	.0235	.0228	32.33
0.98	.0200	.0196	.0192	.0188	.0184	.0181	.0177	.0174	.0170	.0167	49.00
0.99	.0100	.0099	.0098	.0097	.0096	.0095	.0094	.0093	.0092	.0091	99.00

Fig. 15.15 Summary of results for Case I.

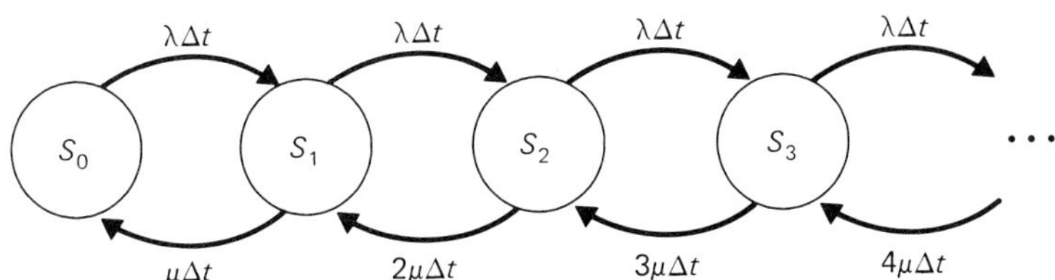

Fig. 15.16 Markov birth and death model for Case II.

Now since

$$\sum_{n=0}^{\infty} \frac{x^n}{n!} = e^x,$$

we have

$$\sum_{i=0}^{\infty} \frac{1}{i!}\left(\frac{\lambda}{\mu}\right)^i P_0 = e^{\lambda/\mu} P_0$$

and thus

$$\boxed{P_0 = e^{-\lambda/\mu}}$$

and

$$\boxed{P_i = \left(\frac{\lambda}{\mu}\right)^i \frac{e^{-\lambda/\mu}}{i!}}$$

and

$$E(i) = \sum_{i=0}^{\infty} i\left(\frac{\lambda}{\mu}\right)^i \frac{e^{-\lambda/\mu}}{i!}$$

$$= e^{-\lambda/\mu} \sum_{i=0}^{\infty} i\left(\frac{\lambda}{\mu}\right)^i \frac{1}{i!} = e^{-\lambda/\mu} \sum_{i=0}^{\infty} \frac{\lambda}{\mu}\left(\frac{\lambda}{\mu}\right)^{i-1} \frac{1}{(i-1)!}$$

$$= e^{-\lambda/\mu}\left(\frac{\lambda}{\mu}\right) \sum_{i=0}^{\infty} \frac{1}{(i-1)!}\left(\frac{\lambda}{\mu}\right)^{i-1} = e^{-\lambda/\mu}\left(\frac{\lambda}{\mu}\right) e^{\lambda/\mu}$$

and thus

$$\boxed{E(i) = \frac{\lambda}{\mu}}.$$

λ/μ	System is idle P_0	Probability of having this number of requests pending P_1	P_2	P_3	P_4	P_5	P_6	P_7	P_8	P_9	Average requests pending $E(i)$
0.1	.9048	.0905	.0045	.0002	.0000	.0000	.0000	.0000	.0000	.0000	0.10
0.2	.8187	.1637	.0164	.0011	.0001	.0000	.0000	.0000	.0000	.0000	0.20
0.3	.7408	.2222	.0333	.0033	.0003	.0000	.0000	.0000	.0000	.0000	0.30
0.4	.6703	.2681	.0536	.0072	.0007	.0001	.0000	.0000	.0000	.0000	0.40
0.5	.6065	.3033	.0758	.0126	.0016	.0002	.0000	.0000	.0000	.0000	0.50
0.6	.5488	.3293	.0988	.0198	.0030	.0004	.0000	.0000	.0000	.0000	0.60
0.7	.4966	.3476	.1217	.0284	.0050	.0007	.0001	.0000	.0000	.0000	0.70
0.8	.4493	.3595	.1438	.0383	.0077	.0012	.0002	.0000	.0000	.0000	0.80
0.9	.4066	.3659	.1647	.0494	.0111	.0020	.0003	.0000	.0000	.0000	0.90
0.91	.4025	.3663	.1667	.0506	.0115	.0021	.0003	.0000	.0000	.0000	0.91
0.92	.3985	.3666	.1687	.0517	.0119	.0022	.0003	.0000	.0000	.0000	0.92
0.93	.3946	.3669	.1706	.0529	.0123	.0023	.0004	.0000	.0000	.0000	0.93
0.94	.3906	.3672	.1726	.0541	.0127	.0024	.0004	.0001	.0000	.0000	0.94
0.95	.3867	.3674	.1745	.0553	.0131	.0025	.0004	.0001	.0000	.0000	0.95
0.96	.3829	.3676	.1764	.0565	.0136	.0026	.0004	.0001	.0000	.0000	0.96
0.97	.3791	.3677	.1783	.0577	.0140	.0027	.0004	.0001	.0000	.0000	0.97
0.98	.3753	.3678	.1802	.0589	.0144	.0028	.0005	.0001	.0000	.0000	0.98
0.99	.3716	.3679	.1821	.0601	.0149	.0029	.0005	.0001	.0000	.0000	0.99

Figure 15.17

Figure 15.17 summarizes the results for Case II. The reader should study Figs. 15.15 and 15.17 carefully to appreciate the differences between the single server and infinite server systems.

In the single server system, if an arriving request finds the disk facility busy, it must wait. In the infinite server system, arriving requests always enter service immediately.

In the single server system, as λ approaches μ, the chance that the system is idle decreases rapidly, and so arriving requests wait. The average number of requests pending grows rapidly. In the infinite server system, the average number of requests pending approaches 1.

SUMMARY

Analytic models are mathematical representations of systems that allow the performance evaluator to draw quick and accurate conclusions about a system's behavior. Queueing models are useful for modeling systems in which requests wait in lines, or queues, until they may be serviced.

Queues may be bounded or unbounded. Customers are supplied to a queueing system from a source which may be finite or infinite. We assumed random arrivals without the possibility of collisions. The times between successive arrivals are called interarrival times. A Poisson arrival process is characterized by the fact that the interarrival times are distributed exponentially. We assume exponential servers to process arriving requests.

Queues may have either infinite capacity, zero capacity, or positive capacity. Queues with zero capacity are characteristic of loss systems.

Systems may be classified as single server systems or multiple server systems. The traffic intensity is the ratio of the mean service time to the mean interarrrival time. It is a measure of a system's ability to service its customers effectively. The server utilization is the traffic intensity per server. It is the probability that a particular server is busy.

Elementary analytic modeling techniques are generally concerned with the steady-state behavior of a system. Transient behavior is a great deal more difficult to model.

Little's result is that the number of customers in the queue is equal to the arrival rate multiplied by the mean time a customer spends in the queue, and that the number of customers in the system is equal to the arrival rate multiplied by the mean time a customer spends in the system.

A process is Poisson if the times between successive arrivals, i.e., the first-order interarrival times, are identically distributed exponential random variables. The sum of two independent Poisson random variables also describes a Poisson process. If independent random erasures are applied to a Poisson process, the new process derived in this manner is also Poisson.

Markov processes are useful for modeling systems that may be in one of a set of mutually exclusive and collectively exhaustive discrete states. Given that a Markov process is in a particular state, its future behavior is not dependent on its past history prior to entering that state. We considered only Markov processes that exhibit steady-state behavior.

An important special case of Markov processes, namely birth and death processes, is particularly applicable in computer systems modeling. Birth and death processes are much easier to solve than general Markov processes.

TERMINOLOGY

analytic model
arrival rate
arrivals
bounded queue
customer population
finite source
infinite capacity queue
infinite source
interarrival time
Kendall notation
Law of Large Numbers
Little's result
loss system
M/M/1 queueing system
M/M/c queueing system
Markov process
multiple server system
Poisson arrivals
positive capacity queue
probability distribution
queue
queue capacity
queue discipline
queueing network
queueing theory
random variable
server
server utilization
service facility
service time
single server system
source
steady state
steady-state solution
traffic intensity
transient solution
unbounded queue
utilization
waiting line
zero capacity queue

EXERCISES

15.1 What are analytic models? Why are they of interest in computer systems performance evaluation?

15.2 Why are queueing models so applicable to operating systems? Give several examples of queueing mechanisms in operating systems.

15.3 Real queueing mechanisms must have bounded rather than unbounded queues. List several problems that might occur in an operating system when bounded queues become full.

15.4 Much of elementary queueing theory relies on the assumption that arrivals and service times are random. Give several examples in operating systems in which this assumption is reasonable. Give several examples in which the assumption is unreasonable.

15.5 Give an example of a loss system that develops in interrupt processing, particularly in real-time systems.

15.6 Give several examples of areas within operating systems that can be modeled by

a) single server systems
b) multiple server systems

15.7 List all of the queue disciplines that have been presented in the text so far. For each, give an example in which it is applicable.

15.8 Why must one be careful when modeling certain quantities with random variables?

15.9 Give several examples in which operating systems may be expected to exhibit

a) transient behavior
b) steady-state behavior

15.10 Give an intuitive argument supporting Little's result.

Note: For exercises 15.11 through 15.16 assume Poisson arrival processes and exponential servers.

15.11 Suppose disk requests arrive at a rate of $\lambda = 10$ requests per second. Use a calculator or write a program to produce the values for Chart 15.1.

t = number of seconds	k = number of arrivals										
	0	1	2	3	4	5	6	7	8	9	10
1											
2											
3											
4	Probability of exactly k arrivals in t seconds										
5											
6											
7											
8											
9											
10											

Chart 15.1

15.12 Two small telecommunications computers each receive requests for service at the rate of $\lambda = 15$ requests per second. These two systems are to be replaced with a single, higher-capacity system. Characterize the arrival process for the new system.

15.13 Requests arrive at a computer network at the rate of λ. They are routed probabilistically to n different network hosts (i.e., computer systems that can perform computation for network users) with probabilities $P_1, P_2, \ldots, P_n$.

a) What is the request arrival rate at each host?

b) What are the merits of using such a probabilistic routing mechanism rather than routing requests in a simple round robin fashion?

c) What are the merits of using such a probabilistic routing mechanism rather than routing requests to the first available host?

d) What potential problems are inherent in probabilistic routing mechanisms? In systems with a large number of hosts servicing a large number of requests would these problems be serious? Explain.

15.14 Jobs arrive at a batch processing computer center at the rate of 24 per hour. From the moment the center opens in the morning

a) how much time should the operator expect to elapse before the first job arrives?

b) how much time should the operator expect to elapse before r jobs arrive?

15.15 A batch processing computer system processes similar compile-and-run jobs. Service times are exponential with a mean of 15 minutes. For a given job what is the probability it will take

a) 5 minutes or less?

b) 15 minutes or less?

c) one hour or less?

d) more than two hours?

15.16 One emerging field in which computer expertise is in demand is called "the factory of the future." Heavily automated factories run by robots and computerized machinery with minimal human supervision will operate 24 hours per day. Real-time process control systems will monitor and control the robots and machinery.

A designer of one such factory is considering the use of four small process control systems vs. the use of one centralized multiprocessor system with several processors of equivalent capacity to the small systems. In this problem you will use queueing theory to help the designer choose the best alternative. Arrivals are Poisson at the rate of 960 per minute. Assume each of the identical processors has exponential service times with a mean of 0.05 seconds.

a) First consider the alternative of using the four small systems. Consider these as M/M/1 queueing systems and characterize their performance as thoroughly as you can using the results from this chapter. Assume each experiences a Poisson arrival rate of 240 requests per minute.

b) Now consider using a single symmetric multiprocessor system with two processors of equivalent capacity to the small systems' processors. Analyze this M/M/2 system as thoroughly as you can using the results of this chapter.

c) Compare the preceding analyses. Which approach would you recommend to the designer? What additional information might you require before making a decision?

15.17 Why are Markov models so applicable to operating systems? Give several examples of activities in operating systems that Markov models might be useful in modeling.

15.18 A computer designer must choose between an architecture with a single powerful processor and an architecture employing multiprocessing, but with less powerful processors.

The computer system being designed must process requests arriving as a Poisson process with an average rate of λ requests per second. If the single processor system is busy, requests are placed in a first-come-first-served queue to await service. In the multiprocessor architecture we shall assume massive parallelism, i.e., there are many more processors than processes, so no arriving process ever waits.

The single processor system has a processor with exponential service times with mean rate μ requests per second. The processors in the massive parallelism architecture are only one-tenth as powerful.

a) Determine for the single processor system and for the massive parallelism system the expected value for the total number of requests pending (i.e., either waiting or in service), and the limiting state probabilities (where states correspond to the number of requests pending).
b) From your preceding analysis, which architecture would you recommend the designer choose? What additional information might you require before making a decision? Is the correct decision sensitive to the arrival and service rates? If so, then how? If not, then why not?

n	$\log_e n$	n	$\log_e n$	n	$\log_e n$
0.0	*	4.5	1.5041	9.0	2.1972
0.1	7.6974	4.6	1.5261	9.1	2.2083
0.2	8.3906	4.7	1.5476	9.2	2.2192
0.3	8.7960	4.8	1.5686	9.3	2.2300
0.4	9.0837	4.9	1.5892	9.4	2.2407
0.5	9.3069	5.0	1.6094	9.5	2.2513
0.6	9.4892	5.1	1.6292	9.6	2.2618
0.7	9.6433	5.2	1.6487	9.7	2.2721
0.8	9.7769	5.3	1.6677	9.8	2.2824
0.9	9.8946	5.4	1.6864	9.9	2.2925
1.0	0.0000	5.5	1.7047	10	2.3026
1.1	0.0953	5.6	1.7228	11	2.3979
1.2	0.1823	5.7	1.7405	12	2.4849
1.3	0.2624	5.8	1.7579	13	2.5649
1.4	0.3365	5.9	1.7750	14	2.6391
1.5	0.4055	6.0	1.7918	15	2.7081
1.6	0.4700	6.1	1.8083	16	2.7726
1.7	0.5306	6.2	1.8245	17	2.8332
1.8	0.5878	6.3	1.8405	18	2.8904
1.9	0.6419	6.4	1.8563	19	2.9444
2.0	0.6931	6.5	1.8718	20	2.9957
2.1	0.7419	6.6	1.8871	25	3.2189
2.2	0.7885	6.7	1.9021	30	3.4012
2.3	0.8329	6.8	1.9169	35	3.5553
2.4	0.8755	6.9	1.9315	40	3.6889
2.5	0.9163	7.0	1.9459	45	3.8067
2.6	0.9555	7.1	1.9601	50	3.9120
2.7	0.9933	7.2	1.9741	55	4.0073
2.8	1.0296	7.3	1.9879	60	4.0943
2.9	1.0647	7.4	2.0015	65	4.1744
3.0	1.0986	7.5	2.0149	70	4.2485
3.1	1.1314	7.6	2.0281	75	4.3175
3.2	1.1632	7.7	2.0412	80	4.3820
3.3	1.1939	7.8	2.0541	85	4.4427
3.4	1.2238	7.9	2.0669	90	4.4998
3.5	1.2528	8.0	2.0794	95	4.5539
3.6	1.2809	8.1	2.0919	100	4.6052
3.7	1.3083	8.2	2.1041		
3.8	1.3350	8.3	2.1163		
3.9	1.3610	8.4	2.1282		
4.0	1.3863	8.5	2.1401		
4.1	1.4110	8.6	2.1518		
4.2	1.4351	8.7	2.1633		
4.3	1.4586	8.8	2.1748		
4.4	1.4816	8.9	2.1861		

*Subtract 10 from $\log_e$, n entries for $n < 1.0$.

Appendix 15.1 Table of natural logarithms.

x	e^x	e^{-x}	x	e^x	e^{-x}
0.00	1.0000	1.0000	2.5	12.182	0.0821
0.05	1.0513	0.9512	2.6	13.464	0.0743
0.10	1.1052	0.9048	2.7	14.880	0.0672
0.15	1.1618	0.8607	2.8	16.445	0.0608
0.20	1.2214	0.8187	2.9	18.174	0.0550
0.25	1.2840	0.7788	3.0	20.086	0.0498
0.30	1.3499	0.7408	3.1	22.198	0.0450
0.35	1.4191	0.7047	3.2	24.533	0.0408
0.40	1.4918	0.6703	3.3	27.113	0.0369
0.45	1.5683	0.6376	3.4	29.964	0.0334
0.50	1.6487	0.6065	3.5	33.115	0.0302
0.55	1.7333	0.5769	3.6	36.598	0.0273
0.60	1.8221	0.5488	3.7	40.447	0.0247
0.65	1.9155	0.5220	3.8	44.701	0.0224
0.70	2.0138	0.4966	3.9	49.402	0.0202
0.75	2.1170	0.4724	4.0	54.598	0.0183
0.80	2.2255	0.4493	4.1	60.340	0.0166
0.85	2.3396	0.4274	4.2	66.686	0.0150
0.90	2.4596	0.4066	4.3	73.700	0.0136
0.95	2.5857	0.3867	4.4	81.451	0.0123
1.0	2.7183	0.3679	4.5	90.017	0.0111
1.1	3.0042	0.3329	4.6	99.484	0.0101
1.2	3.3201	0.3012	4.7	109.95	0.0091
1.3	3.6693	0.2725	4.8	121.51	0.0082
1.4	4.0552	0.2466	4.9	134.29	0.0074
1.5	4.4817	0.2231	5	148.41	0.0067
1.6	4.9530	0.2019	6	403.43	0.0025
1.7	5.4739	0.1827	7	1096.6	0.0009
1.8	6.0496	0.1653	8	2981.0	0.0003
1.9	6.6859	0.1496	9	8103.1	0.0001
2.0	7.3891	0.1353	10	22026	0.00005
2.1	8.1662	0.1225			
2.2	9.0250	0.1108			
2.3	9.9742	0.1003			
2.4	11.023	0.0907			

Appendix 15.2 Table of exponential functions.

LITERATURE

(An78) Allen, A. O., *Probability, Statistics, and Queueing Theory with Computer Science Applications,* New York: Academic Press, 1978.

(An80) Allen, A. O., "Queueing Models of Computer Systems," *Computer,* Vol. 13, No. 4, April 1980, pp. 13–24.

(Bu71) Buzen, J. P., *Queueing Network Models of Multiprogramming,* Ph.D. Thesis, Cambridge, Mass.: Harvard University Press, 1971.

(Bu73) Buzen, J. P., "Computational Algorithms for Closed Queueing Networks with Exponential Servers," *CACM,* Vol. 16, No. 9, September 1973, pp. 527–531.

(Bu74) Buzen, J. P., and P. S. Goldberg, "Guidelines for the Use of Infinite Source Queueing Models in the Analysis of Computer System Performance," *AFIPS Conf. Proc., NCC,* 1974, pp. 371–374.

(Bu76) Buzen, J. P., "Modeling Computer System Performance," *CMGVII Conf. Proc.,* Atlanta, November 1976.

(Bu78) Buzen, J. P., "A Queueing Network Model of MVS," *ACM Computing Surveys,* Vol. 10, No. 3, September 1978, pp. 319–331.

(Gi78) Giffin, W. C., *Queueing,* Columbus, Ohio: Grid, Inc., 1978.

(Kl76) Kleinrock, L., *Queueing Systems, Volume 2: Computer Applications,* New York: Wiley, 1976.

(Ko78) Kobayashi, H., *Modeling and Analysis: An Introduction to System Performance Evaluation Methodology,* Reading, Mass.: Addison-Wesley, 1978.

(Ku79) Kuehn, P. J., "Approximate Analysis of General Queueing Networks, by Decomposition," *IEEE Trans. Comm.,* Vol. COM-27, No. 1, January 1979, 113–126.

(Lu71) Lucas, H. C., Jr., "Performance Evaluation and Monitoring," *ACM Computing Surveys,* Vol. 3, No. 3, September 1971, pp. 79–91.

(Mu75) Muntz, R., "Analytic Modeling of Interactive Systems," *Proc. IEEE,* Vol. 63, No. 6, June 1975, pp. 946–953.

(Pr76) Price, T. G., Jr., "A Comparison of Queueing Network Models and Measurements of a Multiprogrammed Computer System," *ACM Perf. Eval. Rev.,* Vol. 5, No. 4, Fall 1976, pp. 39–62.

(Re76) Reiser, M., "Interactive Modeling of Computer Systems," *IBM Systems Journal,* Vol. 15, No. 4, 1976, pp. 309–327.

(Sa81) Sauer, C. H., and K. M. Chandy, *Computer Systems Performance Modeling,* Englewood Cliffs, N.J.: Prentice-Hall, 1981.

(Sc79) Schardt, R. M., "An MVS Tuning Perspective," *IBM Washington Systems Center Technical Bulletin,* GG22–9023, March 1979.

(Sp79) Spragins, J., "Approximate Techniques for Modeling the Performance of Complex Systems," *Computer Languages,* Vol. 4, No. 2, 1979, pp. 99–129.

Part 7
Networks and Security

16
Network Operating Systems

If the presence of electricity can be made visible in any part of a circuit, I see no reason why intelligence may not be transmitted instantaneously by electricity.

Samuel F. B. Morse

Mr. Watson, come here, I want you.

Alexander Graham Bell

It's currently a problem of access to gigabits through punybaud.

J. C. R. Licklider

Outline

16.1 INTRODUCTION

Originally undertaken as academic research projects, computer networks have reached the status of effective operating utilities. Construction began on Arpanet (Wa79), the grandparent of today's computer networks, in 1968. Today Arpanet links over 100 computer systems, and thousands of computer users are dependent on its reliable operation.

Several commercial networks offer services to the general public. These include Telenet (Du77) in the United States and Datapac (C176) in Canada. These networks offer their users the ability to access a wide variety of computing resources, both hardware and software, distributed among a large number of connected computer systems.

16.2 ELEMENTS OF COMPUTER NETWORKS

A typical computer network (Fig. 16.1) interconnects many computers called *hosts,* each of which is capable of supplying computing services to network users. The networks are connected by a communications subsystem consisting of *communications processors* and various types of communications links such as telephone lines, satellite channels, coaxial cables, and microwave links.

Communications processors are computer systems with three primary functions.

- They effect the communication between the hosts.
- They offload communications tasks from the hosts.
- They define the interface through which the host computers access the communications capabilities of the network.

Each host computer contains an operating system that supports applications processes. This chapter is concerned with operating systems that control computer networks. These operating systems provide many functions including

- supporting terminal access to remote hosts,
- handling file transfer between hosts, and
- handling interuser communications (such as electronic mail).

The primary purpose of computer networks is resource sharing, but many factors have hindered maximal sharing.

- To use many of today's networks, users must be familiar not only with the mechanisms for accessing the network but also with the individual host operating systems.
- One network may have host computers built by several manufacturers. The operating systems of these various hosts may be dramatically different from one another.
- Accounting for resource usage is often handled by the individual hosts. Users wishing to access the resources of a particular host must first establish a sepa-

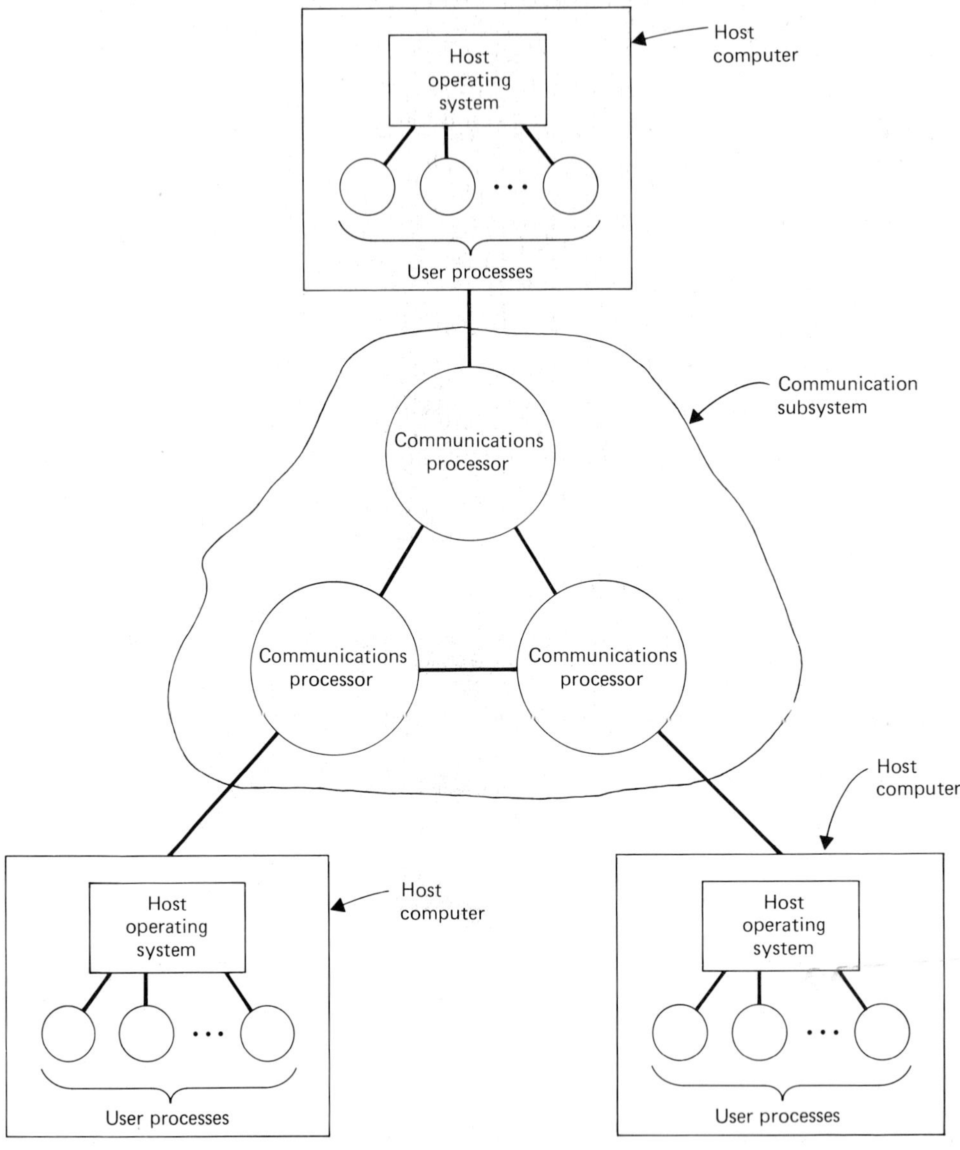

Fig. 16.1 Computer network.

rate account with the organization supporting that host. Thus one user may need to have several different accounts with several different organizations in order to make effective use of a network's resources.

- Documentation about the various hosts and their resources is difficult and costly to obtain.

All of these problems could be solved by the use of an integrated operating system that makes the hosts transparent to the user, and that is controlled by a single organization to which network users subscribe.

16.3 NETWORK CATEGORIES

Networks support various types of distributed processing applications. The nature of these applications greatly affects design, implementation, and operation issues for the networks. Three common categories of networks have evolved. These are (1) *resource sharing networks* (2) *distributed computation networks, and* (3) *remote communication networks.*

16.3.1 Resource Sharing Networks

In resource sharing networks (Fig. 16.2), the resources of the various hosts are made available to other hosts. These may be real devices such as card readers and line printers, or they may be virtual devices such as disk files. The network provides the mechanisms to create the illusion that the remote devices are actually available at the local system. Some resource sharing operations are

- accessing remote files
- transferring files between hosts
- processing data items in a distributed database spread over many of the hosts
- remote printing

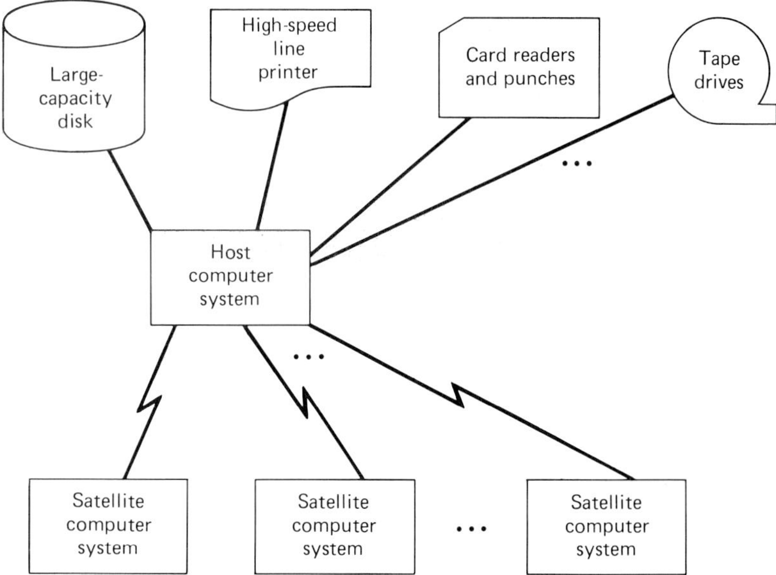

Fig. 16.2 A resource-sharing network.

Communication in resource sharing networks is generally between a process on one host and a resource manager process on another host. In file transfers, the communication involves lengthy streams of data. Accesses to distributed databases generally involve short bursts.

16.3.2 Distributed Computation Networks

On a single computer system, multitasking allows a group of processes to cooperate in accomplishing an activity that can be parcelled into smaller concurrent activities. Distributed computation networks (Fig. 16.3) facilitate such multitasking, but with the individual tasks performed concurrently on several different hosts in the network. Examples of such networks are real-time process control systems, database computers, and parallel processing structures.

Normally, these networks are configured with the resources of particular hosts placed close to the anticipated users of those resources. Applications programs and databases are distributed throughout the network.

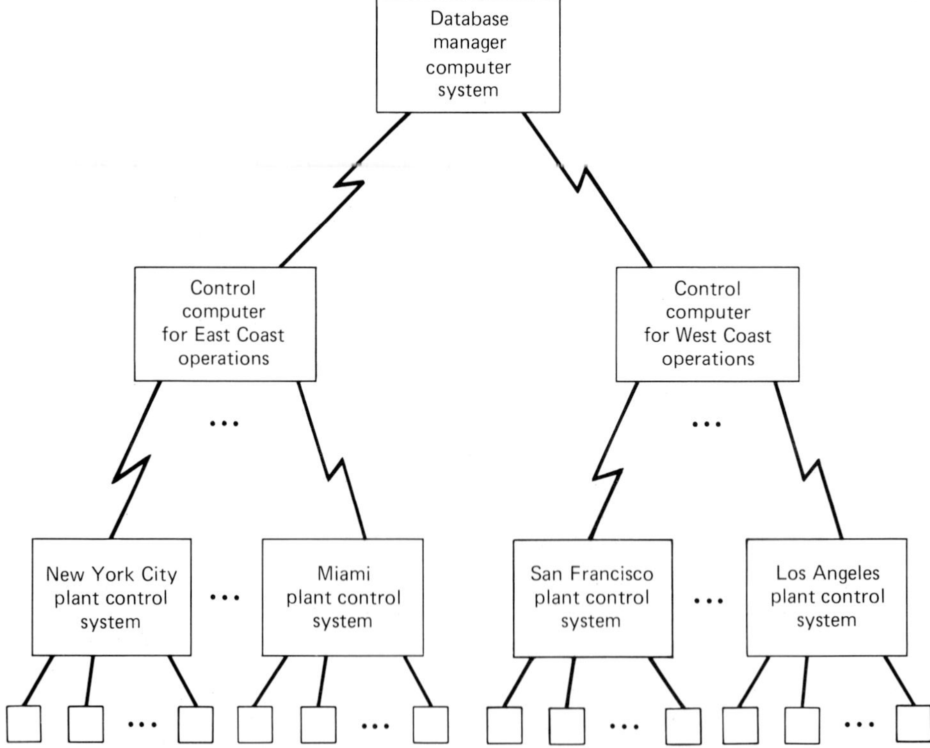

Fig. 16.3 A distributed computation network controlling a company's manufacturing plants nationwide.

16.3.3 Remote Communication Networks

The primary goal of remote communication networks (Fig. 16.4) is to provide the means by which users may access remote computing facilities as economically as possible. Such networks are typically used in remote batch processing systems in which the job defining statements and the input data are entered from a remote site, processed on a distant host, and outputs are returned to the remote site via the network. Such networks often have the databases and applications programs concentrated in one or two large host systems.

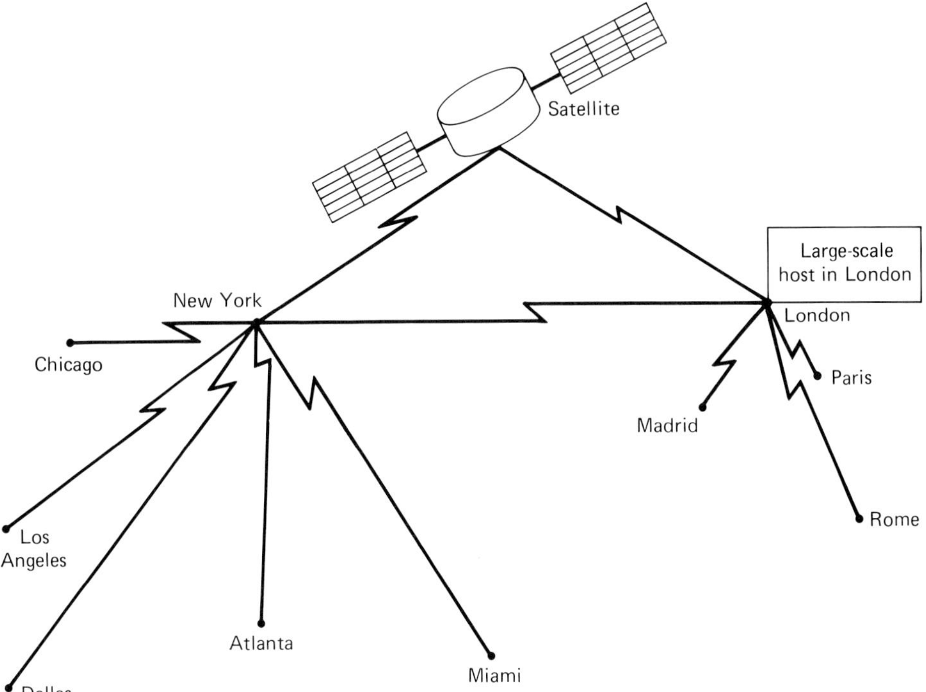

Fig. 16.4 A remote communication network. (From p. 264, *VAX Software Handbook.* © 1981, Digital Equipment Corporation, Maynard, Mass.)

16.4 PACKET SWITCHING

In the late 1960s virtually all data communications occurred over circuit-switched networks like that used by the telephone system. These networks allocate transmission bandwidth (or capacity) for the duration of an entire call—if no one is communicating, the capacity is wasted.

In packet switching, this capacity is allocated dynamically as it is needed to several users who may share the same line. Virtually all new data transmission networks built today use packet switching. In a packet network, messages are divided into packets or fixed length blocks of characters. The actual data is surrounded by error checking information, packet identification, information, routing information, billing information, etc. The key to the scheme is that computers along the path of the packet operate so quickly and can do so much error correction and detection that *it is possible to achieve flawless transmission even over unreliable channels.*

The first published material on what is today considered packet switching was *On Distributed Communications* prepared at the Rand Corporation by Paul Baran in 1964. This study was undertaken for the Air Force to develop a means for communications that would be capable of surviving an attack.

The term *packet* was coined by Donald Davies in a 1966 document that described the 128-byte blocks of data to be transported in a *store-and-forward transmission* system.

In 1967, ARPA (the Advanced Research Projects Agency of the Defense Department) planned the Arpanet to link computing facilities at major universities and research facilities throughout the United States. The plan included the use of packet switching over 50K-bit/second leased lines. Minicomputers were to serve as the packet switches.

As implemented, Arpanet is a completely distributed system. Its dynamic routing algorithm continually examines the load at each network node to determine the best transmission path. Early skeptics claimed that some packets might loop forever in such a network, but these fears soon proved to be unfounded.

In 1975, B.B.N. (Bolt, Beranek, and Newman, Inc.) introduced Telenet, the first public packet network service. By 1978, the network supported 180 host computers across the United States, and had connections to 14 other countries.

16.4.1 ISO OSI Layered Architecture

A layered approach to network architecture is currently being debated by the International Standards Organization (ISO). The Open Systems Interconnection (OSI) proposal (Zi80) includes seven distinct layers of protocol.

1. The Application Layer—This is the highest layer and provides services directly to users. It deals with data exactly as it is generated by and delivered to user processes.
2. The Presentation Layer—This layer resolves differences in formats among the various computers, terminals, databases, and languages used in a network.
3. The Session Layer—This layer provides the means for cooperating presentation-entities to organize and synchronize their dialog and manage their data exchange.
4. The Transport Layer—This layer provides for transfer of messages between end users. The users need not be concerned with the manner in which reliable and cost effective data transfers are achieved.

5. The Network Layer—This layer controls the switching and routing of messages between stations in the network.
6. The Data Link Layer—This layer controls the manipulation of data packets. It handles the addressing of outgoing packets and the decoding of addresses on incoming packets. It detects and possibly corrects errors that occur in the Physical Layer.
7. The Physical Layer—This layer handles the mechanical and electrical details of the actual physical transmission of bit sequences over communication lines.

In addition to these seven layers, the OSI model also provides for a set of functions called *Network Management* that cuts across all layers. This set of functions provides for the control and maintenance of a network. Fault detection and isolation are part of network management.

This layered architecture is typical of the approach in most popular networking schemes like IBM's SNA (Cy79) and DEC's DNA (described at the end of this chapter). The DNA structure uses only six layers. The reader might find it interesting to compare the OSI and DNA schemes as described in this chapter.

16.4.2 Datagrams and Virtual Circuits

Packets are normally transmitted via *datagrams* or *virtual circuits.* In the virtual circuit model, the network provides a perfect channel in which the packets are sent error-free and arrive in the precise order in which they were sent. This mode of transmission is very much like that of the telephone system in which users are given the illusion that they have dedicated point-to-point lines even though their calls are routed by complex switching mechanisms.

In the datagram model, packets are transported as isolated units addressed to a specific destination. The network does no error checking—that is the responsibility of the hosts. A message consisting of several packets may be transmitted in one order and the packets may arrive in a different order—they must be reassembled into correct order by the receiving host. This mode of transmission is like that of the postal service. Several letters sent from one person to another do not necessarily arrive in the order in which they were sent. If a letter is lost or damaged, the postal service does not retransmit a fresh copy.

Each of these transmission modes has its own advantages and disadvantages. The virtual circuit approach has the advantage that it does more of the work associated with correct transmission so there is less of a burden on the hosts. Messages are delivered in correct order. If an out-of-order message arrives, it is automatically delayed until the packets that are supposed to be ahead of it arrive. But there are times when the order of arrival is less important than rapid transmission. Suppose, for example, that a large number of records is being transmitted and that each record has a unique key. With datagram transmission the records will most likely arrive sooner because out-of-order records need not be kept pending.

It is sometimes the case that the automatic error control provided by virtual circuits is actually undesirable. For example, in real-time speech transmission it is probably better to let an occasional garbled packet through than it would be to suffer the delay of retransmitting the packet—the person listening to the speech would probably be able to comprehend it and would probably be less annoyed than if the speech sounded intermittent.

16.4.3 X.25

In 1975, an international effort was mounted to develop a standard user interface to the many networks under development throughout the world. The result of this was the CCITT (Consultative Committee for International Telegraphy and Telephony) Recommendation X.25 adopted in 1976 (Wa79). Since 1976, a family of standards has grown around X.25. These standards include X.29, X.75, and many more. The current packet switching standard (often referred to as X.25) actually includes all of these.

The advent of these standards has permitted the development of *public data networks (PDNs)*. These networks operate like the telephone network; they provide interconnection between users who do not own their own networks, but who wish to communicate with other users.

The X.25 Protocol specifies the manner in which devices should interface to and communicate through public packet switched networks. In the years since it was adopted by CCITT, X.25 has become almost a universal standard. It defines packet format and control procedures in terms of virtual circuits. Control packets are sent for call establishment; data packets are sent over established circuits. Once the network accepts a packet, it assumes responsibility for delivering it to its destination correctly and in correct order with respect to other packets sent over the same virtual circuit.

As in all standardization efforts, there is much controversy over the choice of the virtual circuit approach for X.25. Many users prefer the datagram approach for their particular applications; they merely want the carriers to transmit user-supplied bit patterns. At the present time, serious consideration is being given to extending X.25 to support a datagram option.

16.5 NETWORK OPERATING SYSTEMS (NOS)

Forsdick, Schantz, and Thomas (Fo78) offer the following definition.

> A network operating system (NOS) is a collection of software and associated protocols that allows a set of autonomous computers, which are interconnected by a computer network, to be used together in a convenient and cost-effective manner.

Network operating systems offer many capabilities including

- allowing users to access the various resources of the network hosts
- controlling this access so that only users with proper authorization are allowed to access particular resources
- making the network and the eccentricities of the host computers transparent to the users
- making the use of remote resources appear to be identical to the use of local resources
- providing uniform accounting procedures throughout the network
- providing up-to-the-minute network documentation on-line
- providing a much more reliable operation than possible on a single host, particularly in groups of equivalent hosts

16.6 NOS PRIMITIVES

A communication network provides users with access to various resources. Certainly, programs and data are important resources manipulated by computer networks. Initiating and controlling the movement of programs and data between hosts is called *migration*. Supporting it requires (Ki75) *user communication primitives, job migration primitives, data migration primitives,* and *control primitives.*

16.6.1 User Communication Primitives

User communication primitives support interuser communication, user-to-system and system-to-user communication, and status testing. Interuser communication is very popular and has become one of the most widely used network capabilities. Users may send one another electronic mail, may communicate back and forth as in a spoken telephone dialog, and may even arrange interactive conferences between members of a large group.

Status testing is useful for determining the "health" of the network, the availability of particular systems, and which hosts are temporarily underutilized.

16.6.2 Job Migration Primitives

Job migration primitives are useful for controlling the execution of multistep jobs in which the job steps may be performed by different hosts, balancing the load on the network by moving jobs to underutilized hosts, and moving jobs to the hosts that are best suited to processing those jobs. Job migration functions are best performed by a central network control mechanism.

16.6.3 Data Migration Primitives

Data migration primitives support the remote access of information. When heterogeneous hosts are involved, data translation must be done—data types must be preserved across the boundaries between the hosts, and character translation may need to be performed between possibly different character codes of the different hosts. There are two common approaches to data migration.

- Transmission of a request to a remote host followed by the return transmission of the requested item to the local host
- Retrieval of the entire file containing the requested item from the remote host to the local host with local access to the requested item

The first approach is useful when there are infrequent requests; the second approach is useful when a high density of requests to one file can be expected. One danger associated with the second approach is that it creates multiple copies of the same file. This can lead to problems when the files are modified since it must be assured that all copies of the file are correspondingly updated.

There are two common approaches to transferring information between hosts, namely *direct transmission* and *data transformation.* Direct transmission is transmission of the "raw" data between systems. Data transformation involves a restructuring of the data so that it arrives at the new host in a form more appropriate for its intended application or for residence on the new host.

16.6.4 Control Primitives

Control primitives are required for enforcing subnetwork control, for handling the allocation of communications resources, and for controlling the interaction between the network and its hosts.

16.7 NETWORK TOPOLOGIES

The physical arrangement of the devices and communications lines in a network is called *network topology.* Many network topologies have been implemented (Fig. 16.5) each with its own advantages and disadvantages. The two most common topologies are star networks and ring networks.

16.7.1 Star Networks

In a star network, a central computer communicates with various terminals and other computers over point-to-point lines. The other terminals and computers are directly connected to the central computer, but not to one another. Thus if they wish to communicate with one another, they must do so through the central com-

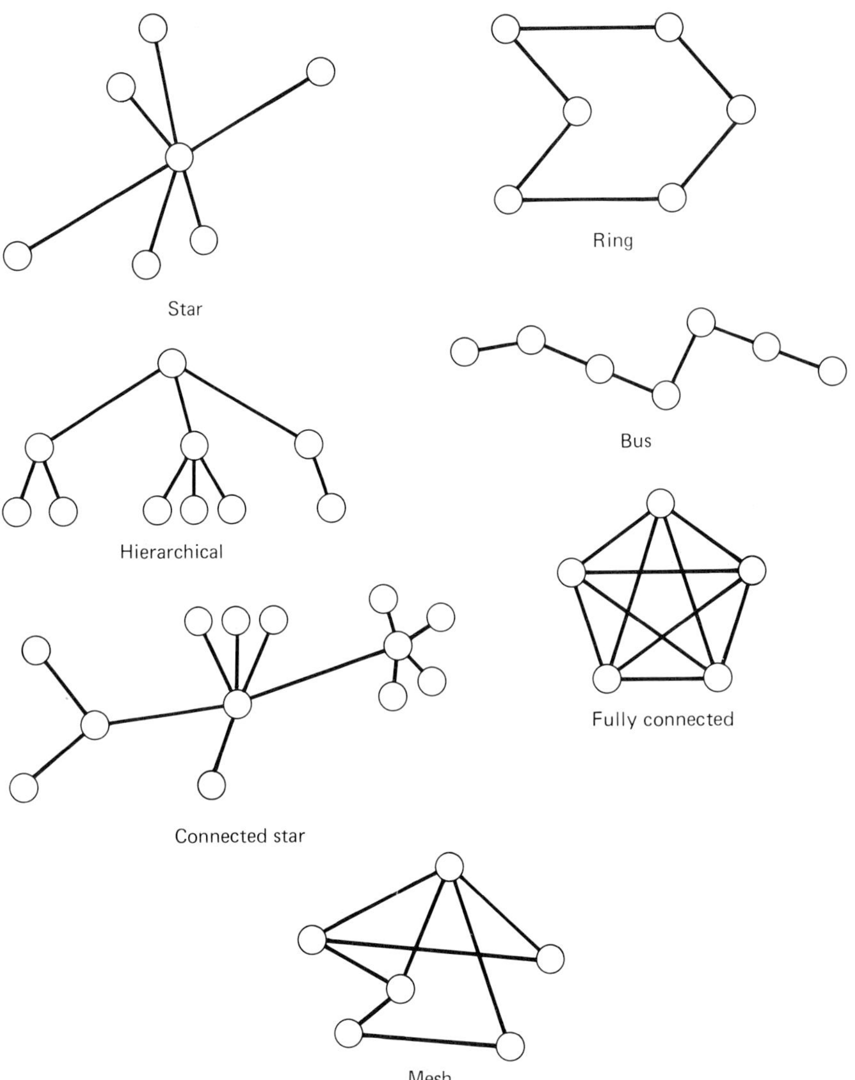

Fig. 16.5 Common network topologies.

puter that functions as the network controller. If the central computer fails, the network fails.

The star topology has the advantage of simplicity. Control is centralized. All of the activity of the network may be monitored through the central computer. Because there is only one network controller, there is no problem of communication and sequencing between separate control stations.

16.7.2 Ring Networks

The ring network topology does not have a central computer system controlling the operation of the entire network. Rather, the various computers in the network are arranged in series around a ring. Each computer may communicate with any other computer in the ring. Messages from one computer to another must be specifically addressed to the destination computer. Because all computers on the ring have access to the message, security becomes more of a problem.

16.7.3 Mesh Networks

In a mesh network topology, each computer (or communications processor) is connected to at least one other processor in the network. Control and data routing functions may be centralized or distributed. The mesh network topology is commonly used for packet networks.

16.8 NETWORK OPERATING SYSTEMS AND DISTRIBUTED OPERATING SYSTEMS

Operating systems for networks are generally classified (Ta81) as either *network operating systems* or *distributed operating systems.* These represent dramatically different structural approaches.

In network operating systems, each of the network hosts runs its own non-network operating system. The networking is controlled by user programs that run on the various hosts. This approach is relatively straightforward to implement and has the advantage that it utilizes the software that already exists for the various hosts. It has the disadvantage, however, that it lacks homogeneity.

In a distributed operating system, the individual operating systems of the hosts are discarded; a single homogeneous operating system is implemented for the entire network. This approach requires considerably more effort than a network operating system, but it offers conceptual integrity of design, an attribute that makes it much easier for designers and implementors to understand the network, maintain it, modify it, etc.

The network operating system approach is generally used when large-scale, architecturally diverse, and geographically dispersed computer systems are connected. Local networks of minicomputers and microcomputers tend to use the distributed operating system approach.

Implementing a network operating system for a group of heterogeneous hosts can be accomplished in several ways. One common approach is to associate with each user an *agent process.* The agent provides the user with a common interface to all hosts in the network.

An agent process can be designed to make the existence of the network *transparent* to the user, or to make the network *visible.* When the network is visible, then the user issues commands like

PERFORM COMMAND A ON HOST B

When the network is transparent, the user issues commands like

PERFORM COMMAND A

and it is the agent process's responsibility to select the host on which that command may be run.

Each agent has a database of information about the various hosts in the network and the programs and data belonging to the user. The information in the database includes accounting information indicating the account numbers to which charges should be posted for each of the hosts, and the limits the user is allowed. The agent's database can be organized to allow a user to access specific files on specific hosts by using each host's naming conventions directly, or it can contain a list of *virtual file names* and the real files to which they correspond.

In one simple strategy for implementing the agents, they act as intermediaries between the users and the hosts. Agents translate the user's commands into the format required by the host processor, and translate outputs from the hosts into the format needed for the user. The agent issues commands to the hosts to ensure that all files are made available where they are needed.

16.9 SECURITY, PRIVACY, ENCRYPTION, AND AUTHENTICATION

Organizations and individuals are entrusting more and more to their computers. Sensitive correspondence is routinely transmitted between computer systems over vulnerable communication lines. Private information is stored in computers and transmitted between them. Electronic banking makes our financial records accessible over communication lines. Computerization of law enforcement agencies makes criminal records accessible. Doctors are computerizing our medical records. The point is that we can no longer afford to transmit information without protecting it from unauthorized access.

Traditionally, *encryption* has been the obvious means for protecting vulnerable communications. A number of political problems are currently developing in this area.

The current "official" encryption standard is *DES (Data Encryption Standard).* Integrated circuit chips are available that perform DES encoding and decoding with a secret key chosen for each application. The United States government has been aggressively promoting this standard.

The real problem with the DES encryption standard is the problem of *key distribution.* The security of the encryption can be no better than the security of the key. This problem of key distribution has led to the development of *public key* encryption algorithms.

One public key encryption–decryption scheme is M.I.T.'s RSA code that uses two keys. One of the two keys is used to encode the data, the other to decode it.

The algorithm is symmetrical; either key may be used for encoding provided the other key is used for decoding. The real value of RSA is that one key cannot be derived from the other in less than a million years of computation with a very powerful processor. There are several important advantages to the two-key RSA scheme.

- An individual can make one of the keys public and thus anybody can use the public key to encode messages and then send them to the individual. Only the individual, however, can decode the message since this takes the other key which, of course, is kept secret.
- It becomes possible to authenticate messages in the following sense. An individual may encode messages with the private key. Anyone possessing the public key may decode the message, thus proving that it must have been originated by this individual.

The RSA code is an incredibly powerful solution to the encryption problem. It requires enormous amounts of computation, however, running about 1000 times slower than DES-based mechanisms.

Encoding the text of messages is only part of the security problem. It is also necessary to encode the identity of the intended recipient of a message. In packet switching networks, this information is contained in the envelopes around the packets, and these are controlled by the network operating system. So there are many levels at which encryption and decryption are needed.

Other desirable features might be the *time-stamping* of all messages with both time of origin and time of receipt. It would also be useful to prove that a message was sent and it was received, in effect creating registered electronic mail.

In electronic mail systems there is a question as to whether all messages should be kept on archival storage for some time for verification purposes. A strong negative argument here is that this would be similar to the United States Postal Service keeping a machine copy of every letter it carries! This information could be safeguarded—encrypted, for example, and physically guarded—but the mere fact that it existed would be an incentive for some persons to try and obtain it, possibly by clandestine means.

16.10 LOCAL NETWORKING

A *local network* is a communications network designed to handle a limited geographic area. Local networks are generally designed to cover a single building or adjacent buildings. The term is also sometimes used when buildings are separated by as much as 50 miles, but this tends to be a different meaning of "local network."

John Connell of the Office Technology Research Group, quoted in *Office Products News,* September 1981, sums up the case for local networking as follows.

> The tendency in the past has been to apply technology to office work by moving the work out of the regular office and into a technology center, such as a

data- or word-processing center. By doing this, companies inadvertently exclude nontechnical personnel from easy accessibility to technological capabilities that could enhance their productivity. With networks, the power and capabilities of all modern technologies are, quite literally, at every manager's fingertips.

Local networks are also justified by the fact that about 90 percent of all business information is distributed within half a mile.

Some of the advantages of local networks are

- data transmission speeds greater than those of the telephone network,
- error rates lower than those of the telephone network,
- greater management flexibility (because the local nets are generally company-owned),
- independence from the constraints of the public telephone system which has a small capacity and simply cannot handle the high data transfer rates required by video and high-speed data communications.

Local Area Networks (LANs) are frequently defined in terms of *topology, media* and *access procedure*. The two most frequently encountered topologies are *broadcast* and *sequential*. In a broadcast topology, all connected devices receive all messages at approximately the same time. A bus and a star network are examples of broadcast topologies. In a sequential topology messages are passed from one device to another. A ring is an example of a sequential topology.

The four most common LAN media are twisted pair, baseband coaxial, broadband coaxial, and fiber optics. Twisted pair is data rate limited, but forms the basis of the most common local network, the PBX. Baseband coaxial distinguishes itself from broadband coaxial only in the method by which the media is used. A baseband coaxial medium permits only a single signal on the medium at a time without interference. A broadband coaxial medium permits multiple simultaneous signals.

The two most common access procedures for LANs are Carrier Sense, Multiple Access with Collision Detection (CSMA/CD) and Token Passing. In a CSMA/CD network, a device with data to transmit listens for other messages in progress (Carrier Sense). If it hears none, it may begin transmitting. While it transmits, it listens to the medium to determine if any other devices are transmitting at the same time (Collision Detection). If so, the device stops transmitting, delays for a period of time, and then attempts to retransmit its message. In a token passing network, only one device is permitted to transmit at any one time. The permission to transmit is controlled by a logical "token" that is passed from one device to another.

Note that while media, topology, and access procedure are independent, some combinations are more common than others. Some of the most common combinations are baseband CSMA/CD broadcast (bus) and baseband token sequential (ring).

LANs that use the bus architecture permit nodes to be hooked onto coaxial cable via taps. Repeaters are placed at the ends of the cable to allow extension of the network or along the cable to permit branching of the network.

With the bus architecture, nodes can be added by tapping the cable while the network continues to function.

16.10.1 CSMA/CD

In CSMA/CD, nodes access the network on a *contention* basis. Before a node begins transmission, it checks that the channel is not busy (carrier sense). If the channel is busy, the node cannot transmit until the channel becomes clear.

When a node begins transmission, it listens for other nodes also beginning transmission. If the transmitted message collides with another message (*collision detection*), then the transmission is aborted and the node waits for a random period of time before attempting to transmit again.

CSMA/CD is a simple concept and is easy to build into inexpensive chips. It works particularly well with lightly loaded channels—the collision probability normally remains below 1 percent. For heavily loaded systems, however, the probability of a collision increases rapidly as the load increases. Collisions can cause unpredictable delays.

Another disadvantage of CSMA/CD is that it is difficult to add a priority mechanism—all messages and nodes typically receive equal treatment in contending for the bus.

16.10.2 Token Passing

In *token passing*, a *message token* is passed node to node. Each node has a designated time at which it can remove the token and either add a message to it or take a message from it. While this occurs, the other nodes can only listen. Token passing can be implemented on either a bus or a ring.

Token passing results in predictable message-transmission times. In a ring structure, the sending node is also the receiving node for acknowledgment. This is used in applications such as process control that require very high reliability. But token passing is not confined to ring networks.

A disadvantage of token passing in a ring network is that a break in the ring prevents messages from returning to their transmitting nodes. It is also more complex than CSMA/CD and more costly to implement. Token passing can be very inefficient when traffic to the different nodes is not balanced. In a bus network, a complex algorithm must be employed to establish a *virtual ring*, and to reestablish a virtual ring when the token is lost. These algorithms require a considerable amount of computational power.

16.10.3 Message Slots

Another strategy particularly well suited to the ring topology is to transmit a series of *message slots* continually around the network. These are bit sequences large enough to hold a message. Each slot may be empty or full. If a node needs to transmit, it waits for an empty slot, marks it as full and places a message in it. The depositing node also enters control information in the slot including its own address and the address of the intended receiver.

16.11 CASE STUDY: ETHERNET

Ethernet (Sh80) (Me76) is a local networking scheme that makes it possible to link various office machines into a single network (Fig. 16.6). It uses a coaxial cable to connect various pieces of information equipment. Information travels over the cable in packets sent from one machine to another. The architecture consists of a CSMA/CD multiaccess bus with distributed control.

Ethernet uses the collision concept to decide which piece of office equipment on the network gets to communicate next. When a transmission is occurring, all other pieces of equipment wait. When the current transmission stops, then any other pieces of equipment may attempt transmission. If these collide, i.e., if two devices

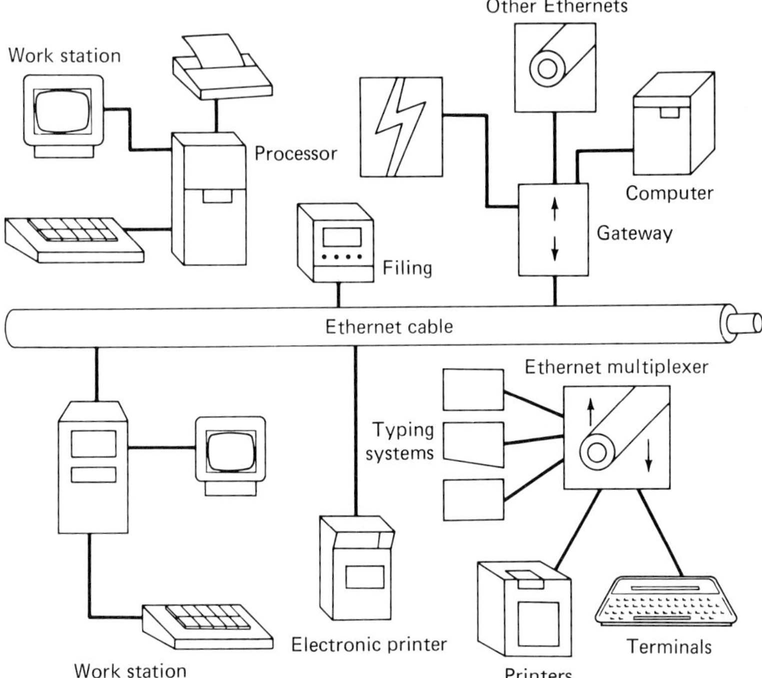

Fig. 16.6 An Ethernet local network. (Courtesy Xerox Corporation.)

attempt to transmit at the same time, they both stop transmitting and wait to start again. Eventually one of the devices begins transmitting again, does not collide with other transmissions, and is able to complete transmission while all other devices wait.

This *collision concept* allows Ethernet to operate without central control, thus making it much easier to add new devices to the network after initial installation.

The Ethernet network (Fig. 16.7) consists primarily of

- *Ether*—a copper and plastic cable with high reliability and low cost
- *Transceivers*—small boxes that insert and extract bits of information as the bits pass by on the cable

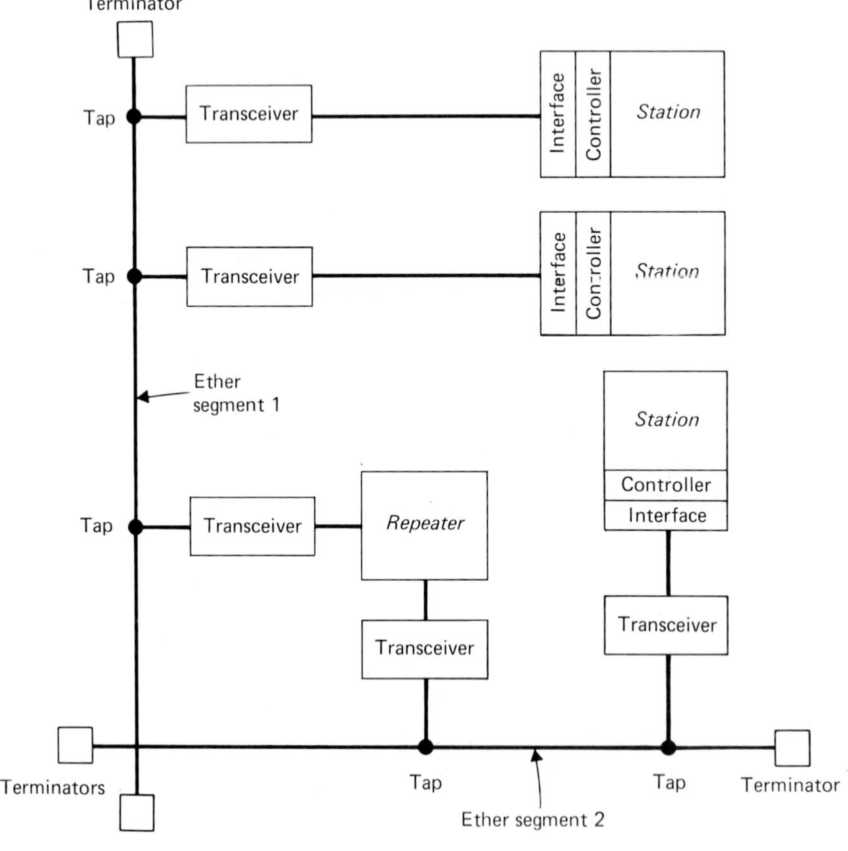

Fig. 16.7 A two-segment Ethernet. (Reprinted from R. Metcalfe and D. Boggs, "Ethernet: Distributed Packet Switching for Local Computer Networks," *COMMUNICATIONS OF THE ACM,* Vol. 19, No. 7, July 1976. Copyright 1976, Association for Computing Machinery, Inc. Reprinted by permission.)

- *Controllers*—large-scale integrated circuit chips that enable all sorts of equipment to connect to the Ethernet
- *Taps*—devices for physically connecting to the Ether while disturbing its transmission characteristics as little as possible

The resulting system is fast, reliable, economical, and is easy to extend with new equipment.

The collision approach to sharing the network may at first seem inefficient. But the network operates so quickly (approximately ten million bits per second), and the packets are so short (maximum packet length is 1500 bytes), that each transmission lasts a maximum of less than a thousandth of a second. Thus the number of collisions is small (unless an installation overloads the network by attaching too many active devices).

Because the control is provided by each individual device or node, the reliability of the network is very high. If an individual node fails, the network will continue to function.

One disadvantage of Ethernet is that it is a *baseband* rather than *broadband* network. As such, it can transmit only on a single channel, and thus it uses only a small percentage of the capacity of the Ethernet coaxial cable. Broadband systems have a much larger capacity, and can transmit over several channels at once. This will make broadband systems more valuable for the multimode transmission environments of the future in which it is expected that voice, data, and video will all be transmitted at the same time. Wang's Wangnet is such a broadband system. Ethernet may have to evolve into a broadband network before it will become widely accepted.

16.12 CASE STUDY: DECnet

In this case study, Digital Equipment Corporation's DECnet system (De80) will be examined in some depth to indicate the range of capabilities provided by a major vendor in a significant network operating system.

DECnet allows computers manufactured by DEC to communicate with one another over a network. DEC provides several *internets* (i.e., protocol emulators) to allow other vendors' computers to be included in a network with DEC equipment.

Different computer systems running different operating systems may interact in a single network. *Physical links* connect adjacent network nodes. The capacity of a single physical link may be shared among several tasks. Each of the individual data paths on a shared physical link is called a *logical link*.

Users in a DECnet system may access many network capabilities including

- *Intersystem file transfer*—A file may be transferred between computer systems.
- *Intersystem resource sharing*—A process executing on one system can access files and devices on other systems.

- *Interprocess communication*—Processes executing on different computer systems may communicate with one another.
- *Routing*—When two systems do not share a physical link, intermediate nodes will direct transmissions from one system to the other.
- *Network command terminal*—A terminal on one system can be made to appear to be connected to another system.
- *Down-line command file loading*—A user may send a command language file to another node in the network. The commands will be executed at that node.

16.12.1 Digital Network Architecture (DNA)

Digital Network Architecture (DNA) consists of the protocols (rules) defining the format, control, and sequencing of message transfers in DECnet systems. DNA controls the data flowing through a DECnet network. It is a layered architecture in which each layer handles specific network functions. The DNA layers and their functions are

- *User layer*—This is the highest layer in the structure. It contains the various functions supplied by the user.
- *Network application layer*—This layer defines the network functions available to the user layer. This layer contains network remote file access modules, a remote file transfer utility, and a remote system loader module.
- *Network service layer*—This layer provides the user layer and the network application layer with a location-independent communication mechanism. It establishes logical links.
- *Transport layer*—This layer provides the network service layer with the capabilities it needs to send a packet from one node to another.
- *Data link layer*—This layer provides the transport layer with the capabilities for sending error-free communications between adjacent nodes.
- *Physical link layer*—This is the lowest layer in the DNA structure. It provides the data link layer with the capabilities for sending communications between adjacent nodes. This layer contains modules specific to each type of communication device in a DECnet.

16.12.2 DECnet-VAX Features

By using DCL (Digital Command Language) statements, users can transfer command files to remote nodes, execute command files at remote nodes, copy files from one node to another, and delete a file at a remote node.

Conventional file operations like open, close, create, delete, and update may be performed on files located at remote nodes. Record-level operations like read, write, update, and delete may also be performed on files at remote nodes.

Programmers may explicitly specify interprocess communication between processes running on different nodes. Such communication may be either *transparent* or *nontransparent.* Transparent interprocess communication utilizes the same calls that are used for accessing files in a high-level language. These include open, close, read, write, etc.

Nontransparent access is available to programmers using DEC's MACRO assembly language. It involves making calls directly to operating system service procedures. Nontransparent access allows programs to monitor network status to have better control over their communications with other processes. It services the following requests.

- CONNECT—establish a logical link (analogous to OPEN)
- CONNECT REJECT—reject a CONNECT attempt
- RECEIVE—receive a message from another process (analogous to READ)
- SEND—send a message to another process (analogous to WRITE)
- SEND INTERRUPT MESSAGE—send a high-priority message to another process
- DISCONNECT—terminate a link (analogous to CLOSE)

An interesting feature of DECnet is that a process may send or receive unsolicited messages to or from another process. The mailbox for unsolicited message traffic is associated with the channel of the logical link rather than with the processes themselves.

Each logical link has two subchannels—one for conventional message traffic and the other for high-priority messages. High-priority messages are written to a mailbox supplied by the receiving process for that purpose.

16.12.3 File Handling

The DECnet-VAX user may invoke the following DCL commands in order to manipulate files stored on a remote node: APPEND, ASSIGN, COPY, DEASSIGN, DEFINE, DELETE, DIRECTORY, and SUBMIT. File specifications are formed as follows:

```
nodename "loginstring"::filename.filetype;version
```

Nodename is the name of the remote node at which the file is located. Loginstring is used for logging in at the remote node. If loginstring is omitted, then default login information is automatically taken from an entry for the remote node in the local configuration database. If loginstring is supplied, it overrides the default string. The double colon (::) separates the nodename from the file specifier. Filename, filetype, and version must conform to the requirements of the remote node's operating system.

Consider the following COPY command.

```
$COPY DALLAS::DBA1:TEST.DAT MIAMI::DMA2:
```

This command causes the file TEST.DAT to be transferred from the disk (DBA1:) at node DALLAS to the disk (DMA2:) at node MIAMI.

The user who wants to execute a command file at a remote node would first copy that file to the remote node and then issue a command like

```
$SUBMIT/REMOTE BOSTON::INITIAL.COM
```

to cause the command file INITIAL.COM to be executed at remote node BOSTON.

16.12.4 Interprocess Communication: A FORTRAN Example

This section discusses how to perform interprocess communication using the regular FORTRAN input/output instructions. Such communication involves (1) establishing a logical link between the communicating processes; (2) one process sending messages to another, and the latter process receiving the messages; and (3) terminating the link upon completion of the communication.

A logical link may be established between processes that specifically agree to cooperate. One process requests that the link be established; the other accepts the request. The requesting process is the *source process*; the accepting task is the *target process.*

A logical link connect request is issued by the source process. It includes a process specifier in its OPEN statement. The process specifier indicates the target process and the node at which it resides. For example,

```
OPEN (UNIT=7,NAME='DALLAS::"TASK=SAM"',ERR=300)
```

requests a logical link connection to the target process (task) SAM at node DALLAS.

Once the logical link has been established, the processes carry on their dialog over the link. Each time the sending process WRITEs a message, the receiving process must READ the message. The processes are responsible for allocating sufficient buffer space to hold the messages, for recognizing when communication is to terminate, and for disconnecting the logical link. Either of the cooperating processes may call CLOSE to disconnect the logical link. The CLOSE causes any pending messages to be aborted, and disconnects the link.

16.12.5 Solicited and Unsolicited Messages

Interprocess communication messages may be either *solicited* or *unsolicited.* A solicited message sent by one process is expected by a cooperating process. Unsolicited messages may be of the following types.

- *Logical link connect request*—This type of message is sent to a target process. The message requests a logical link connection to the source process.
- *Connect accept*—This type of message confirms that a target process accepted a logical link connect request. A connect accept message is received by the source process.
- *Connect reject*—This type of message indicates that a target process rejected a logical link connect request. It is received by the source process.
- *Interrupt message*—Either of two cooperating processes can receive an interrupt message from the other process. The message is placed in the receiving process's mailbox.
- *Synchronous disconnect*—Informs the receiving process that the cooperating process synchronously disconnected the logical link.
- *Abort disconnect*—Informs the receiving process that the cooperating process aborted the link.
- *Network status message*—Informs the receiving process of some event in the network such as the restarting of a data link.

SUMMARY

A computer network consists of host computers connected by a communications subsystem composed of communications processors and communications links. The three most common types of networks are resource sharing networks, distributed computation networks, and remote communication networks.

Most networks transmit data via packet switching. A packet is a block of information containing data to be transmitted between nodes, addressing and routing instructions, billing information, error control information, etc. The grandparent of today's packet switching networks is the Arpanet, designed in 1967 and still in wide use. The first public packet network service was B.B.N.'s Telenet introduced in 1975.

A network operating system, as defined in (Fo78), is "a collection of software and associated protocols that allows a set of autonomous computers, which are interconnected by a computer network, to be used together in a convenient and cost-effective manner."

Supporting the movement of programs and data between hosts requires the use of user communication primitives, job migration primitives, data migration primitives, and control primitives.

Two common approaches to transferring data between heterogeneous hosts are direct transmission in which data is transmitted in raw format, and data transformation in which the data is restructured to a format more appropriate for the new host.

The physical arrangement of the devices and communications lines in a network is called network topology. Some common topologies are star, ring, hierarchical, bus, connected star, fully connected, and mesh. The most common are the star and mesh topologies in long-haul networks, and the bus and ring topologies in local networks.

Operating systems for networks are generally classified as either network operating systems or distributed operating systems. In network operating systems, each of the network hosts runs its own nonnetwork operating system. The networking is controlled by user programs that run on the various hosts. In a distributed operating system, the individual operating systems of the hosts are discarded; a single homogeneous operating system is implemented for the entire network.

Encryption is an important technique for protecting vulnerable communications in networks. The current "standard" is the one key DES scheme. More secure schemes such as M.I.T.'s two-key RSA code are being considered for implementation in computer networks.

A local network is a communications network designed to handle a limited geographic area. Most LANs use the bus architecture with nodes hooked on to a coaxial cable via taps. Repeaters allow extension and branching of the network.

The three most common techniques for accessing local networks are CSMA/CD (carrier-sense, multiple-access/collision detection), token passing, and message slots. In CSMA/CD nodes access the network on a contention basis. When messages collide, they are aborted—the nodes attempt to retransmit aborted messages after a random delay.

In token passing systems, a message token is passed node to node. When a node has the token, it may transmit. Token passing results in transmission times more predictable than those provided by CSMA/CD, but it can be inefficient when traffic to the various nodes is not balanced.

The message slot scheme transmits a series of message slots (bit sequences large enough to hold a message) continually around the network. Each slot may be empty or full. When a message slot arrives at a node, the node may either insert a message into the slot, remove a message from the slot, or pass the message slot to the next node.

Ethernet is a local networking scheme designed for linking various office machines. The architecture uses a coaxial cable bus. The accessing scheme is CSMA/CD. Information is transmitted between nodes in packets. The network consists of Ether (the coaxial cable), transceivers that insert bits onto and remove bits from the cable, controllers that enable machines to connect to the cable, and taps that are the actual physical connections.

Ethernet is currently one of the most widely used local networking schemes. It uses a baseband cable appropriate for data transmission but not useful for carrying real-time voice and video transmissions. Ethernet may expand to include a broadband system as an option. This may be necessary if it is to become a widely accepted standard for local networking.

DECnet is Digital Equipment Corporation's network operating system. With the use of internets, non-DEC equipment may also be used in DECnet networks. A physical link is an actual communications link between adjacent network nodes. A physical link may be shared to create multiple data paths called logical links.

DECnet, among other functions, supports intersystem file transfer, intersystem resource sharing, interprocess communication across nodes, routing, network command terminals, and down-line command file loading.

Digital Network Architecture (DNA) consists of the protocols defining the format, control, and sequencing of message transfers in DECnet systems. DNA is a layered architecture consisting of user, network application, network service, transport, data link, and physical link layers.

Interprocess communication may be either transparent or nontransparent. Transparent interprocess communication uses the normal calls for accessing files in a high-level language. Nontransparent access involves making calls directly to operating system service procedures.

Processes may send or receive unsolicited messages. The mailbox for unsolicited message traffic is associated with the channel of the logical link rather than with the processes themselves.

DECnet allows users at one node to manipulate files on another node. Whole-file operations like copy and delete are possible as well as record-oriented operations like get and put.

A solicited message sent by one process is expected by a cooperating process. Unsolicited messages include logical link connect requests, connect accepts, connect rejects, interrupt messages, synchronous disconnects, abort disconnects, and network status messages.

TERMINOLOGY

agent process
application layer
Arpanet
baseband
broadband
bus network
collision concept
communications processor
CONNECT
CONNECT REJECT
connected star network
control primitives
controller (in Ethernet)
data concentration
Data Encryption Standard (DES)
data link layer (in DNA)
data migration primitives
datagram
Datapac
data transformation
DECnet
direct transmission
DISCONNECT
distributed computation network
distributed operating system
DNA (Digital Network Architecture)
electronic mail
encapsulation
encryption
Ether

Ethernet
fully connected network
hierarchical network
host
internet
job migration primitives
local network
logical link
long-haul network
mesh network
migration
network application layer (in DNA)
network layer (in OSI)
network operating system (NOS)
network service layer (in DNA)
network topology
nontransparent interprocess communication (in DNA)
packet
packet switching
physical layer
physical link
physical link layer (in DNA)
presentation layer
RECEIVE
registered electronic mail
remote communication network
resource sharing network
ring network
RSA code
SEND
SEND INTERRUPT MESSAGE
session layer
SNA (Systems Network Architecture)
solicited message
source process
star network
store-and-forward transmission
tap (in Ethernet)
target process
Telenet
time-stamping of messages
transceiver (in Ethernet)
transparent interprocess communication (in DNA)
transparent network
transport layer (in DNA)
unsolicited message
user communication primitives
user layer (in DNA)
virtual circuit
virtual file names
visible network
Wangnet
X.25

EXERCISES

16.1 What is a computer network?

16.2 What factors have hindered maximal sharing in computer networks?

16.3 Briefly compare and contrast each of the following types of networks: resource sharing, distributed computation, and remote communication.

16.4 List several of the more important capabilities provided by network operating systems.

16.5 Briefly discuss each of the following types of network primitives: user communication, job migration, data migration, and control.

16.6 What are the two common approaches to data migration? Discuss the relative merits of each approach.

16.7 What are the most common network topologies? Which provide the greatest reliability? the greatest security?

16.8 Compare and contrast the network operating system approach and the distributed operating system approach.

16.9 What is an agent process?

16.10 What is a local network? In what ways are the problems of local networks different from those of the long-haul networks?

16.11 Explain the collision concept used in implementing Ethernet.

16.12 A network may be either visible or transparent to the user. Compare and contrast these two approaches to the design of the user/network interface.

16.13 Compare and contrast network operating systems with multiprocessor operating systems.

16.14 List some of the major capabilities of DECnet.

16.15 Most network architectures use a layered approach like that of DNA. What are the merits of a layered network architecture?

16.16 Distinguish between transparent and nontransparent interprocess communication in DNA.

16.17 An interesting feature of DECnet is that a process may send or receive unsolicited messages. In what circumstances are unsolicited messages useful? What problems are more likely to develop with unsolicited messages arriving at a process than with solicited messages?

16.18 Compare the seven-layered OSI architecture with the six-layered DNA architecture. What are the key differences?

LITERATURE

(Ba80) Barak, A. B., and A. Shapir, "UNIX with Satellite Processors," *Software—Practice and Experience,* Vol. 10, 1980, pp. 383–392.

(Cl76) Clipsham, W. W.; F. E. Glave; and M. L. Narraway, "Datapac Network Overview," *Proc. Third International Conf. on Computer Communications,* Toronto, August 1976, pp. 131–136.

(Cr75) Crocker, S. D., "The National Software Works: A New Method for Providing Software Development Tools Using the Arpanet." Presented at Meeting on 20 Years of Computer Science, Pisa, Italy, June 1975.

(Cy79) Cypser, R., *Communications Architecture for Distributed Systems,* Reading, Mass.: Addison-Wesley, 1979.

(Da79) Davies, D. W.; D. L. A. Barber; W. L. Price; and C. M. Solomonides, *Computer Networks and Their Protocols,* New York: Wiley, 1979.

(De80) Digital Equipment Corporation, *VAX Software Handbook,* 1980, pp. 228–253.

(Do79) Donnelley, J. E., "Components of a Network Operating System," *Computer Networks,* Vol. 3, December 1979, pp. 389–399.

(Dv77) Davidson, J.; N. Mimno; R. Thomas; D. Walden; W. Hathaway; and J. Postel, "The Arpanet Telenet Protocol: Its Purpose, Principles, Implementation, and Impact on Host Operating System Design," *Proc. Fifth Data Communications Symposium,* Snowbird, Utah, September 1977, pp. 4.10–4.18.

(Fo78) Forsdick, H. C.; R. E. Schantz; and R. H. Thomas, "Operating Systems for Computer Networks," *IEEE Computer,* January 1978, pp. 48–57.

(Gr79) Green, P. E., "An Introduction to Network Architectures and Protocols," *IBM Systems Journal,* Vol. 18, No. 2, 1979, pp. 202–222.

(Ha79) Halsey, J. R.; L. E. Hardy; and L. F. Powning, "Public Data Networks: Their Evolution, Interfaces, and Status," *IBM Systems Journal,* Vol. 18, No. 2, 1979, pp. 223–243.

(IE78) *Proc. IEEE,* Vol. 66, No. 11, November 1978, special issue on packet communications.

(Ki75) Kimbleton, S. R., and G. M. Schneider, "Computer Communication Networks," *ACM Computing Surveys,* Vol. 7, No. 3, September 1975.

(Ki76) Kimbleton, S. R., and R. L. Mandell, "A Perspective on Network Operating Systems," *AFIPS Conf. Proc.,* Vol. 45, Montvale, N.J.: AFIPS Press, pp. 551–558.

(Ma81) Martin, J., *Design and Strategy for Distributed Data Processing,* Englewood Cliffs, N.J.: Prentice-Hall, 1981.

(Me76) Metcalfe, R., and D. Boggs, "Ethernet: Distributed Packet Switching for Local Computer Networks," *CACM,* Vol. 19, No. 7, July 1976.

(Ne81) Nelson, T., "Mail Chauvinism: The Magicians, the Snark, and the Camel," *Creative Computing,* November 1981, pp. 128–156.

(Ri76) Rinde, J., "Tymnet I: An Alternative to Packet Technology," *ICCC 76,* Toronto, 1976.

(Ro70) Roberts, L. G., and B. D. Wessler, "Computer Network Development to Achieve Resource Sharing," *AFIPS Conf. Proc. 1970,* Spring Joint Conf., Vol. 3G, Montvale, N.J.: AFIPS Press, 1970.

(Sa78) Sanders, R. W., "Comparing Networking Technologies," *Datamation,* July 1978, pp. 88–93.

(Sc77) Schwartz, M., *Computer Communication Network Design and Analysis,* Englewood Cliffs, N.J.: Prentice-Hall, 1977.

(Sh80) Shoch, J. F., and J. A. Hupp, "Measured Performance of an Ethernet Local Network," *CACM,* Vol. 23, No. 12, December 1980, pp. 711–721.

(Ta81) Tanenbaum, A. S., *Computer Networks,* Englewood Cliffs, N.J.: Prentice-Hall, 1981.

(Wa79) Walden, D. C., and A. A. McKenzie, "The Evolution of Host-to-Host Protocol Technology," *IEEE Computer,* September 1979, pp. 29–38.

(We79) Wecker, S., "Computer Network Architectures," *IEEE Computer,* September 1979, pp. 58–72.

(Wr80) Ward, A. A., "TRIX: A Network-Oriented Operating System," *Compcon,* Spring 1980, pp. 344–349.

(Wt80) Watson, R. W., and J. G. Fletcher, "An Architecture for Support of Network Operating System Services," *Computer Networks,* Vol. 4, February 1980, pp. 33–49.

(Zi80) Zimmerman, H., "OSI Reference Model—The ISO Model of Architecture for Open Systems Interconnection," *IEEE Trans. Commun.,* Vol. COM-28, April 1980, pp. 425–432.

17 Operating Systems Security

It is important to note that probably no large operating system using current design technology can withstand a determined and well-coordinated attack, and that most such documented penetrations have been remarkably easy.

B. Hebbard et al. (He80)

A chain is only as strong as its weakest link.

Proverb

A right is not what someone gives you; it's what no one can take from you.

Ramsey Clark

The price one pays for pursuing any profession, or calling, is an intimate knowledge of its ugly side.

James Baldwin

Outline

17.1 Introduction
17.2 Security Requirements
17.3 A Total Approach to Security
17.4 External Security
17.5 Operational Security
17.6 Surveillance
17.7 Threat Monitoring
17.8 Amplification
17.9 Password Protection
17.10 Auditing
17.11 Access Controls
17.12 Security Kernels
17.13 Hardware Security
17.14 Survivable Systems
17.15 Capabilities and Object-Oriented Systems
  17.15.1 Movement and Storage of Capabilities
  17.15.2 Revocation of Capabilities
17.16 Case Study: The Object-Oriented Architecture of the IBM System/38
17.17 Cryptography
  17.17.1 A Cryptographic Privacy System
  17.17.2 Cryptanalysis
  17.17.3 Public Key Systems
  17.17.4 Digital Signatures
  17.17.5 The DES and RSA Schemes
  17.17.6 Applications
17.18 Operating System Penetration
  17.18.1 Generic System Functional Flaws
  17.18.2 Generic Operating System Attacks
17.19 Case Study: Penetrating an Operating System

17.1 INTRODUCTION

As computing has evolved over the last several decades, it has become more accessible. The number of computer installations has increased dramatically over this period. Single-computer timesharing systems and remote access systems introduced the vulnerability of data communications as a key security issue. That vulnerability today is becoming more serious with the proliferation of computer networking (Chapter 16).

Another trend over this period has been to assign computers more of the chores of managing our personal and business activities. Computers are routinely handling the most sensitive correspondence. Electronic funds transfer systems pass our money around in bit streams. Air traffic collision avoidance systems have taken over much of the burden previously handled by air traffic controllers. Microprocessors have been incorporated into a huge variety of devices to provide intelligent control. Computer-controlled artificial body implant devices like pacemakers are in wide use.

It is important to implement security measures to ensure the uninterrupted and uncorrupted functioning of these systems. This chapter discusses the issues of operating systems security. Hardware protection and security are equally important; these issues are treated elsewhere in the text.

The operating system normally represents only a small portion of the total base of software that runs on a particular system. But the operating system controls access to a system's resources; the other software normally requests access to those resources through the operating system. So software security considerations tend to be focused on making the operating system secure.

Operating systems security is only a small part of the total problem of computer security, but it is becoming an increasingly important part. A well-designed security program must address the total picture; operating systems security means little if anyone can walk off with the computer system unnoticed!

There are several reasons why computer security is receiving so much attention today. The availability of personal computers has brought computer savvy to the general public. Millions of people have taken computer courses in universities, read computer books, purchased personal computers, or used computer systems at work. Today, those who would commit fraud are often faced with penetrating a computer system's defenses to achieve their goal.

Millions of computer systems have been tied together via communication networks, most commonly through the telephone system. Where in the past simple physical security might have been sufficient to guard a computer from outside attack, now sophisticated controls must be placed on login attempts from remote terminals.

We have mentioned the notion of user-friendly systems many times in this text; if computer usage is to be brought to the general public effectively, then systems must be made more accessible and easier to use. But by its very nature user friendliness can imply increased vulnerability.

A security program begins with identifying the potential threats. Threats may be from malicious or nonmalicious sources. The best one can hope to do here is identify the vast majority of potential threats; there will always be some that cannot be anticipated.

Sharing and protection are contradictory goals. Programs may be completely isolated from one another by executing them on separate, nonnetworked computers, but this precludes sharing. Programs running on the same computer may be allowed to share resources extensively, but this reduces the amount of protection possible.

Some people might argue that complex systems deter penetration attempts, and that simple systems are more vulnerable because they are easier to understand. In fact, it is easier to verify the security of simple systems; complex systems often leave many security "holes."

The level of security that must be provided in a system is very much dependent on the value of the resources being secured. Information in a banking system may have great financial value. Information in a medical system may have great life-or-death value. Frivolous breaches of security are not to be ignored; the information obtained may be of little value to the intruders but it could be a major source of embarrassment to a system administrator.

17.2 SECURITY REQUIREMENTS

Security requirements for a given system define what it means for that system to be secure. These requirements serve as the basis for determining if the implemented system is secure; without a precise set of security requirements it makes little sense to ask if the system is secure. Similarly, if the requirements are weakly stated (even if the system does meet the requirements), it does not say very much about the true security of the system.

Formulation of security requirements has been of primary concern to the United States Government and the Armed Forces. Each of the following deals with security requirements

- *DOD Directive 5200.28*—Specifies how classified information is to be handled in data processing systems.
- *Computer Security Technology Reference Manual*—Specifies how to evaluate the security of Air Force computer systems.
- *The Privacy Act of 1974*—Requires federal agencies to ensure the integrity and security of information about individuals, particularly in the context of the government's extensive use of computers.

17.3 A TOTAL APPROACH TO SECURITY

Because a total approach to computer security is essential we also discuss some of the areas of computer security other than operating systems security. *External security* is concerned with securing the computer facility from intruders and from disasters such as fire and floods. Once a user is allowed physical access to the computer facility, then the user's identification must be established by the operating system before access is allowed to the programs and data stored on the system; this might be called *user interface security. Internal security* deals with the various controls built into the hardware and the operating system to ensure the reliable and uncorrupted operation of the computer system and the integrity of programs and data.

17.4 EXTERNAL SECURITY

External security consists of *physical security* and *operational security.* Physical security includes *protection against disasters* and *protection against intruders. Detection mechanisms* are important to physical security; smoke detectors and heat sensors can provide early warning in case of fire; motion detectors can determine if an intruder has entered a computing facility at a time when no one is supposed to be there.

Protection against disasters can be expensive to implement and is often treated too lightly. It depends a great deal on the consequences of loss, and most organizations simply can't afford the expense of a thorough disaster protection scheme. The major physical security efforts are directed toward keeping out intruders. For this purpose, installations use various types of physical identification systems such as plastic identification cards with signatures and/or pictures. Fingerprint and voiceprint systems are also popular.

17.5 OPERATIONAL SECURITY

Operational security consists of the various policies and procedures implemented by the management of the computer installation. *Authorization* determines what access is allowed to what entities.

Classification parcels the problem up into subproblems; the data in the system and the users are divided into classes to which various access rights are granted. This is much like the military classification scheme in which only sensitive documents might be classified as *top secret* and only those persons who have been given top secret security clearances may access that information.

Personnel selection and assignment is critical. Can the people be trusted? One common approach here is *division of responsibilities*; people are given distinct sets of responsibilities which they perform without having to know everything about a system. Thus individuals cannot see the total picture. In order to compromise a system, cooperation among many employees might be necessary; this greatly reduces the likelihood of security violations. In large computer installations, for example, only computer operators are allowed access to the computer system; only programmers are allowed to write programs. Operators should not know how to program and programmers should not be familiar with the details of operating the computer system. Similarly, inputs to production systems are controlled by a separate group, and outputs are checked and verified by yet a different group.

A large number of checks and balances should be built into the system to aid in detection of any security breaches. The operational personnel should be kept unaware of the nature of these controls; this reduces the likelihood that they could bypass them. But they should be made aware of the fact that elaborate controls are built into the system; this knowledge is sufficient to deter many people from attempting a security violation.

It is impossible to design effective security measures without first attempting to enumerate and understand the potential security threats. This can require careful and perceptive analysis. What are the available countermeasures? What degree of security is desired?

17.6 SURVEILLANCE

Surveillance deals with monitoring and auditing the system, and authenticating users. Some highly sophisticated user-authentication systems are in use. These systems can be bypassed, but substantial effort is required on the part of the penetrator. An interesting problem inherent in such systems is the possibility of rejecting legitimate users; a voiceprint system might reject a legitimate user who has a cold; a fingerprint system might reject a legitimate user with a cut or a burn.

17.7 THREAT MONITORING

One way to minimize security risks is to have the operating system control sensitive operations rather than to give control directly to a user. If a user wishes to access a critical file, for example, some systems might allow the user to access the file directly. The user would be in control and the operating system would not be able to monitor the activity against the file as it occurs. A more secure technique is called *threat monitoring.*

In threat monitoring, users may not access a resource directly. Only operating systems routines called *surveillance programs* may do so. The user wishing access to a resource requests such access from the operating system. The operating system either grants or denies the access; then a surveillance program actually performs the access to the file and passes the results to the user program. This notion is similar to that of monitors presented in Chapter 5. Threat monitoring is an ongoing activity—penetration attempts are detected at the moment they occur and the system administrator is informed promptly.

17.8 AMPLIFICATION

Sometimes it is necessary to give a surveillance program greater access rights (than users are allowed) so that it may effectively execute certain user requests. Thus to compute the average income of all taxpayers in a town the surveillance program would need access to the individual records of each taxpayer. This is called *amplification.* Clever users might still be able to infer information about individuals by making several different requests and examining the overlap in the results—surveillance programs can be designed to detect such attempts and notify a system administrator.

17.9 PASSWORD PROTECTION

Three classes of items of authentication (Pr75) by which a person's identity may be established are

- *Something about the person*—This includes fingerprints, voiceprints, photographs, and signatures.
- *Something possessed by the person*—This includes special badges, identification cards, and keys, etc.
- *Something known by the person*—This includes passwords, lock combinations, and mother-in-law's maiden name.

The most common authentication scheme in use today is simple *password protection.* The user chooses a codeword several characters long, commits it to memory, and then types it to gain admission to a computer system. Most systems suppress the typing element so that the password does not appear on paper or on a CRT screen as it is typed.

Password protection has many weaknesses. Users tend to choose passwords that are easy to remember such as the name of a friend or relative. Someone who knows the user might try to log in several times using the names of various people this person knows; this might result in a security breach by use of *repeated trials.* Some early systems used short passwords; these systems were easily compromised by simply attempting all possible passwords. Most systems today use longer passwords to thwart such penetration attempts.

Using long passwords is not necessarily wise either; if passwords are difficult to remember, then users will be more inclined to make a note of them; this of course could make it easier for someone to obtain a password. So designers should choose a scheme that uses passwords long enough to make repeated trials futile yet short enough to be easily remembered.

Penetration of an operating system's defenses need not necessarily result in a significant security compromise. For example, suppose someone manages to gain access to the system's master list of passwords. Ordinarily, this would mean that the penetrator would be able to gain access to virtually any information on the system. To make these passwords useless to a penetrator, encryption can be used. Possessing the passwords is then of little use unless the person also possesses the decryption key.

Users of most systems are encouraged to change their passwords often; even if an intruder obtains a password, it may be changed before any real damage can be done.

A simple defense against repeated trials is to limit the number of login attempts that may be initiated in any period of time from a single terminal (or from a single account). Certainly, people make typing errors when attempting to log in. But it is unreasonable for someone who knows the correct password to require tens, hundreds, or thousands of tries. Therefore, the system might allow three or four tries and then disconnect that terminal automatically for several minutes. After a waiting period the terminal may be reconnected. If another series of futile login attempts occurs, the operating system might issue a warning at the terminal that the police are being called, or that an alarm siren in the terminal is about to go off!

17.10 AUDITING

Auditing is normally performed in manual systems "after the fact." Auditors are called in periodically to examine an organization's recent transactions and to determine if fraudulent activity has occurred. Auditing in computer systems can involve immediate computer processing to audit transactions that have just occurred.

An *audit log* is a permanent record of important events that occur in the computer system. It is produced automatically each time such an event occurs, and is stored in a heavily protected area of the system; if the system is compromised, the audit log should remain intact.

The audit log is an important detection mechanism. Even if the system's defenses can be penetrated, people may be discouraged from trying to do so if they fear detection after the fact.

Merely producing an audit log does not guarantee good security. It is necessary to review the log frequently and carefully. Such reviews should be performed both periodically and randomly. Periodic audits give regular attention to security problems; random audits help to catch intruders off guard.

17.11 ACCESS CONTROLS

The key to internal security is to control the access to stored data. *Access rights* define what access various *subjects* have to various *objects.* Subjects make accesses to objects. Objects are information-holding entities. They may be very real objects that correspond to disks, tapes, processors, or storage words; or they may be *abstract objects* that correspond to data structures or processes.

Objects are protected against subjects. Authorizations within a computer system are granted to subjects. Subjects may be many types of entities including users, processes, programs, or other entities.

The most common access rights are *read access, write access,* and *execute access.* A straightforward way of implementing these is to use an *access control matrix.* In such a two-dimensional matrix, the various subjects are listed in the rows and the various objects to which they require access are listed in the columns. Each slot in the matrix contains the access rights that a user has to an object. An access control matrix must, of course, be one of the most closely guarded entities in an operating system.

17.12 SECURITY KERNELS

It is much easier to make a system more secure if security is designed into the system from the beginning rather than retrofitted to an existing system. Security measures should be implemented throughout a computer system. But if one hopes to develop a highly secure system, it is better to concentrate on making the kernel of the operating system secure.

Many *security kernels* have been developed (Mc79) (Wa79) (Po78) (Sc77) (Sc77a) and (Mi76). The most critical security measures are implemented in the kernel. It is intentionally kept as small as possible. This makes it more reasonable to examine the kernel carefully for flaws and to demonstrate its correctness formally.

In the efforts that have been attempted to date, researchers generally found that isolating the various functions that needed to be secured in a large-scale, general-purpose operating system created a large kernel. The security of the system depends especially on securing those functions that perform access control, logging, and monitoring, and that manage real storage, virtual storage, and the file system. These functions ordinarily occupy a large portion of operating system code making it difficult to keep the kernel small. It appears that new approaches to operating system design will be necessary to reduce the size of security kernels to the point that really secure systems can be built.

17.13 HARDWARE SECURITY

As hardware continues to decline in cost and size, it is becoming increasingly desirable to incorporate operating systems functions into the hardware. These functions then become considerably more secure than when they are accessible as easily modified software instructions. Functions incorporated into hardware can run much faster than in software; various monitoring functions may be performed more frequently.

17.14 SURVIVABLE SYSTEMS

One of the reasons for designing highly secure computer systems is to ensure their continued reliable operation and availability. A *survivable computer system* is one that continues to operate even after one or more of its components fail. For computer systems committed to on-line transaction processing, survivability is becoming an increasingly important criterion. An airline stands to lose considerable revenues if its reservations system fails; if a bank's system fails, even briefly, the confidence of its customers could be shaken.

Survivable systems provide for *graceful degradation*; a system with failed components still continues to provide service but at reduced levels. Survivable systems are designed so that a failed component can be taken off-line, repaired, and placed back on-line, all while the system continues to provide uninterrupted service.

One key to survivability is *redundancy*. If a component fails, then an equivalent component picks up the slack. Some systems use a pooled approach in which the identical resources function in parallel. Other systems activate the redundant resources only upon a failure.

Microprocessor architectures have been evolving steadily into more fail-safe designs in recent years. Many of them now use dual bus structures for communication. Multiprocessing is important in any survivable system. Some features for survivability are

- Incorporation of fail-safe mechanisms into the hardware rather than the software
- Use of *transparent multiprocessing*; this allows performance upgrades without software modifications
- Use of multiple input/output subsystems
- Incorporation of major portions of the operating system into hardware
- Incorporation of fault detection mechanisms into the hardware and software

As computing becomes increasingly widespread, users will come to expect the same uninterrupted service from their personal computers that they get from their refrigerators.

17.15 CAPABILITIES AND OBJECT-ORIENTED SYSTEMS

In this section we consider the notion of capabilities and object-oriented systems. These are receiving great interest today as means of achieving secure computer systems. Capabilities were first proposed in a classic paper by Dennis and Van Horn (Dn66).

An *access right* allows some *subject* to access some *object* in a prescribed manner. Subjects are users of computer systems or entities that act on behalf of users or the system. Objects are resources within the system. Subjects may be such things as jobs, processes, and procedures. Objects may be files, programs, semaphores, directories, terminals, channels, controllers, devices, disk tracks, primary storage blocks, etc. Subjects are also considered to be objects of the system so one subject can have rights to access another. Subjects are active entities; objects are passive. Systems must be able to create new types of subjects and objects as they evolve.

A *capability* is a token; the possession of a capability by a subject confers access rights for an object. It is like a ticket which the bearer may use to gain access to sports events. Capabilities are not ordinarily modified, but they can be reproduced. A *protection domain* defines the access rights that a subject has to the various objects of the system. It is the set of capabilities belonging to a subject.

Small protection domains are important if the principle of least privilege is to be enforced. But these imply a large and sparse access control matrix. *Capability-based addressing* is becoming the accepted means for enforcing small protection domains.

A capability is a protected name for an object in the system. The name is unique across the entire system. For a subject to access a particular object, it must possess a capability for doing so. Included in a capability is a statement of the particular access rights that the capability allows its possessor to have to the named object. Capability creation is a function of carefully guarded operating systems routines. Normally, capabilities may not be modified except to reduce the stated access rights. A subject that possesses a capability may perform certain operations including copying it or passing it as a parameter.

Upon creation of an object, a capability for that object is created. This new capability immediately includes all access rights to the new object. The subject that creates the capability may pass copies of the capability to other subjects. A subject receiving a capability may use it (to perform the indicated access to the object), or may create more copies to pass to other subjects. When one subject passes a capability to another, it may reduce the stated access rights. Thus as a capability is propagated throughout the system, its stated access rights can either remain the same or decrease; they cannot increase.

In some systems, capabilities have been integrated into storage addressing hardware. These systems use capabilities on every primary storage reference. This is called capability-based addressing.

In a segmentation system, two-dimensional addresses $v = (s, d)$ are used; s is the segment name, and d is the displacement of the desired address within the segment. An instruction references a storage location within a segment and a capability for the segment. All references to the segment are checked against the stated access rights in the capability. A typical capability would contain an object identifier (or a pointer to the object), the type of the object, and the access rights the possessor of the capability has to the object.

Users must be prevented from creating arbitrary capabilities. This can be accomplished by placing capabilities in special *capability segments* to which the users do not have access. Another approach is to add a *tag bit* to each primary storage location. This bit, inaccessible to the user, is set on if the location contains a capability; if the bit is on, the hardware restricts the manipulation of the location's contents to appropriate system routines.

The identifier in a capability may be implemented as a pointer to the desired object, or it may be a unique code. Pointers make it easier to reach the object, but they must be updated if the object is moved. With the unique code approach, it is not necessary to update the capabilities. The unique code approach does require, however, that on every access to the object, its address must be determined. A hashing mechanism can be implemented efficiently; associative (or cache) storage can be used to reduce the overhead of repeated references to the same object.

The *lost object problem* is inherent in capabilities-based systems; if the last remaining capability for an object is destroyed, that object cannot be used in any manner. So a capabilities-based system must always maintain at least a single capability for each object.

17.15.1 Movement and Storage of Capabilities

Controlling the copying and movement of capabilities is a difficult problem. Systems generally do not allow direct manipulation of capabilities by users; instead capability manipulation is performed by the operating system on behalf of the users.

Keeping track of existing capabilities is an important task of the operating system. It is complicated by the fact that the number of capabilities in a multiuser system can be very large. The operating system must guard the capabilities as well as guarantee rapid access to them. This is often handled by a directory structure that controls all of the capabilities in a system.

17.15.2 Revocation of Capabilities

It is sometimes necessary to revoke capabilities passed to another subject. If a directory system handles all capabilities, this can be relatively straightforward. But without such central control, revoking a capability can be difficult; the capability could have been copied many times.

In an emergency situation, one could copy an object and destroy the original thereby disabling the questionable capability. But this would of course affect many other subjects with capabilities to that object.

Sometimes it is desirable to revoke the capability of a particular subject and also that of any other subject that received the capability from the given subject.

One technique for *selective revocation of capabilities* is to make all capabilities created from an object's primary capability point to the object indirectly through that primary capability. Then a particular capability may be revoked without affecting either the holders of the primary capability or any of the copies.

Capabilities to I/O devices may need to be interpreted differently depending on the type of the device; a capability for a tape drive object might allow rewind, while a capability for a card reader would not.

17.16 CASE STUDY: THE OBJECT-ORIENTED ARCHITECTURE OF THE IBM SYSTEM/38

In the IBM System/38 (IB80), operating systems functions are provided by the Control Program Facility (CPF). The System/38 incorporates a high-level machine architecture that provides many resource management and supervisory functions generally found in software in previous systems.

The architecture provides an object-oriented, uniformly addressable, very large storage. All of the objects in the system are storage-resident. All of the system's storage is addressable by a single device-independent addressing mechanism that performs dynamic integrity and authorization checking.

The System/38 provides high-level machine instructions that directly manipulate objects. The *create* instruction builds a new object according to the attributes in a template.

Some attributes of an object are its name, its owner, and its existence (i.e., whether or not it can be implicitly destroyed). *Generic operations* apply to all objects; *unique operations* apply only to a specific object type.

All System/38 machine objects are *encapsulated*—the internal structure of an object produced by the create instruction is known only to the machine. Figure 17.1 summarizes the objects manipulated by the machine instructions of the System/38.

CPF provides users with an object-oriented interface. All data in the system is stored in object form and manipulated by object-oriented commands. Generic functions handle authorization, moving, renaming, dumping, locking, saving, and restoring objects. Specific functions dictate how an object can be used.

Object	Explanation
Access group	Allows other objects to be grouped for more efficient transfer between primary and secondary storage
Context	Contains the name, type, and subtype of other objects to establish addressability
Controller description	Represents an I/O controller for a cluster of I/O devices
Cursor	Provides addressability into a data space
Data space	Stores database records of one particular format
Data space index	Establishes the logical ordering of records stored in a data space
Index	Stores and orders data
Logical unit description	Represents a physical I/O device
Network description	Represents one of the system's physical network ports
Process control space	Contains process execution
Program	Selects and orders machine instructions
Queue	For communication between processes, and between devices and processes
Space	Stores pointers and scalars
User profile	Identifies a valid user of the machine

Fig. 17.1 System/38 objects. (Courtesy of International Business Machines Corporation.)

When an object is created, CPF places the object's name into a machine object called a *context.* Contexts are seen by users as libraries or catalogs of objects.

CPF uses machine objects as building blocks to construct objects for users. For example, to create a user-oriented object called a database file, CPF combines a data space, a data space index, a cursor, and a space. The user actually sees only a single object, namely the database file. A higher-level object constructed from machine objects and other objects is called a *composite object.*

Each object consists of a functional portion and an associated space. The functional portion might be a program. The associated space is a region of bytes the machine user may manipulate directly. A *space object* has no functional part; it provides storage for buffers, pointers, control blocks, and various other data items.

The System/38 implements capability-based addressing through system pointers. A *system pointer* contains the location of an object and the access rights. System pointers are created and manipulated by special System/38 instructions only; the user cannot create system pointers by bit manipulation.

An *unresolved system pointer* specifies the name of an object but not its location. Once the object is referenced and found, its location is filled in; the system pointer is then *resolved.* Objects are located by searching contexts.

Security is rigidly enforced; every reference to an object is examined to be certain that the user has the right to access the object in the desired manner; if not, the reference is disallowed and a record is made of the attempted security violation.

The System/38 incorporates implicit synchronization into the object access mechanism to prevent simultaneous accesses. When one process is writing an object and another attempts to read it, the accesses are automatically serialized. When simultaneous reads are attempted, however, they are both allowed to proceed.

Users may perform synchronization explicitly with locks. Record-level locks may be used in database references; this greatly reduces the contention that would occur if the entire database were locked.

With CPF, one user is designated as *security administrator.* This user has access to all objects in the system. IBM supplies a standard set of user profiles with CPF; the profile for the security administrator includes all-object authority and the authority to create new user profiles and modify existing profiles.

17.17 CRYPTOGRAPHY

Cryptography was once of interest almost exclusively to the military and the diplomatic communities. Today it is especially important in computing systems. Eavesdropping is easier today. Huge volumes of business are handled over the telephone. Computer networking (Chapter 16) is growing rapidly. Use of electronic mail and electronic funds transfer (EFT) is increasing.

The National Bureau of Standards (NBS) has adopted the Data Encryption Standard (DES) for transmission of sensitive federal information.

Cryptography is the use of data transformations to make the data incomprehensible to all except its intended users. The *privacy problem* is concerned with preventing the unauthorized extraction of information from a communication channel. The *authentication problem* is concerned with preventing one's opponents from modifying a transmission or inserting false data into a transmission. The *problem of dispute* is concerned with providing the receiver of a message with legal proof of the sender's identity, i.e., the electronic equivalent of a written signature.

17.17.1 A Cryptographic Privacy System

In a cryptographic privacy system, the *sender* wishes to transmit a certain unenciphered message (called a *plaintext*) to a legitimate *receiver*; the transmission is to occur over an *insecure channel* assumed to be monitored or tapped by an *eavesdropper.*

The sender passes the plaintext to an encryption unit that transforms the plaintext into a *ciphertext* or *cryptogram*; the ciphertext is not discernible to the eavesdropper. The ciphertext is then transmitted over the insecure channel. At the receiving end, the ciphertext passes through a decryption unit to regenerate the plaintext.

17.17.2 Cryptanalysis

Cryptanalysis is the process of attempting to regenerate plaintext from ciphertext but without knowledge of the decryption key; this is the normal task of the eavesdropper. If the eavesdropper, or *cryptanalyst,* cannot determine the plaintext from the ciphertext (without the key), then the cryptographic system is *secure.*

17.17.3 Public Key Systems

A cryptographic system is only as secure as its keys. Key distribution must be handled over highly secure channels; this can be time-consuming, and sometimes such secure channels are simply not available.

Public key systems circumvent the key distribution problem. In conventional cryptographic systems, enciphering and deciphering are intimately related. Someone who processes the single key to encipher messages can also decipher them. In public key systems, the enciphering and deciphering functions are separated; the enciphering key cannot be used to decipher a message. These systems use an enciphering key, E, and a deciphering key, D, in which it is not computationally feasible (within a "reasonable" time) to determine D from E.

Thus E may be made public without compromising the security of D. This simplifies the problem of key distribution. Every user generates an enciphering key and a deciphering key. The enciphering key is simply made public; the deciphering key is kept secret. Thus anyone can send an encrypted message to a particular user (because the enciphering key is public), but only that user can decipher the message (because the deciphering key is private). E is often called a *public key* and D is called a *private key.*

17.17.4 Digital Signatures

We have grown to accept the use of handwritten signatures as legal proof that a person agrees to the terms of a contract as stated on a sheet of paper, or that a person has authorized a transfer of funds as indicated on a check. But the use of written signatures involves the physical transmission of a paper document; this is not practical if electronic communication is to become more widely used in business.

A written signature can be produced by one person only (although forgeries certainly occur), but it can be recognized by many people as belonging uniquely to its author. A *digital signature*, then, to be accepted as a replacement for a written signature would have to be easily authenticated by anyone, but producible only by its author.

Public key cryptosystems offer a means of implementing digital signatures. The sender uses the private key to create a signed message. The receiver uses the sender's public key to decipher the message.

The receiver saves the signed message for use in resolving disputes. If the sender later denies that the message was sent, the receiver can present the signed message to a court of law where the judge then uses the sender's public key to check that the enciphered message corresponds to a meaningful plaintext message with the sender's name, the proper time sent, etc. Only the sender could have generated the message, and therefore the receiver's claim would be upheld in court.

This technique has one significant disadvantage: It allows an eavesdropper who possesses the sender's public key to determine the message. The defect is easy to correct: The sender can add a second level of encryption to the already encrypted message by using the receiver's public key; the receiver's private key is then used to recover the signed encrypted message and the sender's public key is used to recover the original plaintext.

17.17.5 The DES and RSA Schemes

Two schemes that the reader interested in cryptography might want to explore further are the Data Encryption Standard (DES) (Na77) and the Rivest, Shamir, and Adleman (RSA) scheme (Ri78). DES is a symmetric encryption scheme—the same key is used for both encryption and decryption. RSA is an asymmetric encryption scheme—different keys are used for encryption and decryption. As of this writing, DES is the only scheme to have achieved very wide standardization and acceptance. But its weaknesses will have to be corrected if it is to endure beyond the end of this decade. The Data Encryption Standard publication (Na77) has been reproduced as an Appendix that begins on page 632.

17.17.6 Applications

Cryptography is particularly useful in timesharing systems and computer networks. Passwords should be stored in encrypted form so that even if the operating system is penetrated, the password list will be of no use. This is the most common application of cryptography in today's computer systems.

Cryptography may also be used to protect all stored data in a computer system. But the encryption/decryption overhead would be so large as to make this prohibitive. The advent of special hardware for this purpose will certainly make this practice widespread. File encryption would solve one very serious problem with today's shared systems: Every system has at least one person designated as having unrestricted access to all system files, so users are reluctant to store sensitive information. File encryption would enable users to trust their most sensitive information to computers.

If an encrypted tape or disk pack is stolen, encryption prevents it from being of use. Encrypted backups need not be guarded as heavily as unencrypted ones.

Computer networks have introduced new vulnerabilities into computer-based systems. The layered network protocols discussed in Chapter 16 offer several levels of encryption. In *link encryption* the network assumes the responsibility for encryption/decryption at each node; the data is transmitted between nodes in encrypted form, decrypted at each node to determine where to pass it next, and then reencrypted.

In *end-to-end encryption* a message is encrypted at its source and decrypted only once—at its destination. The message is thus protected throughout its transmission even if security at one of the nodes has been compromised. In a store-and-forward packet switching network with end-to-end encryption, the destination address associated with a packet cannot be encrypted; it must be readable at each node for routing purposes.

Password logins can also be protected with encryption. A *challenge and response procedure* can be helpful here. The user transmits a login request "in clear" (i.e., not encrypted). The system, to authenticate the user, sends a *challenge* string to the user in clear. The challenge string should be one that is guaranteed not to repeat; the date and time carried to millionths of a second would be appropriate. The user's terminal encrypts this challenge using a key supplied by the user (and known to the system) and transmits the result to the system. The system authenticates the user by comparing the response with an internal encrypted version of the challenge. Then all future transmissions during this session are encrypted with the user's key. Because the key is never transmitted, an eavesdropper would have to cryptanalyze the transmissions to understand them or to impersonate the valid user.

17.18 OPERATING SYSTEM PENETRATION

Certainly, a favorite pastime of many people, especially university students, is to call in to a timesharing system, penetrate its defenses, and then happily publicize their success. Instructors have found their student grade files modified, and system administrators have been horrified to discover master lists of all user passwords posted on public bulletin boards! Operating systems students thoroughly enjoy the explanations of complex successful security penetration attempts. At one major university (legend has it) the instructors in the systems courses guaranteed a grade of "A" to any student who could penetrate the university's operating system; a disproportionately large number of "A" grades were awarded that semester!

In some systems, the ultimate penetration consists of flipping the machine state bit from problem state to supervisor state. Once this is accomplished, the penetrator may then execute privileged instructions to gain access to virtually any data protected by the operating system.

Penetration studies are designed to determine if a system's defenses against attacks by nonprivileged users are adequate. Their goal is to expose design deficiences so that they may be corrected.

I/O control is a favorite area for penetration attempts. I/O code is often complex; various types of errors and omissions are often exposed upon detailed analysis. Because I/O channels have access to primary storage, they could modify critical system information. An I/O channel can be forced into an infinite loop thus denying I/O capability to the system; this could be devastating in systems that must operate reliably.

One goal of penetration tests is to estimate the *penetration work factor,* an indication of how much effort and resources must be expended by a potential penetrator to obtain unauthorized access to system resources. A key goal of security mechanisms is to make this factor very large; actual penetration studies may reveal that it is not as large as the system designers intended it to be.

Linde (Li75) describes the results of a number of penetration studies undertaken by System Development Corporation. His paper contains two thorough appendixes summarizing generic flaws and attacks. The material in the next two sections is abstracted from these appendixes.

17.18.1 Generic System Functional Flaws*

Several flaws have been found to be common to many computing systems. These include

- *Authentication*—On many systems, users cannot determine if the hardware and software on which they are running are what they are supposed to be. This makes it easy for a penetrator to replace a program without the user's knowledge. A user might obligingly type a password into a counterfeit login program, for example.
- *Encryption*—The master list of passwords should be stored in encrypted form. It often isn't.
- *Implementation*—A well-thought out design for a security mechanism may be improperly implemented.

---

*R.R. Linde, "Operating System Penetration," Proceedings, 1975. National Computer Conference, Vol. 44, AFIPS Press.

- *Implicit trust*—A common problem; one routine assumes that another is functioning properly when, in fact, it should be carefully examining parameters supplied by the other.
- *Implied sharing*—The system may inadvertently deposit critical system information in a user's address space.
- *Interprocess communication*—The penetrator may use a SEND/RECEIVE mechanism to test various possibilities. For example, the penetrator may request a system resource and supply a password; the return information may indicate "password correct" confirming the penetrator's guessed password.
- *Legality checking*—Quite simply, the system may not be performing sufficient validation of user parameters.
- *Line disconnect*—In timesharing and networking, when the line is lost (for any reason) the operating system should immediately logout the user or place the user in a state such that reauthorization is necessary for the user to regain control. Some systems let a process "float" after a line disconnect. A penetrator may be able to gain control of the process and use whatever resources the process may access.
- *Operator carelessness*—A penetrator may trick an operator into mounting a counterfeit operating system disk pack.
- *Parameter passing by reference vs. by value*—It is safer to pass parameters directly in registers than it is to have the registers point to the locations containing the parameters. Passing by reference can lead to a situation in which the parameters are still in the user's address space after legality checking occurs; the user could thus supply legitimate parameters, have them checked, and then modify them just before the system uses them.
- *Passwords*—Passwords are often easy to guess or to obtain by repeated trials.
- *Penetrator entrapment*—Systems should contain entrapment mechanisms to lure the unskilled penetrator. This is a good first line of detection, but most systems have inadequate entrapment mechanisms.
- *Privilege*—In some systems, too many programs are given too much privilege. This is contrary to the principle of least privilege.
- *Program confinement*—A program borrowed from another user can act as a Trojan Horse; it might steal or alter the borrower's files.
- *Prohibitions*—Often users are warned not to use certain features because the results may be "indeterminate," but indeed these features remain accessible to the users.
- *Residue*—Often the penetrator may find a list of passwords by simply looking in a wastebasket. Residues are sometimes left in storage after a system routine runs. Sensitive information must always be overwritten or destroyed before the media it occupies (storage, paper, etc.) is released or discarded. Paper shredders are popular for this purpose.

- *Shielding*—A current in a wire generates a magnetic field around the wire; penetrators may actually tap a transmission line or computer system without making physical contact. Electrical shielding may be put in place to prevent such "invisible intrusions."
- *Threshold values*—These are designed to discourage repeated login attempts, for example. After a certain number of invalid login attempts, that user (or the terminal at which the logins are being attempted) should be locked out and the system administrator should be notified. Many systems lack this feature.

17.18.2 Generic Operating System Attacks

Certain penetration methodologies have been used effectively on many systems.

- *Asynchronism*—With multiple processes progressing asynchronously it is possible for one process to modify parameters that another has tested for validity but not as yet used; thus one process can pass bad values to another even if the second performs extensive checking.
- *Browsing*—A user searches the computer system attempting to locate privileged information.
- *Between lines*—A special terminal is used to tap into a communication line held by an inactive logged in user.
- *Clandestine code*—A patch is made under the guise of correcting a bug in the operating system; the code contains trapdoors that allow subsequent unauthorized reentry to the system.
- *Denial of access*—A user writes a program to crash the system, set the system into an infinite loop, or monopolize the system's resources. The intent here is to deny access or service to legitimate users.
- *Interacting synchronized processes*—Processes use the system's synchronization primitives to share and pass information to one another.
- *Line disconnect*—The penetrator attempts to gain access to a user's job after a line disconnect, but before the system acknowledges the disconnect.
- *Masquerade*—The penetrator assumes the identity of a legitimate user after having obtained the proper identification through clandestine means.
- *"NAK" attack*—Many systems allow a user to interrupt a running process (such as by pressing the "negative acknowledge" key on a teletypewriter), perform another operation, and then resume the interrupted process. These interrupts may be generated at any time. In some cases the penetrator can "catch" the system in an unprotected state and easily seize control.
- *Operator spoof*—A clever penetrator can often fool a computer operator into performing an action that compromises system security.
- *Piggyback*—The penetrator uses a special terminal to tap a communication line.

The penetrator intercepts messages between the user and the processor, and either modifies the messages or replaces them entirely.

- *Trojan Horse*—The penetrator places code in the system to allow subsequent unauthorized access. The Trojan Horse may be left in the system permanently, or it may erase all traces of itself after a penetration.
- *Unexpected parameters*—The penetrator supplies unexpected values in a supervisor call to take advantage of a weakness in the system's legality checking mechanisms.

17.19 CASE STUDY: PENETRATING AN OPERATING SYSTEM

A graduate-level computer science class at the University of Michigan in Ann Arbor successfully penetrated the Michigan Terminal System (MTS) operating system (He80). The study was concerned only with software security. The goals were for an authorized and knowledgeable but nonprivileged user to gain access to files (to which this user did not have access), and to cause the system to crash.

MTS is a general-purpose operating system for IBM 360/370 compatible computers. It supports both batch and interactive computation. The file system supports extensive sharing. Some 25,000 user accounts are maintained. MTS supports 250 concurrent interactive users.

Team members were regular users of MTS. They were given access to internal system documentation. They performed a comprehensive analysis of the system and produced a report listing all suspected flaws. They employed the flaw hypothesis methodology developed by System Development Corporation. This involves

- *Flaw hypothesis generation*—The team examines well-known system weaknesses, and uses its collective knowledge about the system to list suspected flaws.
- *Flaw hypothesis confirmation*—Tests are run to determine if the suspected flaws are in fact real flaws.
- *Flaw generalization*—The confirmed flaws are carefully studied to determine if they imply other flaws or general design weaknesses. If they do, these cause this cycle to begin again with flaw hypothesis generation.

The team discovered a flaw in some of the system subroutines. The parameter checking mechanisms were weak; they would allow a user to cause arbitrary bit sequences to be stored into the *system segment* that contains much of the system's control information about a task. The flaw made it possible for a user to modify the system's accounting information, and to change the user's privilege level. The MTS protection system's information, also stored in the system segment, could be altered to completely disable the protection mechanisms. The user could switch the system from user mode to system mode and execute privileged supervisor calls. One of these can disable hardware storage protection, allowing the user to modify shared storage segments. The MTS supervisor core resides in such shared segments, and so the user could switch the machine to supervisor state and freely access arbitrary portions of the supervisor and any other software for that matter. Voilà! A total penetration.

The key flaw in the parameter checking mechanism was that after the parameters were checked by the system the user could then modify them before the system used them. The penetrators exploited this flaw to modify an address parameter to point to the system segment rather than user storage. This flaw illustrates the importance of careful synchronization between parameter checking routines and the routines that actually use the parameters. The team found similar flaws throughout MTS.

Another type of flaw exposed was that portions of the system could be forced to store their critical information in user-accessible segments. They were able to obtain free computer time in an interesting way: they forced a job into abnormal termination in such a manner that the system's accounting routines were bypassed. A careful examination of user-accessible shared storage revealed that some highly sensitive information (like passwords) was being stored in these areas. The team was also able to crash the system; they discovered that a certain instruction sequence forced the supervisor into an infinite loop.

The control relationships within the operating system security mechanism were found to depend on one another's correct operation. Once one mechanism was compromised, the group found it relatively easy to compromise other security mechanisms even at higher-privilege levels.

SUMMARY

As computing continues to become more accessible, security problems increase. Data communications and networking greatly increase the vulnerability of computer-based systems. User-friendliness also implies increased vulnerability.

Sharing and protection are conflicting goals. It is easier to verify the security of simple rather than complex systems. Security requirements for a given system define what it means for that system to be secure.

A total approach to computer security is essential. External security deals with protecting the computer system from intruders and disasters. User interface security is concerned with establishing a user's identity before that user is allowed to access a system. Internal security deals with ensuring the reliable and uncorrupted operation of the computer system and the integrity of programs and data.

Authorization determines what access is allowed to what entities. Division of responsibilities gives people distinct subsets of responsibilities; no one employee deals with a large portion of the operation of the system and so a security compromise would have to involve several employees.

Surveillance deals with monitoring and auditing the system, and authenticating users. In threat monitoring, the operating system controls sensitive operations rather than giving control directly to the users. Surveillance programs perform the sensitive operations. When surveillance programs must have greater access than user programs in order to service user requests, this is called amplification.

The most common authentication scheme in use today is simple password protection. Short passwords can often be determined by repeated trials. Encryption of the master list of passwords helps keep passwords secure even if a system is penetrated. Passwords should be changed frequently.

An audit log is a permanent record of events that occur in a computer system; it is heavily protected. The audit log acts as a deterrent to those who would attempt a security violation.

Access rights define what access various subjects have to various objects. Objects are protected against subjects. The most critical security measures are implemented in a security kernel. A survivable computer system is one that continues to operate even after one or more components fail. One key to survivability is redundancy. Survivability is facilitated by incorporation of fail-safe mechanisms into hardware, use of transparent multiprocessing, use of multiple input/output subsystems, incorporation of much of the operating system into hardware, and incorporation of fault detection mechanisms into hardware.

Capabilities-based object-oriented systems are being investigated today as a means of achieving secure computing systems. A protection domain defines the access rights that a subject has to the various objects of a system. Small protection domains are important for enforcing the principle of least privilege. For a subject to access a particular object, it must possess a capability to do so. The lost object problem is concerned with what happens when the last capability to an object is deleted. Revoking capabilities can be difficult; a capability could have been copied many times.

The IBM System/38 provides an object-oriented capabilities-based environment. It provides high-level machine instructions that directly manipulate objects. System/38 machine objects are encapsulated; their internal structure is known only to the machine. All object names are placed in cataloglike objects called contexts. A summary of System/38 machine objects is presented in the chapter.

System/38 implements capabilities through system pointers. Security is rigidly enforced; every reference to an object is examined to be sure the user has the right to access the object in the desired manner. Implicit synchronization prevents simultaneous accesses. The person designated as security administrator has access to all objects in the system.

Cryptography is important to the security of today's computing systems. The National Bureau of Standards has adopted the Data Encryption Standard (DES) for the transmission of sensitive federal information. Some interesting issues in cryptography are the privacy problem, the authentication problem, and the problem of dispute.

A sender encrypts a plaintext to create a ciphertext to send to a receiver over an insecure channel monitored by an eavesdropper. The receiver decrypts the ciphertext to reconstruct the original plaintext. Cryptanalysis is the process of attempting to regenerate a plaintext from a ciphertext, but without knowledge of the decryption key.

In public key systems the enciphering and deciphering functions are separated; each requires a different key. One key is made public; the other is kept private. When a message is encrypted with a user's public key only that user can decipher the message. Using public key systems it is possible to implement digital signatures that guarantee the authenticity of the sender of a message.

Two of the most significant cryptography schemes are the Data Encryption Standard (DES) and the Rivest, Shamir, and Adleman scheme. DES is a symmetric scheme in which a single key is used for encryption and decryption; RSA is an asymmetric scheme in which different keys are used for these purposes.

The most common use of encryption in today's operating systems is to protect a system's master list of passwords. Encryption may also be used to protect data stored in files; this makes a user's files useless to others—even to a system administrator with access to all data on the system.

Encrypted backup tapes and disks need not be guarded as heavily as unencrypted ones. Link encryption is concerned with encryption/decryption at each node of a computer network. With end-to-end encryption, messages are encrypted only at their source and decrypted only at their destination. A challenge and response procedure can enable a system to authenticate a user during login without the need for transmitting a key.

An operating system's defenses should be able to withstand a penetration attempt by a nonprivileged user; making an operating system impenetrable is an impossible task. The best one can hope to do is to make the system highly resistant to penetration. Penetration studies attempt to estimate a system's penetration work factor, that is, how much effort and resources must be expended to penetrate the system.

Studies by many groups have uncovered numerous generic system functional flaws that enable successful penetrations. These were enumerated in the chapter. Operating systems designers should study them carefully to be sure they do not build systems with these flaws.

The chapter also presented an enumeration of generic operating system attacks. Here, too, the operating system designer must be aware of the techniques used by system penetrators if the designer is to attempt to produce a secure system.

The chapter concluded with a discussion of a penetration study performed at the University of Michigan. The Michigan Terminal System (MTS) was successfully penetrated in several ways by a team of students with access to system documentation and source listings, but who could only access the system as conventional nonprivileged users. The students used the flaw hypothesis methodology developed by System Development Corporation; suspected flaws were enumerated, confirmed, and then generalized to expose other flaws and design weaknesses. The key flaw that enabled a total penetration was a defect in the parameter checking mechanisms. After parameters were verified, the user was able to change them before the operating system actually used them.

TERMINOLOGY

abstract objects
access control matrix
access rights
amplification
asymmetric encryption
asynchronous attack
audit log
auditing
authentication problem
authorization
browsing
capabilities list
capability
capability-based addressing
challenge and response procedure
ciphertext
classification
composite object
confinement
context
Control Program Facility (CPF)
create instruction
crytanalysis
cryptography
cryptosystem
Data Encryption Standard (DES)
decryption
denial-of-access
detection mechanisms
digital signature
division of responsibilities
DOD Directive 5200.28
eavesdropper
encapsulation
encryption
end-to-end encryption
external security
flaw generalization
flaw hypothesis confirmation
flaw hypothesis generation
flaw hypothesis methodology
generic operating system attacks
generic operations
generic system functional flaws
graceful degradation
IBM System/38
insecure channel
internal security
legality checking
link encryption
lost object problem
monitoring
NAK attack
object-oriented system
objects
operational security
operating system penetration
operator spoof
password protection
penetration study
penetration work factor
penetrator entrapment
physical security
piggyback
plaintext
principle of least privilege
Privacy Act of 1974
privacy problem
private key
problem of dispute
protection against disasters
protection against intruders

protection domain
public key
public key system
redundancy
repeated trials
resolved system pointer
revocation of capabilities
security
security administrator
security kernel
security requirements
space object
subjects
surveillance
surveillance programs
survivable systems
symmetric encryption
system pointer
threat monitoring
transparent multiprocessing
Trojan Horse
unresolved system pointer
user authentication
user interface security

EXERCISES

17.1 Why is a precise statement of security requirements critical to the determination of whether or not a given system is secure?

17.2 User-friendliness can imply increased vulnerability. Why?

17.3 Sharing and protection are conflicting goals. Give five significant examples of sharing supported by operating systems. For each, explain what protection mechanisms are necessary to control the sharing.

17.4 How are surveillance programs used in threat monitoring? Describe several checks a surveillance program might make to determine if a user is attempting to corrupt a critical file.

17.5 Give several reasons why simple password protection is the most common authentication scheme in use today. Discuss the weaknesses inherent in password protection schemes.

17.6 What is an audit log? What information might an operating system deposit in an audit log? How does an audit log act as a deterrent to those who would commit a security violation?

17.7 One maverick operating systems security expert has proposed the following economical way to implement a reasonable level of security: Simply tell everyone who works at an installation that the operating system contains the latest and greatest in security mechanisms. Don't actually build the mechanisms, the expert says, just tell everyone that the mechanisms are in place! Who might such a scheme deter from attempting a security violation? Who would not likely be deterred? Discuss the advantages and disadvantages of the scheme. In what types of installations might this scheme be useful? Suggest a simple modification to the scheme that would make it far more effective, yet still far more economical than a comprehensive security program.

17.8 What is the principle of least privilege? Give several reasons why it makes sense? Why is it necessary to keep protection domains small to effect the least privilege approach to security? Why are capabilities particularly useful in achieving small protection domains?

17.9 How does a capabilities list differ from an access control list?

17.10 Why is an understanding of cryptography important to operating systems designers?

List several areas within operating systems in which the use of cryptography would greatly improve security.

17.11 What is a security kernel? What types of functions are controlled by a security kernel? Give several motivations for keeping a security kernel as small as possible. What factors tend to force security kernels to be larger than designers consider desirable?

17.12 Why is it desirable to incorporate certain operating systems security functions directly into hardware? Why is it useful to microprogram certain security functions?

17.13 What is a survivable computer system? Why is interest in such systems increasing rapidly? List several design techniques for improving the survivability of computer systems.

17.14 Give brief definitions of each of the following terms.

a) cryptography
b) Data Encryption Standard (DES)
c) privacy problem
d) authentication problem
e) problem of dispute
f) plaintext
g) ciphertext
h) insecure channel
i) eavesdropper
j) cryptanalysis

17.15 Give brief definitions of each of the following terms.

a) public key system
b) public key
c) private key
d) digital signature
e) link encryption
f) end-to-end encryption
g) challenge and response procedure

17.16 Why is input/output such a ripe area for penetration attempts?

17.17 What is a penetration work factor? Why is it so difficult to determine?

17.18 Argue both for and against the incorporation of penetrator entrapment mechanisms in operating systems.

17.19 Asynchronous operating system attacks can occur in a uniprocessor system, but they are a far more serious problem in multiprocessing systems and computer networks. Explain why.

17.20 Why are denial of access attacks of such great concern to operating systems designers? List as many software-oriented means as you can that might be used in a denial of access attack.

17.21 Explain how public key cryptography systems provide an effective means of implementing digital signatures.

17.22 Explain how cryptography is useful in each of the following.

a) protecting a system's master list of passwords
b) protection of stored files
c) protection of vulnerable transmissions in computer networks
d) user authentication in login attempts

17.23 Summarize the results of the case study describing the penetration attack on the Michigan Terminal System.

Term Project

17.24 Design a penetration study for a large computer system with which you are familiar. Adhere to the following.

a) Perform the study only with the full cooperation of the computer center administrators and personnel.
b) Arrange to have ready access to all available system documentation and software (and firmware) source listings.
c) Agree that any flaws you discover will not be made public until they have been corrected.
d) Prepare a detailed report summarizing your findings and suggesting how to correct flaws.
e) Your primary goals are to achieve
   i) total system penetration
   ii) denial of access to legitimate system users
   iii) the crashing of the system.
f) You may access the system only through conventional mechanisms available to nonprivileged users.
g) Your attacks must be software and/or firmware oriented.

LITERATURE

(An75) Andrews, G., "Partitions and Principles for a Secure Operating System," *Proc. ACM,* October 1975.

(At76) Attanasio, C. R.; P. W. Markstein; and R. J. Phillips, "Penetrating an Operating System: A Study of VM/370 Integrity," *IBM Systems Journal,* Vol. 11, No. 1, 1976, pp. 102–118.

(Ba80) Bahad, M., and J. A. Hopper, "Data Element Security and its Effects on File Segmentation," *IEEE Trans. on Soft. Eng.,* Vol. SE-6, No. 5, September 1980, pp. 402–410.

(Bi74) Bisbey, R., and G. Popek, "Encapsulation: An Approach to Operating System Security," *Proc. ACM,* November 1974, Vol. 2.

(Cl81) Cheheyl, M. H., et al., "Verifying Security," *ACM Computing Surveys,* Vol. 13, No. 3, September 1981, pp. 279–339.

(Cr81) "Report of the Public Cryptology Group," *CACM,* Vol 24, No. 7, July 1981, pp. 434–450.

(De77) Denning, D. E., and P. J. Denning, "Certification of Programs for Secure Information Flow," *CACM,* July 1977, pp. 504–513.

(De79) Denning, D. E., and P. J. Denning, "Data Security," *ACM Computing Surveys,* Vol. 11, No. 3, September 1979, pp. 227–249.

(De81) Denning, D., "Secure Personal Computing in an Insecure Network," *CACM,* Vol. 22, No. 8, August 1981, pp. 476–482.

(De81a) Denning, D. E., and G. M. Sacco, "Timestamps in Key Distribution Protocols," *CACM,* Vol. 24, No. 8, August 1981, pp. 533–536.

(Dn66) Dennis, J. B., and E. C. Van Horn, "Programming Semantics for Multiprogrammed Computations," *CACM,* Vol. 9, No. 3, March 1966, pp. 143–155.

(Di79) Diffie, W., and M. E. Hellman, "Privacy and Authentication: An Introduction to Cryptography," *Proc. IEEE,* Vol. 67, No. 3, March 1979, pp. 397–427.

(Do75) Donovan, J. J., and S. E. Madnick, "Hierarchical Approach to Computer System Integrity," *IBM Systems Journal,* Vol. 14, No. 2, 1975, pp. 88–202.

(Fe81) Fernandez, E. B.; R. C. Summers; and C. Wood, *Database Security and Integrity,* Reading, Mass.: Addison-Wesley, 1981.

(Ga78) Gaines, R. S., and N. Z. Shapiro, "Some Security Principles and Their Application to Computer Security," *Operating Systems Review,* Vol. 12, No. 3, July 1978, pp. 19–28.

(Gt78) Gait, J., "Easy Entry: The Password Encryption Problem," *Operating Systems Review,* Vol. 12, No. 3, July 1978, pp. 54–59.

(Go78) Gorski, J., "A Modular Representation of the Access Control System," *Operating Systems Review,* Vol. 12, No. 3, July 1978, pp. 61–78.

(Gu80) Gudes, E., "The Design of a Cryptography-Based Secure File System, *IEEE Trans. on Soft. Eng.*, Vol. SE-6, No. 5, September 1980, pp. 411–420.

(Ha76) Harrison, M.; W. Ruzzo; and J. Ullman, "Protection in Operating Systems," *CACM,* Vol. 19, No. 8, August 1976.

(He80) Hebbard, B., et al., "A Penetration Analysis of the Michigan Terminal System," *Operating Systems Review,* Vol. 14, No. 1, June 1980, pp. 7–20.

(Ho80) Hoch, C., and J. C. Browne, "An Implementation of Capabilities on the PDP-11/45," *Operating Systems Review,* Vol. 13, No. 3, July 1980, pp. 22–32.

(Hs79) Hsiao, D. K.; D. S. Kerr; and S. E. Madnick, *Computer Security,* Academic Press, 1979.

(IB80) *IBM System/38 Technical Developments,* IBM Corporation, General Systems Division, Atlanta, Ga.: G580-0237–1, July 1980.

(Jo80) Jones, A. K., "Capability Architecture Revisited," *Operating Systems Review,* Vol. 14, No. 3, July 1980, pp. 33–35.

(Kr79) Krause, L., and A. MacGahan, *Computer Fraud and Countermeasures,* Englewood Cliffs, N. J.: Prentice-Hall, 1979.

(Kr80) Krieger, M. M., "Current and Proposed Computer Crime Legislation," *Computer Law Journal,* Vol. 2, No. 3, 1980, pp. 721–771.

(La81) Landwehr, Carl E., "Formal Models for Computer Security," *ACM Computing Surveys,* Vol. 13, No. 3, September 1981, pp. 247–278.

(Le79) Lempel, A., "Cryptology in Transition," *ACM Computing Surveys,* Vol. 11, No. 4, December 1979, pp. 286–301.

(Li75) Linde, R. R., "Operating System Penetration," *AFIPS Conf. Proc.,* Vol. 44, 1975.

(Li76) Linden, T. A., "Operating System Structures to Support Security and Reliable Software," *ACM Computing Surveys,* Vol. 8, No. 4, December 1976, pp. 409–445.

(Mc79) McCauley, E. J., "KSOS: The Design of a Secure Operating System," *AFIPS Conf. Proc.,* Vol. 48, 1979, pp. 345–353.

(Mc74) McPhee, J., "Operating System Integrity," *IBM Systems Journal,* Vol. 13, No. 3, 1974.

(Me81) Merkle, R. C., and M. E. Hellman, "On the Security of Multiple Encryption," *CACM,* Vol. 24, No. 7, July 1981, pp. 465–467.

(Mi76) Millen, J., "Security Kernel Validation in Practice," *CACM,* Vol. 19, No. 5, May 1976.

(Mo79) Morris, R., and K. Thompson, "Password Security: A Case History," *CACM,* Vol. 22, No. 11, November 1979.

(My80) Myers, G. J., and B. R. S. Buckingham, "A Hardware Implementation of Capability-Based Addressing," *Operating Systems Review,* Vol. 14, No. 4, October 1980, pp. 13–25.

(Na77) National Bureau of Standards, "Data Encryption Standard," January 1977, NTIS *NBS-FIPS PUB 46.*

(Or72) Organick, E. I., *The Multics System: An Examination of Its Structure,* Cambridge, Mass.: M.I.T. Press, 1972.

(Pi80) Pinnow, K. W.; J. G. Ranweiler; and J. F. Miller, "System/38 Object-Oriented Architecture," *IBM System/38 Technical Developments,* IBM Corporation, General Systems Division, Atlanta, Ga.: G580-0237-1, July 1980, pp. 55–58.

(Po74) Popek, J., and C. Kline, "Verifiable Secure Operating System Software," *AFIPS Conference Proc.,* Vol. 43, 1974.

(Po78) Popek, G. J., and C. S. Kline, "Issues in Kernel Design," *AFIPS Conf. Proc., 1978 NCC,* Vol. 47, pp. 1079–1086.

(Po79) Popek, G. J., and C. S. Kline, "Encryption and Secure Computer Networks," *ACM Computing Surveys,* Vol. 11, No. 4, December 1979, pp. 331–356.

(Pr75) "Computer Security Guidelines for Implementing the Privacy Act of 1974," *NBS FIPS Pub. 41,* May 1975.

(Ri78) Rivest, R. L.; A. Shamir; and L. Adleman, "On Digital Signatures and Public Key Cryptosystems," *CACM,* Vol. 21, No. 2, February 1978, pp. 120–126.

(Sa74) Saltzer, J. H., "Protection and the Control of Information Sharing in Multics," *CACM,* Vol. 17, No. 7, July 1974, pp. 388–402.

(Sr77) Schiller, W. L., "The Design and Abstract Specification of a Multics Security Kernel," Bedford, Mass.: The Mitre Corp., November 1977, *MTR-3 294,* Vol I; *EST-TR-77-259,* Vol. I (NTIS *AD A04876*).

(Sc77) Schroeder, M. D.; D. D. Clark; and J. H. Saltzer, "The Multics Kernel Design Project," Proc. Sixth ACM Symposium on Operating Systems Principles, in *Operating Systems Review,* Vol. 11, No. 5, 1977, pp. 43–56.

(Sc77a) Schroeder, M. D.; D. D. Clark; J. H. Saltzer; and D. H. Wells, *Final Report of the Multics Kernel Design Project,* MIT-LCS-TR-96, 1977.

(Sh77) Shankar, K. S., "The Total Computer Security Problem: An Overview," *IEEE Computer,* June 1977, pp. 50–65.

(Si79) Simmons, G. J., "Symmetric and Asymmetric Encryption," *ACM Computing Surveys,* Vol. 11, No. 4, December 1979, pp. 305–330.

(Sy76) Sykes, D., "Protecting Data by Encryption," *Datamation,* Vol. 22, No. 8, August 1976.

(Wa79) Walker, B.; R. Kemmerer; and G. Popek, "Specification and Verification of the UCLA UNIX Security Kernel," *Proc. Seventh ACM Symposium on Operating Systems Principles,* December 1979.

(Wa80) Walker, S. T., "The Advent of Trusted Computer Operating Systems," *AFIPS Conf. Proc., NCC 1980,* Vol. 49, pp. 655–665.

(Wi81) Wilkinson, A. L., et al., "A Penetration Analysis of a Burroughs Large System," *Operating Systems Review,* Vol. 15, No. 1, January 1981, pp. 14–25.

(Yo81) Young, C. R., "A Security Policy for a Profile-Oriented Operating System," *AFIPS Conf. Proc., NCC 1981,* pp. 273–282.

Part 8
Case Studies

18 Case Study: UNIX Systems*

Small is beautiful.

Schumacher's dictum

. . . the increased productivity fostered by a friendly environment and quality tools is essential to meet ever increasing demands for software.

M.D. McIlroy, E.N. Pinson, and B.A. Tague

*UNIX is a trademark of Bell Laboratories.

Outline

18.1 INTRODUCTION

The field of operating systems has suffered many frustrating and costly failures, but along the way several significant successes have been achieved. The UNIX operating system developed at Bell Laboratories is one of the notable successes (Ri78).

UNIX systems were designed to be *convenient systems for supporting program development.* They have a simple but powerful command language and a *device-independent file system.*

Hundreds of UNIX systems are in use throughout the Bell System, and it is popular in university and industrial environments. Versions for use on personal computers are also available. The minimum configuration needed to support a typical multiuser timesharing system is a 16K-bit processor with 256K bytes of main storage and a fast-access disk drive.

18.2 HISTORY

During 1965–1969, Bell Laboratories participated, with General Electric (later Honeywell) and Project MAC at the Massachusetts Institute of Technology, in the development of the Multics system. Originally designed to be run on the large and powerful GE-645 mainframe, Multics is a large and complex system. It is a general-purpose computer utility built to service the diverse needs of large user communities.

In 1969, Bell Labs withdrew from the Multics effort. Some members of the research staff began to work on a far less ambitious system called UNIX. The group, led by Bell Labs staff member Ken Thompson, sought to create a computing environment for facilitating programming research and development. The first version of the UNIX system was produced for DEC's PDP-7 and was written in assembly language.

The UNIX system effort attracted Dennis Ritchie who was instrumental in rewriting UNIX programs in the C high-level language (Jo78), (Ke78), (Ri78b) by 1972. This helped make UNIX software more *portable* and understandable. The system machine code grew by about a third over the assembly language version, but some of the increase was due to the addition of multiprogramming support and the ability to share reentrant procedures.

The PDP-11 was already popular in the universities when news of Thompson and Ritchie's UNIX system began to spread. In 1973, Western Electric agreed to license the system to nonprofit organizations. It made UNIX systems available to dozens of educational institutions.

By 1975, UNIX systems had become very popular in the universities, and a users' organization developed that evolved into the group now called USENIX. The first release of a UNIX system for public consumption was version five. It looked more like the result of a research project rather than a product development effort.

Version six appeared in 1975, and is still in wide use today. The Seventh Edition System, released in 1979, reflects a great deal of polishing designed to make a UNIX system a valid commercial product.

18.3 VERSIONS OF UNIX SYSTEMS

Although designed for the PDP-11 family of computers, a UNIX system has been successfully implemented on many other systems. In 1977 it was implemented for the Interdata 8/32. It is now available on many large mainframes, and a variety of microprocessor versions have been implemented. The UNIVAC 1100 version was the first large-scale mainframe UNIX system. UNIX systems are also available on DEC's VAX computers (see Chapter 19).

Several versions of UNIX systems are currently in use. In the next several sections, some of the more popular versions are discussed. Later in the chapter, some of the special-purpose versions of UNIX systems are considered.

18.3.1 Standard UNIX Systems

Standard UNIX systems are multiprogramming, timesharing operating systems intended primarily for the DEC PDP-11/34, 40, 45, and 70 computers. They provide the environment of a small-scale computer center supporting up to 40 users. They are currently the most popular UNIX systems. Standard UNIX systems provide a hierarchical file system with full protection, demountable volumes, device independence, and features that facilitate programming simplicity. Any program or group of programs can be run asynchronously in *foreground* (interactive) or *background* (unattended) without change.

UNIX systems do not distinguish user programs from system programs in either capability or usage, except for restrictions imposed by file protection. Input/output buffering, main storage allocation and disk storage allocation are handled automatically by the system and are invisible to the user. Procedural code in all programs produced by the C compiler is reentrant and shareable.

UNIX systems allow users to route the output of one program directly into the input of another. This facilitates the solution of large-scale programming problems by composing available small programs, rather than by developing completely new programs.

Standard UNIX systems are distributed with a set of packaged programs including a text editor, a programmable command language interpreter, several compilers for popular languages, an assembler, a link editor, debuggers, document formatters (with mathematical capabilities), text processing programs, a sorting utility, a status inquiry capability, interuser communication capability, administrative and maintenance programs, standard libraries of system and user routines, and a game package.

The source code for all programs (except for the game package) is supplied with the system. Much of the documentation is made available on-line to interactive users.

18.3.2 PWB/UNIX System: The Programmer's Workbench

The *Programmer's Workbench* is an expanded version of a standard UNIX system. It is a specialized computing facility designed for supporting program development. A PWB/UNIX system provides a set of programming tools to support programming projects ranging in size from one person to several hundred people.

A complete word processing system is provided with editing, text formatting, spelling, typographical error detection, and phototypesetting control facilities.

A Remote Job Entry (RJE) facility allows a UNIX system to send jobs to various large mainframe computers, and to receive job outputs. To the host mainframe, the UNIX system RJE facility appears to be a card reader/punch and line-printer station. As job outputs are received from the mainframe, they are placed in UNIX system files, and the user is notified of the arrival of the output.

One of the most important facilities of a PWB/UNIX system is the *Source Code Control System (SCCS)* designed to maintain all of the source code and text files (such as manuals) on a software development project. SCCS provides facilities for the storing, updating, and retrieving, by version number or date, of all versions of source code modules and documents. SCCS records each software change indicating who made it, when, and why it was made.

18.3.3 MINI-UNIX System

The MINI-UNIX operating system is essentially a scaled-down version of a standard UNIX system. It is designed to provide most of the capabilities of a standard UNIX system to users of smaller computers such as DEC PDP-11/10, 20, 30, and 40 systems. The MINI-UNIX system can support up to four users and 13 concurrent processes.

18.3.4 UNIX/V7: The Seventh Edition System

The Seventh Edition system, for use on DEC PDP-11/45 or 11/70 models, contains a number of significant enhancements over prior versions. Files may be as large as one billion bytes. The system has been made more portable. The C language has been extended. Phototypesetter software has been greatly enhanced (indicating a surge of user interest in text processing). A more powerful *shell* (interpreter of user commands) has been implemented including string variables, structured programming, trap handling, and other features. A new capability has been added for machine-to-machine file transfers.

UNIX system-version seven reflects Bell's efforts to accommodate the diverse needs of an ever increasing base of UNIX system users. The continuing cycle of improvements and new releases of UNIX systems are making UNIX systems more of a commercial product and less of a home-grown system for the convenience of a local programming group. Several other versions of UNIX systems are in use. Some of these are discussed later in this chapter, after the operation of the UNIX operating system is explained.

18.4 DESIGN GOALS

Two aspects of the origin of UNIX systems have contributed greatly to its unique design.

- The first version of a UNIX system was built in just a few work-years primarily by two people.
- The people who built the UNIX system were major users of the system.

The coherence of UNIX systems is attributable to these factors, in much the same manner as the programming language Pascal reflects a unique coherence among languages because it was designed by one person, namely Nicklaus Wirth.

It is possible for an experienced systems programmer to comprehend the entire UNIX system in a matter of weeks, rather than the months or years it can take to learn some of today's mainframe operating systems.

The first design goal was to keep the operating system simple and have it support only a minimum amount of function. User programs are left with the task of providing real sophistication.

The second goal was generality. A single method should serve a variety of purposes. Generality is manifested in UNIX systems in many areas. For example:

- The same system calls are used to read (or write) files, devices, and interprocess message buffers.
- The same naming, aliasing, and access protection mechanisms apply to data files, directories, and devices.
- The same mechanism is used to trap software interrupts and processor traps.

The third goal is to create an environment in which *large tasks may be accomplished by combining existing small programs rather than developing new programs.*

18.5 PROCESS CONTROL

At the heart of the UNIX system is the kernel. It consists of about 10,000 lines of C code and another 1000 lines of assembly code. Of the assembly code, the major portion performs hardware functions not convenient or practical in C. The remainder is frequently executed code and was written in assembly language for execution efficiency. The kernel represents only a small portion of the operating system (between 5 and 10 percent of the code).

The current state of an individual user's *pseudocomputer* is called an *image.* A process is the execution of an image. An image contains

- a storage image
- general register values
- the status of open files
- the current directory

and other information. A process's image resides in main storage during the execution of that process. An image may be swapped out to disk if a higher-priority process needs the space in main storage.

The storage image is divided into three logical segments (Fig. 18.1).

- reentrant procedure segment (beginning at location zero in the virtual address space)
- data segment
- stack segment

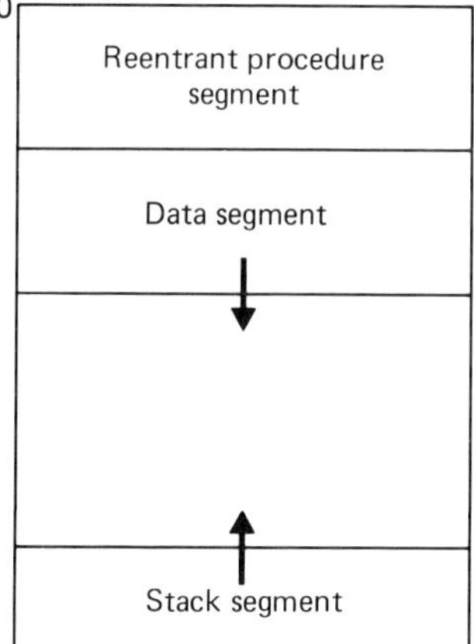

Fig. 18.1 A storage image.

Reentrant procedure segments may be shared between processes—*only a single copy of a shared segment is maintained in primary memory.* The data segment begins after the procedure segment and may grow upward (toward higher storage addresses). The stack segment begins at the highest address in the virtual address space and grows downward as information is pushed onto it by subroutine calls and interrupts.

The read-only text segments in the system are centrally controlled in the *text table* (Fig. 18.2). Each entry contains both the secondary and primary storage addresses of the segment. When a process first executes a shared-text segment, that segment is placed in secondary storage, and a text table entry is created with the

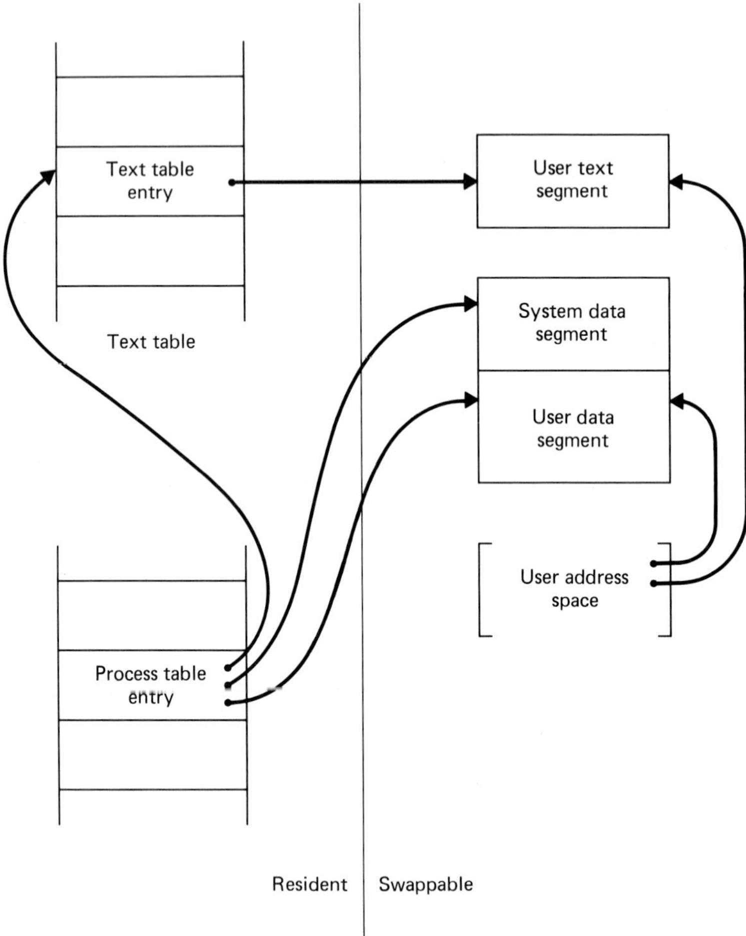

Fig. 18.2 Process control tables. (Adapted with permission from *The Bell System Technical Journal.* Copyright 1978, AT&T.)

appropriate storage addresses and a counter indicating the number of processes sharing the segment. When this counter becomes zero, the entry is freed and the primary and secondary storage occupied by the segment is released.

The data segment in the storage image contains private read-write data for this one process. System data associated with this process is maintained in a separate fixed-size segment. This *system data segment* is swapped with the process. The system segment contains data about the active process such as

- saved registers
- open file descriptors
- accounting data

- scratch data area
- stack for the system phase of the process.

A system data segment is not addressable directly by the process to which it corresponds.

Each process has a *process table* containing the data needed by the system when the process is not active. The process table contains the name of the process, the location of its segments, and scheduling information. It exists for the life of the process. It is addressable by the kernel.

18.5.1 Process Creation

New processes are created by a system primitive called *fork*. This system call causes the current process to split into two independent concurrent processes called a *parent process* and a *child process*. The two processes do not share primary storage, but they do share all open files. Copies of all writable data segments are made for the child. The fork call returns a value so that each process may determine if it is the parent or the child.

18.5.2 Exec

The primitive *exec* enables a process to execute a file. This causes the current text and data segments of the process to be exchanged for the new text and data segments specified in the file. The former segments are lost. This effectively changes the program that the process is executing, but not the process itself. Files that were open before the exec remain open afterward.

18.5.3 Process Synchronization

Synchronization of processes is accomplished by an *event* mechanism. Processes *wait* for events to occur. Process tables are associated with events. Events are represented as the addresses of the corresponding tables. A parent process waiting for one of its child processes to terminate waits for an event that is the address of its own process table entry. A completing process *signals* the event represented by its parent's process table entry. Signaling an event for which no process is waiting has no effect.

At any moment, all but one of the processes has called *event-wait* in the kernel. The remaining one is the executing process. When it calls event-wait, another process whose event has been signaled is dispatched.

18.5.4 Process Scheduling

Processes may run in either of two states, namely *user* state or *system* state. In user state, a process executes user programs and accesses the user data segment. In system state, a process executes kernel code and accesses the system data segment.

The primary objective of process scheduling in a UNIX system is responsiveness for interactive users. Processes are scheduled according to priorities. Initial priorities are assigned by the kernel code that processes event-waits. *Disk events* receive high priority. *Terminal events, time-of-day events,* and *user-process events* receive progressively lower priorities.

User processes are assigned priorities based upon the amount of processor time they have received. Processes that have received a large amount of processor time receive low priorities. Processes that have received only a small amount of processor time receive high priorities. This scheduling method assures good interactive response times. All system processes have higher priority than user processes, so they are always serviced first. A process gets the CPU for a quantum of typically one second. It either finishes voluntarily before the quantum expires, or it is suspended upon expiration of the quantum. Processes of like priority are scheduled in round robin fashion. The scheduling mechanism tends to be fair across all processes.

18.5.5 Swapping

Processes are swapped to and from secondary storage as needed. Both primary and secondary storage are allocated using a first-fit storage placement strategy. If a process needs to grow, it requests more storage. It is given a new section of storage sufficiently large to hold it, and the entire contents of the old storage are copied to the new area. The old storage is then released. If insufficient primary storage is available at the moment for the expansion, then secondary storage is allocated, the process is swapped to secondary storage, and is swapped back into primary storage (with its new size) when a sufficiently large hole becomes available.

The swapping process controls the swapping of all other processes to and from secondary storage. When the swapping process decides to swap in a swapped-out, ready-to-run process, it allocates primary storage for that process, and reads its segments into primary storage. That process then competes for CPU time with all loaded processes. If sufficient primary storage is not available, the swapping process examines the process table to determine which process may be swapped out to make room for the incoming process. Swapped-out processes that are ready-to-run are swapped in on a first-out-first-in basis, i.e., the process residing on the secondary storage longest is swapped in first. Processes in primary storage are selected for swapping out by their age in primary storage as well as by determining if they are waiting for slow events like I/O.

18.5.6 Process Termination

Processes may be terminated voluntarily by the *exit* primitive, or involuntarily as a result of illegal actions or signals or traps generated by the user. *Traps* are usually caused by program faults such as references to bad addresses or attempts to execute undefined operation codes. Involuntary termination causes the process's image to be written on a file. This image can be examined later by a debugging program to determine the reason for the termination.

The *interrupt* primitive may be used to terminate a program. The *quit* primitive functions like interrupt except that it also writes the process's image file.

18.6 INPUT/OUTPUT SYSTEM

The input/output system consists of two distinct components.

- the block I/O or structured I/O system
- the character I/O or unstructured I/O system

Input/output in a UNIX system is handled primarily in five system calls, namely *open, close, read, write,* and *seek.* (Three other calls, *gtty, stty,* and *stat* are used to get and set information about files and terminals.)

To open a file, one uses

```
fd = open (filename, mode)
```

where mode indicates whether reading, writing, or both are to be performed, and fd is the *file descriptor* to be used in subsequent references to the file.

Reading and writing are accomplished by using

```
nobytesread = read (fd, buffer, nobytesdesired)
```

and

```
nobyteswritten = write (fd, buffer, nobytesdesired)
```

In the case of a read, there are three possibilities, each of which involves sequential reading

- If this is the first read, then the read is sequential from the beginning of the file.
- If the file was just read, then the current read obtains the data following the previous data read.
- If a seek (see the following) was just performed, then the read is sequential at the offset specified in the seek call.

The same is true for writing. *All reading and writing is sequential, but the effect of direct access is achieved by using the seek call to adjust the offset within the file* as follows

```
seek (fd, offset, offsettype)
```

in which offsettype specifies

- whether the offset is relative or absolute
- whether the offset is in units of bytes or of 512 byte blocks.

The seek operation works fine on magnetic tape as well as on disk! But, of course, "direct access" programs run much more slowly on tape. Files are closed simply by writing

```
close (fd)
```

For users familiar with large operating systems, the preceding discussion may give UNIX systems the appearance of being a toy system. But even large data management systems have been implemented with these capabilities. The real problem is not functional capability, but performance. Commercial data processing environments supporting the storage and transfer of massive amounts of data often demand much greater capabilities than UNIX systems provide.

These same I/O calls are used for physical devices in the exact same manner in which they are shown here. Physical devices are represented in a UNIX system as *special files* within the file system structure. This means that users cannot write device dependent routines in UNIX systems unless, of course, the dependencies are reflected directly in the I/O stream.

Programs do not ordinarily have to open their standard input or output files, which are normally assigned to the user's terminal. The terminal is opened automatically by the login command.

18.6.1 Stream vs. Record I/O

All input/output in UNIX systems is *stream-oriented* rather than *record-oriented* as in most other systems. A *stream* is a sequence of bytes terminated by a delimiter (i.e., an *end-of stream* character). The stream concept makes it easy to implement device independence and the transparency between files, devices, and pipes (to be discussed shortly). It gives users flexibility in dealing with collections of data, but it does place more of a burden on the user who must now write data management code.

The user interested in record I/O can implement it quite easily. To implement *fixed length record processing,* the user need merely specify the constant length in all reads and writes. *Direct access I/O* with fixed length records is achieved by multiplying the record length by the record number and calling *seek* to position the file to the desired record. *Variable length records* may be implemented by preceding each record with a fixed length record size field. For example, using a two-byte *size field,* variable length records may be read by pairs of reads as follows

```
read (fd, size, 2);
read (fd, buffer, size);
```

18.7 FILE SYSTEM

A UNIX system file is a collection of randomly addressable characters. Its size is exactly the number of characters it contains—up to a maximum of about one billion. *A file contains whatever data the user chooses to put in it, and has no structure other than that imposed upon it by the user.*

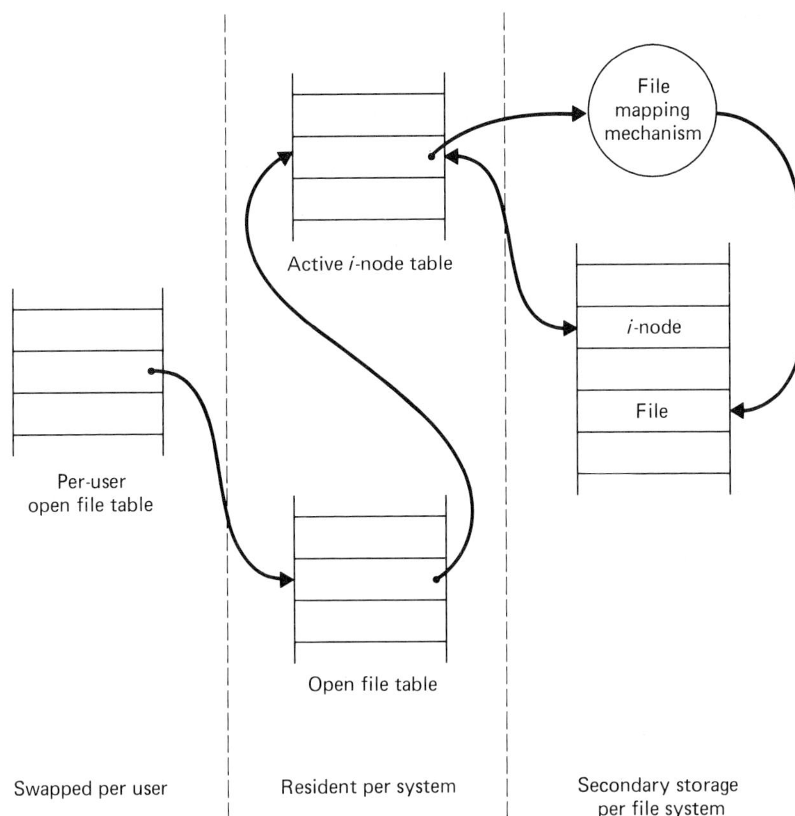

Fig. 18.3 File system data structure. (Adapted with permission from *The Bell System Technical Journal.* Copyright 1978, AT&T.)

The file system (Fig. 18.3) resides primarily on disks composed of blocks of 512 bytes each. A file breaks the disk into four regions (Fig. 18.4).

- an unused block
- *super block* that contains the size of the disk and the boundaries of the other regions
- the *i-list* with a list of file descriptions called *i-nodes*
- storage areas for the file contents.

An *i*-node contains

- owner's *user identification*
- owner's *group identification*
- protection bits

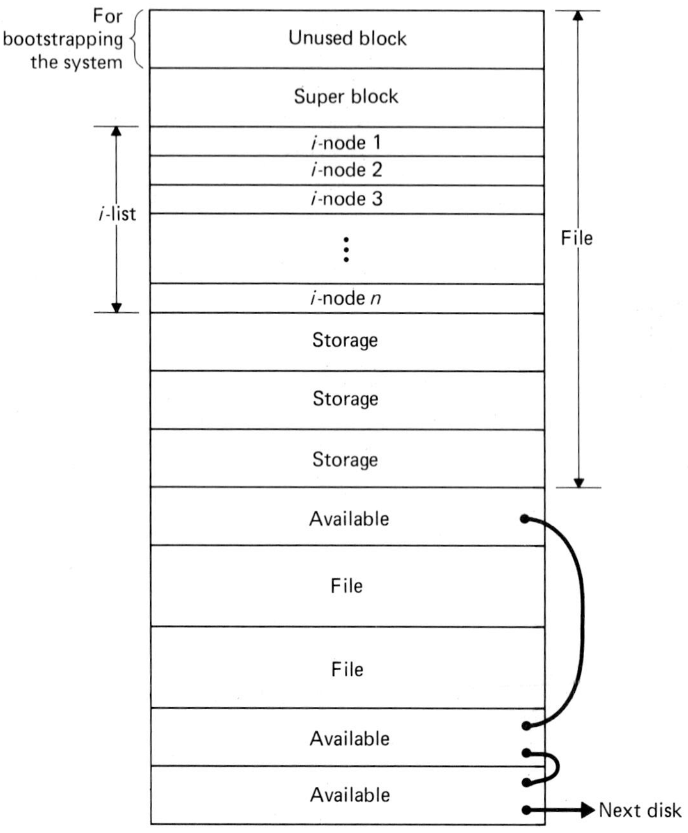

Fig. 18.4 Disk file organization.

- physical disk or tape addresses for the contents of the file
- file size
- time of creation
- time of last use
- time of last modification
- the number of links to the file
- indication of whether the file is a *directory*, an *ordinary file*, or a *special file*

Following the *i*-list are free storage blocks available for holding the contents of files. Remaining free space on the disk after the file is maintained as a linked list of available disk blocks.

Thus a UNIX file system is a data structure resident on disk and containing a super block that defines the file system, an array of *i*-nodes that defines all of the files in the file system, the actual files themselves, and a collection of free blocks. All allocation is performed in fixed size blocks.

Each file is uniquely identified by a *major device number*, a *minor device number*, and an *i-number* (the index of the file's *i*-node in the *i*-node array). When a device driver is called, the major device number is used to index an array containing the driver entry points. The minor device number is used by the device driver to select one of a group of identical physical devices.

Directory files list the names of files, and provide a mapping between these names and the files themselves. Directories are directed graphs arranged in a tree structure. Regular and device files may be linked at various places throughout the graph. Unprivileged programs may not write directories, but with appropriate permission they may read directories. Directories may not be linked.

There are many system directories maintained by UNIX systems for their own use. One of these is the *root directory*, the base of the entire directory structure, from which all other files may be located. Other UNIX system directories contain the programs and commands available for users and device files.

File names are constructed by specifying a sequence of directory names separated by slashes ("/") and leading toward a leaf of a particular tree. When a file name begins with a slash, the path originates at the root directory. File names without a leading slash imply the path begins at the current directory. File names that start with "../" imply that the path begins with the directory that is the parent of the current directory. The file name "stuff" indicates the entry "stuff" in the current directory. The file name "/user1/joe/stuff" searches the root for the user1 directory, then searches the user1 directory for the directory joe, and finally locates entry stuff within directory joe. Slash (/) by itself designates the root. This example shows the typical hierarchical structure in the file system, i.e., user1 may refer to a disk (mounted as user1), joe is a user's directory, and stuff belongs to joe.

A nondirectory file may appear in many different directories under perhaps different names. This is called *linking*. Directory entries for files are called *links*. In UNIX systems, all such links have equal status. Files do not exist in directories. Rather a file exists independently of directory entries and the links in the directories point to the actual physical files. A file "disappears" when the last link to it is deleted. A link may have protection bits different from those in the original file. This solves the problem of restricting access to certain people.

Each supported device is associated with one or more special files. Input/output to special files is done in the same manner as with ordinary disk files, but these requests cause activation of the associated devices. Each special file usually resides in directory /dev. Links may be made to special files exactly as with ordinary files.

The entire file system hierarchy need not reside on the same device as the root. The system request *mount* allows the incorporation of files on a removable volume into the file system hierarchy.

A user identification number and a set of ten protection bits is used to implement file protection. Nine of the bits implement read, write, and execute access for the owner of the file, other members of the owner's group, and for all other users.

18.8 SHELL

The *shell* is the UNIX system mechanism for communication between users and the system. It is a command interpreter that reads lines typed by the user and causes the execution of the requested system features. The shell is not permanently resident in main memory like the kernel—it can be swapped as needed. It is an application program, and custom shells are often written (e.g., a minishell for naive users).

The full command language interpreted by the shell is substantial and somewhat complex, but most of the commands are simple to use and relatively consistent. A command line consists of a *command name* (i.e., the name of any executable file), followed by a list of arguments separated by blanks. The shell breaks up the command line into its components. The file specified in the command is loaded, and the command arguments are made accessible to it. A fork is performed creating a child process containing the shell. The child executes the command while the parent process waits for the child to terminate. Upon termination of the child, the shell types its *prompt* to the keyboard to indicate that the user may type the next command.

The shell gives each program it executes three open files—one for input, one for output, and one for error output. These files are normally assigned to the terminal, but they may easily be redirected as in the following. In the given command line, if an argument is preceded by "<" then it names a file producing input for the command. A file prefixed by ">" is for receiving the standard output of commands. A prefix of "> >" means that the output is appended to the file rather than replacing it. The file names following these prefixes are interpreted by the shell and are not passed to the commands. The importance of this is that *input and output may be redirected to and from files without modifying the program.*

The shell command language includes control flow capabilities. Command language programs may be written using *if/then/else, case, while,* and *for* structures.

Pattern matching facilities are provided for constructing file names or groups of file names. The asterisk (*) indicates any run of characters, and the question mark (?) indicates any single character. Thus the command

```
ls f*
```

(ls means "list") is used to list all files whose names begin with the letter "f." The command

```
ls f?
```

is used to list all files with two character names beginning with "f." Other useful pattern matching facilities are also provided.

18.8.1 Pipes and Filters

One of the most important contributions of the UNIX system is the concept of *pipes. A pipe is an open file connecting two processes.* Information written into the pipe at one end may be read from the pipe at the other end (Fig. 18.5). Synchroni-

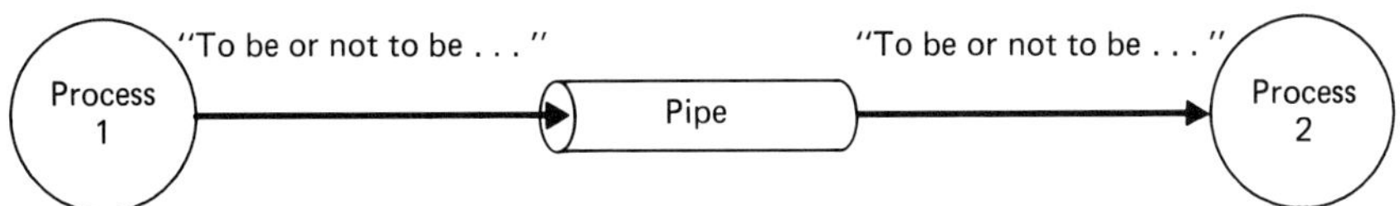

Fig. 18.5 A pipe. Process 1 writes to the pipe. Process 2 reads from the pipe.

zation, scheduling, and buffering are handled automatically by the system. Using the notion of pipes between pairs of processes, a user may create a *pipeline* by connecting several processes by pipes in a linear fashion. The user specifies a pipeline to the shell by a series of filenames separated by vertical bars. The output of the file of the file named at the left of a bar is the input to the file named at the right of the bar. The shell uses linear pipes. Processes may interconnect more generally.

A *filter* in a UNIX system is a program that processes a single input stream to produce a single output stream. UNIX systems provide a large number of filters. For example, the language processors supplied with UNIX systems do not produce listings. Instead, their output is fed into a filter that prints all output listings in a uniform format. Filters and pipes can be used to produce many interesting outputs. Let's consider some examples.

Suppose it is desired to determine how many users are currently on the system. This can be accomplished by feeding the output of the system's *who* command into the utility that determines the number of lines in its input. The command line

```
who ! wc -1
```

causes the output of the system command *who* that might appear as

```
zack     console   Aug 27 18:40
samg     tty00     Aug 27 02:14
bobp     tty01     Aug 26 23:14
suem     tty02     Aug 27 19:20
billy    tty05     Aug 27 17:19
```

to be sent to the program *wc* called "word count." The option −1 indicates that only the number of lines are to be printed. Thus this command prints the number of users on the system as follows.

```
>who ! wc -1
5
>
```

The user can create a file containing this command line and can call the file "users." By typing "users," the user may determine the number of users on the system.

One example frequently given for the use of pipes and filters is the creation of a spelling verifier program. Begin with a program that places every word in a file on a separate line. Connect the output of that program (via a pipe) to a program that sorts lines alphabetically. The output of this program is now a sorted list of all the words in the original file. This list is now fed to a program that removes adjacent duplicate lines. The output of this program contains one line for each different word in the original file. Finally, this is fed into a program that lists words in the list not contained in yet another file (a dictionary). Typing the command line

```
prep file ! sort ! uniq ! comm wdlist
```

in which the four programs, *prep, sort, uniq,* and *comm* perform the functions indicated in the preceding discussion, causes the creation of a list of words present in file but not in wdlist. The beauty of this is that by using pipes and filters we have created a simple spelling verifier program out of some existing utility programs without writing a new program.

Now by creating a file "spell" containing the command line

```
prep $* ! sort ! uniq ! comm /usr/dict/words
```

we have created a new command "spell." The notation $* is replaced by the file name given when the user types

```
spell samsfile
```

to locate spelling errors in samsfile.

18.8.2 Multitasking

The user may specify *multitasking* by following a command with an ampersand (&). In this case, the shell does not wait for the execution of the command to finish. It immediately prompts for a new command while the previous command continues execution in the background. The command specified may be a file containing other commands, so an interactive user can initiate substantial batch processing sequences to be run in the background. As a simple example, the command

```
(cc source; a.out)&
```

causes the two commands (a compile-and-go sequence) to be executed in the background. The semicolon (;) is a statement separator. It indicates that the separated commands are to be executed sequentially. The parentheses are used to group commands, in this case so that the & applies to the entire sequence. Figure 18.6 shows a typical process creation hierarchy with shells for interactive processes and batch processes. The subshell is being used here by a user temporarily leaving BASIC to execute a system command.

18.9 PERFORMANCE VS. USABILITY

At this point, the reader familiar with the problems faced by large-scale commercial data processing installations should be convinced that UNIX systems have little use in such environments. Its designers never intended it for that purpose, so it is diffi-

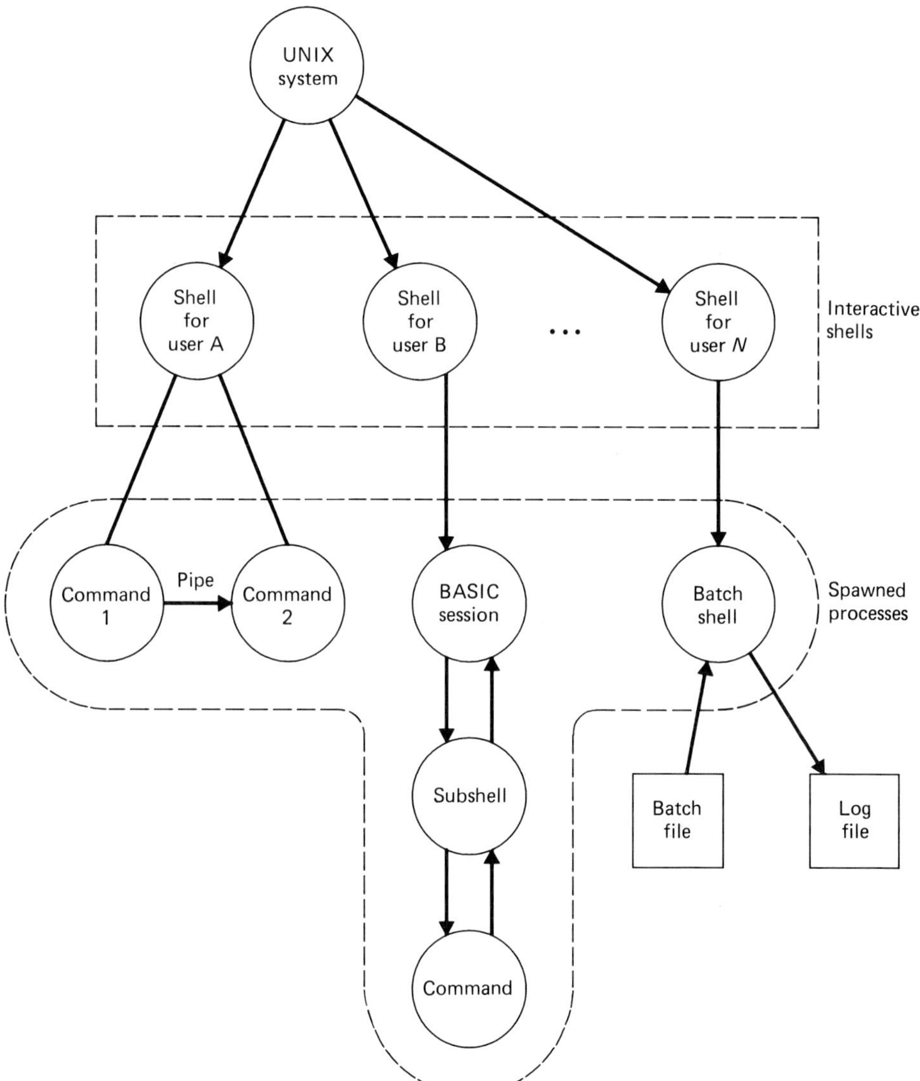

Fig. 18.6 Process hierarchy. (Reprinted with the permission of Microsoft Corporation.)

cult to criticize them for building a system inferior in certain ways to various mainframe operating systems. Hardware performance was simply not one of the design precepts in UNIX systems.

Associated with performance are issues of security, reliability, recoverability, and others also downplayed in UNIX systems. These issues, too, are critical in large-scale commercial systems. It is important to note here that UNIX systems are distributed to user installations with its source code, so customization is rampant. Many UNIX systems installations have systems that bear little resemblance to the supplied source code.

UNIX systems are successful, and in fact phenomenally so, because of their usefulness in program development environments. It meets the needs of programmers building software, and of administrators who must control software development efforts. It gives the interactive user a full range of easily accessible capabilities.

18.10 XENIX: A COMMERCIAL UNIX SYSTEM STANDARD

Microsoft, a software supplier to the microcomputer industry, developed XENIX, an operating system based on the UNIX systems. XENIX is designed to run on 16-bit microcomputers. It promises to be prime competition for the CP/M-based operating systems, now considered by many to be the de facto standard for microcomputers. We consider CP/M (for 8-bit micros) and MP/M (for 16-bit micros) in depth in Chapter 20.

XENIX provides the powerful multiuser timesharing capabilities of the UNIX system. In addition to its UNIX system base, XENIX provides the major high-level languages that have become standards in the microcomputer world (Fig. 18.7).

18.10.1 History of XENIX

As UNIX systems became more widely used during the 1970s, user feedback from hundreds of test sites motivated a series of improvements. The transportability of the system had become well-known. Its designers at Bell Laboratories had made the system so amenable to customization that no single standard for UNIX systems could be claimed. Many incompatible versions existed even within Western Electric.

Because of AT&T's status as a protected monopoly, the government would not allow it to enter the computer industry. There were legal issues preventing Western Electric from marketing UNIX system software, at least as a competitive commercial product. The commercial UNIX system licenses came packaged with some unattractive provisions. Commercial users had to accept UNIX system source code on an "as is" basis with no warranty, support, or maintenance of any kind supplied by Western Electric.

Recognizing both the value of UNIX systems and Western Electric's inability to support and market it commercially, Microsoft announced, in August 1980, that it would provide XENIX, a commercial version of a UNIX system, on 16-bit microprocessors. Since that time Microsoft has worked closely with Western Electric and various commercial users to develop an industry standard version of a UNIX system.

18.10.2 The XENIX System

Microsoft has produced XENIX systems for various 16-bit microprocessors. To improve the viability of a UNIX system as a commercial product, Microsoft included the following additional features in XENIX.

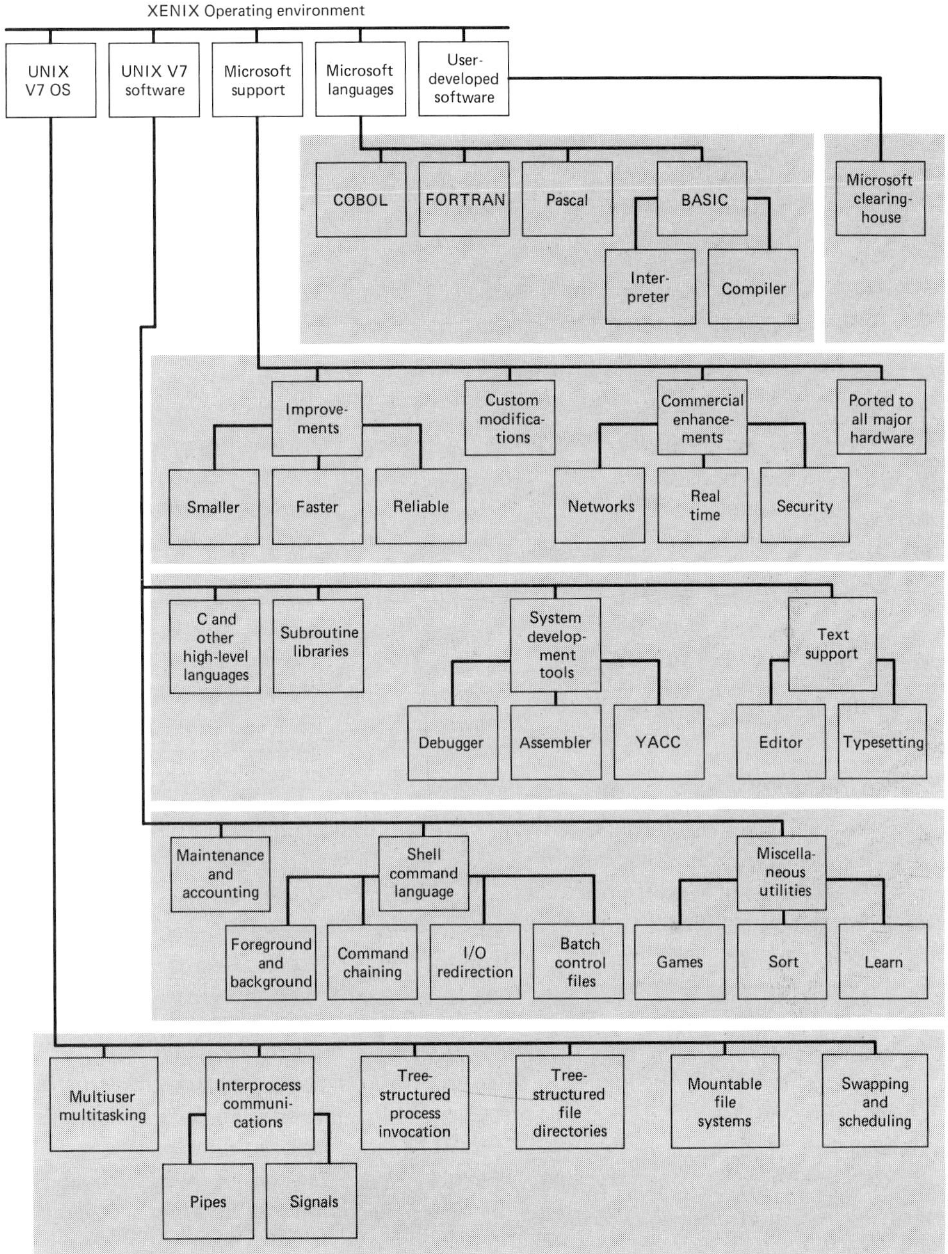

Fig. 18.7 Microsoft's XENIX operating system. The five layers of the XENIX software structure are shown. Each layer depends on the layers beneath it. The bottom two layers represent the latest version of a UNIX system. The remaining three layers are the refinements that combine to make the XENIX system. (Reprinted with the permission of Microsoft Corporation. XENIX is a trademark of Microsoft Corporation. UNIX is a trademark of Bell Laboratories.)

- hardware error recovery
- automatic file repair after crashes
- power-fail and parity error detection
- shared data segments
- improved interprocess communication, and
- the Microsoft versions of BASIC, COBOL, FORTRAN, and Pascal

XENIX will probably experience the same kind of success on 16-bit microcomputers that CP/M has had in the 8-bit market. Microsoft has established a central clearinghouse so that software running under XENIX may be economically distributed.

SUMMARY

A UNIX system is a small operating system developed at Bell Laboratories in the early 1970s. Today, it is in wide use in both academic and commercial environments.

UNIX programs are written in a high-level language, C. This makes the system highly portable. Users may route the output of one program to the input of another making it possible to implement large programs by the composition of existing pieces.

PWB/UNIX systems are specifically oriented to supporting program development. They contain the Source Code Control System for maintaining programs and their documentation on-line.

The coherence of UNIX systems is greatly attributable to the fact that the first version was built in a few years primarily by two people, and the people who built UNIX systems were the major users of the system.

Processes that have received a large amount of processor time receive low priorities; processes that have received only a small amount of processor time receive high priorities. This assures good interactive response times.

Both primary and secondary storage are allocated using a first-fit placement strategy. Processes requiring more storage are moved to a single block of storage large enough to hold their new size. The swapping process controls the swapping of all other processes to and from secondary storage.

The input/output system is especially compact containing only five major calls, namely open, close, read, write, and seek.

All input/output is stream-oriented rather than record-oriented, and all access is sequential. With the UNIX system input/output calls, however, users may simulate either fixed length record processing or variable length record processing. Direct access is simulated with the seek call and works on tape files as well as disk files (albeit more slowly).

UNIX systems use a hierarchical file system structure. Any file may be located by tracing a path from the root directory. Each supported device is associated with one or more special files. Input/output to special files is done in the same manner as with ordinary disk files, but these requests cause activation of the associated devices.

The shell is the UNIX system mechanism for communication between users and the system. It is a command interpreter. Custom shells are often created for the use of naive users.

A pipe is an open file connecting two processes. Information written into the pipe at one end may be read from the pipe at the other end. A filter is a program that processes a single input stream to produce a single output stream. Filters and pipes facilitate the composition of larger programs from existing programs. Multitasking may be specified by following a command with an ampersand (&). This makes it easy for interactive users to initiate substantial batch processing sequences to be run in the background.

XENIX is a version of a UNIX system produced by Microsoft for use on 16-bit microprocessors. It is a prime competitor to CP/M-based systems such as MP/M also designed for the 16-bit micros. Many features not included in the Bell Laboratories versions of UNIX systems have been included by Microsoft in XENIX in order to make XENIX a valid commercial product.

TERMINOLOGY

background
Bell Laboratories
block I/O system
C language
character I/O system
child process
close I/O call
data segment
device files
device-independent file system
/dev
direct access I/O
directory
event
event-wait
exec
exit primitive
file descriptor
file system path
filter
foreground
fork
i-list
i-node
i-number
image
interrupt primitive
link
linking
Microsoft
MINI-UNIX system
mount system request
open I/O call
ordinary files
parent process
pipe
pipeline
portability
process table
program text segment
Programmer's Workbench
pseudocomputer
PWB/UNIX system
read I/O call
reentrant procedure segment
root directory
seek I/O call
shell
signal
Source Code Control System (SCCS)

special files
stack segment
storage image
stream
stream I/O
super block
super user
swapping
system data segment
system directories
text table
trap
UNIX system
UNIX system RJE facility
UNIX/V7 system
unlink
wait
write I/O call
XENIX

EXERCISES

18.1 How is a UNIX system dramatically different from many of the other multimode systems of the late 1960s and early 1970s?

18.2 We have discussed the importance of software engineering. What features of UNIX systems are especially useful from a software engineering standpoint?

18.3 UNIX systems began as a home-grown system. Today it is marketed widely as a commercial product. What notable differences would you expect to find between an early system, and a version of UNIX systems used in industry today?

18.4 What aspects of the origin of UNIX systems contributed greatly to its unique design?

18.5 In a UNIX system, the same system calls are used to read (or write) files, devices, and interprocess message buffers. What are the advantages of this?

18.6 UNIX systems provide an environment in which large tasks may be accomplished by combining existing small programs rather than developing new programs. Why is this important?

18.7 Most of the UNIX system kernel is written in C, but a portion of the kernel is written in assembly language. Why? What portions of the kernel would you expect to be written in assembly language?

18.8 Suppose a process requests more storage. Describe precisely how UNIX systems grant the request. Consider each of the following cases.

a) Sufficient additional storage is available immediately following the process's current storage area.
b) A large block of storage is available elsewhere in primary storage.
c) Sufficient additional primary storage is not currently available.

18.9 What criteria does the swapping process use to determine which process to swap in? to swap out?

18.10 List the calls in the UNIX system I/O system and briefly describe the function of each.

18.11 All input/output in a UNIX system is stream-oriented rather than record-oriented as it is in most other systems. Discuss the advantages and disadvantages of this approach

18.12 Describe how fixed length record I/O and variable length record I/O are implemented in UNIX systems.

18.13 Suppose a particular operating system supports record I/O but not stream I/O. Is it possible to simulate stream I/O on this system? If yes, then state how. If no, then state why not.

18.14 Describe the directory structure of the UNIX file system.

18.15 What are the distinguishing characteristics of the UNIX system shell?

18.16 What are pipes and filters? What is a pipeline?

18.17 List several filters that might be useful in text processing applications. Give an example of how a pipeline may be created by connecting some of these filters to accomplish a complex text processing task.

18.18 Summarize the features of UNIX systems that have made them such phenomenally successful operating systems.

18.19 A UNIX system does not check for processes attempting to "hog" resources. But many installations have added features for doing so. Describe the features you would add to a UNIX system for this purpose.

18.20 What features led Microsoft to develop XENIX? What features have been included in XENIX that are not included in basic UNIX systems?

LITERATURE

(Ba80) Barak, A. B., and A. Shapir, "UNIX with Satellite Processors," *Software—Practice and Experience,* Vol. 10, pp. 383–392.

(Bo78) Bourne, S. R., "The UNIX Shell," *Bell System Technical Journal,* Vol. 57, No. 6, Part 2, July–August 1978, pp. 1971–1990.

(Do78) Dolotta, T. A.; R. C. Haight; and J. R. Mashey, "The Programmer's Workbench," *Bell System Technical Journal,* Vol. 57, No. 6, Part 2, July–August 1978, pp. 2177–2200.

(Gr81) Greenberg, R. B., "The UNIX Operating System and the XENIX Standard Operating Environment," *Byte Magazine,* June 1981, pp. 248–264.

(Ha80) Harland, D. M., "High-Speed Data Acquisition: Running a Realtime Process and a Time-Shared System (UNIX) Concurrently," *Software—Practice and Experience,* Vol. 10, pp. 273–281.

(Jo78) Johnson, S. C., and D. M. Ritchie, "Portability of C Programs and the UNIX System," *Bell System Technical Journal,* Vol. 57, No. 6, Part 2, July–August 1978, pp. 2021–2048.

(Ke76) Kernighan, B. W., and P. J. Plauger, *Software Tools,* Reading, Mass.: Addison-Wesley, 1976.

(Ke78) Kernighan, B. W., and D. M. Ritchie, The C Programming Language, Englewood Cliffs, N.J.: Prentice-Hall, 1978.

(Ke79) Kernighan, B. W., and J. Mashey, "The UNIX Programming Environment," *Software—Practice and Experience,* Vol. 9, pp. 1–15, January 1979, New York: Wiley.

(Lu78) Luderer, G. W. R.; J. F. Maranzano; and B. A. Tague, "The UNIX Operating System as a Base for Application," *Bell System Technical Journal,* Vol. 57, No. 6, Part 2, July–August 1978, pp. 2201–2208.

(Ly78) Lycklama, H., and D. L. Bayer, "The MERT Operating System," *Bell System Technical Journal,* Vol. 57, No. 6, Part 2, July–August 1978, pp. 2049–2086.

(Ly78a) Lycklama, H., "UNIX on a Microprocessor," *Bell System Technical Journal,* Vol. 57, No. 6, Part 2, July–August 1978, pp. 2087–2102.

(Ly78b) Lycklama, H., and C. Christensen, "A Minicomputer Satellite Processor System," *Bell System Technical Journal,* Vol. 57, No. 6, Part 2, pp. 2103–2114.

(Mc78) McIlroy, M.; E. Pinson; and B. Tague, "UNIX Time-Sharing System," *Bell System Technical Journal,* Vol. 57, No. 6, Part 2, July–August 1978, pp. 1899–1904.

(Ma81) Marsh, B.; G. Munsey; K. Myers; and C. Forney, "The UNIX Operating System." In J. Zarrella (ed.), *Microprocessor Operating Systems,* Suisun City, Calif.: Microcomputer Applications, 1981, pp. 8.1–8.15.

(No81) Norman, D. A., "The Trouble with UNIX," *Datamation,* November 1981, pp. 139–150.

(Pl81) Plauger, P. J., and M. S. Krieger, "UNIX-Like Software Runs on Mini- and Microcomputers," *Electronics,* New York: McGraw-Hill, March 24, 1981.

(Ri78) Ritchie, D. M., and K. Thompson, "The UNIX Time-Sharing System," *Bell System Technical Journal,* Vol. 57, No. 6, Part 2, July–August 1978, pp. 1905–1930.

(Ri78a) Richie, D. M., "A Retrospective," *Bell System Technical Journal,* Vol. 57, No. 6, Part 2, July–August 1978, pp. 1947–1970.

(Ri78b) Ritchie, D. M., "The C Programming Language," *Bell System Technical Journal,* Vol. 57, No. 6, Part 2, July–August 1978, 1991–2020.

(St76) Stonebreaker, M., et al., "The Design and Implementation of INGRES," *ACM Trans. on Database Systems,* Vol. 1, 1976, pp. 189–222.

(Th78) Thomspon, K., "UNIX Implementation," *Bell System Technical Journal,* Vol. 57, No. 6, Part 2, July–August 1978, pp. 1931–1946.

19 Case Study: VAX*

It is not best to swap horses while crossing the river.

Abraham Lincoln

Mirrors should reflect a little before throwing back images.

Jean Cocteau

*Major portions of the VAX case study are based upon *Computer Programming and Architecture: The VAX-11* by H.M. Levy and R.H. Eckhouse, Jr., Digital Press, 1980, and *VAX-11 Software Handbook,* Digital Equipment Corporation, 1981; the author is grateful for permission granted to use these materials.
The following are trademarks of Digital Equipment Corporation: VAX, VMS, PDP, DEC, RSX, RMS, UNIBUS, LSI-11 MASSBUS.

Outline

19.1 INTRODUCTION

VAX is a family of 32-bit multiprogramming virtual storage computer systems offered by Digital Equipment Corporation (DEC). The VAX systems are the extension of DEC's popular PDP-11 line of 16-bit minicomputers into the realm of larger scale virtual storage systems.

As hardware costs continue to decline, and as trends toward decentralized processing are reinforced, the market for large system functionality at minicomputer costs continues to grow. This has changed the nature of minicomputers from simple, scaled-down systems to complex systems supporting multimode operation. Today's minicomputer operating systems provide functionality that, just a few years ago, was available only on mainframes. Many minicomputer operating systems simultaneously support batch, real-time, interactive, and program development tasks, and provide a wide variety of high-level languages and utility programs.

This increased functionality for minicomputers has created the need for more powerful virtual storage capabilities in these machines. DEC developed the VAX-11 architecture in response to these needs. VAX represents a *Virtual Address Extension* of the PDP-11 family.

The primary goal of the VAX-11 architecture is to provide a significant increase in the size of the virtual address space available in the PDP-11 (whose larger models were limited to 128K virtual spaces). The possibility of increasing the PDP-11's word size (while essentially preserving the remainder of its architecture) was considered. But because the size of the virtual address is so deeply ingrained in a computer's machine language, it is difficult to extend the size of virtual addresses while still allowing existing programs to take advantage of the extension without substantial program modifications. So the VAX designers chose the route of developing a new architecture.

19.2 VAX DESIGN GOALS

Several major goals influenced the design of the VAX family.

- The architecture had to have a long lifetime because of the huge investments that must be made by the vendor and by users in designing the hardware and software for a new architecture.
- The architecture had to provide very large virtual address spaces.
- The architecture had to provide an environment for the efficient compilation and execution of high-level languages.
- The architecture had to be similar to the PDP-11 to make it convenient for DEC's customer base to convert to the VAX.
- The architecture had to support a complete family of machines with a wide variety of performance, but with compatible functions.

- To provide for more efficient execution of its operating system, the architecture had to include instructions to facilitate the execution of frequently used operating systems functions. (The designers included instructions providing hardware support of queues, variable length bit fields, and saving and restoring program contexts.)

19.3 PDP-11 COMPATIBILITY

The goal of achieving compatibility between VAX and the PDP-11 was achieved in several ways. Both machines use the same data formats and media formats for I/O. Thus data files produced on one machine are readable on the other.

The syntax and mnemonics of the assembly languages on both machines are basically the same. Thus compilers that generate PDP-11 assembly code can be adapted easily to generate VAX-11 code. VAX-11 high-level languages have been designed to be upward compatible with the corresponding PDP-11 versions.

The VAX/VMS (Virtual Memory System) operating system is quite similar in structure to PDP-11 RSX. Many of the key functional areas of both operating systems, such as the file system and record management facilities are identical.

The VAX-11 has a *PDP-11 hardware compatibility mode* that can run many PDP-11 user mode programs directly. A subroutine package called the Applications Migration Executive aids users in converting to VAX by providing emulation of RSX services.

19.4 INSTRUCTIONS AND STORAGE

VAX contains a unique and powerful instruction set. Individual instructions may be as long as 37 bytes and may specify as many as six operands. Six different formats are supported for arithmetic. Instructions are provided for efficient manipulation of bit stings as long as 32 bits and character strings as long as 64K bytes.

Several instructions provide functionality rarely available on competitive machines.

- EMOD performs extra precise range reduction on floating point numbers. It is useful in normalizing arguments of trigonometric functions.
- POLY calculates the value of a polynomial of the form

$$a_n x^n + a_{n-1} x^{n-1} + \ldots + a_1 x + a_0$$

greatly speeding the computation of mathematical functions.

- INDEX examines the value of an index and calculates the location of the corresponding element of an array.
- CASE directly implements the FORTRAN computed GOTO statement with automatic range checking.
- CRC performs cyclic redundancy checks directly (useful in data communications systems for detecting errors in data streams).

Virtual storage management has been incorporated into both the hardware and VAX/VMS. Multiple user programs are supported simultaneously, each with its own virtual address space. Half of the virtual address space is automatically shared by all programs.

Four hierarchical protection levels have been provided. These are (Fig. 19.1) kernel, executive, supervisor, and user. Protection and sharing are handled at the page level. Pages are 512 bytes each, much smaller than on most other paging systems. Page tables aid in the mapping of virtual addresses to physical addresses, and specify the access allowed (none, read-only, read/write) for each of the four protection modes.

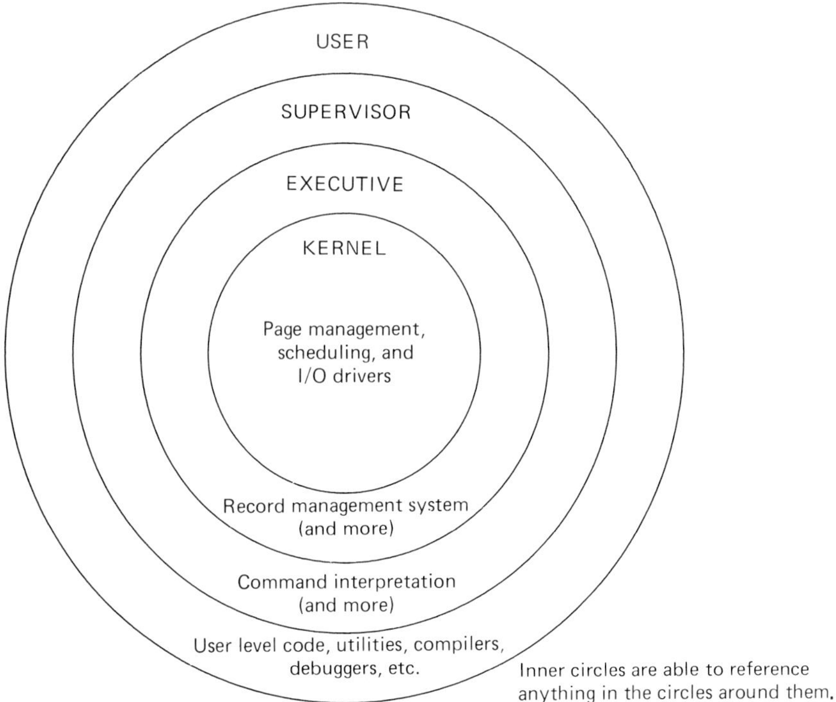

Fig. 19.1 VAX privilege modes.

19.5 THE VAX-11/780

The VAX-11/780 was the first member of the VAX family announced. It consists of a central processing unit, main memory subsystem, I/O subsystem, and a console subsystem (Fig. 19.2). The processor, storage subsystem, and I/O subsystem are interconnected via the *Synchronous Backplane Interconnect (SBI)*, a high-speed bus that is the system's primary path for control and data. The *Unibus* provides a 1.5

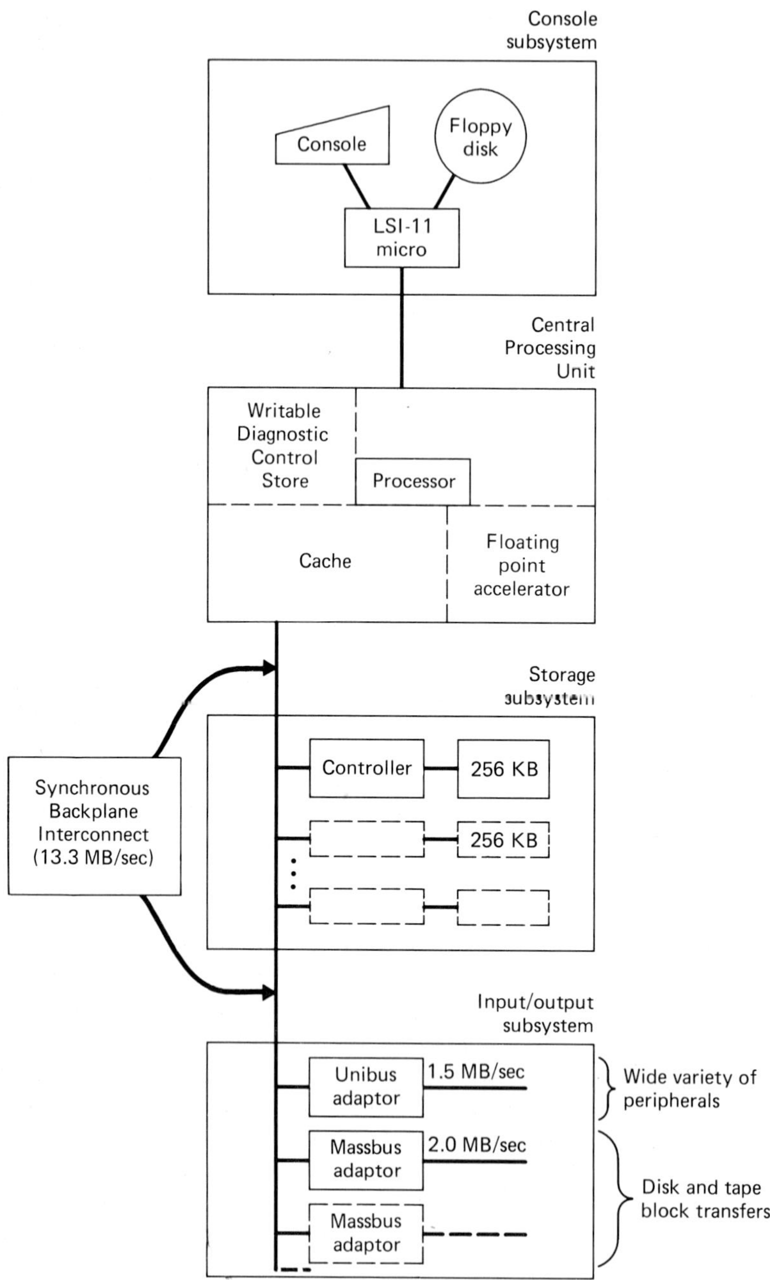

Fig. 19.2 VAX-11/780.

MB/sec path for handling a wide variety of peripherals. As many as four *Massbus* adaptors can be used to provide 2 MB/sec paths for disk and tape block transfers.

The instruction set is implemented in microcode. Cache buffers are used to improve performance. An 8K cache provides ultrahigh-speed access to frequently used data, and considerably reduces traffic on the SBI. A 128-entry cache is used to facilitate high-speed dynamic address translation. An instruction buffer is used so that the processor may fetch and decode the next instruction while the current instruction is executing. A buffer at the SBI–CPU interface allows the CPU to direct storage writes to the buffer, initiate storage transfer, and then continue execution without having to wait for the completion of the write.

Substantial error detection and correction capabilities are provided to improve reliability and maintainability. The operating system can even map around defective storage locations to continue operation.

The intelligent console contains an LSI-11 microcomputer with RAM, ROM, and a floppy disk. The floppy disk is used both for system installation, and for making software updates.

19.6 STORAGE MANAGEMENT

Storage management in VMS consists of two parts, the *pager* and the *swapper*. The pager is responsible for reading in a referenced page when a page fault occurs, and for writing out a modified resident page when it is necessary to make room for an incoming page. The pager executes in the context of the process that called it, and is a subroutine shared by all processes in the system.

The swapper removes or loads entire processes from or into primary storage. It works closely with the scheduler in determining which processes to swap between disk and storage and vice versa.

19.6.1 Paging

Each process is given a limit, called the *resident set limit*, for the number of pages in storage that it may occupy. Those pages a process has in storage at once constitute the process's *resident set* (also called the working set in VMS documentation). The resident set list points to these pages.

When a page fault occurs, the pager gains control. From the virtual address, the pager locates the page table entry for the faulted page. This entry contains information that helps the pager locate the page on disk. The pager locates an empty page of storage and initiates the reading of the page from the disk. The page table entry is modified to indicate the location of the page in storage. Upon completion of the page read, the pager returns control to the user program at the instruction that generated the fault.

As the process continues its execution, it generates page faults each time it references a page not in its resident set. If the process has not as yet reached its resident set limit when a page fault occurs, then the new page is read into an available page in storage. If the resident set limit has been reached, then the process must yield one page from its resident set to make room for the incoming page.

It is interesting that VAX does not use one of the more sophisticated page replacement strategies we have discussed. Rather, pages are selected for replacement in first-in-first-out fashion. But, as will soon become clear, the cost of throwing out a page about to be referenced (certainly a real possibility with FIFO) is kept low by other mechanisms provided by VMS.

The system maintains two lists of physical pages, the *free page list* and the *modified page list.* When a process needs a new physical page for an incoming page, it takes the page at the head of the free page list. The system attempts to keep some pages free at all times, but occasionally all physical pages do become occupied.

When a process must yield a page because it has exceeded its resident set limit, that page is placed at the tail of either the free page list or the modified page list, depending on whether the page is unmodified or modified. Modified pages are not written to disk until the modified list reaches a certain size. Unmodified pages on the free page list remain there until the free pages need to be assigned. A page on either the free page list or modified page list may be reclaimed by a process referencing that page. *Page reclamation* causes a referenced page to be returned to the resident set at relatively little cost, and it also helps to reduce the amount of paging I/O. Actually, such reclamation is somewhat unfair to processes with stable resident sets. In effect, processes that are faulting constantly tend to extend their resident sets into the free page and modified page lists.

Pages are written to disk in *clusters* to minimize the amount of paging I/O. Of course, page reclamation removes many pages from the modified page list reducing even further the paging I/O.

With several pages in the modified page list at once, the system can attempt to write contiguous pages from the same processes to contiguous locations on disk. This allows future reads to bring in clusters of adjacent pages if desired.

Processes first beginning their execution tend to experience a rapid succession of page faults as they accumulate their working sets. VMS attempts to minimize this paging activity by doing clustered reads of many pages for these new processes.

VMS dynamically adjusts a process's resident set size based upon the fault rate the process is experiencing. It increases the resident set size for processes with high fault rates, and decreases the resident set size for processes with low fault rates. This strategy tends to equalize the fault rate across all processes.

19.6.2 Swapping

In addition to paging individual pages, VMS moves the complete resident sets of processes from the *balance set* (i.e., the set of processes that resides in primary storage) to disk and vice versa. Such movement of complete resident sets is called swapping, and is performed by a process called the swapper.

The swapper swaps entire resident sets from the balance set in primary storage to disk to make room for swapping in the resident sets of other processes. VMS differs from many virtual storage systems in this regard. Many other systems require nonresident processes to demand page themselves back into primary storage one page at a time. VMS instead loads a process's entire resident set that was in place at the time the process was last swapped out. This greatly reduces paging disk I/O because resident sets are paged in clusters to and from the disk.

VMS guarantees that a process just swapped into primary storage will receive at least one quantum before being swapped out. Determining the next process to swap in is straightforward—the swapper merely chooses the highest priority nonresident executable process. At this point, the swapper must find a sufficient number of free pages to hold the incoming resident set. Free pages are located in several ways.

- They may be taken from the free storage list.
- The modified page list may be written out to the disk to create more free pages.
- A process of lower or equal priority may be swapped out.

When a large resident set is to be swapped in, it is often necessary to swap out several processes to make room.

19.7 PROCESS SCHEDULING

VAX/VMS uses a priority scheme to schedule executable processes in the balance set. Normal processes are referred to as either *timeshared* or *background* processes; real-time processes are sometimes called *time-critical.*

VAX/VMS uses 32 *priority levels* for scheduling (Fig. 19.3). Priorities 0–15 are allocated to normal processes; priorities 16–31 are reserved for real-time processes.

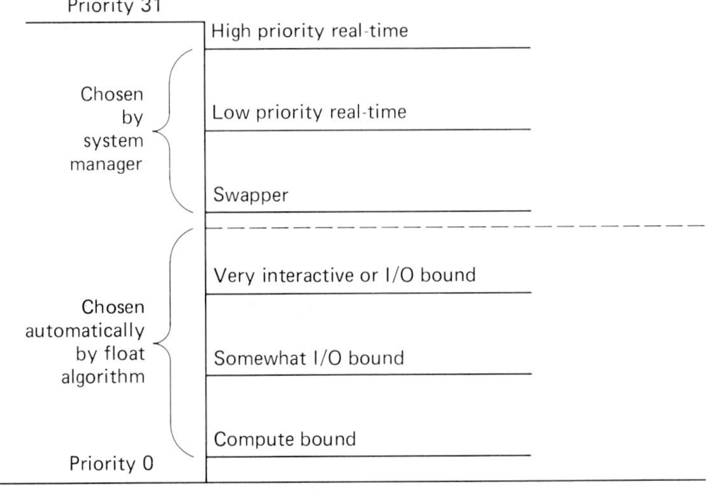

Fig. 19.3 Process priorities.

Higher numbers indicate higher priorities. Real-time processes are scheduled strictly according to priorities—a higher-priority process ready to execute preempts an executing lower-priority process. Priorities of normal processes are varied dynamically to achieve maximal overlap of CPU usage and I/O processing. Each system event has an associated priority increment. When the event occurs, if it causes the process to become executable, the scheduler sets the process's priority equal to the process's base priority plus the increment associated with the event. Each time a normal process is scheduled, its priority decreases but never below its base priority (Fig. 19.4).

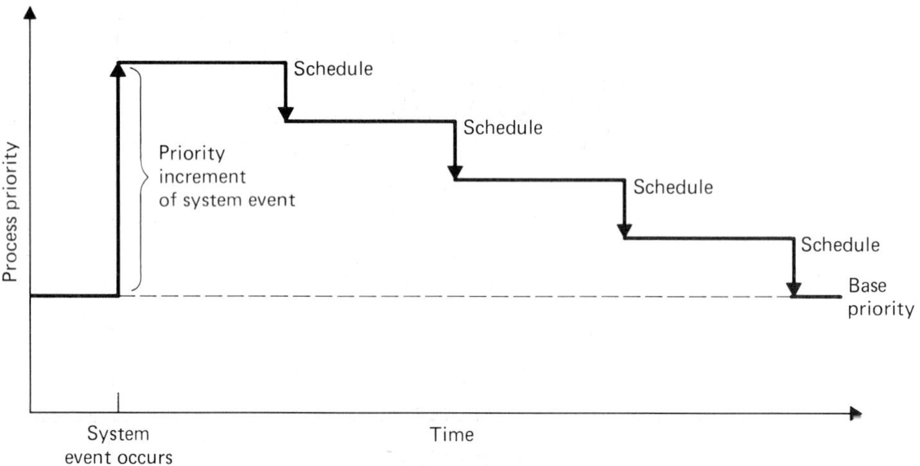

Fig. 19.4 Dynamic priority adjustment for normal processes.

The working set swapper is a system process that moves entire working sets back and forth between primary and secondary storage. Swapping a process from primary storage to secondary storage is called *outswapping*; swapping a process from secondary storage to primary storage is called *inswapping*.

Swapping is necessary in order to

- replace lower-priority executable processes with higher-priority executable processes
- replace nonexecutable processes resident in primary storage with executable processes in secondary storage
- supply the scheduler with executable processes in configurations with insufficient primary storage to contain all active processes' working sets

19.7.1 Scheduling

VAX assures fast response to real-time processes granting them higher priority than the priority granted to normal processes. The next process chosen for execution is always the one with the highest priority in the executable resident state queue.

System events cause the status of a process to change. They can occur synchronously with the process (such as when the process issues a wait) or they can occur asynchronously (such as an I/O completion).

A process can be, at any moment, in any of several mutually exclusive states. State transitions occur as a result of system events. The state of a process is indicated in its software Process Control Block (PCB). The system maintains a queue of processes for each state. Wait queue headers contain a count of processes associated with each queue.

19.7.2 Executable Process State Queues

Figure 19.5 shows a typical queue structure that might exist for executable processes in the balance set. The summary longword contains one bit for each queue. If the bit is zero, then there are no processes in the queue; if the bit is one, then processes are waiting.

Processes are selected from this queue in priority order with the higher-priority processes selected first. Processes of the same priority are selected from that priority subqueue on a first-in-first-out basis.

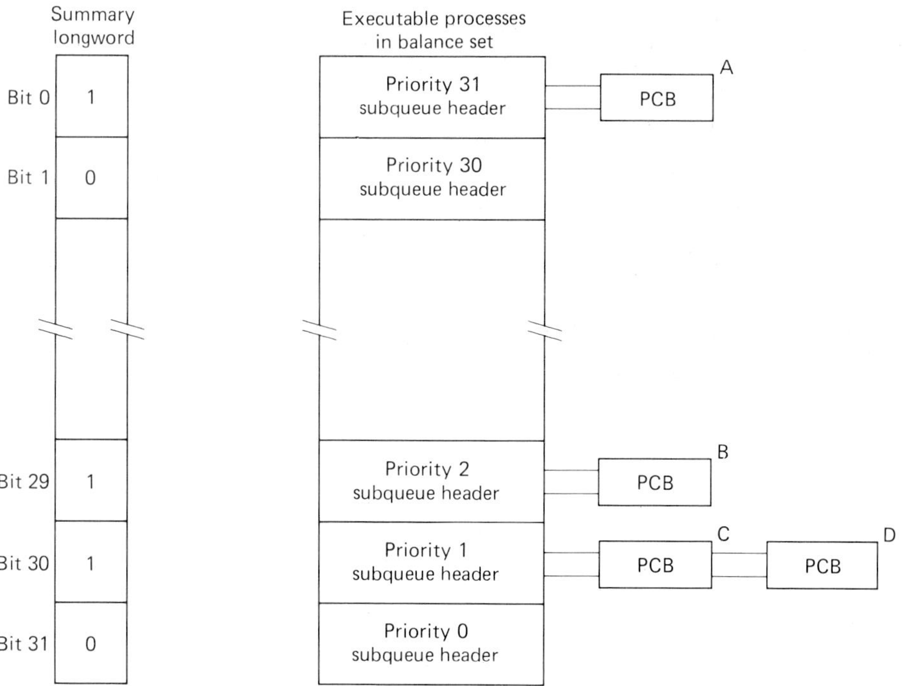

Fig. 19.5 Executable process state queue.

19.7.3 Process State Transitions

Process state transitions occur because of system events reported to the scheduler. These are summarized in Fig. 19.6. A currently executing process that consumes its processor quantum will be rescheduled to the executable state queue for resident processes. Various operations causing a currently executing process to wait for the completion of some event cause that process to enter one of several wait states. A newly created process enters the nonresident executable state.

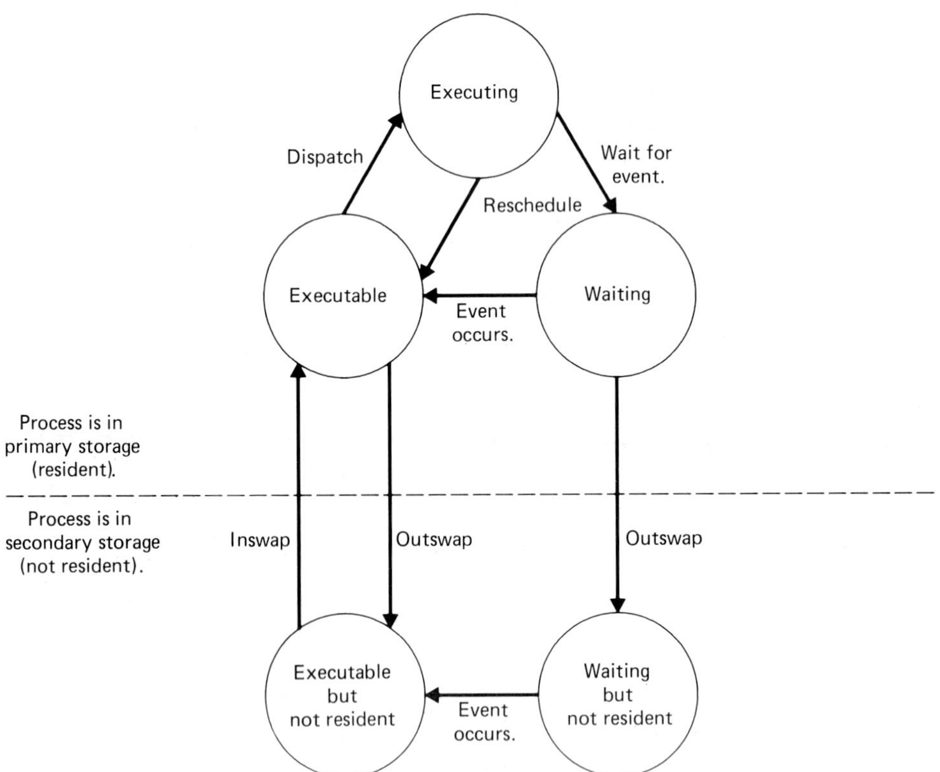

Fig. 19.6 Process state transitions.

19.7.4 Dispatching

Dispatching an executable process is a straightforward operation with minimal decision making. The dispatcher merely chooses the process at the head of the highest priority occupied subqueue of executable processes in the balance set. Scheduling (vs. dispatching) decisions are made as a result of system events that make processes executable.

19.7.5 Quantum Control

Each process is assigned an execution time quantum. The quantum

- provides a minimum amount of time during which work may be performed by the process before it is swapped out of the balance set
- forces compute-bound processes to receive a reasonable share of CPU time

Real-time processes are not subject to quantum expirations. It is important to mention here that the quantum in VAX systems defines primary storage occupancy time rather than processor execution time.

Processes may be preempted many times before receiving their full quanta. But a process will remain in the balance set until its first quantum expires, or until service is required by a nonresident process of higher priority, or until the process enters a wait state.

19.8 VAX/VMS INPUT/OUTPUT

The VMS input/output system is organized into several layers as illustrated in Fig. 19.7. From the highest to the lowest levels, input/output operations proceed from the most logical to the most physical. At the highest levels, VMS is concerned with files, records, and fields. At the lowest levels, it is concerned with the physical operation and organization of the various input/output devices.

VMS I/O is normally asynchronous—once a process issues an input/output request, the process may continue executing while the I/O request is being serviced. Processes may explicitly check for I/O completions, or they may receive notification from the system. Processes desiring to wait for an I/O completion call an operating system routine asking to be suspended. It is important to note that in VMS such suspension does not occur automatically as a result of the issuance of an I/O request.

Data structures are used to describe the state of the I/O system at any moment. Special control blocks are used to describe every

- bus adaptor
- controller
- device unit
- outstanding I/O request

The various control blocks are linked together to form a data structure representing the topology of the I/O system hardware. For example, Fig. 19.8(a) shows a VAX hardware configuration. The data structure in Fig. 19.8(b) represents the state of this hardware and pending I/O requests. The arrows indicate pointers between

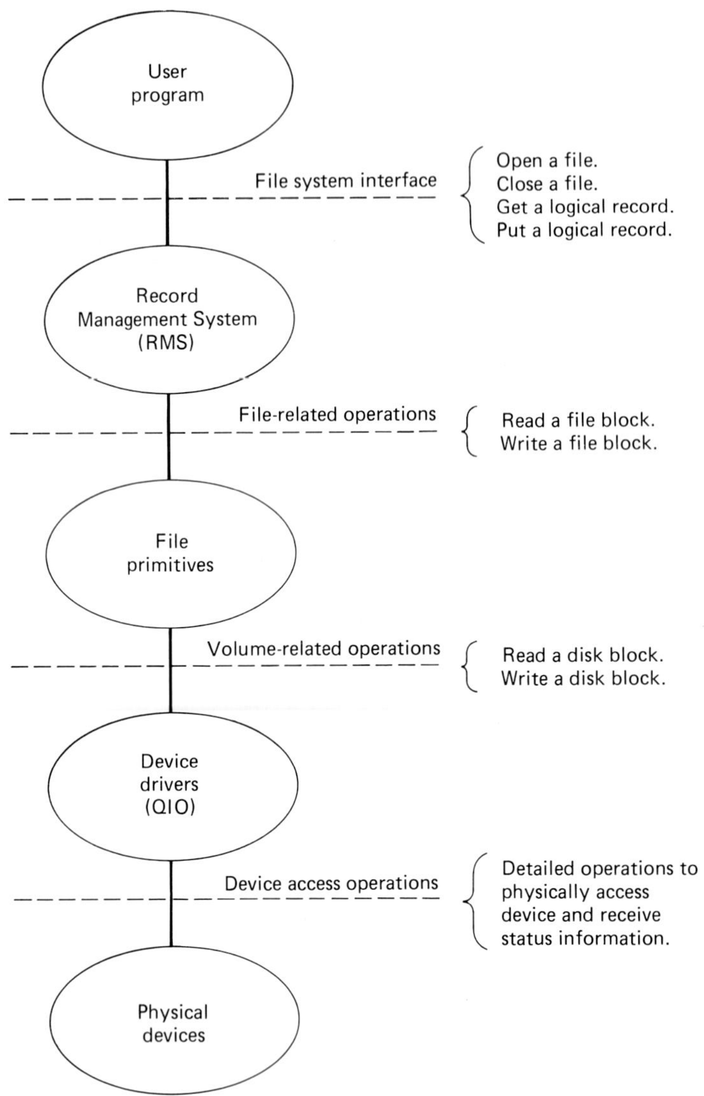

Fig. 19.7 Layered input/output system.

the various control blocks. Six different types of control blocks are illustrated. Briefly, their functions are as follows.

- Device Data Block (DDB)—Contains information common to the various devices of a given type which are all connected to a single controller (e.g., the device name, such as TTA for terminals attached to controller A).

- Unit Control Block (UCB)—Contains the characteristics and state for a single device, and the context of the device's driver process.
- I/O Request Packet (IRP)—Contains all of the information describing a particular I/O request (e.g., the identifier of the process requesting the I/O, the operation to be performed, and the address and length of the user's storage buffer).
- Channel Request Block (CRB)—Contains information describing the state of a controller. It contains the identifier of the device currently transferring data, and the identifiers of those devices waiting for the controller to become available.
- Interrupt Dispatch Block (IDB)—An extension to the Channel Request Block, the IDB indicates what a controller is currently doing, and it is used to determine which device issued a particular interrupt.
- Adaptor Control Block—Contains information about the characteristics and state of a Massbus adaptor or Unibus adaptor.

The contents of these various control blocks indicate the status of all of the hardware in the I/O system at any moment in time.

19.8.1 VMS I/O System Components

I/O in VMS involves three components, namely

- Queue I/O system service (QIO)
- device drivers
- I/O postprocessing routines

QIO is a procedure called by the user program to request any I/O operation. QIO validates the arguments supplied by the user, and builds an I/O Request Packet (IRP) describing the I/O operation to be performed. The IRP contains the data needed by the device driver to perform the actual physical I/O. QIO verifies whether or not the calling process is allowed to issue requests to perform the indicated operation on the device.

The Unit Control Block points to a list of outstanding I/O requests. QIO inserts new IRPs into the appropriate queues for the proper units, and then returns to its caller. It is up to the calling process to continue or to request suspension until the I/O operation is finished.

A device driver process controls the operation of a device. Device drivers execute at high priority in order to ensure high utilization. The Unit Control Block defines a device driver process in the same way that any process is defined by a Process Control Block. Each device has an associated Unit Control Block that indicates the status of the device as well as the status of the device driver process.

I/O postprocessing routines complete I/O operations. They return the final status and data to the user process's storage.

19.8.2 I/O Control Flow

In this section, the flow of a single I/O request through VMS is traced in detail. Every I/O request is initiated by a process calling QIO. QIO validates the request, builds an I/O Request Packet, queues the packet onto the appropriate device's Unit Control Block, and then returns control to the user. The IRP defines the I/O request to the system. In particular, it contains all information needed to allow the request to be serviced asynchronously with the requesting process, and to complete the I/O later in the context of the requesting process.

The precise sequence of events from this point is shown in Fig. 19.9. The user calls the QIO service routine that operates in the user's own process, but in kernel mode. QIO locates the Unit Control Block for the device, and checks any device-independent parameters in the call. It calls various driver subroutines to validate any device-dependent parameters. Then QIO builds the I/O Request Packet, and queues it to the Unit Control Block's request queue, where it remains until the driver process is ready to handle the request.

The driver process eventually dequeues the request and starts the indicated I/O operation on the device. The driver then voluntarily suspends itself by placing its UCB in a wait queue, thus allowing other processing to proceed while the device performs the I/O operation. When the device completes the I/O, it generates an interrupt to the operating system that then resumes the driver process. The driver copies status information describing the outcome of the I/O operation from the device and controller registers, and places this information into the IRP. The IRP is then placed on a queue to wait for the I/O postprocessing routines.

I/O postprocessing checks the IRP to determine how to complete the I/O. It copies any status information from the IRP into the user's memory, and then notifies the process that the I/O operation has completed.

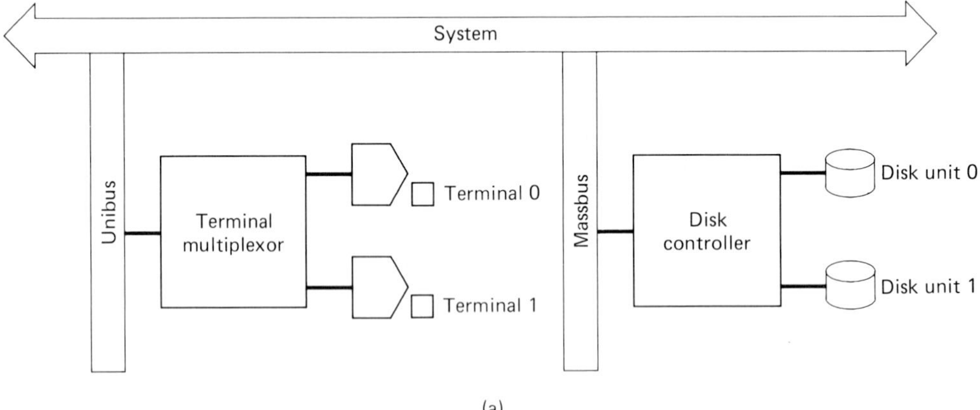

Fig. 19.8 (a) A sample VAX hardware configuration and (b) the corresponding VMS data structures.

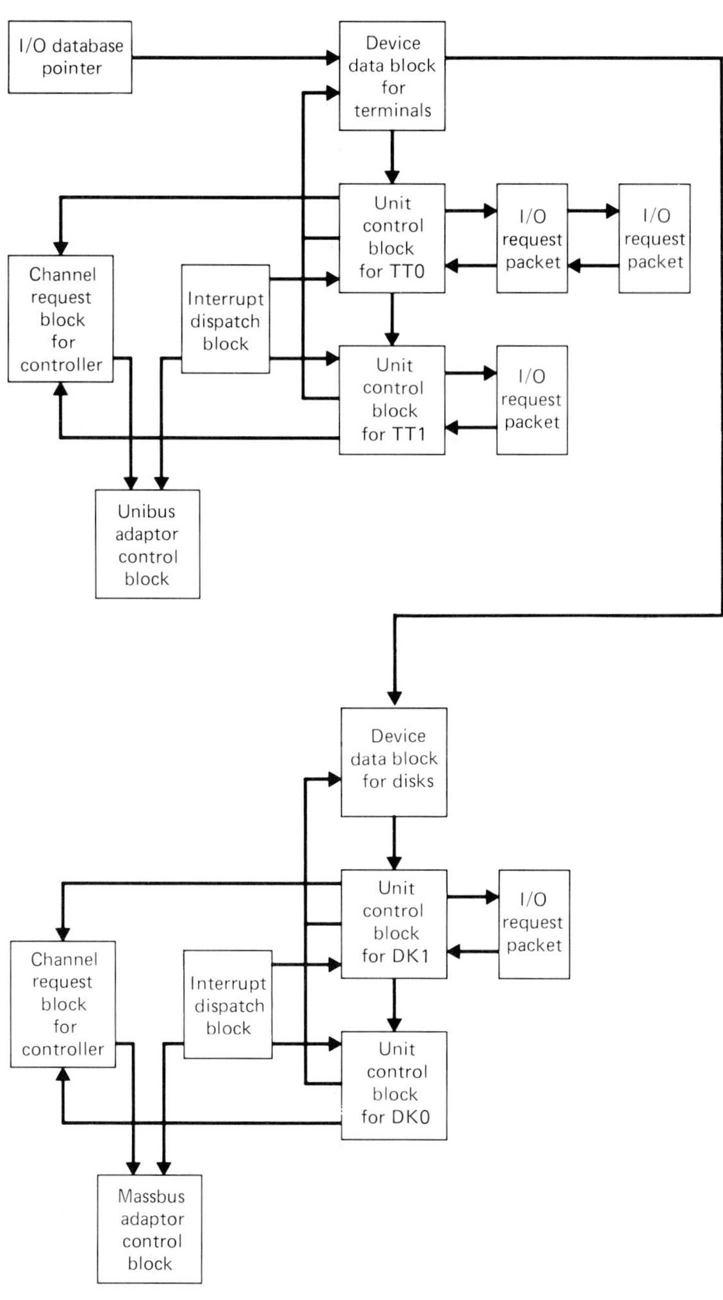
I/O database pointer
Device data block for terminals
Unit control block for TT0
I/O request packet
I/O request packet
Channel request block for controller
Interrupt dispatch block
Unit control block for TT1
I/O request packet
Unibus adaptor control block
Device data block for disks
Unit control block for DK1
I/O request packet
Channel request block for controller
Interrupt dispatch block
Unit control block for DK0
Massbus adaptor control block

(b)

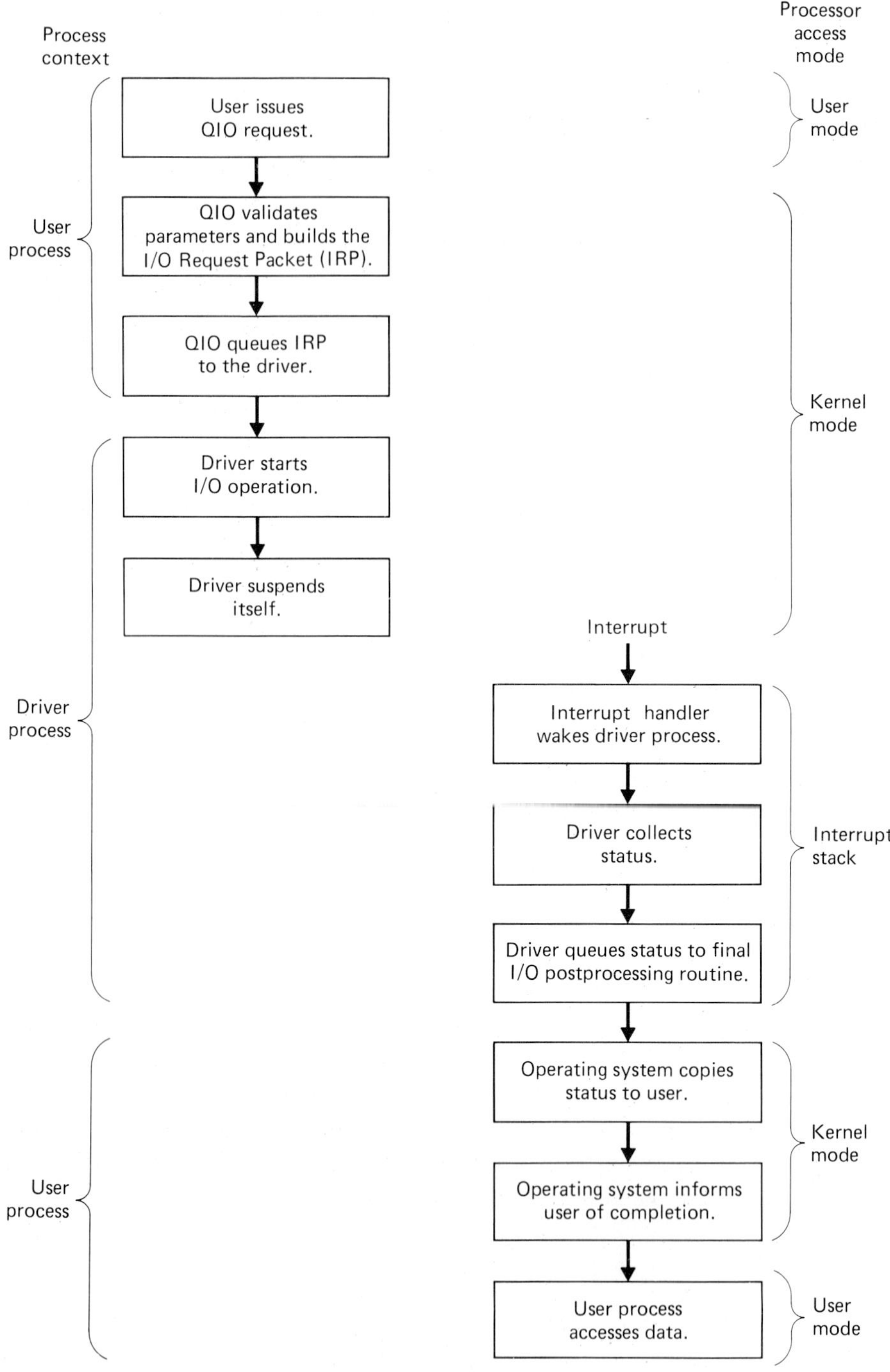

Fig. 19.9 VMS I/O request processing flow (Le80, p. 310).

19.9 RECORD MANAGEMENT SERVICES (RMS)

VAX-11 Record Management Services (RMS) are normally used for input/output requests to mass storage devices. The more complex QIO is for handling input/output to terminals and various special purpose devices such as graphics equipment. RMS facilitates the processing of logical records; it handles record blocking and deblocking automatically in the user's behalf.

RMS can create files of three types: *sequential, relative,* and *indexed.* Three access modes are provided: *sequential, keyed,* and *Record's File Address.*

19.9.1 Sequential File Organization

Perhaps the simplest of the VAX/VMS file organizations, sequential file organization maintains records in consecutive order. The sequence is determined by the order in which the records were written to the file. Figure 19.10 shows a sequential file.

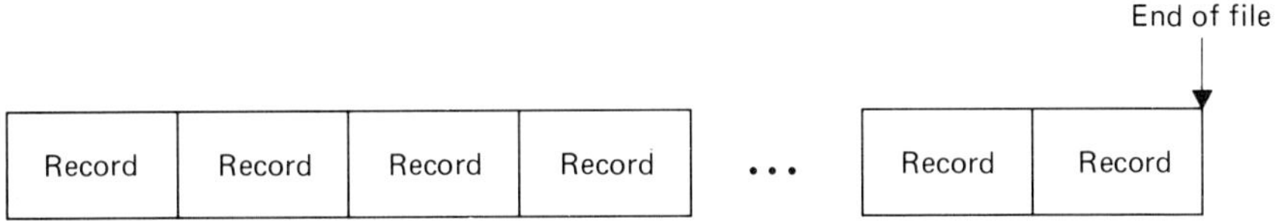

Fig. 19.10 Sequential file organization.

19.9.2 Relative File Organization

In relative file organization (Fig. 19.11) a file consists of a series of fixed size cells. The user specifies the fixed cell size. The cells are numbered sequentially from 1 for the first record to some highest number for the last record. Each cell may contain a single record or may be empty. Empty cells may appear anywhere in the file; they need not be contiguous. Cell numbers are unique and may therefore be used to identify the record occupying a cell as well as the cell itself. A cell number used to identify a record is called a *relative record number.*

Cell 1	Cell 2	Cell 3	Cell 4	Cell 5		Cell 2499	Cell 2500
Record 1	Record 2	Empty	Record 4	Empty	...	Record 2499	Record 2500

Fig. 19.11 Relative file organization.

19.9.3 Indexed File Organization

From the user's standpoint, indexed file organization (Fig. 19.12) facilitates the design of retrieval-oriented applications. The indexed file organization is unique in that accesses may be by data within the records themselves and not just by a record's position within the file. In indexed organization, each record has a *key field.* The length of the key and its position in each record are fixed. RMS uses six different keyfield types: character string, signed 15-bit integer, unsigned 16-bit binary, signed 31-bit integer, unsigned 32-bit binary, and packed decimal.

As each record is added to an indexed file, RMS constructs a tree-structured table called an *index.* The index consists of entries containing key values for records written to the file. Each entry in the index contains a key value and a pointer to the location in the file at which the record with this key may be located. Multiple indi-

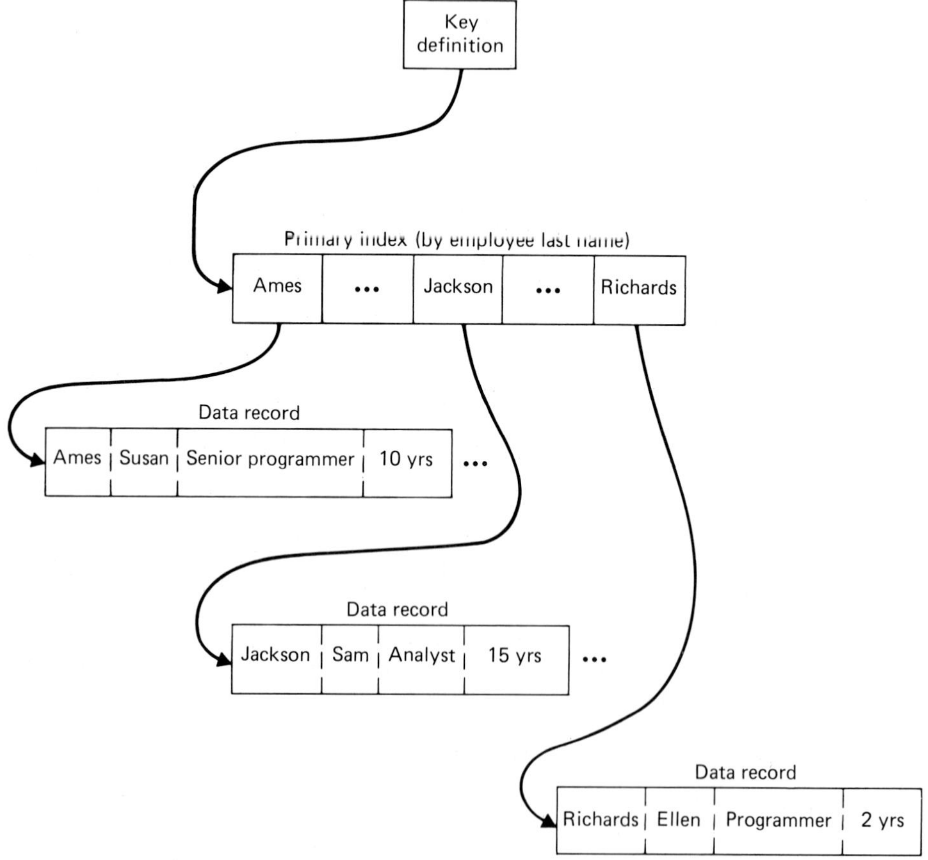

Fig. 19.12 Indexed file organization.

File organization	Advantages	Disadvantages
Sequential	Uses disk and memory efficiently: minimum disk overhead, block-boundary crossing. Provides optimal usage if the application accesses all records sequentially on each run. Provides the most flexible record format. Allows data to be stored on many different types of media, in a device-independent manner. Allows easy file extension.	Some high-level languages allow sequential access only. Allows records to be added only to end of file. Allows write access by multiple, concurrent users, but only at user's risk.
Relative	Allows both sequential and random access for all languages. Provides random record deletion and insertion. Allows records to be write-shared.	Allows data to be stored on disk only. Requires that files contain a record cell for each relative record number allocated; that is, files may not be densely populated. Requires that record cells be the same size.
Indexed	Allows sequential and random access by key value for all languages. Allows random record deletion and insertion. Allows records to be read- and write-shared. Allows variable-length records to change length on update. Allows easy file extension.	Allows data to be stored on disk only. Requires more disk space. Uses more of the central processing unit to process records. Generally requires multiple disk accesses to process a record.

Fig. 19.13 File organizations—advantages and disadvantages. (Courtesy Digital Equipment Corporation.)

ces may be constructed for accessing a single file. Figure 19.13 lists the advantages and disadvantages of sequential, relative, and indexed files.

19.9.4 Sequential Access Mode

The considerations of how records are accessed from a file are separate from the actual file organizations. Normally, when a file is opened, an access method is specified. In some cases a program may change access methods while a file is being processed.

In sequential access mode, records are retrieved in sequence. Sequential access to sequential files occurs in the order in which the records were written to the file. Sequential access to relative files ignores empty slots. Successive reads obtain successive records from occupied slots. Sequential access to indexed files occurs in the order indicated in the index.

19.9.5 Random Access Mode

Random access is common in interactive applications in which access to a particular record must be expedited. Each request may bear no relationship to the previous request: accesses are often scattered throughout the file.

Random access to sequential files is possible when the file consists of fixed length records and the access specifies the relative record number. Random access to relative files is accomplished by specifying the relative record number of the desired record. If an attempt is made to read an empty cell, RMS returns a "record doesn't exist" indication. If an attempt is made to write to an occupied cell, RMS returns a "record already exists" indicator. Random access to indexed records is by key. When RMS matches the search key with that of a key in the index, it returns the record pointed to by the index entry.

19.9.6 Record's File Address Access Mode

This access method may be used with any file organization whenever a record's precise address on disk is known. After each successful read or write, RMS returns the record file address to the program initiating the I/O request. The program may save this address for future use. This access method greatly speeds access to records but does require more effort by the user.

19.10 INTERPROCESS COMMUNICATION AND SYNCHRONIZATION

VAX/VMS provides a variety of interprocess communication facilities for synchronizing execution, sending messages, and sharing common data between cooperating processes. Four different communications techniques are provided.

- common event flags
- mailboxes
- shared areas of storage
- shared files

These techniques offer various speeds and degrees of generality to processes desiring to communicate with one another.

19.10.1 Common Event Flags

The event flag is the simplest interprocess communication mechanism in VMS. An event flag is a status posting bit that can be set or cleared indicating the occurrence of an event. Various event flag service capabilities are provided.

- Set or clear a specific flag.
- Test the current status of a flag.
- Place a program in a wait state where it will remain until a specific flag or group of flags is set.

Each event flag resides in a 32-bit event flag cluster. Each process has access to four clusters numbered 0 through 3. Event flags can be assigned any meaning. Two of the four clusters are for local process functions; two are for interprocess communication.

Event flag clusters 2 and 3 are called common event flag clusters. They are created dynamically by system service request; they can be shared with other processes. Processes must associate with a common event flag cluster; the first process to do so causes the cluster to be created; the remaining processes do so to be able to access the flags.

VMS provides six general event flag services for performing operations on both local and common event flags.

- Set event flag.
- Clear event flag.
- Read event flag.
- Wait for single event flag.
- Wait for logical OR of event flags.
- Wait for logical AND of event flags.

Three VMS services are specific to common event flag clusters.

- Associate common event flag cluster.
- Disassociate common event flag cluster.
- Delete common event cluster.

Figure 19.14 illustrates process synchronization with event flags. Whichever process actually calls the Associate with Common Event Flag Cluster ($ASCEFC) service first creates the cluster, and the other process associates with it. Each of the processes first sets a flag indicating to the other that it is ready; each process then waits for its own flag to be set. The EFN parameter specifies an event flag number.

```
                    Process 1

$ASCEFC_S EFN=#64,NAME=cluster_name   ; create or associate
                                      ; ...cluster 2
$SETEF_S EFN=#65                      ; notify process 2
$WAITFR_S EFN=#66                     ; wait for proc. 2 signal
   .
   .
   .

                    Process 2

$ASCEFC_S EFN=#64,NAME=cluster_name   ; create or associate
                                      ; ...cluster 2
$SETEF_S EFN=#66                      ; notify process 1
$WAITFR_S EFN=#65                     ; wait for proc. 1 signal
   .
   .
   .
```

Fig. 19.14 Process synchronization with event flags.

19.10.2 Mailboxes

Event flags are useful for awaiting events and determining when they have occurred but they do not allow for passing data between processes. For this purpose, VAX provides a more general facility called mailbox communications. A mailbox is a record-oriented virtual device that can be used for interprocess communication. It is read to or written from in the same manner as files and devices.

Messages are inserted at one end and read from the other; so messages are read first-in-first-out. A process reading the mailbox either gets the oldest message it contains or an indication that the mailbox is empty. Processes may request to be notified when a message is placed in a mailbox.

The creator of a mailbox specifies the maximum message size and the maximum number of messages the mailbox can hold. The creator may control which processes are allowed to write to the mailbox. Mailboxes are protected in the same manner as VMS files.

When one process creates another, it may specify a mailbox which is to receive the termination status when the created process is deleted.

19.10.3 Shared Storage

The most general of the interprocess communications mechanisms is shared storage. Processes may share storage in the process portion of their address spaces through *global sections.* A global section is a named area of storage that can be mapped into several processes' address spaces.

Processes using shared storage for interprocess communication use their own agreed-upon protocols for synchronization, thus making this is a very general communications mechanism. Processes using shared storage often use event flags as well as the shared data areas.

Some global sections are permanently installed in the system; others are created dynamically by processes. When a dynamically created global section is referenced, it is mapped into the referencing process; it is deleted when there are no more references to it.

19.10.4 Shared Files

Processes may communicate via shared files. Disk files can be shared by any number of programs that are reading (but not writing) the file. Sequential disk files can be accessed by a single writer or shared by multiple readers. Relative and indexed files, however, can actually be shared by multiple readers and writers.

SUMMARY

VAX represents a Virtual Address extension of the PDP-11 family. VAX was designed to be compatible with the PDP-11. Both machines use the same data formats and media formats for I/O. Their assembly languages are basically the same. The VAX/VMS operating system is quite similar to PDP-11 RSX. The VAX-11 has a PDP-11 hardware compatibility mode.

Four hierarchical protection levels have been provided—kernel, executive, supervisor, and user. The instruction set is implemented in microcode. Caches are used to facilitate address translation and access to frequently used data.

Storage management involves two main components: the pager and the swapper. The pager moves individual pages back and forth between primary and secondary storage; the swapper moves entire processes. Each process has a resident set limit, i.e., the maximum number of pages it may have in primary storage at once. When a process has reached its resident set limit and attempts to page in a new page, it must yield one of its current pages from primary storage. This is a local page replacement policy. Pages are selected for replacement on a first-come-first-served basis. A replaced page is added to the modified page list if it has been changed, and to the free page list if it is has not. Modified pages are paged to the secondary storage only when necessary. Often, modified pages are reclaimed by their processes before they are paged out. Free pages are often reclaimed before they are reassigned. VMS dynamically adjusts a process's resident set size based upon the fault rate the process is experiencing. VMS attempts to equalize the fault rate across all processes. VMS reduces paging disk I/O by paging resident sets in clusters to and from the disk.

VMS uses 32 priority levels for scheduling processes. Real-time processes are scheduled strictly according to priority. Each time a normal process is scheduled, its priority decreases, but never below a certain base priority.

Processes make various state transitions throughout their existence. Notable in VMS is the importance of inswapping and outswapping: the states occur in mirror images depending on whether the process is in primary storage, or has been swapped out.

VMS I/O is normally asynchronous—once a process issues an input/output request, the process may continue executing while the I/O request is being serviced. A data structure describes the state of the I/O system at any moment. This data structure consists of Device Data Blocks, Unit Control Blocks, I/O Request Packets, Channel Request Blocks, Interrupt Dispatch Blocks, and Adaptor Control Blocks. This chapter contains a detailed description of I/O control flow in VMS.

VMS Record Management Services (RMS) are normally used for input/output requests to mass storage devices. RMS can create sequential files, relative files, and indexed files. Three access modes are provided—sequential access, keyed access, and Record's File Address access.

VMS provides a variety of interprocess communication facilities for synchronizing execution, sending messages, and sharing common data between cooperating processes. These are common event flags, mailboxes, shared areas of storage, and shared files.

TERMINOLOGY

Adaptor Control Block
Applications Migration Executive
associate with an event flag cluster
background process
balance set
cell
Channel Request Block
common event flag
Device Data Block
device driver
event flag
event flag cluster
executive protection mode
free page list
global section
index
indexed file
inswapping
interprocess communication
Interrupt Dispatch Block
I/O postprocessing routine
I/O Request Packet
kernel protection mode
key field
keyed access
mailbox
message queue
Massbus
modified page list
nonresident executable process
outswapping
page clusters
page fault rate
page reclamation
pager
PDP-11
PDP-11 hardware compatibility mode
priority levels

Process Control Block (PCB)
Queue I/O (QIO) system service
random access
real-time process
Record Management Services (RMS)
Record's File Address access
relative file
relative record number
resident set
resident set limit
RSX
sequential access
sequential file
summary longword
supervisor protection mode
swapper
swapping
Synchronous Backplane Interconnect
system event
time-critical process
timeshared process
Unibus
Unit Control Block
user protection mode
VAX-11/780
VAX/VMS

EXERCISES

19.1 In VAX systems pages are 512 bytes each, much smaller than on other systems. Give several advantages of having such a small page size. Give some disadvantages.

19.2 VMS guarantees that a process just swapped into primary storage will receive at least one quantum before being swapped out. Why does it do this?

19.3 The quantum in VAX systems defines primary storage occupancy rather than processor execution time. Compare and contrast the two approaches.

19.4 VMS I/O is normally asynchronous; that is, once a process issues an input/output request, the process may continue executing while the I/O request is being serviced. Processes may explicitly check for I/O completions, or they may receive notification from the system. Processes desiring to wait for an I/O completion call an operating system routine asking to be suspended. It is important to note that in VMS such suspension does not occur automatically, as a result of the issuance of an I/O request. Compare and contrast this approach with one in which an I/O request suspends the process that issues it.

19.5 How was compatibility between VAX and the PDP-11 achieved? Why is this compatibility critical to the success of VAX?

19.6 Does VAX use a global or a local page replacement strategy?

19.7 Explain the process of page reclamation. Discuss the use of both the free page list and the modified page list.

19.8 Although page reclamation can greatly reduce the amount of paging I/O, such reclamation can be unfair to processes with stable resident sets. Explain how this can be true.

19.9 VAX/VMS writes pages to disk in clusters to minimize the amount of paging I/O. Explain how this might, however, diminish the effectiveness of the page reclamation mechanism.

19.10 VMS dynamically adjusts a process's resident set size based upon the fault rate the process is experiencing. It increases the resident set size for processes with high fault rates, and decreases the resident set size for processes with low fault rates. This strategy tends to equalize the fault rate across all processes. Is this a global or a local strategy? Does it reward "well-behaved" processes, or does it reward "poorly behaved" processes? Why would processes exhibit different fault rates in the first place? Why do you suppose the VAX designers chose a strategy that tends to equalize the fault rate across all processes? Give an example in which this is not an effective strategy.

19.11 In VAX/VMS, a data structure of control blocks describes the state of the I/O system at any moment. Discuss the purpose of each of the following control blocks.

a) Device Data Block (DDB)
b) Unit Control Block (UCB)
c) I/O Request Packet (IRP)
d) Channel Request Block (CRB)
e) Interrupt Dispatch Block (IDB)
f) Adaptor Control Block (ACB)

19.12 Discuss the functions of each of the following VMS I/O system components.

a) Queue I/O system components
b) device drivers
c) I/O postprocessing routines

19.13 As precisely as you can, trace the flow of a single I/O request through VMS.

19.14 Compare and contrast these VMS interprocess communications and synchronization facilities.

a) common event flags
b) mailboxes
c) shared areas of memory
d) shared files

19.15 Each of the three VMS file organizations allows sequential access and random access. Which file organization(s)

a) provide(s) the most efficient sequential access when all records must be accessed on a given run?
b) generally require(s) multiple disk accesses to process a record?
c) allow(s) records to be added only to the end of a file?
d) allow(s) random record deletion and insertion?
e) provide(s) random access most conveniently from the user's viewpoint?

LITERATURE

(Bh79) Bhandarkar, D.P., and S. Rothman, "The VAX-11, DEC's 32-Bit Version of the PDP-11," *Datamation*, February 1979.

(Bu77) Burr, W.E., and W.R. Smith, "Comparing Computer Architectures," *Datamation*, Vol. 23, February 1977, pp. 48–52.

(Le80) Levy, H., and R.H. Eckhouse, Jr., *Computer Programming and Architecture: The VAX-11*, Bedford, Mass.: Digital Press, 1980.

(Sa81) Satyanarayanan, M., and D. Bhandarkar, "Design Trade-offs in VAX-11 Translation Buffer Organization," *Computer*, Vol. 14, No. 12, December 1981, pp. 103–111.

(St76) Strecker, W.D., "Cache Memories for the PDP-11 Family Computers," *Proc. 3rd Annual Symposium on Computer Architecture, ACM*, January 1976, pp. 155–158.

(St78) Strecker, W.D., "VAX-11/780—A Virtual Address Extension to the DEC PDP-11 Family," *Proceedings of the NCC*, Montvale, N.J.: AFIPS Press, 1978.

DEC Publications

The following publications about the PDP-11 and VAX-11 computer systems are all available from Digital Equipment Corporation, Maynard, Massachusetts.

- *Introduction to VAX-11 Concepts*
- *PDP-11 Peripherals Handbook*
- *PDP-11/04/34/45/55/60 Processor Handbook*
- *Terminals and Communications Handbook*
- *Translation Buffer, Cache, and SBI Control Technical Description*
- *VAX-11 Architecture Handbook*
- *VAX-11 Command Language User's Guide*
- *VAX-11/780 Hardware Handbook*
- *VAX-11 Linker Reference Manual*
- *VAX-11 Macro Language Reference Manual*
- *VAX-11 Primer*
- *VAX-11 Software Handbook*
- *VAX-11 Symbolic Debugger Reference Manual*
- *VAX-11/780 System Maintenance Guide*
- *VAX-11 Technical Summary*

20
Case Study: CP/M®

Suppose for a moment that the automobile industry had developed at the same rate as computers and over the same period: how much cheaper and more efficient would the current models be? If you have not already heard the analogy, the answer is shattering. Today you would be able to buy a Rolls-Royce for $2.75, it would do three million miles to the gallon, and it would deliver enough power to drive the Queen Elizabeth II. And if you were interested in miniaturization, you could place half a dozen of them on a pinhead.

Christopher Evans

In the future, you're going to get computers as prizes in breakfast cereals. You'll throw them out because your house will be littered with them.

Robert Lucky

Get hold of portable property.

Great Expectations
Charles Dickens

Outline

20.1 INTRODUCTION

CP/M® *(Control Program for Microcomputers)* is an operating system originally developed for 8-bit microcomputers. As the microprocessor industry evolved, the system developed into a complete family of highly portable operating systems, software tools, applications packages, and languages.*

The revolution in computing brought on by microcomputers was made possible by several developments.

- the availability of low-cost integrated circuit technology
- the availability of low-cost, highly reliable floppy disks
- ever increasing labor costs that demand improvements in technology in order to improve productivity.

20.2 HISTORY

When the Intel 8080 microprocessor was first developed, Shugart Associates and a number of other companies were developing highly reliable floppy disks. The cassette mechanisms that were in use up to that point were slow and prone to breakdown. The floppy disk drives retailed for about $500 apiece, a price that has remained relatively constant since that time, in spite of inflation. The combination of integrated circuit memory technology, processor technology, and floppy disks made it possible to configure a useful microcomputer for just a few thousand dollars, about a hundred times less than it cost two decades before, and a thousand times less in "real" dollars if inflation is considered.

CP/M was developed by Gary Kildall. Kildall, while employed as a consultant at Intel, wrote the first PL/M compiler. PL/M (Programming Language for Microcomputers) became Intel's software systems implementation language, a significant switch for Intel from the use of assembly languages for writing microcomputer systems software. In 1974, Kildall wrote the first version of the CP/M file system that he designed to support a resident PL/M compiler.

CP/M was licensed for commercial distribution in 1975. At about that time, early versions of the assembler, editor, and debugger were developed. The first major commercial user of CP/M was IMSAI, an early pioneer in the development of microcomputer systems.

CP/M became extraordinarily popular among users of personal computers, and evolved through a series of increasingly powerful versions. The development of hard disk technology for microcomputers provided significantly larger storage capabilities, making CP/M-based microcomputers competitive with low-end minicomputers. *MP/M*™ was designed as a CP/M-compatible system for 16-bit micros; it provides

---

ASM, CP/M-86, MP/M, and MP/M-86 are trademarks of Digital Research Inc.

multiuser timesharing and real-time processing capabilities. *CP/NET*® was released in 1980 to provide networking capabilities for CP/M-based *requestors* with MP/M-based *servers.*

20.3 PL/M

PL/M was developed in 1972 by MAA (Microcomputer Applications Associates), the predecessor of Digital Research, as a systems programming language for use on Intel's 8-bit microprocessor. PL/M is derived from the compiler-writing language XPL, a language derived from Burroughs Algol and full PL/I.

MAA implemented a paper tape editor for the Intel 8008 microprocessor with PL/M, and this program later evolved into the CP/M editor, ED. Intel has successfully implemented PL/M on a variety of microprocessors, and has adopted the language for its software systems development.

MAA saw the possibility of combining Intel 16K byte 8080-based microcomputers with the economical floppy disks being produced by Shugart. The new system would provide a dedicated system for PL/M program development. The idea was rejected at the time because the PL/M development environments available on large timesharing systems were considered sufficient.

20.4 THE CP/M FAMILY

MAA decided to implement the CP/M system anyhow and completed it in 1974. CP/M was built as a single user system with a very reliable file system. File access to floppy disks was much faster than that provided by the cassette drives of the time, and users were able to spread their files among numerous floppy disks, loading and unloading them from the drives as needed.

20.4.1 Portability

The reliability, power, and friendliness of CP/M created an enormous demand for it. By the mid-1970s it had been implemented on many different computer systems. Yet the basic flavor of the system was preserved on each implementation.

CP/M's designers then split the system into two major parts to facilitate its implementation on a diversity of microcomputers, an *invariant* part and a *variant* part. The invariant part contains the disk operating system written in PL/M. The variant part, written in the assembly language of the particular computer for which it is being implemented, contains the I/O device drivers required by the particular local hardware configuration. This split has made it possible for CP/M to become one of the world's two most portable operating systems. The other is the UNIX system.

20.4.2 Table-Driven Systems

The popularity of microcomputers created a demand for new and more powerful peripherals. The industry responded to this with various capacity floppy disk devices and with the Winchester hard-disk drives. Responding to the diversifying base of devices that had to be supported by CP/M, Digital Research completely redesigned the system in 1979 to be *table-driven*. In particular, all of the disk-dependent parameters that were interspersed throughout the invariant portion of the system were moved into tables in the variant portion. When CP/M is implemented for different hardware, these tables must be filled in accordingly. In table-driven systems, parameters that control the operation of the system appear in tables rather than being "hard coded." As the system runs, it references these tables. Table-driven systems are often much easier to modify than are hard-coded systems.

Thus CP/M has become a rather general system much of whose operation is defined by table entries and I/O subroutines written for local implementations. The system is now in use worldwide at several hundred thousand installations with thousands of different hardware configurations.

20.5 STRUCTURE OF CP/M

CP/M consists of three major subsystems (Figure 20.1).

- the *Console Command Processor (CCP)*
- the *Basic Input/Output System (BIOS)*
- the *Basic Disk Operating System (BDOS)*

CCP interprets commands entered by the user and issues responses. It creates the user's view of the microcomputer—a user-friendly one (at least as far as computer hobbyists are concerned) that relieves the user from having to know the internal operation of CP/M and of the computer system. CCP calls upon BIOS and BDOS to perform the actual input/output and file processing.

BIOS contains the various device drivers that send data to and receive data from the devices, and receive status information about the success or failure of input/output operations.

BDOS contains the various utility routines for managing disks. It makes disk file management transparent to the user—certainly a key to any operating system's success since physical manipulation of the disks is a complex and tedious chore. Disk files are often widely scattered in small blocks throughout the surface of the disk, and this complicates information storage and retrieval. BDOS manages these blocks, dynamically allocating and releasing storage as necessary.

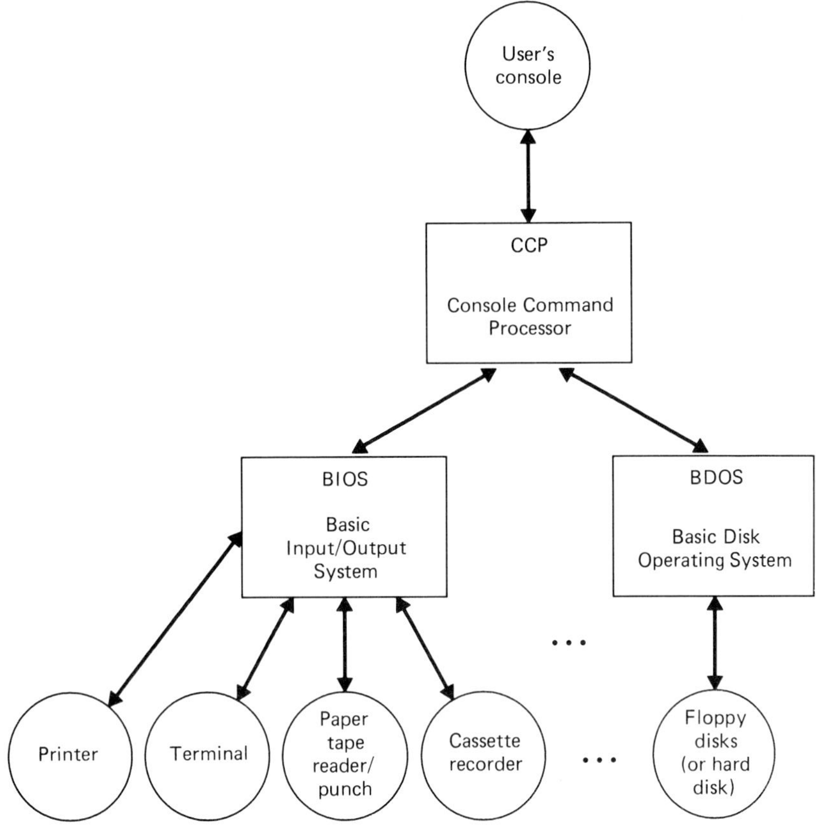

Fig. 20.1 Structure of CP/M.

20.6 MEMORY ALLOCATION

CP/M is a real storage system. Certain areas of primary storage are reserved for the operating system, but the vast majority is available for user programs, especially on larger systems.

Figure 20.2 shows how storage is partitioned in a typical CP/M system. The first 256 bytes (page 0) are reserved for various system parameters. The operating system resides in upper storage. The remaining locations, called the *Transient Program Area (TPA),* are available for user programs. In CP/M terminology, it is common to refer to the combination of BIOS and BDOS as *FDOS (Functional Disk Operating System).* The FDOS and CCP together constitute CP/M. In *S-100 bus* computers like the North Star and Cromemco systems, the TPA ordinarily begins

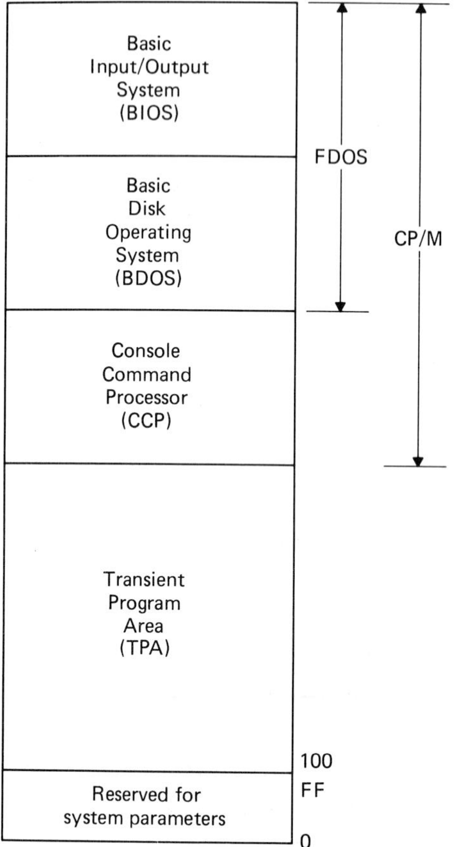

Fig. 20.2 CP/M storage allocation.

after page 0. On other systems, like the Radio Shack TRS-80, with ROM programs in low memory, the TPA begins after the ROM locations.

A user requiring more space than is available in the TPA may overlay much of the CP/M system. But the user's program must reload CP/M before exiting.

20.7 LOGICAL TO PHYSICAL DEVICE MAPPING

CP/M views devices as being either *logical devices* or *physical devices.* A physical device is a real device capable of performing input/output. A logical device is an artifact provided by the operating system to make the user interface more friendly; it doesn't actually exist. Users do input/output via logical devices. It is the assignment of logical devices to physical devices that enables user input/output requests to be satisfied by the operating system.

CP/M supports four logical devices, namely CON:, RDR:, PUN:, and LST: (the colons are part of the names).

- CON: designates a low-speed device for communications between the user and CP/M. It has three *logical device drivers* associated with it: CONIN inputs one character at a time from the console input device, CONOUT outputs one character at a time to the console output device, and CONST examines the console input device to determine its "character ready" or "character not ready" status.
- RDR: designates the logical reader device used for input from mass storage devices. Its logical driver is called READER.
- PUN: designates the logical punch device used for output to mass storage devices. Its logical driver is called PUNCH.
- LST: designates the logical listing device. It normally directs the output of a program to the printer, but in some cases sends the output to a mass storage device other than disk. Its logical driver is called LIST.

Logical devices simplify user programming. Physical devices, however, must be used by the operating system that ultimately performs all input/output in the user's behalf. CP/M supports the physical devices listed in Fig. 20.3

TTY:	Teletype device
CRT:	CRT device
BAT:	Batch mode (RDR input and LST output)
UC1:	User-defined console device
PTR:	High-speed reader device
UR1:	User-defined reader #1
UR2:	User-defined reader #2
PTP:	High-speed punch device
UP1:	User-defined punch #1
UP2:	User-defined punch #2
LPT:	Line printer device
UL1:	User-defined list device

Fig. 20.3 CP/M physical devices.

In the distributed versions of CP/M, each logical device is permanently set to be one particular physical device. When the *IOBYTE function* is implemented, however, each logical device may be set at various times to one of four physical devices.

The mapping of logical to physical devices is controlled by the contents of the IOBYTE (one byte reserved for CP/M at a fixed location in storage) as shown in Fig. 20.4. For example, if bits 7 and 6 are set to the bit pattern "10" then the LST: logical device sends its outputs to the line printer. If these bits are set to "00" then the output is directed to the terminal, and if the bits are "01" then outputs are directed to the CRT.

Bit pattern	(List) LST: bits 7 and 6	(Punch) PUN: bits 5 and 4	(Reader) RDR: bits 3 and 2	(Console) CON: bits 1 and 0
00	TTY:	TTY:	TTY:	TTY:
01	CRT:	PTP:	PTR:	CRT:
10	LPT:	UP1:	UR1:	BAT:
11	UL1:	UP2:	UR2:	UC1:

Fig. 20.4 Logical to physical device mapping via the IOBYTE.

20.8 CONSOLE COMMAND PROCESSOR (CCP)

The Console Command Processor examines command lines typed by the user, performs some simple validation, and calls the appropriate BDOS and BIOS functions to accomplish the desired tasks. A summary of CP/M commands is shown in Fig. 20.5.

Command	Description
ASM	assemble a program
DDT	Dynamic Debugging Tool. This command loads DDT and interprets user-entered DDT commands. Among its capabilities, DDT can
	enter assembly language statements
	display contents of memory
	fill a portion of memory with a hexadecimal constant
	begin program execution at a specific address
	set a breakpoint at a specific address
	disassemble object code to assembly code
	move memory contents to another area
	read a file from disk to memory
	alter the contents of memory
	execute a certain number of instructions and then halt and display register contents
	display register contents
	alter register contents
DIR	display directory

Command	Description
DUMP	display a file in hexadecimal
ED	edit a file. Some of the editor capabilities are
	append lines
	position to beginning of file
	position to bottom of file
	move characters
	delete characters
	end edit and return to CP/M
	find a string
	insert text
	delete lines
	quit editing (without alteration of file)
	get a copy of a library file
	replace a string
	print a certain number of lines
	transfer a block of lines
ERA	erase a file
LOAD	load a program
MOVCPM	construct a new copy of CPM
PIP	perform various file utility operations. PIP can
	copy a file
	concatenate two files
	echo copy to console
	translate uppercase to lowercase characters and vice versa
	add line numbers to lines of text
	insert page feeds every *n* lines
	set tab stops
REN	rename a file
SAVE	save a file
STAT	display status of diskettes, files, devices, etc.
SUBMIT	instruct CP/M to execute commands from a file instead of the console
SYSGEN	create versions of CP/M
TYPE	display the contents of a file on the console
USER	set the user number
x:	change the currently logged disk drive to x (which is "A" through "P")

Fig. 20.5 CP/M commands.

20.9 BASIC INPUT/OUTPUT SYSTEM (BIOS)

BIOS handles input/output to the peripheral devices. Ordinarily it is not supplied by Digital Research or other CP/M vendors. Instead, local vendors supply the appropriate routines to configure a BIOS to handle the particular peripherals on a customer's system.

BIOS can read a character from the console (normally the keyboard), write a character to the console (normally a CRT or printer), read a character from the logical reader device, write a character to the logical punch device, write a character to the printer, get or set I/O status, write a string to the console, read a string from the console, and determine if the console is ready.

Thus the BIOS handles only the most primitive I/O operations. In particular, it has no knowledge of the existence of files.

20.10 BASIC DISK OPERATING SYSTEM (BDOS)

The BDOS handles all disk input/output. BDOS functions are not directly available in the command language; rather they are called either by CCP or a transient program. BDOS can lift the disk head, reset the disk system, select the disk, open a file, close a file, search the directory for a file, search for next extent of a file, delete a file, read a file sequentially, write a file sequentially, create a file, rename a file, determine which disk drives are usable, determine the current disk drive, set DMA (Direct Memory Access) address, get address of disk allocation vector, write-protect a disk, determine which drives are write-protected, set attributes of a file, get the address of the disk parameter block, get or set a user code, read a disk randomly, write a disk randomly, compute the size of a disk file, and set a random record position.

20.11 THE FILE SYSTEM

CP/M's file processing is handled by CCP and BDOS; BIOS operates at a much lower level. CP/M translates the user's logical view of the file into the system's physical view; this depends on the particular storage medium used. CP/M has been implemented for a diversity of disk types including 8-inch floppies and 5 1/4-inch floppies (Fig. 20.6), single-density disks and double-density disks, disks with hard sectoring and disks with soft sectoring. More recently, floppy disks are being superseded by economical Winchester hard disks. *(The disk primitives of these devices vary considerably, so for the purposes of this discussion we shall consider only CP/M Version 1.4 running on a single-density, 8-inch, soft-sectored floppy disk in IBM 3740 format as shown in Fig. 20.7).*

20.11.1 Physical Disk Organization

The disk consists of 77 tracks numbered 0—76. There are 26 sectors per track. Each sector contains 128 bytes. Multiplying these numbers we obtain the capacity of the disk—256,256 bytes. The utilization of this space is indicated in Fig. 20.8.

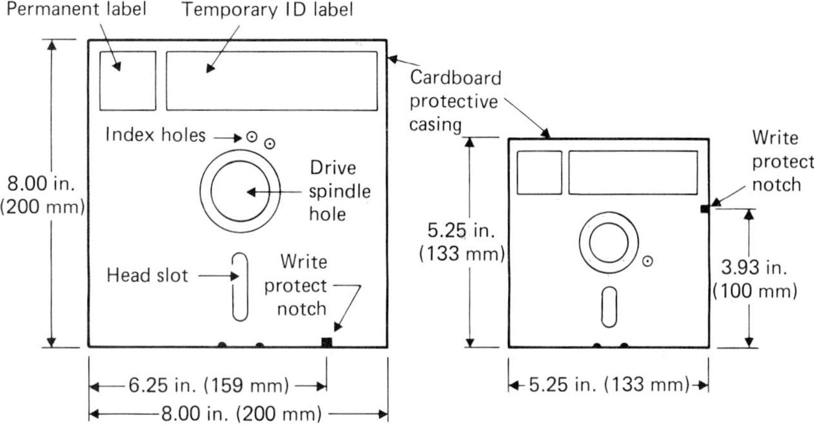

Fig. 20.6 Standard 8-inch and 5 1/4-inch floppy disks. (Courtesy of Shugart.)

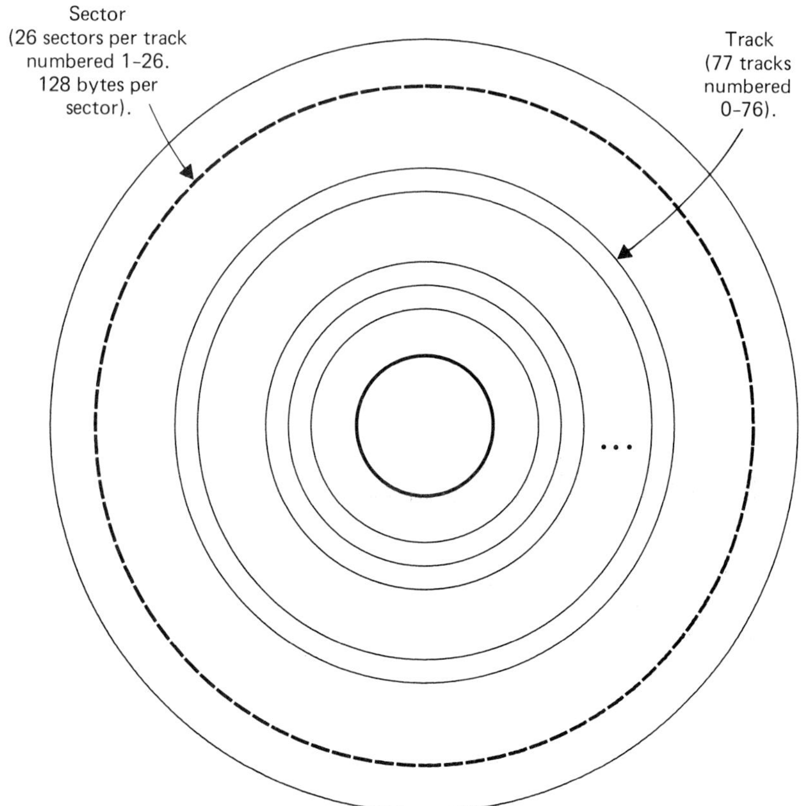

Fig. 20.7 IBM 3740 8-inch floppy disk format.

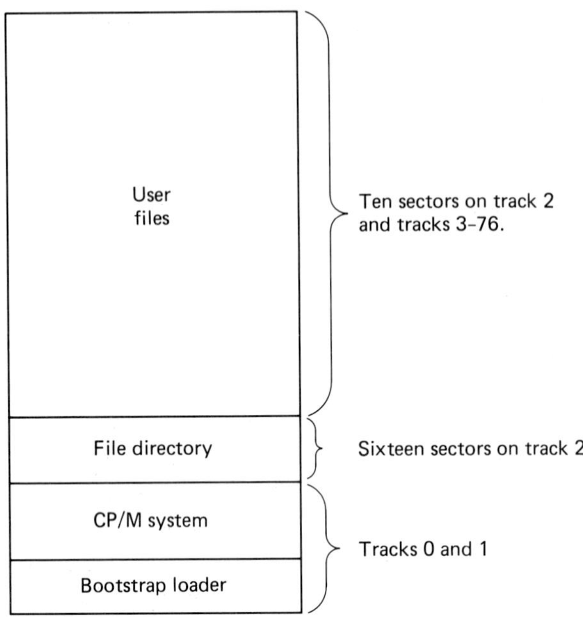

Fig. 20.8 Eight-inch floppy disk utilization.

Tracks 0 and 1 are reserved for the CP/M system including a small bootstrap loader. Sixteen sectors on track 2 contain the directory listing all files stored on the disk. The remainder of track 2 and all remaining tracks (3 through 76) contain user files.

20.11.2 File Organization

Each sector contains 128 bytes. In CP/M, this is called a record. Each file is a collection of records and, most likely, these records are not all contiguous; ordinarily they are spread over the surface of the disk. Some systems use a list structure to keep track of the relationships among the records. CP/M instead keeps a list of all sectors belonging to a file in the *file descriptor* or *File Control Block (FCB).* The layout of the File Control Block will be presented shortly.

Each file may contain as many as 16 *units,* and each unit may have between zero and 128 records (zero to 16K bytes). Thus CP/M may have files as large as 16 times 16K or 256K bytes, a figure slightly larger than the capacity of an IBM 3740 8-inch floppy disk. Each File Control Block represents as much as 16K bytes of a file; 16 File Control Blocks may be linked together to describe a 256K byte file.

File Control Blocks are 33 bytes long. They are stored in the directory area of the floppy disk. When a file is in use, its FCB is brought into the Transient Program Area so that it may be referenced quickly. When a file is closed, its FCB is copied back to the disk.

In CP/M, users reference files by a symbolic name. These symbolic names must be translated by CP/M into precise physical file locations and descriptions. The mapping between logical names and physical files is performed in the File Control Blocks contained in the file directory. The organization of a File Control Block is illustrated in Fig. 20.9; The fields of the FCB are described in Fig. 20.10.

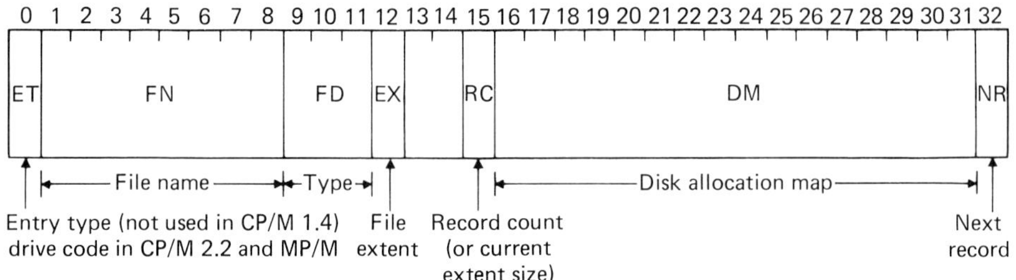

Fig. 20.9 CP/M File Control Block.

Field	Position	Meaning
ET	0	entry type (not used in CP/M 1.4) drive code in CP/M 2.2 and MP/M
FN	1–8	file name
FD	9–11	extension
EX	12	extent, normally 0
	13–14	not used
RC	15	record count (number of records in the current extent of the file)
DM	16–31	disk allocation map
NR	32	next record to be read or written

Fig. 20.10 Fields of the File Control Block.

A logical CP/M record is one sector of 128 bytes. A single file may occupy between zero sectors and a full disk. Logically contiguous records are not normally physically contiguous. If they were, then file processing would be much slower. Let's see why.

After each sector on the disk there are several bytes used for control purposes. After a sector is read or written, these bytes must be processed to confirm the accuracy of the read or write operation and to facilitate certain housekeeping operations. If the next logical record were indeed contiguous to the previous one, then it would probably have passed under the disk's read-write head before the various housekeeping chores were completed. Thus the disk would have to rotate another complete cycle before the record would again be accessible at the read-write head. Reading or writing a sequential file would be intolerably slow. CP/M solves this problem by placing logically adjacent records several physical sectors apart; the standard separation (or *skew*) in CP/M is six sectors. Figure 20.11 shows a typical logical sector to physical sector mapping scheme with a six-sector skew.

Logical sector numbers	Physical sector numbers																									
	01	02	03	04	05	06	07	08	09	10	11	12	13	14	15	16	17	18	19	20	21	22	23	24	25	26
Access on first revolution	01						02						03						04						05	
Access on second revolution					06						07						08						09			
Access on third revolution			10						11						12						13					
Access on fourth revolution		14						15						16						17						18
Access on fifth revolution						19						20						21						22		
Access on sixth revolution				23						24						25						26				

Fig. 20.11 Logical to physical sector mapping with a six-sector skew.

20.11.3 The Allocation Bit Map

CP/M allocates space to disk files dynamically. Users need not specify in advance how much space is to be reserved for a file. Again, for the purpose of this discussion we will discuss only 8-inch floppy disks with 77 tracks, 26 sectors per track, and 128 bytes per sector, i.e., IBM 3740 format.

For each disk drive, BDOS maintains a 243-bit *allocation bit map* to indicate which portions of the disk have been allocated to files, and which portions are available. Each bit in the map corresponds to a group of eight logically contiguous sectors called a *cluster.* Figure 20.12 shows a typical allocation bit map. The 243 bits are numbered (in hexadecimal) from 00 to F2. This map shows that clusters 00 through 74 are currently allocated, and that clusters 75 though F2 are available for allocation to files.

Now let us consider how the allocation bit map is utilized in managing space on a disk. A request to create a file causes BDOS to search the contents of the allo-

First digit	0	1	2	3	4	5	6	7	8	9	A	B	C	D	E	F
0	1	1	1	1	1	1	1	1	1	1	1	1	1	1	1	1
1	1	1	1	1	1	1	1	1	1	1	1	1	1	1	1	1
2	1	1	1	1	1	1	1	1	1	1	1	1	1	1	1	1
3	1	1	1	1	1	1	1	1	1	1	1	1	1	1	1	1
4	1	1	1	1	1	1	1	1	1	1	1	1	1	1	1	1
5	1	1	1	1	1	1	1	1	1	1	1	1	1	1	1	1
6	1	1	1	1	1	1	1	1	1	1	1	1	1	1	1	1
7	1	1	1	1	1	0	0	0	0	0	0	0	0	0	0	0
8	0	0	0	0	0	0	0	0	0	0	0	0	0	0	0	0
9	0	0	0	0	0	0	0	0	0	0	0	0	0	0	0	0
A	0	0	0	0	0	0	0	0	0	0	0	0	0	0	0	0
B	0	0	0	0	0	0	0	0	0	0	0	0	0	0	0	0
C	0	0	0	0	0	0	0	0	0	0	0	0	0	0	0	0
D	0	0	0	0	0	0	0	0	0	0	0	0	0	0	0	0
E	0	0	0	0	0	0	0	0	0	0	0	0	0	0	0	0
F	0	0	0													

First available 1024-byte cluster is number 75.

Fig. 20.12 Allocation bit map.

cation bit map looking for the first 0 bit. This of course corresponds to a free cluster. BDOS sets this bit to 1 and then inserts the hexadecimal cluster number in the mapping area of the new file's File Control Block.

Only write operations can cause BDOS to change the contents of the allocation bit map. After all eight sectors of a cluster have been written to, the next write attempt causes BDOS to search the allocation bit map for the next free cluster. Again, when a free cluster is found, its hexadecimal cluster number is placed in the File Control Block and the bit in the allocation bit map is set to 1.

20.12 CP/M OPERATION

This section provides an overview of the operation of CP/M. CCP displays its prompt and waits for the user to enter a command. CCP uses BIOS to handle the physical transmission of the prompt, and to receive the command typed by the user. BIOS places the command in CCP's buffer.

Some commands are built into CP/M; others are not. *Built-in commands* reside in the portion of storage reserved for the system. If the command received by CCP is built in, CCP executes it directly. If the command is not built in, CCP makes the assumption that the user is requesting a transient program with a file name the same as the command name and with the *extension* "COM." (An extension, like "COM," is concatenated to a file name to indicate that the file is of a certain type.) CCP directs BDOS to locate this file and read it into the TPA. CCP then constructs File Control Blocks for the files to be processed and then terminates, thus making the storage it had occupied available. The files to be processed are either specified explicitly in the command line, or they are implicit in the use of certain commands.

BDOS locates the file to be processed as follows. It finds the filename in the FCB created by CCP. Then it searches the disk where each file has a complete FCB (created by CCP the last time the file was referenced). If the file is present on disk, then BDOS will find an FCB with the matching filename.

When BDOS locates the file's disk FCB, it transfers certain information to the storage FCB created by CCP (the location of the file on disk, for example). Each access to the file results in some changes to the FCB. When the file is finally closed, BDOS makes the last changes (the total number of records written, for example) and then copies the FCB from storage to the disk.

If the user types a command name that is neither for a built-in command nor for a *transient command*, then CCP displays the invalid name followed by a question mark. If the user creates a file with a "COM" extension, and if the user types the name of that file in a command, CCP will try to execute the file regardless of whether it is a program or data.

The file names typed by the user are validated by CCP that then passes them to the designated command processor. Some commands operate only on files with specific extensions. For example, ASM™ operates only on files with extension "ASM," and LOAD requires extension "HEX." If the extensions are not correct, the command causes CCP to prompt the user.

20.13 MP/M

Digital Research designed MP/M (MultiProgramming monitor for Microcomputers) for real-time processing. MP/M contains a nucleus that supports many cooperating sequential processes, and a CP/M-compatible file manager with terminal handling facilities. MP/M functions well as a multiuser, timesharing, multiprogramming system.

MP/M uses an output spooler to print files produced by various users. With only a single printer available on many systems, only one file at a time can be printed. Other printer output files are directed to disk for printing when the printer becomes available.

20.13.1 Structure of MP/M

MP/M is similar in structure to CP/M, containing the following components.

- XIOS (BIOS and extended IOS)
- XDOS (BDOS and extended disk operating system)
- CLI (Command Line Interpreter)
- TMP (Terminal Message Processor)

CP/M is a system in which all of the resources are dedicated to a single user. MP/M is a multiuser system; it accommodates many simultaneous users who share the system resources.

20.13.2 Process Scheduling

Processes are assigned priorities by MP/M; the processor is dispatched to the next ready-to-run process with the highest priority. A process uses the processor until

- it releases the processor voluntarily
- it issues a system call
- it is interrupted, or
- the real-time clock ticks once

The system dispatcher finds the process's priority in the *process descriptor*. The dispatcher stores temporary information about the process in the process descriptor, and deposits state information in the descriptor when the process is interrupted. Processes with equal priority are dispatched first-come-first-served. A real-time clock may be used to facilitate process scheduling and to implement automatic delays.

20.13.3 Process Synchronization

Message queues are used for process synchronization. *A process waiting for a message is suspended until the message arrives from the sending process.* MP/M message queues are special files that can be opened and closed. Information is fed to message queues first-in-first-out.

Message queues are useful for spooling, and for providing mutually exclusive access to shared resources. For example, to synchronize access to the line printer, processes may cooperate as follows: One process (i.e., the process that controls the line printer) can set up a message queue and place a message in it only when the line printer is available; a process desiring to use the line printer would be required to read the message from the message queue before accessing the device. When the line printer is in use, the queue remains empty. Thus the process that wants to use the line printer remains suspended until the line printer becomes available and the line printer control process deposits a message in the message queue.

20.13.4 Command Types

MP/M has no built-in commands. Commands are either

- *transient* (COM extension)
- *page relocatable* (PRL extension) or
- *resident system processes* (RSP extension)

Transient programs use the absolute Transient Program Area. They may only be loaded and executed in the precise locations for which they were compiled. When possible, programs should be made relocatable so that they may be loaded into any available location in storage and still execute properly.

20.13.5 Multitasking

A user may run several programs simultaneously from a single terminal in MP/M. A user may detach a program from a terminal in which case the program's output no longer appears at the terminal. A specific program may be reattached to a terminal (the one from which it was detached) by use of the ATTACH command. Figure 20.13 illustrates the MP/M commands.

DIR S	display a system file directory
ERAQ	erase files using query mode
CONSOLE	display the console number
DSKRESET	change disk if not in use by another user
GENHEX	create HEX file from COM file
PRLCOM	create COM file from PRL file
GENMOD	create PRL file from HEX file
SPOOL	send printer output to spool file
STOPSPLR	terminate spooler output
TOD	display or set time and date
SCHED	schedule a program for future execution
ABORT	abort a running program
ATTACH	attach a console to a detached program
MPMLDR	load, relocate, and execute MP/M
MPMSTAT	display MP/M system status
USER	display and/or change current user area
XSUB	provide input to programs executed in submit file

Fig. 20.13 MP/M commands.

20.13.6 Bank Selectable Memory

The 8080, 8085, and Z80 processors can reference only 64K bytes of memory directly. But it is possible to use more than one bank of storage with MP/M. With two banks of storage, each user may run a very large program that consumes most of storage. MP/M handles this by switching back and forth between the storage banks. Confusion between identical addresses of different users is eliminated by the *bank switching* mechanism that makes only one bank active at a time.

20.14 CP/NET

CP/NET was released by Digital Research in 1980 as a network operating system that distributes operating systems functions throughout a network of nonhomogeneous processors. CP/NET connects many CP/M-based *requestors* (possibly on different types of processors) with many MP/M-based *servers* (again possibly on different types of processors).

CP/NET was designed with the same philosophy as CP/M and MP/M—to be highly portable. It is a very general system and is independent of the actual media used for data transmission in a particular network. CP/NET can use simple low-

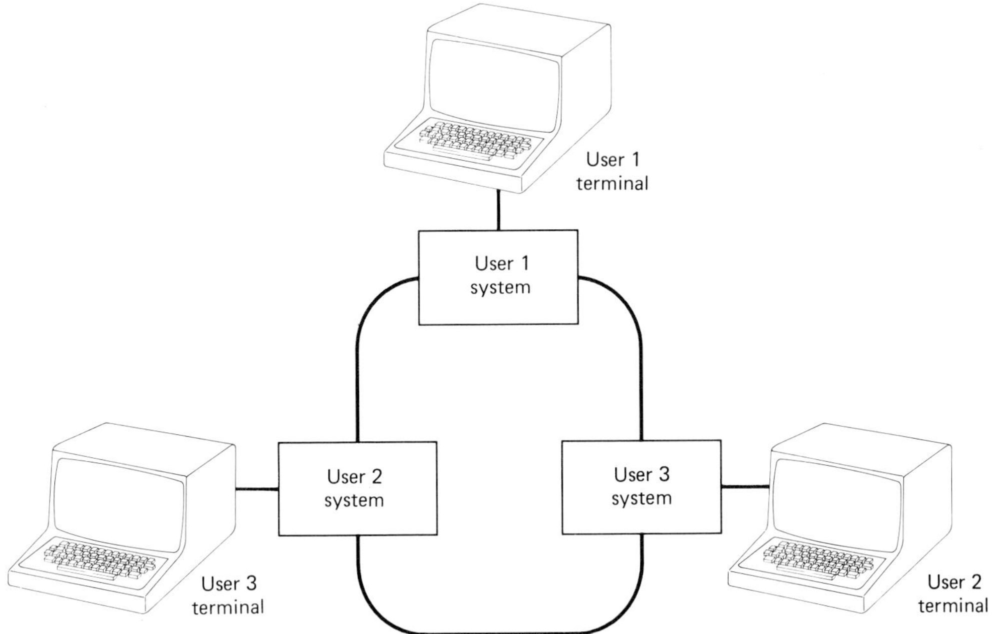

Fig. 20.14 Network without a master node.

speed protocols like the *RS-232C* or high-speed protocols like Ethernet. It can use most common network topologies such as star, ring, and common-bus architectures.

CP/NET's invariant portions operate under CP/M and route system calls over the network to a particular MP/M server. The MP/M server simulates the actions of CP/M. The simulation is made transparent to applications programs running on any CP/M machine.

CP/M runs one user on one computer system; MP/M runs multiple users on one computer system; CP/NET runs multiple users on multiple computer systems.

Some networks connect many relatively independent nodes together (Fig. 20.14). Networks like these are used to foster intercommunication among their

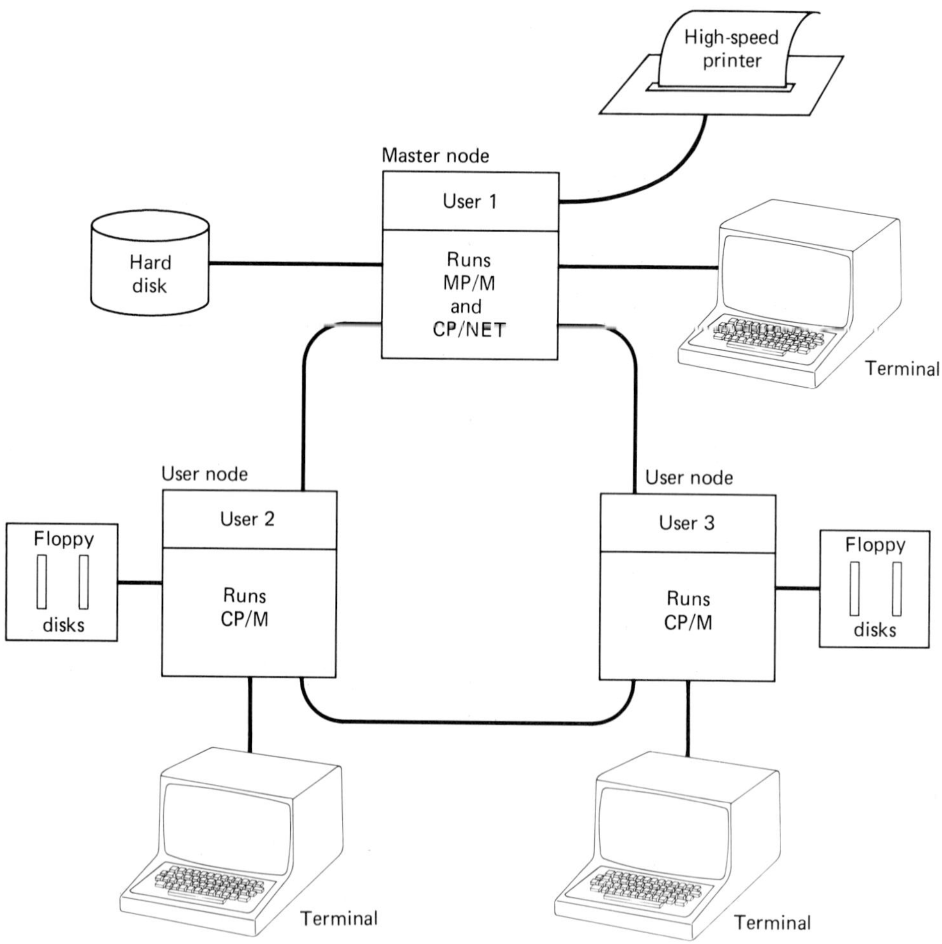

Fig. 20.15 CP/NET system with a master node.

users. Each user can function independently of the network, or can link into the network to communicate with other users. If one user station malfunctions, then the ability of the network to remain in operation depends on the interconnection scheme.

CP/NET operates with at least one *master node* that is responsible for managing the network (Fig. 20.15). The master node runs CP/NET and MP/M and normally has substantial disk storage available. Other nodes may consist only of a processor with as little as 16K of storage, or they may have more storage and local peripherals. CP/NET makes it possible for the various user nodes to share resources, and in some cases to improve their execution speed.

Often, an organization installs CP/NET as a means of giving many user nodes access to a central shared database contained on high-capacity disk drives. Office environments often connect user work stations so that they can share expensive peripherals such as letter quality printers, high-speed printers, and various types of facsimile transmission equipment. In any case, the normal reason for using networking is sharing of resources, and these may be hardware resources, software resources, or information resources.

20.14.1 CP/NET Commands

Nodes in CP/NET networks can use the full power of CP/M and MP/M, and can also use a number of additional commands unique to CP/NET itself. These are summarized in Fig. 20.16.

Command	Description
LOGIN	logs the user into a master node
LOGOFF	allows a user to disassociate from the network
SNDMAIL	allows a user to send a message to any other user in the network
RCVMAIL	displays all messages (and their sources) since the last RCVMAIL was issued
BROADCST	allows a master node to send a message to all of the nodes in the network
MRCVMAIL	the master node uses this command to receive its mail
NETWORK	enables one node to use the network's devices
LOCAL	allows a local node to cancel its association with NETWORK devices
DSKRESET	operates the same as MP/M's DSKRESET command
SPOOL	allows individual users to use the master node's spooler (see MP/M's SPOOL command)
ENDLIST	terminates list output to the network

Fig. 20.16 CP/NET commands.

20.14.2 An Office-of-the-Future Example

Many companies are developing operating systems to support a concept called the *office-of-the-future,* in which most of the paper shuffling associated with today's offices is eliminated by the use of CRT work stations connected via a local network to various devices such as high-speed printers, facsimile transmission devices, mass storage devices, etc. Let us briefly consider how a word processing application might be handled by CP/NET.

In a large law office, contracts are often composed from standard paragraphs with only a small amount of information changing each time a contract is printed. With CP/NET, the standard paragraphs might be stored in a central database managed by MP/M and accessed from any of several CP/M-based word processors in the network. The CP/NET interface is used to assign one local disk drive to the MP/M server. The CP/M-based word processor then reads the standard paragraphs from the assigned drive. This actually causes the paragraphs to be read from the MP/M server since it is not on the local disk. The contract is then composed locally with the CP/M-based word processor. The finished contract may then be printed on the local printer, or the listing device may be assigned to the network in which case it will be printed at the MP/M server.

20.14.3 An Abundance of Software

Because of the popularity of CP/M and MP/M, a huge base of CP/M-compatible and MP/M-compatible software has been developed, most of it by independent entrepreneurs. CP/NET makes it possible for individuals to gain access to this software by cooperating with other users at CP/M-based systems. This distribution of software through networks of cooperating microcomputers promises to be a major influence on the future of personal computing.

20.15 PL/I SUBSET G: THE CP/M APPLICATIONS LANGUAGE

During the late 1970s, industry and the academic community made substantial commitments to the use of Pascal, a concise structured language designed by Nicklaus Wirth in 1969. Some engineering schools dropped FORTRAN. Some industrial users and large numbers of computer science programs dropped PL/I. COBOL kept its position among commercial users; it remains the most widely used language available for file manipulation.

But the trend to Pascal seems to be slowing. Computer science schools are becoming somewhat disenchanted with the "ad hoc mentality" developed in Pascal students; the language is so sparse in some areas that the user is forced to build capabilities which are commonly available in other languages. This, of course, greatly decreases the portability of programs.

In the late 1960s and throughout the 1970s, the universities and many industrial environments provided computing capabilities through timesharing computer systems. Today, many of these same capabilities can be provided far more economically through dedicated personal computer systems, often interconnected in computer networks. The influence of CP/M and CP/M-compatible systems has become a dominant factor in the distribution of computer capabilities among personal computer users. In 1981, both IBM and Xerox entered the personal computing marketplace, each with CP/M-compatible hardware. This underscored the significance of CP/M as the de facto standard microprocessor operating system.

Digital Research had to decide upon the applications language to be supported by CP/M-based systems. The choice was a critical one; the popularity of CP/M was well established, and whatever applications language was chosen might possibly become the international standard for microprocessor systems.

Virtually every microcomputer system manufacturer supports BASIC. But the language is sparse and unstructured. Few manufacturers want to commit themselves to BASIC as the "language of the future." Digital Research carefully considered standard Pascal as the applications language to support. But they rejected it because the language lacks important commercial facilities such as decimal arithmetic, comprehensive file processing capabilities, character string manipulation, and error-exception handling.

The popularity of Pascal was never in question—only its usefulness as a language to meet real computing needs. There was much discussion over the possibility of extending Pascal to include the necessary features. But doing this would have been contrary to Digital Research's desire to choose a broad-based, widely accepted, standardized language.

Digital Research made a rather dramatic choice considering the sentiments among software engineering researchers. It decided upon PL/I Subset G as the applications language for CP/M systems. Full PL/I is too large a language and is considered unacceptable in the software engineering community; the language simply offers too much power to programmers and is too easy to misuse.

PL/I Subset G provides powerful capabilities to both commercial and scientific users. It is a relatively concise subset of full PL/I, consistent, and easy to use. Digital Research began implementing Subset G in 1978 and finished implementing it in 1980. Its compiler runs in three passes. The first two passes produce symbol tables and an intermediate language program acceptable for most target machines. The last pass is machine dependent. It produces machine code and performs code optimization.

It will be interesting to see how the marketplace reacts to PL/I Subset G. Digital Research's commitment to this language will certainly cause renewed interest in PL/I. But Pascal may be too firmly entrenched at this point to be displaced. One indication of this is IBM's decision to supply BASIC and Pascal (and not PL/I) with its personal computer.

20.16 EVOLUTION IN PROCESSOR ARCHITECTURE

One dilemma faced by microcomputer vendors today, and certainly by vendors of microcomputer software, is the decision to emphasize 8-, 16-, or 32-bit architectures. Current systems emphasize 8-bit architecture with 16-bit machines becoming quite popular. The big question that microprocessor vendors are dealing with now is whether to make major commitments to the 16-bit machines, or instead to produce software for the newer 32-bit architectures.

The key issue seems to be that microprocessor vendors are finding themselves competing with the minicomputer manufacturers. The 16-bit minis are already outdated. Most minicomputer manufacturers are making 32-bit products. It seems clear that the real future of microprocessors, certainly in the next decade or so, is with 32-bit architectures.

20.17 CP/M-BASED SOFTWARE

Much of CP/M's popularity is based unquestionably upon the availability of a huge component of applications software. Almost 1000 commercial software packages are currently available for CP/M environments. The large base of CP/M users enables software vendors to offer substantial software products at modest cost, and this causes significant demand. It is a self-perpetuating cycle. The user is the prime beneficiary.

20.18 THE IBM PERSONAL COMPUTER

Now that we have considered both UNIX and CP/M, it is interesting to assess the current state of competition in the microcomputer software industry.

UNIX was developed for minicomputers and is currently "pushing down" into micros via XENIX and other UNIX-based systems. CP/M was developed for 8-bit microcomputers and is currently "pushing upwards" into the 16-bit micro arena with systems like CP/M-86® (single user system for 16-bit micros) and MP/M-86™ (multiuser system for 16-bit micros). It appears as though the battle for supremacy will occur within the 16-bit arena.

The IBM personal computer, announced in 1981, will probably be the machine at the center of the action. At the heart of the machine is the Intel 8088 16-bit microprocessor, a target micro for CP/M-based systems. But IBM opted instead to have Microsoft produce its personal computer operating system that it calls IBM Personal Computer DOS. This system does bear a superficial resemblance to CP/M, but is in fact a scaled-down version of Microsoft's UNIX-based XENIX operating system discussed in Chapter 19. IBM contracted with Digital Research to provide CP/M-86 as an alternative operating system. It will be interesting to discover in the future which operating system becomes the system of choice among IBM personal computer users.

Digital Research claimed 300,000 CP/M installations as of 1981 and at that time forecasted 2,800,000 CP/M-86 based systems by 1986, including a very large number of IBM personal computers. At this writing, there is no way to predict with confidence which of the competitors will eventually dominate in the 16-bit operating system marketplace. All we can say with certainty is that it will be either CP/M-86 or UNIX-based XENIX, and that is precisely why both of these case studies were incorporated into this text.

20.19 THE FUTURE OF CP/M

CP/M and CPM-compatible systems are the most widely used operating systems in the world today, and their numbers are growing quickly. Recent announcements of personal computers by major hardware vendors have for the most part included CP/M-compatible operating systems.

Because its implementors made the system portable, CP/M is now used on an enormous variety of computer systems and hardware configurations. Such popularity will probably prolong the use of CP/M (and CP/M derivative systems) for several decades. Certainly it is the dominant operating system for 8-bit microprocessors. The question remains as to whether it will maintain this popularity among users of 16-bit and 32-bit systems. In this arena, it faces stiff competition from UNIX-based systems and other more powerful operating systems.

SUMMARY

CP/M has become the de facto standard among operating systems for 8-bit microprocessors. Derived from CP/M are the MP/M and CP/NET systems. MP/M is a multiuser timesharing system, and CP/NET is a network operating system for CP/M-based personal computers.

CPM has a variant part and an invariant part. The invariant part contains the disk operating system written in PL/M. The variant part is normally written in the assembly language of the microprocessor to which CP/M is being customized; it contains the I/O device drivers for the local hardware.

CP/M has been made table-driven to facilitate its portability and extendability. It consists of three major portions, namely the Console Command Processor (CCP), the Basic Input/Output System (BIOS), and the Basic Disk Operating System (BDOS). CCP provides a user-friendly interface. BIOS contains the device drivers. BDOS contains the disk file management routines.

CPM is a real storage system. The operating system and the user share primary storage. User programs are transients brought in from the disk when needed.

CP/M offers a reasonably powerful command language for such a small system. The user is given access to an assembler, a debugger, an editor, a loader, a file utility, and an assortment of commands to perform commonly used functions.

BIOS handles input/output to the nondisk peripheral devices, especially the user's console, (normally a keyboard and a CRT or character printer).

BDOS handles disk input/output. It manages files providing operations like open, close, read, write, create, delete, rename, etc.

Files are described by File Control Blocks (FCBs) that are stored in the directory area of the disk. When a file is in use, its FCB is brought to the Transient Program Area so that it may be referenced quickly.

Logically contiguous records are not normally stored contiguously on the disk. This is actually done to speed sequential access.

Commands are either built in, or they are user transients. Builtin commands reside in the system portion of primary storage. Transients must be brought in from the disk.

BDOS locates files by searching the FCBs in the file directory. When it finds a match, it transfers certain data to a corresponding storage FCB. When a file is closed, the FCB is copied back to disk. File name extensions are used to indicate the type of a file.

MP/M contains a nucleus that supports many cooperating sequential processes, and a CP/M-compatible file manager with terminal handling facilities. MP/M functions well as a multiuser, timesharing, multiprogramming system.

In MP/M, each process is described by a process descriptor. State information about a process is deposited in the process descriptor when the process is interrupted. Processes are dispatched on a priority basis with processes of equal priority dispatched first-come-first-served.

MP/M uses message queues for process synchronization. A process waiting for a message is suspended until the message arrives from the sending process.

Multitasking capabilities in MP/M allow a user to run several programs simultaneously from a single terminal. Users may detach a program from a terminal and reattach it when desired.

It is possible to use more than one bank of storage with MP/M. This makes it possible to run very large programs that occupy most of storage. There is no conflict between the common address in the different storage banks because a bank switching mechanism makes only one bank active at a time.

CP/NET is a personal computer network operating system that distributes operating system functions throughout a network of nonhomogeneous processors. It connects CP/M-based requestors with MP/M-based servers. A master node manages the network. CP/NET has several of its own commands many of which are useful for sending and receiving electronic mail.

CP/NET is useful in office-of-the-future applications. Individual work stations are networked together and share access to a common database.

Digital Research bypassed Pascal and BASIC and chose PL/I Subset G as the applications language for its CP/M-based systems. This was a highly controversial decision—even IBM, the creator of PL/I, did not offer PL/I (or the Subset G version) with its first releases of its personal computer.

Because of CP/M's popularity, a huge base of CP/M-compatible software exists. Manufacturers of personal computers have tended toward CP/M-compatible hardware so that purchasers of their computers would be able to make use of the abundance of CP/M software.

CP/M was first implemented for 8-bit microcomputers and has subsequently been implemented for the 16-bit micros. UNIX was originally implemented for 16-bit minicomputers and has subsequently been made available for 16-bit micros, particularly in the XENIX version marketed by Microsoft. These two systems will be the prime competitors in the personal computing operating systems marketplace in the next several years. IBM opted to have Microsoft supply the operating system for the IBM personal computer, but also contracted with Digital Research to supply CP/M-86 as an alternative operating system. It will be interesting to see which operating system ultimately becomes more popular with users of IBM's personal computer.

TERMINOLOGY

8-bit microcomputer
16-bit microcomputer
32-bit microcomputer
allocation bit map
bank switching
Basic Disk Operating System (BDOS)
Basic Input/Output System (BIOS)
builtin commands
cluster
Console Command Processor (CCP)
CP/M
CP/M-86
CP/M-compatible system
CP/NET
device drivers
Digital Research
Ethernet
File Control Block (FCB)
filename extension
floppy disk
Functional Disk Operating System (FDOS)
IBM personal computer
Intel 8080
Intel 8088
invariant part
IOBYTE
IOBYTE function
logical devices
message queue
master node
MP/M (Multiprogramming Monitor for Microcomputers)
MP/M-86
office-of-the-future
page relocatable
physical devices
PL/I Subset G
PL/M
portability
process descriptor
requestor
resident system process (RSP)
RS-232C
sector
sector skew
server
Shugart Associates
table-driven system
transient command
Transient Program Area (TPA)
variant part
Winchester disk drive

EXERCISES

20.1 What developments made possible the revolution in computing brought on by microcomputers?

20.2 Why did CP/M's designers split the system into an invariant part and a variant part? Discuss the advantages and disadvantages of this approach.

20.3 What does it mean for an operating system to be table-driven? How has this approach been incorporated into CP/M?

20.4 What are the major functions of each of the following portions of CP/M?

a) the Console Command Processor (CCP)
b) the Basic Input/Output System (BIOS)
c) the Basic Disk Operating System (BDOS)

20.5 Ordinarily, BIOS is not supplied by Digital Research or other CP/M vendors. Why not? Discuss the advantages and disadvantages of this approach to supplying operating systems software. Consider both the vendor's viewpoint and the user's viewpoint.

20.6 Describe how CP/M manages primary storage.

20.7 Discuss the organization and operation of the CP/M file system.

20.8 Logically contiguous records are not normally physically contiguous on CP/M-managed disks. If they were, then file processing would be much slower. Explain why.

20.9 What is MP/M? How does it differ from CP/M? How is it similar?

20.10 Describe how processes are scheduled in MP/M? Compare this with "process scheduling" in CP/M.

20.11 How is process synchronization implemented in MP/M?

20.12 Explain the operation of bank switching in MP/M.

20.13 Discuss the operation of CP/NET.

20.14 Discuss the importance of networking schemes like CP/NET to small businesses.

20.15 Consider a book distributor. The company receives orders for books either by telephone or by mail. The company operates a warehouse in which many best-selling titles are kept in stock. When a request arrives for a book not in stock, the company orders the book from the appropriate publisher. Customers are billed as soon as requested books are shipped. Bills from the publishers are paid when the books arrive at the warehouse. Discuss the ways in which a multiple-computer network running under CP/NET might be useful in such an environment.

20.16 Explain the influence that personal computer networks are likely to have on the development of personal computing.

20.17 Why did Digital Research choose PL/I subset G as the applications language for CP/M-based systems? Why was BASIC rejected? Why was Pascal rejected?

20.18 Which operating systems are likely to be the primary competitors in the 16-bit microcomputer marketplace in the next several years?

20.19 How is the IBM personal computer likely to influence the battle for supremacy among 16-bit microcomputer operating systems?

20.20 What are the advantages of using a logical-to-physical device mapping mechanism in a small system like CP/M? How does CP/M accomplish this mapping?

20.21 A new file is to be created that will eventually occupy about 10K bytes. Explain precisely how and when BDOS allocates space for this file. Include in your explanation how BDOS will use the allocation bit map, the secondary storage File Control Block, and the disk allocation map in the primary storage File Control Block.

LITERATURE

(Ba80) Ballinger, C, "HDOS or CP/M?" *Interface Age,* September 1980, pp. 88–91.

(Bb80) Barbier, K., "CP/M for Single-Drive Systems," *Kilobaud Microcomputing,* September 1980, pp. 94–98.

(Br80) Brigham, B., *CP/M Summary Guide,* Glastonbury, Conn.: The Rosetta Stone, 1980.

(Ep80a) Epstein, J., "An Introduction to CP/M," *S-100 Microsystems,* January–February 1980, pp. 6–10; March–April 1980, pp. 28–33; May–June 1980, pp. 12–17.

(Ep80b) Epstein, J., and C. Terry, "Introduction to CP/M: The CP/M Connection," *S-100 Microsystems,* September–October 1980, pp. 10–32.

(Fe80) Fernandez, J., and R. Ashley, *Using CP/M,* New York: Wiley, 1980.

(Fr79) Frantz, J.J., "Turn-Key CP/M Systems," *Creative Computing,* December 1979, pp. 104–114.

(Fr81) Friedman, H. "Demystifying CP/M," *Computers and Programming,* September–October, 1981, pp. 57–74.

(Fz80) Fritzon, R., "The New CP/M: Is It Worth It?" *Kilobaud Microcomputing,* July 1980, p. 66.

(Ho81) Hogan, T., "Osborne CP/M User Guide," Berkeley, Calif.: Osborne/McGraw-Hill, 1981.

(Ki81) Kildall, G., "CP/M: A Family of 8- and 16-Bit Operating Systems," *Byte,* June 1981, pp. 216–231.

(La81) Larson, J., "The Ins and Outs of CP/M," *Byte Magazine,* June 1981, pp. 268–298.

(Le81) Lettieri, L., "Digital Research and CP/M Move into the Big Time," *Mini-Micro Systems,* November 1981, pp. 228–230.

(Mi78) Miller, A., "CP/M Part 2 — A Macro Assembler and Other Goodies," *Interface Age,* December 1978, pp. 130–135.

(Mi79) Miller, A., "CBASIC: A Business-Oriented Language for CP/M," *Interface Age,* August 1979, pp. 116–119.

(Mi80a) Miller, A., "Diagnostics Package for CP/M," *Interface Age,* October 1980, p. 104.

(Mi80b) Miller, A., "CP/M for the TRS-80 Model II: Lifeboat and FMG Corp. Versions," *Interface Age,* November 1980, pp. 94–98.

(Mk81) Miastkowski, S., "A Close Look at the IBM Personal Computer," *Popular Computing,* December 1981, pp. 52–58.

(No78) North, S., "The CP/M Disk Operating System," *Creative Computing,* November–December 1978, pp. 52–53.

(St78) Stewart, J.F., "CP/M Primer: A Most Sophisticated Operating System," *Kilobaud Microcomputing,* April, 1978, pp. 30–34.

(Te80) Terry, C., "The CP/M Connection," *S-100 Microsystems,* July–August 1980, pp. 32–35.

(Va80) Van Buer, D., "A Table-Driven Assembler on CP/M," *Dr. Dobb's Journal,* February 1980, pp. 18–25.

(Va81) Vaughn, W.R., "Getting Compatible with CP/M," *Mini-Micro Systems,* August 1981, pp. 173–179.

(Wa76a) Warren, J., "First Word on a Floppy Disk Operating System," *Dr. Dobb's Journal,* April, 1976, p. 5.

(Wa76b) Warren, J., "The Time for Floppies Is Just about Now!" *Dr. Dobb's Journal,* August, 1976, p. 5.

(Wi80) Willoughby, S., "Hardcopy Device Driver Programs for CP/M," *Dr. Dobb's Journal,* September 1980, pp. 34–37.

(Wm82) Williams, G., "A Closer Look at the IBM Personal Computer," *Byte,* Vol. 7, No. 1, January 1982, pp. 36–68.

(Za80) Zaks, R., *The CP/M Handbook with MP/M,* Sybex, 1980.

Digital Research Publications

The following manuals are available from Digital Research, Pacific Grove, California 93950.

- *An Introduction to CP/M Features and Facilities*
- *CP/M 2.0 User's Guide*
- *ED: A Context Editor for the CP/M Disk System*
- *CP/M Assembler (ASM)*
- *CP/M Dynamic Debugging Tool (DDT)*
- *CP/M System Alteration Guide (1.4)*
- *CP/M 2.0 Alteration Guide*
- *CP/M Interface Guide (1.4)*
- *CP/M 2.0 Interface Guide*

21
MVS

One large MVS configuration in the United States has seven interconnected processing units in a single room. This configuration has more than 450 direct access devices and services approximately 15,000 terminals in more than 50 locations. The total instruction execution capacity is over 40 million instructions per second.

M.A. Auslander et al. (Au81)

Overall, the philosophy is to attack the availability problem from two complementary directions: to reduce the number of software errors through rigorous testing of running systems, and to reduce the effect of the remaining errors by providing for recovery from them. An interesting footnote to this design is that now a system failure can usually be considered to be the result of two program errors: the first, in the program that started the problem; the second, in the recovery routine that could not protect the system.

A.L. Scherr (Sc73)

In 1956, it was indeed rare that IBM written software took more than a few cycles of the system. Today it is not at all uncommon for IBM provided software to use 90 percent or more of the capacity of the system, with the user written application programs using the remainder.

M.A. Auslander et al. (Au81)

Outline

21.1 HISTORY OF MVS

The MVS (Multiple Virtual Storage) operating system was introduced by IBM in mid-1974 as the successor to MVT (Multiprogramming with a Variable number of Tasks). It is IBM's operating system for its large mainframe computers. MVT was introduced in 1967 and had outgrown its usefulness. It was originally designed for batch processing but already had TSO (Timesharing Option), IMS (Information Management System), HASP (Houston Automatic Spooling Priority system), and ASP (Asymmetric Multiprocessing system) grafted to it to provide more of the functions demanded by the user community. MVT allowed only 15 jobs to run concurrently. OS/SVS (Single Virtual Storage) was introduced in 1972 as an interim operating system to take advantage of the IBM/370 architecture and virtual addressing. Essentially, SVS was MVT with paging. Figure 21.1 traces the evolution of IBM operating systems that led to MVS.

With the introduction of MVS, many of the functions that had been add-ons to MVT became standard. These included TSO, JES (Job Entry Subsystem), multiprocessing (up to 16 processors) and, most importantly, a resource manager. MVS virtual addressing provides each user with a 16-million byte address space. On some models, the address space has been extended to two billion bytes (two gigabytes). It appears that MVS will remain the premier operating system for IBM's large-scale processors, at least through the coming decade, although it will certainly receive strong competition from VM (Chapter 22).

Logically, up to 9999 concurrent tasks may be supported on MVS, but the practical limit is more like 300 to 400 concurrent interactive users, each in its own address space. The number of users that can realistically be logged on to some application in a single address space is between 500 and 700.

MVS is the culmination of 25 years of operating systems development. Figure 21.2 shows the evolution of operating systems functions over this period.

21.2 MVS DESIGN OBJECTIVES

The design objectives of MVS are to provide performance, reliability, availability, and compatibility for the large system environment. MVS provides a more stable environment than did previous systems. The operating system attempts to recover from errors in programming. There are numerous Functional Recovery Routines (FRR) that are given control in the event of an operating system failure. The system attempts to reconstruct control block chains that have been destroyed. It attempts recovery from hardware errors. If a tape drive generates too many interrupts, for example, the system gives the operator an indication of the offending tape drive and the options the operator may take to recover. In a multiprocessor environment, a failing processor does not ordinarily bring the entire system down. The operating system detects that the processor has failed and lets the remaining processors take over the functions previously performed by that processor.

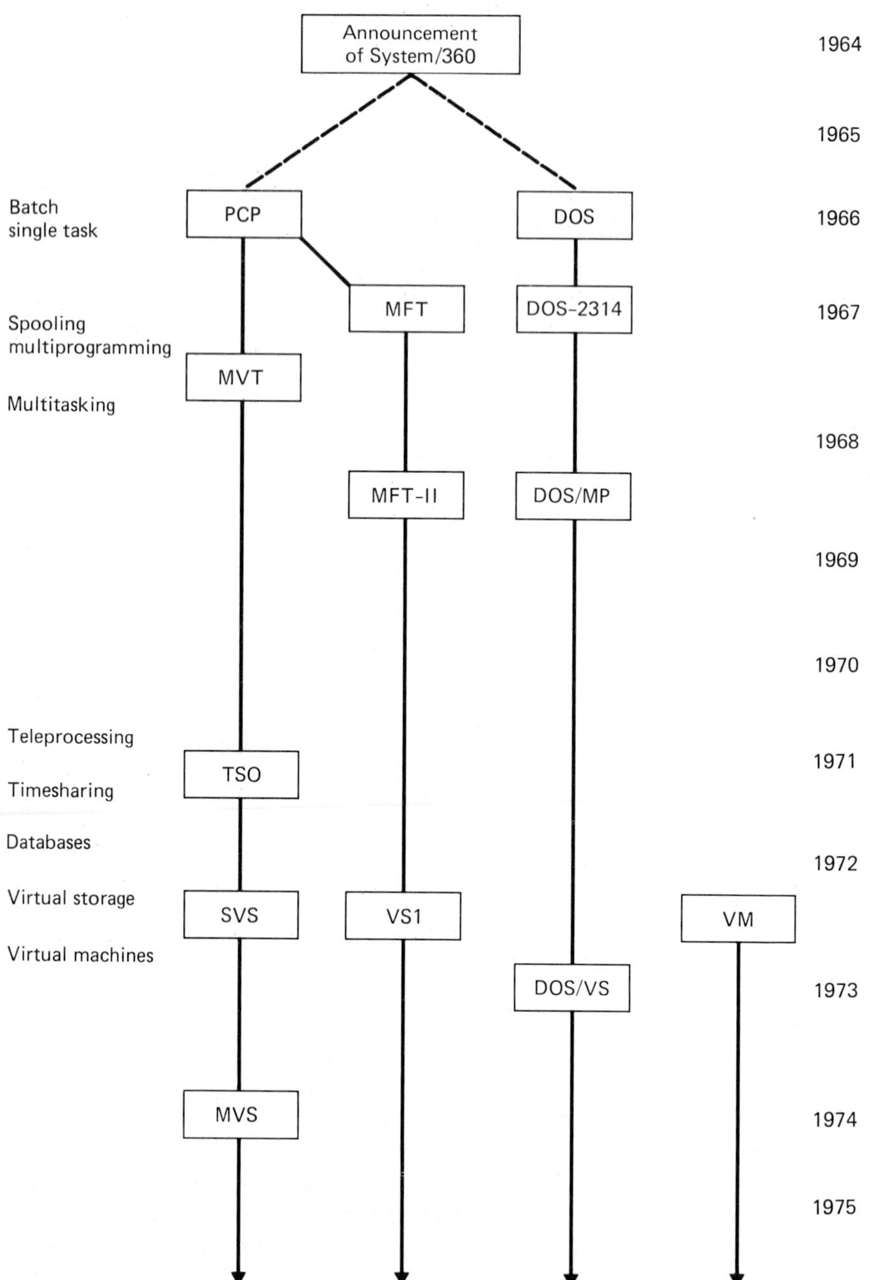

Fig. 21.1 The evolution of OS/360. PCP = primary control program. MFT = multiprogramming with a fixed number of tasks. MVT = multiprogramming with a variable number of tasks. TSO = timesharing option. SVS = single virtual storage. MVS = multiple virtual storage. DOS = disk operating system and VM = virtual machine facility. (Copyright 1981 by International Business Machines Corporation; reprinted with permission.)

The transition from DOS (Disk Operating System) to OS/360 was a painful one for both IBM and its users. Most programs had to be rewritten, files moved, and JCL rewritten before an installation could convert to OS/360. Many installations incurred large costs in this conversion. Many did not convert—IBM still supports DOS and DOS/VSE. It is highly unlikely that IBM will ever force such a dramatic conversion again. It is more likely that it will support current applications in future systems.

21.3 SYSTEM/370 HARDWARE

Before examining the operating system itself, it is important to consider the hardware on which MVS runs.

21.3.1 Virtual Address Translation

The large System/370 models use a virtual address space of 16,777,216 bytes (with 24-bit addressing as in Fig. 21.3). Of this, approximately eight million bytes are for programmer use; the remainder is for the operating system. The real storage addressable by the operating system is up to 32MB on multiprocessors, and 24MB on uniprocessor machines.

Address translation is performed as follows: First the *Translation Lookaside Buffer* (*TLB*) (a special associative storage that helps determine if the segment and page is in primary storage) is checked. If this information is not found in the TLB, the search continues to the segment and page tables maintained in storage. If there is still no hit, a page fault occurs and the Auxiliary Storage Manager (ASM) is called to find the page and bring it into memory. The TLB holds up to 128 translated addresses, and is updated using an LRU algorithm. The segment table points to the page table, the page table indicates the real address of the page frame, and the byte offset is appended to that address for the resulting real address (Fig. 21.4).

There are three address types used in System/370: *absolute, real,* and *virtual.* The differences are in the way the addresses are translated. Virtual addresses are converted to real addresses, and *prefixing* converts real to absolute addresses. Absolute addresses are assigned to real storage addresses, and usually match one for one, but some models of the 370 allow real storage blocks to be assigned to different absolute storage addresses. Absolute addresses are used by processors and channels. A real address identifies a physical location in real storage. A virtual address is an address in virtual storage and may be up to 16MB (with 24-bit addressing). In reality, real and absolute addresses are the same, except when there is more than one processor accessing primary storage. In this case, a special feature called *prefixing* is used. Prefixing assigns real addresses 0 through 4095 to an absolute block of storage. When a processor tries to access that storage, the address is appended to the

Generation	Operations	Extensions of function	
		Hardware functions	Application functions
Pre-operating system (early 1950s) with, e.g., the 701	Manual (e.g., each job step required manual intervention) No multiple-application environment support	Symbolic assembler Linking loader	Subroutine libraries in card tubs, manual retrieval
First generation (late 1950s and early 1960s) with, e.g., FMS, IBSYS on the IBM 704, 709, and 7094	Automatic job batching Manual device allocation, setup, work-load scheduling No multiple-application environment support Off-line peripheral operations	Higher-level languages—FORTRAN, COBOL Primitive data access services with error recovery	Subroutine libraries on tape, automatic retrieval Primitive program overlay support
Second generation (late 1960s) with, e.g., OS/360 on System/360	Multiprogramming Primitive work-load management Primitive tuning (device, core allocation) Spooling, remote job entry	More higher-level languages—PL/I, ALGOL, APL, BASIC Device independence in data access First random access data organizations	DASD subroutine libraries Full facilities for programmed overlays Interactive program development support

	Operator begins to be driven by the system Primitive application protection Initial multiprocessing (loosely and tightly coupled)	Primitive software error recovery, full hardware ERP's Array of hardware function extensions Supervisor call routines	Primitive automatic debugging aids First application subsystems Checkpoint/restart
Third generation with, e.g., MVS OS/VS on System/370	Integrated multiprocessing (loosely and tightly coupled) Work-load management extensions More self-tuning, integrated measurement facilities Less operator decision making, fewer manual operations Full interapplication protection, data and program authorization Primitive storage hierarchies for data	Virtual storage Device independence extended Hardware error recovery extended to CPU, channels Operating system functions begin to migrate to hardware	Growing libraries Overlay techniques obsoleted by virtual storage Symbolic debugging aids Primitive data independence Integration of application subsystems Software error recovery for system and applications

Fig. 21.2 Capabilities of MVS and its predecessors. (Copyright 1981 by International Business Machines Corporation; reprinted with permission.)

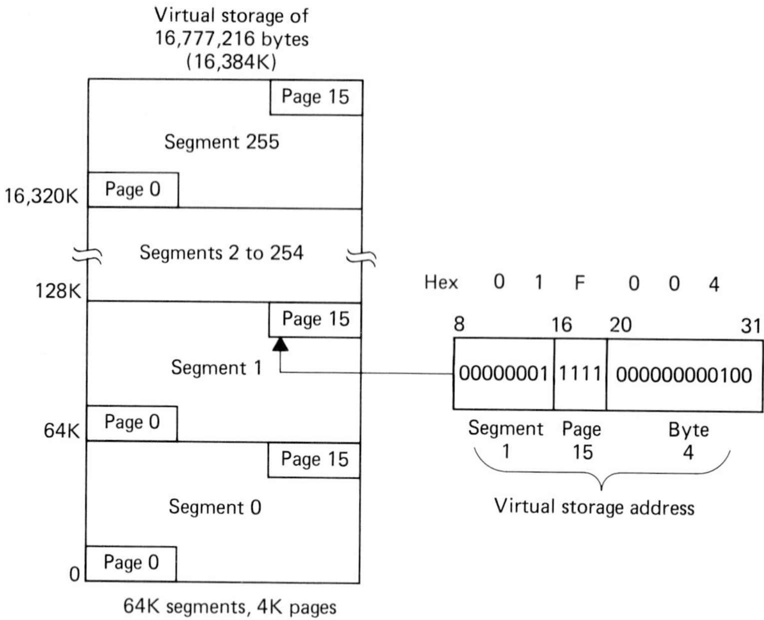

Fig. 21.3 Virtual storage addressing with 16MB address space. (Courtesy of International Business Machines Corporation.)

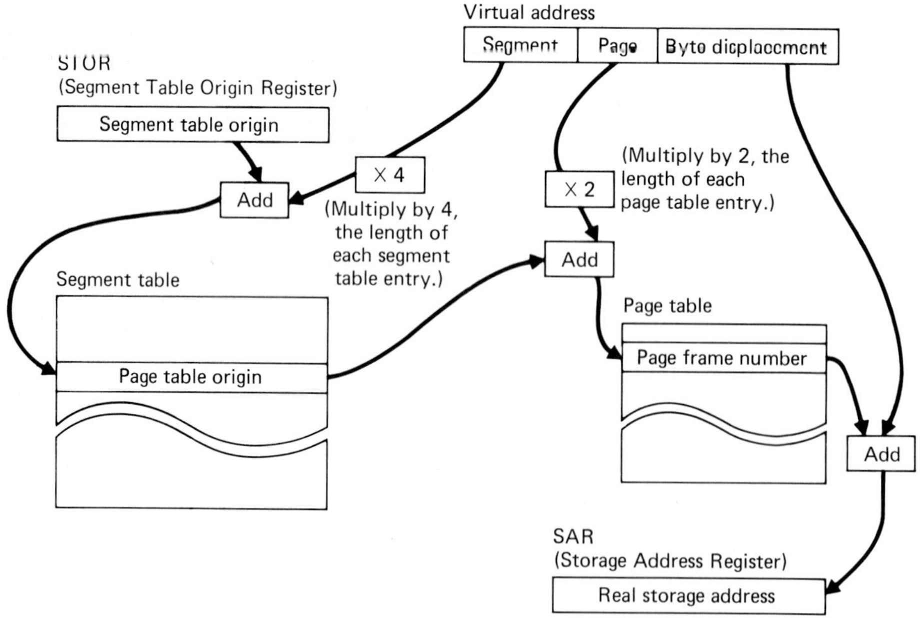

Fig. 21.4 Dynamic address translation. (Courtesy of International Business Machines Corporation.)

prefix that is stored in a control register so that it will access the correct storage area. Each processor has an area called the PSA (Prefixed Storage Area) to hold addresses that the two processors cannot share, such as old and new Program Status Words for the various interrupt types.

21.3.2 Storage Protection

There are three types of storage protection provided by System/370: *key, segment,* and *low-address.* There are 16 keys provided and they are set by the hardware. In key protection, a store operation is permitted only if the access key matches the request for a storage key. A fetch is permitted if the fetch bit is zero and the keys match. Segment protection controls storing in a segment by a bit in the segment table entry being on or off. Low-address storage protection protects bytes 0–511, and is under control of one of the system control registers.

21.3.3 Interrupt Scheme

When an interrupt occurs, the PSW (Program Status Word) is stored as the old PSW, the information needed to decode the interruption is saved, a new PSW is loaded, and processing continues at the location indicated in the new PSW. This new location is the address of the appropriate interrupt handler for the interruption that has just occurred. The unit of work that was executing may or may not have control returned to it after the interrupt handler is complete. If it is a *nonpreemptive unit,* it will be redispatched. Otherwise, the dispatcher will be called to schedule the highest-priority service request or task that is ready to run. (See Chapter 3.)

21.4 MVS FUNCTIONS

MVS is a large operating system, and as such provides many functions to an installation, including

- *Supervisor*—Provides the controls needed for multiprogramming. It creates dispatchable units of work, handles dispatching, and serializes the use of resources (i.e., provides mutual exclusion capabilities).
- Master Scheduler—Is responsible for starting the system and communicating with the operator.
- Job Entry Subsystem—Allows work to be entered into the system and printed output to be returned to the user.
- System Management Facility—Collects information to account for system use, to analyze system performance, and to charge users for system resources.
- System Activity Measurement Facility—Records system events for later reporting.
- Timesharing Option (TSO)—Provides users with interactive editing, testing, and debugging capabilities.

- Data Management—Handles all I/O and file management activity.
- Telecommunications—Provide access to MVS by remote terminal users.
- System Support Programs—Provide linkage editing, loading, and other support functions.
- Utility Programs—Provide utility functions such as copying files and performing catalog updates.
- Service Aids—Provide dump formatting, tracing, and other functions useful to the systems programmer.

MVS requires 2MB of storage for a minimum system. A more realistic system occupies 6MB in support of both TSO and batch processing, and optionally a database system.

21.5 SUPERVISOR

The Supervisor makes the decisions regarding the use of resources through its many subfunctions. These include the Real Storage Manager, Virtual Storage Manager, Resource Manager, and Auxiliary Storage Manager. It also contains the logic to drive a multiprocessing system.

21.6 MASTER SCHEDULER

The Master Scheduler is responsible for initializing the system and responding to commands issued by the system operator. It does this by reading system initialization parameters at IPL (Initial Program Load, or startup) time to set up the environment in which MVS functions. These might include the page data set names, the master catalog name, the names of all volumes to be mounted, a list of program libraries available to all users, and defaults for system storage areas. The *Communication Task* reads commands from the system operator, issues those commands to the appropriate subtasks in the system for execution, and returns responses to the operator. If the Communication Task should *abend (abnormal end)*, the operator loses communication with the system, and the system will most likely have to be restarted.

21.7 JOB ENTRY SUBSYSTEM

The Job Entry Subsystem receives jobs to process and prints and/or punches job outputs. There are two Job Entry Subsystems, JES2 and JES3. They are the descendants of the spooling systems HASP and ASP, respectively. Basically, both JES2 and JES3 provide the same functions, with JES3 additionally providing job scheduling based on the job's requirements (i.e., tapes, disks) and installation scheduling requirements.

JES processing proceeds as follows (Fig. 21.5). Jobs are entered into the system through card readers, from timesharing terminals, or they can be generated by a

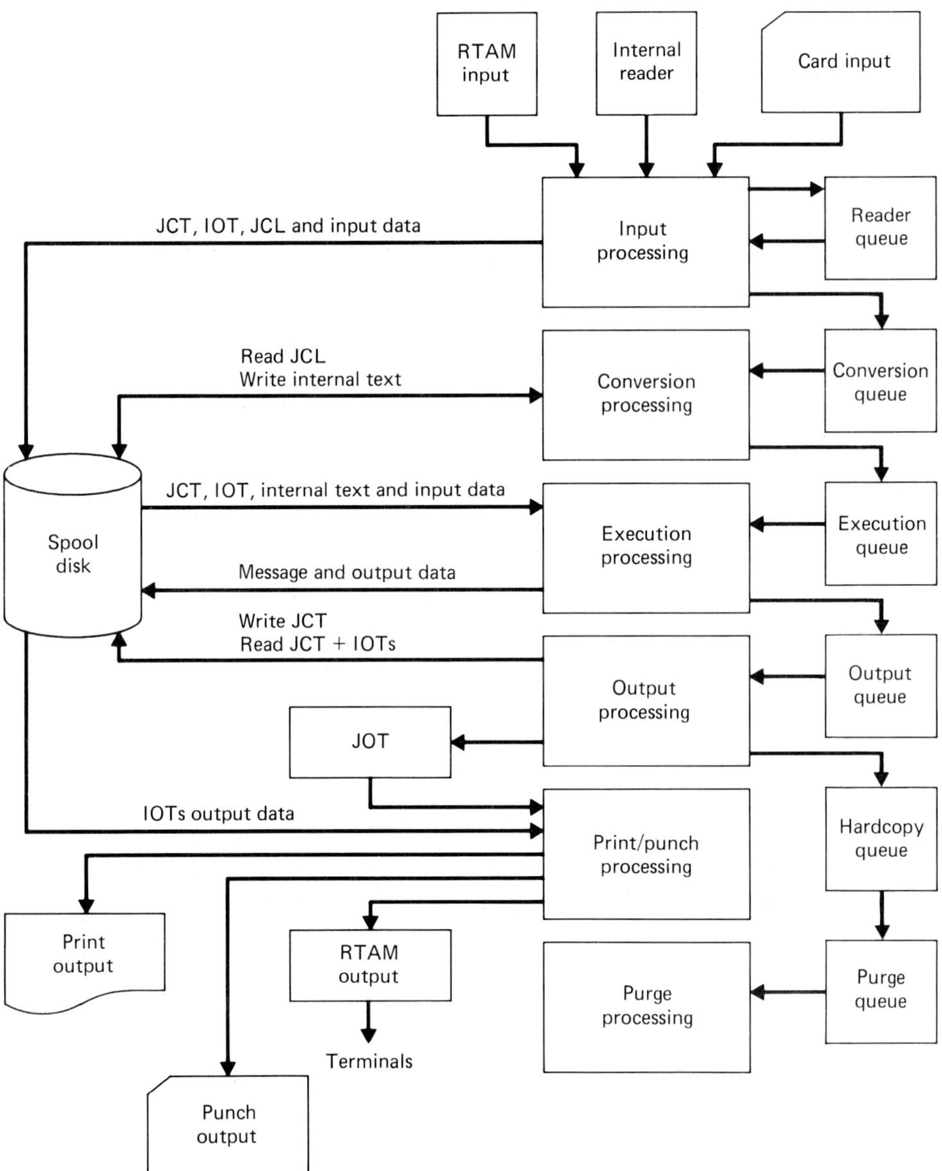

Fig. 21.5 JES processing. (Courtesy of International Business Machines Corporation.)

program and passed to the system. All jobs are scanned for correctness, and then are placed on an appropriate queue. JES provides a means for the installation to schedule work in some orderly fashion based on a class priority structure. The *Converter* converts the job control language statements to an internal form readable by MVS. Other checking also takes place at this point. Errors cause the job to be flushed from the system with appropriate messages to the user.

Next, jobs are sent to MVS for execution, once again based on class and priority. JES then relinquishes control over the job, except for printed output trapped by JES and placed on a spooling disk. At job end, MVS notifies JES of the completion. The job moves to the next JES operation—the output step. Outputs are printed or punched, and the job is purged from the system. Any spool space used by the job is made available for reuse.

A JES3 installation may provide *deadline scheduling,* i.e., the time of day by which a given job should be selected to run may be specified.

Both JES2 and JES3 offer *priority aging.* The longer a job waits to run, the higher the system automatically raises its priority.

21.8 SYSTEM MANAGEMENT FACILITY AND SYSTEM ACTIVITY MEASUREMENT FACILITY

The System Management Facility and the System Activity Measurement Facility (SMF and MF/1) are the means by which the system gathers performance statistics. SMF records important information about every task in the system. This information includes elapsed processor time, number of I/Os completed, files used, lines printed, and working set size. An installation can use this information to bill users for resources, determine average turnaround time, etc. MF/1 records vital statistics about the operating system, such as paging activity, processor activity, and device activity. With this information, the performance analyst can determine how to set performance objectives, and can locate bottlenecks.

21.9 TIMESHARING OPTION

With the TSO facility, users have immediate access to the computer, possibly from remote locations. Users can edit files, and compile and test programs. Once a program has been compiled without errors, it may be executed interactively and debugged. TSO can also be used to view output from a batch job, and to submit work to the system.

21.10 DATA MANAGEMENT

Data Management controls accessing of *data sets* (files) on I/O devices. This includes buffering, scheduling I/O, and performing the I/O. MVS supports many file organizations and access methods. There are several file organizations available.

- *Sequential*—One record follows another, records are stored and retrieved according to their physical order.
- *Indexed Sequential*—Records are logically ordered according to a key, indices are maintained to facilitate retrieval by key.
- *Direct-random access*—The user must provide an address to access a record on a direct access device; the records may be organized in any manner that meets the user's needs.
- *Partitioned*—Multiple subfiles are contained in one file, with a directory to locate each subfile. A data set consists of *members*. Each member is an independent sequential subfile. Partitioned data sets are used to store libraries of programs, macros, etc.

Programs may use either *queued access techniques* or *basic access techniques* to access the records in a data set. With queued access techniques, programs transfer data with GET and PUT macro instructions. Sequential access is assumed. Records are grouped automatically in anticipation of future I/O requests. Control is not returned to the program issuing the I/O request until the operation has completed.

With basic access techniques programs transfer data with READ and WRITE macro instructions. Any record may be accessed at any time. No anticipation of future requests occurs. Control is returned to the program before the I/O operation completes. The program must explicitly test for completion.

These file organizations are accessed by one or more of the following *access methods*.

- BDAM (Basic Direct Access Method)—Records are stored and retrieved by their addresses on direct access volumes.
- BSAM (Basic Sequential Access Method)—This method is used for sequential or partitioned files. Records are sequentially organized and stored and retrieved in physical blocks.
- BPAM (Basic Partitioned Access Method)—This is used for the partitioned file to update the directory (the manipulation of the data is done by BSAM or QSAM).
- QSAM (Queued Sequential Access Method)—This is used for sequential or partitioned files, uses queueing. Performs logical, buffered record operations.
- ISAM (Indexed Sequential Access Method)—This method is used only for indexed sequential files. Access can be either sequential (QISAM) or direct (BISAM).
- VSAM (Virtual Storage Access Method)—A method used only for virtual storage files.

The first four access methods were developed for the early operating systems (MFT and MVT) and carried over to MVS for compatibility reasons. VSAM is entirely new for the virtual storage systems. VSAM is the only access method available on most of IBM's operating systems designed for System/370. By committing to VSAM, the smaller user may make operating system upgrades without major reprogramming changes. VSAM will be discussed in greater detail shortly.

Telecommunications enables an operating system to communicate with users in remote areas. The following are the telecommunication access methods available in MVS.

- BTAM (Basic Telecommunication Access Method)—This method provides basic support for telecommunications applications. It uses READ and WRITE macros.
- TCAM (Telecommunication Access Method)—This method is used almost exclusively by TSO. It is a queued access method, and provides an interface for user-written applications. It allows each application to control its own error checking, message routing, and message editing.
- VTAM (Virtual Telecommunication Access Method)—This is IBM's SNA (System Network Architecture) in working form, at least the host processor portion. Data transfers may occur in either *record mode* via SEND and RECEIVE macros or *basic mode* via READ and WRITE macros. VTAM moves functions that used to be performed on the host processor to the communications controller. Polling terminals for work, for example, must be performed frequently to ensure reasonable response times. Polling takes large amounts of processor time. By allowing the controller to do the polling, more work can be accomplished by the processor. VTAM also uses logical addresses for terminals. This is important for large networks. A channel can have a maximum of 256 devices attached to it. With VTAM, the only address required (other than local terminals) is the address of the communications controller itself.

Figure 21.6 shows the major steps involved in servicing an input/output request. The user program is responsible for defining the operation to be performed. The system performs the operation, handles the completion interrupt, and posts the status of the completed operation.

The virtual storage access method (VSAM) was especially designed to provide high performance access in virtual storage systems. It can process three different types of data sets.

- *Key-sequenced data set*—Each record has a key. Records are loaded in key sequence. New records are inserted in key sequence.
- *Entry-sequenced data set*—Records are loaded into the data set sequentially as they are entered. New records are appended to the end of the data set. When VSAM stores a record in an entry-sequenced data set it returns the *relative byte address* of the record to the user. The user program may optionally create its own index to the file to allow direct access to the records.

User program	Access method	System components
1. Describes data set.		
2. Issues OPEN macro to prepare data set.		
3. Issues I/O request to call the access method.		
	4. Builds control blocks and channel program to describe request.	
	5. Issues EXCP macro to invoke the system components.	
		6. Builds control blocks, fixes pages and translates channel program, schedules or starts operation with an SIO instruction, and returns to the requester.
	7. Waits for operation to complete. (User program waits for completion if using basic access technique.)	
		8. Handles I/O interruption that signals completion of the operation, analyzes and posts the status of the operation, and returns to the dispatcher.
9. Continues processing when I/O operation is complete.		
10. Issues CLOSE macro when all operations on a data set are complete.		

Fig. 21.6 Major steps in processing an input/output operation. (Courtesy of International Business Machines Corporation.)

- *Relative record data sets*—Records are loaded according to a relative record number. If VSAM assigns the relative record number, new records are appended at the end of the data set. If the user program handles the relative record numbering, then new records can be added in relative record sequence.

Records in a relative record data set occupy fixed-length slots. The slots are numbered sequentially from 1 to the number of records in the data set. Storing and retrieving of records is performed by slot number. Records may be accessed either sequentially or directly, but only by relative record number. Direct access to relative record data sets is much faster than direct access to key-sequenced data sets.

VSAM allows the construction of an *alternate index* for either a key-sequenced or an entry-sequenced data set. Alternate indices are used to provide mutiple ways of accessing a single data set, thus eliminating the need for keeping several copies of the same data set for different applications.

21.11 REAL STORAGE MANAGER

The *Real Storage Manager (RSM)* administers the use of real storage and is also responsible for causing pages to be moved to or from the paging device. It receives guidance from the System Resources Manager. Only currently used pages are kept in real storage—the rest are on direct access devices and are under the control of the Auxiliary Storage Manager (ASM). The RSM calls the ASM to move pages to and from storage. The RSM assigns free page frames from a pool, and translates addresses. It also maintains the pool by swapping, reclaiming page frames from terminated jobs, or reclaiming frames freed by a user. The RSM determines working set size for swapping functions. It also allows jobs to run in real storage if necessary. The RSM has service routines for use by the system. These include page fault processing, virtual I/O, and placing real storage off and online.

21.12 AUXILIARY STORAGE MANAGER

The *Auxiliary Storage Manager (ASM)* is responsible for transferring pages between real storage and direct access devices. This movement can occur a page at a time (called a *paging operation*) or a task at a time (called a *swapping operation*).

The Auxiliary Storage Manager maintains the *page data sets.* The page data sets contain virtual pages not currently occupying a real storage frame. Swap data sets contain the pages of swapped out tasks.

The ASM manages the *external page table.* When a page-in is to occur, the RSM locates a free page frame, and the ASM examines the external page table to locate the required page on secondary storage. When a page-out is to occur, the ASM locates a free *page slot* on secondary storage, transfers the page from real storage to secondary storage, and makes appropriate entries in the external page table.

21.13 VIRTUAL STORAGE MANAGER

The *Virtual Storage Manager (VSM)* is responsible for controlling the use of virtual storage being used by a task. Each task is placed in an entity called an *address space* that is created by the VSM during the initialization of the control blocks for the task. The virtual storage within the address space is controlled by the VSM. It is the responsibility of the VSM to satisfy requests for storage if it is available, and to free space when requested. It does this by checking the control blocks in the address space to see if virtual storage is available and, if it is, makes the appropriate entries in the control blocks. The Virtual Storage Manager calls RSM to satisfy requests for real storage.

21.14 SYSTEM RESOURCES MANAGER

The *System Resources Manager (SRM)* determines which task of all the active tasks will be given access to system resources, and at what rate the task will be allowed to consume these resources. The SRM bases its decisions primarily on two objectives: distributing resources in accordance with installation requirements for response and turnaround (i.e., the *Installation Performance Specification* or *IPS*), and optimizing system resource use. The installation tells the SRM what its requirements are through initialization parameters read at system startup time. The SRM balances resource utilization by scheduling more work, or by swapping work out (by a recommendation to the RSM). For instance, if a task is using too much processor time, it can be swapped out to allow other tasks better access to the processor. This can also happen to a task that is overutilizing storage or a channel. The SRM tries to balance channel and device utilization by spreading out requests for their use. It maintains *use counts* on devices—the device with the lowest use count will be allocated. The SRM resolves page frame shortages by swapping a task out of main storage and stopping the initiation of new tasks. The SRM also *steals pages* from tasks to satisfy requests for storage. A page that has not been used for the longest period of time is stolen. Pages will be stolen from all address spaces until the request is satisfied. Page stealing is done on demand only. The SRM makes the following types of decisions.

- Which address spaces (tasks) should be swapped in so that they may compete for the system's resources?
- Which pages should be stolen and at what times?
- When should the dispatching priority of a task be adjusted?
- Which devices should be allocated?
- When should the creation of new tasks be suppressed?

The SRM comprises

- The SRM Control that determines what processing should be performed by the SRM and routes control to the appropriate SRM routines.
- The Work-load Manager that monitors each task's use of resources. Makes recommendations to SRM Control to help keep each task's resource consumption within the range specified in the IPS.
- The Resource Manager that monitors systemwide use of each resource to determine if resources are underutilized or overutilized. It makes recommendations to SRM Control to optimize throughput.

The Work-load Manager measures resource usage rates by tasks in *service units* per second. Service units are computed by considering processor time used, I/O activity, and real storage frames occupied. The *service rate* is then service units per unit time. The Resource Manager has four major components.

- Storage management—This deals with page stealing and preventing the creation of new address spaces.
- I/O management—Concerned with swapping and device allocation.
- Processor management—Concerned with swapping and adjusting dispatching priorities.
- Resource monitoring—Concerned with determining optimal multiprogramming levels.

21.15 STORAGE ORGANIZATION

Once MVS has been initialized, all tasks have the same view of storage (Fig. 21.7). Storage contains operating system code, system control blocks, common storage areas, task control blocks, and application code. The following paragraphs supply a breakdown of those areas and their major functions.

The Nucleus area contains some of the most important control blocks for the system. These include the Communication Vector Table (CVT) that contains the address of the current task, the entry addresses of all important routines in the Nucleus, and pointers to other important control blocks. Much of the operating system itself is in the Nucleus area, especially the important and most frequently executed SVC handlers.

Above the Nucleus area is the Fixed Link Pack Area (FLPA), which contains all of the modules that normally would be in the Link Pack Area but must run fixed or nonpageable. Modules that significantly improve system performance when fixed rather than paged should be in the FLPA.

Next is the user area that contains the program area, Scheduler Work Area (SWA) and Local System Queue Area (LSQA). The SWA holds all the job-related control blocks. The LSQA contains the necessary control blocks to run the task, such as the page and segment tables, and the Task Control Block (TCB).

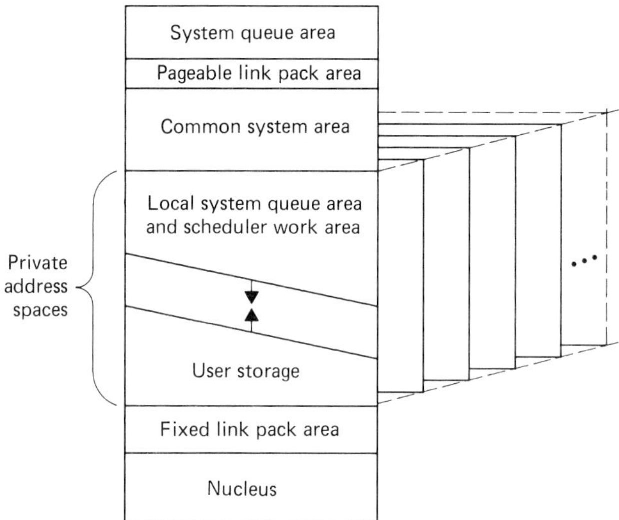

Fig. 21.7 MVS storage map. (Courtesy of International Business Machines Corporation.)

The Common System Area (CSA) is where data needed by all tasks is kept. It is the only area accessible by every task in the system. It is used for passing data between tasks not executing in the same address space.

The System Queue Area (SQA) contains the queues and tables that are needed by the system. This area is fixed and cannot be paged. It contains the page tables that define the system area and the common area.

The Pageable Link Pack Area (PLPA) is where all common system routines reside, as well as some SVC handlers. All of the code in the PLPA is reeentrant—there is no need to page it out should the storage be needed by some other routine. This helps reduce response times in a storage-constrained system. Most installations have special lists of the most frequently used routines to be kept together to reduce paging in the PLPA area. All routines are shareable by any task in the system. The search for modules starts in the FLPA, then goes to the PLPA unless directed otherwise by the user. With large amounts of sharing, the amount of real storage used by all tasks is reduced. A favorite trick of many installations is to place all of the TSO routines into the PLPA to further reduce real storage usage.

21.16 RESOURCE CONTROL

Resource Control is an important consideration in MVS, especially with the multiprocessor feature in effect. In MVT the Enqueue primitive is used to protect a resource from simultaneous use by several tasks. This is essentially a software technique. Enqueue will be discussed shortly.

21.17 LOCKING

There is a *hierarchy of locks* for various resources in the system to prevent simultaneous updating. This is a problem in a multiprocessor in which two tasks—even two subtasks of the same task—can be executing at the same time. The locks in the hierarchy are shown in Fig. 21.8. A task can hold locks while requesting higher locks in the hierarchy, but cannot request a lock lower than it currently holds—this prevents deadlock as per Havender's Standard Allocation Pattern. A *global lock* affects the entire system; a *local lock* affects only a single address space. There are two types of locks: *spin* and *suspend.* If a processor tests a spin lock and finds it unavailable, the unit of work requesting the lock is delayed until the lock is available; it repeatedly tests the lock until the lock is released by the other processor. The requesting processor then obtains the lock and control of the associated resource. If a suspend lock is unavailable, the requesting processor is dispatched to another unit of work.

Class of lock	Name of lock*	Resource protected	Type of lock
Global	DISP	Dispatcher control blocks	Spin
	ASM	ASM control blocks	
	SALLOC	RSM and VSM routines	
	IOSYNCH	Global IOS functions	
	IOSCAT	Channel availability table	
	IOSUCB	Unit control blocks	
	IOSLCH	Logical channel queues	
	TPNCB	VTAM node control blocks	
	TPDNCB	VTAM destination node control blocks	
	TPACBDEB	VTAM data extent blocks	
	SRM	SRM algorithms and control blocks	
	CMS	Cross memory services	Suspend
	CMSEQDQ	Cross memory services (ENQ/DEQ)	
	CMSSMF	Cross memory services (SMF)	
Local	LOCAL	Address space storage and control blocks	

*Locks are listed in hierarchical order, from highest to lowest.

Fig. 21.8 Hierarchy of MVS system locks. (Courtesy of International Business Machines Corporation.)

21.18 ENQUEUE

Another method used to force serialization on a resource is the *Enqueue.* It allows a program to request a resource, and while the program holds that resource it is *uninterruptible,* i.e., other tasks requiring the same resource will be nondispatchable. This can lead to deadlock if the running task requests a service from a nondispatchable task.

21.19 RESERVE

Reserve is similar to Enqueue but it is used exclusively with shared disks (more than one system sharing the same disk). Reserve turns on a hardware lock against the entire volume so that no other processor may access it. On the processor that issued a Reserve, an Enqueue is actually set. Again this may cause deadlock. If two processors reserve two separate volumes and then each requests the volume the other has reserved, both will wait until one of the tasks is cancelled.

21.20 TASKS AND SERVICE REQUESTS

There are two *units of dispatchable work* in MVS, the *service request* and the *task.* The service request is a unit of work designed especially for MVS. It helps to increase parallelism on multiprocessors, and reduces startup overhead for small units of work. A program with independent units of work benefits greatly from this design. A service request is a smaller unit of work than a task, and it is dispatched with a higher priority. The unit can be dispatched to any address space—consequently it is used for communication between tasks. An example of the use of a service request is in the I/O interrupt handler; when enough information is gathered, it schedules a service request that then frees the I/O interrrupt handler to service new interrupts. This increases channel and device utilization.

The other unit of work is the task. Creating a task involves considerable overhead, and this was the primary reason for the creation of service requests. In actuality, all tasks are subtasks of the Master Scheduler and are attached through various control block structures. A batch job is attached by the *Initiator,* the task that starts the job. The *Region Control Task* is the mother task of the Initiator as well as the dump task and the batch task. An application can have as many subtasks as it desires. The application can raise or lower its subtask's dispatching priorities within the address space. Subtasks are good for an application if they are independent of the mother task because they can be executing while the mother task is in a wait state. On a multiprocessor, several tasks may be executing simultaneously.

21.21 DISPATCHER

The *Dispatcher* is part of the supervisor and is responsible for keeping the processors busy with the highest-priority work units available. The dispatching queues are constructed by the SRM based on the installation's requirements for response to various types of work. The dispatcher gives priority to special exits such as *vary processor* (change the status of a processor to available or not available), or *processor recovery* (take a processor logically away from the system or try to recover from a transient processor malfunction). After the special exits, the dispatcher gives priority to the *global service requests*, then the *local service requests*, and then the highest-priority task.

21.22 MULTIPROCESSING

Multiprocessing can help an installation improve throughput, reliability, availability, and serviceability. The multiprocessor (MP) or attached processor (AP—an AP has no channels) is essentially the attachment of more storage and processors to the existing configuration. With multiple processors, MVS can dispatch work to each for simultaneous processing. Several tasks can be active concurrently, or one task can have several subtasks executing simultaneously. There is still only one operating system. Throughput ordinarily increases by a factor of approximately 1.8 to 1.9 on a two processor system.

The processors communicate with one another by using the *signal processor (SIGP)* command to *shoulder tap* a processor (inform the processor it must perform some action). The responding processor decodes the SIGP and performs the indicated operation.

Naturally there is the possibility of several programs updating the same word of storage, so two instructions have been provided to prevent this from occurring—the *Compare and Swap* and the *Compare Double and Swap*. Basically, they allow a programmer to ensure that a field being updated will not be updated concurrently by some other program. They accomplish this by serializing that word (or double word) in storage. Once the instruction is begun and the word fetched, it cannot be changed by the other CPU until the instruction is finished. To use the instruction correctly, a program saves the value to be changed in a register, then issues the Compare and Swap. If the save value and the location to be changed are equal, the storage location is updated. In the event that the save value and the storage location are unequal, the storage location is loaded to the save register and the location is not changed. The register is loaded so a loop may be performed to try the change again. The various orders possible with the SIGP instruction are summarized in Fig. 21.9.

Processor communications occur when

- performing system initialization
- dispatching units of work

Hex code	Order	Explanation
01	Sense	The addressed CPU presents its status to the issuing CPU.
02	External call	An "external call" external interruption condition is generated at the addressed CPU.
03	Emergency signal	An "emergency-signal" external interruption condition is generated at the addressed CPU.
04	Start	The addressed CPU is placed in the operating state.
05	Stop	The addressed CPU performs the stop function.
06	Restart	The addressed CPU performs the restart function.
07	Initial program reset	The addressed CPU performs the initial program reset.
08	Program reset	The addressed CPU performs program reset.
09	Stop and store status	The addressed CPU performs the stop function, followed by the store–status function.
0A	Initial microprogram load	The addressed CPU performs the initial program reset and then initiates the initial microprogram load function (same as that performed in manual initial microprogram loading).
0B	Initial CPU reset	The addressed CPU performs the initial CPU reset.
0C	CPU reset	The addressed CPU performs the CPU reset.

Fig. 21.9 SIGP (Signal Processor) orders. (Courtesy of International Business Machines Corporation.)

- starting I/O operations
- stopping and restarting processors during reconfiguration
- attempting alternate CPU recovery

During system initialization in a tightly coupled multiprocessor, MVS can determine if a processor is online by issuing a SIGP sense. If it is online, MVS can start the processor with a SIGP start (which has the same effect as if an operator pressed START on that processor's console).

When one processor is idle and enters the wait state, another processor may shoulder tap the idle processor to inform it that more work has arrived.

Shoulder tapping is also useful when one processor is running a process that needs to initiate I/O on a device attached to a different processor. One processor can issue a SIGP external call to ask another processor to perform the I/O.

During system reconfiguration one processor may issue a SIGP stop to force the other into the stopped state. The stopped processor may be restarted by the other process issuing a SIGP restart. These SIGPs have the same effect as if an operator pressed the STOP and then RESTART keys on the target processor's console.

Interprocessor communication is particularly important in recovery operations. One processor can force another to perform an operation immediately by issuing a SIGP emergency-alert. A failing processor can issue this instruction to force another processor to initiate alternate CPU recovery activity. The operative processor might issue a SIGP program-reset to reset pending I/O operations on the failing processor. The operative processor can also issue the SIGP stop-and-store-status to record the status of the failing processor.

21.23 PERFORMANCE

Wasted, unused, or hidden capacity can lead an installation to acquire more capacity needlessly. Realistically, not all jobs, timesharing users, and system tasks can be given the same share of the computing resource. Users demand good response, at least within the bounds of the system. For instance, a TSO user should get good response from a trivial transaction but, on the other hand, if the user is doing a job interactively that would be better off in batch, the transaction should receive the same performance as a batch job. Response to the interactive user is usually the fastest in the system (other than the response to the operating system itself), at least for trivial transactions. MVS can ensure through the SRM that response will be good for this type of transaction by giving the user priority in the dispatching queue. But as a TSO user absorbs more than its share of resources, the SRM lowers the user's priority and gives it fewer resources and slower responses. The SRM can completely control the resource that any particular user can absorb. It can even delay responses so that a user will not get used to the fast response of a lightly loaded system. This ensures consistent response times.

21.24 MONITORING SYSTEM ACTIVITY

MVS provides several mechanisms for monitoring the work units in the system. These mechanisms facilitate debugging, provide useful information for evaluating system performance, and record resource usage. We have already discussed several of MVS's monitoring facilities. In this section we consider more of them.

MVS provides comprehensive dumping facilities to provide snapshots of the system's virtual storage locations. A SNAP dump is a snapshot of virtual storage requested directly by a running process.

An ABEND dump is requested by a process that wants to terminate processing because of an unrecoverable error it has encountered.

SVC dumps are the system program's equivalent of user SNAP dumps. Both of these types of dumps return control directly to the source that initiated the dump.

A stand-alone dump is initiated by the system operator when MVS fails. It dumps all of real storage and portions of virtual storage.

MVS provides many facilities for tracing system events. These include *System Trace, Master Trace,* and the *Generalized Trace Facility.* Each of these captures system events by the use of *hooks.* A hook is a sequence of instructions that signals an event to the tracing mechanism, captures event-related data, and makes this data available to the tracing mechanism.

System Trace records external interruptions, start I/Os, I/O completion interrupts, program interrupts, SVC interrupts, and dispatching events.

The Generalized Trace Facility (GTF) traces all of the events normally handled by System Trace, plus many other types of events. It may trace in either *internal mode,* in which it builds trace records in virtual storage, or *external mode,* in which trace records are also written to tape or disk.

Master Trace is used to monitor console traffic and other external system activity such as volume mounting requests and confirmations, status displays, operator requests, and the system responses to these requests. This information is often helpful in debugging system failures, particularly those involving I/O devices.

Dumps present the contents of virtual storage when an error has occurred. Traces supply a chronology of system events. MVS associates these two diagnostic capabilities in its SLIP (Serviceability Level Indication Processing) mechanism. SLIP relates a particular diagnostic action like dumping or tracing with a specific event such as a program interruption or storage reference. In SLIP terminology the specification of a system event to be intercepted and the action that is to be taken when the event occurs is called a *trap.* When a trap is *enabled,* the specified action is indeed taken if the event occurs. If a trap is *disabled,* then the system does not even check for the occurrence of the event. Traps may be enabled and disabled in response to changing system conditions.

In addition to all of the monitoring capabilities discussed so far, MVS provides error recording. It creates a complete system history (from initialization to shutdown) of hardware failures, system software errors, and certain system events. This history is written to the permanently resident logging data set.

21.25 CONCLUSIONS

MVS is a large and complex operating system. Since the earliest releases of MVS, IBM has been issuing improvements to the operating system, usually for performance and reliability purposes. Most of the improvements have been in the form of path reductions for functions performed frequently, movement of high-frequency code into firmware, and improved processing algorithms.

Installations have difficulty keeping up with the new releases of MVS. Finding good systems programmers and operators trained in MVS is very difficult. The *Hydra* concept may help to alleviate this problem. The Hydra machine is a processor located in a remote location that is run by an operator at a central site. The operator can run the remote processor just like a machine at the central site. Many remote processors can be run from a single console at one central site.

Because of the shortage of skilled people and the complexity of the operating system, it is likely that the multiple virtual storage operating system will move into firmware. The systems programmer will use *exit points* to make modifications to the system. Exit points are now the approved way to make modifications to JES2. It is apparent that IBM has discarded revolutionary advances (1401 to 360, DOS to OS), in favor of an evolutionary approach.

There will always be a need for large efficient batch processing. MVS will certainly have its place as the operating system for IBM's large processors for many years to come. There is some possibility that IBM might merge MVS and VM. In all likelihood the two operating systems will continue to exist as separate entities because installations would be unwilling to convert from one to the other. VM is an excellent vehicle for testing a new release of an operating system or for conversion to a different operating system because both the old and the new systems can be run concurrently. MVS allows maximum throughput while both interactive and batch processing tasks co-exist. The next chapter examines VM in depth.

SUMMARY

MVS is IBM's top-of-the-line operating system for its large mainframe computers. It evolved from OS/360, first announced in 1964. It is the virtual storage successor to IBM's MVT real storage variable partition multiprogramming system. MVS was designed to provide performance, reliability, availability, and compatibility for the large system environment.

MVS runs on IBM and IBM-compatible computers with virtual addressing. Models with 24-bit addressing use a 16,777,216-byte virtual address space. With 31-bit addressing, the virtual address space is extended to two gigabytes.

Absolute, real, and virtual address are used. Virtual addresses are converted to real addresses by the dynamic address translation mechanism. Prefixing converts real addresses to absolute addresses and is useful in multiprocessing configurations. Absolute addresses are used by processors and channels.

Key protection uses storage keys to identify blocks of storage that may be referenced by a running process. Segment protection is controlled by entries in the segment tables. Low-address protection guards certain vital information in the locations 0–511.

The interrupt mechanism uses current, old, and new PSWs. When an interrupt occurs, the current PSW is saved as the old PSW for that interrupt type, and a new PSW for that interrupt type is loaded containing the address of the appropriate interrupt handler. When interrupt processing is completed, the current PSW is restored from the old PSW and control is returned to the interrupted unit of work if it is nonpreemptive; otherwise the next ready process is dispatched.

The Supervisor creates dispatchable units of work, handles dispatching, and serializes the use of resources. The Master Scheduler is responsible for initializing the system and responding to commands issued by the system operator. The Job Entry Subsystem receives jobs to process, and prints and/or punches outputs. JES supports deadline scheduling and priority aging.

The System Management Facility and the System Activity Measurement Facility are the means by which the system gathers performance statistics. The Timesharing Option (TSO) provides users with online interactive program development capabilities.

Data Management controls the accessing of data sets on I/O devices. This includes buffering, scheduling, and performing the input/output operations. MVS supports several file organizations including sequential, in which records are stored and retrieved according to their physical order; indexed sequential, in which records are stored according to a key and indices are provided by the system to facilitate retrieval by key; direct, in which users access records on direct access devices by providing the record addresses; and partitioned, in which several sequential subfiles may be located through directory entries.

Queued access techniques use GET and PUT macros, access records sequentially, and anticipate future I/O requests. Basic access techniques use READ and WRITE macros, may access any record at any time, and future requests are not anticipated.

Some of the access methods provided by MVS are Basic Direct Access Method (BDAM), Basic Sequential Access Method (BSAM), Basic Partitioned Access Method (BPAM), Queued Sequential Access Method (QSAM), Indexed Sequential Access Method (ISAM), Queued Indexed Sequential Access Method (QISAM), Basic Indexed Sequential Access Method (BISAM), and Virtual Storage Access Method (VSAM). Three telecommunication access methods are supplied, namely Basic Telecommunication Access Method (BTAM), Telecommunication Access Method (TCAM), and Virtual Telecommunication Access Method (VTAM) which is used with IBM's System Network Architecture (SNA).

VSAM is a comprehensive access method that uses three different types of data sets: key-sequenced, entry-sequenced, and relative record.

The Real Storage Manager administers the use of real storage and causes pages to be moved to or from the paging device. The Auxiliary Storage Manager transfers pages between real storage and direct access devices. Pages may be moved one at a time (paging) or a task at a time (swapping). The Virtual Storage Manager controls the virtual storage of each task.

The System Resources Manager determines which task of all the active tasks will be given access to system resources, and at what rate the task will be allowed to consume these resources. The SRM has two primary objectives—achieving optimal resource usage, and distributing resources in accordance with installation requirements for response and turnaround.

In MVS, storage is divided into areas containing operating system code, system control blocks, common storage areas, task control blocks, and application code. The Nucleus contains some of the most important control blocks for the system, and much of the frequently executed operating system code such as SVC handlers. The Fixed Link Pack Area contains nonpageable modules. The Scheduler Work Area holds job-related control blocks. The Local System Queue Area holds a task's Task Control Block, and its page and segment tables. The Common System Area is used for passing data between tasks executing in different address spaces. The System Queue Area contains system-related queues and tables; it is nonpageable. The Pageable Link Pack Area is where all common system routines reside. Because all code is reentrant, there is no need to page code out should the storage be needed by another routine.

MVS contains many separate locks for preventing simultaneous updating of different system tables. Having many locks makes it possible for more parallel activity to occur. The locks are arranged in a hierarchy. Tasks may hold locks while requesting only higher locks in the hierarchy. This prevents deadlock as per Havender's Standard Allocation Pattern. Locks may be either global (if they affect the entire system), or local (if they affect a single address space). A process loops on a spin lock until it becomes available; a process loses the CPU if it finds a suspend lock unavailable.

MVS uses two different dispatchable units of work. Tasks correspond to processes in non-IBM systems. Creating a task involves a considerable amount of overhead. To achieve more parallelism without the concommitant increase in overhead associated with tasks, MVS designers created the service request. Service requests are designed for small units of work, and are dispatched with a higher priority than tasks.

MVS supports multiprocessing with MP (multiprocessor) or AP (attached processor) configurations. Processors communicate with one another via the SIGP (Signal Processor) instruction. The Compare and Swap instruction prevents simultaneous updating of a location by two processors. Interprocessor communication occurs for many reasons including system initialization, dispatching, input/output, reconfiguration, and recovery.

MVS provides many dumping capabilities to aid in monitoring and debugging activities. These include SNAP dump, ABEND dump, SVC dump, and stand-alone dump.

Several tracing capabilities are provided including System Trace, Master Trace, and the Generalized Trace Facility. These capture information about the system by the use of hooks. A hook is a sequence of instructions that signals an event to the tracing mechanism, captures event-related data, and passes this information to the tracing mechanism.

MVS combines the advantages of dumps and traces in the SLIP (Serviceability Level Indication Processing) mechanism that uses traps. A trap is the specification of a system event to be intercepted and the action to be taken when the event occurs. Traps may be created and then enabled or disabled as conditions change.

Finding skilled MVS personnel is difficult. The Hydra concept may help to alleviate this problem by allowing remote computer systems to be controlled by a central installation.

There is some controversy as to whether MVS will remain IBM's top-of-the-line system. It is receiving strong competition from VM, another large IBM operating system. Because of the inherent advantages of each, it is unlikely that users will be willing to convert from one to the other. VM is examined next.

TERMINOLOGY

abend
ABEND dump
absolute addresses
access methods
address space
alternate index
AP (Attached Processor)
ASM (Auxiliary Storage Manager)
ASP (Asymmetric Multiprocessing System)
basic access techniques
BDAM (Basic Direct Access Method)
BISAM (Basic Indexed Sequential Access Method)
BPAM (Basic Partitioned Access Method)
BSAM (Basic Sequential Access Method)
BTAM (Basic Telecommunications Access Method)
Communication Task
Compare and Swap instruction
CSA (Common System Area)
CVT (Communication Vector Table)
DAT (Dynamic Address Translation)
Data Management
data set
deadline scheduling
direct access file organization
disable a trap
dispatcher
DOS (Disk Operating System)
enable a trap
Enqueue
entry-sequenced data set
exit points
external page table
file organization
FLPA (Fixed Link Pack Area)
FRR (Functional Recovery Routines)
Generalized Trace Facility
global lock
HASP (Houston Automatic Spooling Priority system)
hierarchy of locks
hook
Hydra
IMS (Information Management System)
index sequential file organization

Initiator
IPL (Initial Program Load)
IPS (Installation Performance Specification)
ISAM (Index Sequential Access Method)
JES2 (Job Entry Subsystem 2)
JES3 (Job Entry Subsystem 3)
key protection
key-sequenced data set
local lock
lock
low-address protection
LSQA (Local System Queue Area)
Master Scheduler
Master Trace
MP (Multiprocessor)
MVS (Multiple Virtual Storage)
MVT (Multiprogramming with a Variable number of Tasks)
nonpreemptive unit of work
Nucleus
OS/360
OS/SVS (Single Virtual Storage)
page data set
page slot
paging operation
page stealing
partitioned file organization
PLPA (Pageable Link Pack Area)
preemptive unit of work
prefixing
priority aging
PSA (Prefixed Storage Area)
QISAM (Queued Indexed Sequential Access Method)
QSAM (Queued Sequential Access Method)
queued access techniques
real addresses
Region Control Task
relative byte address
relative record data set
Reserve
Resource Manager
RSM (Real Storage Manager)
Scheduler
segment protection
sequential file organization
service rate
service request
service units
shoulder tap
SIGP (Signal Processor) instruction
SLIP (Serviceability Level Indication Processing)
SNA (System Network Architecture)
SNAP dump
spin lock
SQA (System Queue Area)
SRM (System Resources Manager)
SRM Control
stand-alone dump
supervisor
suspend lock
SVC dump
SWA (Scheduler Work Area)
swap data set
swapping operation
System Activity Measurement Facility
System Management Facility
System Trace
task
TCAM (Telecommunications Access Method)
TLB (Translation Lookaside Buffer)
trap
TSO (Timesharing Option)
use counts
virtual addresses
virtual sequential file system
VSAM (Virtual Sequential Access Method)
VSM (Virtual Storage Manager)
VTAM (Virtual Telecommunications Access Method)
Work-load Manager

EXERCISES

21.1 MVS is designed for very large-scale computer systems. In that regard, how is it different from other systems like UNIX and VAX?

21.2 List several features of MVS designed to improve its reliability, availability, and serviceability.

21.3 Why are the various system locks in MVS arranged hierarchically? Distinguish between spin locks and suspend locks. What types of resources are best protected by a spin lock? What types of resources are best protected by a suspend lock?

21.4 Distinguish between absolute, real, and virtual addresses.

21.5 Discuss each of the following storage protection schemes

a) key b) segment c) low-address

21.6 MVS is a system designed for large installations with substantial data processing requirements. Discuss several MVS features particularly useful in such environments.

21.7 What is the difference between queued access techniques and basic access techniques?

21.8 Describe the major steps in processing an input/output operation under MVS.

21.9 Describe the various types of data sets that may be processed under VSAM.

21.10 In what types of applications might a programmer best access records by relative record number?

21.11 Describe how virtual address translation occurs in systems running under MVS.

21.12 Briefly describe the various file organizations supported by MVS.

21.13 What telecommunication access methods are supported by MVS?

21.14 Compare and contrast the two units of dispatchable work in MVS, namely the service request and the task. Most other operating systems use only a single dispatchable unit. Why did the designers of MVS choose this unique approach?

21.15 What types of decisions are made by the SRM?

21.16 Discuss the functions performed by each of the following components of the SRM.

a) SRM Control b) Work-load Manager c) Resource Manager

21.17 What types of programs and data are kept in each of the following MVS storage areas?

a) Nucleus
b) Fixed Link Pack Area
c) Scheduler Work Area
d) Local System Queue Area
e) Common System Area
f) System Queue Area
g) Pageable Link Pack Area

21.18 How is the SIGP instruction useful to MVS in controlling each of the following situations that arise under multiprocessing?

a) performing system initialization
b) dispatching units of work
c) starting I/O operations
d) performing system reconfiguration
e) attempting alternate CPU recovery

21.19 What are the functions of each of the following MVS trace facilities?

a) System Trace b) Master Trace c) Generalized Trace Facility

21.20 How are each of the following dumps used?

a) SNAP dump
b) ABEND dump
c) SVC dump
d) stand-alone dump

21.21 What is the purpose of MVS's SLIP (Serviceability Level Indication Processing) mechanism? What is a trap? Why is it useful to be able to enable and disable traps?

21.22 In what circumstances might the MVS troubleshooter resort to the use of the error recording file?

21.23 Explain the Hydra concept.

LITERATURE

(Au81) Auslander, M.A.; D.C. Larkin; and A.L. Scherr, "The Evolution of the MVS Operating System," *IBM Journal of Research and Development,* Vol. 25, No. 5, 1981, pp. 471–482.

(Be78) Beretvas, T., "Performance Timing in OS/VS2 MVS," *IBM Systems Journal,* Vol. 17, No. 3, 1978, pp. 290–313.

(Co77) Considine, J.P., and J.J. Myers, "MARC: MVS Archival Storage and Recovery Program," *IBM Systems Journal,* Vol. 16, No. 4, 1977, pp. 378–397.

(Ly74) Lynch, H.W., and J.B. Page, "The OS/VS2 Release 2 System Resources Manager," *IBM Systems Journal,* Vol. 13, No. 4, 1974, pp. 274–291.

(Sc73) Scherr, A.L., "Functional Structure of IBM Virtual Storage Operating Systems, Part II: OS/VS2-2 Concepts and Philosophies," *IBM Systems Journal,* Vol. 12, No. 4, 1973, pp. 382–400.

(Si78) Simpson, R.O., and G.H. Phillins, "Network Job Entry Facility for JES2," *IBM Systems Journal,* Vol. 17, No. 3, 1978, pp. 221–240.

(Wi78) Withington, F.C., "IBM's Future Large Computers," *Datamation,* July 1978, pp. 115–120.

IBM Publications

The following publications, available from IBM Corporation, Data Processing Division, New York 10604, describe various aspects of MVS.

- *OS/VS2 Systems Logic Library,* Volumes 1–7, SY28–0713 to SY28–0720.
- *OS/VS2 MVS System Programming Library: Initialization and Tuning Guide,* GC28–0681.
- *OS/VS2 Systems Programming Library: Supervisor,* GC28–0628.
- *OS/VS2 MVS Performance Notebook,* GC28–0886.
- *OS/VS2 MVS System Programming Library:* JES2, GC23–0002.
- *OS/VS2 MVS JES2 Logic,* SY24–6000.

- *IBM System/370 Principles of Operation*, GA22–7000.
- *A Guide to the IBM 3033 Processor Complex, Attached Processor Complex, and Multiprocessor Complex of System/370*, GC20–1859.
- *Introduction to IBM Direct–Access Storage Devices and Organization Methods*, GC20–1649.
- *OS/VS2 MVS JES3 Overview*, GC23–0038.

22
VM: A Virtual Machine Operating System

Conversation is but carving!
Give no more to every guest,
Than he's able to digest.
Give him always of the prime,
And but little at a time.
Carve to all but just enough,
Let them neither starve nor stuff,
And that you may have your due,
Let your neighbor carve for you.

Jonathan Swift

Outline

22.1 INTRODUCTION

A *virtual machine* is an illusion of a real machine. It is created by a *virtual machine operating system* that makes a single real machine appear to be several real machines (Fig. 22.1). From the user's viewpoint, virtual machines can be made to appear to

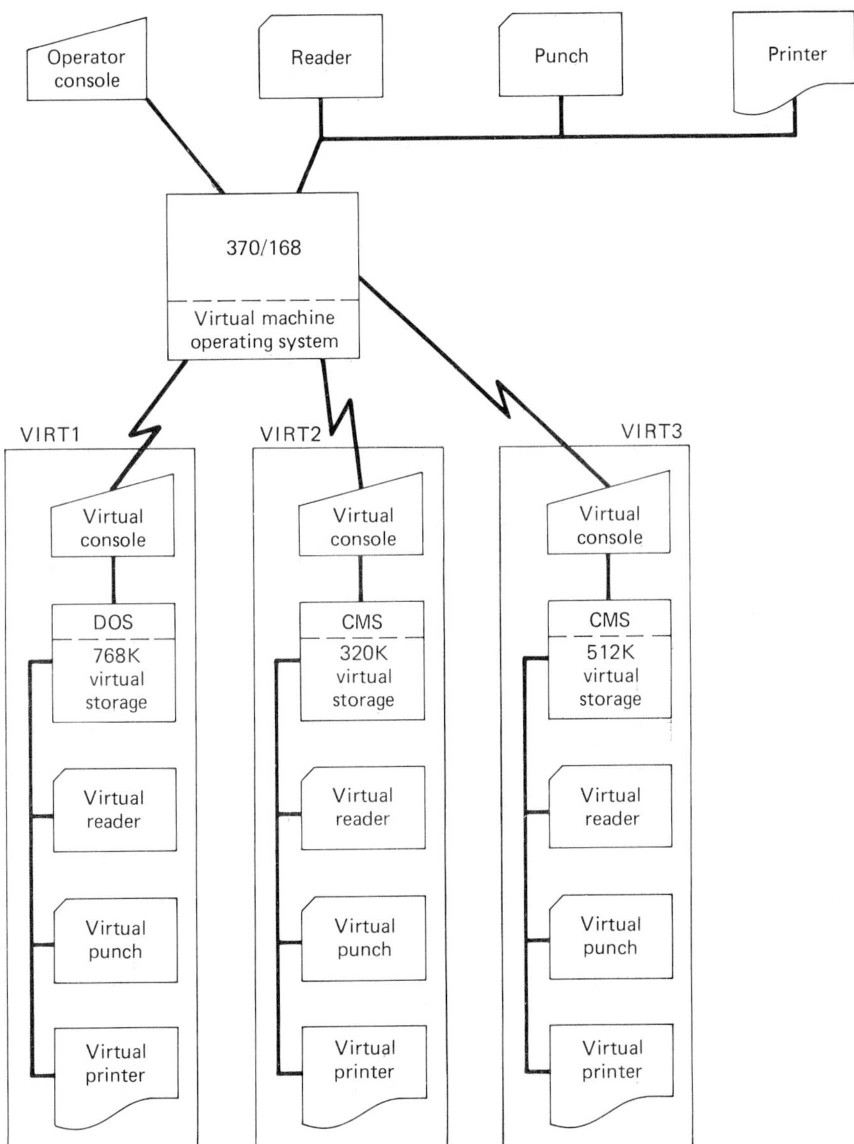

Fig. 22.1 Several virtual machines created by a single real machine.

be very similar to existing real machines, or they can be dramatically different. The concept has proven to be a valuable one and many virtual machine operating systems have been developed. The most widely used of these is *VM/370.* Because this system is now in use on many systems more recent than the IBM/370, we shall henceforth refer to it simply as VM.

VM manages an IBM System 370 computer (or similar hardware), and creates the illusion that each of several users operating from terminals has a complete System 370, including a wide range of input/output devices. *Each user can choose a different operating system—VM can actually run several different operating systems at once, each of them on its own virtual machine.* The VM user may run any of several different IBM operating systems, or a customized or "home-grown" system. Most commonly, VM users run versions of the IBM operating systems listed in Fig. 22.2.

Batch or single users interactive systems
DOS
DOS/VS (and DOS/VSE)
OS/PCP
OS/MFT
OS/MVT
OS/VS1
OS/VS2 (MVS)
OS-ASP
PS44
RSCS
Multiple-access systems
VM/370
Timesharing Option of OS
Conversational system
CMS

Fig. 22.2 Virtual machine operating systems.

Conventional multiprogramming systems (Fig. 22.3) share the resources of a single machine among several processes. These processes are each allocated a portion of the real machine's resources. They see a machine smaller in size and capabilities than the real machine on which they run.

Virtual machine multiprogramming systems (Fig. 22.4) share the resources of a single machine in a different manner. They create the illusion that one real machine is actually several machines. They create virtual processors, storage, and I/O devices, possibly with much larger capacities than those of the underlying real machine.

The main components of VM are

- the *Control Program—(CP)*
- the *Conversational Monitor System—(CMS)*

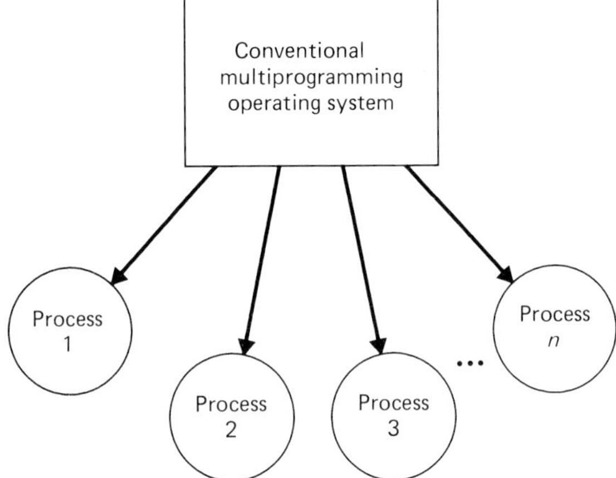

Fig. 22.3 Conventional multiprogramming.

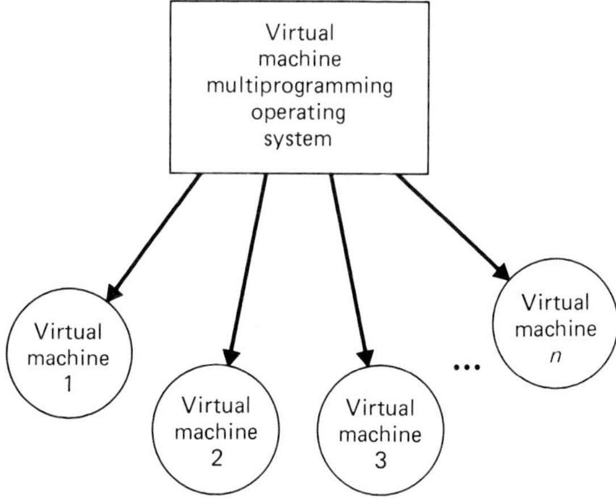

Fig. 22.4 Virtual machine multiprogramming.

- the *Remote Spooling Communications Subsystem—(RSCS)*
- the *Interactive Problem Control System—(IPCS)*
- the *CMS Batch Facility*

CP creates the environment in which virtual machines can execute (Fig. 22.5). It provides the support for the various operating systems normally used to control actual System/360, System/370, and other compatible computer systems.

CMS is an applications system with powerful features for interactive development of programs. It contains editors, language translators, various applications packages, and debugging tools.

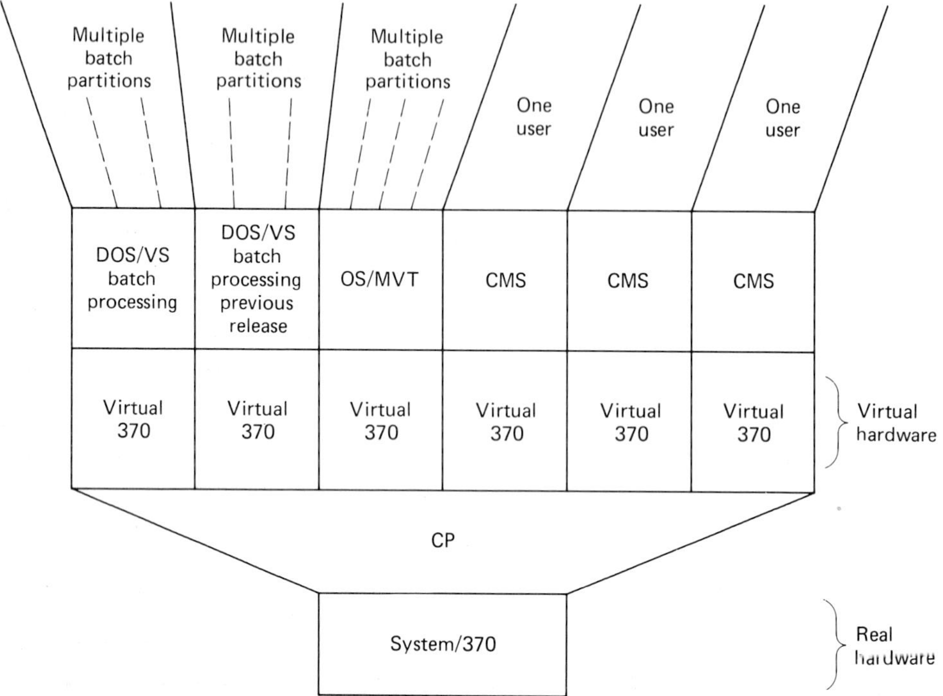

Fig. 22.5 CP creating a multiple virtual machine environment.

CP manages the real machine underlying the virtual machine environment. It gives each user access to the facilities of the real machine such as the processor, storage, and I/O devices. CP multiprograms complete virtual machines rather than individual tasks or processes.

RSCS provides VM with the ability to transmit and receive files over a teleprocessing network. IPCS is used for on-line analysis and for fixing VM software problems. IPCS allows the tracking of problems, and has various statistical capabilities for reporting the frequency of different types of errors.

The CMS Batch Facility allows the terminal user to submit longer jobs for batch processing while the user continues interactive work with a CMS virtual machine. CMS Batch runs in its own virtual machine controlled by the system operator. Job control statements define the processing to be performed. Jobs are input in card-image format; they may actually be punched on cards or they may be supplied as card-image records in a CMS file. Job outputs may be sent either to the system's real output devices or to the virtual machine output devices associated with the user who submitted the job. The CMS Batch Facility notifies the submitter when the job begins, and again when it ends.

Virtual machines running under CP perform much as if they were real machines, except that they operate more slowly since VM generally runs many users simultaneously.

One use of the virtual machine concept is debugging new operating systems or enhancements while the installation continues to run production. CP provides many functions that give a systems programmer control over a virtual machine similar to the control the programmer would have while sitting at the console of a real machine. For example, CP commands may be used to dump virtual storage areas, set instruction stops, monitor changing values in various locations, and perform other functions normally controlled from a real console.

A virtual machine runs programs much the same as they would be run on a real machine. The virtual machine communicates with its operator through a designated console, normally a terminal. The console messages are identical to those that would be printed at the console of the corresponding real machine.

Processes running on a virtual machine are not controlled by CP, but rather by the actual operating system running on that virtual machine. Virtual machines operate independently of one another with conflicts resolved by CP. The operating systems running on virtual machines perform their full range of functions including storage management, processor scheduling, control of input/output, protection of users from one another, protection of the operating system from the users, spooling, multiprogramming, job and process control, error handling, etc.

VM itself may run in any of the virtual machines it creates (Fig. 22.6). This exotic possibility is quite useful. It allows, for example, the debugging of CP itself.

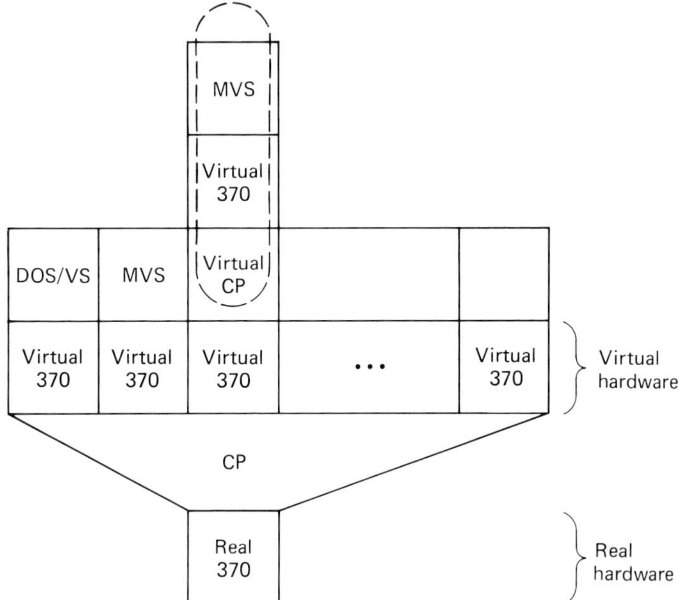

Fig. 22.6 Running VM in a virtual machine created by VM.

22.2 HISTORY

In the late 1940s and the 1950s, most computers were single user, dedicated systems. The computer user sat at the console of the real machine with the full capabilities of the machine visible and available to that user. Running a job was like interacting with today's personal computers—if the machine needed a response, and if the user sat there thinking about it for a while, the machine sat idle. The only real difference was cost, and the costs then were thousands of times what they are today.

This concept of an entire machine dedicated to one user is what is simulated by VM. A user at a VM virtual machine actually sees the equivalent of a complete real machine, a view very different from that ordinarily provided to users of conventional interactive systems.

Batch multiprogramming systems were developed to get better utilization out of expensive computing resources; this made it impractical for individual users to command an entire computer. It became less common to see a programmer sitting at the console of a computer while debugging a program.

In the early 1960s, a group at M.I.T. developed the CTSS timesharing system that allowed users sitting at typewriterlike terminals to command the computing power of a machine (Co62). CTSS ran a conventional batch stream to keep the computer busy while giving fast responses to interactive users doing program editing and debugging. The computing capabilities provided by CTSS resemble those provided to VM and personal computer users today, namely a highly interactive environment in which the computer gives rapid responses to large numbers of relatively trivial requests.

Since CTSS, interactive computing has become enormously popular with millions of people. They use interactive computing capabilities every day on the job, in managing their homes and finances, and even for recreation.

Today's personal computers provide ready access for an individual to a complete machine, much as their progenitors of 30 years ago did. But the big difference is that personal computers can connect with nationwide and worldwide information networks as the society we live in becomes more and more dependent on information.

CP/CMS began as an experimental system in 1964. It was to be a second generation timesharing system based upon the IBM System/360 computers (Ad66). Originally developed for local use at the IBM Cambridge Scientific Center, it soon gained favor as a tool for evaluating the performance of other operating systems.

The first operational version appeared in 1966 consisting of CP-40 and CMS. These components were designed to run on a modified IBM 360/40 with newly incorporated dynamic address translation hardware. At about this time, IBM announced an upgrade to its powerful 360/65. The new system, the 360/67, incorporated dynamic address translation hardware, and was supposed to provide the basis for a general-purpose timesharing, multiprogramming computer utility called TSS/360. The TSS effort, performed independently of the work on CP/CMS, encountered many difficulties (typical of the large-scale software efforts of the mid-1960s). Meanwhile CP/CMS was successfully moved to the 360/67, and eventually superseded the TSS effort. VM/370 became available in 1972 for the virtual storage models of the IBM 370 series. Today, over 2500 large-scale VM systems are operating, and the number is growing quickly (Cr81).

CTSS, successfully used at M.I.T. through 1974, most strongly influenced the design of CP/CMS. Interestingly, the CTSS design group went on to design the Multics system which never achieved much commercial success. The CP/CMS designers found that CTSS was difficult to design and modify. They felt that a more modular approach would be appropriate. So *they split the resource management portion from the user support portion of the operating system resulting in CP and CMS, respectively.* CP provides separate computing environments that give each user complete access to a full machine; CMS runs on a CP-created virtual machine as a one-user interactive system.

There is no question that *the most significant decision made in the design of CP was that each virtual machine would replicate a real machine.* It was clear that the 360 family concept would create a long lifetime for 360 programs; users requiring more power would simply move up in the family to a compatible system with more storage, devices, and CPU speed. Any decision to produce virtual machines different in structure than a real 360 probably would have resulted in the failure of the CP/CMS system. Instead, the concept has been successful, and as we shall see later in this chapter, VM may become IBM's leading operating system for the 1980s.

22.3 THE CONTROL PROGRAM (CP)

CP is the component of VM/370 that creates the virtual machines in which the various operating systems run. Because CP runs on a real machine in the real machine's supervisor state, it has access to all privileged instructions. When CP dispatches a particular virtual machine, that virtual machine runs on the real machine but in the real machine's problem state. There is only a single real processor (assuming uniprocessing, of course), and this machine may be either in its supervisor state or in its problem state. But there are many virtual machines. For each of them, CP keeps a main control block containing the *virtual registers* and the *virtual state word.* The virtual state word indicates (among other items), the current state of the virtual machine and the virtual instruction counter. The virtual machine may be in either *virtual supervisor state* or *virtual problem state.*

The real machine alternates its execution between the real supervisor state and the real problem state. A casual observer at the console of the real machine wouldn't see anything noticeably different from what would be seen if the real machine were running a conventional operating system. *CP, however, runs each virtual machine in real problem state.* It keeps track of what state each virtual machine thinks it is in, namely virtual supervisor state or virtual problem state. CP does this so effectively that the operating system running in a virtual machine cannot ever issue instructions that will determine if CP is running the virtual machine in real problem state.

When CP dispatches a virtual machine, the virtual machine executes real instructions on the real machine. CP gains control because of various types of interrupts. Many interrupts occur because a virtual machine attempts to execute a privileged instruction normally acceptable for an operating system. But since virtual machines are constrained to run in real problem state, interrupts result each time a virtual machine attempts a privileged instruction. Thus *program interruptions are the key to the interfacing between an executing virtual machine and CP.*

When a virtual machine generates a program exception interrupt, CP gains control and determines the cause of the interrupt. The virtual machine may be executing in the virtual problem state. If it is, then CP passes the real program interruption directly to the virtual machine which then processes the interrupt through its conventional interrupt handling procedures.

If, however, the virtual machine is operating in virtual supervisor state, then CP simulates the execution of the privileged instruction. It first determines what the virtual machine is attempting to accomplish. If input/output is being attempted, then CP performs any necessary mapping between virtual and real devices. If disk I/O is involved, then CP maps virtual track addresses to real track addresses. CP then schedules the real I/O operation corresponding to the virtual I/O request, and returns control to the virtual machine's operating system which then continues operation as if it itself had initiated the I/O.

When an I/O operation completes, CP receives the completion interrupt and then transfers control to the operating system of the virtual machine requesting that I/O. To the virtual machines's operating system, this appears the same as if the real hardware itself had indicated I/O completion.

22.3.1 Demand Paging

CP runs on computer systems equipped with hardware to perform demand paging and dynamic address translation. It pages its real storage with the exception of a small *nucleus* that remains in real storage at all times. Figure 22.7 shows how real storage might appear in a VM system running three CMS users, namely CMSA, CMSB, and CMSC, and two OS/VS1 virtual machines, namely VS1A and VS1B.

The consequences of this are quite interesting. For conventional real storage operating systems like OS/MFT and OS/MVT, performance under VM can be dramatically different from what it is on a real machine. CP pages the real storage in these operating systems. It does this in a manner logically transparent to the operating system on the virtual machine. But *the timing delays suffered in a paged environment can invalidate the usefulness of VM for running certain jobs designed to execute in real storage environments, particularly jobs with strict timing dependencies.*

The problems are even more interesting when virtual storage operating systems like DOS/VS and MVS run under VM. These systems are subjected to two levels of paging.

Nonpageable portion of CP					
Pageable portions of CP					
VS1A Nucleus	CMSB	CMSC	VS1A Partition 2	VS1B Partition 1	
CMSA	VS1A Nucleus	CMSC	VS1B Nucleus	VS1B Nucleus	
VS1A Nucleus	CMSB	CMSC	VS1B Nucleus		
CMSA	CMSC	CMSC	VS1B Partition 2		
CMSA	CMSB	VS1A Partition 1	VS1B Partition 2		
CMSB	CMSA	VS1A Partition 1	VS1B Partition 1		

Fig. 22.7 Real storage utilization under VM.

- paging initiated by a virtual machine
- paging initiated by CP

Paging initiated by a virtual machine is handled by CP as normal input/output. Paging initiated by CP is logically transparent to the virtual machine.

Performance is always of concern in paged systems, but it is of particular interest in VM because of the multiple levels of paging. Various actions may be taken to reduce paging overhead.

- A virtual machine may be designated to run in "virtual equals real" mode.
- An individual page frame may be locked into real memory.

- Redundant paging may be eliminated on some virtual machines by *handshaking,* a technique that allows the virtual machine to interface closely with CP and take advantage of CP's mechanisms.

The handshaking option is attractive because it still allows the normal resource allocation mechanisms to make decisions for the benefit of all users. The first two options can severely hinder the functioning of the system, and can greatly reduce the system's capacity. All of these options should be exercised prudently.

22.3.2 Minidisks

A DASD (Direct Access Storage Device) volume may be dedicated to one particular virtual machine, or it may be shared among several virtual machines.

A single DASD may be divided by CP into many *minidisks* (Fig. 22.8), each of which may be allocated to a different virtual machine. Minidisks are subsets of full disks. They each consist of a range of cylinders. Each is treated by a virtual machine operating system as a complete physical disk device but one of smaller capacity than a full disk. CP handles the mapping of minidisks to real disks but the space

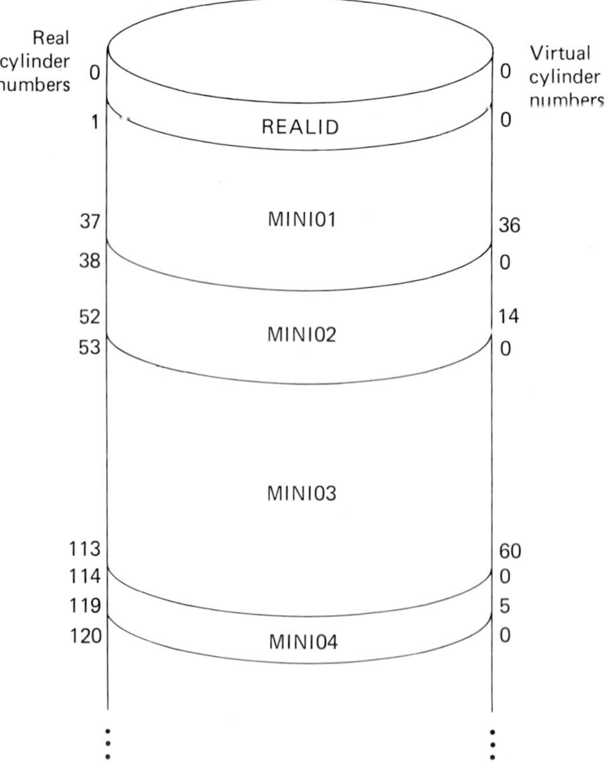

Fig. 22.8 Minidisks on a real disk. Each minidisk is origined to virtual cylinder zero. (Courtesy of International Business Machines Corporation.)

within each minidisk is managed by the operating system running on the virtual machine to which the minidisk is assigned. CP prevents a virtual machine from referencing space on a disk volume outside the boundaries of that machine's minidisk(s). Sharing of minidisks is possible but must be carefully controlled.

A single DASD may be dedicated to a particular virtual machine, or it may be shared among several virtual machines. Each minidisk on a given DASD volume may belong to a different virtual machine.

22.3.3 Console Management

CP supplies a *virtual console* for each virtual machine. Thus in VM, users at terminals can control their virtual machines as if they had a complete physical console to the corresponding real machine. This gives users considerably more power than they normally get in timesharing systems. Some of the CP commands a user may invoke from a terminal are summarized in Fig. 22.9.

ADDSTOP defines an instruction address stop location in virtual storage.

BEGIN resumes execution in the virtual machine (the functional equivalent of pressing the start key on a real computing system).

DETACH removes a specified device from the virtual machine configuration.

DISPLAY displays specified virtual machine registers or virtual storage contents.

EXTERNAL causes an external interrupt.

LINK makes a specified virtual direct access storage device a part of the virtual machine configuration if the device is defined as shared and the user can supply the appropriate password.

QUERY displays certain system information such as log messages, the number of spool files, or the virtual machine configuration.

READY simulates a device end interrupt from a virtual device.

SET establishes certain system values such as the level of error message to be printed or the amount of VM line editing for terminal input lines.

SPOOL alters the spooling control options (such as the number of copies) for one or more virtual unit record devices that are used for spooling. Transfers data files among users and remote stations, and starts and stops console spooling.

STORE inserts data into virtual machine registers or virtual storage.

TERMINAL allows the user to define the VM logical editing symbols and the logical line size of I/O to and from the terminal.

Fig. 22.9 CP commands.

22.3.4 CP User Privilege Classes

Characteristic of large computing environments (such as the typical VM installation) is the need for many different groups of people to interact with the system while it is in operation. Some of these people are applications users. Others are concerned more with the operation, management, and updating of the system. Still others are concerned with hardware repair. Not all of these groups require universal access to the facilities of the operating system; in fact, certain groups must be expressly forbidden to use features that might allow them to corrupt the system. VM uses a scheme of *user privilege classes* to identify these various groups. CP commands are associated with these privilege classes. A user attempting execution of a command not associated with that user's privilege class is denied access to the command. The CP user privilege classes are summarized in Fig. 22.10.

Class	User	Function
A	Primary system operator	Controls availability of VM, system accounting, broadcast messages, performance options, and many other items.
B	System resource operator	Controls all real VM resources, except those controlled by class A and D (a B user can for example DETACH a channel from a particular user).
C	System programmer	Can update certain functions not controlled by other user classes (e.g., make a temporary "fix" to the contents of real storage without bringing down the entire VM system).
D	Spooling operator	Controls spooling data and certain unit record functions (such as the use of single or double spacing on the printer, for example).
E	System analyst	Can examine and save data in VM storage area.
F	Service representative	Can access data concerning real I/O devices. The class F user can extract data from system error records.
G	General user	Can perform various control functions associated with the operation of the user's virtual machine (e.g., start a virtual machine).
H	Reserved	Reserved for IBM use.
Any	Any user	Can gain or relinquish access to VM.

Fig. 22.10 CP user privilege classes.

22.3.5 VM Directory

Access to VM is controlled via information in the *VM directory,* a file containing descriptions of all potential virtual machines allowed to run on a particular VM system. For each user, the directory contains the user identification, the password, the privilege class, and various other items defining that user's virtual machine.

A sample VM directory entry is shown in Fig. 22.11. The user's identification is VIRT1, and so is the password. This virtual machine is allocated 512K bytes of virtual storage with a maximum allowed virtual storage size of 1M (or 1024K bytes). The account number is S5. The console is at virtual physical device address 009 and is a type 3215 device. This virtual machine uses spooled unit record devices including a 2540 reader at virtual physical device address 00C, a 2540 punch at 00D, and a 1403 (printer) at 00E; each of these devices has spool output class A. One 3330 minidisk is assigned to virtual physical device address 191. The LINK entry indi-

```
USER VIRT1 VIRT1 512K 1M G
ACCOUNT S5 SYSPRG
CONSOLE 009 3215
SPOOL 00C 2540 READER A
SPOOL 00D 2540 PUNCH A
SPOOL 00E 1403 A
MDISK 191 3330 001 001 CPR6L1 R
LINK MAINT 194 194 RR
```

Fig. 22.11 Sample VM directory entry.

```
VM/370 online
logon smith
ENTER PASSWORD:

LOGON AT 10:07:36 ON FRIDAY 05/27/83
ipl cms
```

Fig. 22.12 Logging on to VM/370 and then loading CMS.

cates that this virtual machine has been given read-only access to a minidisk belonging to another virtual machine.

Users with a proper directory entry may logon to VM as shown in Fig. 22.12. The user types the user identification. The system checks that this is listed in a directory entry and then prompts for the user's password. The user then enters the password (which the system masks for security purposes). The directory is checked to be sure the password is correct. After logging on to the system, the user may run any supported operating system.

VM provides a *security journaling option* (which must be specified when the system is generated). When this option is in force, unsuccessful logon attempts are recorded and messages are sent to the system administrator documenting the date, time, terminal, user identification, and password involved. The vast majority of unsuccessful logon attempts are normally caused by user typing errors. Efforts at penetrating the system by repeatedly attempting to logon with a series of "likely" passwords will be detected.

22.4 THE CONVERSATIONAL MONITOR SYSTEM (CMS)

Initially, CMS stood for *Cambridge Monitor System*, but more recently it is called *Conversational Monitor System*. It is a disk-oriented operating system that gives the user complete access to what appears to be a dedicated real machine but which is, in fact, a virtual machine created by CP. CMS is a one user system that provides functions quite similar to those in CTSS. When CMS first became operational, it ran on a real 360 serving a user operating the machine from the system console. Eventually, when CP was installed, CMS was recoded to operate strictly in a CP-created virtual machine; current versions of CMS cannot run on a bare machine.

Sharing of data between virtual machines is controlled by CP that provides for multiple virtual machines to access common disks. Also, sharing is accomplished by the transmission of data files between virtual machines by simulated unit record equipment (card readers, card punches, and printers).

All CMS commands available to the user are stored in disk files; they are not actually part of the system. This makes it easy for users to tailor the instruction set of their virtual machines to their own needs by adding, deleting, or changing the command files.

CMS gives the user powerful program development capabilities. A CMS user sees a dedicated virtual machine (Fig. 22.13). VM provides a multiuser timesharing environment by supporting many separate CMS virtual machines.

The user communicates with CMS via a terminal and with a series of commands, rather than with job control statements. CMS presents a user-friendly interface. It provides particularly useful diagnostic messages directly to the interactive user so that errors may be immediately corrected.

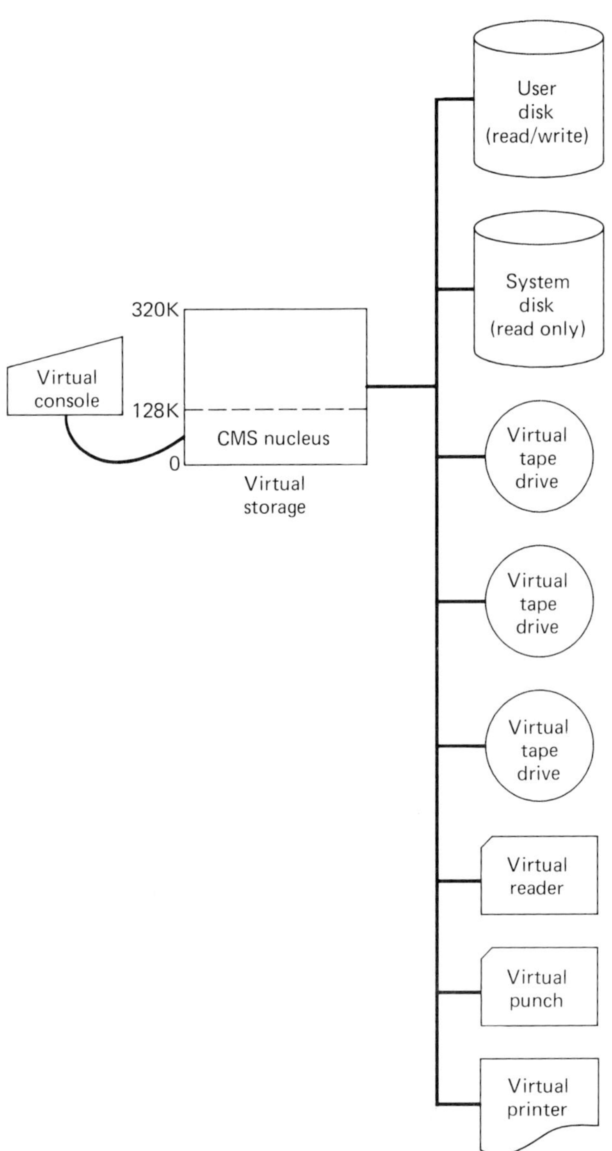

Fig. 22.13 A dedicated virtual machine as seen by a CMS user.

22.5 REMOTE SPOOLING AND COMMUNICATIONS SYSTEM

The Remote Spooling and Communications System, RSCS (He79), supports the transfer of data files between computers and remote work stations in communications networks (Fig. 22.14). It operates in a CP-created virtual machine, and uses

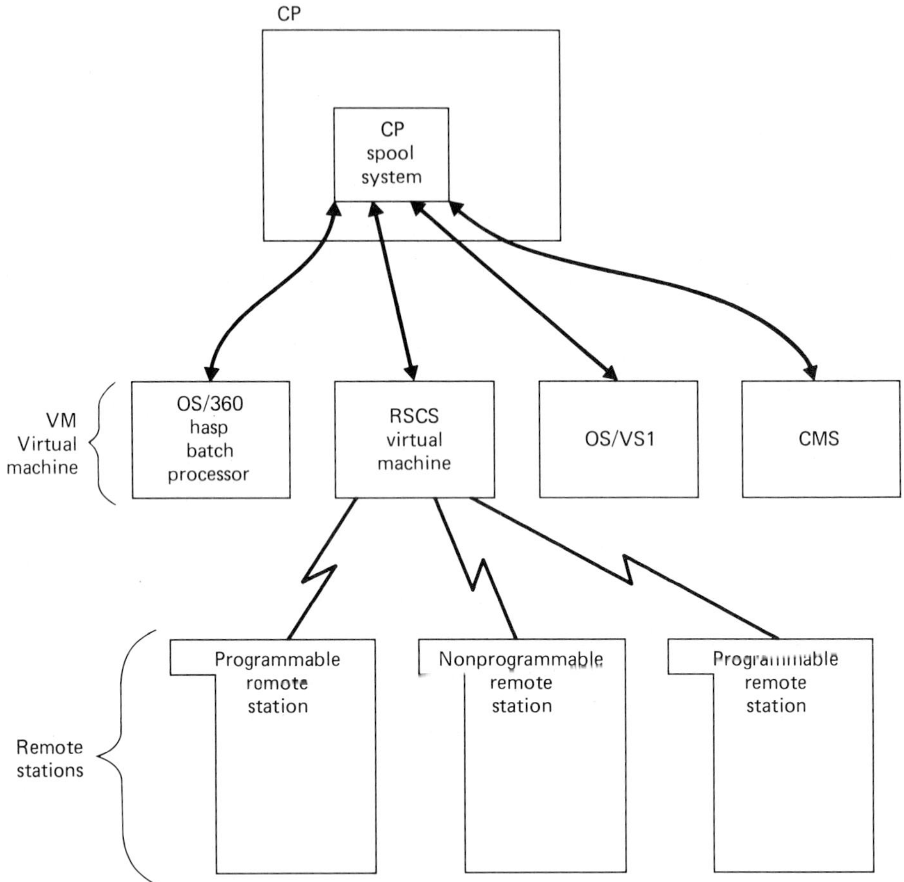

Fig. 22.14 A VM RSCS teleprocessing network.

communications links and unit record equipment to transmit files. It provides a convenient means for transferring files between virtual machines on the same real machine, as well as more conventional transmission between computer systems and remote work stations.

CP itself passes files between virtual machines on a single real machine. It operates as a central node in a star network in which each point of the star is a virtual machine. One virtual machine desiring to send a file to another sends it to CP that then passes it to the destination machine. The files are transmitted by using each virtual machine's virtual card reader and punch.

RSCS operates in a virtual machine connected to communications equipment. Each real computer system has a unique identifier. To transmit to another computer, RSCS sends a file to the RSCS on the next computer, and the next until the file reaches its destination. Within IBM, RSCS is used to address over 50,000 users on 400 computer systems over five continents (Cr81).

22.6 STRENGTHS OF VM

VM can support a diversity of computing applications. It makes one real computer appear to be many virtual computers, and each virtual computer can support a different operating system. An installation running VM can thus create the illusion that it is running many separate computer systems, with different operating systems, emphasizing different capabilities.

VM allows a new operating system to be tested while production work continues. The conversion of programs to the new format, and the testing of these new programs may occur simultaneously with the continued smooth operation of the installation. CMS facilitates the translation to new formats.

Most active installations are dynamic environments with changes constantly being proposed, tested, and instituted. VM makes it possible for these activities to occur simultaneously with continued production.

Sometimes, unique applications require the availability of an operating system different from that currently running at the installation. VM makes it possible to run the application under the appropriate operating system without the need for bringing all other production work at the installation to a halt.

One intriguing application of VM is running multiple copies of the same operating system. Some operating systems limit the number of users that may run. By bringing up VM, the installation desiring to run a particular operating system (but with more users) may run multiple copies of that operating system and thus double, triple, etc. the number of users that may run at once.

VM/370 provides a reliable environment that can operate unattended, unless of course disk or tape volumes must be mounted. In February of 1978, New England suffered a severe blizzard. The entire state of Massachusetts was literally closed down. Only emergency vehicles were allowed to operate on the state's roads. During this period, the VM/370 system at IBM's Cambridge Scientific Center functioned continuously for a week in a locked computer room without an operator. The system was monitored from a remote terminal with operator privileges.

22.7 VM/370 EVOLUTION

VM/370 has continued to evolve since its introduction. Communication between virtual machines has become more popular, and more applications systems tend to exploit the architectural features of the virtual machine environment. Holley et al. (Ho79) discuss the use of multiprocessing in VM/370 environments.

22.8 PERFORMANCE CONSIDERATIONS

The performance of a VM/370 system is affected by many factors including

- the particular computer system used
- the total number of virtual machines executing
- the particular operating systems in use on each of the virtual machines
- the nature of the work load on each of the virtual machines
- the operational characteristics of each of the primary paging devices and the channels over which page transports occur
- the number of channels available
- the types of channels (block multiplexor or selector)
- the amount of real storage available
- the use of the *virtual machine assist feature*
- the use of *VM Extended Control Program Support*

CMS runs efficiently in a CP-created virtual machine. A VM system may run many more CMS virtual machines than MVS virtual machines, so it is difficult to categorize a particular hardware configuration merely by the number of virtual machines it can support.

22.8.1 Virtual Machine Assist Feature

The *Virtual Machine Assist* feature is a performance improvement option available to VM installations. It has both hardware and software components. Virtual storage operating systems such as OS/VS1 and DOS/VS execute in problem state while under the control of VM/370. These operating systems use a large number of privileged instructions and SVCs that generate interrupts requiring VM's attention. Normally, these interrupts are serviced by software routines. But with the VM Virtual Machine Assist feature, the hardware intercepts and services many of these interrupts resulting in significant performance improvements.

22.8.2 Extended Control Program Support Feature

The Extended Control Program Support feature provides *expanded virtual machine assist, CP assist,* and *virtual interval timer assist.*

Expanded virtual machine assist includes hardware emulation of more privileged instructions. Its use increases the percentage of interrupts directly serviced by hardware emulation rather than software simulation.

CP assist provides hardware assist for many of the frequently used portions of CP including virtual machine I/O handling, storage management, page management, privileged instruction handling, and dispatching.

Virtual interval timer assist provides for hardware updating of the interval timer for each virtual machine. Without this feature, the updating is performed by software. The hardware feature makes timer values more accurate.

22.8.3 Performance Measurement and Analysis

The VM control program provides for the use of two commands that measure and report system performance. The incorporation of such capabilities in VM emphasizes both the designers' concerns for the importance of performance monitoring and the users' desires to know how well their systems are performing.

The *MONITOR command* collects performance measurement data on tape for subsequent analysis. The *INDICATE command* displays current performance information at the user's terminal.

VM has a built-in capability for monitoring system performance as CP runs. CMS is designed to run directly under CP and with very little overhead. But other virtual machines do suffer significant overhead running under CP, and designers have addressed this issue. A number of improvements have been made to VM over the years to reduce this overhead.

CP pages even nonpaged systems like OS/MFT and OS/MVT. Some programs designed for nonpaged real storage environments require ultrahigh performance without the associated delays of a paged environment. One option available to VM users allows a single virtual machine to be run in a *virtual equals real mode* so that *the real storage of that virtual machine is not paged.*

It is possible to share procedural code among virtual machines to minimize duplication of frequently used pages in real storage. This yields better storage utilization.

Tetzlaff (Te79) discusses the VM/Monitor program and presents some interesting summaries and analyses of VM/370 performance. MacKinnon (Ma79) discusses the concept of handshaking, changes made to operating systems running under VM/370 to make them aware that they are running in a virtual machine environment. This facilitates the elimination of many redundant operations normally performed because one operating system runs under another in a virtual machine environment. In particular, DOS/VS and VS/1 have been modified in this manner so that they can interface directly with VM. The performance improvements have been significant.

22.9 RELIABILITY, AVAILABILITY, AND SERVICEABILITY

The virtual machine concept provides for the enforced isolation of users from one another with the dividing lines drawn even more sharply than in conventional multiprogramming environments. This isolation has important ramifications upon system reliability, availability, and serviceability.

- CP prevents a virtual machine from addressing any area of storage other than its own.
- Passwords are required for access to the system and to shared disk files.
- Disk files can be made read-only for protection.

- CP detects abnormal termination of a virtual machine and confines any effects to that virtual machine and its user(s).
- The flexible virtual machine environment allows users to test and debug new versions of operating systems while simultaneously executing production work. A real machine does not have to be dedicated to testing a new operating system at the expense of delays in production work.
- Various versions of the same operating system can run simultaneously so programs not as yet converted to the new version may run concurrently with already converted programs.
- Multiple copies of the same operating system may be run simultaneously on the same machine. This feature is particularly attractive to users committed to an operating system, and who used to run the system on a slower machine. With the availability of a more powerful processor, the user may expand by running several copies of the older operating system at once.
- VM/370 provides a solid complement of commands for tracing, examining, and altering the operation of a virtual machine and the contents of its virtual storage. These commands are useful for debugging programs in the virtual machine environment.
- VM/370 provides a number of features that allow a service representative to check out the machine and input/output devices by running special diagnostic programs in one virtual machine while production work continues in others.

22.10 VM: IBM'S LARGE-SCALE OPERATING SYSTEM FOR THE 1980S?

This section argues the case for VM becoming increasingly important over the next decade. There are many reasons why this is likely to occur.

It is not uncommon today for large companies to have programming backlogs of several years. It is expected that throughout the middle to late 1980s, the number of programmers produced will fall 50 percent short of the demand. Clearly, if we are to meet the programming needs of the 1980s, we must improve programmer productivity. The revelation of the 1960s was that interactive program development greatly improved programmer productivity. So operating systems that facilitate interactive program development will be important in the 1980s.

IBM's two main contenders among interactive operating systems for IBM's large-scale computers are TSO (the Timesharing Option) of MVS, and VM. Without question, VM is the superior interactive system, both in capabilities provided and in sheer performance. On a given computer system, it is often the case that VM can support twice as many interactive users as MVS.

MVS is and has been IBM's top-of-the-line batch processing operating system for many years. IBM users have made substantial commitments to MVS, and these cannot be ignored. IBM simply cannot force its huge base of MVS users to convert to a completely different operating system. Here, too, the versatility of VM comes to bear because MVS can run under VM. So the installation committed to MVS can run it under VM while providing the substantial interactive capabilities of VM. The installation will run VM, and under VM it will run MVS and many CMS virtual machines.

IBM created DOS (Disk Operating System) for its smaller installations. DOS is a relatively simple system compared with MVS. It has strong batch processing capabilities, but weak interactive capabilities. Over the years, DOS users have generally resisted converting to MVS for more capabilities. They have instead placed considerable pressure on IBM to provide these additional capabilities in DOS. But there is a limit to the effectiveness of DOS as an installation grows, so many DOS users have reluctantly switched to MVS, in many cases a protracted and painful experience.

Once again, the versatility of VM becomes important. The DOS user may move up to a more powerful processor that runs VM. Then the user may run DOS under VM immediately generating two substantial benefits: better interactive capabilities are provided by VM, and the more powerful processor runs DOS jobs faster. An additional benefit is that the user may run multiple copies of DOS under VM simultaneously, thus removing certain limitations inherent in DOS such as the limited number of partitions it supports.

CMS was specifically designed to be a high-powered interactive system. Its designers decided to support the standard compilers and assemblers running under IBM's large-scale batch processing operating systems of the time. Thus programmers could develop and test their programs under CMS and then compile and execute them under IBM's DOS or OS batch processing systems.

One interesting story about the early years of VM goes something like this: IBM was trying to decide whether to "kill" VM or to release it as a supported product. The president of the company at that time, T. Vincent Learson, went to a presentation offered by the MVS group at which they argued that indeed VM should be killed. At a tour after the presentation, Learson noticed that the MVS development group was running MVS under VM. At that moment (report has it), he decided that if VM was good enough for IBM, it was also good enough for its customers. VM was subsequently released as a supported product.

VM offers an interesting performance improvement to some DOS users. It is reasonable to expect that DOS running on certain hardware will be more efficient than DOS running under VM on identical hardware. But the opposite is often true. How can this be? Quite simply it occurs because VM's virtual storage management is much more efficient than DOS/VS's. Another plus for VM.

VM's popularity has been increasing steadily and there is every reason to believe that it will continue to do so. IBM and other vendors have been releasing a steady stream of performance enhancements. The concept of the virtual machine operating system has proved to be worthwhile. VM, like CP/M and UNIX systems, was built in a "small shop" by designers who saw merit in a unique concept. It is not clear that the designers of any of the systems foresaw the great success their systems would experience.

SUMMARY

A virtual machine is an illusion of a real machine. It is created by a virtual machine operating system. Conventional multiprogramming systems share the resources of a real machine among several processes. Virtual machine operating systems share the resources of a real machine among several virtual machines.

The main components of VM are the Control Program (CP), the Conversational Monitor System (CMS), the Remote Spooling Communications Subsystem (RSCS), the Interactive Problem Control System (IPCS), and the CMS Batch Facility.

CP creates the environment in which the virtual machines execute. CMS is a one user, interactive system. RSCS provides VM with the ability to transmit and receive files over a teleprocessing network. IPCS is used for on-line analysis and for fixing VM software problems. The CMS Batch Facility allows the terminal user to submit longer jobs for batch processing while the user continues interactive work with a CMS virtual machine.

CP provides separate computing environments that give each user complete access to a full machine; CMS runs on a CP-created machine as a one user, interactive system.

CP runs on the real machine in the real machine's supervisor state. Virtual machines dispatched by CP are run in the real machine's problem state. CP keeps track of whether each virtual machine thinks it is in virtual supervisor state or virtual problem state.

Program interruptions are the key to the interfacing between an executing virtual machine and CP. When a program interruption occurs, CP gains control. If the virtual machine was in virtual program state, CP passes the interruption directly to the virtual machine for processing via that machine's own interruption handling procedures. If the virtual machine was in virtual supervisor state, then CP simulates the execution of the privileged instruction.

CP runs on computer systems equipped with hardware to perform demand paging and dynamic address translation. It pages its real storage with the exception of a small nucleus that remains in real storage at all times. When a CP-created virtual machine runs a real storage operating system like OS/MFT or OS/MVT, CP pages the real storage managed by the real storage operating system. When a virtual storage operating system is run in a CP-created virtual machine, paging occurs on two levels and this can cause performance problems.

DASD devices under CP can be divided into minidisks. These are subsets of full disks. CP handles the mapping of minidisks to real disks, but the space within each minidisk is managed by the operating system of the virtual machine to which the minidisk is assigned.

In VM, users at terminals control their virtual machines as if they have a complete physical console to the corresponding real machine.

CP uses a scheme of user privilege classes to identify various groups of users. Users may access only those commands assigned to their user privilege classes.

Access to VM is controlled via information in the VM directory, a file containing descriptions of all potential virtual machines allowed to run on a particular VM system.

CMS (the Conversational Monitor System) is a one user, disk-oriented operating system that gives the user complete access to what appears to be a dedicated real machine. It provides powerful program development capabilities.

RSCS (the Remote Spooling and Communications System) supports the transfer of data files between computers and remote work stations in communications networks.

VM makes one computer appear to be many virtual computers, and each of these can support a different operating system. A new operating system may be tested under VM while the installation's production work continues. Multiple copies of the same operating system may be run under VM. VM can operate unattended for extended periods.

Performance issues are of vital concern in VM environments, especially because of the multiple levels of paging. Microcoded hardware assists are provided to speed the execution of VM systems by directly servicing interrupts with hardware emulation rather than software simulation. VM has a built-in capability for monitoring system performance as CP runs.

VM has many features that have important ramifications upon reliability, availability, and serviceability. Each virtual machine's addressing is carefully constrained. Passwords are required for access to the system and to shared disk files. Disk files can be made read-only. Abnormal terminations are confined to the virtual machines in which they occur. Testing and debugging of new operating systems may occur while production continues. Powerful debugging capabilities are provided. Service representatives may run diagnostic programs in one virtual machine while production work continues in others.

It is likely that VM's popularity will increase greatly over the next decade. It provides more comprehensive and more efficient interactive computing capabilities than MVS. It gives the DOS user a growth path that allows the user to stay with DOS while increasing capabilities and while benefitting from VM's interactive facilities. Since MVS can run under VM, MVS users can add interactive capabilities via VM rather than the less powerful and less efficient TSO.

TERMINOLOGY

CMS (Conversational Monitor System)
CP (Control Program)
CP nucleus
Extended Control Program Support
handshaking
isolation of address spaces
lock a page frame into real storage
minidisk

multiple levels of paging
privileged instructions
problem state
real machine
real problem state
real state word
real supervisor state
security journaling option
supervisor state
VM/370
VM/370 assist
virtual console
virtual equals real
virtual machine
virtual problem state
virtual registers
virtual state word
virtual supervisor state

EXERCISES

22.1 What is a virtual machine? What is a virtual machine operating system?

22.2 List several advantages and disadvantages of the virtual machine concept.

22.3 Distinguish between the manner in which multiple users are serviced on conventional multiprogramming systems and on virtual machine multiprogramming systems.

22.4 What are the main components of VM? Briefly explain the purpose of each.

22.5 The timesharing user under VM runs CMS. But CMS is a one user system. Explain how a multiuser timesharing system is implemented under VM. How does this differ from the implementation of more conventional timesharing systems?

22.6 (*Virtual machine performance anomaly.*) Running an operating system on a bare machine involves certain overhead. Running an operating system under VM additionally involves the overhead of the virtual machine operating system. It is often the case that an operating system running under VM will run more efficiently than when it runs on the same machine but without VM. How is this possible?

22.7 Virtual machines operate independently of one another with conflicts resolved by CP. What are some of these conflicts? How does CP resolve them?

22.8 VM itself may run in any of the virtual machines created by VM. What are the applications of this exotic possibility?

22.9 (*Virtual machine recursion.*) Suppose that a virtual machine operating system could create a virtual machine that could in turn run another copy of the virtual machine operating system that could in turn create another virtual machine, etc.

a) Suggest some applications of this concept.
b) What implementation problems might you expect to encounter? How would you handle them?
c) What performance problems might you expect to encounter? How would you handle them?

22.10 VM is a virtual storage operating system using paging. Many of the operating systems it runs are real storage systems. What are the advantages and disadvantages of running a real storage operating system under VM?

22.11 What is the key to the interfacing between an executing virtual machine and CP?

22.12 Suppose a program running on a virtual machine initiates an I/O request to read a record from disk. Describe precisely how the request is handled via the user's operating system, CP, and the real hardware.

22.13 Paging initiated by a virtual machine is handled by CP as normal input/output. Paging initiated by CP is logically transparent to the virtual machine. Explain.

22.14 What options are available in VM to help reduce performance degradation due to multiple levels of paging?

22.15 What are minidisks? How does CP manage minidisks?

22.16 Why are users separated into various privilege classes in a VM environment?

22.17 All CMS commands available to the user are stored in disk files; they are not actually part of the system. What are the advantages and disadvantages of this scheme?

22.18 Why is it sometimes attractive to run several identical copies of one operating system under VM? What alternatives are available to an installation that does not support VM?

22.19 Discuss the various features of VM that are related to security.

22.20 What are some of the key factors that affect the performance of a VM system?

22.21 Discuss how each of the following can improve performance in a VM system.

a) the Virtual Machine Assist feature
b) expanded virtual machine assist
c) CP assist
d) virtual interval timer assist

LITERATURE

(Ad66) Adair, R.J.; R.U. Bayles; L.W. Comeau; and R.J. Creasy, "A Virtual Machine System for the 360/40," Cambridge, Mass.: *IBM Scientific Center Report 320–2007*, May 1966.

(At79) Attanasio, C.R., "Virtual Control Storage–Security Measures in VM/370," *IBM Systems Journal*, Vol. 18, No. 1, 1979, pp. 93–110.

(BU73a) Buzen, J.P.; P.P. Chen; and R.P. Goldberg, "Virtual Machine Techniques for Improving System Reliability," *IEEE Symposium on Computer Software Reliability*, 1973, pp. 12–17.

(BU73b) Buzen, J.P., and U.O. Gagliardi, "The Evolution of Virtual Machine Architecture," *Proceedings of AFIPS National Computer Conference*, Vol. 42, 1973, pp. 291–299.

(BU73c) Buzen, J.P., and U.O Gagliardi, "Introduction to Virtual Machines," *Honeywell Computer Journal*, Vol. 7, No. 4, 1973, pp. 245–250.

(Ca75) Callaway, P.H., "Performance Measurement Tools for VM/370," *IBM Systems Journal*, Vol. 14, No. 2, 1975, pp. 135–160.

(Ca80) Canon, M.D.; D.H. Fritze; J.H. Howard; T.D. Howell; M.F. Mitoma; and J. Rodriguez-Rosell, "A Virtual Machine Emulator for Performance Evaluation," *Communications of the ACM*, Vol. 23, No. 2, February 1980, pp. 71–80.

(Ca78) Canon, M.D., J.H. Howard; T.D. Howell; M.F. Mitoma; and J. Rodriguez-Rosell, "Virtual Machine Emulation Facility for Performance Evaluation," *IBM Technical Disclosure Bulletin,* Vol. 21, No. 7, December 1978, pp. 3004–3005.

(Co62) Corbato, F.J.; M. Merwin-Daggett; and R.C. Daley, "An Experimental Time-Sharing System," *Proc. Spring Joint Computer Conference (AFIPS),* Vol. 21, 1962, pp. 335–344.

(Cr81) Creasy, R.J., "The Origin of the VM/370 Time-Sharing System," *IBM Journal of R&D,* Vol. 25, No. 5, September 1981, pp. 483–490.

(Do79) Doherty, W.J., and R.P. Kelisky, "Managing VM/CMS System for User Effectiveness," *IBM Systems Journal,* Vol. 18, No. 1, 1979, pp. 143–163.

(Fo76) Forbes, B.; T. Weidner; R. Yoder; and T. Pitchford, "Realizing a Virtual Machine," *Ninth Annual Workshop on Microprogramming,* 1976, pp. 42–46.

(Go71a) Goldberg, R.P., "Hardware Requirements for Virtual Machine System," *Proceedings of the 4th Hawaii International Conference on Systems Sciences,* 1971, pp. 449–451.

(Go71b) Goldberg, R.P., "Virtual Machines: Semantics and Examples," *IEEE Computer Society Conference,* Boston, September 1971, pp. 141–142.

(Go73) Goldberg, R.P., "Architecture of Virtual Machines," *Proceedings of AFIPS Conference,* Vol. 42, 1973, pp. 309–318.

(Go74) Goldberg, R.P., "Survey of Virtual Machine Research," *Computer,* Vol. 7, No. 6, June 1974, pp. 34–45.

(He79) Hendricks, E.C., and T.C. Hartmann, "Evolution of a Virtual Machine Subsystem," *IBM Systems Journal,* Vol. 18, No. 1, 1979, pp. 111–142.

(Ho79) Holley, L.H., R.P. Parmelee, C.A. Salisbury, and D.N. Saul, "VM/370 Asymmetric Multiprocessing," *IBM Systems Journal,* Vol. 18, No. 1, 1979, pp. 47–70.

(Je79) Jensen, R.M., "A Formal Approach for Communication between Logically Isolated Virtual Machines," *IBM Systems Journal,* Vol. 18, No. 1, 1979, pp. 71–92.

(Ke78) Kemen, H., and H.H. Nagel, "Experiments with a Virtual Network Machine Concept for an Inhomogeneous Local Computer Network," *Proceedings of Compcon Fall 78: Computer Communication Networks, IEEE,* 1978, pp. 280–286.

(Ma79) MacKinnon, R.A., "The Changing Virtual Machine Environment: Interfaces to Real Hardware, Virtual Hardware, and Other Virtual Machines," *IBM Systems Journal,* Vol. 18, No. 1, 1979, pp. 18–46.

(Md69) Madnick, S.E., "Time-Sharing Systems: Virtual Machine Concept vs. Conventional Approach," *Modern Data,* Vol. 2, No. 3, March 1969, pp. 34–36.

(Md74) Madnick, S.E., and J.J. Donovan, "Virtual Machine/370 (VM/370)," *Operating Systems,* New York: McGraw-Hill, 1974, pp. 549–563.

(Mu79) Murphy, M., "VM: A Basic Ingredient in Emergency Planning," *Datamation,* December 1979, pp. 167–170.

(Pa71) Parmelee, R.P., "Virtual Machines: Some Unexpected Applications," *Proceedings of IEEE International Computer Society Conference,* 1971, pp. 145–146.

(Pa72) Parmelee, R.P.; T.I. Peterson; C.C. Tillman; and D.J. Hatfield, "Virtual Storage and Virtual Machine Concepts," *IBM Systems Journal,* Vol. 11, No. 2, 1972, pp. 99–130.

(Se79) Seawright, L.H., and R.A. MacKinnon, "VM/370—A Study of Multiplicity and Usefulness," *IBM Systems Journal,* Vol. 18, No. 1, 1979, pp. 4–17.

(Sh77) Shriver, B.D.; J.W. Anderson, and D.M. Hyams, "Virtual Machine Monitor for a Distributed Minicomputer System," *Microprocessors, Microprogramming and Minicomputers,* 1977, pp. 66–83.

(Sr73) Srowdawa, R.J., and Lee A. Bates, "An Efficient Virtual Machine Implementation," *Proceedings of AFIPS Conference,* Vol. 42, 1973, pp. 301–308.

(Ta78) Tang, T., and K. O'Flaherty, "Virtual Machines and the NCR Criterion," *Datamation,* Vol. 24, No. 4, April 1978, pp. 129–134.

(Te79) Tetzlaff, W.H., "State Sampling of Interactive VM/370 Users," *IBM Systems Journal,* Vol. 18, No. 1, 1979, pp. 164–180.

(Ve81) Verity, J.W., "Goodbye 360, Hello VM," *Datamation,* December 1981, pp. 36–42.

(We78) Weegenaar, H.J., "Virtuality and Other Things Like That," *Proceedings of Compcon Fall 78: Computer Communications Networks, IEEE,* 1978, pp. 287–293.

(Wi71) Winett, J.M., "Virtual Machines for Developing Systems Software," *Proceedings of IEEE International Computer Conference,* 1971, pp. 143–144.

IBM Publications

- *Concepts of a Virtual Machine,* (Independent Study Program), IBM, Poughkeepsie, N.Y., 12602, 1979.
- *IBM Virtual Machine Facility/370 Introduction,* IBM Systems Library order number GC20-1800, IBM Corporation, Department D58, P.O. Box 390, Poughkeepsie, N.Y., 12602.

Appendix

FIPS PUB 46

Federal Information Processing Standards Publication 46

1977 January 15

ANNOUNCING THE

DATA ENCRYPTION STANDARD

Federal Information Processing Standards are issued by the National Bureau of Standards pursuant to the Federal Property and Administrative Services Act of 1949, as amended, Public Law 89-306 (79 Stat 1127), Executive Order 11717 (38 FR 12315, dated May 11, 1973), and Part 6 of Title 15 Code of Federal Regulations (CFR).

Name of Standard: Data Encryption Standard (DES).

Category of Standard: Operations, Computer Security.

Explanation: The Data Encryption Standard (DES) specifies an algorithm to be implemented in electronic hardware devices and used for the cryptographic protection of computer data. This publication provides a complete description of a mathematical algorithm for encrypting (enciphering) and decrypting (deciphering) binary coded information. Encrypting data converts it to an unintelligible form called cipher. Decrypting cipher converts the data back to its original form. The algorithm described in this standard specifies both enciphering and deciphering operations which are based on a binary number called a key. The key consists of 64 binary digits ("0"s or "1"s) of which 56 bits are used directly by the algorithm and 8 bits are used for error detection.

Binary coded data may be cryptographically protected using the DES algorithm in conjunction with a key. The key is generated in such a way that each of the 56 bits used directly by the algorithm are random and the 8 error detecting bits are set to make the parity of each 8-bit byte of the key odd, i.e., there is an odd number of "1"s in each 8-bit byte. Each member of a group of authorized users of encrypted computer data must have the key that was used to encipher the data in order to use it. This key, held by each member in common, is used to decipher the data received in cipher form from other members of the group. The encryption algorithm specified in this standard is commonly known among those using the standard. The unique key chosen for use in a particular application makes the results of encrypting data using the algorithm unique. Selection of a different key causes the cipher that is produced for any given set of inputs to be different. The cryptographic security of the data depends on the security provided for the key used to encipher and decipher the data.

Data can be recovered from cipher only by using exactly the same key used to encipher it. Unauthorized recipients of the cipher who know the algorithm but do not have the correct key cannot derive the original data algorithmically. However, anyone who does have the key and the algorithm can easily decipher the cipher and obtain the original data. A standard algorithm based on a secure key thus provides a basis for exchanging encrypted computer data by issuing the key used to encipher it to those authorized to have the data. Additional FIPS guidelines for implementing and using the DES are being developed and will be published by NBS.

Approving Authority: Secretary of Commerce.

Maintenance Agency: Institute for Computer Sciences and Technology, National Bureau of Standards.

Applicability: This standard will be used by Federal departments and agencies for the cryptographic protection of computer data when the following conditions apply:

1. An authorized official or manager responsible for data security or the security of any computer system decides that cryptographic protection is required; and
2. The data is not classified according to the National Security Act of 1947, as amended, or the Atomic Energy Act of 1954, as amended.

However, Federal agencies or departments which use cryptographic devices for protecting data classified according to either of these acts can use those devices for protecting unclassified data in lieu of the standard.

In addition, this standard may be adopted and used by non-Federal Government organizations. Such use is encouraged when it provides the desired security for commercial and private organizations.

Data that is considered sensitive by the responsible authority, data that has a high value, or data that represents a high value should be cryptographically protected if it is vulnerable to unauthorized disclosure or undetected modification during transmission or while in storage. A risk analysis should be performed under the direction of a responsible authority to determine potential threats. FIPS PUB 31 (Guidelines for Automatic Data Processing Physical Security and Risk Management) and FIPS PUB 41 (Computer Security Guidelines for Implementing the Privacy Act of 1974) provide guidance for making such an analysis. The costs of providing cryptographic protection using this standard as well as alternative methods of providing this protection and their respective costs should be projected. A responsible authority then should make a decision, based on these analyses, whether or not to use cryptographic protection and this standard.

Applications: Data encryption (cryptography) may be utilized in various applications and in various environments. The specific utilization of encryption and the implementation of the DES will be based on many factors particular to the computer system and its associated components. In general, cryptography is used to protect data while it is being communicated between two points or while it is stored in a medium vulnerable to physical theft. Communication security provides protection to data by enciphering it at the transmitting point and deciphering it at the receiving point. File security provides protection to data by enciphering it when it is recorded on a storage medium and deciphering it when it is read back from the storage medium. In the first case, the key must be available at the transmitter and receiver simultaneously during communication. In the second case, the key must be maintained and accessible for the duration of the storage period.

Hardware Implementation: The algorithm specified in this standard is to be implemented in computer or related data communication devices using hardware (not software) technology. The specific implementation may depend on several factors such as the application, the environment, the technology used, etc. Implementations which comply with this standard include Large Scale Integration (LSI) "chips" in individual electronic packages, devices built from Medium Scale Integration (MSI) electronic components, or other electronic devices dedicated to performing the operations of the algorithm. Micro-processors using Read Only Memory (ROM) or micro-programmed devices using microcode for hardware level control instructions are examples of the latter. Hardware implementations of the algorithm which are tested and validated by NBS will be considered as complying with the standard. Procedures for testing and validating equipment for conformance with this standard are available from the Systems and Software Division, National Bureau of Standards, Washington, D.C. 20234. Software implementations in general purpose computers are not in compliance with this standard. Information regarding devices which have been tested and validated will be made available to all FIPS points of contact.

Export Control: Cryptographic devices and technical data regarding them are subject to Federal Government export controls as specified in Title 22, Code of Federal Regulations, Parts 121 through 128. Cryptographic devices implementing this standard and technical data regarding them must comply with these Federal regulations.

Patents: Crytographic devices implementing this standard may be covered by U.S. and foreign patents issued to the International Business Machines Corporation. However, IBM has granted nonexclusive, royalty-free licenses under the patents to make, use and sell apparatus which complies with the standard. The terms, conditions and scope of the licenses are set out in notices published in the May 13, 1975 and August 31, 1976 issues of the Official Gazette of the United States Patent and Trademark Office (934 O. G. 452 and 949 O. G. 1717).

Alternative Modes of Using the DES: The "Guidelines for Implementing and Using the Data Encryption Standard" describe two different modes for using the algorithm described in this standard. Blocks of data containing 64 bits may be directly entered into the device where 64-bit cipher blocks are generated under control of the key. This is called the electronic code book mode. Alternatively, the device may be used as a binary stream generator to produce statistically random binary bits which are then combined with the clear (unencrypted) data (1-64 bits) using an "exclusive-or" logic operation. In order to assure that the enciphering device and the deciphering device are synchronized, their inputs are always set to the previous 64 bits of cipher that were transmitted or received. This second mode of using the encryption algorithm is called the cipher feedback (CFB) mode. The electronic codebook mode generates blocks of 64 cipher bits. The cipher feedback mode generates cipher having the same number of bits as the plain text. Each block of cipher is independent of all others when the electronic codebook mode is used while each byte (group of bits) of cipher depends on the previous 64 cipher bits when the cipher feedback mode is used. The modes of operation briefly described here are further explained in the FIPS "Guidelines for Implementing and Using the Data Encryption Standard."

Implementation of this standard: This standard becomes effective six months after the publication date of this FIPS PUB. It applies to all Federal ADP systems and associated telecommunications networks under development as well as to installed systems when it is determined that cryptographic protection is required. Each Federal department or agency will issue internal directives for the use of this standard by their operating units based on their data security requirement determinations.

NBS will provide assistance to Federal organizations by developing and issuing additional technical guidelines on computer security and by providing technical assistance in using data encryption. A data encryption testbed has been established within NBS for use in providing this technical assistance. The National Security Agency assists Federal departments and agencies in communications security and in determining specific security requirements. Instructions and regulations for procuring data processing equipment utilizing this standard will be provided by the General Services Administration.

Specifications: Federal Information Processing Standard (FIPS 46) Data Encryption Standard (DES) (affixed).

Cross Index:

a. FIPS PUB 31, "Guidelines to ADP Physical Security and Risk Management"

b. FIPS PUB 39, "Glossary for Computer Systems Security"

c. FIPS PUB 41, "Computer Security Guidelines for Implementing the Privacy Act of 1974"

d. FIPS PUB—, "Guidelines for Implementing and Using the Data Encryption Standard" (to be published)

e. Other FIPS and Federal Standards are applicable to the implementation and use of this standard. In particular, the American Standard Code for Information Interchange (FIPS PUB 1) and other related data storage media or data communications standards should be used in conjunction with this standard. A list of currently approved FIPS may be obtained from the Office of ADP Standards Management, Institute for Computer Sciences and Technology, National Bureau of Standards, Washington, D.C. 20234.

Qualifications: The cryptographic algorithm specified in this standard transforms a 64-bit binary value into a unique 64-bit binary value based on a 56-bit variable. If the complete 64-bit input is used (i.e., none of the input bits should be predetermined from block to block) and if the 56-bit variable is randomly chosen, no technique other than trying all possible keys using known input and output for the DES will guarantee finding the chosen key. As there are over 70,000,000,000,000,000 (seventy quadrillion) possible keys of 56 bits, the feasibility of deriving a particular key in this way is extremely unlikely in typical threat environments. Moreover, if the key is changed frequently, the risk of this event is greatly diminished. However, users should be aware that it is theoretically possible to derive the key in fewer trials (with a correspondingly lower probability of success depending on the number of keys tried) and should be cautioned to change the key as often as practical. Users must change the key and provide it a high level of protection in order to minimize the potential risks of its unauthorized computation or acquisition. The feasibility of computing the correct key may change with advances in technology. A more complete description of the strength of this algorithm against various threats will be contained in the Guidelines for Implementing and Using the DES.

When correctly implemented and properly used, this standard will provide a high level of cryptographic protection to computer data. NBS, supported by the technical assistance of Government agencies responsible for communication security, has determined that the algorithm specified in this standard will provide a high level of protection for a time period beyond the normal life cycle of its associated ADP equipment. The protection provided by this algorithm against potential new threats will be reviewed within five years to assess its adequacy. In addition, both the standard and possible threats reducing the security provided through the use of this standard will undergo continual review by NBS and other cognizant Federal organizations. The new technology available at that time will be evaluated to determine its impact on the standard. In addition, the awareness of any breakthrough in technology or any mathematical weakness of the algorithm will cause NBS to reevaluate this standard and provide necessary revisions.

Comments: Comments and suggestions regarding this standard and its use are welcomed and should be addressed to the Associate Director for ADP Standards, Institute for Computer Sciences and Technology, National Bureau of Standards, Washington, D.C. 20234.

Waiver Procedure: The head of a Federal agency may waive the provisions of this FIPS PUB after the conditions and justifications for the waiver have been coordinated with the National Bureau of Standards. A waiver is necessary if cryptographic devices performing an algorithm other than that which is specified in this standard are to be used by a Federal agency for data subject to cryptographic protection under this standard. No waiver is necessary if classified communications security equipment is to be used. Software implementations of this algorithm for operational use in general purpose computer systems do not comply with this standard and each such implementation must also receive a waiver. Implementation of the algorithm in software for testing or evaluation does not require waiver approval. Implementation of other special purpose cryptographic algorithms in software for limited use within a computer system (e.g., encrypting password files) or implementations of cryptographic algorithms in software which were being utilized in computer systems before the effective date of this standard do not require a waiver. However, these limited uses should be converted to the use of this standard when the system or equipment involved is upgraded or redesigned to include general cryptographic protection of computer data. Letters describing the nature of and reasons for the waiver should be addressed to the Associate Director for ADP Standards as previously noted.

Sixty days should be allowed for review and response by NBS. The waiver shall not be approved until a response from NBS is received; however, the final decision for granting the waiver is the responsibility of the head of the particular agency involved.

Where to Obtain Copies of the Standard:

Copies of this publication are for sale by the National Technical Information Service, U. S. Department of Commerce, 5285 Port Royal Road, Springfield, Virginia 22161. Order by FIPS PUB number and title. Prices are published by NTIS in current catalogs and other issuances. Payment may be made by check, money order, deposit account or charged to a credit card accepted by NTIS.

Federal Information
Processing Standards Publication 46

1977 January 15

SPECIFICATIONS FOR THE

DATA ENCRYPTION STANDARD

The Data Encryption Standard (DES) shall consist of the following Data Encryption Algorithm to be implemented in special purpose electronic devices. These devices shall be designed in such a way that they may be used in a computer system or network to provide cryptographic protection to binary coded data. The method of implementation will depend on the application and environment. The devices shall be implemented in such a way that they may be tested and validated as accurately performing the transformations specified in the following algorithm.

DATA ENCRYPTION ALGORITHM

Introduction

The algorithm is designed to encipher and decipher blocks of data consisting of 64 bits under control of a 64-bit key. Deciphering must be accomplished by using the same key as for enciphering, but with the schedule of addressing the key bits altered so that the deciphering process is the reverse of the enciphering process. A block to be enciphered is subjected to an initial permutation *IP*, then to a complex key-dependent computation and finally to a permutation which is the inverse of the initial permutation IP^{-1}. The key-dependent computation can be simply defined in terms of a function *f*, called the cipher function, and a function *KS*, called the key schedule. A description of the computation is given first, along with details as to how the algorithm is used for encipherment. Next, the use of the algorithm for decipherment is described. Finally, a definition of the cipher function *f* is given in terms of primitive functions which are called the selection functions S_i and the permutation function *P*. S_i, *P* and *KS* of the algorithm are contained in the Appendix.

The following notation is convenient: Given two blocks *L* and *R* of bits, *LR* denotes the block consisting of the bits of *L* followed by the bits of *R*. Since concatenation is associative $B_1B_2 \dots B_8$, for example, denotes the block consisting of the bits of B_1 followed by the bits of $B_2 \dots$ followed by the bits of B_8.

Enciphering

A sketch of the enciphering computation is given in figure 1.

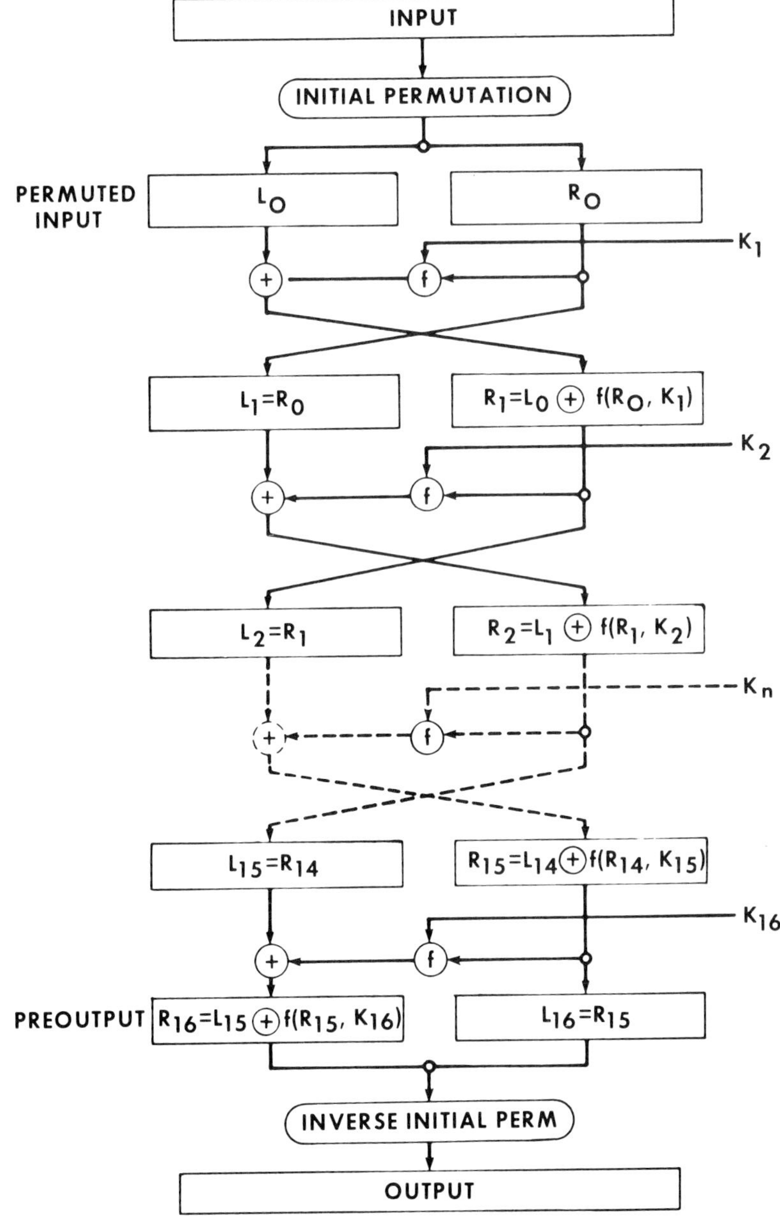

FIGURE 1. *Enciphering computation.*

The 64 bits of the input block to be enciphered are first subjected to the following permutation, called the initial permutation *IP*:

IP

58	50	42	34	26	18	10	2
60	52	44	36	28	20	12	4
62	54	46	38	30	22	14	6
64	56	48	40	32	24	16	8
57	49	41	33	25	17	9	1
59	51	43	35	27	19	11	3
61	53	45	37	29	21	13	5
63	55	47	39	31	23	15	7

That is the permuted input has bit 58 of the input as its first bit, bit 50 as its second bit, and so on with bit 7 as its last bit. The permuted input block is then the input to a complex key-dependent computation described below. The output of that computation, called the preoutput, is then subjected to the following permutation which is the inverse of the initial permutation:

IP^{-1}

40	8	48	16	56	24	64	32
39	7	47	15	55	23	63	31
38	6	46	14	54	22	62	30
37	5	45	13	53	21	61	29
36	4	44	12	52	20	60	28
35	3	43	11	51	19	59	27
34	2	42	10	50	18	58	26
33	1	41	9	49	17	57	25

That is, the output of the algorithm has bit 40 of the preoutput block as its first bit, bit 8 as its second bit, and so on, until bit 25 of the preoutput block is the last bit of the output.

The computation which uses the permuted input block as its input to produce the preoutput block consists, but for a final interchange of blocks, of 16 iterations of a calculation that is described below in terms of the cipher function *f* which operates on two blocks, one of 32 bits and one of 48 bits, and produces a block of 32 bits.

Let the 64 bits of the input block to an iteration consist of a 32 bit block *L* followed by a 32 bit block *R*. Using the notation defined in the introduction, the input block is then *LR*.

Let *K* be a block of 48 bits chosen from the 64-bit key. Then the output *L'R'* of an iteration with input *LR* is defined by:

(1)
$$L' = R$$
$$R' = L \oplus f(R,K)$$

where $\oplus$ denotes bit-by-bit addition modulo 2.

As remarked before, the input of the first iteration of the calculation is the permuted input block. If *L'R'* is the output of the 16th iteration then *R'L'* is the preoutput block. At each iteration a different block *K* of key bits is chosen from the 64-bit key designated by *KEY*.

With more notation we can describe the iterations of the computation in more detail. Let *KS* be a function which takes an integer n in the range from 1 to 16 and a 64-bit block *KEY* as input and yields as output a 48-bit block K_n which is a permuted selection of bits from *KEY*. That is

$$K_n = KS(n, KEY) \tag{2}$$

with K_n determined by the bits in 48 distinct bit positions of *KEY*. *KS* is called the key schedule because the block K used in the n'th iteration of (1) is the block K_n determined by (2).

As before, let the permuted input block be LR. Finally, let L_0 and R_0 be respectively L and R and let L_n and R_n be respectively L' and R' of (1) when L and R are respectively L_{n-1} and R_{n-1} and K is K_n; that is, when n is in the range from 1 to 16,

$$\begin{aligned} L_n &= R_{n-1} \\ R_n &= L_{n-1} \oplus f(R_{n-1}, K_n) \end{aligned} \tag{3}$$

The preoutput block is then $R_{16}L_{16}$.

The key schedule *KS* of the algorithm is described in detail in the Appendix. The key schedule produces the 16 K_n which are required for the algorithm.

Deciphering

The permutation IP^{-1} applied to the preoutput block is the inverse of the initial permutation IP applied to the input. Further, from (1) it follows that:

$$\begin{aligned} R &= L' \\ L &= R' \oplus f(L', K) \end{aligned} \tag{4}$$

Consequently, to ***decipher*** it is only necessary to apply the ***very same algorithm to an enciphered message block,*** taking care that at each iteration of the computation ***the same block of key bits*** K ***is used*** during decipherment as was used during the encipherment of the block. Using the notation of the previous section, this can be expressed by the equations:

$$\begin{aligned} R_{n-1} &= L_n \\ L_{n-1} &= R_n \oplus f(L_n, K_n) \end{aligned} \tag{5}$$

where now $R_{16}L_{16}$ is the permuted input block for the deciphering calculation and L_0R_0 is the preoutput block. That is, for the decipherment calculation with $R_{16}L_{16}$ as the permuted input, K_{16} is used in the first iteration, K_{15} in the second, and so on, with K_1 used in the 16th iteration.

The Cipher Function f

A sketch of the calculation of $f(R, K)$ is given in figure 2.

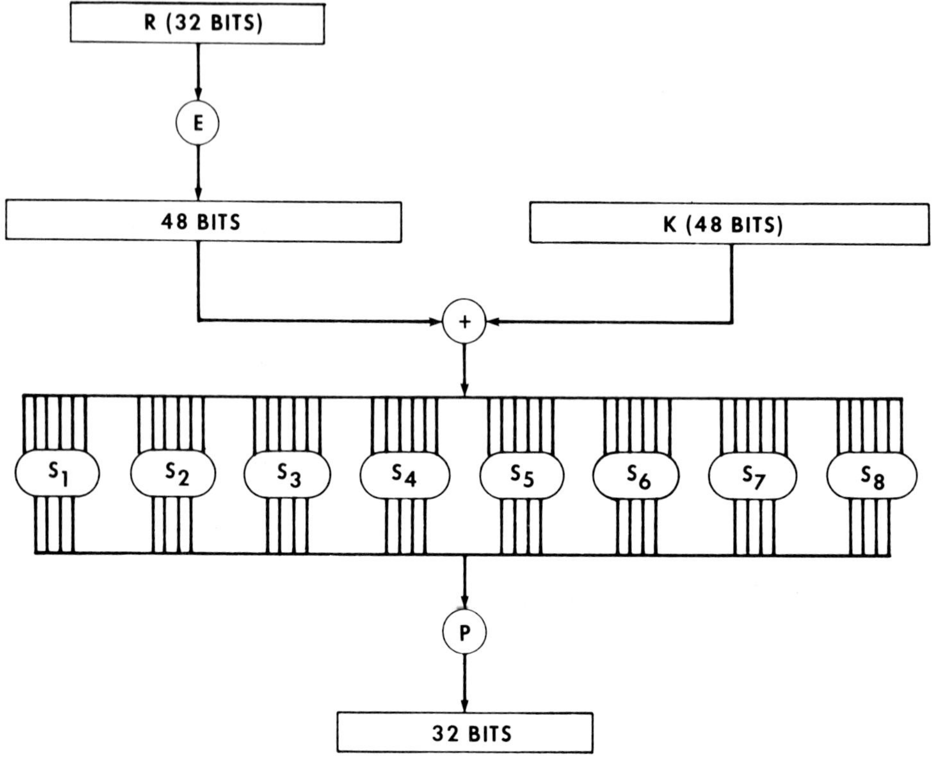

FIGURE 2. *Calculation of* f (R, K).

Let E denote a function which takes a block of 32 bits as input and yields a block of 48 bits as output. Let E be such that the 48 bits of its output, written as 8 blocks of 6 bits each, are obtained by selecting the bits in its inputs in order according to the following table:

E BIT-SELECTION TABLE

32	1	2	3	4	5
4	5	6	7	8	9
8	9	10	11	12	13
12	13	14	15	16	17
16	17	18	19	20	21
20	21	22	23	24	25
24	25	26	27	28	29
28	29	30	31	32	1

Thus the first three bits of $E(R)$ are the bits in positions 32, 1 and 2 of R while the last 2 bits of $E(R)$ are the bits in positions 32 and 1.

Each of the unique selection functions $S_1, S_2, \ldots, S_8$, takes a 6-bit block as input and yields a 4-bit block as output and is illustrated by using a table containing the recommended S_1:

$\underline{S_1}$

Column Number

Row No.	0	1	2	3	4	5	6	7	8	9	10	11	12	13	14	15
0	14	4	13	1	2	15	11	8	3	10	6	12	5	9	0	7
1	0	15	7	4	14	2	13	1	10	6	12	11	9	5	3	8
2	4	1	14	8	13	6	2	11	15	12	9	7	3	10	5	0
3	15	12	8	2	4	9	1	7	5	11	3	14	10	0	6	13

If S_1 is the function defined in this table and B is a block of 6 bits, then $S_1(B)$ is determined as follows: The first and last bits of B represent in base 2 a number in the range 0 to 3. Let that number be i. The middle 4 bits of B represent in base 2 a number in the range 0 to 15. Let that number be j. Look up in the table the number in the i'th row and j'th column. It is a number in the range 0 to 15 and is uniquely represented by a 4 bit block. That block is the output $S_1(B)$ of S_1 for the input B. For example, for input 011011 the row is 01, that is row 1, and the column is determined by 1101, that is column 13. In row 1 column 13 appears 5 so that the output is 0101. Selection functions $S_1, S_2, \ldots, S_8$ of the algorithm appear in the Appendix.

The permutation function P yields a 32-bit output from a 32-bit input by permuting the bits of the input block. Such a function is defined by the following table:

$\underline{P}$

16	7	20	21
29	12	28	17
1	15	23	26
5	18	31	10
2	8	24	14
32	27	3	9
19	13	30	6
22	11	4	25

The output $P(L)$ for the function P defined by this table is obtained from the input L by taking the 16th bit of L as the first bit of $P(L)$, the 7th bit as the second bit of $P(L)$, and so on until the 25th bit of L is taken as the 32nd bit of $P(L)$. The permutation function P of the algorithm is repeated in the Appendix.

Now let $S_1, \ldots, S_8$ be eight distinct selection functions, let P be the permutation function and let E be the function defined above.

To define $f(R, K)$ we first define $B_1, \ldots, B_8$ to be blocks of 6 bits each for which

(6) $$B_1 B_2 \ldots B_8 = K \oplus E(R)$$

The block $f(R, K)$ is then defined to be

(7) $$P(S_1(B_1)S_2(B_2) \ldots S_8(B_8))$$

Thus $K \oplus E(R)$ is first divided into the 8 blocks as indicated in (6). Then each B_i is taken as an input to S_i and the 8 blocks $S_1(B_1)$, $S_2(B_2)$, . . ., $S_8(B_8)$ of 4 bits each are consolidated into a single block of 32 bits which forms the input to P. The output (7) is then the output of the function f for the inputs R and K.

APPENDIX

PRIMITIVE FUNCTIONS FOR THE DATA ENCRYPTION ALGORITHM

The choice of the primitive functions KS, $S_1, \ldots, S_8$ and P is critical to the strength of an encipherment resulting from the algorithm. Specified below is the recommended set of functions, describing $S_1, \ldots, S_8$ and P in the same way they are described in the algorithm. For the interpretation of the tables describing these functions, see the discussion in the body of the algorithm.

The primitive functions $S_1, \ldots, S_8$, are:

S_1

14	4	13	1	2	15	11	8	3	10	6	12	5	9	0	7
0	15	7	4	14	2	13	1	10	6	12	11	9	5	3	8
4	1	14	8	13	6	2	11	15	12	9	7	3	10	5	0
15	12	8	2	4	9	1	7	5	11	3	14	10	0	6	13

S_2

15	1	8	14	6	11	3	4	9	7	2	13	12	0	5	10
3	13	4	7	15	2	8	14	12	0	1	10	6	9	11	5
0	14	7	11	10	4	13	1	5	8	12	6	9	3	2	15
13	8	10	1	3	15	4	2	11	6	7	12	0	5	14	9

S_3

10	0	9	14	6	3	15	5	1	13	12	7	11	4	2	8
13	7	0	9	3	4	6	10	2	8	5	14	12	11	15	1
13	6	4	9	8	15	3	0	11	1	2	12	5	10	14	7
1	10	13	0	6	9	8	7	4	15	14	3	11	5	2	12

S_4

7	13	14	3	0	6	9	10	1	2	8	5	11	12	4	15
13	8	11	5	6	15	0	3	4	7	2	12	1	10	14	9
10	6	9	0	12	11	7	13	15	1	3	14	5	2	8	4
3	15	0	6	10	1	13	8	9	4	5	11	12	7	2	14

S_5

2	12	4	1	7	10	11	6	8	5	3	15	13	0	14	9
14	11	2	12	4	7	13	1	5	0	15	10	3	9	8	6
4	2	1	11	10	13	7	8	15	9	12	5	6	3	0	14
11	8	12	7	1	14	2	13	6	15	0	9	10	4	5	3

S_6

12	1	10	15	9	2	6	8	0	13	3	4	14	7	5	11
10	15	4	2	7	12	9	5	6	1	13	14	0	11	3	8
9	14	15	5	2	8	12	3	7	0	4	10	1	13	11	6
4	3	2	12	9	5	15	10	11	14	1	7	6	0	8	13

S_7

4	11	2	14	15	0	8	13	3	12	9	7	5	10	6	1
13	0	11	7	4	9	1	10	14	3	5	12	2	15	8	6
1	4	11	13	12	3	7	14	10	15	6	8	0	5	9	2
6	11	13	8	1	4	10	7	9	5	0	15	14	2	3	12

S_8

13	2	8	4	6	15	11	1	10	9	3	14	5	0	12	7
1	15	13	8	10	3	7	4	12	5	6	11	0	14	9	2
7	11	4	1	9	12	14	2	0	6	10	13	15	3	5	8
2	1	14	7	4	10	8	13	15	12	9	0	3	5	6	11

The primitive function P is:

16	7	20	21
29	12	28	17
1	15	23	26
5	18	31	10
2	8	24	14
32	27	3	9
19	13	30	6
22	11	4	25

Recall that K_n, for $1 \leq n \leq 16$, is the block of 48 bits in (2) of the algorithm. Hence, to describe KS, it is sufficient to describe the calculation of K_n from KEY for $n = 1, 2, \ldots, 16$. That calculation is illustrated in figure 3. To complete the definition of KS it is therefore sufficient to describe the two permuted choices, as well as the schedule of left shifts. One bit in each 8-bit byte of the KEY may be utilized for error detection in key generation, distribution and storage. Bits 8, 16, . . ., 64 are for use in assuring that each byte is of odd parity.

Permuted choice 1 is determined by the following table:

$PC-1$

57	49	41	33	25	17	9
1	58	50	42	34	26	18
10	2	59	51	43	35	27
19	11	3	60	52	44	36
63	55	47	39	31	23	15
7	62	54	46	38	30	22
14	6	61	53	45	37	29
21	13	5	28	20	12	4

The table has been divided into two parts, with the first part determining how the bits of C_0 are chosen, and the second part determining how the bits of D_0 are chosen. The bits of KEY are numbered 1 through 64. The bits of C_0 are respectively bits 57, 49, 41, . . ., 44 and 36 of KEY, with the bits of D_0 being bits 63, 55, 47, . . ., 12 and 4 of KEY.

With C_0 and D_0 defined, we now define how the blocks C_n and D_n are obtained from the blocks C_{n-1} and D_{n-1}, respectively, for $n = 1, 2, \ldots, 16$. That is accomplished by adhering to the following schedule of left shifts of the individual blocks:

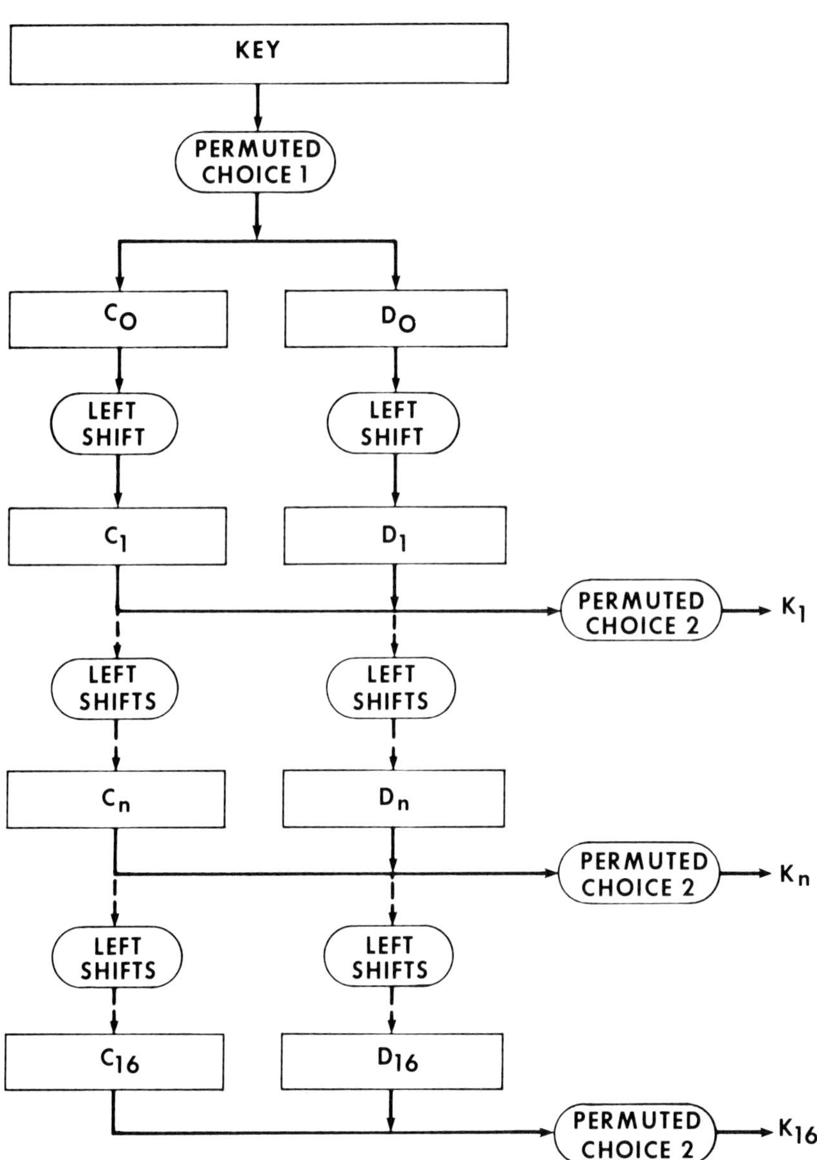

FIGURE 3. *Key schedule calculation.*

Iteration Number	Number of Left Shifts
1	1
2	1
3	2
4	2
5	2
6	2
7	2
8	2
9	1
10	2
11	2
12	2
13	2
14	2
15	2
16	1

For example, C_3 and D_3 are obtained from C_2 and D_2, respectively, by two left shifts, and C_{16} and D_{16} are obtained from C_{15} and D_{15}, respectively, by one left shift. In all cases, by a single left shift is meant a rotation of the bits one place to the left, so that after one left shift the bits in the 28 positions are the bits that were previously in positions 2, 3, . . ., 28, 1.

Permuted choice 2 is determined by the following table:

PC−2

14	17	11	24	1	5
3	28	15	6	21	10
23	19	12	4	26	8
16	7	27	20	13	2
41	52	31	37	47	55
30	40	51	45	33	48
44	49	39	56	34	53
46	42	50	36	29	32

Therefore, the first bit of K_n is the 14th bit of C_nD_n, the second bit the 17th, and so on with the 47th bit the 29th, and the 48th bit the 32nd.

Author Index

Subject Index